UNION COUNTY, SOUTH CAROLINA
MINUTES OF THE COUNTY COURT 1785-1799

by
Brent H. Holcomb, C. A. L. S.

Please Direct all Correspondence & Orders to:

Southern Historical Press, Inc.
P.O. Box 1267
Greenville, S.C. 29602-1267

Originally published: Easley, S.C. 1979
Reprinted :Southern Historical Press, Inc.
Greenville, S.C., 1994
Copyright 1979 by
The Rev. Silas Emmett Lucas, Jr.
Easley, S.C.
All Rights Reserved.
ISBN # 0-89308-159-0
Library of Congress Catalog Card # 79-66945
Printed in the United States of America

To my great-aunt

Mrs. W. E. Greer, Sr.

who taught me to appreciate
genealogy and Union County
from my childhood.

INTRODUCTION

Union was an original county formed in Ninety Six District by the County Court Act of 1785. This court was to sit beginning on the fourth Monday of March, June, September, and December. (Statutes, VII: 212-213). In 1791, the court system was somewhat changed, then called Intermediate Court which was to sit on the first Monday of April and September, and the county court to sit on the 1st day of January and June. (Statutes, VII: 266-267). The minutes of both these court are included in these volumes. The county courts were set up to record deeds, try small cases, take bastardy bonds, etc. By an act of 28 March 1787 (Statutes, VII: 245-246), these court were also made courts of ordinary, proving wills, granting letters of administration, appointing guardians, etc. Proving deeds became a difficult matter--finding two witnesses to come to court--and also took a great amount of court time. By an act of 29 January 1788, a deed could be proved by any one witness before a magistrate (not in open court) or acknowledged in open court by the grantor (Statutes, VII: 247-249). In 1800 the county court system in South Carolina was abolished, and all counties became known as districts.

These volumes are labeled only by years, not by any designation such as A, B, C, or 1, 2, 3. Only the first volume of these minutes is paginated, and this pagination is indicated in the left margin of the page in this transcription. Therefore to locate an entry, one should use the date of the court, with the exception of the first volume. If I mistake not, Union is the only county which has for some years extant both "rough" and "finished" minutes. These do not differ in content. The "finished" minutes are neater, easier to read, and in this case, in better condition. From 27 September 1790 to 6 January 1792, we have extant both the finished and rough minutes. From the middle of the minutes of 6 January 1792 to 8 April 1794, we have only rough minutes. There is an advantage to the rough minutes: they appear to contain actual signatures of judges and parties on bonds, etc. The volumes 1794-1796 and 1796-1799 appear to be rough minutes. One unique feature to the contents of these minutes is the "swearing" or "affirming" of the jurors. Those who "affirm" were likely Quakers, or at least members of some religious group that forbade its members to "swear."

It is hoped that this volume will be a help in locating Union County forebears, and give some insight into their lives and times.

Brent H. Holcomb, C. A. L. S.
Box 21766
Columbia, S. C. 29221
October 14, 1978

South Carolina...........)
Union County To Wit.......)

1   Be it hereafter Remembered One Thousand seven
hundred and Eighty five, and of the Sovereignty and
Independence of the United States of America the Ninth.
That at the House of Alexander McDougal in the State of
South Carolina and County of Union, according to Law and
by appointment assembled together Zachariah Bullock, John
Henderson, William Kennedy, Charles Sims, James Harrison,
Thomas Brandon, and John Birdson Esquires) who having
produced a Commission from his Excellency William Moultrie
Esquire Governor of the State of South Carolina Commission-
ing and authorizing them to be Justices of the Peace in
and for the said County of Union in pursuance to an act
of the Legislature of this State passed the twenty fourth
day of March in the year of Our Lord One thousand seven
hundred and Eighty five, To hold a County Court in and for
the said County of Union as by Law in the said Act Directed..
also the said Zachariah Bullock, John Henderson, William
Kennedy, Charles Sims, James Harrison, Thomas Brandon and
John Birdson Esquires produced Certificates from under the
Hand of the Honourable Henry Pendleton Esquire One of the
associate Judges for this our said State that they had
Taken the Oaths of that Office Required by Law, which said
Commission and Certificates are by them ordered to be
Recorded by the person who shall be appointed Clerk for the
said County of Union.

2 Then the Worshipful Court proceeded to Business nominated
and appointed John Haile Esquire Clerk in and for the said
County of Union who together with Zachariah Bullock and
John Henderson his Securities Entered into and acknowledged
their Bonds for the performance of the said office, and the
said John Haile took the Oath Required and directed by Law,
Then proceeded to Record the aforesaid Commission and
Certificates
State of South Carolina

                By his Excellency William Moultrie Esquire
                Governor and Commander in Chief in and over
                the State aforesaid.
                Know Ye that in pursuance of an act of the
                Legislature of this State passed the twenty
(Seal)   fourth day of March in the year of Our Lord
                one thousand seven hundred and Eighty five
                Entitled an act for Establishing County Court,
                and for Regulating the proceedings therein;
                I do by these presents
Willm.   Commission you the said Zachariah Bullock,
Moultrie   John Henderson, William Kennedy, Charles
                Sims, James Harrison, Thomas Brandon and John
                Birdsong to be Justices of the Peace, in and
                for the County of Union, and you or any three
                of you have full power and Jurisdiction to
                hold the County Court in and for the said
                County by the aforesaid act, Established; and
                you are to pear and determine all Causes,
                and other matters and Controverseys, properly
                appertaining and Referred by Law to your
                Jurisdiction.
                This Commission to Continue and be in force
                during Good Behaviour.

By his
Excellency's
Command
John
Vanderhorst
Secretary

Given under my hand and Seal in the City of
Charleston this twenty fourth day of March
in the year of Our Lord One thousand Seven
hundred and Eighty five, and of the
Sovereignity of the United States of America
the Ninth.

Pursuant to Law the Court nominate and appoint William Farr
Sheriff in and for the County of Union, Ordered by the
Court that he be Recommended to his Excellency the Governor
as a fit person to Execute the Office of Sheriff of this
County for the Ensuing two years.

3 I do hereby Certify that Thomas Brandon, James Harrison
and John Birdsong appointed Justices to set in the County
Court of Union this day took the Oaths prescribed by Law
before me and thereupon Qualified to Enter on the Execution
of their Respective Offices.
April 28th 1785.   H. Y. Pendleton, Judge

I do hereby Certify that John Henderson Esquire this day
took before me the Oaths prescribed by Law as a Justices
of the Peace of the County Court of Union May the 28th.
1785.   H. Y. Pendleton, Judge

On Petition of Major Charles Miles to keep a Publis House
or Tavern which being Considered by the Court, is Ordered
that the petition be Granted and that the petitioner Obtain
a Licence for the same by Complying with Law.

State   Plaintiff)
  against   ) The Defendant William Beckham
William Beckham   Defendant) together with William Farr
                              his security both of the
County Come into Court and undertake Jointly and Severally
that the Defendant shall will and busly appear at the next
Court, whereupon it is Ordered by the Court the Recognizance
be Continued accordingly.

State   Plaintiff)
  against   ) The Defendant Isaac Young together
Isaac Young Defendant) with Colonel Thomas Brandon his
                         Security came into Court and
acknowledged themselves Indebted to the State in the following Sums to Wit the Defendant Thomas Young in the sum of
fifty pounds and his Security in the sum of twenty five
pounds to be lived on their Goods and Chattels. lands
and Tenements for the appearance of the Defendant next
Court.

Ordered by the Court that William White, Evan Thomas &
Nathaniel Henderson be and is hereby appointed Constables
who took the Oaths of Office Required by Law.

4 Major Charles Miles Comes into Court together with Colonel
Thomas Brandon and William Farr his Securities who Entered
and acknowledged themselves bound in Sum of One hundred
pounds for said Charles Miles on which he Obtained Licence
to keep a Tavern or Public house as before Granted in this
Our County.

Pursuant to Law the Court Nominated and appoint William Kenedy Esquire Coroner and for the County of Union, Ordered that he be Recommended to his Excellency the Governor as a fit person to Execute that office for the said County.

Benjamin Woodson is hereby appointed Surveyor or overseer of the High-Way from Loves Ford on Broad River to Sharps Creek and it is Ordered that he keep the same Road in Good Repair.

James Bogan is hereby appointed Surveyor of the High-way from Sharps Creek; to Jones on the Road, Ordered that he keep the same in good Repair.

Jacob Paulk is hereby appointed Overseer or surveyor of the High Way from Jones on the Road to Fairforest, Ordered that he keep the same Road in good Repair.

Turner Rountree is hereby appointed Surveyor or Overseer of the Highway from Fairforrest; to Tygar River at Bobo's Ford, Ordered that he keep the same Road in good Repair.

Peter Renfrow is hereby the Court appointed Surveyor or Overseer of the Highway from Bobo's ford on Tygar River to Jones Mill on Enoree River, Ordered that he keep the same in good Repair.

Matthew Pattern Esquire is hereby the Court appointed Surveyor or Overseer of the Road from the County line near Fairforrest, to the Race paths near Captain Daniel Jackson, and ordered that he keep the same in good Repair.

Captain Thomas Blassingame is hereby appointed Surveyor or Overseer of the Highway from the Race Paths near Captain Daniel Jacksons; to Sugar Creek, and ordered that he keep the same Road in Good Repair.

John Goodwin is hereby the Court appointed Surveyor.
5 or Overseer of the Highway from Sugar Creek to Dining Creek, and Ordered that he keep the same Road in Good Repair.

Joseph Little is hereby appointed Surveyor or Overseer of the Highway from Dining Creek to Adams Mill on Tygar River, and Ordered the same Road in Good Repair.

John Clerk is hereby appointed Surveyor or Overseer of the Highway from Adam's Mill of Tygar River to Kenedy's ford on Enoree River, and Ordered that he keep the same Road in good Repair.

Joseph West is hereby appointed Overseer or Surveyor of the Highway from Colonel Thomas Brandon to Rockey Creek, and Ordered by the Court that he keep the same Road in Good Repair.

Captain James Crawford is hereby appointed Surveyor or Overseer of the Highway from Rockey Creek to Gibbs Old Place, and Ordered by the Court that he keep the same in good Repair.

William White is hereby appointed Overseer or Surveyor, of the Highway from Gibs Old place Crossing the Creek at or near Henderson's Mill...into the Road near Packolate, To Packolate River and Ordered by the Court that he keep the same Road in Good Repair.

John Beckham is hereby appointed Overseer of the Highway leading from Packolate to Henry Long's from Packolate River, to Browns Creek, Ordered that he keep the same Road in Good Repair.

John Brandon is hereby appointed Overseer of the Highway from Brown's Creek to Jolly Creek, and Ordered by the Court that he keep the same Road in Good Repair.

Jeremiah Gregory is hereby appointed Surveyor or Overseer of the Highway from Jolly Creek, to Ottersons Ford on Tygar River, and Ordered by the Court that he keep the same Road in good Repair.

George Little is hereby appointed Overseer or Surveyor of the Highway from Ottersons Ford on Tygar to Enoree River, and Ordered by the Court that he keep the same Road in good Repair.

William McCulloch is hereby appointed Surveyor of Over seer of the Highway (on the Road leading from Smith's ford on Broad River to Grindal's Shoals on Packolate) from said Smith's ford to the old meeting House, and Ordered that he keep the same Road in good Repair.

Charles Miles is hereby appointed surveyor or overseer of the highway from the old Meeting house to Grindal Shoals on Packolate River Ordered that he keep the same Road in good Repair.

6 William Hendley is hereby appointed Surveyor or Overseer of the Highway (on the Road leading from Bullock's Creek ford on Broad River to the Iron Works on Lawson's Fork) from the said Bullocks Creek ford, to the Cross Roads where the Negroe was Hung; and Ordered by the Court that he keep the same Road in good Repair.

Joseph Gault is hereby appointed Surveyor or Overseer of the Highway from the Cross Road where the Negro was hung: to Charles Miles: ordered by the Court that he keep the same Road in Good Repair.

Samuel Littlejohn is hereby appointed Surveyor or Overseer of the Highway from Charles Miles to the County line, Ordered that he keep the same Road in good Repair.

Joseph Hughs is hereby appointed Surveyor or Overseer of the Highway (on the Road leading from Loves Ford on Broad River to Duff's Ford on Tygar River) from said Love's Ford, to Neal's path, and Ordered by the Court that he keep the same Road in good Repair.

James Thomas is hereby appointed Overseer or Surveyor of the Highway from Neal's path, to the lower Fishdam Creek, Ordered by the Court, that he keep the same Road in good Repair.

Benjamin Johnson is hereby appointed Surveyor or Overseer of the Road from the lower Fishdam Creek to Duff's Ford on Tygar Ordered by the Court that he keep the same Road in good Repair.

Phillip Anderson is hereby appointed Surveyor or Overseer of the Highway from Duff's Ford, on Tygar River to Andersons ford on Enoree River, Ordered by the Court that he keep the same Road in good Repair.

Ordered by the Court that Captain James Terrill and Captain John Thompson lay out and Mark a Road from the Cherokee Ford on Broad River the nearest and best way to Grindal's Shoals on Packolate River and Report the same to our next Court.

Ordered by the Court that Robert Lusk Esquire and Samuel Tolbert lay out and Mark a Road from the Scull Shoals the nearest and best way to Hughe's and Report the same at our next Court.

James Bankhead is hereby appointed Surveyor or Overseer of the Highway from the Scull Shoals on Packolate River to Fanning's Creek and ordered that he keep the same Road in good Repair.

Merry Maguire is hereby appointed Surveyor or Overseer of the Highway from Fannings Creek to Hughe's near Love's Ford on Broad River, and Ordered that he keep the same Road in good Repair.

Joshua Palmer is hereby appointed Surveyor of Overseer of the Road from Torbert's Ferry on Borad River to the Road leading to Ninety six, and Ordered that he keep the same Road in good Repair.

7 Pursuant to Law the Court do set. and affix the following Rates of Liquors Diet Lodgings Provender, Stablage Foder Pasturage &C to be paid in the Several Ordinaries and Taverns in this County for this year.

Good west India Rum p Quart	two shillings
Good west India Rum p Pint.................	One Shilling
Good west India Rum pr Half pint...........	Seven Pence
Good west India Rum pr Gill................	Four pence
Common Rum........ pr Quart...............	One Shilling & Four pence
Common Rum........ pr Pint................	Nine pence
Common Rum........ pr Half pint...........	Six pence
Common Rum........ pr Gill................	Three pence.
Wine.............. pr Quart...............	Two shillings & Four pence
Wine.............. pr Pint................	One Shilling & Four pence
Wine.............. pr half Pint...........	Nine pence
Wine.............. pr Gill................	Five pence
Toddy with Loaf Sugar pr Quart............	One Shilling & Two pence
Lodging...................................	Four pence
Stablage for One horse pr night...........	Four pence
Fodder sufficient for twelve Hours........	Four pence

```
Corn................. pr Gallon........... Six pence.
Oats................. pr Gallon........... Four pence
Warm Dinner.............................. One Shilling
Cold Dinner.............................. Nine Pence
Breakfast with Coffee Tea or Chocolate..... Eight Pence
Cold Breakfast........................... Six Pence
Pasturage for Twelve Hours for One Horse... Three pence
```

The Court adjourned untill Court of Course at the same
Place   Zachariah Bullock
                             John Henderson
                             John Birdsong
            Signed by   William Kennedy   Esquires
                             James Harrison
                             Charles Sims

At a Court Begun and Held in and for the County of Union
at the House of Alexander McDougal the twenty sixth day of
September in the year of Our Lord One thousand seven hundred
and Eighty five, and in the tenth year of the Sovereignity
and Independence of the United States of America.

                             John Henderson
            Present   William Kennedy   Esquires
                             Thomas Brandon
                             John Birdson

A Commission from his Excellency William Moultrie Esquire
Governor and Commander in Chief in and over the State of
South Carolina directed to William Farr Esquire to be
Sheriff in and for the County of Union to Continue and be
in force for Two years Which was produced in Court by the
said William Farr and Read, whereupon he together with
Charles Miles and Robert Lusk his Securities Entered into
and acknowledged their several Bonds to the Treasury of the
State in the sum of one thousand five hundred pounds for
the payment of all Public Taxes by him Collected or Other
sum or sums of money; and for the faithful Executing of
the said Office as by the act of assemble directed.
Which said Commissions and Bonds are hereby Ordered to be
Recorded.
State of South Carolina
            By His Excellency William Moultrie Esquire
            Governor and Commander in Chief in and Over the
            State aforesaid.
(Seal)   To William Farr Esquire

            Know Ye that I Reposing a Special Trust and Confi-
            dence in your abilities, Care, Prudence and
            Integrity have by virtue of the power and authority
Willm.   in me vested Commission, Constitute and appoint and
Moultrie   by these presents do Commission Constitute and
            appoint you the Said William Farr to be Sheriff in
            and for the County of Union in the said State. To
            Have Hold Exercise and Enjoy the said office of
            Sheriff together with all Rights Privilages profits
            and Emoluments to the said Office belonging or in
            any wise appertaining.
                This Commission to Continue and be in force for
            two years.

By his   Given under my hand and Seal in the City of
Excel-   Charleston this fourteenth day of July in the
lency   year of our Lord One thousand seven hundred and
Command   Eighty five, and of the Sovereignity and Indepen-
John   dence of the United States of North America the
Vander-   Tenth.
horst
Secretary

Know All Men by these presents that we William Farr, Charles
Miles and Robert Lusk of the State and County of Union are
held and firmly Bound unto the Treasury of the said State
and there Successors in the office of Treasurers in the
sum of One thousand five hundred pounds Sterling, which
payment well and Truly to be made and done we Bind Ourselves our Heirs Executors administrators Jointly and
Severally and firmly by these presents Sealed with Our
Seals, and dated this twenty Sixth day of September One
thousand seven hundred
9 and Eighty five the Condition of the above Obligation is
such that whereas William Farr is appointed high Sheriff
for the County of Union aofresaid by Commission from his
Excellency William Moultrie Esquire now if the said William
Farr shall well and Truly pay or cause to be paid as well
all the public Taxes of the said County as all other sums
or sums of money as may be delivered to him to Called by
virtue of this said Office agreeable to Law and in all
other things faithfully Execute the office of Sheriff of
the County of Union then the above Obligation to be void
otherwise to Remain in full force and Virtue
                                Wm Farr (Seal)
Signed Sealed & Delivered   Charles Miles (Seal)
   In Open Court   Robt. Lusk (Seal)
John Haile C. Clk

Rebecca Johnson infant and Orphan of James Johnson with the
consent and approbation of the Court came and made Choice
of Samuel Otterson her Guardian. Also the said Samuel
Otterson is by the Court appointed Guardian to James
Johnson, Thomas Dougen Johnson, Samuel Otterson Johnson,
Robert Johnson, and Mary Johnson Infants and Orphans of
the said James Johnson Deceased, Whereupon the said Samuel
Otterson together with William Farr and James Orr his
Securities (which is approved of by the Court) Entered
into and acknowledged their Bonds in the Sum of three
hundred pounds for the Securiting of the said Orphans
Estate and indemnifying the Court.

John Albritin Request of the Court to keep a Tavern, which
said Request is Granted on his giving Captain Joshua Palmer
and Benjamin Savage Security in the Sum of One hundred
pounds.

John Albritain together with Joshua Palmer and Benjamin
Savage his Securities came into Court and Entered into and
acknowledged their bonds the sum of One hundred pounds for
the said John Albutain on which he Obtained a Licence to
keep a Tavern or public House at his Own house in this
County as before Granted.

David Dickson Came into Court and proved a Deed of Conveyance from William Orr to James Orr dated the thirteenth

7

day of January One thousand seven hundred and Eighty, whereupon the same is Ordered by the Court to be Recorded.

Ephraim Clerk Comes into Court and present a petition for a Road to be laid Out from Major Charles Miles to Clerk's Ferry on Broad River, which is ordered to be laid Over to be reconsidered next Court.

The Court adjourned from Alexander McDougal's to the place appointed to hold the Court for the said County of Union, at Jone's till the Morrow at ten OClock.
John Henderson
William Kennedy   Esquires
John Birdsong

10 At a Court Continued and held by adjournment at the House of Joseph Jones in and for the County of Union the twenty seventh day of September in the year of Our Lord One thousand Seven hundred and Eighty five, and of Sovereignty and Independence of the United States of North America the Tenth.
Present   William Kennedy
Thomas Brandon   Esquires
John Birdsong

Ordered that the Court House and Other Public Buildings for the Benefit and use of the County be Entered upon Joseph Jones land on the Summet of the Hill between said Jones's and Coldwells, by Order of Zachariah Bullock, Thomas Brandon, John Henderson, Charles Sims, William Kennedy and John Birdsong (Esquires) Justices of the said County Court of Union.

Colonel Thomas Brandon presents the County of Union with two acres of Land on the place nominated and appointed by the Justices of the Court to set the Public Buildings on being the Quantity Required by Law, which is accepted of by the Court and Ordered therefore to be Entered upon the Records of this Court.

Ordered that James Yancey Esquire be duly admitted as a practising attorney in this Court, he having taken the Oaths Required by Law.

An Indenture of Lease and Release Between Thomas Tramble of the One parts and William Farr of the Other Part was acknowledged by the said Thomas Tramble to the said William Farr for one hundred acres of Land, and Ordered to be Recorded.

Present John Henderson Esquire.
The Grand Jury being drawn tried and Sworn to Wit John Thompson Foreman, John Montgomery, Thomas Stribling, Job Hammond, James Thomas, Benjamin Savage, James Savage, John McCooll, John Sarter, John Gregory, William Williams, Adam Goudylock, Alexander McDougal, of Inquest for the Body of this County, and having Received their Charge, Retired from the Barr to Consult their Verdict.

The Court do hereby bind William Hardwick aged Eleven years, and David Hardwick aged seven years, untill they are twenty One years of age, To William Hardwick House Joiner, who is

8

hereby Required to well and truly to Teach and instruct them
in the Trade and Mistry of a House Joiner and that he the
said William Hardwick Shall find the said Intended appren-
tices William and David Hardwicks Sufficient Bed Board and
Cloaths, & also instruct or cause them to be instructed to
Read Write, and Cypher in arithmetic.
                                to
11 to the Rule of Three, Ordered that the same be hereby
Recorded.

Ordered by the Court that John Palmer, William Beckham,
and John Haile do lay Out and Mark a Road from Grindal's
Shoals on Packolate the nearest and best way to the Duck
Pond, between Buffolow and Brown's Creeks and Report the
same to our next Court.

Ordered by the Court that Colonel Thomas Brandon and William
Kennedy Esquires lay Out and Mark a Highway from the Duck
pond between Buffolow and Brown's Creek the nearest and
best way to the Ninety Six Road near Union Court house.

Ordered by the Court that Major Joseph McJunkin and Samuel
McJunkin lay out and Mark a Highway from Union Court house
the nearest and best way to the Charleston Road near
Tinker Creek and Report the same to our next Court.

Ordered by the Court that Major Samuel Otterson and John
Willson lay out and mark a Highway from the Charleston Road
near Tinker Creek where the Highway from Union Court to
the said Charleston Road come to laid Out by Major Joseph
McJinkin and Samuel McJunkin the nearest and best way to
Hamilton's Ford on Tygar River, and Report the same to Our
next Court.

An Indenture of Deed of Conveyance between Charles Jones of
the One part, and Hezekiah Rice of the Other part for two
hundred acres of Land proved in Court by the Oaths of
Thomas Brandon, William Goldsmith and Shadrick Landtrip
witnesses thereunto and Ordered to be Recorded.

State   Plaintiff)
  against   ) Bastardy.
William Beckham Defendant) Hannah Still having been
                     delivered of a Bastard Child
made Oath that the Defendant William Beckham is the Father
of it, the Court after hearing the Council on behalf of
the Defendant, are of Opinion that the defendant is the
Father of the said Child, Whereupon it is Ordered by the
Court that the Defendant William Beckham give Security to
the County for the Support and Maintaince of the same Child,
Whereupon the said William Beckham together with William
Farr Daniel Jackson and Philip Anderson Came into Court and
Entered and acknowledged themselves indebted to the
County the sum of fifty pounds in the same of their
Respective Lands Tenenments Goods and Chattels to be Levied
to and for the use of the said County. Yet upon Condition
that the said William Beckham do well and Reasonably main-
tain and support the aforesaid Bastard Child, untill it be
ten years of age...Ordered that William Beckham pay unto
Hannah Still the sum of four pounds for the Miantenance &
support of her Bastard Child which he stand charged as the
Father thereof for the space of One Year Ensueing.

9

12 An Indenture of Lease and Release Between Nehemiah Howard
of the One part, and Archer Smith of the Other part, was
acknowledged by the said Nehemiah Howard unto the said
Archer Smith for One hundred acres of Land.
Ordered that the same be Recorded.

An Indenture of Lease and Release Between Archibald Smith
of the One part, and Nehemiah Howard of the Other Part, for
One Hundred acres of Land was acknowledge by the said
Archibald Smith to the said Nehemiah Howard.
Ordered that the same be Recorded.

An Indenture of Deed of Conveyance Between William Bryant
of the One part and Jonathan Penall of the Other part for
Eighty four acres of Land, by the Oaths of James Woodson
Senior and James Woodson Junior, Witnesses thereunto and
Ordered to be Recorded.

An Indenture of Lease and Release Between William Edmondson
of the One part and Samuel Torbert of the Other part for
two hundred acres of land was acknowledged by the said
William Edmondson to the said Samuel Torbert, and
Ordered that the same be Recorded.

Hannah Still having been delivered of a Bastard Child
whereof William Beckham is Convicted to be the Father of it;
Ordered that they be fined five pounds Each to be paid into
the Treasury of the County.

Ordered that Archebald Smith take into his Care Six
Children of Rebecca Smith the Orphans of Soloman Smith
Deceased and keep the same in his Care untill December
Court next.

Thomas Brandon   Plaintiff)
    against   )   Attachment
David Adams   Defendant)   In Debt
                                The plaintiff by James Yancy
his attorney on Motion to Court obtained and Order for the
Sheriff to Sell so much of the Estate of the Defendant
David Adams as to Raise the sum of ten pounds fourteen
Shillings and three pence which was awarded to Colonel
Thomas Brandon for a debt due by note also a Sufficiency
to Satisfy all Costs incrued thereon and Retain the same
in his hands.

William Farr high Sheriff of our County pursuant to his
Commission and the Acts of assembly Nominated and appointed
Thomas Stribling Junior Deputy Sheriff in and for the said
County of Union, which meet with the Concurence and
approbation of the Court Ordered that he take the Oaths
Required by Law, Whereupon the said Thomas Stribling Junior
took the Oaths prescribed by Law in the act of assembly and
Entered into the Execution of the Said Office by Order of
Court.
        Signed   John Henderson: William Kennedy   Jno. Birdsong

13 At a Court Continued and held by adjournment at the House
of Joseph Jones in and for the County of Union the twenty
Eight day of September in the year of Our Lord One thousand
Seven hundred and Eighty five, and of the Sovereignty and
Independence of the United States of America the tenth.

10

```
Present                          William Kennedy
                                 Thomas Brandon
                                 James Harrison   Esquires
                                 John Henderson
                                 James Birdsong
```

An Indenture of Lease and Release Between Daniel Plummer of
the One part, and William Plummer of the Other part, for
two hundred and twenty acres of Land was proved by the
Oaths of Renny Belue and Shadrick Landtrip Witness thereunto
and
Ordered to be Recorded.

An Indenture of Lease and Release Between Frances Posey of
the one part, and Caleb Gassaway of the Other part, for
One hundred acres of land was proved by the Oaths of William
Farr and Benjamin Hollingsworth Witnesses thereunto and
Ordered to be Recorded

An Indenture of Lease and Release Between James Hardwick of
the One part and Frances Posey of the Other part, for One
hundred acres of Land being proved before according to Law,
is therefore
Ordered to be Recorded.

An Indenture of Deed of Conveyance Between Adam McCooll of
the One part and Joseph Hughes of the other part, for One
hundred acres of Land was acknowledged by the said Adam
McCooll to the said Joseph Hughes and
Ordered to be Recorded.

An Indenture of Lease and Release Between Isaac Simmonson
of the One part, and James Hardwick of the other part for
one hundred acres of Land the same being proved before
according to Law is therefore
Ordered to be Recorded.

An Indenture of Deed of Conveyance Between David George of
the One part, and William Williams of the other part for
six hundred Acres of Land being proved before according to
Law and is therefore
Ordered to be Recorded.

Ordered by the Court that Rydarus Clark be and is hereby
appointed Constable for the County of Union and that he
take the Oaths Required by Law

14 An Indenture of Deed of Conveyance Between Joseph Jones of
the One part and John McCooll of the Other part, for Two
Hundred acres of Land was acknowledged by the said Joseph
Jones, to the said John McCooll, also Sarah Jones wife of
the said Joseph Jones. She being first Examined privately
as the law directs acknowledged her Right of Dowrey and the
same ordered to be recorded.

An Indenture of Deed of Conveyance Between Thomas Young of
the One part, and Joseph Jones of the Other part, for one
hundred and fifty acres of Land, was acknowledged by the
said Thomas Young, to the said Joseph Jones and the same is
Ordered to be Recorded.

11

An Indenture of Deed of Conveyance Between Thomas Brandon
Esquire of the One part, and Thomas Young of the Other
part for One hundred and forty acres of Land was acknow-
ledged by the said Thomas Brandon Esquire to the said Thomas
Young and the same
Ordered to be Recorded.

Hugh Nelson is hereby appointed overseer or Surveyor of the
Highway from McCooll Ferry on Broad River into Ninety Six
Road the old way Ordered that he keep the same Road in good
Repair.

Robert Montgomery   Plaintiff)
    against   )   In Debt. attachment
George Purvis   Defendant)   John George Comes into Court
                                   and undertakes for the
Defendt. that in Case he shall be Cast he shall pay the
Judgment of the Court, or Render the Body of the Defendant
in discharge thereof; and that he the said John George will
pay the Condemnation of Court for him, whereupon it is
Ordered that he be accepted as Special Bail for the defen-
dant, untill next Court
Ordered that the Cause be continued over accordingly.

Robert Montgomery   Plaintiff)
    against   )   Debt attachment.
Ezekiel Gibbs   Defendant)
                                   This day came the plaintiff
by James Yancy his attorney on the attachment Granted by
Zachariah Bullock Esquire Returned Goods attached in the
Hands of Wilson Jolly; and the Defendant not appearing to
Replevy the same, thereupon came also a Jury To wit Thomas
Vance, Moses Collier, Richard Powell Daniel Jackson Thomas
Shockley, James Woodson Issac White William Beckham, Joseph
Hughs, William Edmondson William McJunkin & John Still who
being duly drawn tried and Sworn well and truly to
enquire of debt, Upon their Oaths do say that the defendant
doth owe to the plaintiff nine pounds ten Shillings besides
his Costs. Whereupon it is considered by the Court, that
the verdict
15 be Recorded, and that the Plaintiff Recover against the
Defendant the debt aforesaid in form aforesaid, and his
costs in and about is suit in this behalf Expended and the
said Defendant in money &C.

State   Plaintiff)
    against   )   Ordered by the Court
James & Martha Bensons   Defendant)   that Writs of Subpoenas
                                       Issue for Elizabeth
Cooper, Isaac Young and Thomas Holden personally to appear
at Our next Court to give Testimony in behalf of the State
against the Defendants, James & Martha Bensons It is
further Ordered by the Court that Defendants James and
Martha Bensons Continue their Recognizance on which they
were bound here, untill next Court, Whereupon the said
James & Martha Bensons together with their Securities Came
into Court...Entered into and acknowledged their Recognizance to appear here next Court and not to depart without
leave of the Court.
Came into Court John Smith James Bogan and William Smith of
the County of Union and acknowledged themselves Indebted
to the County of Union and acknowledged themselves Indebted

12

to the State that is John Smith in the sum of fifty pounds,
James Bogan and William Smith in the sum of twenty five
pounds each; in the same of their respective Lands, Tenements Goods & Chattels to be Levied to the Treasury of the
State of South Carolina, Yet upon Condition that the said
John Smith do appear at our next Court and prosecute in
behalf of the State a suit against James and Martha Benson
then the Recognizance to be void.

John Ewart   Plaintiff)
  against   )   In Debt. attachment
George Purvis   Defendant) This day came the plaintiff by
                              James Young his attorney on the
attachment by Zachariah Bullock Esquire Returned Levied
on two Cows and Calves one Heiffer and some Household
Furniture, also Summonsed John Montgomery a Garnishee to
appear here, the Defendant appearing but Refusing to give
Special Bail to Replevy the same, thereupon Came also a
Jury To Wit Thomas Vance Moses Collier Richard Powell
Daniel Jackson Thomas Shockley James Woodson, Isaac White,
William Joseph Hughs, William Edmondson, William McJunkin &
John Still who being duly drawn tried and Sworn diligently
to Enquire of Debt. Upon their Oaths do say that the defend.
doth Owe to the plaintiff fifteen pounds besides his Cost
Whereupon it is Considered by the Court that the Verdict be
Recorded and that the plaintf Recover against the Defendt.
the debt aforesaid and his Cost in and about his suit in
that behalf Expended...and the said Defendant in money &C.
&C.

16 The Grand Jury having this day Returned into Court and made
the following presentments To Wit We do present that the
Inhabitants of this County are aggrieved by Reason of their
public Dues not being paid, also upon information it appears
that the Overseer appointed upon the Road from the Old
Meeting House to Grindals Shoals have neglected his duty,
also it appears that the Road from the Mouth of Bullocks
Creek ford on Broad River leading to the Iron Works as far
as the Cross Roads where the Negroe was Hung is neglected
also present John Garrat from the Information of Robert
Lusk for Selling and Retailing Strong Liquors Contrary to
Law.   John Thompson Foreman

Ordered that the Sheriff Summons Samuel Otterson, Thomas
Blassingame, Nehemiah Howard, John Goodwin, John Blassingame
James Bell, John Clark, Govin Harrington, George McWhorter
Robert Harris, William Pattent Matthew Pattent Turner Rountree Jos. McJunkin & Wm Young personally to appear here to
serve as a Grand Jury of Inquest for the Body of this County
at our next Court they being nominated and draw according
to Law.

Ordered that the Sheriff Summons Hezekiah Rice, Robert
Montgomery, Drewry Harrington, Moses Guyton, John Montgomery,
William Steen, James Blassingame, James Bankhead, James
Crawford, John Reed, John Steen Junr., Richard Wood, John
McWhorter, Alexander Hamilton, Robert Good, George Story
Junr., James McElwain Junr., John Gregory, Isaac Gregory,
Archibald Smith, William Lawson, Ambrose Wray, John Howard,
John Layton, Stephen Layton, William Smith, John Smith,
John Linenam, James Orr, Jeremiah Hamilton personally to be

13

and appear here to serve as petit jurors, for the Body of
this County at our next Court they being drawn according to
Law.

Thomas Brandon   Plaintiff)
  against   )   In Debt. attachment
David Adams   Defendant)
                           This day Came the plaintiff
by James Yancy his attorney on attachment Granted by William
Kennedy Esquire on Motion of the plaintiff the Defendant
being Solemnly Called came not to Replevy the Goods attached
but makes Default and say nothing in Barr or Defence of
the plaintiffs adion, by which he Remains therein against
him undefended therefore it is Considered by the Court that
the plaintiff Recover against the said Defendant his debt
amounting to twelve pounds. four shillings and three pence
mentioned in the attachment and in the Note on which the
attachment is granted and his Costs in this behalf Expended
and the said Defendant in Money &C. in form aforesaid &C.

James Bell have obtained Licence to keep a public House
and Given Security according to Law, Ordered that the Clerk
make out the same

17 Mark Jackson Plaintiff)
   against   ) Case attachment.
William Meek Defendant) This day Comes the plaintiff into
                       Court by James Yancey his attorney
and Continued Over the said Causes untill next Court.

Charles Miles Plaintiff)
  against   ) In Debt attachment
Soloman Mangham   ) This day came the plaintiff by
                     James Yancey his attorney and
the Defendant, Soloman Mangham in his own proper person,
and says that he Cannot deny the plaintiffs action but that
he Owes him Sixteen pounds and four pence as the Plaintiffs
Complains against him the said Defendant therefore it is
adjudged by the Court that the plaintiff Recover against
the Defendant his debt and Costs in his behalf Expended and
the said Defendant in money &C in form aforesaid &C.

State   Plaintiff)
  against   ) Ordered by the Court that the
John Thompson Defendant) Defendant be dismissed and his
                     Recognizance to be void in
paying cost.

An Indenture and Deed of Conveyance Between Wilson Rogers
of the One part, and John Thompson Junr. of the other part,
for One hundred acres of Land was proved by the Oaths of
John Thompson Senior and John Woods Witnesses thereunto
and Ordered to be Recorded.

State   Plaintiff)
  against   ) The Court on fully hearing the
James Shockley Defendant) Council on behalf of the
                     Plaintiff and also fully
hearing the Defence of the Defendant have Ordered the
Defendant to be Dismissed on paying Costs.

State   Plaintiff)
  against   )   The Court on fully hearing the
Benjamin Long Defendant) Council on behalf of the State,
                        also fully hearing the Defence
of the Defendant have Ordered him to be dismissed and the
Recognizance to be Void on paying Costs.

State   )
  against) The Court on fully hearing the Council on
John Woods) behalf of the State also hearing the Defence
            made by the Defendant have Ordered him to be
Dismissed and Recognizance to be void on paying Costs.

State   )
  against   ) The Court have this Ordered that the
James & Martha Jones) Defendants James and Martha Jones
                Continue their Recognizance on which
they were bound here untill next Court whereupon they
together with their Securities Came into Court Enter into
and acknowledge their Recognizance to appear here next Court
and not to depart without Leave of the Court.

Henry Turner   Plaintiff)
  against   ) Attachment
Wilson Rogers Defendant) Whereupon the same being
                  Returned that there is no
property of the Defendants to be found therefore the
Ordered the Suit to be Discontinued at the Plaintiffs costs.

John Ewart   )
  vs.   ) Debt on an attachment. Whereupon John
George Purvis) Montgomery was Summonded a Garnishee, who
            being Called and Sworn on his Oath do say
that he is Indebted to the Defendant George Purvis twenty
three pounds Six Shilling and Eight pence Sterling and hath
the same in his hands Whereupon Judgment is awarded against
him for as much as will Satisfy the Judgment that the
plaintiff hath obtained against the Defendant and the
Costs of Suit.

Ordered that process Issue against all persons presented
by the Grand Jury that they may appear here at next Court,
to answer respectively to the presentments against them
also Ordered that Subpoeonas Issue for the Informers.

Ordered to be Recorded the Grist and Saw Mills on Harris
Creek on Fairforrest belonging to John Thomas Junior, and
that any person may have the priviledge of Building or
Repairing the same under the Owner or Owners thereof.

Ordered that the Mill on Fairforrest be Recorded belonging
to Colonel Thomas Brandon and that any person may have the
priviledge of Building or Repairing the same under the
Owner or Owners thereof.
                  Signed by   William Kennedy
                            James Harrison   Esquires
                            John Birdsong

December Term 1785

At a Court begun and held in and for the County of Union at the House of John McCooll the twenty Six day of December in the year of Our Lord One thousand Seven hundred and Eighty five, and of the Sovereignity and Independence of the United States of America.

Present   Thomas Brandon
                           John Birdsong   Esquires
                           William Kennedy
                           Charles Sims

Daniel Brown Esquire produced a licence from the Honourable

19 Henry Pendleton ACdamus, Burk, John F. Grimke Esquires Associate Judges of the State of South Carolina to practice as an attorney in the Several Courts in this State, Ordered that he be admitted accordingly to plead in this Court.

William Shaw Esquire produced a Certificate from under the hand of the Honourable Henry Pendleton and the Rest of the associate Judge of the State of South Carolina Certifying that he was admitted to practice the Law as an attorney in the Several Courts in this State, which being Read, Ordered that he be admitted accordingly to plead in this Court.

Jacob Brown Esquire produced a Licence from under the Hand of the Honourable Henry Pendleton Aldamus Burk and J. F. Grimke Esquires associate Judges of the State of South Carolina to practice the Law as an attorney in the Several Court in this State which being Read, Ordered that he be admitted Accordingly to plead in this Court.

Ordered that the Goal and Stokes be Recorded that were let out by the Consent and agreement of the Court, the Goal to Benajah Thompson for the sum of Ninety nine pounds, and the Stocks to John McCooll for the sum of Seven pounds by Order of Court.

Present Zachariah Bullock Esquire
An Indenture of Lease & Release...Between Thomas Brandon of the One part and Thomas Young of the other part, for one hundred and seven acres of Land was acknowledged by the said Thomas Brandon which is Ordered to be Recorded.

An Indenture of Lease and Release Between Thomas Brandon of the one part and James Bell of the other part, for one hundred acres of Land acknowledged by the said Thomas Brandon to the said James Bell which is Ordered to be Recorded.

An Indenture of Lease and Release Between Thomas Brandon of the One part and John Brandon of the Other part for One hundred and twenty five acres of Land acknowledged by the said Thomas Brandon to the said John Brandon Ordered to be Recorded.

16

An Indenture of Deed of Conveyance Between Robert Looney
of the One part and George Marchbanks of the Other part,
Ordered by the Court to be Recorded.

An Indenture of Lease and Release Between John McWhorter
of the One part and John George of the Other part, for
80 acres of Land which is Ordered to be Recorded.

An Indenture and Deed of Conveyance Between Francis
Wilkie of the one part and Nocholes Curry of the Other Part
for two hundred acres of Land which is ordered to be
recorded.

20 An Indenture and Deed of Mortagage Between Davis Wilkie of
the One part and Lewis Aikins of the Other part for two
hundred acres of Land Ordered to be Recorded.

An Indenture of Lease and Release Between Emanuel Stephens
of the One part, and William Lawson of the Other part, for
One hundred acres of Land Ordered that the same be Recorded.

James Woodson together with Aaron Fincher his Security
came into Court who Entered into and acknowledged their
Bonds to the County, in the sum of One hundred pounds. for
the said James Woodson on Which he obtained a Licence to
keep a Tavern or public House in this Our County Ordered
that the same be kept according to Law.

John McCooll together with James Bell has Security came
into Court who Entered into and acknowledged their Bonds
to the County in the sum of One hundred pounds for the said
John McCooll by which he Obtained a Licence to keep a
Tavern or publick house in this Our County. Ordered that
the same be kept according to Law.

Ordered that in future no person be allowed to practice as
a Lawyer or a pleader in this Court without producing his
admission to the Bar from the Judges of the Court of Common
pleas.

Ordered that James Yancy Esqr. having been previously
admitted in this Court be the only Exception to the above
Order and that he produce his Credentials at June Court
next.

An Indenture and Deed of Conveyance Between Daniel McElduff
of the One part, and Robt. Creanshaw of the other part on
Tygar River Bounded on the One Side by Land laid out to
William Hill on the Other side by land laid out to William
Hardwick acknowledged by him the said Daniel McElduff to the
said Robert Creanshaw. Ordered to be Recorded.

An Indenture and Deed of Conveyance Between Thomas Gorden
of the One part, and James Orr of the Other part for One
hundred acres of Land proved by the Oaths of Major Samuel
Otterson and Charles Sims Esquire and Ordered to be
Recorded.

An Indenture and Deed of Conveyance Between Joseph Frankling
of the One part, and James Beuford of the Other part, for
Seventy five acres of Land acknowledged by the said
Joseph Frankling to the said James Beuford which is

Ordered to be Recorded.

An Indenture and Deed of Conveyance Between William Hendley
of the One part, and John Reed of the Other part, for forty
Eight acres of Land acknowledged by the said William
Hendley to the said John Reed Ordered to be Recorded.

21 An Indenture and Deed of Conveyance Between Caleb Gassaway
and wife and Susannah Moore of the One part, and Benjamin
Johnson of the other part four hundred acres of Land
Ordered to be Recorded.

An Indenture of Lease and Release Between Francis Posey
of the One part and Nathan Arthurberry of the other part
for four hundred acres of Land and the Same Ordered to be
Recorded.

State   Plaintiff   ) The Defendant appearing to
   against   ) answer the Complaint of the
William Hendley Defendant) Grand Jury on a presentment
                              is by the Court dismissed on
                              paying Costs.

State   Plaintiff)
   against   ) Bastardy
Ann Stone Defendant) Nehemiah Miller Surrenders the
                       Defendant in discharge of his
Recognizance Ordered that the Sheriff Take the Defendant
into Custody-afterwards she is by the Court discharged
on paying Costs.

A Bond for the Title of Land Between Joseph Robison of the
One part, and Thomas McGrue of the other part for One
hundred acres of Land laying on both sides of Abbingtons
which is ordered to be Recorded.
Proved by the Oath of Moses Guyton an assignment on the
said Bond from the said Thomas McGuire to Robert Whitley
Ordered to be Recorded.

Signed by   Zachariah Bullock
                           John Birdsong   Esquires
                           Thomas Brandon

At a Court Continued and held by adjournment in and for the
County of Union at the house of John McCooll the twenty
seventh day of December in the year of our Lord One
thousand and seven hundred and Eighty five and of the
Independence of the United States of America the Tenth.

Present   Zachariah Bullock
                           William Kennedy
                           Thomas Brandon   Esquires
                           John Birdsong

A Bill of Sale Between Gabriel Brown of the One part and
Colonel William Farr of the Other part for four Negroes
Viz Silvy Chaney Jesse and Dublin proved by the Oaths of
Colonel Thomas Brandon and Samuel Otterson Justices then of
the Peace. Ordered that the same be Recorded.

An Indenture of Lease and Release Between John Brandon
and Mary his wife of the One part and William Kennedy

18

Esquire of the Other part, for two hundred acres of Land, proved by the Oaths of Thomas Vance and Evan Thomas Witness thereunto and Ordered to be Recorded.

22 An Indenture of Lease and Release Between Moses Stevens of the One part and Thomas Blassingame of the Other part for One hundred and Eighty Seven acres and of half of Land Ordered that the same be Recorded.

State   Plaintiff)
  against   )   Ordered that the Defendant
Benjamin Long   Defendant)   Benjamin Long Enter into a
                              Recognizance together with
Henry Long and Colonel William Farr his Securitys and acknowledge the same for the appearance of the said Benjamin Long at next Ninety Six Court.

A Commission from his Excellency William Moultrie Esquire Governor and Commander in Chief in and over the State of South Carolina directed to William Kennedy Esquire to be Coroner in and for the County of Union was produced in Court by the said William Kennedy which was Read. and the Oath administered. Required by Law and the same ordered to be Recorded.

State of South Carolina
             By his Excellency William Moultrie Esquire
(Seal)   Governor and Commander in Chief in and of the
             State aforesaid
                   To William Kennedy Esquire
                            Greeting

William   Know Ye that I Reposing a Special Trust and
Moultrie   Confidence in your abilities Care, Prudince and
           Integrety have Commissioned Constituted and
           appointed and by these presents do Commission
           Constitute and appoint you the said William
           Kennedy to be Coroner in and for the County of
           Union in the said State to Have Hold Exercise
           and Enjoy the said Office of Corner together
           with all Rights Priveledges Profits and Emolu-
           ments to the said Office belonging or in any
           wise appertaining

By his   Given under my hand and Seal this ninth
Excellency's day of October in the year of Our Lord
Command   One Thousand Seven hundred and Eighty five
              and of the Sovereignity and Independence of
              the United States of America the Tenth.

              Present. James Harrison Esquire

State   )
  against) Bastardy
Sarah Page) Upon Examination of the Defendant it appears
              to the Court that the Defendant is guilty
whereupon she is corrected and fined three pounds Eleven Shillings and Costs of Suit to be paid next Court into the Treasury.

23 The Court Nominates and appoints William Kennedy Esquire County Treasurer for this County and the same Office is by him accepted.

Ordered that Seven pounds two Shillings and Six pence be paid into the Treasury be the fines of William Beckham and Hannah Still Received persuant to the Order last Court.

An Indenture of Lease and Release Between John Steen and Martha his wife of the One part and Francis Lettimore of the Other part was by the said John Steen and Martha is wife acknowledge for two hundred acres of Land and Ordered to be Recorded.

The Court proceeded to lay a Tax on the Inhabitants of the County to defray the necessary Expences, it is therefore Resolved that Each Negro Slave Residing in this County is Taxed with the sum of Eight pence per head, the first Quality of land pr Hundred acres One Shilling and one penny half penny the Second Quality at Seven pence, the third Quality five pence the fourth Quality three pence pr Hundred acres. Ordered that a Copy of this Tax be by the Clerk delivered to the Sheriff, and the Sheriff do Collect the same as soon as possible.

Ordered that the Treasurer William Kennedy Esquire Deliver unto Benajah Thompson all the fines that are deposited in the Treasury or in his hands. Whereupon the said William Kennedy paid in Open Court Seven pounds two Shillings and three pence unto the said Benajah Thompson in behalf of the County.

James Hilhouse)
  against   ) Debt.
John Steen   ) The Defendant Came into Court in his Own
                  proper person and acknowledged himself
Indebted to the plaintiff the Sum of Eleven pounds Eleven Shillings and three pence, Whereupon the Court award Judgment against him for the same and Costs of Suit.

Hugh Saxton)
  agt.   ) Debt.
James Gibbs) The Defendant Came into Court and acknowledged
            he owed the plaintiff nine pounds five
Shillings and Eight pence half penny according to Specially & Confesses Judgment for the same with Cost of Suit.

Samuel Farrow   Plaintiff)
  against   ) Debt.
Nathaniel Henderson Defendant) Then Came into Court the
                        plaintiff by James Yancy
his attorney and Complained by his petition that the defendt. Owed him One pound five Shillings, whereupon it is considered by the Court that the Plaintiff Recover against the Defendant the same and Costs of Suit.

Thomas Brandon & Co)
  against   ) Debt.
Daniel Jackson) When Came the Plaintiff by James
              Yancy their attorney, also Came the
Defendant in his Own proper person and acknowledged himself

20

indebted to the plaintiffs the sum of twelve pounds
Eighteen Shillings and one penny, and Confessed Judgment
for the Same with Costs of Suit.

Thomas Brandon & Co.   Plaintiff)
  against   )   Debt.
Daniel Jackson   Defendant)   When Came into Court the
                                             plaintiff by James
Yancey their attorney on their petition, also Came the
Defendant in his Own proper person and confessed Judgment
for One pound three Shillings and Cost of Suit which was by
the Court Decreed accordingly.

James Odare   Plaintiff)
  against   )   Debt.
William Steen   Defendant)   When Came into Court the
                                       plaintiff by James Yancy his
attorney, also Came the Defendant in his own proper person
and acknowledged himself Indebted to the plaintiff fourteen
pounds five shillings according to specially and confesses
Judgment for the same with Costs of Suit whereupon the
plaintiff by his attorney aforesaid agree to Stay.
Execution against the Defendant for three months.

Robert Lusk   Plaintiff)
  against   )   Debt.
James Shockley Defendant)   Came the plaintiff by William
                                       Shaw his attorney on a petition
also Came the Defendant in his own proper person and acknowledged he owed the plaintiff three pounds five shillings
and six pence, and also Confesses Judgment for the same
with Costs of Suit which was by the Court decreed accordingly

John Hampton   Plaintiff)
  against   )   Debt on attachment
David Adams   Defendant)   When came the plaintiff by James
                                       Yancy his attorney and the
Defendant being Solemnly Called but not appearing on a
Writ of Enquiry Judgment is awarded against the Defendant
for Eleven pounds two Shillings and cost of suit.

A Bill of Sale Between Elizabeth Burk of the one part and
Colonel Thomas Brandon of the Other part was proved by the
Oaths of William Farr, also the said Colonel Thomas Brandon
acknowledged the assignment of the said Bill of Sale to
Samuel Cooper and the whole is Ordered to be Recorded.

25 An Indenture of Deed of Conveyance Between Francis
McNamary the one part, and Charles Clanton of the other
part for three hundred acres of Land was proved in Court
by the Oaths of John Ewart and Absolam Petty Witnesses
thereunto and Ordered to be Recorded.

John Bird   Plaintiff)
  against   )   Debt.
William Smith   Defendant)   When Came the plaintiff into
                                       Court also Came the Defendant
in their Own proper persons and there agree to Discontinue
the Suit at the plaintiffs Cost which is by the Court
Ordered accordingly.

James Felse   Plaintiff)
   against   ) Debt
James Blasingame Defendant) When Came the plaintiff into
                              Court in his Own proper
person and the Defendant by Daniel Brown his attorney and
there agree to discontinue the suit at the plaintiffs
Costs which is by the Court Ordered according.
                    Court adjourned untill tomorrow
Signed by   Zachariah Bullock
                            William Kennedy
                            Thomas Brandon
                            Charles Sims

At a Continued and held by adjournment at the House of
John McCooll in and for the County of Union the twenty
Eight day of December in the year of Our Lord one thousand
Eight hundred and Eighty five and of the Independence of
the United States of America the Tenth.

Present   William Kennedy
                            Thomas Brandon   Esquires
                            Charles Sims
                            John Birdsong

Ordered that a Road from Grindal Shoals the directest and
best way to Union Courthouse by John Haile, William Buchan-
nan and John Palmore...it is further Ordered that the same
Road be laid out by the John Hail William Buchannah and
John Palmore from the said Shoal to the Duck Pond and
Ordered that it be laid out from the said Duck Pond by
Colonel Thomas Brandon and William Kennedy Esquire to
Union Courthouse...it is further Ordered that Abner
Colman be appointed Overseer on the said Road from the
said Shoal to the first waters on Brown's Creek, and from
thence on same Road Joseph Jones appointed Overseer to
Union Courthouse.

26 A Bill of Sale Between William Jackson of the One part and
Thomas Brandon of the Other part, for three Negroes Viz
Reachel Ossey and Abraham bearing date the thirteenth day
of September One thousand Seven hundred and Eighty five.
Ordered to be Recorded.

Present   Zachariah Bullock
                            James Harrison   Esquires

Ordered that the Executors of the Estate of Daniel Shaw be
Sited to appear at our next Court in Order to answer the
Complaint of Arthur Simpson Exhibited against them.

State   Plaintiff)
   against   ) When Came the Defen-
James & Martha Bensons Defendant) dants into Court the
                              fully hearing their
defence it is Ordered by the Court that they be dismissed
from their Recognizance on paying Cost which is done
accordingly.

John Hampton)
   against   ) Debt on attachment
David Adams)

22

Tobithia Pearson being Summonded as a garnishee and sworn
accordingly saith that she has of the property of the
Defendant David Adams in her hands nine pounds Eight
Shillings and two pence half penny Sterling forty Eight
yards of Brown Linen being the Balance of a Consideration
money due to the said David Adams for a negroe Boy Named
Bob: Judgment awarded against the said Tobithia Pearson
accordingly for the Same.

Ordered that the following Deposition be Recorded.
State South Carolina)
Union County   )   This day Came into Court James
Hamilton and being duly Sworn according to Law Made Oath
and Saith that he was personally acquainted with James and
Susannah Bole as Husband and Wife, and that he heard it
publickly

26 Report that Susannah Bole had a Son named James Bole and
that he has been acquainted with the same James Bole Junior
part in the State of Pennsylvania and that the said James
Bole Junior was the Reputed Son and heir of the said James
Bole Senior and that he never heard any Report to the
Contrary and that he lived in the same Neighborhood with
the said James Bole in the State of Pennsylvania in Chester
County any thing further he saith not Sworn before us the
twenty Eight day of December One thousand seven hundred and
Eighty five
                        Zachariah Bullock JP
                        William Kennedy JP
                        Charles Sims JP
                        John Birdsong JP

27 Richard Cox   Plaintiff)
     against   )   TrO. &C
   Luke Carrell   Defendant) The plaintiff being Solmenly
                        Called to come and prosecute his
Suit, but came not whereupon the Defendant by Daniel Brown
his attorney On Motion it is Ordered that the plaintiff be
Nonsuited and the Defendant Recover against the plaintiff
five Shillings Damages and Cost of Suit.

   Caleb Gassaway   Plaintiff)
     against   )   Debt.
   Thomas Taylor   Defendant) The Defendant being Solemnly
                        called came not to the defendt
the suit on Motion of the plaintiff by James Yancy his
attorney a Default is awarded against the Defendant.

   Ann Robison   Plaintiff)
     against   )   Slander
   John Steen   Defendant) When came into Court the plaintiff
                        by James Yancy her attorney and
also the Defendant in his Own proper person and Confessed
Judgment for One penny Damages and Costs of Suit which is
Ordered to be Recorded accordingly.

   John Thomas Senr. Plaintiff)
     against   )   Debt
   John Steen   Defendant) When Came the plaintiff into
                        Court by James Yancy his
attorney, also Came the Defendant in his own proper person
and acknowledged that he Owed the plaintiff five pounds

23

One Shilling according to Specially and Confessed Judgment
for the same and Costs of Suit.

Thomas Brandon & Co.   Plaintiffs)
  against   )   Debt.
Merry Maguire   Defendant)   When Came into Court the
                                     plaintiffs by James Yancy
their attorney on petition also the Defendant in his Own
proper person the Court on hearing the Complaint of the
plaintiff also the Defence of the Defendant, Decree
against the Defendant four pounds Seventeen Shillings and
four pence and Costs of Suit.

John Thomas Junr.   Plaintiff)
  against   )   Debt.
John Steen   Defendant)   When Came into Court the
                                 Plaintiff by James Yancy his
attorney, also the Defendant in his Own proper person and
acknowledged that he Owed the plaintiff One pound fifteen
shillings according to specially and confesses Judgment for
the same with Costs of Suit and decreed according.

Thomas Blassingame   Plaintiff)
  against   )   Debt
Archer Smith   Defendant)   When Came into Court the
                                  Plaintiff by his attorney
James Yancy and also the Defendant in his Own proper
person and acknowledged that he Owed the plaintiff four
pounds five shillings and seven pence and Confessed Judgment
for the same according to Note and Costs of Suit.

Thomas Brandon & Co.   Plaintiff)
  against   )   Debt
William McElduff   Defendant)   Came the plaintiffs into
                                    Court by James Yancy their
attorney on petition and the Defendant being Solemnly
Called Not appearing but maketh Default the Court on
hearing the Complaint of the Plaintiff decree against the
defendant four pounds five shillings and six pence with
Costs of Suit.

Thomas Brandon & Co.   Plaintiff)
  against   )   Debt
Job Hammonds   Defendant)   Came into Court the
                                    plaintiff by James Yancy
28 their attorney also came the defendant in his Own person
and acknowledged that he owed the plaintiffs three pounds
and one shilling and also Confessed Judgment for the same
with Costs of Suit.

John Gorden   )
  against   )   Debt
William Mayfield)   Came the plaintiff into Court by his
                    attorney James Yancy by a petition, and
also the Defendant by William his attorney, Whereupon the
plaintiff agree to Suffer a nonsuit whereupon it is
Considered by the Court that the Defendant Recover against
the plaintiff five shillings Damages and Costs of Suit which
is ordered accordingly.

24

Thomas Brandon & Co.   Plaintiff)
  against   ) Debt
Harrison Nicholas   Defendant) Came into Court the plain-
                                   tiff by James Yancy his
attorney and the Defendant being Solemnly called came not
to defend the said Suit Whereupon it is Ordered that there
be a Default Entered up against him.

William Farr   Plaintiff)
  against   ) Debt on attachment
William Wafford   Defendant) Came the plaintiff by William
                               Shaw his attorney and
Complained on the said attachment and the defendant
being Solemnly called Came not to defend or to answer the
Complaint Whereupon the Court awarded Judgment against the
Defendant for one hundred and fifty paper dollars in April
One thousand seven hundred and seventy nine Equal to three
pounds twelve Shillings and three pence half penny and Costs
of suit.

29 John Fondrin   Plaintiff)
     against   ) Case on attachment
   Archibald Rutherford   Defendant) Came the plaintiff by his
                                      attorney Jaceb Brow
into Court and Continue the Suit untill next Court.

State, plaintiff against Gidion Mayfield, Defendant.
Ordered to be dismissed on the Defendant paying Costs.

An Indenture Between Joseph McCord of the One part, and
William McJunken of the Other part when the said Joseph
McCord is bound to the said William McJunkin was proved
by the Oaths of Jeptthah Hollingsworth bearing date the
first day of February One thousand seven and Eighty four.

Merry Maguire Motion to the Court for a Licence to keep a
Tavern or Public House which is granted to him on Giving
Bond and Security to the Clerk.

State   Plaintiff)
  agt   ) Swaring Profanely
Hugh Holland & Defendants) It appearing to the Court
Caleb Gassaway   ) that the Defendants were
                             guilty whereupon the Court
fine each in the sum of four shillings and Eight pence and
Costs whereupon the Defendant Caleb Gassaway paid the said
Fine of four shillings and Eight pence.

Thomas Brandon atty for James Campbell against James
Ainsworth. Debt on attachment. Came into Court Isaac
Bogan being Summonsed a Garnishee and on Oath saith that he
has in his hands Eleven pounds Eight Shillings and four
pence of the property of the Defendant James Ainsworth
being the Balance of a Note of hand for four hundred
pounds former Currency.
          Signed by   William Kennedy JP
                             Thomas Brandon JP
                             John Birdsong JP

At a Court Continued & held by adjournment at the House of
John McCord the 29th day of December 1785 and of the Independence of the United States of America the Twelveth in

25

and for the County of Union.
Present   Zachariah Bullock
                       William Kennedy   Esquires
                       Thomas Brandon
                       John Birdsong

30 State   )
   against   )   Nusance
   John Albritain)   The Grand Jury presented the Defendant for
                      being Drunk & the Defendant Pleaded
guilty and fined by the Court three Shillings and Six
pence Whereupon he paid the same to the Treasurer and
Dismissed.

Joseph & Samuel McJunkin's Report to the Court that in
pursuance of the Order of Court to them directed they
have laid Out the Road from the Court house to Samuel
McJunkens the nearest and best way which is approved of by
the Court. It is therefore Ordered that Isaac Hawkins be
and is hereby appointed Overseer of the same Road laid out
as aforesaid.

Joseph McJunkins is appointed Overseer of the Road from
Samuel McJunkins to the Swift Run and it is Ordered that
he keep the same Road in Good Repair.

John Wilson is appointed Overseer of the Road from the
Swift Run to Hamelton's Ford on Tygar River and it is
Ordered that he keep the same in Good Repair.

John Bankhead appointed Overseer of the Road from Clerk's
Ferry on Broad River to where the same Road will Cross
Thickety Creek it is Ordered that he keep the same in good
Repair.

Hugh Taylor is appointed Overseer of the Road from
Thickety Creek untill it Comes into the Road leading to
Major Charles Miles Ordered that he keep the same Road in
Good Repair.

Ordered that Robert Lusk be and is appointed to lay out the
Road from Clerk's Ferry on Broad River to the Road Leading
to Major Charles Miles's.

James Sims appointed Overseer of the Road from Hollingsworth's old place on Canes Creek to the said James Sims
place where Towns formerly lived on Tygar River. Ordered
that he keep the same in good Repair.

Ordered that James Sims keep a Ferry over Tygar River at
his place where Towns formerly lived and Receive the following Rates Viz for a Waggon and Team One Shilling and Six
pence, for a Man and Horse three pence for a Rowling
Hodgshead and Team nine pence for a loaded cart and Team
One Shilling and Other two Wheeled Carriages the same,
One penney per head for all live Stock Ferried of Sweamed
over by the said Ferryman---Ordered that the same fees be
paid and the same is hereby rated for all persons that well
maintain a good Flat with Such attendance as is allowed by
Law on the said River within our County.
Ordered that Ephraim Clerk be Licenced to keep a public
ferry.

26

31 on Broad River & Receive the following Rates Viz for a
Waggon and Team two Shillings and four pence; for a Man
and horse four pence, for a Rowling Hogdshead and Team One
Shilling for a Loaded Cart and Team and Other two wheeled
Carriages one Shilling and Two pence, for Sweaming Horses
and all other Cattle two pence per head, for Hogs and Sheep
One penny half penny Ordered that all Ferrys on Broad
River be paid the Same Fees, and the same is hereby Rated
for all persons that will Maintain a good Flatt with Such
attendance as is allowed by Law on the said River within
our County Ordered that the Overseers on the Road leading
to the Fords near or at the Ferrys on Tygar and Broad
Rivers be kept Open within Our County.

In the Case of the State against William Beckham for
Bastardy Hannah Still the Prosecutrix it fully appearing
that the said William Beckham having Settled with John
Still Father to the said Hannah Still on her hehalf to the
Satisfaction of the Court, and is by the said Court
acquitted of everything Brought against him by the said
Hannah Still as may appear by his Records.

Ordered that a Way be laid out by John Savage, Isaac
Gregory and William Farr, From Farr's Schoolhouse on the
Waters of Ned's Creek the Best way to Union Courthouse.

Ordered that upon the Resignation and Removal of James
Harrison Esquire One of the Justices of this County. that
John Thompson Junior be and is appointed a Justice of the
said County in the Room of James Harrison Esquire

Ordered that John Birdsong and William Kennedy Esquires be
and is appointed to view & Receive the Goal when Finished
and done According to agreement.

Ordered that the County Treasurer pay all the money that
Comes into his Hands towards the defraying the Expences of
the Building of the Goal.

An Indenture of Lease and Release Between Samuel Farrow
of the One part and William Buchannan of the other part,
for One hundred and fifty acres of Land proved by the Oaths
of Alexander McDougall and Thomas Stribling Junior
Witnesses thereunto and Ordered to be Recorded.

An Indenture of Lease and Release Between Joab Mitchel
of the One part, and Richard Hawkins of the other part for
three hundred acres of Land is ordered to be Recorded

32 An Indenture of Lease and Release Between Samuel Farrow
of the One part and Thomas Stribling of the other part, for
three hundred acres of Land proved by the Oaths of Alexander
McDougal and William Buchannan Witnesses thereunto Ordered
to be Recorded.

Ordered that John Birdsong and Charles Sims Esquires be
and is appointed to Inspect the Clerk's Office.

Joseph Hughes   Plaintiff)
   against   ) Ordered that a Commission or
James Shockley   Defendant) a Dedemus polestatum Issue to

27

Major Johnson and Captain Thompson Justices of the Peace
in the County of Louisa in the State of Virginia to take
the Deposition of Nelson Anderson Junior and James Burley
and that the same be admitted in Evidence on the Trials
on the behalf of the plaintiff.

Grand Jury
1. Samuel McJunkins
2. William Young
3. James Bogan
4. Jeptha Hollingsworth
5. Nathan Glenn
6. Elias Hollingsworth
7. Bird Beuford
8. Philip Anderson
9. Nehemiah Howard
10. James Mays
11. Robert Harris
12. William Tate
13. James Terrill
14. Edward Tilman
15. John Read
16. Benjamin Savage
17. Nicholas Jasper
18. Hezekiah Rice
19. Thomas MacDonald

Petit Jury
1. John Beckham
2. Abner Colman
3. William Shaw
4. Moses Giyton
5. Alexander McDougal
6. Elishia Green
7. William Giles
8. Hugh Nelson
9. Jacob Brown
10. James Thomas
11. Jeremiah Gregory
12. John Alertain
13. Benjamin Johnson
14. Wm. Ragsdale
15. Robert Creanshaw
16. James Gassaway
17. George Lineman
18. William Glen
19. Samuel Cooper
20. John Wilson
21. Ely Cook
22. Thomas Young
23. Thomas Greer
24 John Blassingame Junr.
25. John Story

Ordered that Joseph Jolly be sited to appear before the
Justices of Our said Court and the next Court to be held
for the said County to answer the Compalint Lodged against
him in regard of the Orphans of John Jolly Deceased.

Ordered that John Birdsong and Thomas Brandon Esquires
be and is appointed to Contract with Workman to build a
log house with a
33 Cabin Roof twenty four by Sixteen feet with a Rough plank
foor with doors and windows &C. &C...&C Seals &C &C.

Ordered that the Clerk draw a Deed from the Original for
two acres of Land Given to the County by Colonel Brandon
where the Courthouse is to Stand.

An Indenture and Deed of Conveyance Between John Letta
of the One part and Robert Wallace of the Other part, for
two hundred and seventy eight acres of Land proved by the
Oaths of John Birdsong and John Thomas Witnesses thereunto
and Ordered to be Recorded
Signed by   Zachariah Bullock
                             William Kennedy
                             John Birdsong

At a Court begun and held in and for the County of Union
at the Courthouse of the said County the twenty seventh
day of March in the year of Our Lord One thousand seven
hundred and Eighty six and of the Independence of the
United States of America the Tenth

28

```
Present                    William Kennedy
                           Thomas Brandon    Esquires
                           John Birdsong
```

```
The County to John McCooll Debtor
To Building the Stocks and Pillory                    L7.0..0
To finding plant & doing the Inside of the
   Courthouse                                            4"
           March 27th 1786                      L 11.0..0
```

An Indenture and Deed of Conveyance Between Lewis Ledbetter
of the One part and James Petty of the other part, for two
hundred acres of Land was proved by the Witness thereunto
Subscribed and Ordered to be Recorded.

An Indenture and Deed of Conveyance Between James Terrell
of the One part and Moses Qualls of the other part, for
one hundred and thirty four acres of Land was by the said
James Terrell acknowledged to the said Moses Qualls and
Ordered to be Recorded.

Ordered that James Shockley be and is appointed a Constable
for this County and Took the Oath Required by Law.

An Indenture of Lease and Release Between William Wafford
Senior of the one part and Thomas Brandon fo the Other part
for one hundred and fifty acres of Land proved by the Oaths
of James Yancy and William Shaw Witnesses thereunto and
Ordered to be Recorded.

34 Charles Goodwin Esquire attorney at Law on his producing
his Credentials at Our next Court was admitted to plead in
the Court which is Ordered accordingly.

An Indenture of Lease and Release Between Joseph Little of
the one part and Bazel Wheat of the other part, for one
hundred and fifty acres of Land proved by the Oaths of John
Haild and Jonathan Stokes witnesses thereunto Ordered to be
Recorded.

An Indenture and Deed of Conveyance between Robert Whitley
of the one part, and Moses Guyton of the other part for one
hundred acres of Land is Ordered to be recorded.

An Indenture and Deed of Conveyance between Moses Guyton
of the one part, and John Leek of the other part. for one
hundred acres of Land is Ordered to be Recorded.

An Indenture of Lease and Release between Alexander
Johnson of the one part and Joseph Guyton of the other part
for Sixty acres of Land is ordered to be recorded.

An Indenture and Deed of Conveyance Between Jacob Garner
of the one part, and Isaac Parker of the Other part for
ninety acres of Land proved by the Oaths of Moses Guyton
and John Moorehead as Witnesses thereunto and ordered to
be Recorded.

An Indenture and Deed of Conveyance Between Elias Palmer
and Ann his wife of the one part and John White of the
other part for One hundred and fifty acres of Land is
Ordered to be Recorded.

An Indenture of Lease and Release between Elizabeth
Rinchard of the one part and John McPherson of the other
part, for One hundred acres of Land is ordered to be
Recorded.

Elishia Green be and is appointed Constable for this
County and Took the Oath Required by Law.

An Indenture of Lease and Release between William Pearson
of the one part, and Tobithia Pearson of the other part for
two hundred and Eighty acres of Land proved by the Oaths of
Robert Barns and William Martindale Witnesses thereunto
and Ordered to be Recorded.

An indenture of Deed of Conveyance Between John White of
the One part and William Mays of the other part for two
hundred and fifty acres of Land acknowledged by the said
John White to the said William Mays. Ordered to be
Recorded--also Peggy White wife of the said John White
acknowledged her right of Dower which is Ordered to be
Recorded.

35 An Indenture of Lease and Release Between Edmond Hays and
Jamima his wife of the one part, and John Hames of the
other part, for One hundred and Twenty five acres of Land
proved by the Oaths of Evan Thomas and John Palmore Witnesses thereunto and Ordered to be Recorded.

Charles Johnson   Plaintiff)
  against   )   Debt on attachment
Thomas Smith   Defendant)   On Motion of Jacob Brown
                                  attorney for the plaintiff
Benjamin Johnson Summonsed a Garnishee is Sworn and on
Oath saith that he hath in his hands Sixty pounds Virginia
Money the property of the Defendant Thomas Smith.

An Indenture and Deed of Conveyance Between Robert Looney
of the one part, and John Jefferies of the other part, for
six hundred acres of Land proved by the witness thereunto
subscribed and Ordered to be Recorded.

An Indenture and Deed of Conveyance between William Smith
of the one part and John Foster of the other part, for
two hundred acres of land ordered to be recorded.

An Indenture and Deed of Conveyance between Rydarus Clark
of the one part, and John Foster of the other part, for two
hundred acres of Land ordered to be recorded.

An indenture and Deed of Conveyance between James Love of
the one part and Ryderus Clark of the other part, for
thirty one acres of Land is ordered to be recorded.

An Indenture of Conveyance of Lease and Release between
Henry Clark of the one part and John Foster of the other
part, for one hundred and Eighty acres of Land is ordered
to be recorded.

An indenture and Deed of Conveyance Between John & Daniel
McElduff of the one part and Stephen Creanshaw of the other
part for two hundred acres of Land; proved by the Oaths of
William Farr and William Hardwick & ordered to be recorded.

30

Ordered that Thomas Scales be and is hereby appointed
Guardian to the Orphans of George Scales Deceased on
Giving Bond with Nehemiah Howard Security in the Sum of
One hundred pounds, Whereupon the said Thomas Scales
together with the said Nehemiah Howard his Security
Entered into and acknowledged their Bonds in the sum of
One hundred pounds for Securing the said Orphans Estate.

36 William Farr high Sheriff of our County pursuant to a
Commission and act of assembly Nominated John Gregory
Deputy Sheriff in and for the County of Union which meet
with the Coneroorence and approbation of the Court, where-
upon the said John Gregory took the presscribed by the
act of assembly and entered into the Execution of the said
Office by Order of Court
Signed   William Kennedy
                          Thomas Brandon
                          John Birdsong

A a Court continued and held by adjournment at the Court-
house of the said County the twenty eight day of March
One thousand seven hundred and Eighty six and of the
Independence of the United States of America the Tenth
Present   William Kennedy
                          Thomas Brandon   Esquires
                          John Birdsong

An Indenture and Deed of Conveyance Between Ralph Rogers
of the One part and Henry Smith of the other part, for two
hundred acres of Land Ordered to be Recorded.

An Indenture and Deed of Conveyance Between Robert
Montgomery of the one part and Thomas Kennedy of the other
part, acknowledged by the said Robert Montgomery to the
said Thomas Kennedy for one hundred and seven acres of
Land and Ordered to be Recorded.

An Indenture and Deed of Conveyance Between Robert Montgomery of the one part, and James Kennedy of the other
part, for eighty nine acres of Land acknowledged by the
said Robert Montgomery to the said James Kennedy and
Ordered to be Recorded.

An Indenture of Lease and Release Between James Fannin
of the One part, and Charles Thompson of the other part for
two hundred acres of Land proved by the Oaths of John
Ewart and William Thompson Witnesses thereunto and
Ordered to be Recorded.
                    Fannen Wife to the said James
Fannen acknowledged her Right of Dower to the said Land
which is ordered to be Recorded.

An Indenture of Lease and Release Between Alexander Walker
of the One part and Rydarus Clark of the other part for
one hundred acres of Land Ordered to be Recorded.

37 An Indenture and Deed of Conveyance Between Charles Clanton
of the One part and Absolam Petty of the other part, for
one hundred acres of Land acknowledged by the said Charles
Clanton to the said Absolam Petty and Ordered to be
Recorded.

Zachariah Hammond)   The plaintiff comes into Court by his
   agt.   )   attorney Daniel Brown & Move for an
Robert Montgomery)   Execution against the Defendant Robert
                     Montgomery by Virtue of a Judgment
from the State of North Carolina which is over Ruled by
the Court, and this Motion Ordered to be dismissed at the
plaintiffs Costs.

An Indenture of Lease and Release Between Joseph Burson
and Mary his wife of the one part, and Evan Thomas of the
other part, for One hundred and fifty acres of Land, proved
by the Oaths of William Little and William Nix Witnesses
thereunto and ordered to be recorded.

An Indenture of Lease and Release Between Thomas Briggs
of the one part, and Thomas Tod of the other part, for One
hundred acres of Land by the Oaths of Edward Musgrove and
Thomas Layton Witnesses thereunto and ordered to be
Recorded, Catherine Briggs wife of the said Thomas Briggs
acknowledged her right of Dower which is Ordered to be
Recorded.

An Indenture and Deed of Conveyance Between Aaron Fincher
and Mary his wife of the one part, and Moses Collier of the
other part, for One hundred acres of Land, acknowledged
by the said Aaron Fincher to the said Moses Collier
Ordered to
The said Mary Fincher wife of the said Arron Fincher
acknowledged her Right of Dower to the said Land Ordered
that the same be Recorded.

An Indenture and Deed of Conveyance Between Aaron Fincher
and Mary his wife of the one part, and Ann Esther and Mary
Colliers of the other part, for one hundred acres of Land
acknowledged by the said Aaron Fincher to the said Ann
Esther and Mary Colliers Ordered to be Recorded.
The said Mary Fincher wife of the said Aaron Fincher
acknowledged her Right of Dower to the said Land Ordered
that the same be Recorded.

An Indenture of Lease and Release Between Thomas Blasingame
of the one part, and Bazel Wheat of the Other part, for One
hundred and fifty acres of Land acknowledged by the said
Thomas Blasingame to the said Bazel Wheat and Ordered to
be Recorded.

An Indenture of Lease and Release between Thomas Bishop
of the one part, and William Martindale of the other part,
for two hundred and sixteen acres proved by the Oaths of
Robert Burns and James Campbell Witnesses thereunto and
Ordered to be Recorded.

38 The Grand Jury to Wit Samuel McJunkin (Foreman) James
Terrell, Edward Tillman, Thomas McDaniel, Nehemiah Howard,
William Young, John Read, Bird Beuford, Nathan Glenn,
Barnard Glenn, Hezekiah Rice, James Bogan, Philip Anderson,
having Received their Chairge Retered from the Barr to
Consult their Verdict and attended by Elishia Green
Constable who is Sworn according to Law.

A Deed of Gift Between Daniel Thomas of the One part and
Sarah Thomas of the other part, for One Negroe named Beck,

32

proved by the Oaths of James and William Thomas Witnesses
thereunto and Ordered to be Recorded.

State   Plaintiff)
  against   )   Bastardy
Hannah Brown   Defendant)   Came into Court Robert Gregory
                             who being Returned Bail for the
Defendant, and Surrendered the said Defendant Hannah Brown
in discharge thereof and the same is admitted of by the
Court, Ordered that the Sheriff take the Defendant into
Custody which is done, The defendant pleased Guilty and
is fined by the Court, three pounds ten Shillings and the
Cost of Suit to be paid next Court. &C Upon William Farr
and John Gregory Entering themselves Security to keep her
said Bastard Child from being any charge or Expence to the
parish or County untill it be ten years of age the Defendant is thereby Release out of the Custody of the Sheriff
for the present time.

Elizabeth Bishop administrator   )
of Robert Bishop   Plaintiff)
  against   )   Debt
Henry Long   Defendant)

When Came the plaintiff by her attorney James Yancy and
filed his Declaration against the Defendant wherein he
complains that the defendant owes to the plaintiff thirty
two pounds two shillings and ten pence on Bond Sale in
the year One thousand seven hundred and Seventy nine and
that the defendant doth Refuse to pay the same whereupon
the plaintiff hath Sustance Damage &C
Whereupon came the defendant by her attorneys Daniel Brown
and William Shaw and defends the force and injury and whatsoever else they ought to defend and pleads no demand
according to the act of assembly for the Regulation of
Sheriffs Sales, payment and set off and this he prays may
be Enquired of by the County and the plaintiff prays also
the same. therefore the said parties by their attorneys
aforesaid agree to buy the Issue Joined; Whereupon Came also
a Jury To Wit, Alexander McDougal, George Lineman, William
Shaw, Stephen Creanshaw, Thomas Young, Abner Coleman,
William Glenn, Henry Storey, Christopher Brandon, Robert
Creanshaw, John Wilson, Hugh Nelson, who being drawn tried
and Sworn the truth to speak upon the Issue Joined upon
their Oaths do say that the Defendant doth owe the plaintiff
the sum of thirty two pounds two shillings and ten pence,
with one shilling damage and interest ammounting to
39 thirty four pounds seven shillings and Eleven pence with
Costs of suit whereupon it is ordered that the Verdict be
Recorded and that the plaintiff Recover against the
Defendant the Debt and Damages aforesaid in form aforesaid
and the said Defendant in money &C &C.

Benjamin Clark   Plaintiff)
  against   )   Debt
William Jackson Defendant   Defendant)   Whereupon the Sheriff
                             hath Returned that
the said Defendant William Jackson is not to be found within
his County. Whereupon the plaintiff Benjamin Clark by his
attorney Daniel Brown pray an attachment against the Estate
of the Defendant Returnable to our next Court which is
award him, Ordered that the same Issue

33

In the Case of Elizabeth Bishop administrator of Robert
Bishop against Henry Long wherein their is Judgment
Entered for the plaintiff the Defendant by his attorney
William Shaw Move for an appeal to the Court of Common
Pleas to be held at Ninety Six which is granted on the
Defendant Giving Bond and Security to prosecute the same
according to Law.

An Indenture Between Mary Scales and her son John of the
One part and Luzian Parlor of the other part is by the
Court Ordered to be Recorded.

Robert Lusk   Plaintiff)
  against   )   Debt
Samuel Pattent   Defendant)   Came the plaintiff into Court
                                by his Attorney William Shaw
on a Petition, also Came the Defendant in his own proper
person and acknowledged that he owed the plaintiff three
pounds two shillings and ten pence, and confessed Judgment
for the same with Cost of Suit. Ordered by the Court that
the same be Decreed against the Defendant.

John Montgomery plaintiff)
  against   )   Debt
Jonathan Jones Defendant)   Came the plaintiff into Court
                             by his Attorney Jacob Brown
and Compalined on petition against the Defendant, who being
Solemnly Called but came not to defend the complaint
on motion of the plaintiff by his attorney aforesaid it is
considered and decreed ag by the Court against the
Defendant for four pounds ten shillings and costs of suit.
Signed by   William Kennedy
                             John Birdsong
                             Thomas Brandon

40 At a Court Continued and held by adjournment in and for
the County of Union at the Courthouse of the said County
the twenty ninth day of March in the year of our Lord One
thousand seven hundred and eighty six and of the Independence of the United States of America the Tenth
                             William Kennedy
Present   Thomas Brandon   Esquires
                             John Birdsong

Ordered that the County Treasurer pay unto Archilus
Fore the sum of nine pounds Out of the County Tax that is
or will be Collected for Building the present Courthouse.

An Indenture and Deed of Conveyance Between John Golightly
of the one part, and William Haild of the other part for
one Hundred and Fifty acres of Land acknowledged by the
said John Golightly to the said William Haild and Ordered
to be Recorded.

An Indenture and Deed of Conveyance Between George Gowin
of the one part, and John Foster of the Other part is
Ordered to be Recorded.

An Indenture and Deed of Conveyance Between Michael Crawford of the One part and Lawrence Easterwood of the other
part for two hundred acres of Land Ordered to be Recorded.

An Indenture of Lease and Release Between John Wood and
Martha his wife of the One part, and John McPherson of
the other part, for three hundred and fifty acres of Land
proved by the Oaths of John Golightly and Jacob Holmes and
Ordered to be Recorded.

Charles Johnson   Plaintiff)
  against   )   Debt on attachment
Thomas Smith   Defendant)   When Came into Court the
                                 plaintiff by Jacob Brown his
attorney and Complains in the attachment that the Defendant
is indebted to him fourteen pounds. &C. Whereupon Came
also the Defendant by his attorney William Shaw and defends
the force and Injury of the above Complaintt and pleads
payment of the same, when the said parties by their
attorneys agree to try the said suit &C thereupon came also
a Jury to Wit Alexander McDougal, George Lineman, William
Shaw, Stephen Creanshaw, John Albritain, Abner Coleman,
James Gassaway, Henry Story, Christopher Brandon, Robert
Creanshaw, John Wilson, Hugh Nelson who being Drawn and
Sworn the truth to Speak in the said Suit upon their Oaths
Return their Verdict and say we find for the Defendant
One shilling Damage and Costs, whereupon it is Ordered to
be Recorded and Considered by the Court that the Defendant
Recover against the plaintiff the Damages and
41 and Costs aforesaid in form aforesaid and the same in money
&C &C.

Whereupon on Motion of the said plaintiff Charles Johnson
by his attorney Jacob Brown a New Trial is Granted him
at our next Court and the same Ordered accordingly.

Charles Miles   Plaintiff)
  against   )   Ordered that the Sheriff
Soloman Mangham   Defendant)   Expose the property to Sale
                                 that was attached to satisfy
the Judgment and Execution obtained against the Defendant
Soloman Mangham.

An Indenture and Deed of Conveyance Between Robert Montgomery of the One part, and James Martin of the other part
for two hundred and thirteen acres of Land acknowledged
by the said Robert Montgomery to the said James Martin
Ordered to be Recorded.

An Indenture and Deed of Conveyance Between John Steen
of the one part, and Charles Miles of the other part for
Eight hundred acres of land acknowledged by the said John
Steen to the said Charles Miles and Ordered to be Recorded.

An Indenture and Deed of Conveyance Between Adam Goudylock
and Hannah his wife of the One part, and Charles Miles of
the other part, proved by the Oaths of James Martin and
John Steen Witnesses thereunto and Ordered to be Recorded.
for three hundred acres of Land.

An Indenture of Lease and Release Between Adam Goudylock
and Hannah his wife of the One part, and Robert Lusk of
the other part, for two hundred acres of Land proved by
the Oaths of John Steen and James Martin Witnesses thereunto and Ordered to be Recorded.

Present   Zachariah Bullock Esquire

Thomas Stribling Junr.   Plaintiff)
   against   ) Detence
Throurgood Chambers   Defendant) Came the parties into
                                      Court and then and
there agree to Continue the trial of the Course over untill
the next Court. and the same is Ordered accordingly.

Luke Carrell   Plaintiff)
   against   ) Assault & Battery
Joseph Frankling   Defendant) Came the plaintiff by Daniel
                                 Brown his attorney and pled
his Declaration against the Defendant, wherein he complained
that the plaintiff did on the tenth day of September in the
year of Our Lord One thousand seven hundred and Eighty
five the Defendant with Arms &C did Assault Beat Wound
and ill treat the plaintiff to
42 the damage. of him twenty pounds, &C Whereupon came the
Defendant by Jacob Brown his attorney and Defends the
force and Injury and whatsoever Else he ought to defend and
pleads not guilty and satisfaction and jurtification and
pray this may be enquired of by the Country and the
plaintiff prays also the same therefore they agree to Try
the Issue Joined. Whereupon Came also a Jury To Wit
Robert Lusk, Thomas Blasingame, Joseph Hughes, Samuel
Montgomery, Richard Powell, Cahrles Miles, Daniel Commer,
Adam Goudylock, David Dickson, Richard Hughes, Andrew
Torrance, William Hardwick who being drawn tried and Sworn
the truth to Speak upon the Issue Joined Return their
Verdict and Say that we find for the plaintiff five shilling
Damages whereupon it is ordered that the plaintiff Recover
against the Defendant the damages aforesaid in form afore-
said, and the said Defendant in Money &C &C. Whereupon the
plaintiff by his attorney Daniel Brown aforesaid move for
a new trial which is granted him and Ordered accordingly.

An Indenture and Deed of Conveyance between Aaron Hart
of the One part and Thomas Brandon of the Other part, for
one hundred acres of Land proved by the Oaths of James
Woodson and Joseph Hughs Witnesses thereunto and Ordered
to be Recorded.

An Indenture of Lease and Release Between John Elliot of
the one part and Thomas Hobson Thompson of the other part
fro two hundred acres of Land acknowledged by the said
John Elliot to the said Thomas Hobson Thompson and
Ordered to be Recorded.

Caleb Gassaway   Plaintiff)
   against   ) Slander
Benjamin Johnson   Defendant) Came the plaintiff into
                                 Court by his attorney Daniel
Brown; and the Defendant by his attorney Jacob Brown and
then and there agree to discontinue the said Suit at the
plaintiffs Costs which is ordered accordingly.

John McCooll   Plaintiff)
   against   ) Debt
John Montgomery   Defendant) When Came the plaintiff by
                                 James Yancy his attorney and
Came also the Defendant John Montgomery in his Own proper

person and acknowledged that he owed the plaintiff seven
pounds four shillings and eleven pence, and confesses
Judgment for the same with costs of suit.

Thomas Brandon Sims & Co. Plaintiff)
   against   )   Debt.
John Montgomery   Defendant)   When Came the
                                    plaintiffs into
Court by James Yancy their attorney, also Came the
Defendant in his Own proper person and acknowledged that
he owed the plaintiffs.
43 Eight pounds One shilling and eleven pence and confessed
Judgment for the same with Costs of Suit.

John Fondrun   Plaintiff)
   against   )   Case on attachment
Archibald Rutherford Defendant)   Came the plaintiff by
                                  his attorney Jacob Brown
and on Motion the Defendant was Solemnly Called but came
not to defend the suit of the plaintiff Whereupon it is
Ordered that a Default be entered against the Defendant.

Daniel McElduff Plaintiff)
   against   )   Assault and Battery
Josoas Little   Defendant)   Came the plaintiff by William
                                  Shaw his attorney, also came
the Defendant in his own proper person and then there
agree to Discontinue the said Suit at the Defendants
Costs which is Ordered accordingly.

Ordered that the County line Remain and Stand as it is
agreeable to the lines of the Regiment.
Signed by   Zachariah Bullock
                      William Kennedy
                      Thomas Brandon
                      John Birdson

At a Court Continued and held by adjournment in and for
the County of Union at the Courthouse of the said County
the thirtieth day of March in the year of Our Lord one
thousand seven hundred and Eighty Six and in the Tenth
year of the Independence of the United States of America.
Present   Zachariah Bullock
                      William Kennedy
                      Thomas Brandon   Esquires
                      John Birdsong

A Power of attorney from William Hendricks to Thomas
Brandon and Mary Hendricks Ordered to be Recorded.

State   Plaintiff)
  agt.   )   The defendant appearing to
Robert Montgomery Defendant)   the Charge Exhibited against
                                  him by his attorney and
pleads not Guilty it is therefore Ordered to be Continued
Untill next Court.

State   Plaintiff)
  against   )   Nele Poseque
Thomas Albritain Defendant)   Ordered to be Dismissed
                                  at the Defendants costs.

State   Plaintiff)
   against   )   Bastardy
Elizabeth Hart   Defendant)   Came into Court James Yancy
                             attorney for the State also
the Defendant in her own proper person and then and there
agree to Continue the Trial over untill next Court which is
Ordered accordingly.

44 State   Plaintiff)
    against   )   Bastardy
 Rebecca George   Defendant)   Came James Yancy attorney for
                             the State also came the
Defendant in her own proper person and pleaded Guilty
Whereupon the Court fined her three pounds ten Shillings
and Costs to be paid next Court. Also Came David Hudson
and Entered himself Security to keep the Child from being
Chargeable to the County also for her fine and Costs of
suit to be paid at the time aforesaid.

Aaron Fincher   Plaintiff)
   against   )   Debt on attached.
David Farmer   Defendant)

John Steen   Plaintiff)
   against   )   Debt on attachment
David Stockton   Defendant)   When the plaintiff by Jacob
                             Brown his attorney on Motion
thereof the Defendant was Solemnly Called but Came not to
defend the Suit Whereupon it is ordered that a Default be
entered against the Defendant.

Thomas Brandon
& William Steen   Plaintiffs)
   against   )   Debt
John Bird and   )
John Steen   Defendant))   When Came the plaintiffs
                             by their attorney James
Yancy on a petition came also the Defendants in their
Own proper persons and acknowledged that they Owed the
plaintiffs two pounds eight shillings and eight pence
and Confesses Judgment for the same Costs of Suit the
Court Decree accordingly.

William Lipscomb   Plaintiff)
   against   )   Debt
Robert Montgomery   Defendant)   Came into Court the
John Bird   )   plaintiff by Daniel Brown
45   his attorney on a petition
also the Defendant Robert Montgomery in his Own proper
person and the Court on hearing the Complaint of the
plaintiff also the Defence of the Defendant consider and
Decree against the Defendant two pounds six shillings and
Eight pence and Costs of Suit.

William Lipscomb   Plaintiff)
   against   )
Robert Montgomery   )   Debt
and John Bird   Defendants)   Came the plaintiff into
                             Court by Daniel Brown
his attorney on petition, also came the Defendant Robert
Montgomery in his Own proper person, the Court on hearing

38

the Complaint of the plaintiff, also the Defence of the
Defendant Decree against the Defendant two pounds six
shillings and eight pence with costs of suit.

William Lipscomb   Plaintiff)
  against   ) Debt
Robert Montgomery   ) Came the plaintiff by
and John Bird   Defendants) Daniel Brown his attorney
                     on petition, also the
Defendant Robert Montgomery in his Own proper person the
Court on hearing the complaint of the plaintiff also the
Defence of the Defendant Decree against the Defendant two
pounds Six Shillings and Eight pence and Costs of Suit.

Samuel Farrow   Plaintiff)
  against   )
Shadrick Landtrip &   ) Debt
Lewis Wells   Defendants) Came into Court the
                     plaintiff by James
Yancy his attorney on petition and the Court on hearing
the Complaint of the plaintiff and defendant making no
Defence the Court Consider and Decree against the Defendant
four pounds five shillings and six pence with costs of suit.

46 John Fondrin)
   against   ) Debt
Drewry Jones) Came the plaintiff by his attorney Jacob
               Brown on a petition and Continue the Suit
Over untill next Court. Ordered accordingly.

Thomas Brandon   Plaintiff)
  against   ) Debt
Nathaniel Jeffries Defendant) Came the plaintiff into
                     Court by his attorney
Jacob Brown, and the Defendant in his Own proper person
and then and there agree to Continue the Suit over untill
next Court.

Mark Mitchel)
  against   ) Debt
Jesse Mabray) Came the plaintiff into Court by his
               attorney William Shaw, also Came the defen-
dant by his attorney Jacob Brown and then and there agree
to Continue the Trial of the Suit untill Court, which is
Ordered accordingly.

Mark Mitchel   )
  against   ) Debt
Benjamin and Henry Longs)

Nathaniel Jefferies Plaintiff)
  against   ) Debt
George Roberts   Defendant) Came the plaintiff into
                     Court by his attorney
William Shaw and on Motion of the plaintiff the Defendant,
being Solemnly Called but Came not to defend the Suit
whereupon it is ordered that a default be entered against
the Defendant.

Charles Sims   Plaintiff)
  against   ) Trespass.
William George   Defendant)

39

Came the plaintiff into Court by his attorney Jacob Brown
and filed his Declaration against the Defendant and
Complains that the Defendant about the ninth day of March
One thousand seven hundred and Eighty five became indebted
to the said Charles Plaintiff the sum of ten pounds ten
Shillings and four pence for money Expended for the use
of the Defendant which he Refuseth to pay to the plaintiff
to his Damage ten pounds ten shillings and four pence &C.
Whereupon Came the Defendant by his Attorney Daniel Brown
and defends the force and Injury and
47 whatsoever else he Ought to Defend and Saith that the
Defendant is not Guilty as the plaintiff hath complained
against him in his Declaration and put himself on his
Country and the plaintiff pray the same therefore the Trial
of the Issue Joined is Ordered to be Continued untill next
Court.

Samuel Cooper   Plaintiff)
  against   )
Thomas Woods &   )   Debt.
Davd. Dixon   Defendant)

William Nelson   Plaintiff)
  against   )   Debt
Thomas Biddy   Defendant)   Came the Defendant by William
                                  Shaw his attorney and on Motion
the plaintiff was Solemnly Called but Came not to prosecute his Suit, Whereupon it is Ordered that the plaintiff
be Nonsuited and that the Defendant Recover against him
five shillings Damages and Costs of Suit.

John Steen   Plaintiff)
  against   )
William & Rebecca George   )   Debt
Admrs. of Davd. George   Defendant)

John Gregory   Plaintiff)
  against   )   Trover
Jeremiah Hamilton   Defendant)

48 William Love   Plaintiff)
  against   )   Debt
John Montgomery   Defendant)   Came into Court the plaintiff
                                  in his Own proper person also
the Defendant by Jacob Brown his attorney and then and
there the plaintiff agree to Discontinue the suit at his
Own Costs which is Ordered accordingly.

James Rogers   Plaintiff)
  against   )   Debt
William Massey   Defendant)   Came into Court the plaintiff
                                  by Jacob Brown his attorney
also the Defendant in his Own proper person and then and
there agree to Discontinue the Suit at the Defendants
Cost which is Ordered accordingly.

John Means   Plaintiff)
  agt   )   Case
Robert Montgomery   Defendant)   Came into Court the plain-
                                  tiff by Daniel Brown his
attorney and filed his Declaration against the Defendant
wherein he complains that the Defendant on the Twenty fifth

day of December One thousand Seven hundred and Eighty five
Received of the plaintiff two hodgsheads of Tobacco his
property to Deliver to Wadsworth and Turpin which the
Defendant never done tho' he promised so to do to the
damage of the said plaintiff fifty pounds &C &C. Whereupon
the Defendant by Jacob Brown his attorney Comes also into
Court and Defends the force and Injury and what ever Else
he Ought to Defend and plead the same with Leave to give
all Special Matters in Evidence and puts himself on the
County and the plaintiff does the same therefore it is
Ordered that the Trial of the Issue Joined be Continued
untill next Court.

Haney Taylor   Plaintiff)
  against   )   Trover
John Montgomery   Defendant)   Came the plaintiff into Court
                                   by her attorney James Yancy
and filed her Declaration against the Defendant wherein
that on the twenty fifth day of February One thousand seven
hundred and Eighty One the plaintiff lost a black Gelding
of the Value of forty pounds and by finding Came into the
hands and possession of the Defendant which the said
Defendant Converted to his own proper use to the damage of
the plaintiff fifty pounds &C &C
Whereupon came the Defendant by Jacob Brown his attorney.

Sarah Gist   Plaintiff)
  against   )   Debt
Zadock Robison &   )   Came the plaintiff by William
Ambrose Barret   Defendant)   Shaw her attorney and filed
                                   her declaration against the
Defendant wherein she complains that the Defendants are
Indebted Seven pounds three shillings and four pence and
Interest and on Motion of the Plaintiff the Defendants
is Solemnly called but came not
49 to defend the Suit it is ordered that a Default be Entered
against them.

Robert Lusk   Plaintiff)
  against   )   Case
Matthew Robison   Defendant)   Came the plaintiff into Court
                                   by William Shaw his attorney
and pled his declaration against the Defendant wherein
he Complains that on the fifteenth day of July in the year
of Our Lord one thousand seven hundred and Eighty three the
Defendant promised to pay to the plaintiff two Cows and
Calves to the Value of Six pounds. which the Defendant hath
not hitherto paid &C. &C Whereupon the Defendant by his
attorney Jacob Brown Comes also into Court and defends the
force and Injury and whatsoever Else he Ought to defend
and saith he is not guilty as the plaintiff hath complained
against him in his Declaration and of this he puts himself
on the County and the plaintiff doth the same, Wherefore
it is ordered that the Issue Joined be Continued untill
next Court.

Caleb Gassaway   Plaintiff)
  against   )   Trover
John Moore   Defendant)   Came the plaintiff into Court
                                   by his attorney Daniel Brown
and On Motion the Defendant was Solemnly Called, but came

41

not to defend the suit, Whereupon it is Ordered that a
Default be Entered against the Defendant.

Moses Collier   Plaintiff)
   against   )   Trover
Daniel Jackson   Defendant)   Came the plaintiff by his
                               attorney Daniel Brown into
Court and filed his Declaration against the Defendant
wherein he complains that on the twenty fifth day of
November One thousand seven hundred and Eighty he lost a
Certain Gray horse of the Value of fifty pounds, and by
finding Came to the hands and possession of the Defendant
who Converted him to his Own use to the plaintiffs damage
fifty pounds &C &C Whereupon the Defendant Came by his
attorney James Yancy and defends the force and Injury and
whatsoever Else he Ought to defend as Saith that he is not
Guilty as the plaintiff hath complained in his declaration
and this he prays may be Enquired of by the County; and the
plaintiff doth the same therefore it is ordered that the
Trial of the Issue Joined be continued untill next Court.

Francis Fincher   Plaintiff)
   against   )   Slander
William & Jean Lees &   )   Came the Defendants by
Ann & James Jackson   Defendant)   William Shaw their
                               attorney and on Motion
the Plaintiff was Solemnly called but came not to prosecute
his Suit whereupon it is ordered that the plaintiff be
nonsuited and that the Defendant Recover against the
plaintiff five shillings damages and Costs of suit.

Abner Robison   Plaintiff)
   against   )   Slander Came the parties into
William Gilkie   Defendant)   Court

50 William Williams Plaintiff)
   against   )
John Towns   Defendant)

George Legget.   Plaintiff)
   against   )
Nathaniel Gorden   Defendant)

Luke Carrell   Plaintiff)
   against   )   Assault & Battery
James Hogans   Defendant)   When Came into Court the
                              plaintiff by his attorney Daniel
Brown and filed his declaration against the Defendant wherein he complains that about the first day of December One
thousand Seven hundred and Eighty three the defendant did
Beat Bruse Wound and ill treat the plaintiff to his Injury
and Damage twenty pounds &C &C. Whereupon the Defendant
by his attorney Jacob Brown Comes and Defends the force and
Injury and whatsoever Else he ought to defend and Saith he
is not guilty as the plaintiff hath complained against him
also pleads a former Judgment in Barr, and puts himself on
his Country and the plaintiff pray the same therefore the
Trial of the Issue Joines is Referred &C.

William Giles   Plaintiff)
   against   )   Case
William Pearson   Defendant)

42

Came the parties into Court in their Own proper persons and there agree to discontinue the Suit at the Defendants Costs which is Ordered accordingly.

51 John Montgomery   Plaintiff)
   against   )   The Sheriff having Returned
   Peter Edwards   Defendant)   that the Defendant is not
                                    to be found within this the
County on Motion of the Plaintiff by Jacob Brown his attorney an alias is awarded him and Ordered accordingly.

Joseph Adare   Plaintiff)
   against   )   Debt
Shadrick Landtrip   Defendant)   Whereupon the Sheriff hath
                                   Returned that the Defendant
is not to be found within his County, On Motion of the plaintiff by his attorney James Yancy who prays a Juditial attachment against the Estate of the Defendant which is awarded him and Ordered to Issue accordingly.

George Salmons   Plaintiff)
   against   )   Debt
Shadrick Landtrip   Defendant)   Whereupon the Sheriff hath
                                   Returned that the Defendant
is not to be found within his County, On motion of the plaintiff by James Yancy his attorney who prays a Judicial attachment against the Estate of the Defendant Returnable to our next Court which is awarded him and Ordered to Issue accordingly.

Jeremiah Hamilton   Plaintiff)
   against   )   Case
Francis Hawkins   Defendant)   Whereupon the Sheriff hath
                                   Returned that the Defendant
is not to be found within his County On Motion of the plaintiff by Jacob Brown his attorney who pray a Judicial attachment against the Estate of the Defendant Returnable to our next Court which is awarded him, and Ordered to Issue accordingly.

Hollin Sumner   Plaintiff)
   against   )   Whereupon the sheriff hath
Caleb Lanstone   Defendant)   Returned that the Defendant
                                 is not to be found within his
County, it is Ordered that the Suit be Dismissed at the plaintiffs Cost.

Holland Sumner   Plaintiff)
   against   )   Whereupon the plaintiff
Caleb Lanstone   Defendant)   hath Returned that the
                                 Defendant is not to be found
within his County it is Ordered that the Suit be Dismissed at the plaintiff costs.

John Montgomery   Plaintiff)
   against   )   Debt.
Wilson Jolly   Defendant)   Whereupon the Sheriff hath
                                 Returned that the Defendant
was not to be found within his County, On motion of the plaintiff by his attorney Jacob Brown who pray a Judicial attachment against the Estate of the Defendant Returnable to next Court which is awarded him Ordered that the same

43

Issue accordingly.

52 James Rogers   Plaintiff)
      against   ) Debt
   William Massey Junr.   Defendant) Came into Court the
                                     plaintiff by Jacob
   Brown his attorney on petition also the Defendant in his
   Own proper person and there agreed to Discontinue the Suit
   at the Defendants Costs which is Ordered accordingly.

   William Farr   Plaintiff)
      against   )
   Edward McNeal   Defendant)

   James Harrison   Plaintiff)
      against   ) Debt on attachment
   Thomas Bishop   Defendant) Came the plaintiff into Court
                                by James Yancy his attorney
   also Came the Defendant in his Own proper person and there
   agree to Discontinue the Suit at the Defendants Costs which
   is Ordered accordingly.

   Thomas Brandon   Plaintiff)
      against   ) Trover on attachment
   Samuel Gray   Defendant) Came the Plaintiff into Court
52   by his attorney Jacob Brown
   and filed his Declaration against the Defendant, wherein he
   Complains that about the tenth day of November One thousand
   Seven hundred and Eighty the plaintiff lost a Brown horse
   and also One Bay mare the Value of twenty five pounds, and
   by finding Came to the hands and possession of the Defendant and converted them to his own use to the damage of
   the plaintiff fifty pounds &C &C. On Motion of the
   plaintiff by his attoryney aforesaid the Defendant is
   Solemnly Caled but Came not to defend the suit whereupon
   it is ordered that a Default be entered against him.

   William Giles   Plaintiff)
      against   ) Trover
   George Avery   Defendant) Whereupon the Sheriff hath
                               Returned that the Defendant is
   not to be found within his County on Motion of the plaintiff by his attorney James Yancy who pray a Judicial
   attachment against the Estate of the Defendant Returnable
   to our next Court, which is awarded him and Ordered
   accordingly.

53 John Thomas   Plaintiff)
      against   ) Ordered that the Sheriff Expose
   John Steen   Defendant) To Sale the Land he hath already
                               Executed to Satisfy the Judg-
   ment Obtained against the Defendant.

   John Thomas Junr.   Plaintiff)
      against   ) Ordered that the Sheriff
   John Steen   Defendant) Expose to Sale the Land
                                   he hath already Executed
   to Satisfy the Judgment and Execution Obtained against
   the Defendant.

44

James Hillhouse)
  against   ) Ordered that the Sheriff Expose to Sale
John Steen   ) The Land he hath already Executed to
                   Satisfy the Judgment and Execution
Obtained against the Defendant.

State   Plaintiff)
  against   ) Assault & Battery on Luke
James Hogans Defendant) Carrel & his Wife Martha Carrell
                     Came into Court James Yancy
attorney for the State and Complained on a Bill of Judgment
found against the Defendant by the Grand Jurorers of this
County that the Defendant on the third day of December One
thousand seven hundred and Eighty three at the house of
the said Luke Carrell with force of arms did Beat Bruse
Wound and Evilly Entreat the said Luke Carrell and Martha
his wife that their lives were greatly Dispared of to the
Great damage of the said State Whereupon Came also a Jury
To Wit Alexander McDougal, Thomas Vance, James Gassaway,
Robert Creanshaw, Edward Ragsdale, Henry Story, Christopher
Brandon, William Shaw, Thomas Young, John Wilson, George
Lineman, Hugh Nelson who being duly drawn tried and Sworn
the Truth to Speak wherein the State of South Carolina is
plaintiff and James Hogans Defend and Upon their Oaths
Return their Verdict and say that the Defendant is Guilty
which is Ordered to be Recorded. Whereupon it is Considered
by the Court that the Defendant pay unto the State Nineteen
pounds Nineteen Shillings for a fine and the Costs of the
prosecution. Also Ordered that an Execution Issue against
the Defendants Goods and Chattels for the Same.

Thomas Brandon Plaintiff)
  against   ) Debt
Thomas Vance   Defendant) Came the Plaintiff into Court
                     by James his attorney also
the Defendant in his Own proper person and then and there
agree to discontinue the Suit at the Defendants Costs which
is Ordered accordingly.

Robert Glover   Plaintiff)
  against   )
James Hogans &   ) Case
Daniel McElduff Defendants) Came into Court the
                     plaintiff by
54 Charles Goodwin his attorney, also came the Defendants by
Jacob Brown their attorney and then and there agree to
with draw the said Suit as to the Complaint against the
Defendant Daniel McElduff on which the Court Ordered a
Discontinuance on the part of Daniel McElduff at the
plaintiffs Costs and on Motion of the Defendant James
Hogans by his attorney Jacob Brown aforesaid also on a
Motion of the plaintiff Robert Glover by his attorney
Charles Goodwin the Court on fully hearing the Council on
both Sides the plaintiff agree to Suffer a Nonsuit on the
part of the Defendant James Hogans. which is Ordered by the
Court to be Entered and Considered that the Defendant James
Hogans Recover against the plaintiff five Shilling Damages
and Costs of Suit.

Colonel William Farr informed the Court that he had a Bill
of Sale from Thomas Crosby to him for One Negro Woman Named
Jane about twenty one or two years of age at this time also

45

Major Otterson made Oath in Court that he Saw a Bill of
Sale in the possession of Colonel William Farr for a Negro
Woman Named Jane or Jin he could not tell which, he further
Saith on Oath that on the Back of the said Bill of Sale
there was a Copy of said Crosby Oath. Setting faith that
the said Negroe Woman Named Jane was his lawful Right and
property, and that She was Clandestatly taken from him,
and that he never Sold her to any person but to said William
Farr.

Thomas Vance   Plaintiff)
   against   ) Case
John Steen   Defendant) Came the plaintiff into Court
                               by James Yancy his attorney
also came the Defendant in his Own proper person and then
and there agree to Refer the said Suit to Colonel Thomas
Brandon and William Kennedy Esquires as arbitrators. with
liberty to Choose a third person in Case the said arbitrators do not agree and the award of the said arbritrators
to be the Judgment of Court.

William Hardwick   Plaintiff)
   against   ) Case
William George   Defendant) Came into Court the said
                               parties in their own proper
person and their agree to Continue the said Suit over
untill next Court which is Ordered accordingly.

Luke Carrell   Plaintiff)
   against   ) Assault & Battery
Humphries Posey   Defendant) When came into court the
                               plaintiff by Daniel Brown
his attorney, also the Defendant by William Shaw his
attorney and then and there agree to Discontinue the
suit at the Defendants cost which is Ordered Accordingly.

55 Thomas Stribling &   )
   William Buchannan   Plaintiff)
      against   ) Debt on attachment
   William Gist   Defendant) Came the plaintiffs
                                    into Court by their
attorney Daniel Brown and filed their Declaration against
the Defendant where--in they Complain that the Defendant
owes them One hundred and Eighty seven pounds fourteen
Shillings and five pence half penny due by Bond whereon
they have Sustained Damages &C. Whereupon Came Sarah Gist
wife of the Defendant by William Shaw her attorney and
interpleaded and Claimed the property that the Sheriff had
Returned attached, whereupon the Court Ruled the said Sarah
Gist to Enter Special Bail, Then Came into Court Aaron
Fincher in his Own proper person and Entered himself
Special Bail for the said Sarah Gist. Ordered that the
Cause be Continued.

Merry Maguire   Plaintiff)
   against   ) Debt.
John Steen   Defendant) Came into Court the plaintiff
                               by James Yancy his attorney,
also Came the Defendant by William Shaw his attorney and
then and there agrees to Submit the said Suit to arbitration Over to Colonel William Farr and his award to be the

Judgment of Our said Court. which is Ordered Accordingly.

Luke Carrell   Plaintiff)
  against   )   Assault and Battery
Nehemiah Posey Defendant)   Came the plaintiff into Court
                             by Daniel Brown his attorney and
Came also the Defendant by Jacob Brown his attorney and
then and there agree to dismiss the said Suit at the
Defendant's Costs which is Ordered accordingly.

Luke Carrell   Plaintiff)
  against   )   Assault and Battery
David Hudson   Defendant)   Came the plaintiff into Court
                             by Daniel Brown his attorney
also Came the Defendant by Jacob Brown his attorney and
then and there agree to Continue the Cause untill next
Court at the plaintiff's Costs which is Ordered accordingly.

Luke Carrell   Plaintiff)
  against   )   Assault and Battery
Nehemiah Posey Defendant)   Came the plaintiff into Court
                             by Daniel Brown his attorney
and Came also the Defendant by Jacob Brown his attorney
and then and there agree to dismiss the said Suit at the
Defendant's Costs which is Ordered accordingly.

Luke Carrell   Plaintiff)
  against   )   Assault and Battery
David Hudson   Defendant)   Came the plaintiff into Court
                             by Daniel Brown his attorney
also came the defendant by Jacob Brown his attorney and
then and there agree to Continue the Cause untill next
Court at the plaintiff's Costs which is Ordered accordingly.

Luke Carrell   Plaintiff)
  against   )   Assault and Battery
James Beuford   Defendant)   Came the plaintiff by Daniel
                             Brown his attorney into Court,
also Came the Defendant by Jacob Brown his attorney and
then and there agree to Continue the said Cause over untill
next Court at the plaintiff Costs which is Ordered
accordingly.

Luke Carrell   Plaintiff)
  against   )   Assault and Battery
Caleb Gassaway Defendant)   Came the plaintiff by Daniel
                             Brown his attorney into Court
also the Defendant by Jacob Brown and agree to Discontinue
the said Suit at the Defendants Costs which is Ordered
accordingly.

56 Luke Carrell & Wife   Plaintiff)
     against   )   Assault and Battery
   James Hoggans   Defendant)   Came the parties into
                                    Court by their attorney
aforesaid thereupon Came also a Jury Wit. Alexander McDougal
Thomas Vance, James Gassaway, Robert Creanshaw, Edward
Ragsdale, Henry Story, Christopher Brandon, William Shaw,
Thomas Young, John Wilson, George Lineman, Hugh Nelson who
being duly drawn and Sworn the truth to Speak upon the
Issue Joined upon their Oaths do say that the Defendant is

47

Guilty as the plaintiff hath complained and do assess
damages by Occasion thereof Nineteen pounds Nineteen
Shillings and Eleven pence and Costs of Suit whereupon it
is considered by the Court that the Verdict be Recorded
and that the Plaintiff Recover against the Defendant in
form aforesaid, and the said Defendant in money &C.

Soloman Mangham   Plaintiff)
  against   ) Debt
John Montgomery   Defendant) Came the parties by their
                                attorneys aforesaid and for
Reasons annexed it is Ordered to be Continued at the
Defendants Costs.

Ann Robison admx.   )
of Joseph Robison   Plaintiff) Debt
  against   ) Came the plaintiff into
John Steen   Defendant) Court by James Yancy his
                                attorney also the Defen-
dant in his Own proper person and there agree to discontinue
the said Suit at the Defendants Costs which is Ordered
accordingly.

George Gordon   Plaintiff)
  against   ) Debt
John Montgomery   Defendant) Came the plaintiff into Court
                                by James Yancy his attorney
also Came the Defendant in his Own proper person and
acknowledged he owed the plaintiff five pounds Seven
Shillings and three pence and Confessed Judgment for the
same with Costs of suit Whereon the plaintiff agreed to
Stay Execution for Six months, which is Ordered accordingly.

Thomas Brandon   Plaintiff)
  against   ) Trover and Coversion on
Samuel Gray   Defendant) attachment. Came the plain-
                                tiff by his attorney aforesaid
on a Default on of the said plaintiff by his attorney
the Defendant was again Solemnly called but came not to
defend the said Suit Whereupon Came also a Jury To Wit
Alexander McDougal, Henry Story, William Shaw, John
Brandon, Christopher Brandon, James Bell, Thomas Young,
William Steen, Hugh Nelson, James Martin, Thomas Vance,
John Montgomery who being duly drawn and Sworn Upon a Writ
of Enquiry the truth to Speak upon their Oaths do say that
the Defendant is Guilty of the Trover and Conversion as
Mentioned in the Declaration and do assess damages by
Occasion thereof to twenty five pounds and costs of Suit
Whereupon it is Considered by the Court that the Verdict
be Recorded and that the plaintiff Recover against the
Defendant his damages aforesaid, and in form aforesaid and
the said Defendant in Money &C. &C.

57 Proceeding brought up and Signed by
                        Zachariah Bullock
                        William Kennedy
                        Thomas Brandon
                        John Birdsong

At a Court Continued and held by adjournment in and for the
County of Union at the Courthouse the thirty first day of
March in the year of Our Lord One thousand Seven hundred

and Eighty Six, and of the Independence of the United
States of America the Tenth.
Present   William Kennedy
                           Thomas Brandon
                           Charles Sims   Esquires
                           John Birdsong

Came John Haile Clerk of said County Recommended John
Ewart as Deptuty Clerk of this County; who by and with
the Consent and approbation of the Court was appointed
accordingly who took the Oath Required by Law.

An Indenture and Deed of Conveyance Between Edward McNeal
of the one part, and Charles Sims of the other part, for
three hundred and fifty acres of Land Ordered to be
Recorded.

James Fannin   Plaintiff)
   against   )   Debt.
John Bird   Defendant) Came the plaintiff into Court
                            by James Yancy his attorney
and filed his Declaration against the Defendant wherein
he complains that on the seventeenth day of February in
the year of Our Lord One thousand Seven hundred and Eighty
three that the Defendant became indebted to the plaintiff
One hundred and fifteen pounds former Currency by Note
to the plaintiff damage &C. &C. Whereupon the Defendant
Comes by his attorney Jacob Brown his attorney and Defends
the force and Injury and whatsoever else he Ought to Defend
with leave to give all Special Matters in Evidence and
this he prays may be enquired of by the Country and the
plaintiff doth the same therefore they agree to Try the
Issue Joined. Whereon there came also a Jury To Wit.
Alexander McDougal, George Lineman, John Brandon, Thomas
Vance, Edward Ragsdale, Robert Creanshaw, Hugh Nelson,
John Wilson, James Bell, Luke Carrell, Joseph McJunkin,
Richard Powell who being drawn and sworn the truth to
Speak upon the Issue Joined upon their Oaths do say we
find for the plaintiff Sixteen pounds Eight Shillings
and three pence with Interest from the first of October
One thousand seven hundred and Eighty three to the thirty
first of March One thousand Seven hundred and Eighty Six
and Costs of Suit whereupon it is considered by the Court
that the Verdict be Recorded and that the plaintiff
Recover against the Defendant in form aforesaid and the
said Defendant in Money &C. &C.

58 Ordered that Jacob and Daniel Brown's have leave to built
an attorneys Office twelve feet square in the clear on the
Courthouse Lot and have free access and Regress to and from
the same at all times so long as the said Office shall last.

Robert Smith   Plaintiff)
   against   )   Debt
William Steen   Defendant) Came the plaintiff by James
                            Yancy his attorney and the
Defendant by William Shaw his attorney and for Reasons
annexed it is Ordered that this Course be Continued untill
next Court.

49

Luke Carrell   Plaintiff)
    against   )   Assault and Battery
Micajah Hoggan   )   Whereupon the Sheriff hath
Humphrey Posey Defendants)   Recommed that the Defendants
Francis Posey   )   were not to be found within
                                his County Whereupon the
plaintiff by his attorney Daniel Brown prays a Judicial
attachment against the Estate of Micajah Hogan and an
alias's against the Rest of the Defendants which is awarded
him and Ordered accordingly.

Abraham Lipham   Plaintiff)
    against   )   Debt.
John Campbell   Defendant)   Came the plaintiff into Court
                                by Daniel Brown his attorney
also the Defendant by William Shaw his attorney Thereupon
Came also a Jury to Wit Alexander McDougal, George Lineman,
John Brandon, Thomas Vance, Edward Ragsdale, Robert
Creanshaw, Hugh Nelson, John Wilson, James Bell, Luke
Carrell, Joseph McJunkin, Richard Powell, who being duly
drawn Tried but not Sworn, When Came into Court the
Defendant in his own proper person and acknowledged he
Owed the plaintiff five pounds fourteen shillings and
three pence farthing and confessed Judgment for the same
and Costs of Suit. Whereupon the plaintiff agree to Stay
Execution for the Debt for three months and Execution to
Issue for the Costs.

James Hawkins   Plaintiff)
    against   )   Case
James Hogans   Defendant)   Came into Court the plaintiff
                                by James Yancey his attorney
and filed his declaration against the Defendant, wherein
he Complains that the Defendant did on the fifteenth day
of February in the year of our Lord One thousand Seven
hundred and Eighty five became indebted to the plaintiff
by promise and assumption the sum of thirty pounds for a
certain Horse to the plaintiffs damage fifty pounds &C
whereupon came the Defendant by Jacob Brown his attorney
and defends the force and Injury and Whatsoever Else he
Ought to Defend and the Defendant is not Guilty as the
plaintiff
59 hath Complained against him in his Declaration and further
pleads the General Issue with Leave. and this he prays may
be Enquired of by the Country and the plaintiff pray the
same a Jury to Wit Alexander McDougal, George Lineman,
John Brandon, Thomas Vance, Edward Ragsdale, Robert
Creanshaw, Hugh Nelson, Richard Powell, John Wilson,
James Bell, Luke Joseph and McJunkin who being duly drawn
Tried and Sworn the truth to Speak upon the Issue Joined
upon their Oaths do say we find for the plaintiff fourteen
pounds five shillings and Eight pence also we do assess
five Shillings Damage and Costs of Suit. Whereupon it is
ordered by the Court that the Verdict be Recorded and that
the plaintiff Recover against the Defendant the Damages
aforesaid and in form aforesaid and the same in Money &C &C.

George Purvis   Plaintiff)
    against   )   Case
John Ewart   Defendant)   Came the plaintiff into Court
                                by William Shaw his attorney
also the Defendant in his Own proper person and then and

there the plaintiff agrees to Discontinue the said Suit at
his the said plaintiff's own Costs which is Ordered
accordingly.

Joseph Hughes   Plaintiff)
  against   )   Ordered that a Commission
James Shockley   Defendant)   a Dedimus potestatum Issue
                                 to Major Johnson and Captain
Thompson, or any two Other Justices in the County of
Luazia in the State of Virginia. to take the Depositions
of Nelson Anderson Junr. and James Burley in the part and
behalf of the plaintiff and that the same be admitted in
Evidence on the trial.

Ordered that for the year One thousand Seven hundred and
Eighty Six there be assessed for a County Tax. One Shilling
and One penny on Every Negro Slave on the first Quality
of Low Grounds. One Shilling and Six pence pr hundred
acres One Shilling pr hundred acres, on the second
quality of Land, Nine pence pr hundred acres on the third
quality of Land Six pence pr Hundred acres, and a pole
Tax on all free men from twenty one years of age to fifty
they having no land or Negroes. two Shillings and four
pence Each.

Elizabeth Bishop   Plaintiff)
administrators of   )
Robert Bishop   )
  against   )   Whereas the Defendant
Henry Long   Defendant)   moved for and appeal
                                  to the Court of Common
Pleas. at Ninety Six which was Granted him by giving Bond
with Security Whereupon the Defendant Came into Court by
his attorney and Withdraw the said appeal.

60 Ordered that the Sheriff Summons the following persons to
serve as a Grand Jury for a Body of Inquest for this
County at our next Court.

1. John Montgomery   11. Thomas Stribling
2. Adam Goudylock   12. William Pallent
3. John Goodwin   13. John Davis
4. James Crawford   14. Henry Clark
5. William Buchannan   15. Obadiah Howard
6. Joseph McJunkin   16. Thomas Greer
7. George Story   17. Bazel Wheat
8. Samuel Kelsa   18. Benjamin Halcomb
9. John Layton   19. Jeremiah Stokes
10. James Thomas   20. Isaac Gregory

Ordered that the Sheriff Summons the following persons
to serve as petit Jurors at our next Court.

1. Turner Rountree   10. Richard Hughes
2. Archibald Howard   11. Joseph Hughs
3. Richardson Rountree   12. William Sharp.
4. Avery Breed   13. Williams Giles
5. Benjamin Savage   14. Clayton Stribling
6. Jepthah Hollingsworth 15. William Williams
7. Thomas Vance   16. George Wadkins
8. James Bell   17. Caleb Gassaway
9. George Newton   18. Samuel Skelton

51

19. John Brandon   21. William Williams Broad
20. William Johnson   River
                                    22. John Brandon Junr.

William Farr high Sheriff of our County pursuant to a
Commission and act of assembly Nominated and appointed
John Ewart Deputy Sheriff in and for the County of Union
which meet with the Concurrence and approbation of the
Court Whereupon it is ordered that he take the Oath
Required by Law Whereupon it is ordered that he take the
Oath Required by Law Whereupon the said John Ewart took the
Oath Prescribed by the act of assembly and entered into
the Execution of the said Office by Order of Court.

Ordered that any two of the Justices of the Court bind out
any of the poor orphans that is within the County and it
shall be Lawful
Signed   William Kennedy
                               Charles Sims
                               Thomas Brandon
                               John Birdsong

61 At a Court Begun and held by Adjournment in and for the
County of Union at the Court house of the said County the
twenty sixth day of June in the year of Our Lord one
thousand seven hundred and Eighty Six and in the Independence of the United States of America the Tenth.
Present   Thomas Brandon
                               William Kennedy   Esquires
                               Charles Sims

An Indenture and Sheriff's Deed of Conveyance Between
William Farr Sheriff of the One part and Thomas Brandon
of the Other part, for One hundred acres of Land dated
the twenty third day of October One thousand seven hundred
and Eighty five was acknowledged by the said William Farr
to the said Thomas Brandon and Ordered to be Recorded.

James Yancy Esquire produced a Licence from the Honourable
the associate Judges of the Court of Common Pleas authorizing to plead the Law as an attorney in the Several Courts
of this Ordered that he be admitted accordingly in this
Court.

Thomas Stribling motion to the Court for a Licence to keep
a Tavern or public House and Offered Joseph Hughs and William
Johnson Security which is approved of by the Court, on
which he has Obtained a Licence and the Same Ordered
accordingly.

Charles Goodwin Esquire produced a Licence or his Certificate from the Honourable the Judges &C to practice the
Law in this State Ordered that he be admitted in this Court
accordingly.

        Present   Thomas Blassingame Esquire
        Absent   Thomas Brandson   Esquire

State   Plaintiff)
   against   ) Bastardy
Ami Hollingsworth Defendant) Presented by the Grand Jury
and Dismissed on paying Costs.

52

```
State            Plaintiff)
  against              )    Bastardy
Sussannah Moore  Defendant)  Came the Sheriff into Court
                             and Delivered up the Defendant
who is Dismissed on her giving Bond and Security to keep
the Child from being Chargeable to the County and for the
Costs of Suit  Whereupon the Defendant together with John
Stokes her Security Entered into and acknowledged their
Bond for the same Ordered to be dismissed and the Costs to
be paid next Court.
```

```
Present    Zachariah Bullock   Esquires
           John Henderson
```

62 Ordered to be Recorded the Grist Mill belonging to Mark
Murphy on Tygar River near Lewis Bobo's Ford.

```
State     Plaintiff)
  against        )    Bastardy
Ann Lee   Defendant)  Information of the Grand Jury
                      Dismissed on paying Costs.
```

Ordered that the Sheriff Summons the following persons to
serve as Petit Jurors at our next Court the same being
drawn out of the Taxable Inhabitant of this County according
to Law.

1.	William Littlefield	16.	Robert Glover
2.	Jacob Segar	17.	Benjamin Hawkins
3.	Hugh Tollison	18.	John Cane
4.	John Cook	19.	Thomas Lamb
5.	Richard Addas	20.	William White
6.	Jacob Paulk	21.	Fredrick Jackson
7.	Benjamin Darbey	22.	Robert Burns
8.	John Townsend	23.	Moses Hames
9.	Philip Anderson	24.	William Jenkins
10.	John Thomas	25.	James Benson
11.	Jesse Young	26.	John Sission
12.	Joseph Gault	27.	Robert Dunkin
13.	John Burgess	28.	John Kennedy
14.	William Morgan		
15.	William Cooper		

An Indenture and Deed of Conveyance Between William
Wafford on the One part, and Robert Woodson of the Other
part, for fifty acres of Land proved by the Oaths of James
Woodson and Turner Rountree Witnesses thereunto and Ordered
to be Recorded.

Ordered that the Sheriff Summons the following person to
Serve as Grand Jurors for a Body of Inquest for this
County at Our next Court they being Recommended and
drawn according to Law.

1.	Robert Lusk	10.	Robert Creanshaw
2.	Nathaniel Jeffries	11.	John Beckham
3.	Jpethath Hollingsworth	12.	James Petty Junr.
4.	John Goodwin	13.	Nehemiah Howard
5.	Elishia Green	14.	Hugh Means
6.	James Crawford	15.	Isaac Hawkins
7.	George Ashford	16.	William Means
9.	Turner Rountree	17.	Nathan Glenn

18. Moses Guyton
19. Aaron Fincher
20. Joseph Guyton

63 Francis Fincher   Plaintiff)
    against   )
William Lee James &   ) Slander
Ann Jacksons   Defendants) Came into Court John
                                   Stokes who being Bail
for the Defendants James and Ann Jackson to the Sheriff
and Surrendered them to the Court. Ordered that he be
discharged of the Bail accordingly.

Luke Carrell   Plaintiff)
  against   ) Assault and Battery
Barnerd Glenn   Defendant) Came into Court Thomas Shockley
                             as Bail to the Sheriff for the
Defendant and on Motion thereof he is discharged and the
same Ordered accordingly.

Henry Fondrin   Plaintiff)
  against   ) Debt
Drewry Jones   Defendant) Came the plaintiff into Court
                             by his attorney Daniel Brown
on a Summons and Petition, also Came the Defendant on his
Own proper person and acknowledged that he Owed the
plaintiff three pounds fifteen shillings and Confessed
Judgment for the Same and Costs of Suit, Whereupon the
plaintiff agree to Stay Execution until the fifteenth of
November next for the Debt, and an Execution to Issue for
the Costs.

An Indenture and Deed of Conveyance Between James Vernon
of the one part, and Aaron Harlin of the other part Ordered
to be Record for fifty acres of Land.

Sarah Gist   Plaintiff)
  against   ) Debt
Holland Sumner   Defendant) Came the plaintiff into Court
                             by his attorney William Shaw
and then and there agree to Discontinue the suit at his
the plaintiffs costs Ordered accordingly.

An Indenture and Deed of Gift Between Obediah Howard of
the one part and his son Joseph Howard of the other part
for one hundred acres of land was acknowledged by the said
Obediah Howard to the said Joseph Howard ordered to be
Recorded.

64 Thomas Brandon Plaintiff)
    against   ) Detinue
Goven Gorden   Defendant) Ordered that there Issue a
                             Dedimus to Newberry County to
take the Deposition of Colonel Levy Cassy to be taken
before Colonel Lindsay or any other Justice on the said
County.

An Indenture and Mortgage Deed Between Richard Burgess of
the one part, and Thomas Brandon of the other part, bearing
date the thirty first day of December One thousand seven
hundred and Eighty five proved by the Oaths of James Woodson

54

and Sarah Gist. Witness thereunto and Ordered to be
Recorded.

An Indenture and Deed of Lease and Release Between Thomas
Young of the one part and Colonel Thomas Brandon of the
other part, for five hundred and fifty acres of Land proved
by the Oaths of James Woodson and Sarah Gist Witnesses
thereunto Ordered to be Recorded.

Nathaniel Jefferies   Plaintiff)
  against   )   Come the plaintiff into
George Roberts   Defendant)   Court by William Shaw
                                  his attorney and then and
there agreed to Discontinue the said Suit as his the said
plaintiffs own Cost which is Ordered accordingly.

James Terrell   Plaintiff)
  against   )   Debt
George Purvis   Defendant)   Came George Bailey into Court
                             and Surrendered the Defendant
to the Sheriff in Discharge of his Bail and the Same
Ordered accordingly.

Signed   Zachariah Bullock
                          John Henderson
                          Charles Sims
                          Thomas Brandon
                          Thomas Blassingame

At a Court. Continued and held by adjournment in and for
the County of Union at the Court house of the said County
the twenty seventh day of June in the year of Our Lord
One thousand Seven hundred and Eighty Six and in the Tenth
year of the Independence of the United States of America.

65 Present   Zachariah Bullock
                          John Henderson
                          Charles Sims   Esquires
                          John Birdsong
                          Thomas Brandon

A Petition being presented for a Road from Hill's Ford to
Colonel Hopkins Ordered to be laid Over untill next Court.

An Indenture and Deed of Conveyance Between William Wafford
on the One part and Turner Rountree of the other part,
for two hundred acres of Land proved by the Oaths of
James Woodson Senior and James Woodson Junior Witnesses
thereunto and Ordered to be Recorded.

An Indenture and Deed of Lease and Release Between John
Steen and Martha his wife of the One part and Francis
Drake of the Other part, for three hundred and fifty
acres of Land Ordered to be Recorded.

John Fondrin   Plaintiff)
  against   )   Debt on attachment
Archibald Rutherford   Defendant)   Drewry Jones being
                                       Summonsed a Garnishee
Came into Court, and being Sworn, the Court Condemn in his
hands Seven pounds Sixteen Shillings Virginia Money equal to
five pounds seven Shillings and five pence half penny.

55

State   Plaintiff)
  against   ) Bastardy
Rhody Prince Defendant) Came the Defendant into Court
                       and Made Oath on which she
declares she is not Worht Enough to pay or Satisfy the
Costs and is therefore discharged by the Court.

State   Plaintiff)
  against   ) Whereas the Defendant was
James Hogans Defendant) fined at March Term One
                       thousand Seven hundred and
Eighty Six in the sum of Nineteen Pounds Nineteen Shillings
and Eleven pence it is Ordered that he be Released from
the said Fine on paying Costs.

Daniel McElduff Plaintiff)
  against   ) Debt.
Luey Inlow   Defendant) Came the plaintiff into Court
                       and then and there agree to
discontinue the said Suit at his the plaintiffs own costs
which is Ordered accordingly.

66 Wilson Jolly   Plaintiff)
  against   ) Debt
Jonathan Jones Defendant) Came the Plaintiff into Court
                       also Came the Defendant,
and then and there agrees to Discontinue the said Suit at
the Defendants Costs, also Came into Court Nathaniel
Jeffries in his Own proper person and assumed to pay the
costs of suit. and the same Ordered accordingly.

John Montgomery Plaintiff)
  against   ) Debt.
William Hodge Defendant) Came the plaintiff into
                       Court by Jacob Brown his
attorney on a petition and Summons, and Complained that
the defendant was indebted to the plaintiff the sum of
Six pounds the Balance due by a Bond and Interest. Whereupon Judgment was awarded against the Defendant for Six
pounds and One year's Interest amounting to in the whole
Six pounds Eight shillings and four pence three farthings,
and Costs of Suit on the plaintiff giving Bond that the
said Bond on which the above Judgment is Obtained that it
shall never appear against the defendant Ordered that the
said plaintiff's Bond be lodged in the Clerk's Office.

Robert Montgomery Plaintiff)
  against   ) Came the plaintiff into
Soloman Mangham Defendant) Court by his attorney
                       Jacob Brown and the Defen-
dants by James Yancy his attorney and for Reasons assigned
by Defendant by his attorney aforesaid a Nonsuit is awarded
for the Defendant, and it is further Considered by the
Court that the Defendant Recover against the plaintiff
five shillings damage and Costs of suit and the same
Ordered accordingly.

Absent. Thomas Brandon Esquire)
Thomas Brandon & Co. plaintiff)
  against   ) Debt.
Henry McCardin   Defendant) Came the plaintiff into
                             Court by James Yancy their

attorney on a Petition and Summons and Complains that
Defendant is indebted to them the sum of three pounds
Seventeen Shillings and two pence Decreed against the
Defendants for the same and Costs of Suit.

Jonathan Jones)
  against   ) Debt
John Montgomery) Came the parties into Court and then
                   and there agree to Continue the suit
                   until next court.
67 at the plaintiffs costs, which is ordered accordingly.

Charles Clanton Plaintiff)
  against   ) Case
Joseph Jolly   Defendant) Came the plaintiff into Court
                   by his attorney William Shaw
also the Defendant by James Yancy his attorney and then
and there agree to Continue the Trial by Consent untill
next Court, and the same ordered accordingly.

Philip Shivertaker Plaintiff)
  against   ) Debt
George Purvis   Defendant) Came the plaintiff into
                   Court by his attorney
Jacob Brown and the Defendant by William Shaw his attorney
and then and there agree to Continue the Trial untill
next Court which is Ordered accordingly.

James Terrill   Plaintiff)
  against   ) Debt.
George Purvis   Defendant) Special Bail Entered John
                  Montgomery of this County Comes
into Court and undertakes for the Defendant that in case
he is Cast in the Suit he will pay the Judgment of Court
or Render the Defendants Body in Discharge thereof.

Joseph Alexander Plaintiff)
  against   ) Debt
Lark & Phebe Wells Defendant) Came the plaintiff by his
                  attorney Jacob Brown and
the Defendants by William Shaw their attorney and then
and there agrees to Continue the Trial untill the next
Court at the plaintiffs Costs. Ordered accordingly.

Richard Hoss   Plaintiff)
  against   )
Joshua Petty admr. of) Debt.
John Nuckols   ) Came the Defendant by William
                  Shaw his attorney and the
plaintiff being solemnly called but came not to prosecute
his suit, on Motion of the Defendant by his attorney aforesaid a Nonsuit is awarded against the plaintiff and it is
also Ordered by the Court that the Defendant Recover against
the plaintiff five shillings Damage and Costs of Suit.

Archer Howard   Plaintiff)
  against   ) trover
Samuel Simpson Defendant) Came the plaintiff into Court
                  by Jacob Brown his attorney on
a petition and Summons Came also the Defendant by his
attorney James Yancy Move for a
68 Trial by a Jury which Granted him also it is Ordered to be

Continued at the plaintiff's Costs untill next Court.

Samuel Farrow   Plaintiff)
    against   )   Debt
Richard Burgess Defendant)   Came into Court the Defendant
                             by his attorney James Yancy
on petition, also came the Defendant in his Own proper
person and acknowledged that he Owed the plaintiff two
pounds Six Shillings and Eight pence & Confessed Judgment
for the same with Costs of Suit & Decreed by the Court
accordingly.

James Hogans   Plaintiff)
    against   )   Debt
John Inlow   Defendant)   Came the plaintiff by Jacob
                             Brown his attorney on a petition
and Summons. and the Defendant being Solemnly called but
came not to defend the suit whereupon the plaintiff complains that the Defendant is indebted to him the sum of
three pounds four shillings and eight pence. Whereupon
the Court Consider and Decree against the Defendant for
the same with Costs of Suit.

Isaac Gregory   Plaintiff)
    against   )   Debt
Handcock Porter Defendant)   Came the parties into Court and
                             then and there agree to Continue
the trial untill next Court which is Ordered accordingly.

Samuel Farrow   Plaintiff)
    against   )   Debt
Richard Burgess   Defendant)   Came the plaintiff into
                             Court by James Yancy his
attorney on petition and Summons also Came the Defendant
in his own proper person and acknowledged he owed the
plaintiff four pounds four shillings and Confessed Judgment
for the sae with costs of suit and Decreed by the Court
accordingly.

John Inlow   Plaintiff)
    against   )   Debt
James Hogans Defendant)   Came the Defendant into Court by
                          Jacob Brown his attorney and on
    Motion of the Defendant
69 by his attorney aforesaid the plaintiff was solemnly
called but came not to prosecute his suit. Whereupon it
is Ordered that the plaintiff be Nonsuited and it is
further considered by the Court that the Defendant recover
against the Plaintiff five shillings and costs of suit.

Robert Lusk   Plaintiff)
    against   )   Case on an attachment
John Jones   Defendant)   John Montgomery being summonsed
                             as a Garnishee appeared in open
Court and Sworn.

Robert Montgomery   Plaintiff)
    against   )   On an attachment
David Shipman   Defendant)   Ordered to be Continued
                                 untill next Court

Luke Carrell   Plaintiff)
  against   )   Assault & Battery on attachment
Micajah Hogan   Defendant)   Came the plaintiff into Court
                                 by his attorney Daniel Brown.
Whereupon the Sheriff hath Returned that Caleb Gassaway
a Garnishee on Motion of the plaintiff by his attorney
aforesaid a ferefieias is awarded against the Garnishee to
appear next Court. Which is ordered accordingly.

Robert Montgomery   Plaintiff)
  against   )   Debt on attachment
Davis Wilkie   Defendant)   Came into Court John Leek
                                 being summonsed as Garnishee
being Sworn saith that he hath in his hand a Cow and Calif
which is valued by the Court to One pound twelve shillings
and eight pence.

Jeremiah Hamilton   Plaintiff)
  against   )   On attachment
Francis Hawkins   Defendant)   Whereupon the Sheriff
                                 hath Returned that the
Defendant hath not any Goods Chattels Lands or Tenements
within his Country it is Order that the Suit be Dismissed
as the plaintiffs Costs.

William Giles   Plaintiff)
  against   )   Trover on attachment
George Avery   Defendant)   Came into Court William Farr
                                 who being summonsed a Garnishee
Ordered that he be
70 Sworn which is done accordingly on his Oath saith he has
in his hands nine pounds Old Currency Equal to one pound
five shillings and Eight pence half penny Sterling.

A Receipt Signed by John McElduff to Stephen Creanshaw
for three hundred and fifty six pounds ten shillings
proved by the Oaths of Robert Creanshaw and William Hardwick
Witness thereunto and Ordered to be Recorded.

George Salmons   Plaintiff)
  against   ) Debt on attachment
Shadrick Landtrip Defendant)   Whereupon the Sheriff hath
                                 Returned that he Levied the
said attachment on one Brown Mare Saddle and Bridle...Came
into Court Aaron Fincher and Inter pleads and Claims the
property attached pursuant to a Morgtage from the Defendant
Shadrick Landtrip.

John Montgomery   Plaintiff)
  against   )   Debt on attachment
Wilson Jolly   Defendant)   Whereupon the Sheriff hath
                                 Returned that the Defendant
hath not any Lands Tenements within his Country it is
Ordered that the Suit be Discontinued at the plaintiffs
Costs.

Thomas Brandon & Sims Plaintiff)
  against   ) Debt on attachment
David Shipman   Defendant) Whereupon the Sheriff
                                 hath Returned that the
Defendants hath not any Lands Tenements Goods or Chattels

59

within my County Whereupon it is Ordered that the Suit be discontinued at the plaintiffs Cost.

George Salmon   Plaintiff   )
   against   )   Debt on attachment
Shadrick Landtrip Defendant)   Came the plaintiff by James
                                Yancy his attorney and filed
his Declaration against the Defendant Wherein he Complains
that the Defendant on the Seventeenth day of March Seventeen
hundred and Eighty three became indebted to the plaintiff
the sum of five hundred pounds Current money of South
Carolina to the Plaintiff's Damage twenty pounds &C...Where-
upon the Defendant by his attorney Jacob Brown.

71 George Head   plaintiff)
   against   )   Debt on attachment
   Isaac Holman   Defendant)   Ordered to be Continued at
                                Equal Cost

Merry Maguire   Plaintiff)
   against   )   Debt
John Steen   Defendant)   Whereas this Suit was Referred
                                to William Farr by Order of
Court at March Term last who Return his award which is
Ordered to be Recorded. I do hereby decree that the said
John Steen pay to Said Merry Maguire Six pounds fourteen
Shillings and Costs of Suit. Given under my hand and
Seal the twenty seventh day of June one thousand seven
hundred and Eighty Six
                              Wm. Farr
Whereupon it is Considered by the Court that the plaintiff
Recover against the Defendant according to the above award
in form aforesaid and the said Defendant in Money &C &C.

Gabriel Brown   Plaintiff)
   against   )   Debt on attachment
Michael Mattocks Defendant)   Whereupon the Sheriff Returned
                                that he attached of the
Estate of the Defendant three Cows and Calves, Eight head
of Hoggs, two Feather Beds, and One Waggon one horse and
Geers. Whereupon it is Ordered that the Sheriff Expose
the property to Sale agreeable to Law.

Turner Rountree   Plaintiff)
   against   )   Debt on attachment
James Ainsworth   Defendant)   Whereas Joseph Wafford was
                                by the Sheriff Returned
Summonsed as a Garnishee and failed to appear on Motion of
the plaintiff by Charles Goodwin his attorney it is Ordered
that there Issue a Siere facias against the said Joseph
Wafford to appear at next Court to Show Cause why Judgment
Should not be entered against him.

State   Plaintiff)
   against   )   Came the Defendant into
Benjamin Johnson Defendant)   Court by his attorney Jacob
                                Brown and no person appear-
ing to prosecute is Ordered that the Defendant be dismissed
on paying costs.

72 State   Plaintiff)
      against   )   Bastardy
   Catherine Petty   Defendant)   Ordered by the Court that the
                                      Defendant be discharged on
                                      her paying the costs.

An Indenture and Deed of Conveyance Between Jacob and Ruth
Brown's of the One part, and John Mayfried of the Other
part for three hundred acres of Land proved by the Oaths
of William Grant and John Haile Witnesses there--unto
and Ordered to be Recorded.

Adam Goudylock   Plaintiff)
      against   )   Debt
Lewis Bobo   Defendant)   Came into Court the plaintiff
                                   in his own proper person, also
Came the Defendant in his Own proper person and acknowledged
he owed the plaintiff the Condition of a Certain Bond and
Confessed Judgment according to the same with interest and
costs of suit untill paid Whereupon it is considered but
the Court that the plaintiff Recover against the Defendant
the Condition of the said Bond with Interest untill paid
and costs of suit & in form aforesaid and the said
Defendant in Money &C.

Obediah Howard is hereby appointed Overseer of the Road in
the Room and Place of Jacob Paulk. and it is Ordered that
he keep the said Road in Good Repair.

Thomas Stribling &   )
William Buchannan   Plaintiffs)
      against   )   Debt on attachment
William Gist   Defendant)   Ordered that Colonel
                                      Thomas Brandon take the
Deposition of Giles Turley tomorrow at Twelve O'Clock on
behalf of the plaintiff, and that the same be admitted in
Evidence Notice being given to the Defendants attorney
accordingly.

Thomas Vance   Plaintiff)
      against   )   Case
John Steen   Defendant)   Whereas this Suit at March Term
                                last was Referred to Thomas
                                Brandon and
73 William Kennedy who Return their award which is Ordered
to be Recorded Pursuant to the Order of Court We Thomas
Brandon and William Kennedy having heard the Aligation and
Losses of the Plaintiff. Master Thomas Vance made, declare
this our Judgment that the Defendant John Steen pay to the
said Thomas Vance the sum of twenty five pounds two
Shilling and all the costs of suit. Given under our hands
this twenty six of June one thousand seven hundred and
Eighty Six.   Thomas Brandon
                       William Kennedy
Whereupon it is considered by the Court that the plaintiff
Recover against the Defendant according to the above award
in form aforesaid and the said Defendant in money and
Soforth.

An Indenture of Deed of Conveyance Between Nathaniel
Jeffries of the One part and John Jefferies of the Other
part, for two hundred acres of Land, acknowledged by

61

the said Nathaniel Jeffries to the said John Jeffries and
Ordered to be Recorded.

John Gregory   Plaintiff)
  against   ) Trover
Jeremiah Hamilton Defendant) Came the parties into Court
                               by their attorneys afore-
said and then and there agree to Refer the said Suit to
Colonel William Farr, Colonel John Lindsay, Jeremiah
Williams and William Smith and their award to be the
Judgment of Court and the same Ordered accordingly.

John Ewart Come into Court and Resign his Office as Deputy
Shff. which is ordered to be Recorded.

Philip Anderson   Plaintiff)
  against   ) Debt on attachment
Daniel McElduff   Defendant) Came into Court Robert
                               Creanshaw who was returned
by the Sheriff Summonsed a Garnishee Ordered that he be
Sworn and on his Oath saith that all the Effects, Debts
Dues or demands of the said Daniel McElduff in his hands
at the time of the Levying the said attachment were as
follows, that he gave on the third of April One thousand
Seven hundred and Eighty Six his note to the said McElduff
for Six thousand Weight of Merchantable Tobacco (one
Hodgshead of which Weight unknown
74 was paid before the attachment lieved as pr Receipt on
the note, that on the fifth day of April One thousand
Seven and Eighty Six the said Daniel McElduff assigned the
said note to William Farr, and that the attachment was
levied on the thirteenth day of April, also this Deponant
paid on note on the third of April to the said McElduff
nine pounds thirteen Shillings Virginia money, he owed to
the said McElduff some time before the attachment levied he
was informed it was assigned to William Hollingsworth, of
both which assignments the Deponomt had notice before the
attachment levied in his hands...and lastly this
Deponant had at the time of Issuing the attachment in
his hands Eight Bushels the property of said McElduff which
was Condemned under an attachment from Newberry County
Court.

Soloman Mangham   Plaintiff)
  against   ) Debt.
John Montgomery   Defendant) Came the parties by their
                               attorneys aforesaid and
then and there agree to Refer the said Suit to John
Thompson, Francis Lettimore and Adam Potter and any two
of them to be the Judgment of Court and Ordered accordingly.

Daniel Brown Esquire is by the Court Nominated and appoint
attorney in and for the State in this County which is
accepted of by the said Daniel Brown Esquire Ordered
accordingly.
Court adjourned untill tomorrow at eight o'Clock
Signed by   Thomas Brandon
                             Zachariah Bullock
                             Thomas Blassingame
                             William Kennedy
                             Charles Sims

75 Ordered that the County Treasurer pay unto Colonel William
Farr the sum of forty nine pounds Seven Shillings.

Benjamin Clark   Plaintiff)
   against   )   Debt on attachment.
William Jackson   Defendant)   Whereas the Sheriff Returned
                                 that he Summonsed Colonel
Thomas Brandon a Garnishee. Ordered that the said Col.
Brandon be Sworn. Who on Oath saith that he hath nothing
in his hands of Said Defendants Jackson's Property...it
is further Ordered that the suit be Dismissed at the
plaintiffs costs.

William Farr high Sheriff in and for the County of Union
pursuant to a Commission and act of assembly Nominated
and appointed Benjamin Woodson Deputy Sheriff in and for
the County of Union which meet with the Concurrence and
approbation of the Court. Whereupon it is Ordered that the
said Benjamin Woodson take the Oath Required by Law.
Whereupon he took the same prescribed be the act of
assembly and Entered into the Execution of the said Office.

John Little is hereby appointed Overseer or Surveyor of
the Highway in the Room and place of John Goodwin Ordered
that he keep the same Road in Good Repair.

Joshua Petty is hereby appointed Overseer or Surveyor of
the Highway in the Room and place of Samuel Littlejohn
Ordered that he keep the same Road in Good Repair.

Captain William Young and Jesse Young is hereby appointed
Overseer or Surveyor of the Highway in the place and Room
of John Clark Ordered that he keep the said Road in Good
Repair.

Elishia Green, Evan Thomas, William Savage, John Little
and James Mabray be and is hereby appointed Constables in
and for the County of Union Ordered that they take the
Oaths Required by Law.

George Harlin, farmer is hereby appointed Overseer or
Surveyor of the Highway in the Room and place of Thomas
Blassingame Esquire Ordered that he keep the same Road
in Good Repair.

State   Plaintiff)
   against   )   The Court having yesterday
James Hogans   Defendant)   made an order that the fine
                                 of Nineteen pounds Nineteen
Shillings and Eleven pence which was Inflicted on the
76 Defendant James Hogans at the last Court for an assault
and Battery on Luke Carrell and his wife be Remitted, and
it appearing to the Court this day that said Order was
made without Maturely Considering of the matter and the
Court being in doubt whither they had a power to Remit
said Fine will take further time to Consider the matter
fully. Ordered therefore that the Consideration of said
Matter be Referred to next Court and that the Order of
yesterday be Considered of no force untill further Reconsidered and that James Hogans be Served with a Copy of this
Order. Ordered also that the Sheriff proceed to Collect

the Costs on the said Indictment, and that Execution be
stayed for the fine.

Court adjourned untill Court of Course
Signed by   Zachariah Bullock
                             Thomas Blasingame
                             William Kennedy
                             Charles Sims
                             John Henderson

At a Court begun and held in and for the County of Union
at the Court house of the said County the twenty fifty
day of September in the year of Our Lord One thousand
seven hundred and Eighty Six and in the Eleventh year of
the Independence of the United States of America.
Present   Thomas Brandon
                             John Birdsong
                             Charles Sims   Esquires
                             Zachariah Bullock
                             Thomas Blasingame
                             William Kennedy

Ordered that the Sheriff summons, the following persons to
Serve as Grand Jurors for a Body of Inquest for this
County at Our next Court they being nominated and Drawn
according to Law.

1.	David Hudson	9.	Joseph Wood
2.	Isaac Parker	10.	William Lawson
3.	Robert Dunkin	11.	George Harlin, Farmer
4.	Hezekiah Rice	12.	Benjamin Halcomb
5.	Thomas Mays	13.	Drewry Murrell
6.	John Jeffries	14.	Nathaniel Jackson
7.	Robert Burns	15.	HandCock Porter
8.	James Crawford		

Ordered that the Sheriff Summons the following persons
77 to serve as petitt Jurorers for the said Court at our
next Court they being drawn out of the Taxable Inhabitants
of this County according to Law.

1.	John Hope	16.	Alexander McDougal
2.	Samuel Cooper	17.	Avery Breed
3.	William Skelton	18.	William Hawkins
4.	Thomas Williams	19.	Charleton Shockley
5.	Ralph Jackson	20.	Henry Clark
6.	Isaac Hawkins	21.	William Plummer
7.	Joseph West	22.	John McKee
8.	David Harris	23.	John Harrington
9.	George McWhorter	24.	Renney Belue
10.	Samuel Thompson	25.	John Sission
11.	George Harlen (Hatter)	26.	William Sission
12.	John McPherson	27.	Nathaniel Jeffries
13.	John Hamilton	28.	Nathaniel Davis
14.	Charles Clanton	29.	John Jenkin
15.	James Hawkins	30.	Edward Dinney

An Indenture and Deed of Conveyance Between Elizabeth
Marten of the One part and John Little of the other part
for One hundred acres of Land acknowledged by the said
Elizabeth Martin to the said John Little and Ordered to
be Recorded.

64

An Indenture and Deed of Conveyance Between Gabriel Brown of the One part and Richard Barret of the Other part for one hundred acres of Land acknowledged by the said Gabriel Brown to the said Richard Barret, Ordered to be Recorded.

An Indenture of Lease and Release Between Ambrose Ray and Elizabeth his wife of the One part and Elizabeth Dunkin of the other part for two hundred acres of Land and the same ordered to be recorded.

An Indenture and Deed of Conveyance Between James Martin of the one part, and George Harlin of the other part, for one hundred acres of Land ordered to be recorded.

An Indenture of Lease and Release Between Joseph Robison and Ann Robison of the other part, and William Faucett of the other part, for three hundred acres of Land Ordered to be Recorded.

An Indenture of Lease and Release Between John Woods of the one part, and Drewry Harrington of the other part, for one hundred and Seventy acres of Land proved by the Oaths of John Moorehead and Absalom Petty Witnesses thereunto and Ordered to be Recorded.

An Indenture of Deed from Hugh Quinn to James Terrill for 150 acres Ordered to be Recorded.

78 An Indenture and Deed of Conveyance Between Moses Qualls of the one part and James Terrell of the other part for one hundred and fifty acres of Land proved by the Oaths of Abner Robison and John Robison Witnesses thereunto and ordered to be Recorded.

An Indenture and Deed of Conveyance Between Moses Qualls of the one part, and James Terrill of the Other part, for one hundred acres of Land proved by the Oaths of Abner Robison and Henry Smith Witnesses thereunto and Ordered to be Recorded.

An Indenture and Deed of Conveyance Between Daniel Lipham of the One part, and William Jinkins of the other part, proved by the Oaths of Josiah Darby and Benjamin Darby Witnesses thereunto and Ordered to be Recorded.

An Indenture and Deed of Conveyance Between William Smith and Martha Smith of the one part, and William Lockard of the Other part for One hundred and fifty acres of Land proved by the Oaths of James Terrell and Abner Robison Witnesses thereunto and Ordered to be Recorded.

An Indenture and Deed of Conveyance Between John White and Peggy White of the One part and Henry Milhouse of the other part for three hundred acres of Land acknowledged by the said John & Peggy White to the said Henry Milhouse and Ordered to be Recorded also the said Peggy White wife of the said John White acknowledged her Right of Dower to the said three hundred acres of Land and Ordered to be Recorded.

An Indenture and Deed of Conveyance Between Jeremiah Routh of the one part, and Daniel Jackson of the other part, for

two hundred acres of Land proved by the Oaths of William
Plummer witness thereunto and Ordered to be Recorded.

An Indenture and Deed of Conveyance Between George Crosley
Senior of the One part, and George Crosley Senior of the
other part, for one hundred acres of Land proved by the
Oaths of Uriah Paulk and Ezekiel Springer witnesses
thereunto and Ordered to be Recorded.

79 An Indenture of Lease and Release Between Theophelus Faver
and Elizabeth Faver of the one part, and John Moorehead
of the other part, for eighty acres of Land proved by the
Oaths of William Moorhead and John Moorhead Witnesses
thereunto and Ordered to be Recorded.

An Indenture and Deed of Conveyance Between William George
of the one part, and William Sharp of the other part for
one hundred acres of Land proved by the Oaths of Richard
Hughs. and Richard Faucett. Witnesses thereunto and
Ordered to be Recorded.

An Indenture and Deed of Conveyance Between John Huglar
of the one part and John Gorden of the other part for
fifty acres of Land Ordered that the same be Recorded

An Indenture and Deed of Conveyance Between Edward Nixon
of the one part and Benjamin Darby of the Other part, for
two hundred acres of Land. Ordered to be Recorded.

An Indenture and Deed of Conveyance Between Samuel Poston
of the One part, and Richard Hughes of the Other part for
One hundred and twenty five acres of Land proved by the
Oaths of William Giles and Richard Faucett Witnesses thereunto and Ordered to be Recorded.

An Indenture and Deed of Conveyance Between John Ham and
Mary Ham of the one part,and Benjamin Darby of the other
part, for fifty acres of Land proved by the Oaths of Josiah
Darby and Samuel Jenkins Witnesses thereunto and Ordered
to be Recorded.

An Indenture and Deed of Conveyance Between David Pruit and
Sarah Pruit of the one part and Benjamin Darby of the other
part, for fifty acres of Land proved by the Oaths of Josiah
Darby and William Jenkins Witnesses thereunto and ordered
to be Recorded.

An Indenture and Deed of Conveyance of Lease and Release
Between Mark Mitchel of the One part and Marsharshallbary
Lile of the other part, for two hundred acres of Land,
proved
80 by the Oaths of John Haile Esquire and Adam Potter Witnesses
thereunto and Ordered to be Recorded.

An Indenture of Lease and Release Between Aurther Simpson
of the One part, and Robert and Thomas Barrons of the
other part, for two hundred acres of Land proved by the
Oaths of Adam Potter and Samuel Shaw Witnesses thereunto
and Ordered to be Recorded.

An Indenture and Deed of Conveyance Between Vardy McBee

of the one part, and Peter Peterson of the Other part for
two hundred acres of Land proved by the Oaths of Drewry
Harrington and James Petty Witnesses thereunto and Ordered
to be Recorded.

An Indenture and Deed of Conveyance Between Vardy McBee
of the one part and James Petty of the other part, for one
hundred and Twelve acres of Land proved by the Oaths of
Duuary Harrington and Peter Peterson. Witnesses thereunto
and ordered to be Recorded.

An Indenture of Lease and Release between Matthew Robinson
of the one part and William Saffold of the other part, for
two hundred and Sixty acres of Land Ordered to be Recorded.

A Title Bond Between John Steen of the one part and
Elijah Wells of the other part, for one hundred acres of
Land Ordered to be Recorded.

The Grand Jury Called by the Sheriff is Namely Robert Lusk,
Jephthath Hollingsworth, John Goodwin, George Ashford,
Turner Rountree, Robert Creanshaw, John Beckham, James
Petty Senior, Nehemiah Howard, Hugh Means, Joseph Guyton,
Isaac Cook who be Sworn and Received then Charge Retired
from the Barr to Consult their Verdict

The Petitt Jury Called by the Sheriff, Jacob Paulk, Benjamin
Darby, John Townsend, Philip Anderson, John Thomas, Joseph
Gault, John Burgess, William Cooper, Robert Glover, Benja-
min Hawkins, John Cane.

81 An Indenture and Deed of Gift Between Alexander Cane of
the one part, and his Son Isaac Cane of the other part
proved by the Oaths of Handcock Porter and John Ewart also
a Skedule of the Articles Contained in the said Deed and
a memorandum proved also by the said Handcock Porter and
John Ewart. Witness thereunto the whole and Ordered to
be Recorded.

Ordered that Mary Barron Widow of Thomas Barron have a
Certificate from this County to Receive a Pension from
the Treasury She being Examined on Oath.

Thomas Peter Carnes Esquire produced a Licence from the
Honourable Judges of the State of South Carolina to
practice the law as an attorney and ordered admitted in this
Court accordingly.

Peter Carnes Esquire Ordered to be admitted to Practice
the Law an an attorney in this Court, on his producing
his Licence for the same at our next Court.

An Indenture and Deed of Conveyance Between Thomas Taylor
of the one part and David Johnson for three hundred acres
of Land acknowledged by the said Thomas Taylor to the said
David Johnson Ordered to be Recorded.

An Indenture and Deed of Conveyance of Lease and Release
Between William and Dorcas Hills of the One part and
Robert Creanshaw of the Other part for one hundred acres
of Land proved by the Oaths of Edward Ragsdale and

67

William Mays Witnesses thereunto and Ordered to be Recorded.

Moses Collier is hereby appointed Overseer or Surveyor of the Highway from Rockey Creek to Elishia Green Plantation Ordered that he keep the same Road in good repair.

Joseph West is hereby appointed Overseer of the Road from Elishia Green's Plantation to Colonel Thomas Brandon's Shoals on Fairforrest. Ordered that he keep the same Road in good Repair.

John McNeal Son of Edward McNeal Deceased came into Court and made Choice of Colonel Thomas Brandon his Guardian.

82 Thomas Brandon & Co.   Plaintiff)
     against   ) Debt
   Francis Clayton   Defendant) Whereupon the Sheriff
                                   Returned that the Defen-
dant was not to be found within his County the said Suit Ordered to be Discontinued at plaintiffs Costs.

Thomas Brandon & Co.   Plaintiff)
   against   ) Debt
Isam Clayton   Defendant) Whereupon the Sheriff
                                 Returned that the
Defendant was not to be found within this County it is Ordered that the suit be discontinued at the plaintiffs Costs.

Archer Howard plaintiff)
   against   ) Trover
Samuel Simpson Defendant) Came the parties by their
                          attorneys aforesaid and then and
there agree to Discontinue the said Suit at the Defendants costs which is ordered accordingly.

Rhodrick McCullock   Plaintiff)
   against   ) Debt
Thomas McDonald   Defendant) Came the plaintiff by
                               Jacob Brown his attorney
on Petition and Summons also Came the Defendant by Charles Goodwin his attorney the Court on fully hearing the complaint of the plaintiff and the Defence of Defendant. Ordered the suit to be discontinued at the Plaintiffs Costs.
Whereas Josiah Wood being Summonsed on Evidence for the plaintiff prove one days attendance thereon.

John Sission being Summonsed a petitt Jurorer he maketh Oath that he is not able to attendit is Ordered that he be Discharged.

An Indenture of Lease and Release Between Archer Smith of the one part and Thacker Vivion of the Other part, for forty acres of Land acknowledged by the said Archer Smith to the said Thacker Vivion Ordered to be Recorded.

An Indenture and Deed of Conveyance Between Thacker Vivion of the one part and Stephen Layton of the other part for One hundred acres of Land acknowledged by the said Thacker Vivion to the said Stephen Layton Ordered to be Recorded.

83 Joseph Alexander   Plaintiff)
      against   )   Debt
   Luke and Phebe Wells   Defendant)   Came the plaintiff into
                                          Court by his attorney
   Jacob Brown aforesaid and there agree to discontinue the
   suit at the plaintiff's costs which is ordered accordingly.

   William Smith   Plaintiff)
      against   )   Debt
   James Oliphant   Defendant)   Came the plaintiff into Court
                                    by James Yancy his attorney
   and there agree to discontinue the suit at the Plaintiffs
   Costs which is Ordered accordingly.

   Signed by   Zachariah Bullock
                                 William Kennedy
                                 Charles Sims
                                 Thomas Brandon

   At a Court Continued and held by adjournment in and for the
   County of Union at the Court house of the said County the
   twenty Sixth day of September in the year of Our Lord One
   thousand Seven hundred and Eighty Six and in the Tenth year
   of the Independence of the United States of America.

   Present   Zachariah Bullock
                                 John Henderson
                                 Thomas Blasingame
                                 John Birdsong   Esquires
                                 Charles Sims
                                 William Kennedy
                                 Thomas Brandon

   Adam Goudylock on Motion thereof it is ordered that the said
   Adam Goudylock have the Mark of all his cattle Recorded.
   That is as followeth a Cross and two Slits in each ear.

   An Indenture and Deed of Conveyance Between Laurence Easterwood of the One part, and John Beckham of the other part,
   for two hundred acres of Land proved by the Oaths of John
   Beckham Junior and Adam Potter Witnesses thereunto and
   Ordered to be Recorded.

   An Indenture and Deed of Conveyance Between Rydarus Clark of
   the one part and John Foster of the other part for thirty
   one acres of Land acknowledged by the said Rydarus Clark to
   John Foster and Ordered to be Recorded.

   Proved an Indenture from John Steen to John Hope for 300
   acres of Land Ordered to be recorded.

84 John Hodge   Plaintiff)
      against   )   Debt
   Robert Montgomery   Defendant)   Came the plaintiff into Court
                                      by Daniel Brown his attorney
   and filed his declaration against the defendant. Wherein
   he complains that on the Eighteenth day of December in the
   year of Our Lord One thousand Seven hundred and Eighty
   three became indebted to the plaintiff by Note the sum of
   Seventy Six pounds Sterling to the plaintiffs damage &C
   &C. Whereupon came also the Defendant by Jacob Brown his

attorney and defends and saith that the said plaintiff ought
not to maintain his said Suit &C. for that the plaintiff is
indebted to the said Defendant the sum of four hundred
pounds pleads by Bond a part which Bond the said Defendant
sets off against the Defendants demand, that is so much of
it as will Blance the plaintiff's Demand.
Whereupon came also a Jury and then and there the plaintiff
by his attorney aforesaid agree that the plaintiff be nonsuited which is Ordered accordingly and it is further
Considered by the Court that the Defendant Recover against
the plaintiff five Shillings damages and costs of Suit and
the said in form aforesaid and the said plaintiff in Money
&C &C.

An Indenture of Lease and Release Between Isaac Cruse of
the one part, and William McJunkin of the other part for
one hundred and fifty acres of Land proved by the Oaths
of Thomas Brandon and Samuel Pattent Witnesses thereunto
and Ordered to be Recorded.

An Indenture Between William Willison of the One part and
John Young of the other part, proved by the Oath of William
Shaw and Ordered to be Recorded.

David Vincin   Plaintiff)
  against   ) Debt
William Head   Defendant) Whereupon the Sheriff hath
                              Returned that the Defendant is
nto to be found within his County. Whereupon the plaintiff
prays a Judicial attachment against the Estate of the
Defendant which is awarded him and Ordered accordingly.

Thomas Brandon   Plaintiff)
  against   ) Detinue
William Lea   Defendant) Where as the parties agree to
                              submit the
85 Suit to arbritation. Ordered the award of the said
arbritrators to be the Judgment of Court by the Consent of
the parties.

James Hogans   Plaintiff)
  against   ) Debt
Luke Carrell   Defendant) Came the plaintiff into Court
                              by his attorney Jacob Brown
and the Defendant by his attorney Daniel Brown his attorney
and then and there agree to Discontinue the said Suit at
the plaintiff's Costs. and the same Ordered accordingly.

William Hardwick Plaintiff)
  against   ) Case
William George   Defendant) Came the parties into Court
                              in there own proper persons
and then and there agree to discontinue the said Suit at
the Defendants Costs which is Ordered accordingly.

Luke Carrell   Plaintiff)
  against   ) Assault and Battery
James Beuford   Defendant) Came into Court the plaintiff
                              by his attorney Daniel Brown
and also the Defendant by his attorney Jacob Brown and
then and there agree to Discontinue the said Suit at
Defendant Costs which is Ordered accordingly.

70

Luke Carrell   Plaintiff)
   against   )   Assault & Battery
David Hudson   Defendant)   Came into Court the plaintiff
                             by his attorney Daniel Brown
also came the Defendant by Jacob Brown his attorney and
then and there agree to discontinue the said Suit at the
Defendant Costs which is Ordered accordingly.

John Towns plaintiff   )
   against   )   Debt
William Williams   Defendant)   Came the plaintiff into
                                 Court by his attorney
William Shaw also came the defendant by Daniel Brown his
attorney and then and there agree to Discontinue the said
suit at the plaintiffs costs which is ordered accordingly.

Robert Smith   Plaintiff)
   against   )   Debt
William Steen   Defendant)   Came the plaintiff into Court
                             by his attorney James Yancy
and filed his Declaration against the Defendant wherein
he complains that on the sixteenth day of May
86 in the year of Our Lord one thousand Seven hundred and
Eighty four, the defendant became Indebted to the plaintiff
the Sum of nine pounds Sixteen Shillings Sterling to the
plaintiffs damage &C. Whereupon Came the Defendant by
William Shaw his attorney and defends &C. saith that the
defendant did not assume at the plaintiff hath Compai--
nec in his Declaration. Whereupon came also a Jury and
then and there the plaintiff agree by his attorney aforesaid to be nonsuited which is Ordered accordingly and it is
Considered by the Court that the Defendant Recover against
the plaintiff five shillings Damages and Costs of Suit--
in form aforesaid &C &C.

Charles Johnson   Plaintiff)
   against   )   Debt on attachment
Thomas Smith   Defendant)   Came the parties into Court
                                 by their attorneys Jacob
Brown and William Shaw aforesaid and then and there agree
to Discontinue the said Suit at the plaintiffs Costs which
is Ordered accordingly.

Caleb Gassaway   Plaintiff)
   against   )   Debt
Thomas Taylor   Defendant)   Came the plaintiff by Daniell
                               Brown his attorney, and the
Defendant in his Own proper person and then and there
agree to Discontinue the said Suit at the Defendants Costs.

John Gregory   Plaintiff   )
   against   )   Trover
Jeremiah Hamilton   Defendant)   Came the parties into Court
                                 by their attorneys aforesaid
and then and there again agree to Refer the said Suit to
William Farr John Lindsay Jeremiah Williamsand William
Smith and their award to be the Judgment of this Court and
the same again ordered accordingly.

Caleb Gassaway   Plaintiff)
   against   )   Trover
John Moore   Defendant)

71

Came the plaintiff by his attorney Daniel Brown aforesaid
and the Defendant in his Own proper person and then and
there agree to Discontinue the said Suit at Equal Costs
which is Ordered accordingly.

Sarah Gist   Plaintiff)
  against   )   Debt on a Default
Zadock Robison &   )   Came the plaintiff into
Ambrose Barnett   Defendants)   Court by William
87 Shaw her attorney on Motion the Defendnats were again
Solemnly Called but Came not to Defend the said Complaint
Whereupon Came also a Jury to Wit Jacob Paulk, John Townsend,
Benjamin Darby, Philip Anderson, John Thomas, Joseph Gault,
John Burgess, William Cooper, Robert Glover, Benjamin
Hawkins, John Canes, Thomas Lamb who being duly drawn and
Sworn the Truth to Speak upon a Writ of Enquiry upon their
Oaths do Say we find for the plaintiff Seven pounds ten
Shillings and four pence with Costs of Suit. Whereupon
it is considered by the Court that the Verdict be Recorded
and that the plaintiff Recover against the Defendant in
form aforesaid and the said Defendant in Money &C &C.

Luke Carrell   Plaintiff)
  against   )   Debt
James Hogans   Defendant)   Came into Court the plaintiff
                              by Daniel Brown his attorney
also the Defendant by Jacob Brown his attorney and then
and there agree to Discontinue the said Suit at the
plaintiffs costs which is Ordered accordingly.

Luke Carrell   Plaintiff)
  against   )   Assault and Battery on attachment
Micajah Hogans Defendant)   Came the plaintiff into Court
                              by his attorney Daniel Brown
and on Motion the plaintiff the defendant is solemnly
called but came not to defend the said suit. Whereupon
it is Ordered that a Default be Entered against him.
Also Caleb Gassaway being Returned by the Sheriff Summonsed
a Garnishee Ordered that he be Sworn acko on Oath saith
that he hath in his hands five pounds Virginia Currency in
good Trade for the Defendants.

Robert Montgomery   Plaintiff)
  against   )   Debt on attachment
Davis Wilkie   Defendant)   Came the plaintiff into
                              Court by his attorney Jacob
Brown and on Motion the Defendant is Solemnly called but
came not to defend the said suit whereupon it is ordered
that a Default, be entered against him.

Gabriel Brown   Plaintiff)
  against   )   Debt on attachment
Micheal Mattocks   Defendant)   Came the plaintiff into
                              Court by his attorney Jacob
Brown his attorney aforesaid and then and there agree to
Discontinue the said Suit at his the plaintiffs own costs
which is ordered accordingly.

88 Rowland Conelius   Plaintiff
  against   Debt
William & James Thomas Administrars of Daniel Thomas
Defendant

72

Came the plaintiff into Court by Jacob Brown, also the
Defendants by James Yancy their attorneys and then and there
the said parties agree to Refer the said Suit to John
Blasingame and Thomas Vance and their award to be the
Judgment of this Court and the Same Ordered accordingly.

Luke Carrell   Plaintiff)
  against   ) Assault and Battery
Barnerd Glenn   Defendant) Came the plaintiff into Court
                             by his attorney Daniel Brown
his attorney, also Came the Defendant by William Shaw his
attorney and then and there agree to Discontinue the said
Suit at the Defendants costs which is ordered accordingly.

George Purvis   Plaintiff)
  against   ) Debt
Robert Montgomery Defendant) Came the parties into Court
                               and then and there agree to
Refer the said Suit to Charles Miles and Joseph Gault
and their award to be the Judgment of Court which Ordered
accordingly.

Robert Montgomery Plaintiff)
  against   ) Case
William Liles   Defendant) Came the parties into Court
                               and then and there agree
to Refer the said Suit to Charles Miles and Joseph Gault
and their award to be the Judgment of Court and the same
Ordered accordingly.

John Montgomery Plaintiff)
  against   ) Debt on attachment
Peter Edwards   Defendant) Whereupon the Sheriff hath
                             Returned that the Defendant
hath not any Lands Tenements Goods or Chattels within
his County Whereupon it is Ordered that the suit be discontinued at the Plaintiffs Costs.

John Foster   Plaintiff)
  against   ) Debt
Francis Wilkie Defendant) Came the plaintiff into Court
                            by James Yancy his attorney
also Comes the Defendant in his Own proper person and then
and there agree to Discontinue the said Suit at the Defendants Costs which is Ordered accordingly.

89 James Terrill Plaintiff)
     against   ) Debt
   George Purvis Defendant) Came into Court the plaintiff
                              by Jacob Brown his attorney
also Came the Defendant in his Own proper person and
acknowledged that he Owed the Plaintiff according to
Specialty produced in Court by the said plaintiff and
confessed Judgment for the same with Interest amounting in
the whole to fourteen pounds fifteen Shillings and costs
of suit...Whereupon the plaintiff agree to Stay Execution
against the said Defendant for two months which is Ordered
accordingly. Whereupon it is Considered by the Court that
the plaintiff Recover against the Defendant the Judgment
aforesaid in form aforesaid and the said Defendant in
Money &C...Also Came into Court John Montgomery who having
Entered himself Special Bail for the defendant and

delivered the said Defendant in Discharge thereof, it is
also Ordered that the Sheriff Discharge the Defendant out
of his Custody on the plaintiffs' attorney aofresaid
staying all proceedings against him the said George Purvis
for two Months as aforesaid.

```
State                          Plaintiff )
  against                               ) Assault &
Nancy Clark wife of James Clark         ) Battery on
Elizabeth Bird wife of John Bird   Defendants) Ann Collins
Sarah Gilham wife of John Gilham        )
```

The Defendants being Bound here in Recognizance to appear
hereby have failed in their Several appearances it is
Ordered that a Siereficias Issue against them to appear
at next court to Shew Cause why their said Recognizances
should not be forfeited.

```
William Liles      Plaintiff)
  against                   )  Case
Philip Shivertaker Defendant)  Came the plaintiff into
                               Court by Daniel Brown
his attorney also the Defendant by Jacob Brown his attorney
```
and then and there agree to Discontinue the said Suit at
the plaintiffs Costs which is ordered accordingly.
Signed by   Zachariah Bullock
                          John Henderson
                          Thomas Blasingame
                          William Kennedy

At a Court continued and held by adjournment in and for
the County of Union at the Courthouse of the said County
the twenty Seventh
90 day of September in the year of Our Lord One thousand Seven
hundred and Eighty Six and of the Independence of the
United States of America.
Present   Zachariah Bullock
                          John Henderson
                          John Birdsong
                          William Kennedy   Esquires
                          Thomas Brandon
                          Charles Sims
                          Thomas Blasingame

An Indenture and Deed of Conveyance Between James Wilkinson
of the One part, and William McGowen of the other part, for
two hundred acres of Land proved by the Oaths of Margaret
Barron and John Barron Witnesses thereunto and Ordered to
be Recorded.

An Indenture and Deed of Conveyance Between John Cochren
of the one part, and William McGowin of the other part, for
two hundred acres of Land proved by the Oaths of John
Barron and Margaret Barrons. Witnesses thereunto and
Ordered to be Recorded.

An Indenture of Lease and Release Between Charles Jones of
the One part and John Fincher of the other part for one
hundred and forty acres of Land acknowledged by the said
Charles Jones to the said John Fincher, and ordered to be
recorded.

74

William Smith   Plaintiff)
  against   ) Debt
Mark Jackson   Defendant) Came the plaintiff into Court
                             by James Yancy his attorney
on a Petition and Summons, also Came the Defendant in his
Own proper person and acknowledged he owed the plaintiff
the sum of one pound thirteen Shillings and one penny
and Confessed Judgment for the same and Costs of Suit.
Whereupon the plaintiff agree to Stay Execution for three
months. The Court Decree against the Defendant accordingly
also it is considered by the Court that the plaintiff
recover against the defendant in form aforesaid and the
said Defendant in Money &C &C.

Turner Rountree plaintiff)
  against   ) Trover
George Wadkins   Defendant) Came the plaintiff into Court
                             by Charles Goodwin his attorney
also Came the Defendant in his own proper person and then
and there agree to Discontinue
91 the said Suit at the Defendants Costs which is Ordered
accordingly Elizabeth Cooper being Summonsed a Witness
proved two days attendance which is ordered to be Taxed
against the Defendant accordingly.

Luke Carrell   Plaintiff)
  against   ) Slander
Caleb Gassaway Defendant) Came the plaintiff by his attor-
                             ney Daniel Brown also Came the
Defendant in his Own proper person and then and there
agree to Discontinue the said Suit at Equal Costs which
is Ordered accordingly.

Thomas Holden   Plaintiff)
  against   ) Debt
David Adams   Defendant) The plaintiff being solemnly
                             called but came not to pro-
secuted his suit it is ordered that the plaintiff be
nonsuited.

Thomas Holden   Plaintiff)
  against   ) Debt
Samuel Cooper   Defendant) The plaintiff being solemnly
                             called came not to prosecute
his suit it is therefore ordered that the plaintiff be
nonsuited.

An Indenture and Deed of Conveyance Between Gabriel Brown
of the One part and James Gassaway of the other part, for
two hundred and twenty acres of Land acknowledged by the
said Gabriel Brown to the said James Gassaway and ordered
to be recorded.

Joseph Hughs plaintiff   )
  against   ) trover
James Shockley Defendant) Ordered that there Issue a
                             Commission or Dedimus protes-
tatium to George Brown Esquire in the State of North
Carolina in Burk County to take the Deposition of Elab
Vincin and Daniel Vincin at the plantation of the said,
George Brown on the first of November next to be Read in

Evidence on the Trial at December Term next by the consent
of the parties.
Ordered that the Deposition of agnass Telshaw be taken and
that the same be admitted on the said Trial in Evidence
by the Consent of the Parties.

92 Richard Speaks & Co.   Plaintiff)
   against   ) Debt on attachment
   Robert Montgomery   Defendant) The sheriff hath
                                    Returned that John Bird
Summonsed a Garnishee who failed to appear on Motion of the
plaintiffs by Charles Goodwin their attorney a Siere
facias is awarded against the said Garnishee to appear
next Court to Shew Cause why Judgment should not be
Entered against him. Ordered that the same Issue accordingly

   State   Plaintiff)
   against   ) The
   Nancy Clark wife of James Clark   ) prosecutor
   Elizabeth Bird wife of John Bird Defendant) failed to

appear to prosecute is Ordered that the Defendants be
Released from their Recognizances on paying Costs.

   Moses Coller   Plaintiff)
   against   ) Trover
   Daniel Jackson Defendant) Ordered that a Dedimus protesta-
                              tum Issue to Edward Good Esquire
in the State of Georgia Burk County to take the depositions
of Mark Jackson and John High on behalf of the plaintiff
to be Read in Evidence on the Trial of the said Cause on
Giving fourteen days Notice to the Oppostive party of the
time and place accordingly.

   Isaac Gregory   Plaintiff)
   against   ) Debt
   Handcock Porter Defendant) Came the plaintiff into Court
                               by his attorney Jacob Brown
and the Defendant in his Own proper person and the parties
then and there agree to discontinue the said Suit at the
defendant cost which is ordered accordingly.

   Charles Clanton   Plaintiff)
   against   ) Came the plaintiff into Court
   Joseph Jully   Defendant) by William Shaw his attorney
                                and complained on petition
and summons. that the defendant is indebted to the plaintiff
the sum of Eight pounds eleven shillings by assumpsit for
a Certain Horse, Whereupon came also the Defendant by
James Yancy his attorney and defends the force of the
said Complaint the Court on hearing the Council of both
sides decree against the Defendant for Eight pounds Eleven
Shillings and Costs of Suit and it is further Considered
by the Court that the plaintiff Recover
93 against the Defendant in form aforesaid &C
Mary Lusk being Summonsed on Evidence for the plaintiff
Prove four days attendance Ordered that the same be
Taxed in the Bill of Costs against the Defendant.

   John Means   Plaintiff)
   against   ) Debt
   Robert Montgomery Defendant)

76

William Giles being Returned Common Bail for the Defendant
Comes into Court and Surrenders the Body of the Defendant
in Discharge thereof. Ordered that the Sheriff take the
Defendant into Custody untill he give other Bail.

George Kennedy   Plaintiff)
  against   ) Debt
Daniel Jackson   Defendant) Came the parties into
                            Court and then and there
agrees to Refer the said Suit to Thomas Blassingame and
John McCooll with liberty for the said arbritrators to
Choose a third person in Case they do not agree and their
award to be the Judgment of Court and the same Ordered
accordingly.

An Indenture of Deed of Conveyance Between Archer Smith
of the One part and James Harrison of the other part,
for 370 acres of Land acknowledged by the said Archer
Smith unto the said James Harrison Ordered to be Recorded.

State   Plaintiff)
  against   ) Dismissed on the Defendant
John Holman   Defendant) paying Costs

John Steen   Defendant)
  against   ) Debt on attachment
David Stockton Defendant) Adam Potter of this County
                            Comes into Court, and under-
takes for the Defendant that in case he shall be cast, in
this Suit he will pay the Judgment of Court, or Render the
Body of Defendant in Discharge thereof Whereupon it is
Ordered that he be accepted as Special Bail for the
Defendant that the Cause be continued.

State   Plaintiff)
  against   ) Dismissed on the Defendants
David Adams   Defendant) paying costs

94 Jonathan Jones   Plaintiff)
   against   ) Debt
John Montgomery Defendant) Came into Court the plaintiff
                           by Charles Goodwin his
attorney, and also the Defendant by Jacob Brown his attorney and then and there agree to discontinue the said Suit
at the Defendants Costs which is Ordered accordingly.

John Steen   Plaintiff)
  against   ) Debt
Joshua Petty Administrators   ) Came into Court
of John Nicholas   Defendant) the plaintiff by
                                      Jacob Brown his
attorney and the Defendant by William Shaw his attorney
and then and there agree to Discontinue the said Suit at
the plaintiffs Costs which is Ordered accordingly.

John Steen   Plaintiff)
  against   )
Joshua Petty administrator   ) Debt
of John Nuckols   Defendant) Came the plaintiff
                                    into Court by his
attorney Jacob Brown also Came the Defendant by William
Shaw his attorney and then and there agree to Discontinue

the said Suit at Defendants Costs which is Ordered
accordingly.

Thomas Brandon   Plaintiff)
  against   ) Detinue
Elias Mitchel   Defendant) Ordered by Consent of the
                              parties that there Issue a
Didimus potestatum to Jesse Herd Esquire in the State of
Georgia Wilks County do take the Depositions of any
Evidence whatsoever on the part of the plaintiff and that
the same be Read and admitted in Evidence on the said Trial.

A Bill of Sale Between John Smith of the one part and
William Miles of the other part for One Negroe Woman Slave
Named Rosse and a Still proved by the Oaths of Richard
Speaks and Robert Montgomery Witnesses thereunto and
Ordered to be Recorded.

An Indenture of Lease and Release Between William Steen
of the one part, and John McWhorter of the other part, for
one hundred acres of Land proved by the Oaths of
95 Adam Potter and William Hendley Witnesses thereunto and
Ordered to be Recorded.

An Indenture of Lease and Release Between Elinor McWhorter
of the One part, and John McWhorter of the other part, for
two hundred acres of Land proved by the Oaths of Adam
Potter and William Hendley Witnesses thereunto and
Ordered to be Recorded.

An Indenture of Lease and Release Between John Portman
of the One part and Nicholas Jasper of the other part,
for two hundred acres of Land proved by the Oaths of John
Henderson and John Beckham Junior Witness thereunto and
Ordered to be Recorded.

An Indenture of Lease and Release Between Elinor McWhorter
of the one part and Daniel Crownover of the other part for
fifty acres of Land proved by the Oaths of John McWhorter
and George McWhorter witnesses thereunto and ordered to
be recorded.

An Indenture and Deed of Conveyance Between Duncan McCreevan
of the one part and Joseph Hughes of the other part for
one hundred acres of Land Ordered to be Recorded.

Aaron Fincher   Plaintiff)
  against   ) Ordered that the Sheriff
David Farmer   Defendant) Expose to Sale the land Executed
                              the property of the Defendant
David Farmer at the Instance of the plaintiff Aaron
Fincher pursuant to a Judgment Obtained March Term One
thousand seven hundred and Eighty six according to Law.

James Mabrey Sworn in Constable and took the Oath of
Fedility to the State and the Oath Required by Law.

John Means   Plaintiff)
  against   ) Debt
Robert Montgomery Defendant) Came into Court John
                              Montgomery of this County
and Undertakes for the Defendant that in Case he is Cast

78

in the suit he will pay the Judgment of the Court or
Render the Body of the Defendant in discharge thereof
Whereupon it is ordered that he the said John Montgomery
be accepted as Special Bail for the Defendant and the
Defendant is thereby Released out of the Custody of the
Sheriff

96 Luke Carrell   Plaintiff)
     against   )   Slander
   Caleb Gassaway   Defendant)   Came the plaintiff by his
                                 attorney Daniel Brown also the
Defendant in his Own proper person and then and there the
parties agreed to Discontinue the said Suit at Equal Costs
which is Ordered accordingly.

Ordered that Aaron Fincher John Clark, Henry Clark, Ralph
Hunt, Daniel Lipham and Goven Gorden be and is hereby
appointed to Lay out a Road from Adam's Ford on Tygar
River to Bookter's Ferry on Enoree River.

John Clark is hereby appointed Overseer or Surveyor of
the highway from Adam's Ford on Tygar River to the Black
Rock on the Road leading to Bookter's Ferry on the River
Enoree Ordered that the said Overseer keep the same Road
in good Repair.

Stacy Cooper is hereby appointed Overseer or Surveyor of
the highway from the Black Rock to Liphams on the Road
leading from Adam's Ford on Tygar River to Bookter's
Ferry on Enoree River Ordered that the said Overseer keep
the same in good Repair.

James Colwell is hereby appointed Overseer or Surveyor of
the highway from Liphams to the County line on the road
leading from Adam's Ford on Tygar River to Bookter's
Ferry on Enoree River Ordered that the said Overseer keep
the same in Good Repair.

Joseph Hughes is hereby appointed Overseer or Surveyor
of the Highway from the said Joseph Hughe's Creek to
Edward McNeals Creek. Ordered that the same Road be
Repaired and that the said Overseer keep the same into
good Repair.

   Luke Carrell   Plaintiff)
      against   )   Slander
   James Beuford   Defendant)   Came the plaintiff into Court
                               by Shaw his attorney Daniel
Brown also came the defendant by William Shaw his attorney
and then and there agree to discontinue the said suit at
the Defendant's costs which is ordered accordingly.
Signed by   Thomas Brandon
                             William Kennedy
                             Thomas Blassingame

97 Rules and Orders of the County Court of Union in the
   State of South Carolina to be held the twenty fifth day
   of December one housand seven hundred and Eighty six 1st
   that all persons Summonsed and appearing to answer as
   garnishees in attachment, shall give in their return upon
   oath in writing.

79

2ndly. That no Writ of Enquirey after an Interlocutory
Judgment Shall be Executed, nor a Judicial attachment be
granted, nor an Order for Sale under an attachment made,
nor a decree upon a summons and petition where the defendant
maketh default pronounced nor Judgment against a garnishee
for non appearance given, without the sheriff return being
first Sworn to before a Majestrate and Indorsed on the
Writ or other prossess.
3rdly. That the Sheriff do make all his returns at Least
three days before the Court to which the Writ or other
prossess shall be returnable.
4thly. That no execution shall be issued on any Judgment
obtained in this Court untill the adjournment of the then
Court has taken place without a special order for that
purpose.
5thly. That a copy of every deed, Bond, Bill or Other
writing declared on shall be filed at the Clerks Office
at the time of filing the declaration and the Defendant
or his attorney shall have Oyer of the Original is he
thinks fit to demand it.
6th. That no attorney be permitted or Suffered to be Bail
for any person whatsoever to the Sheriff on pain of such
Censure as the Court shall think proper and the Sheriff is
hereby directed not to take any such Bails or the Bail of
any officer of the Court onbeing Severely fined.
7thly. That where more than One attorney Shall be Employed
on One side, the one that is Generally Employed shall be
Entitled to the Tax Fee.
8thly. That the plaintiff in any suit shall always be at
Liberty to Reply in Evidence but Shall not be allowed in
such reply to Introduce Testimoney foreign to that which
the defendant may have produced in his defence.
9th. That the plaintiff shall aways be entitled to the
last word.
10thly. That no attorney shall be allowed to speak more
than once in a cause where more than one attorney is
employed.
11thly. That the Civil Docket in future shall be called
twice over, and the parties shall not be Ruled to Trial
untill the second calling provided that this will not
extend to summons and petitions. which shall be first
placed on the Docket and heard at the first calling.
12. That when the Justices on the Bench proceed to give
their Judgments or Opinions the youngest Magistrate shall
begin.
Ordered that the said Rules be adoopted for the Layessers
of this Court.

98 At a Court Begun and held by adjournment in and for the
County of Union at the Courthouse of the said County the
twenty fifth day of December in the year of our Lord
One thousand Seven hundred and Eighty Six and in the Tenth
year of the Independence of the United States of America.
Present   Charles Sims
                           John Birdsong   Esquires
                           Thomas Blasingame
                           Thomas Brandon

The Court proceed to nominate and draw the Grand Jury out
of the Taxable Inhabitants of this County. Ordered that
the Sheriff summons the following persons to serve for

Grand Jurorers for a Body of Inquest for this County at
our next Court.

1.	John Jenkins	11.	Hugh Dollison
2.	Isaac Cook	12.	William Beckham
3.	Turner Tountree	13.	Alexander Carter
4.	James Hawkins	14.	Nathaniel Guyton
5.	Isaac Hawkins	15.	John Goodwin
6.	John Clark	16.	Joseph Jones
7.	John Cook	17.	Robert Lusk
8.	John Wilson	18.	Jeremiah Hamilton
9.	Henry Darby	19.	Hugh Means
10.	George Story	20.	John Bankhead

The Court proceeded to draw the petitt Jury Indiscreminately
out of the Taxable Inhabitants of this County. Ordered
that the Sheriff Summons the following persons to Serve
as petitt Jurorers for this County at our next Court
they being drawn according to Law.

1.	Francis Wilkie	16.	John Netherman
2.	Henry Youngerman	17.	Alexander Hamilton
3.	William Mays	18.	William Pearson Senior
4.	John Beckham	19.	Thomas Skelton
5.	William Skelton	20.	James Story
6.	Nathan Glenn	21.	Caleb Gassaway
7.	John White	22.	David Dixon
8.	Obediah Howard	23.	James Petty Junr.
9.	William Lawson	24.	Lewis Turner
10.	William Cooper	25.	John Gaston
11.	William McJunkin	26.	Samuel Otterson
12.	Samuel Thompson	27.	Ralph Jackson
13.	Stacy Cooper	28.	William Hawkins
14.	Jacob Segar	29.	Joseph Little
15.	Joseph Jolly Junior	30.	Goven Gorden

99 acknowledged an Indenture of Deed of Conveyance Between
William Johnson of the one part, and Charles Sims of the
other part by the said William Johnson to the said Charles
Sims for two hundred acres of Land ordered to be Recorded.

An Indenture and Deed of Conveyance Between Thomas Brandon
of the One part, and Christopher Young of the other part
for one hundred acres of Land acknowledged by the said
Thomas Brandon to the said Christopher Young and Ordered
to be recorded.

An Indenture and Deed of Conveyance between George Crosley
of the one part and Aurther Brandon of the other part, for
Eighty six acres of Land acknowledged by the said George
Crosley to the said Aurthur Brandon and Ordered to be
Recorded.

An Indenture and Deed of Conveyance Between George Crosley
of the one part and James Bell of the other part, for
Eighty Six acres of Land acknowledged by the said George
Crosley to the said James Bell and Ordered to be Recorded.

An Indenture and Deed of Conveyance Between Christopher
Brandon of the one part and Thomas Brandon Esquire of the
other part for one hundred acres of Land acknowledged by
the said Christopher Brandon to the said Thomas Brandon
and Ordered to be Recorded.

An Indenture of Lease and Release Between Daniel Oglesby
of the one part and James Hoggat of the other part, for
three hundred and fifty acres of Land laying on Enoree
which was acknowledged by the said Daniel Oglesby to the
said James Hoggat before the Justices of the County Court
of Davison in the State of North Carolina at the July
Sessions One thousand seven hundred and Eighty five and
the same Ordered to be Recorded in this County.

An Indenture and Deed of Conveyance between William Bryant
of the one part and George Harlin of the other part for
twenty five acres of Land proved by the oaths of Thomas
Brandon and John Murrell Witnesses thereunto and ordered
to be recorded.

An Indenture of Lease and Release between James Hoggat of
the one part and Marlor Prior of the other part, for three
hundred and fifty acres of Land proved in Court by the
Oaths of Thomas Blassingame Esquire and the same Ordered
to be Recorded.

100 An Indenture and Deed of Conveyance Between Francis
Fincher of the one part and John Fincher of the other part
for one hundred and fifty acres of Land ordered to be
Recorded.

An Indenture and Deed of Conveyance Between Francis
Fincher of the one part and John Fincher of the other part,
for one hundred acres of Land ordered to be recorded.

William Farr high Sheriff of this County pursuant to a
Commission and the act of assembly nominated and appointed
William Birdsong Deputy Sheriff in and for the said County
of Union which meet with the Concurrence and approbation
of the Court, Whereupon it is Ordered that he take the
Oath Required by Law, the said William Birdsong took the
oath prescribed by Law and by the act of assembly and
entered into the Execution of the said Office accordingly.

Ordered that the petitt Jury be drawn to serve this Court
which is done accordingly.
1. George Harlin   7. John Sission
2. Charles Clanton   8. Nathaniel Jeffries
3. Renney Belue   9. Isaac Hawkins
4. Samuel Thompson   10. William Skelton
5. Alexander McDougal   11. John McKee
6. Ralph Jackson   12. John Harrington

An Indenture and Deed of Gift Between Mary Feemster of
the one part and Samuel Feemster of the other part for
one hundred and fifty acres of Land Recorded in Tryon
County in North Carolina and Ordered to be Recorded here
in Union County.

An Indenture of Lease and Release Between John Grindall
and his wife of the one part and John Watson and Adam
Chesham of the other part, for four hundred and thirty
acres of Land proved by the Oaths of David Chisham and
Jesse Mabray Witnesses thereunto and ordered to be Recorded.

82

An Indenture and Deed of Conveyance Between James Huey
of the one part and John Grindal of the other part for
one hundred acres of Land Ordered to be Recorded.

101 John McCooll proved an accompt of two pair of Iron shokels
for Prisoners for the use of this County. Ordered that
he be allowed eighteen shillings and eight pence out of
the County Treasury for the same.

Ordered that William Hughes be allowed to Establish and
keep a Ferry on Broad River on said William Hughes Land
Opposite John Loves Land.

An Indenture and Deed of Conveyance Between Ferdinand
Hopkins of the one part, and Daniel Lipham of the other
part acknowledged by the said Ferdinand Hopkins to the
said Daniel Lipham and Ordered to be Recorded.

John Birdsong Esquire appointed Overseer of the Road from
Elishia Green Fence to Thomas Brandon's Shoals on Fairforrest in the Room and place of Joseph West, Ordered that
the said Overseer keep the same Road in good Repair.

An Indenture and Deed of Conveyance between Thomas Brandon
of the one part and Christopher Brandon Senior of the other
part, for three hundred acres of Land acknowledged by the
said Thomas Brandon to the said Christopher Brandon and
Ordered to be Recorded.
Signed by   John Birdsong
                             Charles Sims
                             Thomas Blassingame
                             William Kennedy

At a Court continued and held by adjournment in and for
the County of Union at the Court house of the said County
of Union the twenty six day of December one thousand seven
hundred and eighty six and of the Independence of the
United States of America the Eleventh.
Present   William Kennedy
                             Charles Sims   Esquire
                             Thomas Blasingame
                             John Birdsong

An Indenture and Deed of Conveyance Between William
Gilham and Jean his wife of the one part, and John Hamilton
of the other part, for eighty acres of Land Ordered to be
Recorded.

John Harrington and Joseph Jolly is hereby appointed to
lay out a Road from the old Meeting house to Smith's
Ford on Broad River the said Road leading from said
Smith's Ford to Major Charles Miles's the same Ordered
accordingly.

102 John Harrington is hereby appointed Overseer of the
Road from Smith's Ford on Broad River to the Old Meeting
house the said Road leading from said Smith's Ford to Major
Charles Miles in the Room and place of William McCullock.
Ordered that said Overseer keep the same Road in good
Repair.

83

A Bond Between John Weidman of the one part and George
Purvis of the part for a Title for three Hundred acres
of Land and a Mill proved by the Oaths of Thomas Brandon
Esquire and Robert Lusk and Ordered to be Recorded.
An assignment on the said Bond Between the said George
Purvis of the One part and John Ewart of the other part
for the said three hundred acres of Land and Mill, proved
by the Oaths of John Hope a Witness thereunto and Ordered
to be Recorded.

Present   Thomas Brandon Esquire

An Indenture and Deed of Conveyance Between William Cotter
and wife of the one part and James Martin of the Other
part for one hundred and fifteen acres of Land proved by
the Oaths of Charles Miles and Robert Lusk Witnesses
thereunto and Ordered to be Recorded.

An Indenture of Conveyance of Lease and Release Between
William Gault of the one part and John George of the other
part, for one hundred acres of Land proved by the Oaths of
Nicholas Jasper and John George Junior Witnesses thereunto
and ordered to be recorded.

An Indenture of Lease and Release between John McWhorter
of the one part and John George of the other part, for
proved by the Oaths of Nicholas Jasper and John George
Junior Witness thereunto and Ordered to be Recorded.

A Receipt between Thomas Wright of the one part and
Temperance Saffold of the other part for four negroes
proved by the Oath of Adam Thompson Witness thereunto and
ordered to be Recorded.

An indenture and Deed of Conveyance between John Steen
and Martha his wife of the one part and John Thompson of
the other part for two hundred and eighty four acres of
Land proved by the Oath of Francis Lettimore also came the
said John Steen and acknowledged the same to the said John
Thompson and ordered to be recorded.

An Indenture of Lease and Release Between Archer Smith
103 of the one part and John Putman of the other part for
two hundred acres of Land acknowledged by the said Archer
Smith to the said John Putman and Ordered to be Recorded.

John Pearson   Plaintiff)
    against   )   Came the parties into Court
William Johnson Defendnat)   and then and there agree to
                              discontinue the said suit at
the plaintiff's costs which is ordered accordingly.

Joseph Jones plaintiff)
    against   )   Debt on attachment
David Adams   Defendant)   Whereas William Farr being
                           Summonsed as a garnishee, sworn
and on oath saith he hath in his hands of the property of
the Defendant David Adams two pounds Eleven shillings and
Eleven pence Judgment awarded against the said William
Farr as garnishee for the same.

84

Ordered that the County Treasurer pay to Joseph Jones
Geoler Sixteen Shillings and Eight pence for Goal Fees
on account of Adam Moore.

Thomas Brandon attorney   )
for James Campbell   Plaintiff) Debt on attachment
     against   ) Came the plaintiff
James Ainsworth   Defendant) into Court by Jacob
                                     Brown his attorney
on Motion the Defendant waa Solemnly called but came not
to Defend the said suit whereupon final Judgment is
ordered against the defendant for fifty pounds former
currency equal to seven pounds two shillings and ten pence
sterling & costs, of suit also Judgment awarded against
Isaac Bogan as garnishee in the said Suit as confessed in
his hands.

Thomas Brandon   Plaintiff)
     against   ) Debt
Nathaniel Jeffries Defendant) Came the plaintiff into
                               Court by his attorney
aforesaid and the Defendant in his own proper person and
then and there agree to discontinue the said suit at the
defendants csots which is ordered accordingly.

William Farr   Plaintiff)
     against   ) Ordered that the said suit
Edward McNeal   Defendant) abate on account of the defen-
                              dants death at the plaintiffs
                              costs.

104 Philip Shivertaker Plaintiff)
     against   ) Debt.
George Pruvis   Defendant) Came the plaintiff into
                                    Court by Jacob Brown his
attorney on petition and summons and complains that the
defendants owes him four pounds two shillings due by
accompt also come the defendant by William Shaw his
attorney and defends the said suits the Court on fully
hearing the Council on both sides consider and decree
against the defendant for three pounds and costs of suit,
and it is further considered by the Court that the
plaintiff recover against the defendant in form aforesaid
&C.

Luke Carrell   Plaintiff)
     against   ) Assault & Battery
Micajah Hogan   Defendant) Came the plaintiff into Court
                             by Daniel Brown his attorney
aforesaid and then and there agree to Discontinue the said
suit at his the said plaintiff's own costs which is
Ordered accordingly.

William Farr   Plaintiff)
     against   ) Trover
Charles Humphries Defendant) Came into Court the plaintiff
                              by his attorney Jacob Brown
also came the defendant in his own proper person and they
then and there agree to discontinue the said suit at the
defendant's costs which is ordered accordingly.

Ordered that William Farr Sheriff take into his Charge the
Body of John Inlow.

John Ewart assignee of Nathaniel   )
Briggs and William Williams   Plaintiffs)
    against   )
Rebecca and William George   )   Debt
Administrators of David George   Defendants)

Came the plaintiffs into Court by James Yancy his attorney
and complains that the defendants are indebted to him on
petition and summons the sum of twenty five pounds former
currency due by note and interest amounting to six pounds
one shilling sterling, also came the defendants by their
attorney Jacob Brown and defends the said suit the Court
on fully hearing the Council on both sides consider
and decree against the Defendants according to Specialty
and Interest due thereon amounting to
105 to Six pounds one Shilling and costs of suit, and it is
further considered that the plaintiff Recover against the
Defendant in form aforesaid...Julama Pucket being
Summonsed as on Evidence on behalf of the plaintiff
proves two days attendance ordered that the same be taxed
in the bill of costs.

Ordered that the Sheriff summons six tallismen for the Grand
Jury.

An Indenture of Lease and Release between Abgail Padget
of the one part and Ralph Hunt of the other part for one
hundred acres of Land proved by the Oath of James
Addington as Witness thereunto.

Ordered that Summons issue against the Defaulters of the
Grand Jury to appear at next Court to Shew Cause why they
should not be fined.

Sarah Davison   Plaintiff)
    against   )   Case
Moses Guyton   Defendant)   Came the plaintiff into Court
                              by her attorney Daniel Brown
also the Defendant by James Yancy his attorney and then
and there agree to Refer the said Suit to Joseph Guyton,
Isaac Parker, William McCullock, Robert Lusk and John Hope
and there award to be the Judgment of this Court to be
Returned by next Court and the same Ordered accordingly.

Thomas Brandon   Plaintiff)
    against   )   Debt
David Adams   Defendant)   The body of the defendant
                              moved by a Heabes Corpas to
Ninety Six Ordered that the Suit be discontinued at the
plaintiffs costs.

The Sheriff Returned John Brandon, Hugh Nelson, Daniel
Jackson, James Caldwell, John White, John Story as
Tallismen on the Grand Jury by him summonsed.

Caleb Gassaway)
    against   )   Case
Thomas Taylor)   Came the parties into Court in there own

106 proper persons, and then and there agree to discontinue
the said suit at the defendant's costs which is ordered
accordingly.

The Grand Jury Impounded and Sworn
1. Jame Crawford, foreman   8. Handcock Porter
2. David Hudson   9. John Brandon
3. Isaac Parker   10. Hugh Nelson
4. Thomas Mays   11. Daniel Jackson
5. William Lawson   12. James Caldwell
6. Drewry Murrell   13. John White
7. Nathaniel Jackson

Who having Received their Charge Returned from the Barr to
consult their verdict.

John Woods   Plaintiff)
   against   )   The parties having agreed to
Hugh Means   Defendant)   Refer the said Suit to arbitra-
                            tion and the award of the said
arbitrators to be the Judgment of Court, as appears by the
said parties the same is therefore Ordered accordingly.
Signed by   Thomas Brandon
                            John Birdsong
                            William Kennedy

At a Court conintued and held by adjournment in and for
the County of Union at the Court hosue of the said County
the twenty seventh day of December in the year of Our
Lord One thousand seven hundred and Eighty six, and of the
Independence of the United States of America the Twelvth.
Present   Thomas Brandon
                            John Birdsong
                            Thomas Blassingame   Esquires
                            Charles Sims
                            William Kennedy

An Indenture and Deed of Conveyance Between James Gray
of the one part and Robert Woodson of the other part,
for one hundred and fifty acres of Land proved by the
Oaths George Gray and William Woodson Witnesses thereunto
and Ordered to be Recorded.

107 Robert Montgomery Plaintiff)
    against   )   Debt on attachment
George Purvis   Defendant)   Comes the parties into
                                Court and then and there
agree to Continue the said suit untill next Court which is
Ordered accordingly.

Ordered in all cases Referred to arbitration that they
stand over untill next Court if the awards are not
Returned this term, and to be returned next Court, and of
then not returnable to go on as if the same had not been
Referred.

Thomas Gorden and Gabriel Anderson   )
Administrators of Joshua Anderson   Plaintiffs)
Deceased   )
   against   ) In Debt
Tobithia Pearson Executrix of   )
Enoch Pearson Deceased   Defendant)

Came the plaintiffs into Court by James Yancy their attorney
and pled their declaration against the Defendants wherein
they complain that on the fifty day of July in the year
of our Lord one thousand seven hundred and Sixty nine the
said Enock Pearson Deceased became indebted to the
plaintiffs as administrators of the said Joshua Anderson
the sum of six pounds ten shillings sterling and that the
said Enoch Pearson nor the Defendant as Executrix of the
said Enoch Pearson hath not paid the same to the Damage of
the plaintiff &C. Whereupon Came also the Defendant by
her attorney William Shaw and Defends &C. and pleads the
Statutes of Limitations of this State. Whereupon came also
a Jury To Wit Alexander McDougal George Harlin Charles
Clanton Samuel Thompson, Ralph Jackson, John Sission,
Nathaniel Jeffries, Isaac Hawkins, John McBee, John
Harrington, William Plummer and John Jinkins who being
duly drawn and sworn the truth to speak upon an issue joined
upon their Oaths do say we find for the plaintiff six
pounds ten shillings and interest. Whereupon it is
considered by the Court that the Verdict be recorded and
that the plaintiffs recover against the defendant in form
aforesaid and the said defendant in Money &C &C. Whereupon
the said Defendant by his attorney William Shaw aforesaid
from the said Judgment prays an appeal to the Court of
Common Pleas Oyer &C. to be held at Ninety Six on the
twenty sixth day of June next for Reason's filed the
Same...which said appeal was granted to the Defendant. on
giving Bond and Security to the plaintiffs for the prosecuting of the said appeal with effect according to Law,
Whereupon the said Tobitha Pearson Together with John
Bogans and James Gibbs her Security Entered into and
acknowledged their Bonds to the said appellee and filed the
same. Which is ordered accordingly.

108 Luke Carrell   Plaintiff)
       against   )   Assault and Battery
Daniel McElduff Defendant)   Came the plaintiff by his
                                   attorney Daniel Brown also
Came the Defendant by his attorney William Shaw and then
and there agree to Discontinue the said suit at Defendants
costs except an attorneys fee which is ordered accordingly.

Warran Hall   Plaintiff)
   against   )   In Debt
James Sims   Defendant)   Came the plaintiff into Court
                              by Charles Goodwin his attorney
and filed his declaration against the Defendant. Wherein
he complains that on the ninth day of January One thousand
seven hundred and eighty six the defendant became indebted
to the plaintiff the sum of seventeen pounds seventeen
shillings whereupon came also a Jury To Wit Alexander
McDougal George Harlin Charles Clanton Samuel Thompson
Ralph Jackson John Sission Nathaniel Jefferies Isaac Hawkins John McKee John Harrington, William Plummer and John
Jenkins. Who be duly drawn and sworn the truth to speak
upon their oaths do say we find for the seventeen pounds
seventeen shillings also we do say that the plaintiff pay
the cost of suit. Whereupon the plaintiff agree to stay
an execution against the Defendant for three months...
Whereupon it is considered by the Court that the plaintiff
Recover against the Defendant inform aforesaid and the said
Defendant in Money &C &C.

88

Luke Carrell   Plaintiff)
  against   )   Assault and Battery
Daniel McElduff   Defendant)   Came the plaintiff by his
                                attorney Daniel Brown, also
Came the Defendant by his attorney William Shaw and then
and there agree to Discontinue the said suit at the
Defendants Costs Except an attorney's fee which is Ordered
accordingly.

Thomas Blassingame   Plaintiff)
  against   )   Tresspass
William Lee   Defendant)   Came the plaintiff into
                                Court by his attorney
James Yancy and filed his Declaration against the Defendant
wherein he complains that about the twenty eight day of
November one thousand Seven hundred and Eighty the Defendant did with force of Arms at the plantation of the plaintiff take twenty Grown hoggs to the Value of twenty pounds
to his damage &C...Whereupon came the Defendant by William
Shaw his attorney and Defends the force and Injury and whatsoever Else he Ought to Defend and saith he is not guilty
as the plaintiff hath complained.
109 against him in the Declaration and this he praymay be
Enquired of by the Country and the plaintiff prays the same.
Whereupon the parties by their attorney aforesaid agree
to try the Issue Joined Whereupon came also a Jury to Wit.
Alexander McDougal George Harlin, Charles Clanton, Samuel
Thompson, Ralph Jackson, John Sission, Nathaniel Jefferies,
Isaac Hawkins, John McKee, John Harrington, William Plummer,
and John Jinkins who being duly drawn tried and sworn the
truth to speak upon the Issue Joined Upon their Oaths do
say we find for the Defendant One shilling damage and costs
of suit. Whereupon it is considered by the Court that the
Verdict be Recorded and that the Defendant Recover against
the plaintiff in form aforesaid &C &C.
Whereupon the plaintiff by his attorney move for a new
trial, the consider the refer the motion until the
morrow at nine OClock.

The Grand Jurors for the State aforesaid upon their
Respective Office Oaths do make and Return the Following
Bills and presentments We do present Joseph Jolly for
an assault and battery on the body of James Clark. We
also present John Steen for Cow-Stealing Adam Goudylock
the prosecutor. We also present Thomas Moody. We also
present Isaac Holman for Dealing with Negroes Philip
Trammel the prosecutor, We also present Lewis Bobo for
getting Drunk and Swaring. & Signed by
1. James Crawford foreman   8. Handcock Porter
2. David Hudson   9. John Brandon
3. Isaac Parker   10. Hugh Nelson
4. Thomas Mays   11. Daniel Jackson
5. Drewry Murrell   12. James Colwell
6. William Lawson   13. John White
7. Nathaniel Jackson
Signed by   William Kennedy
                           Thomas Brandon
                           John Birdsong

At a Court Continued and held by adjournment in and for
the County of Union at the Courthouse of the said County
the twenty eight day of December in the year of Our Lord

One thousand Seven hundred and Eighty Six and of the
Independence of the United States of America the Eleventh.
Present   William Kennedy
                                 Charles Sims   Esquires
                                 John Birdsong
                                 Thomas Blasingame

Thomas Brandon   Plaintiff)
   against   )   In Detinue
Goven Gorden   Defendant)

110 Came the plaintiff into Court by his attorney Daniel
Brown also Came the Defendant by his attorney William
Shaw...Whereupon John Grier Margaret Grier and Margaret
Montgomery being Legally Summonsed as Evidences on behalf
of the plaintiff Thomas Brandon failed to appear on being
Solemnly Called on which the plaintiff was under the
necessity to suffer a nonsuit which is ordered accordingly
and considered by the Court that the Defendant Recover
against the plaintiff five shillings damage and costs of
suit. &C. Colonel Levey Casey proved six days attendance
and twenty miles to the Courthouse from Newberry County on
the part of the Defendant which is Ordered to be Taxed in
the Bill of Costs..Edward Finch proved nine days attendance
and thirty miles to the Courthouse from Newberry County
on the part of the Defendant, Ordered that the same be
Taxed in the Bill of Costs, John Dunkin proved Eight
days attendance and twenty miles from Newberry County to
the Courthouse Ordered that the same be Taxed in the Bill
of Costs against the plaintiff &C.

Ordered that in future there be no claims of Witnesses
Received in this court any other way but in writing.

Thomas Stribling Junior   Plaintiff)
   against   )   In Detinue
Thorowgood Chambers   Defendant)   Came the plaintiff
                                        into Court by his
attorney William Shaw and filed his Declaration against
the Defendant Wherein he complains that on the twenty fifth
day of October in the year of Our Lord One thousand seven
hundred and Eighty five he was possessed of a Certain
Molatoe Man Slave aged about twenty nine years Named
Charles which the Defendant detains to the plaintiffs
Damage &C. Whereupon came also the Defendant by his
attorney Charles Goodwin and defends the force and Injury
and whatsoever he ought to defend and pleads the same with
leave to give all Special matters in Evidence and this he
prays maybe Enquired of by the Country and the plaintiff
prays also the same therefore the parties agree to Try
the Issue Joined. Whereupon came also a Jury To Wit
Alexander McDougal, George Harlin, Charles Clanton, Samuel
Thompson, Ralph Jackson, John Sission, Nathaniel Jefferies,
Isaac Hawkins, John McKee, John Harrington, William Plummer,
and Avery Breed who being duly drawn tried and sworn the
truth to speak upon the Issue Joined upon their oaths do
say we find the defendant doth detain. Whereupon it is
Considered by the Court that the Verdict be Recorded and
that the plaintiff recover against the defendant in form
aforesaid &C. &C.

90

111 From which said Judgment the Defendant Througood Chambers
by his attorney Charles Goodwin his attorney aforesaid prays
an appeal to the Court of Common Pleas Oyer &C. to be held
at Ninety Six on the twenty sixth day of April next for the
Reasons certified & filed &C. Which said appeal was
Granted to the Defendant on Giving Bond and Security to
the plaintiff for the prosecuting of the said appeal
with Effect according to Law...Whereupon the Defendant
together with John Hampton and Joshua Palmer Entered into
and acknowledged their Bonds to the said appealee and filed
the same, which is ordered accordingly.

Robert Montgomery   Plaintiff)
   against   )   Came the plaintiff by his
Soloman Mangham   Defendant)   attorney Jacob Brown also
                                 Came the Defendant by his
attorney James Yancy his attorney and on Motion of the
Defendant by his attorney aforesaid it is Ordered that the
plaintiff be nonsuited. also it is considered by the Court
that the Defendant Recover against the plaintiff five
shillings Damage and costs of suit and the same Ordered
accordingly.

State South Carolina Plaintiff)
   against   )   Petitt Larcency
John Steen   Defendant)   Came into Court Daniel
                                   Brown attorney for the
State aforesaid in this County and filed a Bill of Indictment found by the Grand Jurors of this County against the
Defendant wherein the attorney for the State aforesaid
Saith that the Defendant did with force of arms privately
and feloniously Steal take and Carry away a Certain Cow,
about three years old of the Value of Thirty Shillings of
the property and from the possession of Adam Goudylock
against the Pease and Dignity of the said State, and to
the Evil Example of all others...Whereupon the Defendant
in his Own proper person Defends and Saith he is not Guilty
as is Mentioned against him in the said Indictment and
further saith he is not Ready for Trial Whereupon it is
Ordered that he the said Defendant Give Good Bail two
securities in the sum of fifty pounds each, and the
Defendant in the sum of one hundred pounds, and on failure
thereof to be committed to Goal & the same Ordered
accordingly.

Daniel Brown   Plaintiff)
   against   )   debt on attachment
Jesse Rackstraw Defendant) William Steen being Summonsed
                             as a Garnishee personally
appeared and being Sworn Saith that he is Indebted to the
Defendant Jesse Rackstraw a Negroe Boy between Eight and
Twelve years of age...Came also the plaintiff and
Complains by his attorney Thomas Peter Carnes on the said
attachment that the Defendant is Justly indebted to him
the sum of ten
112 pounds due by Note bearing date the twenty second day of
September One thousand seven hundred and Eighty Six
Whereon the Court Decree against the Defendant for ten
pounds and Cost of Suit also decree the same against
the garnishee with Stay of Execution until the fifteenth
of February next and then to Issue against the garnishee
for debt and costs.

Thomas Brandon attorney   )
for William Cunningham   Plaintiff)
    against   ) Debt on attachment
David Adams   Defendant) Came the plaintiff
                                      into Court on a
Default and Complains by his attorney William Shaw in his
declaration that on the twenty sixth day of February One
thousand Seven hundred and seventy seven the Defendant
became indebted to John Cunningham the sum of five hundred
pounds by the Condition of a Certain Bond Which afterwards
became the legal Right and property of the said William
Cunningham to the damage of the plaintiff &C. Whereupon
Came also a Jury To Wit Alexander McDougal, George Harlin
Charles Clanton, Samuel Thompson, Ralph Jackson, Nathaniel
Jefferies, Isaac Hawkins, John McKee, John Harrington,
William Plummer and Avery Breed who being duly drawn Tried
and Sworn the Truth to Speak upon a Writ of Enquiry upon
their Oaths do say we find for the plaintiff five hundred
pounds South Currency with Interest amounting in the whole
to One hundred and nineteen pounds five shillings and eight
pence Sterling and Costs of Suit Whereupon it is Considered
by the Court that the Verdict be Recorded and that the
Plaintiff Recover against the Defendant in form aforesaid
and the said Defendant in Money &C &C.

Joseph Hughes   Plaintiff)
    against   ) Trover
James Shockley   Defendant) Came the plaintiff into Court
                             by James Yancy his attorney
and filed his Declaration against the Defendant wherein
that Benjamin Jolly in his lifetime on or about the twentieth day of November in the year of Our Lord one thousand
seven hundred and Eighty One was possessed of a Certain
Brown bay Horse, and the said Benjamin Jolly lost the said
Horse out of his hands; and by finding came to the hands and
possession of the defendant who refuseth to deliver up the
same to the plaintiff as attorney for Joseph Jolly to his
damage fifty pounds &C. Whereupon came also the Defendant
by Charles Goodwin his attorney and defends the force and
Injury and whatsoever else he ought to defend and saith
that he is not Guilty . The plaintiff hath complained
against him in his declaration and
113 this he prays may be enquired of by the Country and the
plaintiff doth the same, then and there they agree to try
the Issue Joined...Whereupon came also a Jury toWit
Alexander McDougall, George Harlin, Charles Clanton,
Samuel Thompson, Ralph Jackson, John Sission, Nathaniel
Jeffries, Isaac Hawkins, John McKee, John Harrington,
William Plummer and Avery Breed who being duly drawn
Tried and Sworn the Truth to Speak upon the Issue joined
upon their Oaths do say we find the Defendant Guilty of
the Trover and Conversion in the declaration mention and
do assess damages by occassion thereof to twenty Eight
pounds Eleven Shillings besides his Costs of Suit. Wherefore it is considered by the Court, that the plaintiff
Recover against the defendant the damages in form aforesaid and his costs by him in this behalf expended and the
said defendant in Money &C &C.
Signed by   William Kennedy
                          Thomas Brandon
                          Thomas Blasingame

92

At a Court continued and held by adjournment in and for
the County of Union at the Courthouse of the said County
the twenty ninth day of December in the year of Our Lord
One thousand Seven hundred and Eighty Six and in the
Twelvth year of the Independence of the United States of
America.
Present   William Kennedy
                           Thomas Brandon   Esquires
                           Charles Sims

An Indenture and Deed of Conveyance Between Robert Bishop
and Elizabeth his wife of the one part and Walter Holmes
of the other part, for one hundred and thirty acres of
Land proved by the Oaths of James Woodson and Daniel
Jackson Witnesses thereunto and Ordered to be Recorded
also the said Elizabeth Bishop acknowledged her right of
Dower in Open Court which is ordered to be Recorded.

James Barron   Plaintiff   )
   against   ) Debt
Benjamin Long & Wife   ) Came the plaintiff
Administrator of Isaac King Defendant) into Court by his
                                      attorney Jacob
Brown and complains in petition and summons that the Defendants are indebted to the plaintiff one pound seventeen
shillings and four pence also Came the defendant by his
attorney Daniel Brown and Defends &C. The Court on hearing
the Council on both sides consider and decree against the
Defendant one pound seventeen shillings and four pence and
costs of suit.
Whereupon the plaintiff agree to stay execution against
the Defendants for three months.

114 John Fondrin   Plaintiff)
      against   ) Debt on attachment
   Archibald Rutherford Defendant) Came the plaintiff into
                                    Court on a Default and
Complained on petition and summons the Court on fully
hearing the same Decree against the Defendant for four
pounds five shillings and eight pence and costs of suit
ordered that an Execution Issue against Drewry Jones as
garnishee for the money Condemned in his hands.

Thomas Stribling &   )
William Buchannon   Plaintiffs)
   against   ) Debt on attachment
William Gist   Defendant) Came the plaintiff into
                                    Court and filed there
Declaration against the Defendant by their attorney
Daniel Brown Wherein they complained that on the first day
of January in the year of Our Lord One thousand seven
hundred and seventy nine the defendant became indebted to
the plaintiff the sum of ten thousand pounds equal to one
hundred and Eighty seven pounds fourteen shillings and five
pence sterling.
To the Damage of the plaintiffs and so forth...Whereupon
the aforesaid Sarah Gist Wife of the said William Gist
comes in Court by his attorney William Shaw as aforesaid
and pleads for the said Sarah Gist as followeth ToWit
1st by an act of this State passed the twenty sixth day of
February One thousand Seven hundred and Eighty two the
person of the said William Gist was Banished from this

State all the Estate both Real and personal of the said
William Gist was confiscated and the same vested in
Commissioners for the Uses and purposes in the said act
mentioned and contained...that by the twenty third section
of the said Law all persons subject or this or any of the
United States who had demands against the Estate of the
said William Gist Should lay a State and proof of such
demands before the said Commissioners on or before a
Certain Day there...in mentioned who were thereby Required
Empowered to Examine into the Justice and Validity of the
said Demands and make Report to the General assembly at
their next Meeting to the use and that the Legislature
might direct with Respect to such Creditors what to Justice
Should appertain and that the amount of Sales of the
Estate of the said William Gist was made liable to satisfy
the said Demand.
2ndly. That by Virtue of the aforesaid Confiscation act a
very considerable part of the Real Estate of the said
William Gist was sold and disposed of and the proceeds
thereof Lodged in the public Treasury of this State for
the purposes of satisfying all legal demands against the
said William Gist and the use of the State, and that there
still remains in the public Treasury a considerable balance
thereof.
3dly. That by an act of this State passed the nineteenth
day of March One thousand Seven hundred and Eighty five.
Stating that whereas it was but consistant with Justice
and humanity that a suitable maintanance should be made
to the said Sarah Gist wife of the said William Gist's
Estate confiscated. It was enacted that five hundred
acres of any lands late the property of the said William
Gist not sold
115 by the Commissioners of forfeited Estates the said Sarah
Gist should choose should be, and the said was thereby
vested in the said Sarah Gist and her children by the said
William Gist their heirs and assigns forever the said
act further enacted that all the personal property under
Confiscation not disposed of for public purposes lately
belonging to the said William Gist should be and the same
was thereby vested in the said Sarah Gist and her children
4thly. That the Effects and property attached as aforesaid
by the said Thomas Stribling and William Buckannon is not
the property of the said William Gist but is the absolute
Right and property of the said Sarah Gist as a feme sole
free and Independant of the said William Gist as a feme
Sole and this She is Ready to Verify.
5thly. That the said Sarah Gist further alledges that the
Bond on which the attachment is granted is defective and
void first because it is given to William Gist who cannot
sue on said Bond he being an Outlaw and a banished person
and secondly because the condition of the said Bond is only
to prosecute the said Suit against the said William
Gist with Effect. Whereas it ought to have Been to pay
Costs and Damages in Case the said Stribling and Buckannan
discontinue or are cast in their suit.
6thly. The said Sarah Gist further alledges that as the
Goods and Chattels attached are her property and given to
her use as a feme sole, if said goods are liable to the
payment of the debts of William Gist She ought to have
had Notice of the Debt according to the Law for Regulations
of Sheriffs Sales...and also if the debt declared for is
due the plaintiff ought to have demanded Security according

94

to the act of assembly for the Recovery of Old Debts
passed in the year of Our Lord one thousand seven hundred
and Eighty four. Whereupon came also a Jury ToWit
Alexander McDougal, George Martin, Charles Clanton, Samuel
Thompson, Ralph Jackson, John Sission, Joseph West, Isaac
Hawkins, John McKee, John Harrington, William Plummer,
Avery Breed who being drawn tried and Sworn the truth to
speak upon the Issue Joined Upon their Oaths do say that
the Defendant pay unto the plaintiffs one hundred and
twenty pounds and costs of suit Wherefore it is considered
by the court that the Verdict be Recorded, and that the
plaintiffs Recover against the defendant the Debt aforesaid
and their Costs of Suit in this behalf Expended in form
aforesaid and the said Defendant in Money &C &C. From
which said Judgment the Defendant Sarah Gist by her
attorney William Shaw aforesaid prays an appeal to the
Court of Common Pleas to be held at the Town of Cambridge
on the Twenty Sixth day of April next for the District of
Ninety six Oyer &C. for the Reasons, filed &C. Which said
appeal was granted to the Defendant on giving Bond and
Security to the plaintiffs for the prosecuting the said
appeal with Effect according to Law Whereupon the Defendants
Sarah Gist together with John Woodson Benjamin Woodson
116 and Thomas Layton her securitys who entered into and
acknowledged their Bonds in the sum of one hundred pounds
to the said appealee and filed the same which is ordered
accordingly.

An Indenture of Lease and Release Between Colonel William
Farr of the One part and Henry Long of the Other part for
three hundred and Seventeen acres of Land was acknowledged
by the said William Farr to the said Henry Long and
Ordered to be Recorded.

John McCooll   Plaintiff)
   against   )   Debt on attachment
John Cansler   Defendant)   Wherein the Sheriff Returned
                                 that he summonsed Alexander
Cane a garnishee who be being solemnly called but came not
on Motion of the plaintiff by his attorney Daniel Brown
a Siere ficias is awarded against him to appear at our
next Court to Shew Cause why Judgment should not be entered
against him.

Robert Leveret   Plaintiff)
   against   )   trover
Thomas Brandon   Defendant)   Came the plaintiff into
                                 Court by his attorney
Daniel Brown also the Defendant in his own proper person
and then and there agree to discontinue the said suit
at the plaintiff's costs which is ordered accordingly.

Adam Thompson   Plaintiff)
   against   )   Debt
Benjamin Crownover Defendant)   Came into Court the
                                 Defendant by his attorney
Jacob Brown and on Motion of the said Defendant by his
attorney aforesaid the plaintiff was solemnly called but
came not to prosecute his suit Wherefore it is Ordered that
he be nonsuited and considered by the Court that the
Defendant Recover against the plaintiff five shillings
damages and costs of suit.

Thomas Brandon   Plaintiff)
  against   ) Debt
Epaphriditus Paulk   Defendant) Whereupon the Sheriff
                                  hath Returned that the
defendant was not to be found in this his County Whereupon
the plaintiff by his attorney Jacob Brown pray a Judicial
attachment against the Estate of the Defendant which is
awarded him and Ordered accordingly.

State   Plaintiff)
  against   ) Dealing with Negroes
Isaac Holman   Defendant) Came the Defendant into Court
                                  in his Own proper person and
pleaded Guilty Whereupon the
117 Court consider and fine the defendant fifteen shillings
and costs of suit and to stand committed to Goal until the
same Judgment be paid by the said Defendant.

William Plummer   Plaintiff)
  against   ) Debt on attachment
Daniel Plummer   Defendant) Ralph Jackson being
                                  summonsed a Garnishee says
on Oath that as administrator to his Father Ralph Jackson
he believes there is money due to the said Defendant but
what sum is not assertained. Ordered by this Court that
all moneys Goods or Chattels that are in his hands or at
time of being summonsed as garnishee be condemned in
Garnishees hands, not exceeding fifty pounds.

William Farr   Plaintiff   )
  against   ) Debt
John Steen and   ) Came the plaintiff into
Francis Lettimore Defendant)   Court by his attorney
                                  William Shaw also Came the
defendant on their own proper persons and acknowledged
that they owed the plaintiff one hundred pounds due by
Bond, and confessed Judgment for the same with costs of
Suit. Wherefore it is considered by the Court that the
plaintiff recover against the defendants the debt aforesaid
and his costs on this behalf expended, in form aforesaid
and the said defendant in Money &C &C.

State   Plaintiff)
  against   ) Assault and Battery on
Charles Miles   Defendant) Nicholas Jasper
                                  Came into Court Daniel Brown
attorney for the said State in this County on a Bill of
Indictment found by the Grand Jurors of this County against
Defendant, and Complains that with force of arms on the
___ day of September One thousand seven hundred and
Eighty five the defendant did on the Body of the said
Nicholas Jasper Commit on assault beat Wound abuse and ill
treat the said Nicholas Jasper against the peace and
Dignity of the said State &C. Whereupon came also a Jury
ToWit Alexander McDougal, George Harlin, Charles Clanton,
Samuel Thompson, Ralph Jackson, John Sission, Joseph
West, Isaac Hawkins, John McKee, John Harrington, William
Plummer and Avery Breed who being duly drawn tried and
Sworn the truth to speak upon the said Bill of Indictment
upon their Oaths do say we find the defendant Guilty.

96

```
State          Plaintiff)
  against            )      Came into Court the Defendant
John Steen   Defendant)     Together with Robert Lusk and
                            John Montgomery his Securitys
```
and Entered into and acknowledged their Bonds Viz the said
118 Defendant John Steen in the sum of one hundred pounds and
the said Robert Lusk and John Montgomery in the sum of
fifty pounds each for the said Defendant John Steen's
appearance at our next court.

```
John Means         Plaintiff)
  against               )    Case
Robert Montgomery  Defendant)  Came into Court the
                            plaintiff by his attorney
```
Daniel Brown aforesaid also Came the defendant by his
attorney Jacob Brown aforesaid thereupon came also a Jury
ToWit. Alexander McDougal, George Harlin, Charles Clanton,
Samuel Thompson, Ralph Jackson, John Sission, Joseph West,
Isaac Hawkins, John McKee, John Harrington, William
Plummer and Avery Breed who being duly drawn Tried and Sworn
the Truth to Speak upon the Issue Joined upon their Oaths
do say we find for the plaintiff thirty nine pounds two
shillings and eight pence damages and costs of suit.
Wherefore ti is considered by the Court that the plaintiff
recover against the defendant the damages assessed as
aforesaid and his costs in this behalf expended and the
said defendant in Money &C &C.
Signed by   Thomas Brandon
                          William Kennedy
                          John Birdsong

At a Court continued and held by adjournment in and for
the County of Union at the Courthouse of the said County
the thirtieth day of December in the year of Our Lord on
thousand seven hundred and Eighty six and of the Independence of the United States of America the Eleventh.
Present   William Kennedy
                          Charles Sims   Esquires
                          John Birdsong
                          Thomas Brandon

An Indenture and Deed of Conveyance Between Joseph Jones
of the one part and John McCooll of the other part for
one hundred and fifty acres of Land acknowledged by the
said Joseph Jones to the said John McCooll Ordered to be
Recorded.

Ordered to be Recorded the Deposition of Thomas Pearson and
William Young taken by John Johnson Esquire the Sixteenth
day of April one thousand seven hundred and seventy seven.

Ordered that the Sheriff Expose to Sale the land under
attachment the property of David Adams pursuant to a final
Judgment Obtained at the Instance of Thomas Brandon.

Ordered that Executions Issue against all persons brought
into this
119 Court on Recognizances or Otherwise and by presentment and
were dismissed on payment of Costs While James Yancy
Esquire acted as County attorney and Render him his fees
and the Treasurer the fine.
```
```

State   Plaintiff)
  against   )   Ordered that Execution Issue
James Hogans   Defendant)   against the defendant James
                           Hogans for the fine inflicted
on him at March Court. that is to say nineteen pounds
Nineteen shillings and eleven pence, and that due Return
be made at next Court.

State   Plaintiff)
  against   )   Ordered that the defendant
Charles Miles Defendant)   Charles Miles be fined one
                           pound one shilling and nine
pence for the assault and Battery of which he was yesterday
foudn Guilty and the costs of the prosecution.

William Farr   Plaintiff)
  against   )   William Kennedy Esquire
William Wafford Defendant) Coroner having returned an
                           order of sale for a tract
of one hundred acres of Land attached as the property of
the defendant William Wafford at the Instance of the
plaintiff William Farr that the said Tract of Land
Remains unsold for want of Buyers a Writ of Venditione
Esepona is awarded him, and it is Ordered that the said
Land be exposed to sale anew.

John McCool   Plaintiff)
  against   )   Debt on attachment
John Cansler   Defendant)   Came into Court Alexander Cane
                           a Garnishee on the said
attachment Sworn and On Oath saith that he is indebted to
the Defendant John Cansler the price of a Cow and Calf
which the Court adjudge to be worth two pounds six shillings
and eight pence and Condemn the same in the hands of the
said Alexander Cane, the Court on fully hearing the
Complaint of the plaintiff by his attorney Daniel Brown
aforesaid decree against the defendant for four pounds
ten shillings and costs of suit.

An Indenture and Deed of Conveyance Between Briant White
and Judith his Wife of the one part and Avery Breed of
the other part, for two hundred acres of Land Ordered to
be Recorded.

David Vincen   Plaintiff)
  against   )   Debt on attachment
William Head   Defendant)   Ordered that the Sheriff

120 a Certain Horse attached the property of the Defendant at
the Instance of the plaintiff David Vincen and have the
Money before the Justices at our next Court.

Benjamin Savage is hereby appointed Surveyor or Overseer
of the Road from Love's Ford on Broad River to James
Bogan's Creek in the place of Benjamin Woodson Ordered that
he keep the same Road in Good Repair.

Thomas Vance is hereby appointed Overseer of the Road from
James Bogans Creek to Union Courthouse, Ordered that he
keep the same Road in Good Repair.

Jacob Paulk is hereby appointed Overseer of the Road from Union Court house to Fairforrest Creek at Colonel Thomas Brandon's Shoals ordered that he keep the same road in Good Repair.

Nehemiah Howard is hereby appointed Overseer of the Road from Brandon's Shoals on Fairforrest to Tygar River Ordered that he keep the same Road in Good Repair.

Andrew Torrence is hereby appointed Overseer of the Road from Tygar River to Enoree River ordered that he keep the same road in Good repair.

Ordered that William Farr and John Sorter be and is hereby appointed to lay out a Road from the Dry pond on the Charleston Road to Gregory's Creek, and the said William Farr and John Sorter is hereby appointed Overseers of the same Road Ordered that they keep the same in good Repair.

Ordered that Jeremiah Gregory and John Savage lay out a Road from Gregory's Creek to Union Courthouse and the said Jeremiah Gregory and John Savage is hereby appointed Overseer of the same Road and it is Ordered that they keep the same Road in Good Repair.

Ordered that the Clerk Issue Order to Each of the Overseers of the Road to Examine and Clear out their Respective Roads and keep them in good Repair.

Ordered that the County Treasurer pay to Joseph Jones one pound sixteen shillings and three pence for fees due for keeping David Adams in Goal.

121 Ordered that the following Rates be Recorded and those who keep Taverns be allowed to Sell accordingly and no higher Rum two shillings and four pence pr Quart
        ditto one shilling and six pence pr pint.
        ditto Ten pence pr Half pint
        ditto Six pence pr Gill

Common West India Rum	two Shillings.......	Quart
ditto	one shilling	pr pint
ditto	eight pence pr half pint	
ditto	five pence pr Gill	
Country Rum	One shilling & Six pence pr Quart	
ditto	Ten pence pr pint	
ditto	E pence pr Half pint	
ditto	four pence pr Gill	
Jamacia Toddy with Loaf Sugar one shilling & four pence		pr Quart
Common West India ditto One Shilling & two pence pr Quart		
Madera Wine	four Shillings & Eight pence pr Quart	
Teneriff Wine	two shillings & Ten pence pr Quart	
Clarett Wine	two shilling pr Quart	
Port Wine	two shillings & four pence pr Quart	
Dinner	one shilling and two pence	
Breakfast or Supper	ten pence	
Hony or Blades	Eight pence pr Night	
Corn	Six pence pr Gallon	
Lodging	three pence pr Night	

Court adjourned untill Court of Course

Signed by   William Kennedy
                                Charles Sims
                                Thomas Brandon
                                John Birdsong

At a Court Begun and held in and for the County of Union
at the Courthouse of the said County the twenty Sixth day
of March in the year of our Lord One thousand Seven hundred
and Eighty Seven and in the Eleventh year of the Indep-
pendence of the United States of America.
Present   Charles Sims
                                John Birdsong   Esquires
                                Thomas Blassingame
                                William Kennedy

Ordered that the Sheriff Summons the following persons to
serve as grand Jurors for a Body of Inquest for this County
at our next Court they being Nominated and drawn according
to Law.

1. John Putman   6. James Bell
2. Samuel Harris   7. James Thomas
3. Robert Burns   8. Thomas Skelton
4. William Hardwick   9. Levy Hollingsworth
5. Avery Breed   10. Samuel Crawford

122 11. John Murrell   16. Nehemiah Posey
     12. John Brandon   17. William Savage
     13. Alexander McCarter 18. Benjamin Hawkins
     14. Joseph Wood   19. Nicholas Curry
     15. Samuel Littlejohn 20. Moses Guyton

Ordered that the Sheriff Summons the following persons
to Serve as petitt Jurors at our next Court the same
being drawn according to Law.

1. John Wilson   16. Bird Beuford
2. Daniel Burmmet   17. Landlot Porter
3. Jesse Young   18. Robert Bell
4. Zion Murphy   19. Jesse Jinkins
5. Lewis Turner   20. John Hopkins
6. George McWhorter   21. James Doane
7. Thomas Bishop   22. William Littlefield
8. William Shaw   23. John McWhorter
9. William Hawkins   24. William Sharp
10. William Smith   25. William Pattent
12. Matthew Jones   26. William Smith
13. James Hawkins   27. William Spencer
14. Benjamin Johnson 28. John Hawkins
15. Thomas Scales   29. William McCullock
                    30. John Story

A Release Between Hannah Brown of the One part, and Colonel
William Farr of the other part proved by the Oaths of
Charles Sims Esquires Witness thereunto and Ordered to be
Recorded.

Ordered that the Treasurer pay unto the Sheriff and Clerk
their arrears of their annual salarys for their Extra
Services out of the first money receives of the county.

An Indenture and Deed of Conveyance Between Jacob Brown
of the one part and John Jolly of the other part for one

hundred acres of Land proved by the Oaths of John Ewart
and John McCooll Witness thereunto and Ordered to be
Recorded.

An Indenture of Lease and Release Between Obediah Howard
of the One part and Zachariah Bell of the other part, for
one hundred acres and fifty acres of Land proved by the
Oaths of John Ewart and John McCooll Witnesses thereunto
and ordered to be Recorded.

An Indenture and Deed of Conveyance Between Jesse Fore
of the One part and Thomas Palmer of the other part for
one hundred and fifty acres of Land proved by the Oaths

123 of Henry Coldwell and Abraham Jones Witnesses thereunto
and Ordered to be Recorded.

An Indenture and Deed of Conveyance Between Edward and
Ann Musgrove of the One part and Robert Creanshaw for
One hundred acres of Land proved by the Oaths of Stephen
Creanshaw and Edward Ragsdale Witnesses thereunto and
Ordered to be Recorded.

An Indenture and Deed of Conveyance Between William and
Dorcas Hills of the one part and Edward Ragsdale of the
other part, for two hundred acres of Land proved by the
Oaths of Stephen Creanshaw and Francis Creanshaw
Witnesses thereunto and Ordered to be Recorded.

An Indenture and Deed of Conveyance Between Avery Breed
of the one part and Aaron Harlin of the other part, for
two hundred acres of Land acknowledged by the said Avery
Breed to the said Aaron Harlin and Ordered to be Recorded.

An Indenture and Deed of Conveyance Between John Haile
of the One part and George Harlin of the Other part, for
twenty acres of Land acknowledged by the said John Haile
to the said George Harlins Ordered to be Recorded.

An Indenture and Deed of Conveyance Between John Haile
of the one part and Thomas Blassingame of the other
part, for five hundred and five acres of Land acknowledged
by the said John Haile to the said Thomas Blassingame
Ordered to be Recorded.

An Indenture and Deed of Conveyance Between James Hall
of the one part and Nathan Sandwich of the other part, for
one hundred acres of Land proved by the Oaths of William
Kennedy and Richard Pruit Witnesses thereunto and
Ordered to be Recorded.

An Indenture and Deed of Conveyance Between James Hall of
the one part and Richard Pruit of the other part for one
hundred acres of Land proved by the Oaths of Kennedy and
Nathan Sandwick Witnesses thereunto and Ordered to be
Recorded.

An Indenture and Deed of Conveyance Between Thomas Gorden
of the one part and John McNeal of the other part acknowledged be the said Thomas Gorden to the said John McNeal
and ordered to be Recorded.

101

An Indenture and Deed of Conveyance Between Thomas Gorden
of the one part and Rebecca McNeal of the Other part,
acknowledged by the said Thomas Gorden to the said Rebecca
McNeal and Ordered to be Recorded.

An Indenture of Lease and Release Between Robert McWhorter
of the one part and James Wood of the other part for five
hundred acres of Land proved by the Oath of Matthew a
Witness thereunto and the hand writing of John Nuchols
another Witness to the same proved by the Oath of John
Haile and Ordered to be Recorded.

An Indenture and Deed of Conveyance Between Joseph Breed
and Catherine his wife of the One part and John Birdsong
of the other part, for one hundred acres of Land proved by
the Oaths of George Harlin and Avery Breed Witnesses
thereunto and Ordered to be Recorded.

An Indenture of Lease and Release Between William Orr of
the one part and William Rogers of the Other part for two
hundred acres of Land ordered to be Recorded.

An Indenture and Deed of Conveyance Between Lewis Bobo and
Sarah his wife of the one part and Drewry Murrell of the
other part, for two hundred acres of Land proved by the
Oaths of Samuel Murrell and John Murrell Witnesses thereunto and Ordered to be Recorded.

An Indenture of Lease and Release Between Mark Jackson
and Elizabeth his wife of the one part and Patrick Shaw
of the Other part for two hundred acres of Land proved by
the oaths of Samuel Noblet a Witness thereunto &C.

An Indenture and Deed of Conveyance Between Francis Posey
and Mildred his wife of the one part and Benjamin Hollingsworth of the other part for one hundred acres of Land
proved by the Oaths of Josiah Wood and John Wood Witnesses
thereunto and Ordered to be Recorded.

An Indenture and Deed of Conveyance Between Francis Posey
and Mildred his wife of the one part, and John Wood of the
other part, for one hundred acres of Land proved by the
Oaths of Josiah Wood and Benjamin Hollingsworth.
124 Witnesses thereunto and Ordered to be Recorded.

An Indenture and Deed of Conveyance Between David Hopkins
and Mary his wife of the one part and James Sims of the
other part for six hundred acres of Land proved by the
Oaths of Nathan Glenn, and Ferdinand Hopkins Witnesses
thereunto and Ordered to be Recorded.

An Indenture of Lease and Release Between Joseph Howell
of the one part and James Oliphant of the other part for
four hundred and ninety three acres of Land acknowledged
by the said Joseph Howell to the said James Oliphant
and Ordered to be Recorded.

A Bill of Sale between Robert Liveritt of the one part and
Bartholomew Brooks of the other part for one negro Woman
Slave named Jude, proved by the oath of William Rogers and
Ordered to be Recorded.

A Bill of Sale between Robert Leveret of the One part and
William Rogers of the other part for one negro man named
Jame also One Still, proved by the Oaths of Jeremiah
Hamilton and John Malone Witnesses thereunto and Ordered
to be Recorded.

Moses Collier   Plaintiff)
  against   ) Trover
Daniel Jackson   Defendant) Came the parties by their
                          attorneys aforesaid then and
there agree to Continue the Suit until Wednesday next and
there to be tried the first Cause which is ordered
accordingly.

An Indenture and Deed of Conveyance Between Ralph Humphreys
of the one part, and Isaac Hawkins of the other part, for
one hundred acres of Land ordered to be recorded.

An Indenture and Deed of Conveyance Between John McCooll
of the one part and Joseph Jones of the other part, for
one hundred acres of Land acknowledged by the said John
McCooll to the said Joseph Jones and Ordered to be Recorded.

John Still   Plaintiff)
  against   ) This suit being before
William Beckham   Defendant) Discontinued at the plaintiffs
                          Costs and on an execution
against the said plaintiff came into court Isaac Edwards
as a garnishee and on Oath saith he hath in his hands
three flax wheels the property of the said John Still and
the Court Condemn the same in his hands of said Edwards.

125 Sarah Davision   Plaintiff)
    against   ) Case
    Moses Guyton   Defendant) This suit being submitted by
                          agreement and Order of
Court to arbitration that is to say to Joseph Guyton,
Isaac Parker, William McCullock, Robert Lusk and John Hope
who Return the following award To Wit to the Worshipful
Court of Union to Whom this present writing Indented of
award Shall come Greeting Whereas there are several
accounts depending and Divers Controverseys and Disputes
have lately arose Between Sarah Davison of the County of
Union and Moses Guyton of the said County &C...all which
Controverseys and Disputes are Chiefly Touching and
Concerning an action of Trespass on the Case Damage fifty
pounds Sterling and whereas for the puting an End to the
said Suit the Worshipful Court of Union hath appointed
Joseph Guyton, Isaac Parker, William McCullock, Robert
Lusk and John Hope as arbitrators to arbitrate adssudge
and Determine the said Controversey
Now know ye that we the said arbritrators whose names are
hereunto subscribed and seales affixed taking upon us the
Burshing of the said award and having examined and duly
Considered the proffs and allegations of both the said
Parties, do for the sethling amity and friendship between
them make and publish this our award by and between the
said parties in Manner following that is to say we do also
award and order that the said Moses Guyton shall pay or
Cause to be paid to the said Sarah Davison the sum of
forty pounds ten shillings sterling. with interest until
paid and Costs of Suit in Witness Whereof we have hereunto

set our hands and seals this fifteenth day of January 1787
(Joseph Guyton (Seal)
(Isaac Parker (Seal)
(William McCullock (Seal)
Robert Lusk (Seal)
John Hope (Seal)

Which said award is by the Court Ordered by the Court to
be Recorded also Considered that the plaintiff Recover
against the defendant according to the same in form
aforesaid and the said Defendant in Money &C &C.

Joseph Walker   Plaintiff)
   against   ) Debt
Jeremiah Stokes Defendant) Came the plaintiff into Court
                           by his attorney James Yancy
and complains on a petition and summons that
126 the Defendant is indebted to him the sum of six pounds
two shillings and ine pence and Interest due by note,
whereupon came also the defendant in his own proper
person and acknowledged the owed the plaintiff according
to specialty and confessed Judgment for the same with
costs of suit whereupon came William Shaw Esquire and
acknowledged payment for debt and costs whereon the
plaintiff by his attorney aforesaid agree to Exonerate
the Defendant from the same which is ordered accordingly.
that the Defendant is Indebted to him the sum of six pounds
two shillings and nine pence and Interest due by note,
Whereupon came also the Defendant in his Own proper person
and acknowledged he owed the plaintiff according to
Specialty and confessed judgment for the same with costs
of suit..Whereupon came William Shaw Esquire and acknowledged payment for debt and Costs whereon the plaintiff
by his attorney aforesaid agree to exonerate the Defendant
from the same which is Ordered Accordingly.

Ordered that Stacy Cooper be served with an order to be
Overseer of the Road on that where he was appointed at
December Term last.
Signed by   Charles Sims
                             John Birdsong
                             Thomas Blasingame

At a court continued and held by adjournment in and
for the County of Union at the Court house of the said
County the twenty seventh day of March in the year of our
Lord One thousand Seven hundred and Eighty Seven and of the
Independence of the United States of America the Twelvth.
Present   William Kennedy
                           Charles Sims   Esquires
                           Thomas Blassingame

A Bill of Sale Between Thomas Poultress of the one part
and William Farr of the Other part, for a Negroe Woman
Slave Named Doll and One Molatoe Boy Named Will proved by
the Oath of William Beckham Witness thereunto and Ordered
to be Recorded.

Ordered to be Recorded a power of attorney from Noah
Williams and Mary his wife to the said Thomas Poultress.
Present   John Birdsong Esquire

Benjamin Purkins Esquire produced a Licence or Certificate from the Honourable Henry Pendleton, Thomas Heyward and Aedamus Burk Judges of the State of South Carolina to practice as an attorney in the several courts in this State, Ordered that he be admitted accordingly.

James G. Hunt, is allowed to Practice as an attorney in this Court, on his producing his Credentials at our next Court which is ordered accordingly.

127 An Indenture and Deed of Conveyance Between William Grant of the one part and John Palmer of the other part for One hundred acres of land acknowledged by the said William Grant to the said John Palmer Ordered to be Recorded.

An Indenture and Deed of Conveyance Between Isaac Chapman of the one part and Benjamin Jones of the other part for one hundred acres of Land acknowledged by the said Isaac Chapman to the said Benjamin Jones and Ordered to be Recorded.

An Indenture of Lease and Release Between Robert Coleman of the one part and Abner Coleman of the other part, proved by the oaths of John Haile a witness thereunto and Ordered not to be Recorded untill proved by the Oaths of Zachariah Bullock or John Henderson Esquires.

An Indenture and Deed of Conveyance Between Gabriel Brown of the one part and James Gassaway of the other part for two hundred acres of Land proved by the oaths of Daniel Brown and John Gregory Witnesses thereunto and Ordered to be Recorded.

An Indenture of Lease and Release Between Isaac Sampson and Phebe his wife of the one part and Colonel William Farr of the other part for four hundred acres of land proved by the Oaths of William Thomas and James CarOeal Witnesses thereunto and ordered to be Recorded.

James Gibbs is hereby appointed Overseer of the Road from Fairforrest Creek to Tygar River on the Ninety six Ordered that he keep the same Road in good Repair.

Julaina Pucket   Plaintiff)
 against   ) Trover on Petition & Summons
John Montgomery Defendant) Came the plaintiff into Court
          her attorney Daniel Brown and
complains that he did take away from her a certain horse and converted the same to his own use. Whereupon came also the defendant by his attorney Daniel Brown and defends &C. Whereon the Court on fully hearing the Council on both sides Ordered the said Suit to be dismissed at the Plaintiff's Costs. Whereupon it is considered be the Court that the Defendant Recover against the plaintiff in form aforesaid and the said plaintiff in Money &C &C.

128 An Indenture and Deed of Conveyance Between William George of the one part and William Whitlock of the other part, for Eight hundred acres of Land proved by the oaths of Job Hammond and Handcock Porter Witnesses thereunto and Ordered to be Recorded.

State South Carolina   Plaintiff)
    against   )   Petty Jury drawn and
John Steen   Defendant)   sworn namely Samuel
                                          Otterson foreman
James Petty, Samuel Thompson, William Pearson, Caleb
Gasaway, Obediah Howard, Stacy Cooper, James Story, Joseph
Little, John White, William Lawson and Nathan Glenn return
their Verdict on their Oaths Say that the defendant is
Guilty.

Acknowledged in open Court a Deed of Conveyance from
Turner Kendrick to William Hendley by the said Kendrick
for 200 acres of Land and Ordered to be recorded.

An Indenture and Deed of Conveyance Between John Weed-
ingham of the one part and Turner Kendrick of the other part
for two hundred acres of Land acknowledged by the said
Jno Weedengman to the said Turner Kendrick and Ordered to
be recorded.

An Indenture and Deed of Conveyance Between Jno Weedengman
of the one part and Turner Kendrick of the other part
for one hundred acres of Land acknowledged by the said
Jno Weedingman to the said Turner Kendrick and Ordered to
be Recorded.

An Indenture of Lease and Release Between Wm. Scisson of
the one part and John Weedingman of the other part for
one hundred and Ninety five acres of Land proved by the
Oaths of Christopher Weediman and William Kennedy proved
the hand Writing of John McDonnell one of the Evidences
to the said Lease and release and Ordered to be Recorded.

An Indenture and Deed of Conveyance Between John McCooll.
of the one part and Thomas Evans of the other part for
ninety four acres of Land acknowledged by the said John
McCooll to the said Thomas Evans and Ordered to be recorded.

Robert Montgomery proved Two days attendance as an Evidence
for the Deft in the Suit Juliana Pucket agat. Jno Montgomery
Junr. also Hugh Taylor Two days attendance for the defendant

An Indenture and Sheriffs Deed of conveyance Between
William Farr Sheriff of the one part and Aaron Fincher of
129 the Other part for one hundred and fifty acres of Land
acknowledged by the said Wm. Farr Shff to the said Aaron
Fincher and Ordered to be Recorded.

State S. Carolina Plff   )
    agt   )   Nusance
Lewis Bobo   Defendt.)   Ordered to be Discontinued at
                                     the Deft. paying all costs.

John Gregory   Plaintiff)
    vs   )   Refered to Cold. Wm. Farr
Jeremiah Hamilton Defendant)   William Smith Cold. John
                                     Lindsey and Jeremiah
Williams to be determined on the Third Saturday in April
next and their award to be the Judgment of the Court.

106

Archd. Fore   Plaintiff)
  vs   )   Agreed to be Refered to William
Jno Holeman   Defendant) Farr and John Ewart with
                          Liberty to chose a 3d man and
their award to be the Judt. of the Court.

Mark Jackson   Plaintiff)
  agt   )   Abner Coleman Summoned as a
William Meek   Defendant) Garnishee filed the Deposition

The Grand Jury being Sworn and returned to consult their
Oppinion returned on their respective oaths and brother
in the following bills the State against William Steen
an Indictment for Hog Stealing the State against Thomas
Cox an Indictment the state against John Steen an
Indictment the State against Thomas Shockley an Indictment
the State against William Brownon an Indictment also
returned the presentments which is ordered to be recorded
and prosses to issue against those who are presented.
Present   Wm Kennedy
                           Chas. Sims   Esquires
                           Jno Birdsong
                           Thos. Blasingame

At a Court continued and held by adjournment in and for
the County of Union on the Twenty ninth day March one
thousand Seven hundred and Eighty Seven
Present   Charles Sims   Esquires
                           John Birdsong
                           Thos. Blasingame

An Indenture and Lease and Release Between Mark Murphy
and Holly Murphy of the one part and Bird Murphey of the
other part for one hundred and fifty acres of Land proved
in Open Court by the Oaths of William Jackson and Ralph
Jackson and Ordered to be Recorded.

130 Moses Collier Pltf)1Nathan Glen foreman)7Stacy Cooper
      agt (Trover)   )2James Petty   )8James Story
    Daniel Jackson Deft)3Saml. Thompson   )9Joseph Little
    William Jackson   )4William Pearson   )10John White
    Sworn on Evidence   )5Cleb Gasaway   )11William Lawson
    for Defendant   )6Obediah Howard   )12Job Hughes
    Mark Jackson for Deft. Ruth Jackson for Deft. Nancey
    McCone for Deft. Fanny Blassingame for pltf & Deft.
    Christian Plumer for Plff & Deft. the Jury find for the
    Plaintiff Fifteen pounds & with Costs of Suit Nathan
    Glenn Foreman.

John Lusk   Plaintiff)
  agt.   )   Ordered to be Continued untill
Mark Jackson   Defendant) next Court.

On Motion of John McCool Leave is Given him to keep a
Tavern or public House by giving bond with Security to
the Clark and complying with the Law wherefore William
Young and Cold. William Entered themselves Security
accordingly.

Ordered that all the Causes now depending be Continued
Over Until next Court.

Robert Lusk being bail for John Steen has delivered him up and is thereby acquited and released of his bail.

Ordered that John Steen receive on his bair back fifteen lashes by the Sheriff with a hickory switch for stealing a Cow the property of Adam Goudylock to the Value of Thirty Shillings Sterling whereof he is Convicted.

Ordered that the Sheriff take in Custody Harrisson Bell for an atrocious assault to the Court.

Moses Collier   Pltf)
  agt.   )   William Jackson proved Twelve days
Daniel Jackson   )   attendance Fanny Blasingame proved
                                five days attendance Christian
Plummer proved Eleven days attendance as Witnesses in this Suit for the Pltf. which is Ordered to be Taxed in the bill of Cost;
Ordered that the Harrisson Bell be released on paying of Cost.

Present.   John Birdsong
                                    Thos. Blasingame   Esquires
                                    William Kennedy

The Worshipful Court met according to adjournment the Thirtieth day of March one thousand seven hundred and Eighty seven

Present   John Birdsong
                                    Thos. Blasingame   Esquires
                                    William Kennedy

Stacy Cooper is hereby appointed Overseer of the Road from

131 The black Rock to Danl Liphams and that he be authorized to take the said Road the Nearest and best way and that he keep the same in Good repair according to Law.

Samuel Otterson is appointed Overseer of the Road in the placed of John Wilson on the Road where the said John Wilson was formerly appointed and that he keep the same in Good Repair &c.

An Indenture and Deed of Conveyance from John Letta of the one part and Robert Wallace of the other part for two hundred and Twenty eight acres of Land proved by the Oath of John Birdsong and Ordered to be recorded and this by John Thomas Junr. also an acknowledgement of Sarah Letta wife to the said Jno Letta to the said Land of 270 acres conveyed, and Ordered to be recorded.

William Giles   Ptlf)
     vs   )   George Awbrey being called according
George Awbrey   Deft)   to Law by the Sheriff and not
                                appeared the said Wm. Giles pray a
Default which is Granted and the Jury Sworn on a writ of enquirery ToWit.
1. Nathan Glenn Foreman   5. Caleb Gasway
2. James Petty   6. Obadiah Howard
3. Samuel Thompson   7. James Story
4. William Pearson   8. Stacy Cooper

108

```
9.  Joseph Little          11.  William Lawson
10. John White             12.  Ralph Jackson
The Jury find for the Pltf. Ŀ 15, 10, and Costs of Suit.
```

Robert Lusk   )
  agt   ) Awrit against Bradly Collins being
Bradley Collins) returned Nothing found the plaintiff
                  prays a Judicial attachment which is
                  awarded him.

Ordered that the Evidence in the Suit William Giles against
George Anbrey determined prove their attendance; which
William Beckham proved Seven days attendance for the
plaintiff.

Ordered that the Sheriff expose to sale the property of Thos.
Lantrip taken by an Execution at the Instance of Saml.
Farrow according to Law.

Mark Jackson)
  vs   ) Attachment the same Jury do before sworn
William Meek) who say on their oaths they find for the
                Pltf five pounds with costs of Suit &C.

Ordered that there be a Stay of Execution in the Cases
yesterday determined between Moses Collier against Danl.
Jackson for three month from this Day by consent of the
parties.

Ordered that Archelous Fore Receive from the Treasury four
shillings for mending the Joal.

132 State S. Carolina)
  agt   ) The prosecutors being Solemnly called
Soloman Mangham   ) failing to appear on which the Court
                      Ordered that his recognizance should
be forfeited also Ordered that a Citation Issue against the
forfeited recognizance to appear at Our next Court, and this
Suit dismissed at Deft. Costs.

State S. Carolina)
  agt   ) Assault and Battery on Soloman
Robt. Montgomery) Mangham Whereupon Came a Jury The same
                    as William Giles against George Anbry
who being Duly sworn to try the Issue Joined Return their
Verdict & Say we find him Guilty. Whereas the Court
Ordered him fined One pound and Costs of Suit. and ordered
that Capias. Issue against his body.

Zachariah Bell presented by the Grand Jury for Over
Selling Spirituous Liquors Over the Rates allowed by Law.
Whereupon the Court fined him One Shilling and Six pence
and Costs of the presentment.

State So. Carolina)
  against   ) Assault & Battery on David Stogdon
John Steen   ) the Defendant pled Guilty Whereupon
                     The Court fined him One pound and
Cost of Suit.

Luke Carrell   )
    vs.   ) Debt.
Joseph Franklin) Came the Plaintiff into Court by his
                attorney James Yancey and the Defendant
by Jacob Brown his attorney Whereupon Came a Jury ToWit.
James Petty, Samuel Thompson, William Pearson, Obadiah
Howard, James Story, Stacy Cooper, Joseph Little, John
White, William Lawson, Ralph Jackson, Joseph Jones and
David Stogdon who being duly drawn and Sworn Return their
Verdict on their Oaths & Say we find for the Plaintiff
Eight pounds and costs of Suit. Which verdict was ratifyed
by the Court.

Ordered that the Clerk at next September Term present the
Court with an exact List of all fines inflected by this
Court since the Sheriff was sworn in with what sums have
been paid of said fines and also what persons that have
been Licenced to keep public house and what dutys have been
paid and also a List of the present Overseers of the Road
in this County.

Ordered that processes Issue against all persons presented
by the Grand Jury at this Term.

On the application of Zachariah Bell Lease is Given him to
Keep Tavern in this County on his Giving Bond with Robert
Lusk and James Bell his Securety according to Law.

On Motion of James Yancey atto. for John Thomas that
Judgment be entered against William Farr Sheriff of this
County for the amount. of Debt and Costs of a Judgment
John Thomas Obtained against. John Steen the Sheriff
Confessed no tuce according to Law. and also Confessed
Judgment agreeable to the above Monteon for the amount
of the execution that Thomas obtained against. Steen Which
is made a Judgement of this Court.

133 William Farr Sheriff of this County appointed Herman Howard
his Deputy Sheriff which met with the approbation of the
Court, when he took the necessary Oaths of Office prescribed
by Law.

Ordered that the following alteration be made in the Tavern
Rates for the Year 1787.
                            SD
Jamaica Rum pr Gallon 9-4   Northward Rum &
           pr Quart   2-4   Taffia pr Gallon   5
           pr pint   1-0   pr Quart   1-6
           pr gill   -6   pr pint   -10
           pr ½ pint   10   pr ½ pint   6
West India Rum pr Gallon 8   pr gill   4
           pr Quart   2-
           pr pint   1-2 Jamaica Toddy with Loaf
           pr ½ pint   8   Sugar pr Quart   12
           pr gill   5   West India pr Ditto 11
Mederia Wine pr Bottle 48 Teneriffe pr Bottle 2/10
Port Wine pr Bottle   24 Clarrett wine pr Bottle 21
Dinner one shilling breakfast and supper ten pence
Horse Keeping pr night on good fodder with four quarts
of Corn 11 Corn pr Gallon Six pence Good Lodgeing pr Night
three pence.

Ordered that the Clerk Send a Copy of the above rates with
each Tavern Licence.
French Brandy pr pint 10d. and Other Quanties same as
Jamaica Rum Holland Ginn the same Whisky four pence pr
half pint pr pint seven pence pr quart one shilling pr
gallon three shillings peach Brandy Six pence pr ½ pint
ten pence pr pint eighteen pence pr. Quart and four
shillings pr gallon.

Ordered that a Seiri facias issue against the Garnishees
in the Suit Mark Jackson against William Meek to appear at
our next Court to shew cause if any they have why Judgment
should not be entered against them for not answering
Defending & Clearing themselves.

William Cureton   Plaintiff)
     vs   )   Debt.
William Brummet   Defendant)   The Defendants attorney Moved
                               for a Non suit which was
granted by the court.

Ordered that the Treasury of this County pay John Ewart.
Eleven shillings and eight pence for a Table provided by
him for the Court.

Signed   William Kennedy
                          Thomas Blasingame   Esquires
                          John Birdsong

134 At a Court Begun and held in and for the County of Union
    at the Court House this Twenty Sixth day of June in the
    Year of Our Lord one thousand seven hundred and Eighty
    Seven and the Eleventh year of the Independence of the
    United States of North America.

Present   John Henderson
                          William Kennedy
                          Charles Sims
                          Thomas Blasingame   Esquires
                          Thomas Brandon
                          Zachariah Bullock

Ordered that the Sheriff Summons the following persons to
serve as Grand Jury for a body of inquest next Court the
same being drawn according to Law as follows-Viz.

1. George McWhorter   11. Henry Milhouse
2. Robert Goode   12. Jas. McElvane
3. Charles Clanton   13. John Haile
4. William Plummer   14. John Thompson
5. John Stokes   15. Benj. Savage
6. James Bankhead   16. John Brandon
7. George Newton   17. James Putman
8. Joseph Little   18. Robert Woodson
9. Richd. Powell   19. Nicholas Currey
10. Henry Foster   20. Joseph East

Ordered that the Sheriff Summon the following persons to
serve as a Petty Jury next Court the same drawn according
to Law Viz.

111

1. Walter Roberts	16. Thomas Skelton
2. Lot Wood	17. John Palmore
3. Jeri. Hamelton	18. Isaac Smith
4. Jesse Young	19. Moses Harris
5. Bathw. Baker	20. Saml. Crawford
6. James Davis	21. Robert Millhouse
7. Jno Goodwin	22. James Bankhead
8. David Harris	23. John Wilson
9. Ralph Hunt	24. Joseph Howard
10. John Clark	25. John Jefferies
11. Philip Anderson	26. Jacob Hollingsworth
12. William Brandon	27. George Wadkins
13. William Williams	28. Isaac Chapman
14. John Cole	29. Frances Wilkie
15. Alexd. Hamelton	30. Daniel Young

An Indenture and Deed of Conveyance from Thomas Brandon Esqr. To Robert Talkington for one hundred acres of Land acknowledged in Open Court by the said Brandon to said Talkington and Ordered to be Recorded.

An Indenture and Deed of Conveyance from John Pearson and Sarah Pearson his wife to William Johnston for Six hundred acres of Land Proved in Open Court by the Oaths of Benj. Burnes John Townsend & M. Pearson and Ordered to be recorded.

A Deed of Conveyance from William Wafford and Abigal Wafford to Thos. Tod Proved in open Court Jeremiah Wilson and Ambrose Yarborough and Ordered to be Recorded

A Deed of Conveyance from George Little to Joseph Little proved in open Court by the oaths of John Thomas and Samuel Little and ordered to be recorded.

135 A Deed of Conveyance from Andrew Jones and Elizabeth Jones to Samuel Shiply proved in Open Court by the Oaths Joshua Petty & Thomas Littlejohn and Ordered to be Recorded.

A Deed of Conveyance Proved in Open Court by the Oaths of Joshua Petty and Thomas Littlejohn from Andrew Jones and Elizabeth Jones to Samuel Shiply and Ordered to be Recorded.

A Deed of Conveyance from Joseph Breed and Catharine Breed to Avery Breed proved in Open Court by the Oaths of George Harlin and Obadiah Howard and Ordered to be Recorded.

A Deed of Conveyance from Obadiah Howard to Jacob Paulk acknowledged in Open Court and Ordered to be Recorded.

A Deed of Conveyance from Peter Inlow to Benjamin Johnston proved in Open Court by the Oaths of John Wood & James Hogans and Ordered to be Recorded.

A Deed of Conveyance from Thomas Kennedy to James Kennedy acknowledged in Open Court and Ordered to be Recorded.

A Deed of Conveyance from Jonathan Pennal to John Little acknowledged in Open Court and Ordered to be Recorded.

A Bill of Sale from John Inlow to John Jenkins proved in

Open Court for Seven hed of Black Cattle two Beds and
Furniture five head of hogs and Ordered to be Recorded.

Acknowledged in Open Court a Deed of Conveyance from Daniel
Lipham to William Rogers and Ordered to be Recorded.

A Deed of Conveyance from John Palmore and Patty his wife
to Evan Thomas acknowledged in Open Court by John Palmore
and his wife being privately examined by Thomas Brandon
Esqr. who Report to the Court she freely without any fear
or Dread of her heirs being Renounce her Right her Right
of Dower to the said Tract of Land which was ordered to be
Recorded.

A Deed from Samuel Feemster to William Beckham acknowledged
in Open Court and Ordered to be Recorded.

Ordered that a Commission issue to Joseph Brown Esqr. and
some other Justice in the County of Chester to examine Mary
the wife of Samuel Feemster Relative to the Renounciation
of her Right of Dower to a Tract of land Conveyed to
William Beckham.

A Lease and Release from William Farr to William Hollingsworth acknowledged in Open Court and Ordered to be Recorded.

A Lease and Release from Elizabeth Walker and John Harden to
Thomas Blasingame Junr. proved in Open Court by the Oaths
of Daniel Pruet and Obadiah Pruet also proved by the said
Pruet that Elizabeth Walker Signed the same as her Right of
Dower to said Land in the said lease and release and
ordered to be recorded.

A Lease and Release from Elizabeth Walker & John Harden to
Obadiah Pruet proved by the Oaths of Thomas Blasingame &
Daniel Pruet which they proved that Elizabeth Walker Signed
the same as a relenquishment of her right of dower to the
Land & Ordered to be recorded.

136 A Deed of Conveyance from John Palmore & Patty his to Joseph
Thomas acknowledged by John Palmer and his wife being
privately examined by Col. Thos. Brandon who reports to
the Court that she freely and volentarily renounce her
Right of Dower to the Said Land & Ordered to be Recorded.

A Deed of Conveyance from Wm. Farr to Richard Cox acknowledged in open Court and Ordered to be Recorded.

A Deed of Conveyance from Elijah McGuire to Robert Smith
acknowledged in Open Court and Ordered to Record.

A Lease and Release from Nehemiah Posey to Joseph Comer
proved in Open Court by the Oaths of Richard Cox & James
Hawkins and Ordered to Record.

A Deed from John Henderson to John Haile acknowledged in
Open Court and Ordered to Record.

A Bill of Sale from Holland Sumner to Thomas Brandon for
household & furniture Cattle & four Negroes proved in Open
Court by the Oaths of James Woodson and Ordered to Record.

113

A Deed of Conveyance from Thomas Brandon to Abner Cane
acknowledged in Open Court and Ordered to be Recorded.

James Hogans   Pltf)
  against   )   The Parties Came into Open
Josiah Wood & Wife   Defts)   Court and agree to discontinue
                              the suit at the Defendants
Costs which is Ordered by the Court.

A Deed of Conveyance from Laurance Pearson to William
Martindale proved in Open Court by the Oaths of Thomas
Bishop & Jesse Young and Ordered to be Recorded.

A Deed of Conveyance from Stephen Howard to George Harlin
acknowledged in Open Court & Ordered to be Recorded.

A Deed of Conveyance from Jacob Paulk to Zachariah Bell
acknowledged in Open Court & Ordered to Record.

A Deed of Conveyance from Charles Jones to John Fincher
proved in Open Court by the Oaths of Frances Fincher &
Ordered to Record.

A Deed of Conveyance from Thomas Bishop to William Martindale acknowledged in Open Court and Ordered to be
Recorded.

A Deed of Conveyance from Lacy McBee & Ann McBee to Hannah
Armond proved in Open Court by the Oaths of George Harlen
and Renny Ballow & Ordered to Record.

137 A Lease and Release from Thomas Bishop to William Young
acknowledged in Open Court and Ordered to Record.

A Deed of Gift from Sarah Cook to George & John Cook proved
in Open Court by the Oaths of John Cook and John Haile
and Ordered to be Recorded.

A Deed of Conveyance from Handcock Porter to Lusian Porter
by the Oaths of Thomas Brandon & William Kennedy in Open
Court and Ordered to be Recorded.

Stephen Howard Last Will and Testament proved in Open
Court by the Oaths of Nehemiah Howard & Edy Howard and
Ordered to be Recorded.

A Lease and Release from David Farmer and Elizabeth Farmer
to William Newman proved in Open Court by the Oaths of
James Gibbs & William Young & Ordered to Record.

A Lease and Release from David Farmer and Elizabeth Farmer
to William Newman proved in Open Court by the oaths of James
Gibbs & William Young & ordered to Record.

Charles Sims and John Birdsong Esquire was appointed by
the Court to Inspect the Clerks Office. Who have reported
to the Court that they have Viewed & Inspected it and find
all papers Regularly filed & Recorded according to Law.

A Lease and Release from David Farmer and Elizabeth Farmer
to John Stokes proved in Open Court by the Oaths of William
Young & William Newman and Ordered to be Recorded.

Ordered that the Overseer of the Road from Bogans Creek on
the Ninety Six Road carry the said Road a long a Ridge to
where it will inersect the Ninety Six Road at the Cross
Roads toward the Court house.

William Brandon   Plaintiff)
     vs   ) A Writ hath been Issued
William Boyd   Defendant) against the Defendant and
                                 The Sheriff returns not to
be found with in his County which the plaintiff prays a
Judicial attachment against the Estate of the said Defendant which is awarded him.

Ordered that William Buckhannan be Overseer of the Road
from Browns Creek that Runs Down by Clayton Striblings to
where it interesects the Old Road that Lead from Henry
Longs to Grindels Shoals & that he keep the same in good
repair according to law.

138 Ordered that Joseph Jones be Overseer of the Road from
Union Court House to where it will Cross Brown Creek it
is also Ordered that all Male hands from fifty to sixteen
within five miles of said Road work on it.

Catharine Jenkins applied for Letters of administration on
the Estate of William Jenkins Deceased which was granted
her by the Court and she took the necessary Oaths of
administration and entered into bond with Jeremiah Hamilton
& William Rogers her Securities in the sum of two hundred
pounds according to Law & she Return on Inventory of all the
estate Real & personal of the said Desd. & Render it to our
next Court.

A Deed of Conveyance from Duncan McCrevan to Josep Hughes
acknowledged in Open Court and Ordered to Record.

John Ham appointed Constable in the Room of John Little and
Took the Necessary Oaths in Open Court.

Mr. James Thomas is appointed by the Court Guardian to
the children of Daniel Thomas Desd. to Wit, Leah, Ann,
Elijah Caty and James Minor Age

Ordered that the Orphans of Sarah Strawn be brought to this
place at our next Court by Bird Buford as the Court may do
for them as they may think right.

Ordered that the Clark issue and order to James Thomas to
receive & take in charge the Orphan children of Dan
Thomas Desd.

The Court proceeded to the Election of a Sheriff by Ballot,
When Mr. John Blasingame was unanimously elected. Ordered
that the Clerk Deliver a Certificate to John Blasingame of
his being Elected Sheriff for the County of Union for the
Ensuing two years to be delivered to his Excellency the
Governor for the purpose of obtaining a commission.

John Jinkins and Phillip Anders are appointed Praisers of
the Estate of William Jenkins Deceased to be Sworn by some
Magistrate of this County.

```
Signed                          Zachariah Bullock
                                Thomas Brandon
                                Thomas Blasingame    Esquires
                                William Kennedy
```

139 At a Court begun and held in and for the County of Union
at the Court House on the 24. Day of September in the Year
of our Lord One thousand Seven Hundred and Eighty Seven and
of the Independence of the United States of North America
the Twelvth.

```
Present                         Thomas Brandon
                                Thomas Blasingame    Esquires
                                Charles Sims
```

Ordered that the Sheriff Summons the following persons to
serve as Petty Jury for Next Court which was drawn according to Law as follows that is to say

1.	Renny Ballew	16.	Wm. Hollingsworth
2.	Lewis Turner	17.	Reuben Ballew
3.	William Savage	18.	John Bankhead
4.	Richard Wood	19.	James Colwell
5.	William Smith	20.	Renny Ballew Jun.
6.	Ezekiel Stone	21.	Lewis Ledbetter
7.	Wm. Goldsmith	22.	Samuel Harlin
8.	Zacha. Ballew	23.	Josiah Wood
9.	Joseph Jones	24.	James Harklar
10.	Isaac Cook	25.	William Shaw
11.	William Mays	26.	Robert Woodson
12.	James Pattent	27.	Nicholas Harris
13.	John Ballege	28.	Joseph Hollingsworth
14.	Hugh Means	29.	Jacob Shaw
15.	Alex McDougal	30.	Charles Hames

John Blasingame Esqr. produced a Commission from his
Excellency the Governor appointed him a Sheriff in and
for the County and Took the Oath required by Law who
Together with Colonel William Farr and William Plummer his
Securities who entered into and acknowledged their Bonds
in the sum of One thousand five hundred pounds for the
Execution of said Office which were approved of by the Court.

A Deed of Gift from William Smith to John Smith acknowledged
in Open Court by the said Wm Smith & Ordered to be Recorded.

A Deed of Gift from William Smith to Joseph Smith acknowledged in Open Court by the said Wm. Smith and Ordered to
be recorded.

A Deed of Conveyance from Mery McGuire to Drewry Going
acknowledged in Open Court and Ordered to be recorded.

A Deed of Conveyance from Archer Smith to George Harlin
Hatter acknowledged in Open Court and Ordered to be
recorded.

A Bill of Sale from Daniel Tramell to Charles Sims for seven
Negroes Named Cook Dinah Cate Jame Luise & Sue and their
Issue proved in Open Court by the Oaths of John Ewart and
William Birdsong and Ordered to be recorded.

116

139 A Deed of Conveyance from George Blanton to Mathew Caldwell
for two hundred acres of Land proved in Open Court by the
Oathes of Nathaniel Guiton and William Lankford and Ordered
to be Recorded.

A Deed of Conveyance from John Steen Senr. to John Steen
Junr. for 400 acres of land proved in open Court by the
Oaths of Absalom Petty and Charles Clanton and Ordered to
be Recorded.

A Deed of Conveyance from John Weedinman to John Cole for
200 acres of Land proved in Open Court by the Oathes of
John Reed and William Scission and Ordered to be recorded.

A Deed of Conveyance from Henry Goode to Robert Goode for
162 acres of Land acknowledged in Open Court and Ordered
to be recorded.

A Lease and Release from William Coleman to Nicholas Harris
for 197 acres of Land and Mary Coleman his wife acknowledged for Right of Dower to the same, and Ordered to be
Recorded.

The Last will of George Martin Deceased was presented in
Court by Susannah Martin and Philimon Martin Executors
thereon Named and proved in Court by the oaths of John
Harrington and Richmond Terrell Witnesses thereunto and on
motion of said Executors a Certificate is Granted and
Obtaining abrobate of said Will in due form and Ordered to
be recorded.

A Deed of Conveyance from John Putman and Mary his wife to
Clement and Michael Margarets proved in Open Court by the
oath of John Little and Jonathan Pennill and Ordered to
be Recorded.

A Deed of Conveyance from Thomas Brandon to Robert Woodson
for 200 acres of Land acknowledged in Open Court & Ordered
to be recorded.

A Deed of Conveyance from Thomas Brandon to Mary Mayfield
acknowledge in Open Court and Ordered to be Recorded.

A Lease and Release from Thomas Brandon and Abbazal his wife
to Ralph Jackson acknowledged in Open Court and Ordered to
be Recorded.

A Deed of Conveyance from John Foster and Nelly Foster to
John Reed proved in Open Court by the Oaths of Josiah Smith
and Miles Smith and Ordered to be Recorded.

A Deed of Conveyance from James Terril to Thomas Wright.
acknowledge in Open Court & Ordered to be Recorded.

A Deed of Conveyance from Ephraim Clark and Mary his wife to
John Bankhead proved by the Oaths of by Henry and Robert
Goode and Ordered to be Recorded.

A Deed of Conveyance from William Lindsey Jonathan Pennal
proved in open Court by the Oaths of Peter Pennal & Samuel
Coson & Ordered to be Recorded.

117

[No page numbered 140]

141 A Deed of Conveyance From Samuel McJunkin to John Howel acknowledged in Open Court and Ordered to be Recorded.

A Deed of Conveyance Francis Holland & John Holland to Frances Whilchel proved in Open Court by the Oath of James Terril and John Wilkie and ordered to be recorded.

A Deed of Conveyance from John Wood to William Horrel proved by the Oaths of William Horrel and Josiah Wood and Ordered to be Recorded.

A Deed of Conveyance from Uriah Paulk to Joseph Redier proved by the Oath of James Bele and Duncan McCuvan and Ordered to Record.

Robert William Johnson Orphan of William Johnson Deceased came into Open Court and made choice of James Gibbs for his Guardian Which was approved of by the who entered into bond with Richard Powel his Security in Sum of Fifty pounds for his True performance of his Guardian Ship to the said Orphans Estate.

The Last Will and Testament of John Waters was present in Court by Moses Waters the Executor therein Named and proved in Open Court by the Oaths of James Terrill & Samuel Shippy and Ordered to be Recorded and On Motion of the said Executor for a Certificate of the proving of said Will which was Granted him.

A Deed of Conveyance from John Savage of Joseph Hughes acknowledges in Open Court and Ordered to be Recorded.

A Deed of Conveyance from Gabriel Brown to Joseph Hughes proved in Open Court by the Oaths of Thomas Brandon & John McCooll & Ordered to be Recorded.

A Deed of Conveyance from William Martindale to Daniel Young acknowledged in Open Court & Ordered to be Recorded.

A Deed of Conveyance from Solomon Mangham to William Tate acknowledged in Open Court and Ordered to be Recorded.

A Deed from Thomas Bishop and Mary his wife to Daniel Young proved in Open Court by the Oaths of John Pearson & William Martendale and Ordered to be Recorded.

A Deed of Conveyance from Charles Shockly to William Brummet acknowledged in Open Court and Ordered to be Recorded.

A Deed of Conveyance from Jacob Earnest and Agness his wife to William Addington proved in Open Court of Thomas Brandon and Jesse hust. and Ordered to be Recorded.

A Bill of Sale from Thomas Brandon to James Adams McCool for One negroe boy named Abraham and Ordered to be Recorded.

A Deed of Conveyance from John Foster to Georege McWhorter prove in Open Court by the oaths of John Crew Foster and Jmaes Davvin and Ordered to be Recorded.

118

142 A Deed of Conveyance from William Comer to Daniel Comer acknowledged in Open Court and Ordered to be Recorded.

Deed of Conveyance from James Addington to John Addington acknowledged in open Court and Ordered to be Recorded.

Moses Collier resigned his appointment of being Overseer of the Road and Evan Thomas appointed in his Room by the Court.

On the Application of Samuel Simpson for a citation to Execute all the Kindred and Creditors of John Simpson Deceased by Letters of Admor. to Shew cause if any they have why Letters of administration should not be granted him on the Estate of the said Deceased which is awarded him by the Court.

The following persons are sworn in open Court to serve this Court as Grand Jurors.

John Thompson	Henry Milhouse
William Plummer	James Portman
Henry Foster	George Newton
Benjamin Savage	Robert Goode
Joseph East	Joseph Little
George McWhorter	John Haile
John Stokes	Robert Wootson

John Blasengame Sheriff Recommend Andrew Torrance as his Deputy Sheriff which the Court appointed him and he took the necessary Oaths of Office prescribed by Law.

The following persons are sworn to serve as Pettit Jurors for this Court

1.	John Jeffries	7.	Walter Roberds
2.	Daniel Young	8.	Lot. Wood
3.	Ralph Hunt	9.	Isaac Smith
4.	John Palmer	10.	Thomas Skelton
5.	Frances Whilchel	11.	Philip Anderson
6.	Moses Hains	12.	Robert Milhouse

The Court adjourn untill tomorrow 9 O'Clock

Signed   William Kennedy
                          Thomas Blasingame   Esquires
                          Thomas Brandon

At a Court continued and held in and for the County of Union on the 25 day of September 1787

Present   Thomas Brandon
                          William Kennedy   Esquires
                          Thomas Blasingame

A Deed of Conveyance from Thomas Brandon to John Thomas acknowledged in Open Court & Ordered to be Recorded.

143 A Deed of Conveyance from John Steen to Wilson Jolly proved in Open Court & Ordered to be Recorded.

119

A Deed of Conveyance from George Crosby to Jacob Haile acknowledged in Open Court and Ordered to be Recorded.

On Motion of William Shaw attorney for William Farr on a Judgment Obtained by him against John Steen and Frances Lattemore at Last December Court for one hundred pounds and Costs of Suit the Plaintiff having Demanded Security according to Law and the Defendants have not complyed Ordered that an Execution Issue for the Debt and Costs or the former Judgment.

A Deed of Conveyance from Robert Lewis Senr. to William Rogers acknowledged in Open Court and Ordered to be Recorded.

A Bond from John Steen to Charles Miles for Six hundred acres of Land proved in Open Court by the Oaths of Frances Lattimore and Phillip Shaver Taker & Ordered to Record.

Archilus Fore)
    vs.   )   This suit is Ordered by the Court to be
Holland Sumner)   discontinued at the Plaintiffs costs.

State   Plaintiff)
    agt.   )   The Defendant being brought into
Joseph Jones   Defendant)   Court and entered into bond with
                            Zachariah Bell his Security for
the penalty of One hundred pounds and his security in fifty for his appearance at our next Court.

John Compty & Co.   Plaintiff)
  against   )   The Defendant came into
William Steen Junr. Defendant)   Court in his On Proper
                          person and Confessed a
Judgment according to Specialty with Interest and Costs of Suit which the Court Decreed for the Same.

John Compty & Co.   Plaintiff)
  against   )   The Defendant being
William Steen Senr. Defendant)   Solemnly Called and failing
                          ing to appear and Defend
his Suit. Judgment was entered against him according to Specialty with Interest and Costs of Suit.

A Lease and Release from Mathew Robison and Susannah his wife to John Waters proved by the Oath of John Thompson and Joshua Petty and Ordered to be Recorded.

William Bostick   Plaintiff)
  against   )   The defendant being solemnly
John Steen   Defendant)   called failing to appear to
144   Defend his suit Judgment was
entered up against him according to Specialty with Interest and costs of Suit which the Court Decreed from the same.

Present Charles Sims John Henderson & Zachariah Bullock Esqr.

Abel Kendrick   Plaintiff)   Debt on attachment. Ordered to
  against   )   be continued at the Defendants
David Sisson   Defendant)   Costs.

```
State          Plaintiff)
  vs                    )    Dismissed at the Defendants costs
Thomas Elliot  Defendant)
```

```
John Gregory   )
  vs           )    this Suit being refered by and Order
Jeremiah Hamilton)  of Court & by the Consent of the parties
                    ToWit
```
We the arbitrators appointed by the Worshipfull Court have
met and Duly aribtrated a certain Matter of Controversy
between John Gregory Plaintiff & Jeremiah Hamilton Defendant have awarded that each man pay his own costs & the
suit to lease.

```
Samuel Cooper          )
  vs                   )    Ordered by the Court to be
Thos Wood & David Dixon)    Dismissed at the Plaintiffs costs.
```

```
George Head )
  vs        )    The plaintiff being solemnly called came
Isaac Holman)    not to prosecute the Suit Ordered by the
                 Court that he be nonsuited.
```

```
John Campbell        )
  vs                 )    Ordered to be Dismissed at the
Samuel & Betsy Cooper)    plaintiffs costs.
```

```
Frances Fincher)
  vs           )    Declaration & Plea Entered Issue Joined
Lee and Others )
```

```
John Wood )
  vs      )    Award Returned & Ordered to be Recorded and
Hugh Means)    Judgment agreeable to the award
               We the Subscribers Chosen arbitrate in Matter
```
in Law Between John Wood Plaintiff & Hugh Means Defendant
having Called in Colld. Henry White an umpire do award and
agree that the Sale was unjust and do further Say that the
Plaintiff shall pay all cost upon said Suit
April 12, 1787   John Golightly
                          John Thompson
                          H. White

```
Robt. Montgomery)
  vs            )    Tresspass Dismissed at the Plaintiffs
William Gilkie  )    Costs.
```

145 Susanah Terril Orphan of John Terrell Deceased Came into
Open Court and made Choice of Susannah Martin her Guardian
which met the approbation of the Court She together with
John & Drewry Arrington her Security Entered into and
acknowledged a Bond of the sum of one thousand pounds for
her performance of her Guardianship & she taking care of
the said Orphan & her Estate.

A Deed of Conveyance from George Newton to William Williams
acknowledged in Open Court & Ordered to be Recorded.

Mrs. Ursla Newton Wife of the aforesaid George acknowledged
her Right of Dower which is Ordered to be Recorded.

121

```
Turner Rountree      Plaintiff)
   vs.                        )   Debt. attachment
James Hainsworth     Defendant)   Came the plaintiff by C
                                  Goodwin his attorney and
the Defendant not appearing Whereupon Came a Jury John
Jeffries foreman, Frances Whilchel Phillip Anderson, Sol.
Wood Isaac Smith Ralph Hunt Moses Haynes, Walter Roberts
Thomas Shelton Robert Milhouse John Palmore Daniel Young
Who being Duly Drawn & Sworn do say on their Oaths We
find for the Plaintiff One hundred & Eleven pounds and
Costs of Suit which Verdict is Ratifyed by the Court &
ordered to be recorded.
```

A Deed of Conveyance from John Still to Thomas Howel proved
in Open Court by the Oaths of Joseph Hughes and William
Clark and Ordered to be Recorded.

A Lease and Release from John Towns to William Hardwik
for 250 acres of Land Ordered to Record.

On the application of William Darby leave is Given him
to keep a Tavern or public house in his County on his
Giving bond with Nehemiah Howard Security according to Law.

A lease and Release from Larkin Wells to John Ewart proved
in Open Court by the Oaths of Thomas Ballew Abner Wells and
Hezekiah Salmon and Ordered to be Recorded.

```
Turner Rountree      Plaintiff)
   against                    )   Whereas the Plt. hath
James Hainsworth     Defendant)   Recorded a Judgment. against
                                  the Defendant agreeable to
Law On an attachment Joseph Wafford Summonsed as Garnashee
confesd On Oath that he is Indue the said Defendant thereby
one pounds Eight Shillings and Seven pence with 32 months
amounting to D 37. 5.11. Interest agreeable to the disposi-
tion filed Judgt. awarded against him for the Same Ordered
that Execution Issue against the Said Garnashee according
to Law.
```

146 A Bond from John Steen to David Stogden proved by the
    Oath of John Thompson and Frances Lattemore in Open Court &
    Ordered to be Recorded.

```
John Baily       Plaintiff)
   vs                     )   Debt.  The Plaintiff being
Abraham Lipham   Defendant)   Solemnly called came not to
                              prosecute his suit.  Ordered by
the Court the Suit be Discontinued at the plaintiffs costs.
```

```
William Nelson   Plaintiff)
   vs                     )   Continued by the Court at
Thomas Beddy     Defendant)   Plaintiff Costs.
```

```
Thomas Brandon   Plaintiff)
   against                )   Discontinued at the plaintiffs
Elias Mitchell   Defendant)   Costs Except the attorneys
                                 fee.
Robert Montgomery  Pltf)
   against               )   Debt on attachment. Ordered to be
Charles Harrington Deft)  Dismissed at the Pltfs Costs.
```

122

William Plummer   Plaintiff)
  against   )   Debt on attachment. Ordered
Daniel Plummer   Defendant)   to be Dismissed at Plaintiffs
                                Costs.

John Elliot   Plaintiff)
  against   )   Ordered to be Dismissed at
James & Sarah McWhorter)   Plaintiffs Costs.

State   Plaintiff)
  against   )   The Defendant Came into Open
Joseph Jolly   Defendant)   Court and Confessed himself
                              Guilty of the charge against him
Whereupon the Court fines him One Shilling & Costs of Suit.

Sarah Johnson   Plaintiff)
  against   )   The plaintiff not appearing to
Charles White   Defendant)   prosecute his Suit Ordered to be
                               Dismissed at his Costs.

Jacob Brown   Plaintiff)
  against   )   Ordered to be Dismissed at
Montgomery &   )   Plaintiff Costs the Clerks fees
Thos Kenney   Defendants)   only to be Taxed.

William Frazier   Plaintiff)
  vs   )   Dismissed at the Defendants own
William Johnson   Defendant)   Costs by his Consent

Thomas Cox   )
  vs.   )   Dismissed at the plaintiffs Costs by
Caleb Gassaway)   Consent of the parties.

Drewry Herrington   Plaintiff)
  against   )   Continued at Equal Costs
Charles Clanton   Defendant)   by Consent of the parties

Mary Palmore   Plaintiff)
  against   )   Discontinued at Defendants Costs
Henry Long   Defendant)

147 Thomas Cox   Plaintiff)
      against   )   Ordered to be Dismissed at the
    Caleb Gassaway   Defendant)   Plaintiffs Costs by Consent

Henry Long   Plaintiff)
  vs   )   Ordered to be Dismissed at
Charles Humpries   Defendant)   the Plaintiffs Costs by
                                 Consent.

James Clark Plaintiff)
  against   )   Ordered to be Dismissed at
Joseph Jolly Defendant)   Defendant Costs.

Archilus Fore Plaintiff)   This Suit being Referred the
  vs   )   arbitrators Return their award
John Holman   Defendant)   which is Ordered to be Recorded
                             and Judgment accordingly the
Debt Satisfyed Ordered that the Same be Record.

The Grand Jury having Received their Charge Withdrew to

123

Consult their minds. and Return the following Bills the
State against William Steen Junr. True Bill On an indict-
ment for an assault Battery State against Josep Jones an
Indictment for Escape True Bill. State against John Foster
Larceny No Bill. State against William Whitlock Tresspass
True Bill. Ordered that the presentsments of the Grand
Jury be Recorded. Ordered that process Issue against On all
the Indictments & presentements of the Grand Jury Ord that
the Grand Jury be Discharged for this Court.

Abil Kindrick   Plaintiff)
     against   ) Debt on attachment.
David Scisson   Defendant) The Defendant Came into Court in
                            his Own proper person and Con-
fessed a Judgment for two pounds Six Shillings & eight pence
& costs of Suit with Stay of Execution for two Months which
is awarded.

John Ewart   Plaintiff)
     against   ) Tresspass
Thomas Moore   Defendant) award Returned by the arbitrators
                            Ordered by the Court to be
Recorded and Judgment according to award and that Execution
Issue.

The Last Will and Testament of Henry Addington was presented
by William Addington & John Odel Executors therein Named
and proved by the Oaths of John Garret and Jesse Rush and
Ordered to be Recorded on Motion of the said Executors a
Certificate is awarded them that they have Taken the
necessary oaths prescribed by Law the Court adjourn until
Tomorrow 9 O'Clock

Signed by   Zachariah Bullock
                            John Henderson   Esquires
                            Thomas Blasingame

148 At a Court Continued and held at the Court House in and
    for the County of Union on the Twenty Sixth Day of
    September 1787.

    Present   Zachariah Bullock
                            John Henderson
                            William Kennedy   Esquires
                            Charles Sims
                            Thomas Brandon

William Bostick &)
     against   ) Ordered that an Execution Issue against
John Steen   ) the Defendnat agreeable to a Judgment
                       Entered against him for Debt and Costs.

James Hill   Plaintiff)
     vs   ) Trespass the Defendant not
Robert Duncan Defendant) appearing to prosecute his Suit
                            Ordered that he be nonsuited.

David Wincen   Plaintiff) Dismissed at the Plaintiffs Costs
     vs   ) and Colld. Brandon assumed to pay
William Head   Defendant) the same in Open Court.

124

Stephen White   Plaintiff)   Ordered that the Plaintiff
   vs   )   file his Declaration before
Mark Jackson   Defendant)   the Court adjourn Till Court
                                  in Course if not Ordered that
                                  he be nonsuited.

Daniel Brown   Plaintiff   )   Ordered that this Suit be
   against   )   Dismissed at the plaintiffs
Benjamin Thompson   Defendant)   Costs.

Dudley Rede   Plaintiff)
   vs   )   Dismissed at Holland Sumners
Thomas Palmore   Defendant)   Costs having Examined this
                                  Suit without the Order of the
Plaintiff Execution Ordered vs Sumner.

Robert Smith   Plaintiff)   This Suit the plaintiff
   against   )   discontinue at his Own Costs.
George Taylor   Defendant)

Robert Lusk   Plaintiff)   Case attachment
   agt   )   Ordered that the Defendant
Bradley Colliers   Defendant)   plead within the time
                                  limited by Law.

Drewry Embry   Plaintiff)   The Plaintiff being called
   vs   )   Came not to prosecute his
Ambrose Yarborough   Defendant)   Suit Ordered that he be
                                  Nonsuited.

Holland Sumner   Plaintiff)   Ordered at this Suit be
   agt.   )   Dismissed at the Defendants
Ambrose Yarborough   Defendant)   Costs by the Consent of the
                                  parties.

149 Ambrose Yarborough   Plaintiff)   Ordered to be Dismissed
   against   )   at the Plaintiffs Costs.
Drewry Embry   Defendant)

Thomas Brandon   Plaintiff)   The parties came into Open
   against   )   Court and agree to Dismiss
George Crossley   Defendant)   this Suit at the Defendants
                                  Costs which is Ordered by the
                                  Court.

John Mullins   Plaintiff)   The parties Came into Court and
   against   )   agreed to Dismiss this suit at
Thomas Cost   Defendant)   the Defendants Cost

Robert Montgomery   Pltf   )   Ordered that this Suit be
   against   )   Discontinued at the
George Perves   Defendant)   Plaintiffs Costs

Thomas Brandon   Plaintiff)   The parties agree to Refer this
   vs   )   Suit to arbitration to Nehemiah
William Lee   Defendant)   Howard Samuel Otterson with
                                  Liberty they do not agree to
Chose a Third person On the fourth Monday in October next
at the house of William Newmans and return their award to
our next Court which said award to be the Judgment of the
Court.

Thomas Brandon   Plaintiff)   Issue Joined by the Parties
  against   )   on Declaration Plea & Replica-
Henry Thickpenny Defendant)   tion whereas Came a Jury Towit
John Jeffries Frances Wilkie
Philip Anderson Lot Wood Isaac Smith Ralph Hunt Moses Hains
Walter Roberts Thomas Skelton Robert Millhouse John Palmer
Daniel Young who Return their Verdict on their Respective
Oaths and say we find for the Plaintiff Ten pounds fourteen
Shillings and four Pence and costs of suit which is Ratified
by the Court on Motion of the Defts. attorney for an appeal
to the Superior Court Ordered that the Defendant file his
reason for his appealling.

Stephen White   Plaintiff)   Came Patrick Shaw who being
  against   )   Summoned as a Garnshee Ordered
Mark Jackson   Defendant)   that he be sworn which was
                                done and deposition filed.

A Lease and Release from Archer Smith to Jas. Olliphant
for One hundred and fifty acres of Land acknowledged in
Open Court by the said Archer Smith and Ordered to be
recorded.

A Deed of Conveyance from William Bishop and Jean Bishop
of the One part and James Johnston of the other part for
Three hundred acres of Land proved in Open Court and Ordered
to be Recorded.

150 William Lawson   Plaintiff)
      against   )   Continued by the parties at
    Jonathan Newman Defendant)   Equal Cost

    Thomas Weaver   Plaintiff)
      against   )   Ordered that this Suit be
    George Earnest Defendant)   Discontinued at Plaintiffs cost.

    William Smith   Plaintiff)   Debt.
      against   )   Decree for the Plaintiff Four
    James Olliphant Defendant)   pounds Eleven shillings and one
                                    penny and costs of suit.

Ordered that William Young and William Martindale be
appointed appraizers of the Estate of Henry Haddington
Deceased in pursuance of a Will recorded; and return the
same to Our next Court.

The Worshipful Court adjourn Untill Tomorrow at Nine
O'Clock
Present   Zachariah Bullock
                               Thomas Blasingame   Esquires
                               Thomas Brandon

At a Court Continued and held by adjournment at the Court
House for the County of Union the Twenty seventh day of
September in the year of Our Lord One thousand seven
hundred and Eighty seven

Present   Zachariah Bullock
                               John Henderson
                               Thomas Brandon   Charles Sims
                               Charles Brandon   William Kennedy
                                        Esquires

126

On petition of the Court Ordered that Walter Robert and Ambrose Ray be and is thereby appointed to Lay Out a road from Blackstocks ford on Tyger River to Townsend Old Shop on the Charleston Road; Ordered that William Smith be appointed Overseer on the same from the said Blackstocks ford to Andrew Torrences; Then Ambrose Ray be appointed Overseer from said Andrew Torrences to the Quaker Meeting House; Then Walter Roberts from thence to Townsends old Shop on the said Road Ordered that all persons Lyable to work on said Road Between the Rivers of Tyger and Enoree Work on the said Road as high as the County Line & as Low as the said Townsends Shop.

State So Carolina   Pltf)   Assault and Battery on the Body
    agt.   )   of Davis Goudylock who came into
William Steen   Defendant)   Court and Pleades Guilty and
                                  fined four shillings and Eight
pence and Costs of Suit. Thos. Brandon enters himself
Security for the fine and Costs of Suit which is Ordered
accordingly.

151 State of South Carolina Pltf)   Nusance
    against   )   appearing to the Court that
James Bell   Defendant   )   the Defendant having removed
                                       the Nusance Ordered that the
Defendant be Dismissed on paying Six pence fine and Costs
of Suit.

State So. Carolina   Plaintiff)   An Obstruction of the Road
    against   )   Ordered that John Goodwin
William Browning   Defendant)   and George Harlin and John
                                      Little be appointed to
Examine the Obstruction on the road and report the same
at our next Court; and to lay out said Road the Defendant
having pleaded Guilty the Court fine him six pence on
removing the Obstruction if the said persons shall think
proper; which the Suit is Dismissed at the Defendants
Costs and fined six pence.

State of So. Carolina Plaintiff)   An Obstruction of the
    against   )   Road the Defendants
Thomas & James Shockley Deft.   )   pleads Guilty Ordered
                                       that the Defendant be
appointed Overseer of the same Road from the Fish Dam
Creek to Cane Creek and that he remove the Obstruction
Complained of and Dismissed at Defendants Costs and fined
six pence.

Ordered that Joseph Joseph Hollingsworth be Overseer of the
Road from Canes Creek on the same Road to Duffs Ford on
Tyger and that he keep the same in Good Repair &c.

State So. Carolina   Plaintiff)   No Bill found by the Grand
    agt.   )   Jury Ordered that it be
John Foster   Defendant)   Dismissed at Defendants
                                      Costs.

State So. Carolina Plaintiff)   Presented for Bastardy
    against   )   Ordered that a Capias Issue
Rhody Prince   Defendant)   against the Defendant to

at our next Court ot the said Charge and that she be held
to Bail in the Sum of Ten pounds.

State S. Carolina   Plaintiff)   Presentment for Basterdy
  against   )   Ordered that a Capias Issue
Betsey Hunt   Defendant)   against the Defendant to
                                 answer at our next Court to
the said presentment and give Bail in the sum of ten pounds.

Ordered that Jeremiah Hamelton be appointed Overseer of the
Road Leading from his ford on Tyger River to Hawkins Old
Mill and William Hollingsworth from thence to the Fish dam
ford on Broad River--Ordered that William Rogers be
appointed Overseer of the Road from Hameltons Ford on the
said River to Hendricks Mill on Enoree.

152 John Steen   Plaintiff)   This Cause Continued untill next
    against   )   Court Ordered that a Dedimus
  David Stocdon Defendant)   potestatum Issue to any of the
                                 Justices of the County of Henry
in the State of Virginia to take the Deposition of Richard
Stockton in the County aforesaid at the Court House of said
County, on the first Monday in December next which Deposition to be admitted in Evidence on the above Trial Ordered
that the Defendant give notice to the plaintiff of the
time and place aforesaid.

John McNail Orphant of Edward McNail Deceased Came into
Open Court and made Choice of Cold. Thomas Brandon his
Guardian with the approbation of the Court who Together with
John McCooll his Security Entered into bond and acknowledged
the same for one hundred pounds for securing the said
Orphans Estate.

State So. Carolina   Plaintiff)   Pettit Larcency Hog
  against   )   Stealing. Whereon Came a
William Steen   Defendant)   Jury Towit John Jefferies
                                 Frankes Wilkie Philip
Anderson Lot Wood, Isaac Smith Ralph Hunt Moses Hains Walter
Roberts Thomas Skelton Robert Millhouse John Palmer & Daniel
Young who Return their Verdict on their Respective Oaths
and say we find the Deft. no Guilty and is thereby
acquitted on paying of Costs. John Jefferies Foreman

Davis Goudylock proved four Days attendance in the above
Suit which Steen is ordered to pay all costs.

Frances Fincher   Plaintiff)   Continued by Consent of
  against   )   the parties at Equal
William Lee & Others Defendants)   Costs.

A Lease & Release from William Trammel & Isaac Trammel to
William Farr proved in Open Court and Ordered to Record.

State So. Carolina   )   The Defendant Came into
  against   )   Ooen Court and Offered
Joseph Jones   Defendant)   WilliamFarr and Luke Carrel
                                 for his Securities which was
approved of by the Court and Entered into a bond that is
the Said Jone in the Sum of One Hundred pounds & each of
his securities in fifty pounds for the said Jones
appearance at Our Next court.

128

```
State So. Carolina    Plaintiff)  This Suit is Dismissed
     against              )       at the Defendants Costs
William Whitlock      Defendant)   by Order of Court

153 State              Plaintiff)  Ord by the Court that the
     against              )        Suit be Dismissed at Defendants
Robert Montgomery Defendant)       Costs.
```

Court adjourn Untill Tomorrow 9 O'Clock
Signed   Zachariah Bullock
                          John Henderson   Esquires
                          William Kennedy

At a Court Continued and held by adjournment at the Court
House the Twenty eighth day of September One thousand seven
hundred and Eighty Seven and the Twelfth year of American
Independancey.

Present   Zachariah Bullock
                          Thomas Brandon   Esquires
                          Charles Sims

```
Charles Sims       Plaintiff)  Case the same Jury sworn as the
     against          )        State against William Steen
William George     Defendant)  who return their Verdict on
                               their respective Oaths & Say
we find for the Plaintiff Ten pounds Ten Shillings and Four
Pence with Interest from the ninth day of March One
Thousand Seven hundred and Eighty Four and Costs of Suit.
```

```
William Gilkie     Plaintiff)  Debt.
     against          )        The Same Jury Sworn return
John Steen         Defendant)  their Verdict and say we find
                               for the Pltf Sixteen pounds
one shilling and six pence sterling & Costs of Suit.
```

```
James Bell         Plaintiff)  Came the Plaintiff by William
     against          )        Shaw his attorney and the
John Steen &         )         Defendant by Jacob Brown his
John Gregory       Defendant)  Counciller Whereupon Came a
                               Jury ToWit John Jefferies
Frances Wilkie Philip Anderson Lot Wood Isaac Smith Ralph
Hunt Moses Haines Walter Roberts Thomas Skelton Robert
Millhouse John Palmore Daniel Young Who being Duly drawn
and sworn Do say on their respective Oaths we find for
the Plaintiff fifteen pounds Ten shillings and costs of
Suit--John Jefferies Foreman Which the above Verdict is
ratified by the Court & Ord to Record
```

Ordered that Stephen White be granted Letters of administration on the Estate of Stephen White Junior Deceased on
his giving Bond and take the necessary Oath prescribed by
Law.

```
John Ewart         Plaintiff)  Debt  Decree for the Plaintiff
     against          )        and that he recover the sum of
Holland Sumner     Defendant)  Ten pounds and Cost of Suit
                               ordered that an Execution
Issue agt. the Defendant for the same.
```

154 Thomas Stribling &   Plaintiff) Agreeable to the Judgment
    William Buckhannon   )   of the Court of Common
       against   )   Pleas held at Ninety Six
    Sarah Gist   Defendant)   on the Twenty Sixth day of
                                      November Last on an appeal
from this Court; On Motion of William Shaw Judgment of this
Court as it stands for the Pltf Ordered that the Judgment be
reversed and the same Entered for the Defendant which was
done accordingly.

Sarah Gist   Plaintiff) Ordered that this Suit be
   agt.   ) Discontinued at Plaintiffs
Holland Sumner   Defendant) Costs Except the Defts.
                                 attorneys fee by Consent of
Colonell Thomas Brandon.

Holland Sumner   Plaintiff) Ordered that this Suit be
   agt.   ) Discontinued at the Plaintiffs
James Woodson   Defendant) Cost.

Frances Dod & Wife Plaintiff   ) The Defendant James
   agt.   ) Clark Came in his Own
James & Ridarous Clark Defendant) proper person and
                                    Confessed a Judgment
on the Said Note for four pounds Thirteen Shillings and Two
Pence half penny with Stay of Execution Untill Next March
and no attorneys fee to be Taxed; and the Clerks and
Sheriffs fees to be paid at Mutual Expence.

Mark Mitchell   Plaintiff) Came the Defendant by Jacob
   agt.   ) Brown his attorney and the
Jesse Maberry   Defendant) Plaintiff being solemnly Called
                                but came not to prosecute his
suit on motion of the Defendant by his attorney aforesaid
a nonsuit is awarded him against the Plaintiff and it is
also Ordered that the Defendant recover five Shillings for
Damage and Costs of suit.

John Steen   Plaintiff) Came the Plaintiff into
   against   ) Court by William Shaw his
Wm & Rebecca George   Defendant) attorney also Came the
                                  Defendant by Jacob Brown
his attorney and agree to Continue said suit at Mutual
cost.

Mark Mitchell   Plaintiff) Notice Given to the Defen-
   agt.   ) dant to Give Security to John
Ben & Henry Long   Defendant) Henderson Esquire to pay
                                the Debt agreeable to the
                                Instalment act

155 Robert H Hughes. Plaintiff) Ordered that his suit be
    against   ) Discontinued at the Plaintiffs
    Richard Burgess   Defendant) Costs.

William Liles   Plaintiff) The Parties Came in their
   agt.   ) Own Proper person and agree
Philip Shivertaker   Defendant) to refer this suit to
                                 arbitration to Daniel
Jackson and Shadrack Landtrip and their award to be the
Judgment of this Court and return the said award to Our
next Court.

130

A Deed of Conveyance from William Young and Margaret Young his wife to Peter Braselman and Cushman Edson for Two hundred and Nine acres of Land by the Oath of Luthar Smith Ordered to Lay Over for the Other Proof.

Hanney Taylor   Plaintiff)   Came the Plaintiff by James
   against   )   Yancy her attorney & Likewise
John Montgomery   Defendant)   Came the Defendant by Jacob
                                Brown his attorney and then
and there agree to Discontinue the said suit at the Defendants Cost Except the attorney fee which is Ordered by the Court accordingly.

Robert Lusk   Plaintiff)   Came the Plaintiff by William
   against   )   Shaw his attorney also Came the
Mathew Robinson Defendant)   Defendant by Jacob Brown his
                                attorney Whereupon came a Jury
ToWit John Jefferies Frances Wilkie Philip Anderson Lot Wood Isaac Smith Ralph Hunt Moses Haines Walter Roberts Thomas Skelton Robert Millhouse John Palmer and Daniel Young. Who return their Verdict on their Respective Oaths and say we find for the Defendant on Motion of Wm Shaw attorney for the Plaintiff.   John Jefferies Foreman
A new Trial is awarded him &c.

Thomas Blasingame   Pltf)   Judith Little proved Twelve days
   against   )   attendance in this Suit Ordered
William Lee Defendant   )   that the Defendant Thos
                                Blasingame pay the same.

William Giles   Plaintiff)   The parties came into Court
   agt.   )   in their own proper person
William Pearson   Defendant)   and agree to refer this suit to
                                the arbitration of William
Farr and John Stokes and their award to be the Judgment of the Court and returned the said award to our next Court.

156 Ordered on Motion of James Yancey attorney and Friend to the heirs of Joseph Redd Deceased that a sitation Issue to Holland Sumner and Ann Sumner his wife administrators of Joseph Redd Deceased to appear at December Term Next to render a true accompt calculation and Reckoning of the rights and Credits of Joseph Redd &c. and that the Court request John Thomas Junior Esquire Late Ordinary of this District to furnish this Court with such Papers and records as concern the said Estate of the said Joseph Redd Decd.

James Olliphant   Plaintiff)   Case
   against   )   Ordered that a Dedimus
Jonathan Newman   Defendant)   protestation Issue to any
                                Two or three convenient
Justices in the State of Georgia to Examine Joseph Rush on the Fourth Monday in November Next on Oath and that his deposition be admitted on the above Trial on behalf of the Plaintiff Notice being Given to the Defendants attorney of the Time accordingly.

Luke Carrell   Plaintiff   )   Ordered that Thomas Biddy
   agt.   )   be Discharged of his bail
Thomas Biddy Bail   )   at the Plaintiff cost.
for Jos. Franklin   Defendant)

131

John Steen   Plaintiff) Ordered that William
    agt   ) Steen be Discharged of
William Steen Bail   ) his bail at the plaintiffs
for Robt. Montgomery Defendant) Costs.

William Brandon Plaintiff)   The Defendant being Called not
    against   )   appearing is Ordered that it
William Boyd   Defendant)   be Gazzerteed and that the
                               Defendant plead to the
Plaintiffs Declaration within the time limitted by Law.

Ordered that the State Docket be first settled for the
Future.

In the Suit Determined William Gilkie against John Steen
Ordered that the Execution Issue against the Defendant
Estate and that the Plaintiff demand Security according to
the Installment act. Before Zachariah Bullock Esquire if
not complyed with the property to be sold to satisfy the
said Judgment.

Thomas Blasingame Plaintiff) The Defendant being solemnly
    against   )   Called and not appeared to
Holland Sumner   Defendant) Defend the Suit Ordered that
                               a Default be entered against
him.

157 William Whitlock Plaintiff) The Defendant being Called
    against   )   but not appeared to defend the
Hold. Sumner   Defendant)   Suit Ordered that a default
                                  be entered against him which
                                  was done accordingly.

Joseph Jones   Plaintiff)   Came the parties into Court and
    agt.   )   agreed to continue said suit
John Holeman   Defendant)   untill next Court which was
                             ordered by the Court accordingly.

John & Jinney Young Plaintiff) Dbt.
    against   )   Arther Crawford who being
Samuel Shaw   Defendant)   Summoned as a Garnashee
                                 who was duly sworn in
Open Court according to Law and his deposition filed.

John Fincher   Plaintiff)   Case.
    agt.   )   Came the Plaintiff by W. Goodwin
David Newman   Defendant)   his attorney and the Defendant
                             being solemnly called to defend
the suit but not appearing it is ordered to be continued
untill next court.

John Foster   Plaintiff)   Came the Plaintiff by W. Goodwin
    agt.   )   his atto. and the Defendt. in
Henry Holcum   Defendant)   his Own proper person and agree
                             to continue said suit untill
next Court which is Ord. accordingly.

John Foster   Plaintiff)   Came the parties in their own
    agt.   )   proper person and agree to Dis-
Caleb Brigs   Defendant)   continue said suit at the
                             Defendts. cost which is ordered
by the Court accordingly.

John Foster   Plaintiff)   Came the plaintiff W. Goodwin
   agt.   )   his attorney and the Defendant
Joseph Randle   Defendant)   by Daniel Brown his Counseller
                          and then agreed to continue said
suit untill next Court which is Ord: accordingly.

William Whitlock   Plaintiff)   Came the Plaintiff by W.
   against   )   Goodwin his attorney and the
Landlot Porter   Defendant)   Defendant by Daniel Brown his
                          attorney and then and there
agree to Continue the said Suit untill next court which is
ordered accordingly.

158 William Bostick   Plaintiff)   Came the Plaintiff by Daniel
     against   )   Brown his attorney and the
John Bird and   )   Defendant by W. Goodwin his
James Derven   Defendant)   Counceller and then and
                          there agree to Continue said
suit untill next Court which is ordered accordingly.

Frances Latemore   Plaintiff)   Came the Plaintiff by Daniel
   against   )   Brown his attorney and the
James Bell   Defendant)   Defendant by William Shaw
                          his Councellor and then and
there agree to Continue said suit untill next Court which
is ordered accordingly.

George Taylor   Plaintiff)   Came the Plaintiff by W. Goodwin
   agt.   )   his attorney and the defendant
Robert Smith   Defendant)   by Jacob Brown his Counceller
                          and then and there agree to
Continue said suit untill next Court; which is Ordered
accordingly.

Andrew Gosset   Plaintiff)   Came the Parties in their Own
   against   )   proper person and agree to
Randal Holbrook Defendant)   continue said suit untill next
                          Court which is Ordered
                          accordingly.

Robert Lusk attorney for   Plaintiff)   Came the Plaintiff by
Ann Robinson   )   Danl. Brown his
   against   )   attorney and the
Joshua Petty   Defendant)   Defendant by Wm Shaw
                                 his Counceller and
then and there agree to Continue said suit untill next
Court which is Ord. accordingly.

William Morehead Came into Open Court and made Oath that
one half of the Corn Except six Bushells and five rows
belongs to John Steen on the plantation where he now lives
and Likewise as Plow and some Geers

State So. Carolina   Plaintiff)   The Defendant appearing to
   against   )   answer the Complaint of the
James Clark   Defendant)   Grand Jury on a presentment
                          and is by the Court Dis-
missed on paying all costs.

A Deed of Conveyance from John McCooll to William Kennedy
Esqr. For One hundred and nine acres of Land acknowledged

in Open Court by the Said John McCooll and Ordered to be recorded.

William Kennedy Esquire recd. of John Henderson Esquire Four Shillings and Eight pence as a fine collected by him for the Use of the County.

159 Robert Glover   Plaintiff)   Ordered that this Suit be
      against   )   referred to William Farr and
    James Hogans   Defendant)   Samuel Otterson with Liberty
                                    to Chose a third person in case
they do not agree and return their award to our next Court
which said award to be the Judgment of the Court.

    Stephen White   Plaintiff)   Came the Defendant by Charles
      agt.   )   Goodwin his attorney and the
    Mark Jackson   Defendant)   pltf being solemnly called but
                                 came not to prosecute his suit;
On motion of the Defendant by his attorney a nonsuit is
awarded him against the Plaintiff and it is also Ordered by
the Court that the Defendant recover against the Plaintiff
five Shillings Damage and Costs of Suit.

    William Sharp   Plaintiff)   Came the Plaintiff by Charles
      against   )   Goodwin his attorney and the
    John Inlow   Defendant)   Defendant by Jacob Brown his
                                Counceller and then and there
agree to refer this suit to the arbitration of William
Farr and Samuel Otterson and return their award to our next
Court which said award to be the Judgment of the Court.

Ordered that the Court adjourn untill tomorrow 9 O'Clock.

Signed by   Zachariah Bullock
                        Thomas Blasingame   Esquire
                        Thomas Brandon

At a Court continued and held in and for the County of
Union on the twenty ninth day of September in the year of
our Lord one thousand seven hundred and eighty seven.

Present   Thomas Brandon
                        William Kennedy   Esquires
                        John Birdsong
                        Zachariah Bullock

Ordered that Drewry Murrell be appointed Overseer of the
Road from Bobo's ford on Tyger River to James Mills on
Enoree in the place of Andrew Torrence who with the appro-
bation of the Court Resigned.

Ordered that the Clerk deliver a List of all the persons who
are Lyable to pay for Tavern Licence Obtained since the
first of March One thousand seven hundred and Eighty Six;
Unto the Sheriff to Collect and that he make a due return
of the same at Our next Court.

160 Thomas Brandon   Plaintiff)   Ordered that the Evidences
      agt.   )   in this Suit prove their
    Henry Thickpenny   Defendant)   attendance for the Plaintiff;
                                    and Ordered that the same
be Taxed in the Bill of Costs against the Defendant which

William Ainsworth proved Thirteen Days attendance Ord. that
the Same be Taxed in the bill of Costs Thomas Hart proved
Eleven Days attendance for the Plaintiff. Ordered that the
same be Taxed in the Bill of Costs John Willard proved
Twelve Days attendance for the Plaintiff one to prove a
Different point in the said Trial Ordered that the Same be
Taxed in the Bill of Costs against the Defendant aforesaid.

William Brandon	Plaintiff)	The Sheriff returned a writ
agt.	)	that the Defendant was not
Jeremiah Stokes	Defendant)	be found with this County an
		alias is awarded against him.

Ordered that Joseph Jones be paid his fees for the time he
supported Trasey in Joal and that the Treasury pay the same.

Ordered that Benajah Thompson who late built the County Goal
be sited to repair and Finish the said Joal before the next
Court and the same be approved of by William Kennedy and
John Birdsong Esquires and on failour thereof the County
attorney file a bill of an Indictment against the said
Benajah Thompson for a Cheat.

Ordered by the Court that William Brandon Jeremiah Gregory
James Bell Richard Burgess and John Ham be and is hereby
appointed Constables for this County who took the Oaths of
Office required by Law.

Thomas Brandon	Plaintiff)	In this suit determined this
against	)	term whereon the defendant
Henry Thickpenny	Defendant)	made a motion for an appeal to
		the Court of Common Pleas it

is Ordered that the Defendant file his reasons for the
same which he refuseth on which it is ordered that the
Verdict of the Jury be confirmed and the motion

Ordered that the Overseers of the Road that is to say Jacob
Paulk and James Gibbs make the bridge Over Fairforest at
Colonell Thomas Brandons Shoals sufficient that Loaded
Waggons may Pass and to be Under the Direction of Colonel
Thos. Brandon Esq. in the same.

161 Ordered that the Court adjourn untill Court in Course.

Signed by   Zachariah Bullock
                             Thomas Brandon
                             William Kennedy   Esquires
                             Charles Sims
                             John Birdsong

At a Court begun and held in and for the County of Union
at the Court house of said County the Twenty fourth day of
December in the year of Our Lord one thousand seven hundred
and Eighty seven and of the Independence of the United
States of North America the Twelfth.

Present   Thomas Brandon
                             Charles Sims   Esquires
                             Thomas Blasingame

Ordered that the Sheriff Summons the following persons to
serve as a body of Inquest for this County at Next Court

135

they being nominated and drawn according to Law as follows.

1	George Parks	11.	A Goudylock
2.	John Beckham	12.	Joseph Guiton
3.	Charles Clanton	13.	Neh. Howard
4.	Charles Miles	14.	James Crawford
5.	Joshua Petty	15.	William Hawkins
6.	Drewry Murrel	16.	John Harrington
7.	John Hope	17.	Isaac Smith
8.	Joseph Howard	18.	Isaac Parker
9.	William Means	19.	George McWhorter
10.	Henry Goode	20.	John Jenkins

Ordered that the Sheriff summon the following persons to serve as Pettit Jury at our next Court for this County they being Drawn according to Law Towit.

1.	William Morgan	16.	Caleb Gasway
2.	Joseph Gault	17.	David Hudson
3.	Wm. Beckham	18.	John Leek
4.	James Moseley	19.	Hugh Donaldson
5.	John Fincher	20.	Joshua Scisson
6.	Benj. Hawkins	21.	John McPherson
7.	John Howard	22.	John Springer
8.	Joseph West	23.	John Clark
9.	John Smith	24.	James Petty
10.	David Prewet	25.	Thomas Skelton
11.	John Stokes	26.	James McElwain
12.	John Reed	27.	John Shippy
13.	Robert Milhouse	28.	Andrew George
14.	John Townsend	29.	John Wilson
15.	John Hughey Junr.	30.	Duncan McCrevan

A Deed of Conveyance from Thomas Brandon to Hezekiah Rice acknowledged in Open Court by Thomas Brandon and Ordered to be Recorded.

162 A Deed of Conveyance from John Fincher to John Sanders acknowledged in Open Court and Ordered to be recorded.

A Deed of Conveyance from Thomas Brandon to Robert Gregory acknowledged in Open Court and Ordered to be Recorded.

A Deed of Conveyance from Robert Gregory to Jeremiah Gregory acknowledged in Open Court and Ordered to be Recorded.

A Deed of Conveyance from Robert Woodson to James Woodson acknowledged in Open Court and ordered to be recorded.

A Deed of Conveyance and from Robert Stark late Sheriff of Ninety Six District to Daniel Lipham Ordered to be Recorded.

A Deed of Conveyance Between John McCooll of the one part and John McKibben of the other part for one hundred and sixty acres of Land acknowledged by the said John McCooll and Ordered to be recorded.

A Deed of Conveyance between Robert Stark late Sheriff of ninety six district of the one part & Daniel Lipham of the other part for two hundred acres of Land and Ordered to be Recorded.

A Deed of Conveyance from John McCooll to John McKibbin for one lot of Land containing one half acre Lying at this Court House acknowledged and Ordered to be recorded.

A Deed of Conveyance from John McCooll to John McKibbin for two lots of land laying at this court house containing one half acre each acknowledged by the said John McCooll & Ord. to record.

A Deed of Conveyance from Lewis Bobo and Sarah his wife of the one part and Caleb Edmondson of the other part for three hundred acres of Land proved by the Oaths of Archer Smith & Andee. Torrence Witnesses thereunto and Ordered to be recorded.

On the application of Cushman Edson Leave is given him to retail spirituous liquors on his Giving John McCooll his Security who entered into bonds according to Law.

On the application of Walter Goodman Leave is given him to retail Spirituous Liquors on his giving Bernard Glenn his security according to law.

A Deed of Conveyance from Nezekiah Gentry & Catherine Gentry to James Hogans for One hundred and Ninety six acres of Land proved by the Oaths of John Jenkins and Rige Hogans Witnesses thereunto and Ordered to be Recorded.

163 Ordered that Samuel Simpson be Granted letters of Administration on the Estate of John Simpson decd. he having returned a Citation Certified by John Pulman and it appearing to the Court that no person having any Objection who Together with Archer Smith and William Martindale his Security intered into bonds and acknowledged the same in the sum of One hundred pounds for the said administration which was approved by the Court and Ordered accordingly.

A Deed of Conveyance from John McPhearson and Sarah McPhearson to Nathan Glenn for Two Hundred and fifty acres of Land; also a memorandom receipt on the back acknowledged and ordered to be recorded.

Ordered that Nathan Glenn and William Hollingsworth be appointed to view the road from the Fishdam ford to the Ninety six Road and report the same to our next Court.

William Plummer   Plaintiff)   Dbt   Came the Plaintiff by
  against   )   atto.   Daniel Brown his atto.
Daniel Plummer   Defendant)   and the Defendant in
                                      Own proper person and
agree to reinstate this suit which was dismissed by a mistake and Geen for Trial which was Ordered by the Court accordingly.

Ordered that Joseph Howard be and is hereby appointed Overseer of the Road from Union Court House to Brandons Shoals on fairforest in the place of Jacob Faulk who with the apporbation of this Court resigned.

Ordered that James Crawford Adam Potter and Arthur Cunningham be appointed to View the best way that a road can

be laid out from Woffords Irons Work's to Union Court House
and report the same to our next court to the County Line.

Ordered that the Court be adjourned untill Wednesday the
Twenty sixth of this Instant at Nine o'clock.

Signed by   Thomas Brandon
                             Charles Sims   Esquires
                             Thos. Blasingame

At a Court continued and held by adjournment at the Court
House of the County of Union the Twenty sixth day of
December One thousand seven hundred Eighty seven

Present   Thomas Brandon
                             William Kennedy   Esquires
                             John Birdsong

164 A Bond from John Nuckols to John Davison deceased proved
by the Oath of John Gilham one of the Evidences thereunto
and Ordered to be recorded.

A Receipt from John Nuckols to John Davison dated the
thirteenth day of August 1774 proved by the Oath of John
Haile Esqr. and Ordered to be recorded.

A Receipt from John Nuckols to John Davison dated the
Twentieth day of October 1774 proved by the Oath of John
Haile Esquire and Ordered to be recorded.

James Fannin produces a Certificate for Susannah Bailey
widow of John Bailey deceased allowing him free Liberty
to administrate of the said John Baileys Estate whereon
Letters of administration was awarded him whereupon he
together with Charles Thompson entered into and acknowledged
their bonds in the sum of one hundred pounds for securing
the said Estate and Took the Oath required by Law which
was Ord. by the Court.

Ordered that John Read William Hendley and Turner Kendrick
be appointed appraisers of the said Estate of John Bailey
decd. and that a true Inventory be returned to our next
Court.

A Deed of Conveyance from William Farr late Sheriff of our
County to Thomas Miles for three hundred acres acknowledged
by the said William Farr and Ordered to be recorded.

A Deed of Conveyance from William Farr late Sheriff of
Our County to cold. Thomas Brandon for One hundred acres
of land acknowledged by the said Wm Farr and Ordered to be
recorded.

A Deed of Conveyance from Joshua Saxton to Moses Guiton
for one hundred and fifty acres proved by the Oaths of
Andr. and John Rodgers Witnesses thereunto and Ordered to
be recorded.

A Deed of Conveyance from John Steen Seniour to Gedion Smith
for two hundred acres of Land proved by the Oathes of
Abraham and John Smith Witnesses thereunto and Ord. to
record.

138

A Deed of Conveyance from William Kennedy to John Kennedy
for one hundred and thirty five acres of Land acknowledged
by the said William Kennedy and Ordered to be recorded.

A Deed of Conveyance from Thomas Brandon to Thos. Kennedy
for one hundred and thirty five acres of Land acknowledged
by the said Thomas Brandon and Ordered to be Recorded.

165 A Deed of Conveyance from Thomas Brandon to William Steen
for three hundred acres of Land acknowledged by the said
Thomas Brandon and Ordered to be recorded.

A Deed of Conveyance from William Rodger of the one part and
Henry Smith of the other part for one hundred acres of Land
proved by the Oath of William Bostick also proved the
hand of Dennis Dempsey who is said to be deceased and
Ordered to be recorded.

A Lease and Release from John Hames to Robert Gaot for one
hundred acres of Land proved by the Oath of John and Thomas
George Witnesses thereunto and ordered to be recorded.

A Deed of Gift Between Thomas Brandon of the one part and
the County of Union of the other part for two acres of Land
acknowledged by the said Thomas Brandon and Ord. to record.

A Deed of Conveyance from John McCooll to John DYoung for
one half acres of Land acknowledged by the said John McCooll
and ordered to be recorded.

Ordered that the County Line be recorded as laid down in
the Platt of a scale of Twenty four miles to an Inch by
James Smith Surveyor.

Ordered that the County Treasury pay unto James Smith
Surveyor Three pounds fourteen shillings and eight pence.

A Deed of Conveyance from Patrick Earley to Thomas Greer
for O Fifty four acres of land acknowledged by the said
Patrick Earley and ordered to be recorded.

A Deed of Conveyance from John Beckham to Robert Thompson
for one hundred acres of Land acknowledged in Open Court by
the said Jno Beckham and Ordered to record.

State of So. Carolina Plaintiff)   Ordered that his Suit
   against   )   be continued over untill
Joseph Jones   Defendant)   next court and then to be
                                   peremptly Tried.

John Young   Plaintiff)   Attachment served in the hands of
   agt.   )   Arther Crawford Judgment against
Samuel Shaw Defendant)   Garnashe according to his deposi-
                          tion filed the Defendant Confessed
a Judt. for six pounds six shillings and costs of suit.

166 State of So. Carolina Plaintiff)   Ordered that the
   against   )   Defendant give security
James Hogans   Defendant)   for his Good behaviour
                                   in the sum of fifty
pounds and for his appearnce at our next Court to answer

a Bill of Indictment to be performed against him for an
assault and battery on one Sarter and Jeremiah Gregory a
Constable.

A Bill of Sale from William Thomas to William Hendley for
One Negro Girl named Sarah proved by the Evidence & Ord.
to record.

Drewery Harrington   Plaintiff)   Case
  agt.   )   Came the Plaintiff by
Charles Clanton   Defendant)   Charles Goodwin his
                                  attorney also came the
Defendant by William Shaw his Counceller and then and there
agree to refer the suit to William McCullock and James
Terrell and their award to be the Judgment of the Court.

Robert Glover   Plaintiff)   Came the Plaintiff by Charles
  agt.   )   Goodwin his attorney also
James Hogans   Defendant)   the Defendant by Jacob Brown
                              his Counciller which there was
an award returned by Samuel Otterson and William Farr and
Ordered to be recorded and Judgment accordingly and the
Defendant is entitled to the benefit of the Installment
Law which said award is made a Judgment of This Court.

William Lawson   Plaintiff)   Trover
  against   )   Declaration filed and plea
Jonathan Norman   Defendant)   entered and the Issue Joined
                               whereupon came a Jury Towit.
Alexander McDougal, Renny Belew, Renny Belew Junior, Zachariah Belew, Reuben Below, William Smith, Hugh Means,
Lewis Turner, Isaac Cook, William Hollingsworth, Jepthah
Hollingsworth, Lewis Ledbetter Who return their verdict
on their respective Oathes and Say we find for the Defendant the Costs of Suit. Alexr. McDougal foreman Which
said Verdict is Ratified by the Court and Ordered to record.

A Deed of Conveyance from Joseph Jones to John Ewart for
one hundred and fifty acres of Land proved by the Oaths of
Jacob Brown and Henry Bailey Witnesses thereunto and
Ordered to be recorded.

John Young   Plaintiff)   Came the Plaintiff by Daniel Brown
  agt.   )   his attorney also the Defendant
John Hames   Deft.   )   by Jacob Brown his Counciller and
                           agree to dismiss this suit at the
Defendants Cost which is Ordered by the Court accordingly.

167 William Bostick Plaintiff)   Ordered that the Sheriff Expose
  agt.   )   to Sale the Lands Executed to
John Steen   Defendant)   Satisfy this debt and Costs.

Ordered that Charles Burton be appointed Constable for this
County the Term of Six month who took the Oath of Office
required by Law.

Thomas Brandon Plaintiff)   Detinue
  agt   )   Came the Plaintiff by Jacob
William Lee   Defendant)   Brown his attorney also the
                             Defendant William Shaw his
Counciller then and there agree that Sarah Hopkins Depositi-
tion be admitted in evidence on this trial which was taken

140

by Consent.

```
Richard & Sarah Penell Exors Plaintiff)   Trover
of James Martin Deceased            )   Came the Plaintiff
   agt.                             )   by Charles Goodwin
Absalom Petty              Defendant)   their attorney also
                                        came the Defendant
```
by William Shaw his Counceller and then and there agree to
refer this Suit to John Thompson Soloman Mangham Robert
Lusk Joseph Guiton and Moses Guiton and their award to be
made a Judgment of the Court-which was ordered accordingly.

Ordered that the Court adjourn untill tomorrow at Nine
O'Clock.

```
Signed by              William Kennedy
                       Thomas Brandon     Esquires
                       Charles Sims
```

At a Court continued and held by adjournment at the Court
House of said County the Twenty seventh day of December One
thousand seven hundred and Eighty seven and of the Inde-
pendencey of the United States of America the Twelfth

```
Present                William Kennedy
                       John Birdsong      Esquires
                       Thomas Blasingame
```

A Deed of Conveyance from Isaac Bogan to Daniel Comer for
one hundred and fifty acres of Land acknowledged by the
said Isaac Bogan to the said Daniel Comer and Ordered to
be recorded.

```
Robert Worster   Plaintiff)   Dbt.
   agt                    )   Came the Plaintiff by Jacob
William Wilson   Defendant)   Brown his attorney and the
                              Defendant being Solemnly
```
called came not to defend his suit; decreed for the
laintiff seven pounds fifteen shillings agreeable to a
proved accompt filed in the Clerks Office and Costs of
Suit which is ordered accordingly.

```
168 John Fincher   Plaintiff)   Case
       agt                  )   Came the Plaintiff by Charles
    David Norman   Defendant)   Goodwin his attorney and the
                                Defendant in his own proper
```
person and then and there agreed to Discontinue the said
Suit at the defendants costs, which is ordered by the Court
accordingly.

```
His Excellency     Plaintiff)   Dbt.
Thomas Pinckney             )   Came the Defendant into Open
   against                  )   Court in his Own proper person
David Stocdon &             )   and confessed Judgment
Jonathan Gilkie    Defendant)   according to Specialty and
                                Costs of Suit with Stay of
```
Execution for Three months which is ordered accordingly.

```
Betsey and John Oliver)   Dbt.
   agt                )   Came the plaintiff by William
John and William Steen)   Shaw his attorney and the
                          Defendant by his Councellor and
```

141

the Defendant being solemnly called came not to prosecute his suit; decree for the plaintiff six pounds nine shillings and costs of suit which is ordered accordingly.

A Deed of Conveyance from Joseph Jones to John Springer for three hundred and forty six acres of Land acknowledged by the said Joseph Jones and Ordered to be recorded.

Thomas Brandon   Plaintiff)   Case
  agt.   )   Declaration filed plea intered
William Lee   Defendant)   and Issue Joined by the parties
                             and ordered for Trial came the
plaintiff by Jacob Brown his attorney also came the Defendant by William Shaw his attorney whereupon came a Jury toWit Alexander McDougal Renny Ballew Senr. Renny Balew Junr. Hugh Means Reuben Belue Jeptha Hollingsworth William Hollingsworth Isaac Cook Lewis Turner Lewis Ledbetter William Smith Nicholas Harris who return their Verdict on their Respective Oathes and say we find for the Defendant with costs of suit.   Alexr. McDougal fr.

William Giles   Plaintiff)   Trover
  agt.   )   The arbitrators return their
William Pearson Defendant)   award William Farr and John
                             Stokes which said award is
ordered to be recorded and Judgment accordingly.

John Mullin   Plaintiff)   Debt on attachment
  against   )   Ordered that the Sheriff expose
Thomas Cox   Defendant)   the property to sail under
                             attached and the Money remain in
his hands untill further orders.

Thomas Brandon   Plaintiff)   Case
  agt.   )   Ordered that the Witnesses in
William Lee   Defendant)   this Suit prove their atten-
                             dance according to law on
behalf of the Defendant and that the same be
169 Taxed in the bill of Cost. Lewis Wells proved Twenty eight days attendance also Seven pounds Three Shillings and four pence for mileage John Clark proved seven days attendance and is allowed seventeen shillings and six pence Ann Jackson proved Thirteen Days attendance and is allowed One pound thirteen shillings and six pence Jean Lee proved Ten days attendance and is allowed one pound five shillings Sarah Hopkins proved 5 days attendance and is allowed Twelve Shillings and Six pence Ordered accordingly.

Thomas Brandon   Plaintiff)   Ordered that the Evidences in
  agt.   )   this suit on the part of the
William Lee   Defendant)   plaintiff prove their attendance
                             according to Law which Rebeccah
Stedham proved Seven days attendance and allowes Seventeen Shillings and Six pence ordered that the same be taxed in the bill of Costs.

Ordered that the Court adjourn untill tomorrow Nine O'Clock
Signed by   William Kennedy
                            John Birdsong   Esquires
                            Thomas Blasingame

At a Court Continued and held by adjournment at the Court
House of the County of Union in and for the said County
the Twenty eighth day of December in the Year of Our Lord
one thousand Seven hundred and eighty seven and of the
Independance of the United States of North America the
Twelfth.
Present   Thomas Brandon
                 Thomas Blasingame   Esquires
                 William Kennedy

A Deed of Conveyance Between Thomas Brandon of the One
part and Thomas Palmer of the other part for two hundred
acres of Land acknowledged by the said Thos. Brandon and
Ord. to record.

John Steen   Plaintiff)   Debt on attachment
   agt.   )   Came the plaintiff by Jacob
David Stocdon   Defendant)   Brown and William Shaw his
                          attorneys also the Defendant by
James Yancey his attorney and then and there agree to
Continue said Suit at Equal Costs which is Ord. accordingly.

Mark Mitchell   Plaintiff)   Debt.
   agt.   )   Came the Plaintiff by William
Benjamin and   )   Shaw his attorney and the
Henry Long   Defendant)   Defendant by Jacob and Daniel
                          Brown their attorney. Which
the Defendant having givin Security according to the act
of assembly for paying of Debts by Instalment whereupon
it is considered by the Court that the Suit be Discontinued at the Defendants Cost and Ordered accordingly.

170 John Steen   Plaintiff)   Debt
    agt   )   Came the Plaintiff by William
Rebecca and   )   Shaw his attorney and the
Wm. George   Defendant)   Defendant by Jacob Brown their
                          attorney and then and there agree
to Continue the said Suit Untill Next Term also Ordered that
the Defendant give security to the plaintiff before our next
court agreeable to Law.

Gabriel Smothers   Plaintiff)   Debt on a petition and
   against   )   summons decreed according to
William Steen   Defendant)   specialty with interest and
                          costs of suit against the
Defendant the plaintiff agree to Stay Execution the Term
of Three months.

Robert Lusk   Plaintiff)   Case
   agt   )   Came the Plaintiff by William
Mathew Robinson   Defendant)   Shaw his attorney also Came
                          the Defendant by Jacob Brown
his Counceller and then and there agree to Continue this
Suit at the Defendants cost which was ordered accordingly.

William Williams   Plaintiff)   Dbt.
   agt.   )   Came the Plaintiff by Daniel
John Towns   Defendant)   Brown his attorney also the
                          Defendant by William Shaw
his Counceller and then and there agree to Discontinue the
said suit at the defendants cost on the affidavit of

143

Daniel Brown attorney for the plaintiff which is Ordered
accordingly.

George Leggat   Plaintiff)   Debt
   agt.   )   Came the plaintiff by Daniel
Nathaniel Gorden Defendant)   Brown his attorney and the
                               Defendant by Jacob Brown his
attorney and for Certain reasons assigned by the Defendant
by his attorney aforesaid a nonsuit is awarded for the
Defendant and it is further considered by the Court that
the Defendant recover against the Plaintiff five shillings
for his Damage and Costs of suit which is ordered accordingly

Robert Montgomery)   Assault and Battery
   agt.   )   Declaration Filed and plea entered
Soloman Mangham)   the parties Join Issue Ordered for
                     Trial Came the Plaintiff by Jacob Brown
his attorney and the Defendant by Daniel Brown his attorney
Whereupon came a Jury towit Alexander McDougal Renny Belew
Senr. Renny Belew Junr. Hugh Means Reuben Belue Jeptha
Hollingsworth William Hollingsworth Isaac Cook Lewis
Turner Lewis Ledbetter William Smith Nicholas Harris Who
say on their respective oaths and say we find for the
defendant cost of suit   Alexr. McDougal foreman
Which said verdict is ratifyed by the Court and Ordered to
be recorded.

171 Robert Lusk Plaintiff)   Case
    agt   )   Came the Plaintiff by William Shaw
    John Jones Defendant)   his attorney also the Defendant by
                             Charles Goodwin his attorney and
then and there agree to Continue said Suit at Mutual Costs
which is ordered accordingly.

Robert Montgomery Plaintiff)   On Attachment
   aginst   )   Came the Plaintiff by Jacob
Davis Wilkie   Defendant)   Brown and William Shaw his
                                attorney also Came the
Defendant in his own proper person and agree to Continue
said suit untill next Court which is Ordered accordingly.

George Sammons   Plaintiff)   Debt on attachment
   agt.   )   Came the plaintiff by James
Shadrack Landtrip Defendant)   Yancey his attorney and the
                               Defendant by Jacob Brown his
Counceller and then and there Confessed a Judgment for
Twenty pounds and Costs of Suit Ordered that Execution
Issue against the Defendant unless he appear before William
Kennedy Esquire and Give Security according to the Instaul-
ment Law that the Said William Kennedy shall seem meet.

George Sammons   Plaintiff)   Ordered that the Evidences in
   agt.   )   this Suit prove their atten-
Shadrack Lantrip Defendant)   dance according to Law which
                               John Howard proved Eight
days attendance on the part of the plaintiff and is
allowed one pound for the same Ordered that the same be
Taxed in the Bill of Costs.

Rowland Cornelias   Plaintiff)   Debt
   agt.   )   Came the plaintiff by
William & Jas. Thomas Defendant)   Jacob Brown his attorney

144

also Came the Defendant by Robert Goodlow Harper his Counceller and then and there agree to Discontinue said Suit at
the Plaintiffs Costs which is Ordered accordingly.

Caleb Gasway   Plaintiff)   Debt.
  agt.   )   Came the Plaintiff by James
Thomas Taylor   Defendant)   Yancey and Daniel Brown his
                               attorney also Came the Defendant
in his own proper person and then and there agree to continue said suit at the Plaintiffs cost which is ordered
accordingly.

Robert Montgomery Plaintiff)   Case
  against   )   Came the Plaintiff by Jacob
William Liles   Defendant)   Brown and William Shaw his
                                attorney also came the
Defendant by Daniel Brown his atto. Ordered that a nonsuit
be awarded the defendant against the plaintiff for not
prosecuting his suit also that the Defendant recover five
shillings damage and costs of suit.

172 George Pervis   Plaintiff)   Case
    agt   )   Came the Defendant by Jacob
Robert Montgomery Defendant)   Brown his attorney and the
                                    Plaintiff being solemnly
called according to Law came not to prsecute his suit
wherefore it is ordered that the plaintiff be nonsuited also
considered by the Court that the Defendant recover five
shillings for Damage and costs of suit which is ordered
accordingly.

William Liles   )   Case
  agt   )   Came the Defendant by William Shaw his
Robert Montgomery)   attorney and the Plaintiff being
                      solemnly called came not to prosecute
his suit wherefor a nonsuit is awarded the Defendant against
the plaintiff and that he recover--the sum of five shillings
for his damage and costs of suit.

William and Rebecca George)   Case
  against   )   Came the Defendant by William
John Steen   Defendant)   Shaw his attorney and the
                              Plaintiff being Solemnly
called came not to prosecute this suit wherefore a nonsuit
awarded the Defendant against the plaintiff also considered
by the Court that he recover the sum of five shillings
damage and Costs of Suit which is Ordered accordingly.

Francis Fincher   Plaintiff)   Slander
  agt.   )   Came the Plaintiff in his
James and Ann Jackson Defendant)   Own proper person and
                                     the Defendant Charles
Goodwin W Harper and William Shaw   Whereupon came a
Jury towit Alexander McDougal Renny Belew Junr. Zachariah
Belew Renny Belew Senr. William Smith Lewis Turner Isaac
Cook William Hollingsworth Jeptha Hollingsworth Lewis
Ledbetter and Nicholas Harris who return their Verdict on
their respective Oaths and say we fine for the Defendant
with costs of Suit.   Alexd. McDougal   foreman
Which Verdict is ratifyed by the Court and Ordered to be
recorded.

145

Turner Rountree   Plaintiff) Debt
  against   ) Came the parties into Open
Joseph Wofford   Defendant) Court and then and there
                               agree to refer the said Suit
to John and Thomas Blasingame and their award to be the
Determination of the Execution Issued against the said
Joseph Wofford which is Ordered by the Court accordingly.

State So. Carolina Plaintiff) Pettit Larcency
  against   ) the Defendant waved all
Daniel Howel   Defendant) advantages on this Bill of
Indictment or any other form pointed out by Law. On
prosecution and pleads Guilty
of Stealing a Handkerchief and prays the Mercey of the Court
and that the Court proceede to Judgment Whereupon the Court
Ordered that the Sheriff Inflict the punishment of five
lashes on his bare back at the publick whipping post and
that the Defendant be Discharged on paying of costs which
is ordered accordingly.

Ordered that the Court adjourn untill tomorrow at Nine
O'Clock
Signed by   William Kennedy
                            Thomas Brandon   Esquires
                            Thomas Blasingame

At a Court Continued and held by adjournment at the Court
house of Union County in and for Said County on the
Twenty ninth day of December One thousand Seven hundred and
Eighty seven and of the Independence of the United States of
North America the Twelfth.

Present   William Kennedy
                            John Birdsong   Esquires
                            Thomas Blasingame

A Bill of Sale from Robert Senn to Adam Thompson for
Cattle & proved by James Thompson an Evidence to the Same
Ordered to be recorded.

The Executors of Henry Addington returned and Inventory
of the said Addington Ordered to be recorded and the same
filed.

Mary Williams Plaintiff) Debt Petition and Summons Came
  against   ) the parties in their Own proper
Daniel Jackson Defendant) person into Open Court and then
and there agree to Continue said Suit untill next Court
which is ordered accordingly.

John McCooll   Plaintiff) Debt Petition and Summons
  against   ) Came the parties into Open
John Montgomery   Defendant) Court in their Own proper
                              person and then and there
agree to continue said suit over untill our next Court
which is Ordered accordingly.

William Farr   Plaintiff) Debt on attachment
  against   ) Dismissed at the plaintiffs
John Steen   Defendant) costs Comes Thomas Vance into
                              open Court and assumed to pay

146

the Costs of This Suit on behalf of the plaintiff Judgment
against Thomas Vance accordingly.

174 William Shaw   )   Debt on attachment.
    against   )   Joseph Jolly being summoned as a
    Robert Montgomery) Garnashee being solemnly called
                            whereon it is ordered that a Scere
facias Issue against the said Joseph Jolly to appear at our
next Court to shew cause why Judgment should not be entered
against him as Garnishee aforesaid.

Nathaniel Jefferies Plaintiff) Debt. attachment
    against   ) Came the parties into Open
John Steen   Defendant) Court in their Own proper
                                 person and then and there
agree to Discontinue this suit at the Ptlfs Cost which was
ordered accordingly.

James Laswell   Plaintiff) Came the Parties into Open
    against   ) Court in their Own proper
James Terrell   Defendant) person and then and there
                              agree to Discontinue said
suit at the Plaintiffs Cost which is ordered accordingly.

William Plummer   Plaintiff) Debt on attachment
    against   ) Came the Plaintiff by James
Daniel Jackson   Defendant) Yancey his attorney also
                              Came the Defendant in his Own
proper person; whereupon came a Jury and writ of Enquiry on
a Default the Declaration filed Towit Alexander McDougal
Renny Belew Junr. Zachariah Belew Renny Belew William Smith
Lewis Turner Isaac Cook William Hollingsworth Jepthah
Hollingsworth Lewis Ledbetter Aaron Fincher who being duly
drawn and sworn do on their respective oaths say we find
for the Plaintiff fifty pounds and costs of suit Judgment
entered against the Garnashe for the Money Condemned in
his hands.   Alexr. McDougal

Ruth Brown   Plaintiff) Ordered that a Dedimus Issue
    against   ) to the State of Georgia to take
Walter Roberts   Defendant) the deposition of David Wilkie
                              the time and place be made
by the Plaintiff and that the deposition be admitted in
evidence in the Trial on the part of the Plaintiff Ordered
that the plaintiff give due and Legal Notice to the Defendant of the time & place aforesaid according to Law.

John Bird Plaintiff) Came the Defendant in his Own
    against   ) proper person and the plaintiff
John Steen Defendant) being solemnly called but came
                        not to prosecute his suit wherefore
a nonsuit is awarded the Defendant against the Plaintiff
and that he recover the sum of five shillings damage and
costs of suit which is ordered by the Court accordingly.

Ordered that Thomas Brandon Lay and Clear out a Road from
Union Court House to the said Cold. Brandons the nearest
and best Way &C.

175 Thomas Vance   Plaintiff) Debt on attachment
    against   ) Ordered that the Sheriff
John & William Steen Defendant) Take the Negroe into

147

possession and expose the Same to Saile. at public auction
and that the Money remain in his hands untill further order
and that the Land attached be Gazzeeted according to Law &c.

John McKibbin   Plaintiff)   Debt on attachment
  against   )   Richard Burgess Came into Open
Jesse Dodd   Defendant)   Court and Undertakes for the
                              Defendant that in Case the
Defendant shall be cast he will pay the Judgment of the
Court or render his body in prison in discharge thereof he
the said Richard Burgess will pay the Condemnation for him
Whereupon on Motion of the Defendant by his attorney it is
Ordered that the Judgment Obtained against him and the said
Richard Burgess Security for his appearance or his Common
Bail the defendant now pleading the General Issue and
Ordered to be Continued.

John Mullins   Plaintiff)   Debt on attachment
  against   )   Came the Plaintiff in his own
Thomas Cox   Defendant)   proper person and the Defendant
                              being solemnly called failed to
appear to prosecute his suit. Wherefore it is Ordered that
Judgment be entered against him by default for 12 pounds
& costs and Interest which is Ord; accordingly.

William Shaw   Plaintiff)   Debt on attachment
  against   )   Declaration filed and plea
Robert Montgomery   Defendant)   entered whereupon came a
                                 Jury Towit on Alexander
McDougal Renny Belew Junr. Zachariah Belew Renny Belew
William Smith Lewis Turner Isaac Cook William Hollingsworth
Jeptha Hollingsworth Lewis Ledbetter and Aaron Fincher who
return their Verdict and writ of enquiry and say on their
respective oaths and say we find for the Plaintiff Sixteen
pounds four shillings with interest and costs of suit
which verdict is ratified by the Court &0 to R.
                                        Alexr. McDougal

Philip Anderson Plaintiff)   Debt on attachment
  against   )   Came the parties into Open
James Hogans   Defendant)   Court and then and there agree
                             to continue said suit untill
next Court which is ordered accordingly.

Stephen White   Plaintiff)   Debt on attachment.
  against   ). The parties agree to continue
Mark Jackson   Defendant)   this suit untill next Court
                              which is Ord. accd.

176 Ralph Jackson   Plaintiff)   Debt on attachment
  against   )   Came the parties into Open
William Jackson Defendant)   Court and then and there agree
                              to Continue the said suit
untill next Court at the plaintiffs Cost which is ordered
accordingly.

John Ewart   Plaintiff)   The Sheriff returned that the
  against   )   Defendant was not to be found
John Weediman   Defendant)   whereon the plaintiff has a
                              Judicial attachment awarded him
against the defendant.

148

Thomas Vance   Plaintiff)   Debt on attachment
   against   )   Whereupon Came a Jury on a
John & Wm. Steen   Defendant)   writ of Enquiry Towit
                                 Alexander McDougal Renny
Belew Junr. Zachariah Belew Renny Belew William Smith
Lewis Turner Isaac Cook William Hollingsworth Jeptha
Hollingsworth Lewis Ledbetter and Adam Fincher who return
their Verdict on their respective Oathes and say we find
for the plaintiff seventy pounds with Interest and Cost of
suit.   Alexander McDougal
Which said Verdict is ratified by the Court and Ordered
to Record.

William Gilkie   Plaintiff)   Debt.
   against   )   Came the plaintiff by Daniel
William Steen   Defendant)   Brown his attorney on a summons
                                 and Petition and the Defendant
by Charles Goodwin his Counseller and after this Court
having fully heard the matter argued on both sides Decred
for the plaintiff three pounds Ten Shillings and cost of
suit.

William Brandon   Plaintiff)   Trover on a petition and
   against   )   summons the Defendant pray
Jeremiah Stokes   Defendant)   a Trial by a Jury which was
                                 awarded him at hiy Costs
whereupon came a Jury Towit.   Alexr. McDougal Renny Belew
Zachariah Belew Renny Belew William Smith Lewis Turner
Isaac Cook William Hollingsworth Jeptha Hollingsworth Lewis
Ledbetter and Aaron Fincher who return their Verdict on
their Respective Oathes and say we find for the Defendant
with costs of suit.   Alexr. McDougal

Luke Carrell Came into Court as a Evidence in the Suit of
William Brandon against Jeremiah Stokes and appearing to
be drunk is by the Court fined Five Shillings for insult-
ing the Court and the above Crime and Costs and the same
Ordered accordingly.

177 Robert Gregory   Plaintiff)   Debt on attachment
      agt   )   Ordered that Sheriff Expose
   Thomas Holden   Defendant)   to Sale the property attached
                                 and that the Money Remain in
his hands untill next Court.

Kirkland &Co.   Plaintiff)   Debt
   against   )   On Motion of the plaintiff an
John Inlow   Defendant)   alias Capias awarded him on a
                                 nonesinventis Return and
Ordered accordingly.

James Minnis   Plaintiff)   Came the parties into Court and
   against   )   agreed to Continue said Suit
Gabriel Brown   Defendant)   over untill next Court which is
                                 Ord. accordingly.

David Stocdon   Plaintiff)   Case
   against   )   Ordered that this Suit be
John Steen   Defendant)   Continued over untill next court

```
Gabriel Brown    Plaintiff)   Debt
   against               )   Ordered that his Suit be
Thomas Biddy     Defendant)   Continued untill next
                              Court

John Thompson    Plaintiff)   Slander
   against               )   Ordered that this Suit be
Adam Goudylock   Defendant)   Contd. untill our next Court.

Daniel White     Plaintiff)   Debt on attachment
   agt.                  )   Ordered that the Sheriff expose
Daniel Howel     Defendant)   the property to Sail attached
                              and that the money remain in his
hands untill further orders and cotinued which is ordered
accordingly.
```

Ordered that the Sheriff expose to Sale all the Estrays
that has been advertised at the Court House the term of
Six Months according to Law.

```
George Kennedy   Plaintiff)   Came the Defendant into Open
   against               )   Court and the plaintiff being
Daniel Jackson   Defendant)   Solemnly called but failed to
                              appear to prosecute his suit
Ordered that it be Discontinued at the plaintiffs cost for
a Default which is ordered accordingly.
```

Ordered that the Evidences in the suit of Frances Fincher
against James and An Jackson prove their attendance and
that the same be taxed in the Bill of Costs according to
three Bills made out and proved and filed in the Office.

```
178 James Olliphant   Plaintiff)   Ordered that the Commission
       against               )   to the State of Georgia to
    Jonathan Norman   Defendant)   take the Deposition of Moses
                                   Rush be Renewed and that
    the time be mentioned by the plaintiff and legal notice
```
given to the defendant of time and place of Taking his
examination and his Deposition So taken Shall be admitted
notwithstanding he being under the age of twenty one years
and the Justices who shall examine the said Rush Shall
Certify from under their hands and seals the age of his the
said Moses Rush at the time he is Examined.

```
William Bostick Plaintiff)   Debt
   against               )   Came the Plaintiff by Daniel
John Bird and          )   Brown his attorney and the
James Darvin    Defendants)   Defendant James Darvin being
                              Solemnly Called Came not to
defend his suit Ordered that a Default be entered against
him.
```

Joseph Jones Goaler, Came into Open Court and Delivered up
the Keys of the Goal to the high Sheriff of this County and
was Discharged from the Care of the Goal any longer.

Ordered that a Citation Issue against all the Defalters
of the Jury who being Called and not answered to appear at
our next Court to Shew Cause if any they have why they
should not be fined.

The Court adjourn Untill Tomorrow Untill the fourth Monday
in March next Which is Court in Course

Signed   William Kennedy
                        Thomas Brandon   Esquires
                        John Birdsong

179 At a Court begun and held in and for the County of Union
at the Court House the Twenty fourth day of March in the
year of Our Lord One thousand Seven Hundred and Eighty
eight and of the Independence of the United States of
America the Twelvth.

Present   Thomas Brandon
                        Charles Sims   Esquires
                        John Birdsong

Ordered that the Sheriff Summons the following persons to
serve at our next Court as Pettit Jurrors they being Drawn
according to Law

1.   Samuel Cooper   16. Scion Murphy
2.   William Scisson   17. Richard Cos
3.   William Hollingsworth 18. Philip Anderson
4.   John Neaderman   19. John Jefferies
5.   Thomas Mays   20. Robert Glover
6.   Robert Woodson   21. George Little
7.   James Gibbs   22. Francis Lattimore
8.   John Wilson   23. Thomas Williams
9.   Joseph Bates   24. William White Tyger
10. Thomas Inlow   25. Joseph Means
11. John Bird   26. Nehemiah Miller
12. Geo. Harlen Farmer   27. Robert Haris
13. Nicholas Harris   28. Aaron Fincher
14. Nathaniel Jeffries   29. Robert Lusk
15. Benjamin Darby   30. Daniel Young

Ordered that the Grand Jury be Drawn to Serve this Court
which are as follows

1.   Samuel Crawford   7.   Henry Goode
2.   Charles Clanton   8.   Joseph Guiton
3.   Charles Miles   9.   Nehemiah Howard
4.   Drewry Murrel   10.   John G.
4.   James Petty Junr.   11.   John Harrington
     [two jurors numbered 4] 12. Isaac Parker
5.   Joseph Howard   13.   Joshua Petty
6.   George Park

A Deed of Conveyance from John Gordon to Christopher
Brandon acknowledged in Open Court and Ordered to be
Recorded

A Deed of Conveyance from Thomas Shockly to Charleton
Shcokley proved in Open Court by the Oaths Salathiel
Shockly & James Shockly and Ordered to be Recorded.

A Deed of Conveyance from John Palmore to Daniel Holden
acknowledged in Open Court and Ordered to be Recorded.

151

A Deed of Conveyance from Thacker Vivion to John Layton proved in Open Court by the Oaths of Turner Rountree and John Howard and Ordered to be Recorded.

A Deed of Conveyance from James Hogans Junr. and wife to James Hogans Senr. proved in Open Court by the Oaths of William Hogans and Thomas Canister and Ordered to be Recorded.

180 Laurance House is hereby appointed Overseer of the Road in the place of John Harrington who Resigned with the approbation of the Court.

Samuel Harlin is hereby appointed Overseer of the Road in the Room of John Birdsong who with the approbation of the Court Resigned.

On the application of John McKibbin Leave is Given him to Keep a Tavern or public House who Gave Bond with Joseph Jones his Security according to Law.

A Deed of Gift from Matthew Sims proved in Open Court by the Oaths of the witnesses thereunto Subscribed and Ordered to be Recorded.

A Deed of Conveyance from Phillip Anderson to James Guthries and Ordered to be Recorded.

An Indenture of Mortgage Deed Between William Newman of the one part and Aaron Fincher of the Other part acknowledged in Open Court and Ordered to be Recorded.

A Deed of Conveyance from William White and Elizabeth White to Hancock Porter Ordered to be Recorded.

A Deed of Conveyance from Shadrack Landtrip to Sarah Gist proved in Open Court by the Oaths of Witnesses thereto and Ordered to be Recorded.

A Deed of Conveyance from John McCooll to Cushman Edson acknowledge in Open Court and Ordered to be Recorded.

Benjamin Jolly Orphan of James Jolly Desd. Came into Open Court and maid Choice of Colo. Thomas Brandon for his Guardian who was appointed by the Court and Entered into and acknowledged his bond with Daniel Comer his Security in the Sum of One hundred pounds for the Taking Care of the Said Orphan and his Estate.

Ordered that the Pettit Jury be Drawn to Serve this Court which is done and are as follows

1.	John McPherson	7.	John Stark
2.	John Springer	8.	Francis Fincher
3.	Hugh Donaldson	9.	William Buckhannan
4.	David Hutson	10.	John Townsand
5.	James McElwain	11.	Joseph Gault
6.	John Wilson	12.	Joseph West

Ordered that a Citation Issue against the following persons as Defaulters of the Pettit Jury to appear at our next

152

Court to Shew if any they why they Should not be fined.
William Morgan, Benjamin Hawkins John Smith David Pruet
John Reed Caleb Gassaway John Leek Joshua Scisson & James
Petty Senr.

181 Thomas Cook is hereby appointed to be Overseer of the
Road in the Room of Charles Miles who with the approbation
of the Court Resigned and that he Clear and Keep the Same
in Good Repair according to Law.

Ordered that a Scitation Issue against the following
persons as Defaulteers of the Grand Jury to appear Next
Court and Shew Cause if any they have why they Should not be
fined. John Beckham John Hope William Means William Hawkins

David Hopkins	Plaintiff)	On attachment
against	)	James Sims Summoned as a
Daniel McKee	Defendant)	Garnashee being Sworn--and
		Deposition

On the application of John High for letters of administration On the Estate of John Lenster deceased Ordered that a
Citation Issue to execute all the Kindred and Creditors
of the said deceased to appear at Our next Court and Shew
Cause if any they have why Letters of administration Should
not be granted to the said John High.

A Lease and Release from Abner Coleman and Susannah his
Wife & William Coleman to Nathaniel Gorden acknowledged in
Open Court and Ordered to be Recorded.

A Deed of Conveyance from William Plummer and wife to
George Harlen (Hatter) acknowledged in Open Court and
Ordered to be Recorded.

A Deed of Conveyance from William Plummer & his wife to
George Harlen (Farmer) acknowledged in Court & Ordered to
be Recorded.

Court adjourn untill Tomorrow Eight O'Clock

Signed	Thomas Brandon	
	John Birdsong	Esquires
	Thomas Blasingame	

At a Court Continued and held in and for the County of
Union at the Court house on the Twenty fifth day of March
1788

Present	Thomas Brandon	
	Charles Sims	Esquires
	Thomas Blasingame	

A Deed of Conveyance from William Kennedy to Joseph
Pearson proved in Open Court by John Brandon and Ordered
to be Recorded.

182 Present William Kennedy Esquire

Ordered that a Citation Issue to George and John Parks
administrators of John Parks decead. to appear at Our
next Court and produce a Copy of Will of the said deceased

153

Together with the appraisement of the Estate Together with
their doings there on in Order to Settle the Same with the
Court.

A Deed of Conveyance from Jonathan Gilkie to William Gilkie
acknowledged in Open Court and Ordered to Record.

A Deed of Conveyance from Samuel Young to William Gilkie
proved in Court by the Witnesses thereto and Ordered to be
Recorded.

Hanney Taylor   Plaintiff)   Michael Asford proved his
   against   )   attendance and Milage Ordered
John Montgomery Defendant)   that the defendant pay him two
                              pounds eight shillings and
eight pence Sarah Asford proved her attendance Ordered that
the defendant pay her Seventeen Shillings & Six pence for
the same.

County of Union   Plaintiff)   Came the Plaintiff by his
   against   )   attorney Daniel Brown & the
Samuel McJunkin   Defendant)   Defendant by Jacob Brown his
                              attorney and the Court
after hearing the Matter argued on both sides Ord. that the
Plaintiff be nonsuited and pay all Costs.

William Kennedy and Thomas Brandon Esquires absent
Zachariah Bullick Esquire Present

John Hampton   Plaintiff)   The Plaintiff by James Yancey
   against   )   Came into Court on a petition
Merry McGuire   Defendant)   and Summons Whereupon the Court
                              Decreed for the Plaintiff for
the Sum of Four pounds three shillings with Interest from
the thirty first of May one thousand seven hundred & eighty
five with Costs of Which is Ordered accordingly.

A Deed of Conveyance from Daniel Plummer of the One part
and Stephen White Ordered to be Recorded.

Robert Lusk   Plaintiff)   Trover on attachment
   against   )   Ordered by the Court that this
John Jones   Defendant)   Suit be Dismissed at Defendants
                              Costs

Stephen White)   Debt on attachment
   against   )   Daniel Jackson Came into Court and Repleved
Mark Jackson)   the property attached and entered himself
                 Special Bail which was ordered by the Court
accordingly.

183 Robert Montgomery   )   Debt on Attachment
      against   )   Came the Plaintiff by Jacob
   Davis Wilkie Defendant)   Brown his attorney Whereon Came
                              a Jury on a Writ of Enquiry Joseph
West forem John McPherson Hugh Donaldson David Hudson James
McElvaine John Wilson John Stokes Frances Fincher William
Buckhannan John Townsand Joseph Gault and John Springer.
Who being duly drawn and Sworn on this Writ of Enquiry do
on their Respective Oaths Say we find we find for the
Plaintiff fifteen pounds with Interest from the March One

154

thousand Seven Hundred and Eighty four. Judgement against
the Garnashee for the Money Condemnd in his hands which is
One pound Twelve & eight pence.

John Ewart   Plaintiff   ) Came the Defendant into Court
  against   ) in their Own proper persons
Rebeckah & William George) and confessed Judgment accord-
                              ing to the Balance of the
Specialty with Interest and Costs of Suit which Ordered
accordingly Ordered that an execution Issue accordingly.

Jacob Brown   Plaintiff   ) Case
  against   ) Came the Plaintiff in his
Robert Montgomery   ) Own proper person and the
and John Bird   Defendants) Defendants by Wm Shaw
                               their attorney Whereupon
Came a Jury Joseph West foreman John McPherson Hugh Donaldson David Hudson James McElwain John Wilson John Stokes
Frances Fincher William Buckhannan Joseph Gault John
Townsand and John Springer who being duly drawn and sworn
do on their respective Oaths say we find for the plaintiff
sixteen pounds six shillings and three pence and costs of
suit Which Verdict is Ratifyed by the Court and Ordered to
be Recorded.

James Barron   Plaintiff) Debt on Petition Summons
  against   ) Came the Defents into Court
Robert Lusk and   ) and Confessed Judgment
Samuel Davison   Defendants) according to Specialty with
                               Interest and Costs of Suit
with stay of Execution three months which is ordered
accordingly.

John McCrary   Plaintiff) Trover on a Petition Summons
  against   ) Came the Defendant into Court
Thomas Bishop   Defendant) and confessed a Judgment for
                            two pounds Sixteen Shillings
and Costs of Suit with Stay of Execution Six months which
is Ordered accordingly.

184 John Ewart   Plaintiff) Debt on Petition and Summons
    vs.   ) Dismissed at the Plaintiff Costs
    John Strange Defendant)

John Thomas   Plaintiff) Case
  vs.   ) Ordered to be Dismissed at the
Jess Fore   Defendant) Pltfs Costs

William Head   Plaintiff) Debt
  against   ) Ordered that the Plaintiff be
David Vincent   Defendant) Nonsuited for not filing
                            his Declaration agreeable to Law

Mary Williams   Plaintiff) Debt on Petition & Summons
  against   ) Came the Plaintiff by Robt.
Daniel Jackson   Defendant) G. Harper her attorney and
                             the Defendant by Charles Good-
win and then and there agree to Dismiss the Suit at the
Defendants Costs which is Ordered accordingly.

155

```
John McCooll        Plaintiff)    Debt on Petition & Summons
   against               )        Came the Plaintiff by
John Montgomery     Defendant)    Daniel Brown his attorney
                                  an the Defendant by Jacob
Brown his Counseller and Confessed a Judgment according to
Specialty with Interest and Costs of Suit which is Ordered
accordingly.

Drewery Harrington  Plaintiff)    Case
   against               )        Came the Defendant into
Charles Clanton     Defendant)    Court by William Shaw his
                                  attorney and Confessed
a Judgment for Seven pounds & three shillings and costs of
suit except the attorneys fee which is ordered accordingly.
```

Samuel Simpson Sworn as administrator of the Estate of
John Simpson deceased. Ordered that Ambrose Ray William
Woolebanks and William Jackson be Sworn to appraise the
Estate of Said deceased and that an Inventory be Returned
to Our next Court.

William McCullock being appointed a Justice of the Peace
for this County Took the Oath Required by Law and Entered
into the Executing of his Office
Court adjourn Untill Tomorrow Nine O'Clock.

```
Signed          John Henderson
                William Kennedy        Esquires
                William McCullock
```

185 At a Court Continued and held for the County of Union at
the Court House on the Twenty Sixth day of March 1788.

```
Present         Zachariah Bullock
                Thomas Blasingame      Esquires
                Thomas Brandon
                John Birdson
```

James Fannin administrator of John Bailey Deceased Returned
an Inventory of the Estate appraised by James Bankhead
William Hendly and Turner Kendrick which was ordered to be
filed in the Clerks Office.

A Deed of Gift from Garland Hardwick to Nancy Hardwick for
one negro Girl named Moriah acknowledged in Open Court and
Ordered to be Recorded.

The Grand Jury Reviewed the Charge with Drew from the Barr
to Consult their Verdict Who Return the following Bills
The State against Gabriel Brown True Bill the State vs
Pharoah Dobb a True Bill the State against George Russel no
bill Ordered that the presentments of the Grand Jury be
Recorded.

```
Thomas Brandon  Plaintiff)    Came the plaintiff by Daniel
   against           )        Brown his attorney on a Pet
Robert Lusk     Defendant)    and Summons and there dis-
                              continued the suit at the
Plaintiffs Costs.
```

156

John Steen   Plaintiff)   Ordered to be Continued by
    against   )   Consent of the Parties
David Stogdon Defendant)

William Liles   Plaintiff)   Case
    against   )   John Montgomery came in
Phillip Shavertaker Defendant)   his Own proper person
                                  Came into Open Court and
Entered himself Special Baile for the Defendant Came the
Plaintiff by Daniel Brown his attorney and the Defendant
by Jacob Brown his Counseller Whereup Came a Jury Towit
Joseph West foreman John Springer John McPherson David
Hudson James McElwain John Wilson, John Stokes Frances
Fincher William Buckhannon John Townsand and Joseph Gault
who been duly drawn and Sworn on their Respective oaths
say we find for the plaintiff Eleven pounds One Shilling
and Costs of Suit which Verdict as Ordered to be Recorded.

Allen Degraftenreed)   Debt on Petition & Summons Came
    against   )   the Defendant Josiah Wood in his
John and Josiah Wood)   Own proper person into Open Court
                        and Confessed a Judgement for ten
pounds and Costs of Suit which is Ordered accordingly.

186 Robert Smith   Plaintiff)   Debt on Petition & Summons
        vs   )   Came the Plaintiff by James
    William Steen   Defendant)   Yancey his atto. and Complains
                                  that the Defent is Justly
Indebted to the Plaintiff Nine pounds Sixteen Shillings
which the Court Decreed for the Plaintiff with Costs of
Suit and Interest from the Sixth day of May 1784. Which is
Ordered accordingly.

A Lease and Release from William Henderson Desd. to
Abner Coleman an proved by John Henderson and Ordered to
be Recorded.

Ruth Brown   )   Trover
    against   )   Ordered by the Court to be Dismissed
Walter Roberts)   at the Plaintiffs Costs.

John Ewart   Plaintiff   )   Debt
    vs   )   Came the Defendant into
John Holman   )   Open Court and Confessed a
William Whitlock Defendants)   Judgment according to
                                 Specialty with Costs of
Suit and Interest with Stay of Execution two Months by the
plaintiff then Execution to Issue for Debt and Costs which
is Ordered by the Court.

Caleb Gassaway   Plaintiff)   Ordered to be Dismissed at
    against   )   the Defendants Costs.
Thomas Taylor   Defendant)

Thomas Brandon   Plaintiff)   Slander
    against   )   Ordered by the Court to be
William Lee   Defendant)   Dismissed at the Plaintiffs
                              Costs.

Thomas Brandon   Plaintiff)   On attachment
    against   )   The Defendant Gave Daniel
George Goodwin   Defendant)   Jackson for Special Bail who

157

was accepted by the Court and the Goods Replyvied and the
attachment to be Dissolved & the suit to be Continued
untill next Court.

Elisha Greer Resigned his office of Constable with the
Leave of the Court.

John Means   Plaintiff) Debt
  against   ) The parties agree to Continue
Robert Montgomery Defendant)   this suit untill next Court
                                at Equal Costs which is
Ordered accordingly.

James Hogans   Plaintiff) Debt
  vs   ) Came the Plaintiff by Jacob
John Liles   Defendant) Brown his attorney and the
                              Defendant by his Counseller
187 Whereupon Came a Jury to wit Joseph West John Springer
John McPherson David Hudson James McElwaine John Wilson
John Stokes Francis Fincher William Buckhannan John Townsand
Joseph Gault Hugh Donaldson Who being duly drawn and Sworn
on their Respective Oaths Say we find for the Plaintiff
seven pounds nine shillings and four pence and costs of
suit.   Joseph West foreman
Which verdict was Ratifyed by the Court and Ordered to be
Recorded.

Ruth Brown   Plaintiff) Ordered that the Witness in this
  vs   ) Suit prove their attendance
Walter Roberts Defendant)   Towit John Gregory Jonathan
                              Roberts and Sarah Randolph
prove each of them Six days attendance which is fifteen
shillings each which is Ordered to be Taxed in the bill of
Costs.

Phillip Anderson   Plaintiff) Came the plaintiff by
  against   ) Chas. Goodwin his attorney
Daniel McElDuff   Defendant)   and the defendant being
                               solemnly called came not to
Defend his Suit Ordered by the Court that the Plaintiff
take a Judgment by Default against him

Richard Speaks & Co. Plaintiff) Debt on attachment
  vs   ) the Plaintiff being
Robert Montgomery   Defendant) Solemnly Called Came
                                  not to prosecute his Suit
Ordered that the Suit be discontinued at his Costs.

Holland Sumner   Plaintiff) Slander
  against   ) Came the Plaintiff by
Thomas Blasingame   ) Charles Goodwin his
Jeremiah Bashiers Defendants) attorney and the Defen-
                               dants by William Shaw
their Counsellor and there agreed to Discontinue the suit
at the Defendants Costs which is Ordered accordingly.

Jacob Brown   ) Ordered that the Plaintiff in this
  against   ) Suit have a new Trial at our next
Robert Montgomery) Court.
& John Bird   )

158

```
John Gilham      Plaintiff)  Case
    vs                     )  Came the Defendant in his own
Thos. Taylor     Defendant)  proper person and Confessed a
                             Judgment for twenty nine pounds
and Costs of Suit Which is Ordered by the Court acc.g.
```

```
Holland Sumner   Plaintiff)  Debt
    vs                     )  Cotninued by Consent of the
Archer Smith     Defendant)  Parties
```

```
188 Holland Sumner   Plaintiff)  Assault and Battery
        vs                     )  Ordered the Plaintiff be
    Archer Smith     Defendant)  nonsuited for not prosecuting
                                 his suit
```

```
William Sharp    Plaintiff)  Case
   against                )  Came the Plaintiff by
John Inlow       Defendant)  Charles Goodwin his attorney
                             and the Defend by Jacob Brown
his Counceller Whereupon Came a Jury, To wit, Joseph West
John Springer, John McPherson David Hudson James McElwain
John Wilson John Stokes  Frances Fincher William Buckhannan
John Townsand Joseph Gault Hugh Donaldson Who being duly
drawn & Sworn who on their respective oaths Return their
Verdict and say we find for the plaintiff fourteen pounds
five shillings & Ten pence and costs of suit
                         Joseph West foreman
```

```
Soloman Mangham  )  Debt
    vs           )  the Parties Came into Open Court and
Robert Montgomery)  agree to Continue this Suit which is
                    Ordered by the Court
```

```
John Anderson )  Debt
   against    )  Ordered to be Continued by Consent at
William George)  the Plaintiffs Costs
```

```
John Steen          )  Debt
    vs              )  Ordered to be Continued by Consent of
Joshua Petty Admrs)  the parties
of John Nuckols     )
```

```
John Hodge       )  Debt
    vs           )  Ordered to be Continued by Consent
Robert Montgomery)  of the Parties
```

```
Robert Lusk)  Trover
    vs     )  Ordered to be Discontinued at the
John Gilham)  Defendants Costs
```

```
Thomas Brandon &        )  Debt
John Gregory Admrs of )  Came the Defendant in his Own
Edward McNeale          )  proper person and Confessed
   against              )  a judgment according to specialty
Caleb Gassaway & wife )  with Interest and Costs of Suit
                           with Stay of Execution three months
then to Issue agreeable to the Installment Law for the
payment of Debt
```

```
189 Jesse Dodd       Plaintiff)  Debt on attachment
        vs                   )  Whereupon the Sheriff hath
    Robert Skelton   Defendant)  Returned levied in the hands of
```

                              159

Robert H. Hughes and him Summoned as Garnashee to Declare
on Oath What he hath in his hands of the Said Skeltons who
being duly Sworn in Open Court, Saith that he haith now in
his hands a certain note of hand Given by Jesse Dodd to
Tabatha Pearson for two hundred pounds all South Currency
in Which said note Robert Skelton was Security for the said
Jesse Dodd, Robert Skelton paid the note and took it up
he then sold it to this deponent for one fourth part of
What Should be Recovered on it from the said Jesse Dodd
this note hath not been Recovered nor any part of it nor
has any money been paid to Skelton in Consequence of this
assumsit except One Dollar & he further Saith that except
what has been above mentioned he this Deponent Saith
that he hath not in his possession any property of the Said
Skelton of any Kind.

Peter Knowlanderder   Plaintiff)   Case
        vs   )   Ordered to be Discontinued
James Gassaway   Defendant)   at the Plaintiffs Costs.

The Court adjourn untill tomorrow 9 O'Clock
Signed   William Kennedy
                        Thomas Brandon   Esquires
                        William McCullock

At a Court Continued & held in and for the County of Union
at the Court House on t he Twenty Seventh day of March One
thousand Seven Hundred and Eighty Eight

Present   Zachariah Bullock
                        Thomas Brandon
                        Charles Sims
                        Thomas Blasingame   Esquires
                        John Birdsong
                        William McCullock

Ordered that Thomas Brandon and John Birdsong Esqrs. lay
out a Road from a Road from Bogans Creek to Brandons Shoals
On Fairforest to Run between the present Court House and
the Goal and that the Overseer of the Road Clear and Keep
them in Good Repair agreeable to Law.

190 William Whitlock   Plaintiff)   Debt on Attachment
        against   )   The Parties Came into Open
    Landlot Porter   Defendant)   Court and then and there
                                     agree to Leave it to arbi-
tration and appointed Thomas Brandon and William Kennedy
Esquires to arbitrate and Settle the Same and their award
to be the Rule of Court and their award to be Returned to
our Next

    William Whitlock   Plaintiff)   Slander
        vs   )   The Parties Came into
    Landlot Porter   Defendant)   Open Court and then and
                                     there agree
190 to leave their Suit to the arbitration of Thomas Brandon
& William Kennedy and their award to be that Rule of this
Court and their award to be Returned to Our next Court.

    Daniel Brown   )   Debt on Petition and Summons
        against   )   Came the Plaintiff by Jacob
    Rydarous & James Clark)   Brown his attorney and the ⑴

160

Defendant by his Councellor and the Court after hearing
the matter fully argued on both sides Decreed for the
Plaintiff three pounds five Shillings and three pence with
Interest and Costs of Suit which is Ordered accordingly.

John Steen   ) Debt.
   vs   ) Came the parties into Court by
Wm. & Rebeckah George) their attorneys whereupon came
                       a Jury to Wit, Joseph West John
Springer John McPherson David Hudson James McElwain John
Wilson John Stokes Francis Fincher William Buckhannan John
Towsand Joseph Gault Hugh Donaldson who being duly drawn &
Sworn to try the Issue Joind. do On their Respective
Oaths Return their Verdict and Say we find for the Defen-
dant Joseph West William Shaw for the Plaintiff Moved for
a New Tryal which was Granted him.

Fanny Whitesides Orphan Came into Open Court and appointed
James Irvin her guardine with the approbation of the Court
who entered into bond with William Blackstock his Security
in the sum of One thousand pounds Sterling for the Taken
Care of the said Orphans person & Estate.

Zachariah Bell   ) Case Debt
   vs   ) Ordered that the Suit be Dismissed
Josep & Abel Pearson) gainst Joseph Pearson and that
                       Judgment be Entered up against Abel
Pearson for five pounds thirteen shillings and costs of
Suit.

William Nelson) Case, Came the Parties into Court by
   vs   ) their attorneys and Whereupon Came a
Thomas Biddy) Jury (towit.) Joseph West foreman John
                 Springer John McPherson David Hudson
Jas. McElwain John Wilson.

191 John Stokes Francis Fincher William Buckhannan John
    Townsand Joseph Gault and Hugh Donaldson Who being Duly
    Sworn to Try the Issue Joind Return on their Respectives
    Oath & Say We find for the Defendant.

John Fincher) Ordered that a Dedimus Potestatom Issue to
   vs   ) the State of North Carolina Rutherford
Bazel Wheat) Directed to any two of the Justices of the
                peace in said County to take the Examination
of Caleb and Reuben Biggs at the Court House of the said
County on the first Monday in June next and the same to
take & Directed to Our Court Under their hands & Seals Shall
be Admitted in Evidence on this Trial.

In the Case of James Oliphant against Jonathan Norman a
New Trial is Granted and the Costs of the Suit to Rest
the determination of said Trial.

Charles Burton) Debt on attachment
   vs   ) Came the plaintiff by Charles Goodwin
Robert George) his attorney and the defendant being
                  Solemnly Called but came not to replevy
the Goods attached it is ordered that a default be entered
against him and that the Sheriff expose to Sale the property
attached that is parrishable and render the Money at our
next Court.

Robert Gregory) Debt on attachment
vs) The parties Came into Court by their
Thomas Holdon) attorneys and the Court after hearing
the matter fully Investigated on both
sides decreed against the defendant for the sum of seven
pounds eleven shillings & eight pence and costs of suit.

Daniel McElduff) Debt on Petition Summons
vs) William Giles Came into Open Court
Thomas Bishop) and undertook to pay the costs of the
Plaintiff be cost in this suit.

Ordered that Thomas Brandon & James Thomas lay out a Road
from the Waggon Road the most Conveniest way to Cold.
Hopkins mill on Broad River & that James Thomas be Overseer
of the Same in Good Repair according to Law. the court
adjourn Untill Tomorrow 9 0'Clock.

Signed   Zachariah Bullock
                William Kennedy   Esquires
                Thomas Brandon
                William McCullock

192 At a Court begun and held in and for the County of Union
    at the Court House on the Twenty Eight day of March in the
    Year of Our Lord One thousand Seven Hundred & Eighty Eight.

Present   Zachariah Bullock
                William Kennedy
                Thomas Blasingame
                Thomas Brandon   Esquires
                William McCullock

Jechoniah Sanstone) Case
   against   ) The parties came into Open Court in
John Montgomery   ) their own proper person and there
                       agreed to leave their suit to the
arbitration of Thomas Brandon James Harrison and Andrew
Torrance and their award to be the Rule of this Court.

Nicholas Lazarus) Case
vs   ) Came the Plaintiff by Daniel Brown his
Catharine Young) attorney and the Defendant by Charles
                   Goodwin his atto. Whereupon came a
Jury (towit) Joseph West Foreman John Springer John McPher-
son David Hudson James McElwaine John Wilson John Stokes
Francis Fincher William Buckhannan John Towsand Joseph
Gault and Hugh Donaldson Who being duly drawn & Sworn to
try the Issue Joind. the Plaintiff with the advise of his
Counsellor agree to suffer a nonsuit which Ordered accord-
ingly.

State   Plaintiff) Assault & Battery
vs   ) Ordered by the Court that the
Joseph Jones Defendant) Recognizance be Continued Untill
                         next Court.

The State   Plaintiff) Col. Thomas Brandon Came into
  against   ) open and entered himself
Gabriel Brown Defendant) Security for the Defendants
                         appearance at our next Court.

162

The State   Plaintiff   )   Ordered to be Dismissed at
  vs   )   the Defents Costs
George Russel   Defendant)

State South Carolina)   Ordered by the Court that the
  vs   )   Recognizance Continue untill next
Vollenture Harlen and)   Court
Sarah Ballue   )

193 John Leek   Plaintiff)   The Parties Came into Open Court
    vs   )   and there agreed to Dismiss this
Mark Jackson   Defendant)   Suit at Equal Costs which is
                         Ordered by the Court.

Thomas Kennedy   Plaintiff)   The Plaintiff by his attorney
  against   )   Came into Open Court and the
Samuel Felps   Defendant)   Defendant being Solemnly
                         Called came not to defend his
Suit Ordered that a Default be Entered against him.

John Means   Plaintiff)   Debt on attachment
  against   )   Ordered to be Dismissed at
Robert Montgomery Defendant)   the Plaintiffs Costs.

Samuel Jackson   Plaintiff)   Debt on attachment
  against   )   The Sheriff Return Levied
William Jackson   Defendant)   in the hands of John
                         McCooll & him Summoned
as Garnashee Who being Duly Sworn in Open Court Saith that
he has not in his hands any thing belonging to the Said
Samuel Jackson nor had at the time of levying of said
attachment.

Thomas Brandon and   Plaintiffs)   Trover
John Gregory administrators   )   Order that this
of Edward McNeal Deceased   )   Suit be Dismissed
  against   )   against Rebeckhah
Abel Pearson and   )   McNeal and the
Rebeekah McNeal   Defendants)   parties by their
                         attorneys came
into Court Whereupon Came a Jury (Towit) Joseph West foreman
John Springer John McPherson David Hudson James McElwaine
John Wilson John Wilson John Stokes Francis Fincher William
Buckhann John Townsand Joseph Gault John Reed

Robert Lusk   Plaintiff)   Ordered that a Dedimus potes-
  vs   )   tatum Issue to any two Justices
Hugh Means   Defendant)   in Rutherford County in the
                         State of North Carolina to take
the Deposition of Charles McClain   Oates & Clerk
On behalf of the Plaintiff and that the Plaintiff Give the
Defnt. timely notice of time & place of Taking Said
Deposition and the Justices before Whom they are to be
examined and their examination to be admitted on this
Trial

194 Ordered that the Evidences in the Suit of Thomas Brandon
and John Gregory administrators of Edward McNeal prove
their attendance Ordered that the Same be Taxed in the bill
of Costs according to the affidavit.

Francis Lattimore   Plaintiff)
  against   )   Debt
George Pruvis and   )   Ordered that a Default
John Steen   Defendants)   be Entered against George
                                  Purvis.

John Steen came into Open Court and Confessed a Judgment
for nine pounds twelve Shillings and ten pence with
Interest and Costs of Suit which is Ordered accordingly.

Daniel McElduff   Plaintiff)   Debt
  vs   )   On Petition & Summons the
Thomas Bishop   Defendant)   Court Hearing the Council
                                on both sides Jacob Brown
Entered himself Security for Costs of Suit and William
Giles former Security for the said Costs is Discharged
by Consent of the parties No attornies fee to be Taxed.

Robert Bell   Plaintiff)   Trover
  vs.   )   the parties by their
Francis Lattermore &   )   attornies came into
Adam Goudylock   Defendant)   Court Whereupon came a
                                  Jury (towit) Joseph
West foreman John Spriger John McPherson David Hudson
James McElwain John Wilson John Stokes Frances Fincher
William Buchhannan Joseph Gault John Reid. Who being duly
drawn & Sworn to try the Issue Joind. Return their Verdict
and Say we find for the Plaintiff thirty seven shillings
and four pence & Judgment accordingly.

John Ewart assignee of)   Debt on Petition and Summons
John Montgomery Senr.)   Ordered thatthis Suit be
  against   )   Dismissed at the Defendants
John Montgomery   )   Costs by Consent of the Parties.
)
Ordered that Joseph Jones be Overseer of the Road from
Union Court House to Grindals Shoals on Packolate River
and that he Clear and Keep the Same in Good Repair agree-
able to Law.

Thoroughgood Chambers)   The Plaintiff being Solemnly
  vs   )   called came not to prosecute his
James Sims   )   suit ordered that he be nonsuited.

Joseph Alexander   )   Came the Parties by their attorneys
  vs   )   and the Court after hearing the
Mark & Pheby Wells)   Matter fully argued on both sides
                       Decreed that the Plaintiff should
Recover Seven pounds ten shillings with interest and costs
of suit Judgment accordingly.

195 Thomas Stribling)   Ordered to be Continued by the Consent
      vs   )   Parties
    James Mabry   )

Humphry Bates)   The Defendant being Solemnly called came
  against   )   not to Defend his Suit Ordered that a
Joseph Bates)   Default be Entered against him.

Thomas Mays   )   Ordered to be Continued by Consent untill
  vs   )   next Court
Charles Burton)

164

John Hodge   ) Ordered the Plaintiff be nonsuited
vs   )
Zachariah Bullock)

Peter Brasselman & Co.) The Defendants being Solemnly
   against   ) called came not to prosecute their
Josiah & John Woods   ) Suit Ordered that they be nonsuited

Jonathan Gilbert Plaintiff) Ordered to be Continued
vs   )
Walter Roberts   Defendant)

John and George Parks) Ordered to be Continued untill
   against   ) next Court
Daniel Jackson   )

Kirkland & Co.   Plaintiff) Debt
vs   ) The Defendant failing to appear
John Inlow   Defendant) to prosecute his Suit Ordered
                             to be nonsuited.

John Moore   Plaintiff) Case Continued by Consent
vs   )
Isaac Parker Defendant)

Holland Sumner   Plaintiff) The Parties Came into Open
vs   ) Court nand there agree to
Thomas Blasingame   Defendant) Refer their Suit to John
                                Montgomery William Farr
Thomas Greer Nehemiah Howard and Stephen Layton and their
award to be the Rule of this Court and their award to be
Returned to Our next Court.

Robert Bell   ) Ordered that the Witnesses in this
vs   ) Suit prove their attendance and that
Francis Lattimore &) the Same be Taxed in the Bill of
Adam Goudylock   ) Costs according to the Deposition
                        filed.

196 A Deed of Conveyance from Daniel White to William Williams
acknowledged in Open Court and Ordered to be Recorded.

A Deed of Conveyance from William Williams to Nicholas
Waters acknowledged in Open Court and Ordered to be
Recorded.

A Lease & Release from Thomas Blasingame Daniel Palmore
acknowledged in Open Court and Ordered to Record.

A Lease & Release from John Hames to William Harris
acknowledged in Open Court and Ordered to Record.

State So. Carolina) William Giles Security his
   against   ) Recognizance forfeited the Court
James Hogans   ) Indulges him with Stay of Execution
                     Six Months.

The Court adjourn untill tomorrow 9 o'clock
Signed   William McCullock
                      Thomas Blasingame   Justices
                      John Birdsong

At a Court Continued & held in & for the County of Union
at the Court House on the Twenty ninth day of March 1788
Present   Zachariah Bullock
                         William Kennedy
                         Thomas Brandon
                         Charles Sims   Esquires
                         Jno Blasingame
                         William McCullock
                         John Birdsong

A Deed of Conveyance from John Hughey and Mary Hughey to
Joseph Tucker Ordered to be Recorded.

A Deed of Conveyance from Joseph McJunkin to Daniel McJunkin
Ordered to be Recorded.

A Deed of Conveyance from Alexander Cain to Wm Whitlock
and Ordered to be Recorded.

197 Ordered that the former Sheriff Give a list of those who
have not paid their County Tax for the Years 1785 and 1786.
to the present Sheriff of this County.

Ordered that the Sheriff Deliver up Robert Montgomery if
he should be in Our County Goal to John Montgomery &
Daniel Jackson as they are Security for his appearance
at our Ninety Six Court on State Matters on the 26 day of
April Next.

Robert Woodson appointed Constable and Took the Necessary
Oath prescribed by Law.

John Gilham   Plaintiff)   The Plaintiff hath Leave to
     vs   )   take out Execution in this Case
Thomas Taylor   Defendant)   by the Court.

Ordered that William Farr late Sheriff be summoned to appear
at the Court House On the fourth day of April next to
Shew what has Gone with a negro Man Slave Committed to his
Charge by Majr. Zachariah Bullock Esqr.

John Haile Clerk of this Court appointed John Sanders his
Deputy who met with the approbation of said Court who took
the necessary Oaths of Office.

John Ewart   Plaintiff)   Debt on attachment
     vs   )   Ordered to be Discontinued at
John Wedingman Defendant)   the plaintiffs costs in person

The County Treasury is allowed two & one half percents
for all Money for all Money Received for the use of the
County and the Same for paying away.

Ordered that the Court adjourn untill Court in Course
Signed   Zachariah Bullock   Thomas Blasingame
                         Thomas Brandon   John Birdsong
                         William Kennedy   William McCullock
                         Charles Sims
                                         Esquires

166

At a Court begun and held in and for the County of Union
at the Court house of said County the Twenty third day of
June 1788 Present. Zacha Bullock Thomas Brandon Charles
Sims Thomas Blasingame & William McCullock, Gentl. Justices

Acknowledged in Open Court a bill of Sale from Thomas
Brandon to Daniel White for One negro woman named Darkis
and Ordered to be Recorded.

A Deed from Henry Long & wife to William White proved by
John and William White and Ordered to be Recorded.

A Deed from Geo McWhortor and Wife to Jesse Patty acknowledged by George & Proved as to his wife and Ordered to be
Recorded

Ordered that the following Persons be summoned to attend
next Court to serve as Grand Jurors for this County towit.

Jesse Maberry	1	Jacob Paulk	13
Isaac Smith	2	Hezekiah Rice	14
Jos. Little	3	Samuel Tolbert	15
Jonas Little	4	Samuel Otterson	16
Peter Sartor	5	William Speers	17
Richd. Powell	6	John Foster	18
Jereh. Hamelton	7	Joseph Galt	19
Wm. Browning	8	William McKown	20
John Fincher	9		
Danl. McJunkin	10		
Federick Jackson	11		
Jacob Haild	12		

Ordered that the following persons be summoned to attend
next Court to serve as Pettet Jurors for this County
Towit.

Alexr. McCarter	1	Edward Denny	16
Isaac Hawkins	2	Beryr. Hawkins	17
Jno. Bullege	3	Geo Harlen (Hatter)	18
Thos. Shockley Jr.	4	William Mays	19
Wm.Hardwick	5	William Jenkins	20
Job Hammond	6	Thomas Minton	21
David Harris	7	James Hawkins Jr.	22
Saml. Thompson	8	John Cole	23
Nathan Glenn	9	William Giles	26
Nathan Hawkins	10	William Smith	24
William Mclellin	11	Joseph Hughes	25
Thomas Lamb	12	Leonard Smith	27
Jacob Hollingsworth	13	Jno. McPhearson	28
William Littlefield	14	Chas. Brandon	29
Thomas Skelton	15	Jesse Young	30

Ordered that the Pettit Jury be drawn to Serve this Court
who are as follows towit.

Nathl. Jefferies	1	Frances Latemore	7
Philip Anderson	2	Richd. Cox	8
John Jefferies	3	Sion Murphey	9
John Bird	4	Nicholas Harris	10
Joseph Means	5	William White Tygar	11
Jno. Neederman	6	Wm. Hollingsworth	12

An Inventory of the Estate of John Bailey decd. returned
and Ordered to be Recorded.

On the motion of John High administration is Granted him
on the Estate of John Leinster Deceased who gave bond
according to Law.

Ordered that Reuben Ballew be bound to appear at Next Court
in the sum of Ten Pounds and his Securities in Five Pounds
each Whereupon Robert Woodson and Ralph Jackson came into
Court and Severally acknowledged themselves indebted to the
State in the above Sum for his appearance.

A Deed from John Steen to George McWhorter proved by
Jno McWhorter and ordered to be Recorded.

A Deed from William Williams to Charles Humpharies acknowledged in Open Court and Ordered to be Recorded.

The Last Will and Testatment of William Wofford was proved
by the Oath of Thomas Todd and Ambrose Yarborough and
Ordered to be Recorded.

A Deed from William Bickhannon to Page Pucket acknowledged
in Open Court and Ordered to be Recorded.

A Deed from Daniel Lipham to David Brewit acknowledged &
ordered to be Recorded.

A Deed from William Williams to Ephraim Pucket acknowledged
and Ordered to be Recorded.

On Motion of Thomas Brandon & Jos. Hughes administration
is Granted them on the Estate of Joseph Jolley Decd. who
entered into bond according to Law.

On the Motion of Thomas Brandon & Joseph Hughes administration is Granted them on the Estate of Benjamin Jolly Decd.
who acknowled. their bond according to Law.

William Bostick)   Ordered that a Vendition Exponas Issue
     vs.   )   in this Case.
John Steen   )

A Bargain and Sale from Pheby & Larkin Wells to George
McWhortor Proved by John McWhortor & Ordered to be recorded.

200 Hugh McBride   ) Debt
       vs   ) Ordered & by Consent of the Parties this
    Parks Adminrts) case is referred to Andrew Thompson and
                      John Birdsong so far as a Settlement of
the said John Parks state respects the Said McBride in right
of his Wife Margaret a Legaice of the Said John and if
refers disagree they are to Chose a Third Person and
their award to be the Judt. of the Court.

Abner Coleman is appointed Overseer of the Road from Rockey
Creek to the Charleston Road near Grindals Shoals and keep
the same in good repair according to Law.

David Smith is allowed 6 days attendance as a witness for
Tabitha Pearson at the Suit of Gordon & Anderson.

Thomas Vance   Plaintiff)
    vs   )   Ordered that Venditis
Jno & William Steen   Defendant)   Exponas Issue.

John Beckham, John Hope, Wm. Means, Wm. Hawkins defaulters
of the Grand Jury are excused for non attendance with
costs.

William Morgan Benja. Hawkins John Smith David Prewit
John Reed Caleb Gasaway John Leek Joshua Scisson & James
Petty Defaulters of the Pettit Jury are Excused for non
attendance with costs.

A Lease & Release from Joseph Hughes to Thomas Brandon
Esqr. acknowledged by the said Jos. Hughes to Thos. Brandon
and Ordered to be Recorded.

Ordered that a Road be laid out the nearest and best way
from Smiths ford on Broad river to the Skull Shoals on
Pacolate River from thence the nearest and best way to
Union Court House by John Reed William McCullock James
Petty Junr. Wm. Hendley Jos. Guiton John Palmer and Geo
McWhorter and make Return to next Court.

A Deed from William Young & Uxor to Peter Braselman &
Cushman Edson Proved before a Justice of the Peace and
Ordered to be recorded.

A Lease and release from Richard Chesney of the One Part
and John Garrot being Proved before a Justice of the Peace
and Ordered to be Recorded.

201 A Lease and Release from Robert Coleman to Abner Coleman

Proved by John Haile & Zacha. Bullock and Ordered to be
Recorded.

A Deed from Joab Mitchell to Peter Copeland Proved by
Zachariah Bullock and Ordered to be recorded.

A Lease & Release from Adam Gillchrest of the One Part
and Henry Millhouse. John Cook & William Hawkins of the
Other Part. Proved by Nathan Hawkins & Ordered to be
recorded.

John Fincher   Plaintiff)   Ordered that this case be
    vs   )   Referred to Nehemiah Howard and
Bazel Wheat   Defendant)   James Woodson by Consent of the
                            Parties. and if they disagree
to Chose a third Person and their award to be the Judt. of
this Court.

Isaac Hawkins is Continued Overseer of the Road from Union
Court House to Samuel McJunkens and Ordered that the male
Tithes within five mile on each Side of Said Road assist
in Clearing and Keeping the Same in Good Repair according
to Law.

A Lease & Release from John Weedyman to John Reed proved
according to Law and Ordered to be Recorded.

On the Motion of Wm. McCullock Esquire John Herrington

is appointed Constable for this County who was duly Qualifyed according to Law.

Ordered that John Sanders Joseph McJunkin and John
Montgomery appraise the Estate of Benjamin Jolly Decd. and
make due return thereof to Our next Court.

Ordered that Samuel Jackson Daniel Jackson and Joseph
East appraise the Estate of John Leenster Decd. and make
due Return thereof to our next Court.

Holland Sumner   Plaintiff)   By Consent of the Parties
  vs   )   Ordered that this Case be
Thomas Blasingame Defendant)   referred to William Farr
                                Nehemiah Howard Thomas Greer
John Montgomery and Stephen Layton and their award to be
the Judgment of the Court.

John Henderson is appointed Overseer of the Road from
Grindale Shoals to the Court House Road and it is Ordered
that he keep the same in good repair with his own hand.

Adam Potter is appointed Overseer of the Irons Work Road
from the County Line unto the Road near
202 Grindle Shoals with the male Tithes Convenient thereto.

Ordered that the Court be adjourned Untill Court in Course
and Signed by
                         John Henderson
                         Wm. Kennedy   Esquires
                         Charles Sims

At a Court begun and held in and for the County of Union
on Monday the 22d. day of September 1788.
Present   Thomas Brandon
                      Charles Sims
                      Wm. Kennedy   Gentl. Justices
                      John Birdsong
                      Wm. Mc.Cullock

Ordered that the following persons be summoned to attend
next court to serve as Pettit Jury for this County Towit.

Henry Thickpenny	1	John Bird	16
Alexander Hamilton	2	Robert Harris	17
Frances Latemore	3	James Gibbs	18
Daniel Covinhovin	4	Benjamin Darby	19
John Sartor	5	Daniel Young	20
Joshua Sisson	6	John Townsend	21
John Beckham	7	Duncan McCrevan	22
Mallon Pearson	8	Nehemiah Miller	23
Andrew George	9	James Barron	24
Benja. Jones	10	Benjamin Gregory	25
Abner Coleman	11	James Petty Junr.	26
Samuel Cooper	12	Jacob Seegar	27
William Buckhannon	13	Hugh Donaldson	28
Geo Little	14	Moses Haynes	29
Thomas Vance	15	Amos Hawkins	30

George Walker Produced a Commission from the Honble. the
associate Judges of the Court of Common Pleas authorizing
him to Plead the Law as an attorney in the several courts

of this State Ordered that he be admitted to Practice in
this Court accordingly.

The following Persons are Sworn as a Grand Jury of Inquest
for the body of this County Towit.
Samuel Tallbert, foreman.   Joseph Little, Richard Powell,
Wm. Browning, Daniel McJunkin, Jacob Haile, Hezekiah Rice
Wm Speers Joseph Gault. Jesse Maberry Jonas Little Jeremiah
Hamelton John Fincher, Frederick Jackson, John Paulk,
Samuel Otterson, John Foster & William McCown.

A Lease and Release from Samuel Otterson of the One part
and Amos Hawkins of the other Part acknowledged in open
Court and Ordered to be Recorded.

An Inventory appraisement and Sale of the Estate of John
Simpson Decd. returned by Samuel Simpson administrator
and ordered to be Recorded.

203 A Deed of Conveyance from Charles Sims of the One Part
to Thomas McDaniel of the Other Part acknowledged in Open
Court and Ordered to be Recorded.

A Deed of Conveyance from Charles Sims to Thomas McDaniel
acknowledged in Open Court & Ordered to be Recorded.

The Last Will and Testament of Thomas Yarborough Deceased
was Presented by Stephen Layton and Peter Pennell on Oath
and Proved by the Oathes of Elijah Alvison and Thomas Todd
and Ordered to be Recorded probate granted and Bond
acknowledged.

A Deed from Charles Hames to James McWhorter acknowledged
in Open Court and Ordered to be Recorded.

A Deed of Conveyance from John Nix to Tully Davit acknowledged in Open Court and Ordered to be Recorded.

A Deed from Jeptha Hollingsworth to Handcock Porter Proved
in Open Court by Landlot Porter and Ordered to be Recorded.

 A Deed from John Gordon to Handcock Porter Proved in Open
Court by the Oath of Landlot Porter and Ordered to be
recorded.

 A Deed from Merry McGuire to John McGuire acknowledged
in Open Court and Ordered to be Recorded.

A Deed of Conveyance from Robert Talkington to Handcock
Porter acknowledged in Open Court & Ordered to be recorded.

A Deed from John McWhortor to Charles Hames acknowledged
in Open Court and Ordered to be Recorded.

John Campbell came into Open Court and made choice of
William McCullock his Guardian who entered into Bond
according to Law.

Ordered that John Bailey Robert Wilkie, Nehemiah Howard
& Drewry Nurrell or any three of them appraise the Estate
of Ambrose Yarborough Deceased and make due return of the
appraisement to our next Court of Union.

A Lease & Release from Nathaniel Jackson of the One Part to Joseph Kelley of the Other Part Proved in Open Court by John Lawson and Ordered to be Recorded.

A Deed of Conveyance from Job Hammond to Thomas Williams acknowledged in Open Court & Ordered to be Recorded.

204 Charles Miles   Plaintiff)   Attachment
         vs   )   Richmond Terrell and James
    Benjr. Burner   Defendant)   Terrell came into Open Court
                                 and entered themselves Special
    bail in this Suit. which was ordered accordingly.

A Lease and Release from John Nederman & Frances his wife to Moses Haines Proved by Lewis Bobo in Open Court and Ordered to be Recorded.

An Assignment Indorsed on a Grant from Peter Frenau and Francis Breman to Mary Robuck Proved by John Blasingame and Ordered to be Recorded.

Ordered that the Court be adjourned untill tomorrow 9 o'clock.
and Signed by   Thomas Brandon
                     Wm McCullock
                     John Birdsong
                     Charles Sims

The worshipful Court of Union met according to adjournment at the Court House of said County on the 23d day of June 1788.
Present   Thomas Brandon
                     Charles Sims   Esquires
                     Thomas Blasingame
                     William McCullock

A Lease & Release from William Wofford to Thomas Wright Proved by Robert Walker and Ordered to be Recorded.

Thos. Holden   Plaintiff)   Debt
       vs   )   It appearing to the Court that
Samuel Cooper Defendant)   Stacy Cooper a witness for the
                            Plaintiff not having attended
when regular subpoenied it is ordered by the Court that he do attend at the Next Court on Pain of Punishment for a Contempt of the Order of Court and the damages that may Ensue.---and that he be served with a copy of this Order.

A Deed from Soloman Mangham to Josiah Tanner Proved before a Justice and Ordered to be recorded.

James Oliphant   Plaintiff)   Case
   against   )   by Consent of the Parties by
Jonathan Norman Defendant)   their attorneys this suit is
                              continued untill the next
Court at the Defendants Cost and assent of the Court.

Jacob Brown   Plaintiff)   Case
   against   )   The Plaintiff Came into
Jno Bird & Montgomery Deft.)   Open Court and then and
                              there agreed to withdraw
his motion for a New Tryal in the above Case.

172

205 Holland Sumner, Plaintiff)   Case
         vs   )   Came the Plaintiff by Charles
    Archer Smith   Defendant)   Goodwin his attorney and also
                                 came the Defendant by James
    Yancey his attorney Whereupon came a Jury Towit Nathan
    Glenn foreman, Isaac Hawkins David Harris Nathan Hawkins
    Thomas Lamb James Hawkins Alexr. McCarter Junr. Job Hammond
    Samuel Thompson William Mclellin Edward Denney and Thomas
    Menton who being duly sworn do say we find for the Plaintiff
    Thirty five pounds fourteen shillings and two pence half
    penny with Interest from the 10th April 1786 which Said
    Judgment or Verdict was Ratifyed by the Court and Ordered
    to be Recorded.

    A Lease and Release from Jeremiah Brashies to Robert Walker
    Proved before a Justice and Ordered to be recorded.

    The Grand Jury having Received their Charge and withdrew

    John Fincher   Plaintiff)   Dismissed at the Plaintiffs
         vs   )   Costs according to the award
    Bazel Wheat   Defendant)   returned by the arbitrators, to
                                whom the determination of the
    Matter Indefferance between the Parties were submitted by
    the Court, which is ordered accordingly.

    Caleb Edmondson   Plaintiff)   Petr.& Summons
         vs   )   by consent of the Parties
    Nathl. Jefferies   Defendant)   and by their attorneys this
                                    Suit is Discontinued at the
    Defendants Cost which is Ordered accordingly.

    Charles Burton   Plaintiff)   Attachment
         against   )   The Defendant Confessed a
    Dempsey Raby   Defendant)   Judgment for the Sum of Fifteen
                                  Pounds Virginia Money, which is
    Ordered accordingly.

    A Lease and Release from John Elver to Samuel Farrow Proved
    before a Justice and Ordered to be Recorded.

    A Deed from Samuel Porter to William Porter Proved before
    a Justice and Ordered to be Recorded.

    A Deed from John McCooll of the One Part to John DYoung of
    the other Part acknowledged in Open Court and Ordered to be
    Recorded.

    John Steen   Plaintiff)   By Consent of the Parties by
         against   )   their attorneys this suit is
    David Stockdon Defendant)   Contd. over untill next September
                                Court at the Defendants Cost
    and assent of the Court which was Ordered accordingly.

206 Philip Anderson   Plaintiff)   Debt on attachment
         against   )   This Suit is discontinued by
    Daniel McElduff   Defendant)   Consent of the Parties by
                                   their attorneys at the
    Plaintiffs Cost which is Ordered accordingly.

Robert Glover   Plaintiff)   The arbitrators to whom the
   vs   )   determination of the matter
James Hogans   Defendant)   Indefferance between the
                               aforesaid Parties were sub-
mitted by a rule of this Court. Return their award in
Confirmation thereof Viz. the Defendant is to Pay Unto the
Plaintiff the Sum of Forty Seven Pounds Ten Shillings in
horse flesh to be Valed by persons hereafter Chosen and the
said Defendant to Pay his attorneys fee and Sheriff and the
Plaintiff his attorneys & Clerks fees which is a Judgment
of this Court according to the above award.

Robert Lusk   Plaintiff)   Case
   agt.   )   Came the Plaintiff by William
Mathew Robinson   Defendant)   Shaw his attorney and the
                               Defendant by Jacob Brown his
attorney, Whereupon Came a Jury Towit Nathan Glenn Foreman
Isaac Hawkins David Harris Nathan Hawkins Thomas Lamb
James Hawkins Junr. Job Hammond Alexr McCarter Samuel
Thompson William McLellin Edward Denny and Thomas Mention
who was duly Sworn do Say on their Oathes Verdict for the
Plaintiff for the Sum of Four Pounds and Costs of Suit and
Judgment accordingly.

On the Motion of Daniel Jackson Ordered that a Scitation
Issue for administration on the Estate of Henry Duke
Deceased.

William Bostick   Plaintiff)   Debt
   agt   )   By Consent of the Parties
Jno. Bird & Darvin Defendant) and by their attorneys this
                               Case is Dismissed at the
Defendants Cost which is Ordered by the Court accordingly.

John Meanes   Plaintiff)   Debt
   against   )   Came the Plaintiff by Daniel
Robert Montgomery Defendant)   Brown his attorney and the
                               Defendant by Jacob Brown his
attorney whereupon came a Jury Towit. Joseph Hughes foreman
John Cole Geo Harlan John McPherson John Howel Wm Newman
Wm Jenkins William Smith Wm Giles Jesse Young John Savage
& John Gregory who was duly Sworn do say on their oathes
Verdict for Plaintiff according to Specialty with Interest
and Costs of Suit and Judgment according being Ratifyed
by the Court Ordered to be Recorded.

207 A Deed of Conveyance from John Henderson of the One Part
to John Jasper of the Other Part acknowledged in Open
Court and Ordered to be Recorded.

On the motion of James Woodson Leave is given him to retail
Spiritous Liquors on his Giveing Bond according to Law.

Ordered that Robert Lusk Pay Redarous Clark One days
attendance as a witness against Robinson.

A Deed from William Wofford to Daniel Langstone and Bennet
Langstone proved before a Justice and Ordered to be
recorded.

A Deed from James Cambell to Abraham Smith proved before
a Justice and Ordered to be Recorded.

Daniel Prince   Plaintiff)   By Consent of the Parties this
  agt   )   Case is Discontinued by agree-
Thomas Holden   Defendant)   ment and Ordered that each
                                 Party Pay his own costs.

A Deed from Jame McJunkin to Joseph McJunkin acknowledged
in Open Court and Ordered to be Recorded.

Hugh McBride in right of his wife Margaret McBride a
Legatee of John Parks deceased Plaintiff
  against
George Parks administrator of the said Jno. Parks Decd.
Deft. the Said McBride is allowed the sum of sixty six
pounds Fourteen shillings and eight pence in right of his
wife aforesaid interest not included the award and final
Settlement of the whole Estate in this Case as Settled by
William Kennedy John Birdsong and Andrew Thompson refferrers
is Ordered to be recorded in this Court and to Stand as a
Settlement of the Estate of the Said John Parks Deceased
and that the Defendant Pay all Costs.

The Last Will and Testament of John ___ Deceased was
Proved by the Oath of Isaac Bogan and Moses Collier and
Ordered to be recorded, Thomas Blasingame & Andrew Torrence
Executors thereun Named Took the Oath Required by Law.

Adam McCooll   Plaintiff)   Debt
  agt.   )   The Defendant came into Open
Hezk. Salmon & Uxer Deft.)   Court and Confessed a Judgment
                                 with Stay of Execution three
months. which was Ordered accordingly.

Spencer Brummet   Plaintiff)   William Farr being summoned
208 against   )   in this Case as Garnashee
Cordial Hogan   Defendant)   Says that he has a Negroe
                                   Woman of the Defendants
Property in his hands and something for her hire which he
cannot assertain at Present.

Ordered that the Court be adjourned untill tomorrow Nine
o'clock and signed by
                         John Henderson
                         Thomas Blasingame   Esquires
                         Charles Sims
                         William Kennedy

At a Court Continued and held in and for the County of
Union at the Court House on Wednesday the 24th September
1788.
Present   Thomas Brandon
                    William McCullock
                    Thomas Blasingame

The Grand Jury returned with a List of their Presentments
as follows
We Present the Overseer of the Road from Tolberts ferry
that Leads out of Ninety Six Road Out of Repair.

We Present the Overseer of the Road from the Court house to
Hamiltons ford Out of Repair.
We Present the Overseer from Grindals Shoals to Cold
Brandons out of Repair.

175

We Present the Overseer of the Road from Skull Shoals to
James McCrackens out of Repair.

We Present as a Greviance that the Circuit Court are not
made Courts of Record and that people are obliged to appear
in Charles-town on the return of any Process which is to be
tried in Ninety Six and Ordered that this Presentment be
Published in the State Gazette and Laid before the Legislature.

State So. Carolina   Plaintiff   ) Pettit Larcency
  against   ) Whereon the Grand
Jno Fincher & Bryan White Defendant) Jury Returned No
                                          Bill Whereof he is
                                          Dismissed on Paying
                                          Costs.

State So. Carolina   Plaintiff) Tresspass
  vs   ) Whereon the Grand Jury
James Spray   Defendant) returned their Verdict
                                  A True Bill which was
ordered accordingly by the Court.

209 State South Carolina   Plaintiff) Tresspass asst. & Battery
      against   ) Whereon the Grand Jury
    Cushman R Edson   Defendant) Returned their Verdict,
                                        a True Bill

On Motion of John Hughey Ordered that a Scitation Issue
for administration on the Estate of William Hughey Decd.

Isaac Parker is appointed Overseer of the Road from Smith
ford to the Bridge on Thickety and Ordered that he Clear and
Keep the same in Good Repair according to Law with the hand
convenient thereto as laid out by Gentlemen appointed by
the Court.

Moses Meek is appointed Overseer of the Road from the Bridge
on Thickety to the Skull Shoal and Ordered that he Clear
and Keep the same in good repair according to Law with
the hands convenient thereto as laid out by Gentlemen
appointed by this Court.

Richard Cole is appointed Overseer of the Road from Skull
Shoals to Fannins Creek and Ordered that he clear and keep
the same in good repair with the hands convenient thereto
as laid out by Gentlemen appointed by this Court for that
purpose.

Thomas Ballew is appointed Overseer of the Road from
fannins Creek to Hollingsworths Mill and Ordered that he
Clear and Keep the Same in Good repair according to Law
with hands Convt. thereto as laid out by Gentlemen appointed
by Court.

George Newton appointed Overseer of the Road from Hollingsworth Mill to the new Road that Leads from Grindel Shoals
to the Court house and Ordered that he Clear and keep the
same in Good Repair according to Law with the hands Convenient thereto as Laid out by Gentlemen appointed by this
Court.

176

Ordered that the Several Persons Presented by the Grand
Jury be Summoned to appear at next Court.

Robert Lusk   ) Ordered that the Plaintiff Pay Thos Cane
  against   ) Forty Five Shillings for Eighty days
Mathew Robinson)   attendance for him also John Montgomery
                    Forty five shillings for eighteen days
attendance as a witness for him on the above suit.

Humphrie Bates   Plaintiff) Attachment
  against   ) Ordered that the Land attached
Joseph Bates   Defendant) in the above Case be adver-
                              tised according to Law.

210 Soloman Mangham   Plaintiff) Came the Plaintiff into
      against   ) Open Court and then and there
    John Montgomery   Defendant) dismissed this Suit at his
                                  cost and no attorney fee to
    be charged which was ordered accordingly.

State So. Carolina) Ordered that the Defendant be
  agt.   ) Dismissed on Paying of Costs
Reuben Ballew   )

John Anderson   Plaintiff) By Consent of the Parties
  agt.   ) by their attorneys Ordered
William George   Defendant) that this case be conintued
                              over untill next Court for
the Plaintiff.

John Steen   Plaintiff) By Consent of the Parties by
  against   ) their attorney they agree to
Joshua Petty   Defendant) Continue this Suit over untill
                            next Court.

Jeh: Langston Plaintiff) By Consent of the Parties
  agt.   ) by their attorneys Ordered
John Montgomery Defendant)   that this case be continued
                             over untill the next Court.

Robert Lusk atty for Robinson Pltf) By Consent of the
  against   ) Parties by their
John Nuckols admrs.   Defendant   ) attorneys Ordered
                                      that this case be
Continued over untill next Court.

Spencer Brummet Plaintiff) Came into Open Court William
  against   ) Farr, Esqr. and Humphrey Bates
Cordial Hogan   Defendant) and then & there Entered
                            themselves Special Bail which
was Ordered accordingly and Continued by Consent of the
Parties Untill next Court.

A Deed of Conveyance from Dudley Red to Richard Berry
acknowledged in Open Court and Ordered to be Recorded.

Thomas Brandon   Plaintiff) By Consent of the Parties
  agt.   ) Ordered that this Case
Epahroditus Paulk Defendant) be continued over untill
                               next Court for the
                               Plaintiff.

177

Ordered that the Sheriff Expose to Sale a Stray Mare
entered before John Henderson Esquire according to Law.

211 Robert Lusk   Plaintiff)   Slander
     against   )   Came the Plaintiff into Open
    John Liles   Defendant)   Court by Daniel Brown his attorney
                                 and the Defendant being Solemnly
Called Came not Judgt. by default was intered whereon came
a Jury Towit. Nathan Glenn foreman Isaac Hawkins David Hanes
Nathan Hawkins Thomas Lamb James Hawkins Jnr. Alexander
McCarter Job Hammond Samuel Thompson William McLellin
Edward Denny & Thomas Minton who being duly Sworn do Say
Verdict for Plaintiff and Judgment for Twenty Pounds
accordingly   Nathan Glenn Foreman
which was ratifyed by the Court and Ordered to be recorded.

Thomas Mays   Plaintiff)   Fals Imprisonment.
 agt.   )   By Consent of the Parties by
Charles Burton Defendant)   their attorneys all matters
                             Indefference between them are
referred to the determination of William Kennedy Esquire and
Edward Good and if they disagree to chose a third Person
and their award to be made the Judgment of the Court and
the same is Ordered accordingly.

Robert Lusk   )   Ordered that the Defendant Pay John
 vs   )   Thompson Thirty two Shillings and Six
Mathew Robinson)   pence for Thirteen days attendance as
                     a witness for him also Francis Latemore
Thirty two Shillings and Six pence as a Witness also for him
in the above Suit.

Daniel Brown   Plaintiff)   Dismissed the Defendant
 vs   )   having run away he is to
Saml. Montgomery Defendant)   recover no costs of the
                              Plaintiff which was Ordered
                              Accordingly.

William Steen   Plaintiff)   By Consent of the Parties by
 against   )   their attorneys this case is
William Gilkie   Defendant)   Continued over untill next
                             Court which was ordered
                             accordingly.

William Steen   Plaintiff)   By Consent of the Parties by
 agt.   )   their attorneys ordered that
Adam Goudylock   Defendant)   this case be continued over
                             untill next Court.

Robert Lusk   Plaintiff)   By Consent of the Parties by
 agt.   )   their attorneys Ordered that
Nuckols Admrs. Defendant)   this affidavit of the
                             Witnesses be Taken and Con-
tinued untill next Court.

John Towns   Plaintiff)   Debt
 agt.   )   Came the Defendant by William
William Williams Defendant)   Shaw his attorney and the
                             Plaintiff being Solemnly
Called came Not to Prosecute his said suit. on motion of
the said defendant by his attorney it is considered by the
Court.

212 that the Plaintiff be nonsuited and that the Defendant
recover against him five shillings damages and Costs of
Suit by him in this behalf expended which was ordered
accordingly.

James Olliphant   Plaintiff)   By consent of the Parties by
   agt.   )   their attorneys Ordered that
Jno Martindale   Defendant)   this case be continued over
                                untill next Court.

Drewry Gowing   Plaintiff)   Debt on attachment
   agt.   )   Came into Open Court Thomas
William Johnston   Defendant)   Canee and Joseph Hughes and
                                entered them-selves Special
Bail for the Defendant that in case he shall be cast they
will pay the Judgment of the Court or render his body in
Prison in discharge thereof which was Ordered accordingly
and Continued over untill next Court by Consent of the
Parties.

Robert Lusk)   Ordered that the Plaintiff Pay Daniel
   vs   )   Jackson Seven Shillings and Six Pence
John Liles)   for three days attendance as a witness
                for him against Liles in the above Suit.

Daniel Jackson   Plaintiff)   Debt on attachment
   against   )   Came the Plaintiff by Charles
Zachariah Estes   Defendant)   Goodwin his attorney and the
                               Defendant by William Shaw
his attorney Whereupon Came a Jury Towit. Nathan Glenn
Foreman Isaac Hawkins David Harris Nathan Hawkins Thomas
Lamb James Hawkins Junr. Alexr. McCarter Job Hammond Samuel
Thompson William McLellin Edward Denny & Thomas Minton who
being duly Sworn do say on their Oaths we find for the
Plaintiff according to Specialty with Interest and cost
of suit.   Nathan Glenn Foreman
Ordered that the Property attached in the above Suit be
Sold according to Law.

A Deed of Conveyance from Robert H Hughes to Walter
Roberts acknowledged and Ordered to be Recorded.

Robert Lusk)   Ordered that the Plaintiff Pay William
   agt.   )   Cotter Two Shillings and Six pence for
John Liles)   One Days attendance as a Witness for him in
                the Above Suit.

Richard Speaks   Plaintiff)   Nathaniel Jefferies being
   agt.   )   summoned as a Garnashee was
John Bird   Defendant)   Sworn according to Law and
                               his deposition filed in Court.
Ordered that this case be Continued over untill next Court
by Consent of the Parties.

213 Thomas Taylor   Plaintiff)   Debt. attachment
   agt.   )   Came the Plaintiff into Open
James McDoan   Defendant)   Court by Jacob Grown his
                               attorney and the Defendant
being called came not to Prospcute his Said Suit on motion
of the plaintiff by his attorney Ordered by the Court that
Judgment go against him by default.

179

Daniel Prince   Plaintiff)   Debt on attachment
  agt.   )   Came the Parties into Open
Thomas Holden   Defendant)   Court by their attorneys and
                               then and there dismissed this
Said Suit on each Party Paying half of the Costs--which
was Ordered accordingly.

Daniel Jackson is appointed Overseer of the Road from
Jacksons Race Pathes to the County Line and Ordered that
he Keep the Same in Good repair according to Law with the
hands Convt.

James Holland   Plaintiff)   It is considered by the Court
  against   )   that a not Suit be Granted in
John Steen   Plaintiff)   this Case for Want of Security
                             for Cost and the Defendant Living
in North Carolina which was Ordered accordingly.

James Armstrong Plaintiff)   Case
  against   )   Came the Plaintiff by Charles
John Steen   Defendant)   Goodwin his attorney and the
                              Deft. by Jacob Brown his
attorney Whereupon Came a Jury Towit Nathan Glenn foreman
Isaac Hawkins David Harris Nathan Hawkins Thomas Lamb
James Hawkins Junr. Alexr. McCarter Job Hammond Samuel
Thompson Wm McLellin Edward Denney and Thomas Minton who
being sworn do Say on their Oathes we Dissmiss the said
suit at the Plaintiffs Cost.   N. Glenn foreman

On the motion of Julias Salmon, George McWhorter and
William Williams is appointed Guardian to her daughter
Nancey Pucket and that they Give bond with Wm Buckhannon
his Security in the Sum of Fifty Pounds. Sterling.

It is Ordered that William Farr Late Sheriff have Credit
for all the moneys he has Paid to the County Treasury
agreeable to the accompt Settled by a Former Order of this
Court and that John Sanders Deputy Clerk of this Court
deliver the said William Farr the books delivered to him
and Mr. Jno Ewart for the said settlement.

214 Robert Hnery Hughes   Plaintiff)   By Consent of the Parties
  against   )   by their attorneys all
Jesse Dodd   Defendant)   matters Indifference
                                     Between them are refered
to the determination of Moses Haines John Martindale and
Thomas Greer and their award to be made the Judgment of
this Court and the Same is Ordered accordingly.

Holland Sumner   Plaintiff)   The Arbitrators to whom
  agt.   )   the determination of this
Thos. Blasingame Jr. Defendant)   cause were submitted to
                                   and the same refusing to
serve Ordered that this case be contd. over Untill next
Court for the Defendant.

William Whitlock   Plaintiff)   By Consent of the Parties
  against   )   and by their attorneys all
Landlot Porter   Defendant)   matters of Indeference
                                 Between them are referred
to the determination of Thomas Brandon and William McCullock
Esquires and their award to be made the Judgment of this

180

Court and the Same is Ordered accordingly.

The Same)   and the Same Order as above
   agt.   )
The Same)

Ordered that the Court adjourn Untill Tomorrow nine o'clock
and Signed by   John Henderson
                           William Kennedy
                           Thomas Brandon

At a Court Continued and held for Union County at the
Court House on Thursday the 25th day of September 1788
Present   William Kennedy
                        John Birdsong
                        Thomas Brandon   Esquires
                        Charles Sims
                        Thomas Blasingame

It is Ordered that John Birdsong Thomas Blasingame Esquires
Samuel Jackson & John Springer lay out a road from Jordon
Jackson to William Plummers ford on Fairforest by Renny
Ballews Joseph Littles and there to Union Court House and
make their report to our next Court.

Ordered that the County Treasury Pay Thomas Brandon Twenty
One Shillings and three Pence for repairs done by him to the
Geoal. Present John Henderson Esqr.

215 State So Carolina   Plaintiff) Tresspass asst. & Battery
       against   ) Whereupon came a Jury Towit
    Cushman R Edson   Defendant) Nathan Glenn foreman &
                                      who being duly sworn do
Say on their Oathes Verdict for the Defendant not Guilty
and Dismissed on Paying of Costs.

State So. Carolina   Plaintiff) Bastardy
   agt.   ) Ordered by the Court that
Valentine Harlen   Defendant) the Deft. be fined the
                                  Sum of Three Pounds Eleven
Shillings and four pence.

State South Carolina Plaintiff) Basterdy
   against   ) Ordered by the Court that
Sarah Ballew   Defendant) the Defendant be fined the
                                 Sum of Three Pounds Eleven
Shillings and Four pence--and Ordered that Valentine Harlan
and Sarah Ballew enter into a Joint Bond with Security
each in the sum of Fifty Pounds to maintain the said
Child and to Indemnify the County from its maintainance
thereof.

Sarah Ballew having been Solemnly called and failing to
appear Ordered that a Scere facias Issue against her
Security.

State South Carolina   Plaintiff) Tresspass assault and
   against   ) Bettery on the body of
Pharoah Cobb   Defendant) Cushman R Edson Whereon
                                    Came a Jury Towit Nathan
Glenn Foreman & c. who being duly sworn do say on their
Oaths we find the Defendant Guilty.

181

It appearing to the Court that there is an Error in the
Settlement of the Estate of John Park Deceased Ordered
that the Same Gentlemen formerly appointed do proceed to
resettle the Same and make their report to next Court.

State South Carolina   Plaintiff)   Tresspass asst. & Battery
   against   )   Continued by Consent until
Gabriel Brown   Defendant)   next Court.

State South Carolina   Plft)   Obstruction the Passage of
   against   )   Fish Ordered that the
James Hawkins   Deft.)   Defendant be fined the sum
                                of Four Pounds and Costs of
Suit and that he be Committed in Custody untill he Pay
the costs.

Thomas Mays   Plaintiff)   Fals Imprisonment
   agt.   )   Judgment according to the award
Charles Burton   Deft)   filed in Court by the Said
                           arbitrators to whom the Deter-
mination of the matter Indefference were submitted to

216 George Taylor   Plaintiff)   Came the Plaintiff into Open
    agt   )   Court and then and there
    Robert Smith   Defendant)   Dismissed this Suit at his
                                 Own Costs which is ordered by
    the Court accordingly.

Bernerd Glenn Took the Oaths of Office as a Justice of
the Peace as an appointed and prescribed by Law
Present Bernard Glenn

State South Carolina Plaintiff)   Bastardy
   against   )   Capias Ordered on this case
Ann Posey   Defendant)

George Taylor)   Ordered that the Plaintiff Pay James
   vs   )   McCracken Twelve Shillings and Six Pence
Robert Smith)   for five days attendance as a witness for
                 him in the above suit.

Evan Thomas is appointed Constable for this County and
was duly Qualifyed according to Law.

A Deed from Thomas Brandon Esquire to Job Hammond
acknowledged in Open Court by the said Thomas Brandon to
the said Job Hammond and Ordered to be Recorded.

State South Caroline Plaintiff)   Presentment
   against   )   Ordered that this case
John Cook   Defendant)   be discontinued at the
                                Defendants costs.

State South Carolina   Plaintiff)   Presentment
   against   )   Ordered that a copy of
John Hope   Defendant)   this presentment be
                                delivered to the
representatives to Lay before the assembly.

State South Carolina Plaintiff)   Presentment Ordered that
   against   )   this case be discontinued
John Cook   Defendant)   at Defendants costs.

182

State South Carolina   Pltf)   TressPass
   against   )   Ordered that this case be
Reuben Ballew   Defendant   )   dismissed at the Defendants
                                cost

State South Carolina)   Bastardy
   vs   )   Ordered that she Give Security in
Mary Hammond   )   the Sum of Twenty Pounds
                         Prock to appear at our next Court
                         of Union.

State South Carolina)   Bastardy
   against   )   Ordered that he give security in the
William Hughes   )   Sum of Twenty Pounds Proe to appear
                         at next Court.

State South Carolina)   Ordered that a Scere facias Issue
   against   )   on the Recognizance.
Reuben & Sarah Ballew)

217 George Taylor   Plaintiff)   Ordered that the Plaintiff Pay
    against   )   Samuel Tolbert Ten Shillings for
Robert Smith   Defendant)   four days attendance Richard
                                Eddice Seventeen shillings and
six pence for seven days. Richard Fauset Twenty two
shillings and six pence for nine days attendance William
Sharp Twenty Shillings for Eight days and John Allbutton
Thirty five shillings for fourteen days attendance as
Witnesses for him in the above suit.

William Hughes Came into Court and acknowledged himself
Indebted to the State in the Sum of Twenty Pounds Proe
Richd. Hughes his Security in the Sum of Ten Pounds like
money for his the said William Hughes appearance next
Court and abide the Order thereof.

The Last Will and Testament of William Young Decd. was
Proved in Open Court by Jeremiah Moore and Ordered to be
Recorded.

Ordered that the Court adjourn untill tomorrow 9 o'clock
and Signed by   Thomas Brandon
                         Bernd C Glenn   Esquires
                         Charles Sims

At a Court Continued and held for the County of Union at
the Court house on the Twenty sixth day of September 1788.

Present   Thomas Brandon
                     Thomas Blasingame
                     William Kennedy   Esquires
                     Charles Sims

A Power of attorney from William White administrators of
Christopher Coleman Deceased to Thomas Stribling Junr.
Proved by Clayton Stribling and Ordered to be recorded.

A Bill of Sale from William White to Thomas Stribling Jr.
Proved in Open Court by Clayton Stribling and Ordered to be
Recorded.

183

State South Carolina) Larceny
   agt   ) Ordered that the Defendants be
Fincher & White   ) discharged on paying of costs.

Joseph Meanes   Plaintiff) Trover
   agt   ) Came the Plaintiff by Daniel
Hugh Meanes   Defendant) Brown his attorney and the
                      Defendant by William Shaw his
attorney Whereupon came a Jury Towit
218 Nathan Glenn Foreman David Harris Nathan Hawkins Isaac
Hawkins Thomas Lamb James Hawkins Jr. Alexander McCarter
Job Hammond Samuel Thompson Wm. McLellen Edward Denny and
Thomas Minton who being duly sworn do say on their oathes
We find for the Plaintiff Thirty five pounds and costs of
suit and Judgment accordingly.   Nathan Glenn Foreman

James Bell   Plaintiff) Atta.
   agt   ) Judgment for Plaintiff according
Mathew Bass   Defendant) to Note filed which is Five pounds
                      seven shillings & Eight pence
which was ordered accordingly.

William Grant   Plaintiff) The arbitrators to whome the
   vs   ) determination of the matter
William Williams Defendant) indefferance between the
                      Parties were submitted to this
day returned their award and was entered rep by Consent
of the Parties viz. We John McCooll & Jacob Brown having
heard the Evidences on both sides in the above suit have
awarded that the sum of Twelve Pounds five Shillings
Sterling shall be entered up in the suit brought by said
Grant against the said Williams in Union County as a
Judgment in said suit together with costs of Suit and that
the said Wm Williams shall have three months stay of
Execution Provided that he shall enter special to the said
action before the Court shall adjourn which is now
setting.
Signed   Jacob Brown
               John McCooll

John Savage   Plaintiff) Petr. & Summons
  against   ) This day came the Parties by
Robert Lusk   Defendant) their attorney and did thereupon
                      agree to Put themselves Upon a
Judgment without a Jury whereupon it is considered by the
Court that the Plaintiff recover against the defendant the
sum of Six Pounds and Interest on the same Six months and
Costs of Suit.

Kirkland & Co.   Plaintiff) By Consent of the Parties
   agt.   ) Ordered that this Case be
John Mullins   Defendant) Continued over untill next
                      Court which is ordered
accordingly.

John Means Plaintiff) Dbt.
  against   ) Came the Defendant into Open
Daniel Lipham Defendant) Court in his Own Proper Person
                      and then and there confessed a
Judgment according to the said Note with Stay of Execution
untill the 1st Day of December next which is Ordered
accordingly.

219 Ordered that the Land of John Steen Executed at the
Instance of Frances Latemore be Sold in behalf of the
Execution Issued by Cold. William Farr. Pryor to Latemore
and that a Venditio Exponas Issue.

Robert Lusk   Plaintiff)   On attachment
   agt   )   Came the Plaintiff by Daniel
Bradley Collins Defendant)   Brown his attorney and the
                             Defendant being solemnly
Called but failed to appear Whereupon Came a Jury towit.
Nathan Glenn Foreman Isaac Hawkins David Harris Nathan
Hawkins Thomas Lamb James Hawkins Jr. Alexr. McCarter Job
Hammond Samuel Thompson William McLellin Edward Denny
Thomas Minton who being duly Sworn do say on their oaths
we find for the Plaintiff the sum of eighteen pounds
and costs of Suit   N. Glenn Foreman

Which was Ratifyed by the Court & Ordered to be Recorded
Ordered that the attached Land in the above case be sold
according to law.

Pheby Wells   Plaintiff)   Debt
   vs   )   This day came the Parties
Nicholas Lazerous Defendant)   by their attorneys into
                             Open Court did then and there
agree to Put themselves upon the Judgment without a Jury
thereupon it is considered by the Court that the Plaintiff
recover against the Defendant the sum of Nineteen shillings
and two pence and costs of suit.

Present William McCullock and Bernerd Glenn Esquires.

Ordered that the Treasury of the County Pay Joseph Jones
late Goaler Two Pounds Seven Shillings and Four Pence
for keeping John Kingsley and Adam Moore in Goal.

Thomas Holden   Plaintiff)   Came the Plaintiff into open
   vs   )   Court by his attorney and &c.
Samuel Cooper   Defendant)   and the Defendant being
                             Solemnly called came not to
prosecute his Suit it is considered by the Court that
Judgment Go against him by Default which was ordered
accordingly.

David Normon   Plaintiff)   Came the Parties into Open
   against   )   Court by their attorneys and
Enoch Floyd   Defendant)   then and there agreed to Dismiss
                             this Suit at the Defendants
Cost which is ordered accordingly.

Samuel Cathcart   Plaintiff)   Petn. & Summons
   against   )   Nonsuit the Defendant
Duncan McCrevan   Defendant)   Paying Clerks fees

220 Daniel Jackson   Plaintiff)   Ptr. & Sums.
   against   )   Continued by Consent of the
William Jackson   Defendant)   Parties untill next Court.

Hugh Quinn   Plaintiff)   Attachment
   against   )   Continued by consent of the
Abraham Floyd   Defendant)   Parties untill next Court.

Jonathan Gilkie   Plaintiff)   Atta.
vs   )   Continued Over untill next
John Turker   Defendant)   Court by Consent of the
                                      Parties

John Motley   Plaintiff)   Atta.
against   )   Continued over untill next
Mark Mitchell   Defendant)   Court by Consent of the Parties.

Kirkland & Co.   Plaintiff)   Continued Over by Consent of
against   )   the Parties untill next Court.
James Sims   Defendant)

John Sanders   Plaintiff)   Case
against   )   Continued by Consent of the
William Clark   Defendant)   Parties until next Court.

Caleb Gasway   Plaintiff)   Case
against   )   Came the Parties into Open
Bud Booker   Defendant)   Court by their attorneys and then
                                      and there agreed to dismiss the
said Suit at the Defendants cost. except an attorneys fee
not to be taxed which is ordered accordingly.

John Bird assa.   Plaintiff)   Dbt
against   )   Cotninued by Consent of the
John Steen.   Defendant   )   Parties untill next Court.

John Bird   Plaintiff)   Dbt
against   )   Continued by Consent of the
John Steen Defendant)   Parties untill next Court.

John Bird   )   Dbt
against   )   Continued untill next Court by
Steen & Montgomery)   Consent of the Parties.

John Meanes   Plaintiff   )   Dbt
against   )   Continued untill next Court
Philip Anderson   Defendant)   by Consent of the Parties.

Minor Winn   Plaintiff)   Debt
against   )   Continued by Consent of the
Caleb Gasway   Defendant)   Parties Untill next Court.

221 James Minnis   Plaintiff)   Asst. & Battery
against   )   Continued by Consent of the
Gabriel Brown   Defendant)   Parties Untill next Court.

Robt. Henry Hughes   Plaintiff)   Case
against   )   By consent of the Parties
Jesse Dodd   Defendant)   this case is continued
                                         over untill next court.

Jonathan Gilkie assa.   Plaintiff   )   Dbt
against   )   By Consent of the
John Steen and Henry Smith   Defendant)   Parties continued
                                               over untill next
                                               Court.

Nathaniel Davis   Plaintiff)   Debt By consent of the
against   )   Parties this case is Contd.
Samuel Austen   Defendant)   over untill next Court.

186

John Gregory   Plaintiff)   Attachment
   against   )   Ordered that the Defendant
John Steen   Defendant)   be served with a copy of the
                               Declaration and Contd. over
untill next Court.

Charles Burton   Plaintiff)   Attachment
   against   )   Came the Plaintiff into
Dempsey Rabey   Defendant)   Open Court and then and there
                               Confessed a Judgment.

William White admrs. Plaintiff)   Dbt
   against   )   Continued by Consent of
Bozan & McWhorter   Defendants)   the Parties Untill next
                                   Court.

Mark Mitchell   Plaintiff)   Debt
   against   )   By Consent of the Parties
Giles and Palmore Defendant)   this case is Continued Over
                               Untill next Court.

Samuel Saxon   Plaintiff)   Petr. & Sums
   against   )   Continued over untill next
William Jackson   Defendant)   Court by Consent of the Parties

Holland Sumner   Plaintiff)   Petr. & Summons
   against   )   The Sheriff having made his
John Tollerson   Defendant)   return on this writ Nonest
                               Inventas Ordered that an alias
Issue against the aforesaid John Tollerson.

222 Charles Miles & Co.   Plaintiff)   Petr. & Summons
   against   )   Continued by Consent of
James Lindsey   Defendant)   the Parties untill next
                                      Court.

Thomas Brandon   Pl aintiff)   Petr. & Sums
   against   )   Continued Untill next Court
James Davis   Defendant)   by Consent of the Parties.

Thomas Brandon   Plaintiff)   Petr. & Summons
   against   )   Continued Untill next Court
James Davis   Defendant)   by Consent of the Parties.

Samuel Jackson   Plaintiff)   Case
   against   )   By Consent of the Parties
William Jackson   Defendant)   Ordered that this case be
                               Continued over untill next
                               Court.

Holland Sumner   Plaintiff)   Debt
   against   )   By consent of the Parties this
Dudley Redd   Defendant)   case is continued over untill
                               next court.

Samuel Saxon   Plaintiff)   Debt
   against   )   Continued untill next Court
William Jackson   Defendant)   by Consent of the Parties.

William Philpeck   Plaintiff)   Case Continued untill
   against   )   next Court by Consent of
Nicholas Tassinier   Defendant)   the Parties.

187

Graaff & Co.   Plaintiff)   Case
  against   )   Continued untill next Court by
Thomas Bishop   Defendant)   Consent of the Parties

Jasper Tommerlin   Plaintiff)   Case
  against   )   Continued Over untill
John Mullins   Defendant)   next Court by Consent of
                                   the Parties.

William Steen   Plaintiff   )   Trover
  against   )   By Consent of the
Benj. Clark & John Steen Defendant)   Parties this case is
                                        Contd. over untill
                                        next Court.

William Patten   )   Trover
  against   )   Continued untill next Court by
Elias Floyd   )   Consent of the Parties
Jno Little Deft.)

Charles Miles   Plaintiff)   Attachment
  against   )   Richmond Terrell and James
Benjamin Burnet   Defendant)   Terrell came into Open Court
                                  and entered themselves Special
Bail--and Cont. untill next Court.

Drewry Gowing   Plaintiff)   Attachment
  against   )   Continued over untill next
William Johnston   Defendant)   Court by consent of the
                                  Parties.

223 John Motley   Plaintiff   )   Debt on Attachment
     against   )   Continued untill next Court
William Cox & Mark Mitchell)   by consent of the Parties.
        Defendant   )

Robert Lusk   Plaintiff)   Case
  against   )   Came the Plaintiff by Daniel
Hugh Meanes   Defendant)   Brown his attorney and the
                                  Defendant by his attorney &c
Whereupon came a Jury Towit. Nathan Glenn Foreman Isaac
Hawkins David Harris Nathan Hawkins Thomas Lamb James
Hawkins Jr. Alexander McCarter Job Hammond Samuel Thompson
William McLellin Edward Denny and Thomas Minton--who being
duly sworn do say on their oathes we find Verdict for
Defendant and Judgment accordingly.

Thomas Brandon   Plaintiff)   Ordered that a Dedimus
  against   )   Potestatum Issue to the
George Goodwinn   Defendant)   State of Georgia to take the
                                  Deposition of Joel Barnet.

Richard Speaks & John Montgomery)   Debt attachment
  against   )   Came the Plaintiff into
John Bird   )   Open Court by his
                                       attorney and the Defen-
dant being Solemnly called came not to prosecute his Suit--
Whereupon it is considered by the Court that Judgment be
entered up against him according to Note hand by default
with Stay of Execution three months which is Ordered
accordingly.

188

Isaac Hawkins   Plaintiff) Ordered that a Dedimus Potes-
   against   ) tatum Issue to take the
William Hughes   Defendant) Deposition of George Russle
                             Debeneesse on Giving the
Defendant ten days notice of the time and place of takeing
the same.

Joseph McJunkin one of the overseers of the Road Presented
by the Grand Jury and he making it appear to the Court that
his Part of the Road is in Good repair Ordered that the
Clerk do not Issue any Process against him.

Isaac Hawkins one of the Overseers of the Road Presented
by the Grand Jury and he makeing it appear to the Court
that his Part of the road is in good repair Ordered that
the Clerk do not Issue any Process against him.

State So. Carolina   Plaintiff) his Securitys recognizance
   against   ) Forfeited and a Scere
Pharoah Cobb & Co. Stribling) facias Ordered.
Deft.   )

224 A Bond from Samuel Scotcher to Joseph McJunkin was Proved
in Open Court by the Oath of C R Edson & Ordered to be
recorded.

Ordered that Thomas Brandon William Kennedy and John
Birdsong Esqrs do contract with such person as they may
think most convenient for the interest of the County for
the building of a Court House at this Place Thirty Feet
Long and Twenty Feet Wide with the necessary Apartments
therein as they may suppose convenient and that the said
Contract be paid by the Treasury of the County Out of the
Moneys arising by fines and Strays.

Thomas Brandon Esquire was duly Qualified in Open Court
as an Executor to the Last Will and Testament of Wm. Young
Deceased.

Thomas Blasingame   Plaintiff) Case
   against   ) Refered to such men as they
Samuel Jackson   Defendant) may chose between this and
                                next Court and their report
to be the Judgment hereof which is Ordered accordingly.

Ordered that the Court be adjourned untill Court in Course.
Signed by: William Kennedy
                    Charles Sims
                    Wm. McCullock   Esquires
                    Thomas Brandon
                    Bernerd Glenn

At a Court begun and held in and for the County of Union
at the Court House of Said County on Monday the 22d Day
of December 1788 and was thence adjourned to Mr. Edsons
Tavern
Present   Wm Kennedy
                    Thomas Brandon   Esquires
                    John Birdsong

The Court Proceeded to draw a Grand Jury to Serve March
Term 1789. To wit.

189

Laurence House 1. Nehemiah Howard 2. Daniel Jackson 3.
William Smith 4. John Hope 5. William Young 6. William
Martindale 7. Thomas Greer 8. William Newman 9. William
Jackson 10. John Cole 11. Robert Crenshaw 12. Jeptha
Hollingsworth 13. Robert Bailey 14. Benjamin Savage 15.
William Speers 16. James Hawkins 17. Nathaniel Jefferies 18.
John Jefferies 19. John Savage 20.

Ordered that the following Gentlemen be summoned to attend
next Court to Serve as Pettit Jurors Towit.
Nathaniel Davis 1 John Martindale 2 James Maberry 3
Hezekiah Rice 4 Handcock Porter 5 William Steen 6 John
Bailey 7 James Woodson Jr. 8 Charles Miles 9 John Thompson
10 Ambrose Ray 11 Bird Beuford 12 Charles Hames 13 Thomas
Young 14 John Fincher 15 Nathan Glenn 16 Moses Guiton 17

225 William Hughes 18 Walter Roberts 19 Archabald Kennedy 20
John B-andon Jr. 21 John Brandon 22 William Barron 23
Robert Lusk 24 William Beckham 25 Lewis Turner 26 Richard
Faucett 27 William White 28 James Bogan 29 David Norman 30

A Deed of Conveyance from Samuel Smith and Wife to Alexander
Hamelton Proved before a Justice and Ordered to be
Recorded.

Hugh Means Took the Oaths Prescribed by Law for the
Execution of a Justice of the Peace for this County
Present Hugh Meanes Esquire

The Court Ordered that the appearance Docket Should be
called the first time which was done accordingly.

A Deed of Conveyance from John McCooll of the One part to
James McClure of the Other Part acknowledged in Open Court
and Ordered to be Recorded.

On the Motion of John McCooll Leave is given him to keep
Tavern on Public House on his Giving Bond with Danel Jackson
his Security according to Law.

On the Motion of William Darby Leave is Given him to
keep Tavern or Public House on his Giving Bond with John
Montgomery his Security according to Law.

A Lease and Release from William Wofford to John Hames
Proved in Open Court by the Oathes of Charles Hames
& Nicholas Waters and Ordered to be Recorded.

Ordered that the Court adjourn untill tomorrow 9 o'clock
Signed by   Thomas Brandon
                     William Kennedy
                     Hugh Meanes

At a Court Continued and held according to adjournment on
Tuesday the 23d day of December 1788 at the Court house of
Union County.
Present   William Kennedy
                 Thomas Brandon
                 John Birdsong   Esquires
                 Charles Sims
                 Wm McCullock
                 Zacha. Bullock

190

226 A Deed from Samuel Beaks and Sarah his wife to William
Hawkins Proved before Bernard Glenn Esqr. & Ordered to
be Recorded.

James Dohertee Produced a Commission from the Honourable
the associate Judges of the Court of Common Pleas authorizing him to Plead the Law as an attorney in the several
Courts of this State. Ordered that he be admitted to
Practice in this Court accordingly.

Isaac Parker is appointed Constable for this County who
was duly Qualifyed according to Law.

George Taylor   Plaintiff)   Came the Parties into Open
   against   )   Court by their attorneys and
John Filpeck   Defendant)   then and there agreed to dis-
                               miss this Suit at the Defendants
Cost which is ordered by the Court accordingly.

John Sanders came into Open Court in this own proper
Person and then and there resigned his appointment as
Deputy Clerk of this Court which is Ordered accordingly.

On the motion of John Haile Clerk Richard Mitchell is
appointed Deputy Clerk of this Court and Took the Oath
Prescribed by Law.

Joseph McJunkin and William Hendley came into Open Court
and took the Oaths appointed by Law for the Executions of
Justices of the Peace and Took their Seals accordingly.

State So. Carolina Plaintiff)   Pettit Larcency
   against   )   The Defendant came into
John Hunt   Defendant)   Open Court and Waved all
                               advantages of a bill of
Indictment or any other form pointed out by Law for the
regular Conviction of Offenders and Pleasds Guilty to the
Charge Exhibited against him and prays that Judgment may be
passed on him in Mercey Whereupon the Court Ordered that
the Said John Hunt receive Twenty five lashes on the bare
back at the Publick Whipping Post and that he be discharged
on Paying Costs.

Thomas Blasingame   Plaintiff)   Case
   against   )   This case being refered the
Samuel Jackson   Defendant)   return of the arbitrators
                               by their award is as follows
Towit. that the Defendant shall Pay to the Plff Twenty
three pounds Elevel shillings and five pence & Costs Six
months after the Date hereof which is made a Judgment of
this Court and Ordered accordingly.

Ordered that all the Proceedings of the appearnace and
Tryal Dockets be continued over untill Court in Course.

227 A Deed from Nehemiah Howard to Archer Howard acknowledged
in Open Court and Ordered to be Recorded.

Ordered that William Hendley be released of being Overseer
of the Road from the ford of Bullocks Creek to the Cross
Roads where a Negroe was hung and John Reed be appointed
in his Room.

Ordered that Charles Humpharies be appointed Overseer
of the Road from Clayton Striblings Path to McDougals to
the old road that Leads to Grindal Shoals in the Rom of
William Buckhannon who is released thereof.

Luke Carrell is appointed Constable for this County and
took the Oathes of Office Prescribed by Law.

Samuel Harlan Overseer of the Road being Presented by the
Grand Jury for not keeping the same in Good repair and he
making it known to the Court that the same in Good Order
and from his Presentment is Released.

Richard Hughes is appointed Overseer of the Road from
Loves ford to Begans Creek in the Room of Benjamin Savage.

Ordered that William Plummer be appointed Overseer of the
Road from Jorden Jacksons across Fairforest to the Road
Leading to Grindal Shoals.

Ordered that Richard Powell be Overseer of the above said
Road to Union Court House.

Ordered that John Birdsong Esqr. John Murrell and John
McKibbin be appointed to appraise the Estate of John Ewart
Deceased and make due return of the same thereof.

Ordered that James Crawford be appointed Overseer of the
road from Gibbs Old Field to Rockey Creek.

Ordered that James McCracken be Overseer of the Road from
Cedar Shoals on Fannins Creek to Capt. Hughes Road.

On the motion of Samuel Simpson leave is given him to
retail spiritous Liquors who gave bond in the sum of fifty
pounds with Richard Burgess his Security according to Law.

A Lease and Release of John Martindale and Uxor to Thomas
Dodd Proved before Thomas Blasingame Esquire & Ordered to
be Recorded.

228 Its Ordered that Fielding Curtis be Overseer of the Road
from Mitchells Creek to dining Creek in the Room of John
Little.

Ordered that Robert Crenshaw be Overseer of the Road from
Hills ford on Tyger River to the Cross Road Leading from
the Fish Dam to Ninety six.

Its Ordered that John Sartor and James Thomas View the road
from the Cross Roads near Thomas Miles to McNeals bigg
Creek and report the same to our next Court.

Ordered that Caleb Gasaway be Overseer of the road from the
fish dam Ford to Cain Creek.

Ordered that John Montgomery be Overseer of the road from
Samuel McJunkins to Swift Run Creek.

Its Ordered that the Old road be cleared and keep in
Good repair that leads from Ottersons old field crossing
Tygar at Potts old ford the nearest and best way to

Liphams and William Rogers be Overseer of the Same.

John Motley   Plaintiff   )   Debt on attachment
   against   )   John Haile Came into Open
Wm. Cox & Mark Mitchell Deft.)   Court and entered himself
                                  Special Bail.

Ordered that the Sheriff Expose to Sale a Stray mare in
the hands of Thomas Blasingame also a Stray heifer in the
hands of Moses Coltier the Thirty first day of this Instant
at this place by advertising the Same.

Ordered that Jacob Haild be allowed the Sum of Twelve
Shillings and Six Pence for keeping a stray Colt and that
the Treasury Pay the Same.

Ordered that the Court adjourn Untill Court in Course
Signed by   John Birdsong
                       William Kennedy
                       Thomas Brandon

At a Court begun and held in and for the County of Union
at the Court house of Said County the Twenty third day of
March 1789
Present   John Birdsong
                       Thomas Blasingame   Esquires
                       William Hendley
                       Hugh Meanes

229 Ordered that the Following Persons be Summoned to serve
next Court as Pettit Jurors Towit.
Charles Thompson 1. Samuel Simpson Jnr. 2. Jonathan Newman
3. Isaac Hawkins 4. Jeduthan Porter 5. Hugh Nelson 6.
Wm. Martendale Junr. 7 William Whitlock 8. Edward Tilman 9.
Aaron Fincher 10. Benja. Hawkins 11. John Whitlock 12.
James Ray 13. William Coleman 14. Robert Goode 15. Spilsby
Glenn 16. William Right 17. John Conner 18. George Bailey
19. William Buckhannon 20. William Lawson 21. William
Springer 22. Nicholas Jasper 23. James Savage 24. John
Netherman 25 William Giles 26. James Kennedy 27. James
Moseley 28. Nicholas Currey 29. Josshua Scisson 30.

Zachariah Talefero Produced a Commission from the Hnob.
the associate Judges of this State authorizing him to Plead
the Law in the Several Court of this State   Ordered that he
be Licensed to Practice in this Court accordingly.

Spencer Brummet   Plaintiff)   Attachment
   against   )   Came the Parties into Open
Cordial Hogans   Defendant)   Court by their attorney and
                                then and there Dismissed this
Said Suit at the Defendants Costs which is Ordered
accordingly.

Thomas Greer foreman Nehemiah Howard Daniel Jackson William
Newman William Jackson John Bal Robert Bailey William
Speers Nathaniel Jefferies John Jefferies John Savage
James Hawkins William Martendale--Who being duly Sworn
according to Law as a Grand Jury of Inquest for the body
of this County and received their Charge and withdrew
accordingly.

On the motion of Samuel Simpson he is appointed Constable for this County who took the Oaths of Office according to Law.

The Last will and Testament of John Henry Keiser Decd. Proved in Open Court by the Oath of James Callwell and Ordered to be accorded also Proved an Inventory of the Estate of the Said John Henry Keeser Deceased.

The Court Ordered the appearance Docket to be called the first time which was done accordingly.

230 John Fincher   Plaintiff)   Came the Parties into Open Court
    against   )   by their attorneys and then and
   David Norman   Defendant)   there dismissed this Suit at
                             the Defendants Costs which is
Ordered by the Court accordingly.

Joseph Jones   Plaintiff)   Came the Parties into Open
  against   )   Court by their attorneys and
John Holdman   Defendant)   then and there Dismissed this
                       Suit at the Plaintiffs Costs.

William Filpeck   Plaintiff)   Came the Parties into Open
  against   )   Court by their attorneys and
Nathl. Tessineer   Defendant)   then and there dismissed this
                       Suit at the Plaintiffs cost.

Robert Lusk Foreman 1. John Martindale 1. Hezekiah Rice 3. William Steen 4 John Bailey 5. Ambrose Wray 6. Bird Booker 7. John Fincher 8. Moses Guiton 9. Walter Roberts 10. Archilus Kennedy 11. William Pearson 12. William White 13. David Norman 14. John Brandon 15. Lewis Turner 16. The foregoing Giving Persons to serve this Court as Pettit Jurors for this County.

On the application of James Gibbs leave is given him to keep a tavern or public house on giving Bond with D R Edson according to law.

Federick Jackson is appointed Overseer of the Road from Cold. Brandons on Fairforest to bobos on Tyger in the Room of James Gibbs.

An Indenture and Deed of Conveyance from Andrew Jones of the One Part and William Lipscomb of the Other Part Proved before Zacha. Bullock Esquire and Ordered to be Recorded.

A Deed of Conveyance from John Mullins to James Hall Proved before a Justice and Ordered to be Recorded.

On the Application of Hugh Means Leave is Given him to keep Tavern or Public House on his giving bond with William Thompson his Security according to Law.

A Deed of Conveyance from Geo Corrsley of the One Part and John McCooll of the Other Proved before a Justice & Ord. to be recorded.

A Deed of Conveyance from John Mullins to Philip Bass was Proved before a Justice and Ordered to be Recorded

231 A Deed of Conveyance from George McCullock and Margaret his wife to John Massey Proved before a Justice and Ordered to be Recorded.

A Deed of Conveyance from Thomas Brandon to Jeremiah Lucas Proved before a Justice and Ordered to be Recorded.

A Deed of Conveyance from John Martindane and Wife to John Garret Proved before a Justice and Ordered to be recorded.

Its Ordered that the Sheriff Expose to Sale a Stray horse Taken up by Charles Brock according to Law.

A Deed from Theodoleous Prigmore to Nicholas Jasper Proved before a Justice and Ordered to be Recorded.

A Deed from James Hill and wife to Leroy Bewford Proved in Open Court by the Oath of Robert Crenshaw and Ordered to be Recorded.

A Deed of Conveyance from James Savage to Elijah McGuire acknowledged in Open Court and Ordered to be Recorded.

Ordered that Thomas Miles be Overseer of the Road from the Cross Roads to Joseph Hollingsworth mill and that he keep the same in good repair according to law.

Ordered that William Hogans be Overseer of the Road from Hollingsworths Spring to Hills ford on Tyger River and that he keep the Same in Good Repair according to Law.

Ordered that Arther Thomas be Overseer of the Road from the Neals Bigg Creek to the Cross Roads Leading to Thomas Miles in the Room of John Salter and that he keep the Same in Good repair according to Law.

Ordered that Selah Beverley and Sarah Beverley Poor Orphans be bound to Abel Pearson Towit. the Said Silah Beverley Ten Years and Sarah Beverley Eleven Years to be Under his jurisdiction and discretion and to be dealt with as Orphans are according to Law.

Its Ordered that Samuel Otterson be Overseer of the Road from Swift Run to Ottersons Old ford on Tyger River and that he keep the Same in Good Repair according to Law.

Its Ordered that Henry Millhouse be Overseer of the Road from Samuel McJunkins to Swift Run Creek and that he keep the same in Good Repair according to law.

232 On the Application of John McKibbin leave is given him to keep Tavern or Public house on giving Bond with John Haile his Security according to Law.

Ordered that William Hall Serve as Constable for this County he taking the Necessary Oath of Office in Open Court.

Ordered that James Hall Serve as Constable for this County upon his Comeing into Open Court and taking the necessary Oathes of Office accordingly.

A Deed of Conveyance from John Layton to Robert White
being duly Proved and Ordered to be Recorded.

A Deed of Conveyance from Joseph Parks to Richard Say
being Proved before a single Justice and thereupon admitted
to Record.

A Deed of Conveyance from Samuel Jackson to Jordon Jackson
acknowledged in Open Court and Ordered to be Recorded.

Ordered that William Brandon bring all the Children of John
Bates Deceased to Court tomorrow to be dealt with as they
see Cause.

The minutes were Read & Signed by
                    Thomas Brandon
                    William McCullock
                    Joseph McJunkin
                    Wm Hendley
The Court then adjourned untill tomorrow 9 o'clock.

Tuesday the 24th day March 1789 the Worshipful Court met
according to Last Evenings adjournment
Present   Thomas Brandon
                    William McCullock   Esquires
                    Hugh Means

Its Ordered that the Distressed Children of John Bates
decd. be bound Out according to Law Towit W. Zachariah
Bell Take Charge of the Eldest named Samuel also George
M. Joseph Jones take Charge of Alexander and Salley untill
next Court.

233 James Harrison   Plaintiff)   Came the Parties into Open
      against   )   Court by their attorneys and
    Thomas Fletchall Defendant)   then and there Dismissed this
                                     Said Suit at the Plaintiffs
    Cost which is ordered accordingly.

    John Steen   Plaintiff)   Attachment
      against   )   Came the Parties into Open
    David Stocdon   Defendant)   Court by their attorneys and
                                    then and there agreed to
    Continue this said suit untill next Court at the Defendants
    Cost Which is Ordered accordingly.

On the Application of Cushman R Edson Leave is Given him
to keep Tavern or Public House who entered into bond
according to Law with Capt. Daniel Comer his Security.

    James Olliphant   Plaintiff)   Case
      against   )   Came the Plaintiff by
    Jonathan Norman   Defendant)   William Shaw Esquire his
                                    attorney and the Defendant
    by James Dohertee Gentlemen his attorney Whereupon came
    a Jury Towit. Robert Lusk Hezekiah Rice William Steen
    John Bailey Ambrose Ray John Fincher Moses Guiton Walter
    Roberts Thomas Young John Brandon Jnr William Beckham &
    Lewis Turner who being Elected Tried and Sworn to well and
    truly try this Issue Joined on their Oathes do say--We find
    Eleven pounds thirteen shillings and four pence for the

196

Plaintiff with Interest for the Same from June 1785.
Robert Lusk foreman.
Whereupon it is Considered by the Court that the Plaintiff
recover against the Defendant according to Verdict.

A Lease and Release from Thomas Blasingame and wife to Daniel
Palmore acknowledged in Open Court by the Said Thomas
Blasingame, and his wife being Privately examined by a
Justice who report that she freely renounces her Right of
Dower Ordered to be Recorded.

On the application of Aaron Cates Leave is Given Rooff
Goodman & Company to keep tavern or public house on giving
bond with Samuel Otterson according to Law.

A Deed of Conveyance from Frances Posey and Wife of the One
Part and Joseph Comer of the Other part, Proved before a
Justice and Ordered to be Recorded.

234 John Anderson   Plaintiff) Case
    against   ) Came the Defendant by Jacob
    William George   Defendant) Brown his attorney and the
                                   Plaintiff being Solemnly
    Called Came not to prosecute
234 his Said Suit where fore a nonsuit is awarded the Defendant
    against the Plaintiff aforesadi also Ordered that he
    recover five Shillings for his damage and Costs of Suit--
    Which is Ordered accordingly.

A Deed of Conveyance from Ecledas Longshore and wife of the
One Part and John Farrow of the Other Part. Proved before
a Justice of the Peace and Ordered to be Recorded.

John Hodge   Plaintiff) Debt
    against   ) Came the Defendant into Open
Robert Montgomery Defendant) Court by Jacob Brown his atty.
                               and then and there withdrew
his Plea; and a Judgment entered according to Specialty
with Interest and Cost of Suit.

Jeho. Langston) Case
    against   ) The Plaintiff being Dead the Suit
John Montgomery) abated at his Cost and Execution to
                   Issue against His Estate--which is
Ordered accordingly.

John Steen   Plaintiff) Debt
    against   ) By Consent of the Parties by their
Joshua Petty   Defendant) attors. Ordered that this Case
                            be Continued Over untill next
Court.

John Steen   Plaintiff) Case
    against   , Continued by Consent of the
Joshua Petty   Defendant) Parties Untill next Court.

Thomas Brandon   Esquire Plaintiff) Debt on attach-
    against   ) ment. Came the
Epaphroditus Paulk   Defendant   ) Plaintiff by Jacob
                                        Brown Esquire his
attorney and the Defendant in his Own proper Person.
Whereupon came a Jury Towit. John Thompson foreman

197

Nathaniel Davis Handcock Porter James Woodson Archebald
Kennedy William Pearson Richard Fasset William White
David Norman John Martindale James Maberry and William
Lawson. Who being Elected Tryed and Sworn to well and truly
Try this Issue Joined On their Oathes do Say we do find
Fifty Pounds for the Plaintiff with Costs of Suit and
Judgment accordingly.   John Thompson   foreman

A Bill of Sale from John Weedingman to William Hendley
Proved in Open Court by the Oath of Ezekiel Stone and
Ordered to be Recorded.

235 William Steen   Plaintiff)   Slander
      against   )   Came the Plaintiff by Charles
    William Gilkey   Defendant)   Goodwin his attorney and the
                                    Deft. by Daniel Brown Esqr.
    his attorney. Whereupon Came a Jury Towit John Thompson
    Nathaniel Davis Handcock Porter James Woodson Archibald
    Kennedy William Pearson Richard Trussett William White
    David Norman John Martindale James Maberry William Lawson
    who being Elected Tried and Sworn to well and truly Try
    this Issue Joinedon their Oaths do say we do find Verdict
    for Defendant and Judgment accordingly.

    Nathaniel Jefferies   Plaintiff)   Attachment
      agt.   )   Came the Defendant into
    John Steen   Defendant)   Open Court and Confessed
                                      a judgment for the sum
    of Twenty Pounds and Costs of Suit which is Ordered
    accordingly.

    A Lease and Release from Mark Love and wife to Samuel Spray
    Proved before a Justice of the Peace and Ordered to be
    Recorded.

    William Steen   Plaintiff)   Slander
      against   )   Came the Plaintiff into Open
    Adam Goudylock   Defendant)   Court by Mc.Carner Esqr. his
                                    atty. and the Defendant by
    Daniel Brown Esqr. his attorney Whereupon came a Jury
    Towit, Hezekiah Rice foreman Handcock Porter William
    Beckham Archilous Kennedy John Bailey Ambrose Wray Thomas
    Young John Fincher Moses Guiton Walter Roberts John
    Brandon Junr. and Lewis Turner who being Elected tried and
    sworn to well and truly Try this Issue Joined on their
    Oathes do say we find for the Plaintiff one pound fifteen
    shillings with Costs and Judgment accordingly. Hezekiah
    Rice Foreman which said Judgment was Rattfyed by the Court
    and Ordered to be Recorded.
    Wm Shaw atto. Gave notice on the Part of the Defendant of
    moveing in arreast of Judgment.

    Samuel Jackson   Plaintiff)   Debt on attachment
      against   )   Came the Parties into Open
    William Jackson   Defendant)   Court by their attorney and
                                    then and there agreed to
    Leave all matter of Indefferance or Contract to Thomas
    Blasingame Esqr. and Isaac Bogan and their award to be
    the Judgment of this Court which is Ordered accordingly.

236 Robert Lusk   Plaintiff)   Debt
    agt.   )   Continued by Consent of the
    Joshua Petty   Defendant)   Parties untill next Court on
                                September on Wednesday.

A Deed of Conveyance from Joseph East to Samuel Clouney
for three hundred acres of Land Proved by the Oaths of
James Yancey and Samuel Jackson before Thomas Blasingame
Esquire and Ordered to be Recorded.

Jesse Dodd   Plaintiff)   Case
    agt.   )   Came the Parties into Open
Isaac Edmondson Defendant)   Court and then and there agreed
                             to refer this Said suit to the
Arbitration of James Woodson Moses Haines Jacob Ducket and
John Fincher and their award to be the Judgmt. of this
Court which is Ordered accordingly.

A Bond from John Journey to Joseph East Bond by Alexander
McDougal and Ordered to be Recorded.

State So. Carolina   Plaintiff)   Bastardy
    agt.   )   The Defendant being
Elizabeth Addington   Defendant)   brought into Open Court
                                   and on her Examination
refuseth to discover the Father of the Child Ordered that
she be committed to Goal.

Harrisson Bell   Plaintiff)   Petr. & Summons
    agt.   )   Came the Plaintiff into Open
George Pervis   Defendant)   Court and then and there
                                Dismissed this Said Suit at
his Costs, which is Ordered accordingly.

William Bostick   Plaintiff)   On Replevey Warrant
    against   )   James Kennedy Came into
Drewery Herrington Defendant)   Open Court and Entered
                                himself Special Bail in
Behalf of the appellant which is Ordered accordingly.

Ordered to be filed in the Clerks Office an Inventory of
the Estate of John Linster Deceased.

The Court adjourned untill Tomorrow 9 o'clock which is
Ordered accordingly &
Signed by   Thomas Brandon
                     William McCullock
                     Joseph McJunkin
                     William Hendley

At a Court Continued and held according to adjournment
on Wednesday the 25th March 1789 at the Court House of
Said County Present   Thomas Brandon, Thomas Blasingame
William McCullock Joseph McJunkin and William Hendley
Esquires

237 Proved in Court a Deed of Conveyance from John Foster to
    Frances Whitlock for two hundred acres of Land and
    Ordered to be Recorded.

James Thomas a Minor of the age of fourteen years son of

199

Daniel Thomas, came into Open Court and Petitioned that
a Guardian might be appointed for him, and nominated his
Uncle William Thomas, Whereupon the Court do appoint the
Said William Thomas, Guardian over the Person and Estate
of the Said James Thomas untill he attains the age of
Twenty one years, the said James Thomas giving Bond and
Security in the Sum of Two hundred Pounds Sterling for
the faithful discharge of his duty hereof.

William Bostick   Plaintiff)   On a replevey Issue Joined
     against   )   Came the Plaintiff by James
Drewry Herrington Defendant)   Cohertee his attorney and
the Defendant by William Shaw his attorney Whereupon Came
a Jury Towit Hezekiah Rice Foreman Robert Lusk Handcock
Porter Archelous Kennedy John Bailey Ambrose Wray
Thomas Young Moses Guiton Walter Roberts John Brandon
William Beckham & Lewis Ledbetter who being duly Sworn to
well & truly try this Issue Joined do seay on their Oathes
we find for the Plaintiff and the Goods Executed to be
sold according to Law.

John McCooll   Plaintiff)   Debt on Attachment
    vs   )   Thomas Henderson being
John Montgomery   Defendant)   summoned as a Garnashee to
                              declare what Property he had
in his hands do say on Oath that he gave one note for
Ten pounds payable in November Next and another for nine
pounds payable that day Twelve Months to the said John
Montgomery.

State So. Carolina   Plaintiff)   Pettit Larcency
    agt.   )   Cushman R Edson Sworn on
Robert Gibson   Defendant)   the behalf of the State to
                              Give Evidence before the
Grand Jury returned a true Bill

State So. Carolina   Plaintiff)   Indictment Riot
    agt.   )   James Benson Senr. and
Saml. David & Elizabeth Cooper)   James Benson Junr. Sworn
                              to give evidence before
the grand Jury returned a True Bill.

State So. Carolina   Plaintiff)   Indictment T. A. &
    agt.   )   Battery
Robert Gibson   Defendant)   Jesse Liles and William
                              Jackson Sworn the Grand
                              Jury returned a true bill

238 James Olliphant   Plaintiff)   Trover
     against   )   Whereupon came a Jury Towit.
John Martindale   Defendant)   Robert Lusk foreman Hezekiah
                              Rice William Steen John
Baley Ambrose Ray Thomas Young Moses Guiton Walter Roberts
John Brandon Junr. William Beckham Lewis Turner & Handcock
Porter who being duly Sworn do say on their Oathes we find
for the Deft.   Robt. Lusk

On the application of James Pucket Leave is Given him to
keep Tavern or Public house on giving bond with John
Fincher and Thomas Vance according to Law. his Security
in the Sum of One hundred pounds sterling.

State So. Carolina   Plaintiff) Indictment for marking &
   agt.   ) Disfiguring Horses
Hez: Salmon   Defendant) Wm Williams Daniel White
                                 Godfrey Fowler William Hall
and Archibald Fore Sworn to give evidence before the Grand
Jury, Returned a True Bill.

It is Ordered that John Herrington, Drewry Herrington and
James Petty appraise the Estate of George Martin Deceased.

Thomas Stribling Plaintiff) Petr. & Sums.
   against   ) Came the Parties into Open
James Maberry   Defendant) Court and Discontinued this
                              Said Suit to which is Ordered
                              accordingly.

State So. Carolina   Plaintiff) Indictment for marking
   against   ) hogs Martin Conner &
Philip Bass & Geo Russel Defendants) William Conner
                                       Sworn to give evi-
dence before the Grand Jury. Returned No Bill.

Thomas Taylor   Plaintiff) Judgment against Josiah Wood
   vs   ) as Garnashee for the Sum of
James McDean   Defendant) Four pounds eighteen
                              shillings and three pence
according to his Oath as Garnashe aforesaid, which is
ordered accordingly.

The State So. Carolina   Plaintiff) Bastardy
   agt.   ) The Defendant being
Elizabeth Haddington   Defendant) Called into Court to
                                       answer to the said
Charge and having refused to discover the Father of her
Bastard Child, the Court doth fine her forty pounds
Proclamation Money---Aaron Fincher and John Martindale
came into Open Court and acknowledged themselves Jointly
and Severally to be Indebted to the Justices of the County
of Union in the Said Sum of Forty Pounds Proclamation
money.

239 Money on account of the said fine and they do hereby
    Jointly and severally bind and Oblige their and each of
    their goods and Chattles Lands and Tenements for the Pay-
    ment of the Said fine of Forty Pounds Proclamation money
    in three Months from this date, Aaron Fincher (Seal)
    Witness Ł 40, Proclamation   Jno. Martindale (Seal)
      Money
    W. Shaw.

Hugh McBride   Plaintiff) This Suit being referred to
   against   ) Persons appointed by this Court
Parks Admr.   Defendant) who have returned their award
                            Towit. Judgment for Forty nine
pounds three shillings and three pence which is the
Judgment hereof and ordered to be Recorded.

Holland Sumner   Plaintiff) Case
   against   ) Came the Parties into Open
Thomas Blasingame Defendant) Court and then and there
                              Dismissed this suit at the
Plaintiffs costs which is ordered accordingly.

201

Cushman R. Edson   Plaintiff)   Petr. & summons
   against   )   Came the Parties into Open
John DYoung   Defendant)   Court and then and there
                                agreed to leave all matter
of Controversy Between them to the Arbitration of William
Kennedy Esqr. and John McKibbin and their award to be made
the Judgment of this Court.

William Whitlock   Plaintiff)   Slander
   against   )   Came the Plaintiff into Open
Holland Sumner   Defendant)   Court and then and there
                                dismissed this said suit
at his cost which is ordered accordingly.

William Whitlock   Plaintiff)   Slander
   against   )   Came the Plaintiff into Open
Landlot Porter   Defendant)   Court and then and there
                                Dismissed this Suit at his
costs which is ordered accordingly.

Thomas Blasingame Plaintiff)   Slander
   against   )   Came the Plaintiff by
Holland Sumner   Defendant)   Charles Goodwin his
                                attorney and the Defndt.
by William Shaw Esq: his attorney whereupon came a Jury
Towit Robert Lusk foreman Hezekiah Rice John Bailey Ambrose
Wray Thomas Young Moses Guiton Walter Roberts John Brandon
Jnr. Lewis Turner Handcock Porter   Wm Steen

240 William Steen and William Beckham who being duly Sworn to
well and truly Try this Issue Joined on their Oaths do
say we find for the Plaintiff the Sum of Twenty Pounds
and costs of Suit and Judgment accordingly.
                                Robt Lusk   Foreman

John Foster   Plaintiff)   Slander
   against   )   Came the Parties into Open
Joseph Randolph Defendant)   Court and then and there agreed
                                to Discontinue this Suit at
the Defendants cost which is Ordered accordingly.

William Brandon   Plaintiff)   Debt on attachment
   against   )   Came the Parties into Court
William Boyd   Defendant)   by their attorneys and Continued this Suit over untill next Court.

William Steen   Plaintiff)   Slander
   against   )   Came the Parties into Open
Adam Goudylock   )   Court and then and there agreed
                                for a new Tryal to be granted
which is ordered accordingly.

State So. Carolina   Plaintiff)   Tresspass asst. & Battery
   against   )   Whereupon came a Jury Towit
Gabriel Brown   Defendant)   Robert Lusk foreman Hez.
                                  Rice John Bailey Ambrose
Wray Thomas Young Moses Guiton Walter Roberts John Brandon
Jnr. Lewis Turner Handcock Porter William Steen and
William Beckham who say on their oathes we find him guilty
and fine him four Shillings and Eight Pence and costs of
suit.   Robt. Lusk foreman

202

```
State So. Carolina     Plaintiff)   Escape
      vs                       )   Thomas Blasingame and
Richd. Burgess         Defendant)   John Martindale Sworn
                                    the Grand Jury returned
                                    a True Bill.
```

The Grand Jury Returned a List of their Presentments as
follows Towit. We Present to the Court that Lucy Crossley
is an Object of Charity
We Present the Road that Leads from Tyger River to Kennedys
ford on Enoree River Out of repair for want of an Overseer.
which we recommend George Wadkins for that Purpose.
Also the Road Leading from the Iron Works to Blackstocks
ford out of repair and recommend Nathaniel Langstone Overseer from said ford to the County Line
Also leading from the Iron Works to Union Court House be
Opened and recommend Arther Cunningham as an Overseer for
that Purpose

241 We Present that by Information that Daniel Meanley and a
Certain Timpey Nelson lives in a Very Disorderly way also
the   to the Widow Meanley and her Daughter (Their
Names Unknown) for further Information.

Also we present William Merchant and Hannah Bryant Living
in a Very Disorderly Manner.

```
James Yancey      Plaintiff  )   Debt on an appeal from the
   against                   )   Judgment of a Justice of
William Dalefield  Defendant)   the Peace Judgment according
                                 to note and reversing the
Magistrates Judgment which is Ordered accordingly.
```

```
State So. Carolina      Plaintiff )   Sce fa on Forfeited
   agt                            )   recognizance Judgment
Pharoah Cobb & C Stribling  Defts)   for five pounds ste.
                                      and the costs of both
prosecutions and that the remainder of the recognizance be
remitted.
```

Its Ordered that a Stray mare Taken up by John Jefferies
and Posted before Wm McCullock Esquire be sold according
to Law.

Its Ordered that the accompt brought in by Jno Birdsong
Esquire for Scantling Plank Nails &c. amounting to Forty
three pounds three pence half penny be filed in the Clerks
Office and that the Treasury Pay the same.

```
The State So. Carolina)   Sie. fa. on forfeited recogn.
   against            )   Judgment for five pounds procla-
Sarah & Reuben Ballew )   mation money and cost of the
                          prosecution for bastardy and also
on the recognizance and that Judgment Issue which is
Ordered accordingly.
```

John Bennet is appointed Constable for this County who
came into Open Court and Took the Oathes Prescribed by
Law.

John Thompson   Plaintiff) Came the Parties into Open
   agt.   ) Court by their attorneys &c and
Adam Goudylock   Defendant) then and there agreed to refer
                            all matter of dispute between
them to the arbitration of Zacha. Bullock.

242 John Henderson Esqr. Nicholas Currey and James Kennedy
Gentlemen if they disagree to Chose a fifth Person and their
award to be made the Judgment of this Court, To be arbitrated
at Thomas Cooks on the Sixth of April which is Ordered
accordingly.

Ordered that the Court be adjourned Untill Tomorrow 9
o'clock
Signed by   Joseph McJunkin
                     Hugh Meanes
                     Wm Hendley

At a Court continued and held according to adjournment at
the Court house of Said County on Thursday the 26th day
March. One thousand Seven hundred and eighty nine
Present   Thomas Brandon
                     William McCullock   Esquires
                     Hugh Meanes
                     John Birdsong

Robert Lusk attorney for Ann Robinson   ) Continued until
   against   ) Wednesday in
Joshua Petty Admrs. of Jno. Nuckols Decd) September Court
                                           by consent of
the Parties which is Ordered accordingly.

Isaac Hawkins   Plaintiff) Case Issue Joined and a Jury
   against   ) Sworn Towit Robert Lusk
William Hughes   Defendant) Foreman &c. and the Plaintiff
                            by his attorney Wm. Carnes
Plead the Defendn. Declaration Out of the Jurisdiction of
this Court and Plead a Nonsuit which was granted him
accordingly.

Fincher Exors.   Plaintiff) Trover Issue Joined
   against   ) Came the Plaintiff by Robt
John Thomas   Defendant) Gouldloe Harper his attorney
                            and the Defendant by Jacob
Brown his attorney whereupon Came a Jury Towit. Robert
Lusk foreman Hezekiah Rice Handcock Porter Thomas Young
Moses Guiton Lewis Turner William Steen John Bailey Walter
Roberts James Woodson James Gibbs & John Savage who being
duly Sworn on their Oaths do well and truly try this Issue
Joined do say we find for the Plaintiff Twenty Pounds and
Judgment accordingly.

James Duncan Proved five days as a Witness for Pltf in the
above Case Joseph Evins Proved five days attendance as a
Witness aforesaid and Miliage one hundred and Eighty miles
which sums are ordered to be Taxed in the bill of cost.

Frances Lattimore Plaintiff) Slander
   against   ) Whereupon came a Jury Towit
Robert Bell   Defendant) Robert Lusk foreman
                              Hezekiah Rice Handcock
Porter Thomas Young John Fincher Moses Guiton

Lewis Turner William Steen John Bailey Walter Roberts
James Woodson and James Gibbs who being duly Sworn to will
and truly try this Issue Joined do say on their Oathes we
find for the Plaintiff forty shillings and Judgment
accordingly.   Robt. Lusk F.Man

Frances Latemore)   Harrisson Bell Proved Seven days
    agt.   )   attendance which is 17/6 in this Suit
Robt. Bell   )   which is Ordered to be Taxed in the bill
                       of Costs, On motion of Frances Latimore
Ordered that the Damages that he recovered against Robt Bell
be Given by the Court to the Poor of the County.

Nathan Glenn is Exonerated from any fine or Costs for
non attendance as a Petty Juror.

William & Ann Thompson   Plaintiff)   Attachment
    agt.   )   Ordered that the
Saml. & Daniel Jacksons   Defendant)   Defendants give special
                                        bail immediately or
                                        that a Capias Issue

State So. Carolina   Plaintiff)   Indictment for marking and
    against   )   Disfiguring Horses the
Hezekiah Salman   Defendant)   Defendant is surrendered by
                                   Edward Tillman his bail in
Open Court and Ordered into the Custody of the Sheriff the
said Tillman is therefore discharged of his bail and thereupon came a Jury Towit. Robert Lusk Foreman Hezekiah Rice
Handcock Porter Thomas Young John Fincher Moses Guiton
Lewis Turner William Steen John Bailey Walter Roberts James
Woodson Jnr. and John Martindale who being duly sworn to
well and truly try this indictment who return their verdict
on their Oaths do say we find the Defendant Guilty-and fine
him Eight Pounds Proclamation Money & Costs of Suit.

State So. Carolina   Plaintiff)   Indictment
    against   )   Quashed and Ordered that
James Spray   Defendant)   this suit be dismissed at
                                   the Defendants Costs.

244 Thomas Cook   Plaintiff   )   Attachment
    against   )   Came the Plaintiff into
Alexander Chesney   Defendant)   Open Court in his Own
                                   Proper Person and then and
there dismissed this suit at his Costs which is Ordered
accordingly.

Frances Latemore   Plaintiff)   Ordered that the Plaintiff
    against   )   Pay Adam Goudylock Twenty two
Robert Bell   Defendant)   Shillings and six pence for
                                 nine days attendance for him
in the above suit.

State So Carolina)   Ordered that the Defendant Pay John
    agt.   )   Smith Fifteen Shillings for six days
James Spray   )   attendance also William Smith Seventeen
                     Shillings and Six Pence for Seven days
attendance as witnesses for him in the above Suit which is
Ordered to be Taxed in the bill of Costs.

Ordered that Samuel Bates George Bates Alexander Bates and
Sarah Bates be delivered up Immediately on Demand to
their Mother Margaret Bates.

Ordered that the Court adjourn untill Tomorrow 9 o'clock
Signed by   William Kennedy
                         Thomas Brandon
                         Wm McCullock
                         Bernard Glenn

At a Court Continued and held according to adjournment at
the Court house of said County on Friday the 27th Day of
March one thousand seven hundred and eighty nine.
Present   Zachariah Bullock
                      Thomas Brandon   Esquires
                      William McCullock

Its ordered that Richard Crossbeys ferry be on the same
footing and regularity as other ferrys are in this county
above the fish dam ford on Broad River and the Rates be
given him by the Clerk of this Court.

Its Ordered that Federick Eison furnish the Goal doors
with Good and Sufficient Locks and repair the doors and
that the Treasury of this County Pay the same and Wm. Birdsong to Judge the Value of the work thereof.

245 Ordered that the Overseer of the Road from Smiths ford on
Broad River to this Place that lives on each side of
Thickety Towit Moses Meek and Isaac Parker Collect their
hands and repair the Bridge on Thickety and William McCullock to Inspect the said bridge to see whether it is done in
a workmanlek manner and substantial or not.

A Deed from David Dixon to Joseph McJunkin proved before
a Justice of the Peace and Ordered to be Recorded.

Its Ordered that the Treasury of this County Pay John
DYoung the sum of five shillings for furnishing a lock to
the Goal.

William Steen   Plaintiff) Ordered that the Plaintiff
   agt.   ) William Steen Pay Frances
Adam Goudylock   Defendant) Latemore Twenty Five shillings
                              for ten days attendance as a
Witness for him in the above suit.

John Thompson)   Ordered that the Plaintiff Jno Thompson
   agt.   )   Pay Frances Latimore Twenty Shillings for
Adam Goudylock)   Eight Days attendance as a witness for
                  him in the above suit.

John Steen   Plaintiff)   Ordered that the Plaintiff
   agt.   )   John Steen Pay Frances Latemore
David Stockdon Defendant)   the sum of Four Pounds Ten
                            Shillings for thirty days
attendance as a witness for him in the above suit also Pay
Adam Goudylock Four pounds ten shilliṅgs for thirty days
attendance as a witness for him in the above suit.

Ordered that all Tavern Keepers in this County Sell
Spirituous Liquors at the following rates and no other

Under the Penalty of the Law that may accrue &c. West India
Rum pr Pint 7. Northerd Rum pr ½ Pint 4d. Franch Brand
7d. Holland Ginn pr ½ Pint 7. Wine pr Quart 2/4 Whiskey pr
½ Pint 4d.

Burton & Hopkins   Plaintiff)   Debt
   agt.   )   Came the Defendant by his
Edmond Cradock   Defendant)   attorney William Shaw and
                                   moved for a nonsuit but was
Over ruled, and Richard Mitchell Came into Open Court and
Entered himself Security for the Costs of Suit in behalf of
the Plaintiff and Continued by consent of the Parties
Untill next Court which is ordered accordingly.

246 A Lease and Release from Saffold Executors to Thomas
Wright Proved before a Justice and Ordered to be Recorded.

A Deed of Conveyance from John Foster to Francis Whilchel
Proved before a Justice and Ordered to be Recorded.

A Deed of Conveyance from Joab Mitchell to Susannah
Bullock Proved before a Justice and Ordered to be recorded.

A Deed of Conveyance from Kirkounell Deceased to Zachariah
Bullock Proved before a Justice and Ordered to be recorded.

Braselmin & Co.   Plaintiff)   Dbt. Issue Joined and a Jury
   against   )   Sworn Towit Robert Lusk
Josiah Wood   Defendant)   Foreman Hezekiah Rice Thomas
                                Young Walter Roberts William
Steen David Norman John Fincher Moses Guiton Lewis Turner
John Bailey John Martindale and Archer Kennedy who return
their Verdict on their Oaths do say we find for the Plain-
tiff Twenty three pounds seventeen shillings and Nine
Pence with Interest and Judgment accordingly.
                         Robt. Lusk   foreman

Which said Judgment was Ratifyed by the Court and Ordered
to be Recorded.

A Deed of Conveyance from John Steen and Martha Steen to
John Thompson Proved before a Justice and Ordered to be
recorded.

Thomas Holden   Plaintiff)   Ordered that the plaintiff
   agt.   )   pay Sarah Pearson Seven shillings
Samuel Cooper   Defendant)   and Six Pence for three days
                              attendance as a witness for him
in the above suit.

State So Carolina   Plaintiff)   Indictment for marking and
   against   )   disfiguring horses the
Hezekiah Salmon   Defendant)   Defendant being fined and
                                 not able to Pay his fine
the Court Ordered that he shall stand in the Pillery one hour
and shall receive Twenty five Lashes on his bare back and
then be discharged on Paying of Costs which is ordered
accordingly.

State So Carolina   Plaintiff)
   agt   )   Indictment for
Saml. David & Elizabeth Cooper   Deft)   Rioting Continued

on the same recognizance on paying costs immediately.

State So. Carolina   Plaintiff)   Pettit Larcency Continued
   against   )   also his recognizance
Robert Gibson   Defendant)   Contd. by the Consent of
                                                the Parties.

247 State So Carolina   Plaintiff)   Indictment for marking
   against   )   hogs No Bill being found
Philip Bass & Geo Russel   )   he is therefore dismissed
                   Defendant)   at the defendants costs
                                                which is ordered
                                                accordingly.

State So. Carolina   Plaintiff)   Tresspass assault &
   against   )   Battery Ordered that this
Mill Sumner   Defendant)   Suit be discontinued at
                                                the Defendants Cost.

State So. Carolina   Plaintiff)   Indictment Escape
   against   )   Continued Untill next Court
Richard Burgess   Defendant)   by Consent which is
                                                Ordered accordingly.

Ordered that James Gibbs be overseer of the road from
Wm. Darbys Store to Leonard Smiths and John Lancaster from
there to the County Line Ordered that they keep the same
in Repair according to Law.

Mr. Daniel Meanley is discharged from his presentment of
the Grand Jury on Paying of Costs.

Ordered that Mr. Joseph East be appointed Constable for
this County who came into Open Court and took the Oathes
according to Law in Exor of his said office.

John Motley   Plaintiff)   On Attachment
   against   )   Came the Plaintiff by Wm.
Wm. Cox and Mark Mitchell   )   Carnes his attorney and the
                 Defendant)   Defendant by William Shaw
                                              their attorney Whereupon
Came a Jury Towit Robert Lusk foreman Hezekiah Rice Thomas
Young Walter Roberts William Steen David Norman John Fincher
Moses Guiton Lewis Turner John Bailey John Martindale and
Archer Kennedy who being duly sworn to well and truly try
this Issue Joined return their verdict on their oathes do
say we find for the Plaintiff one hundred dollars with
interest from the first day of October 1784 and Judgment
accordingly.   Robt. Lusk   foreman

Which said Judgment was ratifyed by the Court and Ord. to
be Recorded.

Major John Birdsong Brought in a bill for sixty three pounds
Six shillings and eight pence which the Treasury is
ordered to pay for covering in the Court House which there
is a Bill of Shantlery and Work filed in the Clerks Office.

248 Ordered that the Court House be Painted with YellowOcre
and White Led to be done at the Expence of the County.

A Deed of Conveyance from Thomas Farrow Sheriff of Ninety
Six District to Daniel Brown Esqr. and Cushman Edson for
Six hundred and thirty Eight acres of Land Proved in Open
Court by the Oath of John Haile and Ordered to be recorded.

Ordered that the Court be adjourned untill tomorrow 9
o'clock
Signed by   Thomas Brandon
                   William McCullock
                   John Birdsong

The Worshipful Court of Union Met according to adjournment
at the Court House of Said County on Saturday the 28r. Day
of March One thousand Seven hundred and Eighty Nine
Present   Zachariah Bullock
                   Thomas Blasingame   Esquires
                   John Birdsong

Ordered that Henry Trevilla be Overseer of the Road from
Union Court House to Samuel McJunkins Senr. in the Room of
Isaac Hawkins and that he keep the same in good repair
according to Law with the hand Convt. thereto.

Ordered that Joseph East William Hall & Thos. Blasingame
Constable for this County be Summoned to attend next Court.

Robert Lusk   Plaintiff) Debt on attachment
   against   ) Ordered that a Siefa Issue
John Liles   Defendant) against Richard Speaks of New-
                             berry County to Shew Cause if any
why Judgment should go against him as Garnashee.

Ordered that Bennet Langston be Overseer of the Road from
Blackstocks ford on Tyger River to the County Line and that
he keep the Same in Good repair according to Law.

A Lease and release from Peter Johnston Exors to Benjr.
Crownover acknowledged before a Justice and Ordered to be
Recorded.

William Lee   Plaintiff) Trover
   agt.   ) Came the plaintiff into
Thomas Blasingame Defendant) Open Court and then and there
                             Discontinued this suit at
his Costs which is Ordered accordingly.

249 Peter Knowlander Plaintiff) Trover
     against   ) Came the Plaintiff into Open
    James Gasway   Defendant) Court and then & there
                               Dismissed this suit at his
Costs which is Ordered accordingly.

Shadrack Landtrip Plaintiff) Petn & Summon
   against   ) Came the Plaintiff into
Samuel Farrow   Defendant) Open Court and Dismissed
                               this said Suit at his Costs
which is ordered accordingly.

Thomas Mays   Plaintiff) Fals Imprisonment
   against   ) This Case being refered by an
Charles Burton   Defendant) Order of Court to the deter-
                             mination of William Kennedy

and Edward Good. by the Consent of the Parties and the Said
Arbitrators return their Award Towit that the Defendant
Pay the Plaintiff Two pounds Sterling and costs of suit with
Stay of Execution three months and the Defendant if
required; to give Security and this said Suit to dismissed
according and no further prosecuted which is a Judgment of
this Court and Ordered to be Recorded.

A Mortguage for a negroe from William Clayton to Thomas
Blasingame Esquire Proved in Court by the Oath of Daniel
Brown and Ordered to be Recorded.

Chestnut & Co.   Plaintiff   )   The Plaintiff moved for
   against   )   leave by his attorney Daniel
James Steens Exors Defendant)   Brown to discontinue this
                                   said suit as to Vance and
Wife on Payment of Costs the wife not appearing to be an
Executrix.

John Chestnut & Co. Pltf.) Same motion as above which
   against   ) was granted by the Court
James Steen Exors   Deft.) accordingly.

Ordered that Cold. Thomas Brandon be Sworn in a Certain
Case concerning certain conveyances &c Towit from Walter
Holmes to George Crossley from Crossley to Joseph Jones
& Thomas Young, Whereupon Came Colo. Thomas Brandon into
Open Court and being duly Sworn according to Law doth say
on his Oath, that he seen Conveyances from Walter Holmes
Deceased to George Crossley Deceased for a tract of Land
Containing four hundred and fifty acres on the waters of
Fairforest also seen conveyances from said Crossley to
Joseph Jones for Two hundred acres also Said Crossleys
Conveyance to Thomas Young for one hundred and fifty acres
being the part where John Ewart lived last as the owner.

250 Also a Conveyance, Also Seen said Joseph Jones convey his
Right to Capt. John McCooll and Thomas Young his to Said
Joseph Jones, and believes he seen all the old conveyances
Delvd. to Capt John McCooll, at the time he and his wife
conveyed the said two hundred acres and farther saith not--
taken in open Court.   Thomas Brandon

Ordered that the Sheriff Expose to Public Sale the Old
Court House and give the money to the Treasury of this
County on giving three months Credit.

The Worshipful Court adjourned untill Court in Course.
Signed by   Zacha. Bullock
                     Thomas Brandon
                     Thomas Blasingame
                     John Birdsong

At a Court begun and held in and for the County of Union
at the Court House of said County on Monday the Twenty
Second day of June one thousand seven hundred and eighty
nine
Present   Thomas Brandon
                     Thomas Blasingame   Esquires
                     Charles Sims
                     John Birdsong   Joseph McJunkin
                     Hugh Meanes   Zachariah Bullock

210

Ordered that the Grand Jury be drawn to serve next Court
Towit
Benjamin Holcomb 1. Jos. Palmore Thomas Vance, Alexr.
McDougal, Bird Bluford, Jacob Paulk, James Woodson, Patrick
Shaw, William Young, Zacha. Bell, Joseph Meanes, Robert
Harris, Henry Millhouse, Thomas Young, Avery Breed, William
Gilham, Benjamin Gregory, Daniel Comer Samuel McJunkin,
Robert Lusk.

Ordered that the following Persons be summoned to serve
next Court as Pettit Jurors Towit.
Thomas Weaver, James Harlen, John High, Samuel Woods,
William Nix, Joseph Gault. Joseph Randolph, Richd. Prince,
Thomas Harris, Thomas Allbritten, Nathl Jackson, Jesse
Holcome, Stephen Howard, William Woolbanks, John Smith,
Frances Wood, John Martindale, Daniel White, William Moor-
head, James Gibbs, Robert White, David Norman, John Hill,
John Young, John Addengton, Benjamin Jones, Randolph
Alexander Jeremiah Cain, James Jackson and Jesse Lyle.

251 A Deed from Thomas Shockley and Wife to Jeptha Hollingsworth
proved before a Justice and Ordered to be recorded.

A Deed from Lewis Ledbetter and wife to John Grittenden
proved before a Justice and Ordered to be recorded.

A Deed of Gift from Colo. William Farr to William Steen
Jnr. for one negroe ordered to be recorded.

A Deed from Jedithan Porter to Joseph Hart proved before
a Justice and Ordered to be Recorded.

Ordered that the Treasury of this County Pay Federick Eisin
thirteen shillings for repairing the Goal Door.

On the application of William Rountree Leave is given him
to keep Tavern or Public House in this County on giving
Bond with Daniel Comer and Jeremiah Gregory his security
according to Law.

Ann Tanner (widow) of Lewis Tanner Deceased applied for
Letters of Administration on the Estate of the Said
Lewis Tanner Deceased to Shew Cause Gohy Letters of
Administration Should not be Granted unto her on the
Said Deed Estate.

A Deed of Conveyance from Aaron Fincher and wife and
William Morgan and Wife to Esther Insco for three hundred
acres of Land. Proved before a Justice and Ordered to be
Recorded.

Delilah Langstone and Levinah Langston Minor of the age of
thirteen and the other Eleven years of age daughters of
John Langstone Deceased came into Open Court and Petitioned
that a Guardian might be appointed for them, and nominated
William Bennet their Step-father Whereupon the Court doth
appoint the said William Bennit Guardian over the Persons
and Estates of the said Delelah and Levenah Langston until
they attain the age of Eighteen years the said William
Bennit giving bond & Security in the sum of two hundred
pounds sterling for the faithful discharge of his duty.

The Court Proceeded to the Election of a Sheriff by Ballot When Colo. William Farr was unanimously Elected for the ensuing two years.

Ordered that the Clerk do Deliver to Colo. William Farr a Certificate of his being Elected Sheriff for the County of Union for the Ensuing Two years to be delivered to his Excellency the governor for the purpose of obtaining a Commission.

252 The Court Ordered that the appearnace Docket to be Called for the first time, which was done accordingly.

Ordered that a Road be laid out from the Waggon Road on Ned Neals Bigg Creek to or near the Ninety six Road where it intersects the Charleston Road, and James Thomas and Colo. William Farr is appointed to lay out the same and the overseer is ordered to work on the same with the hands convenient thereto immediately.

On the Application of John Watson Junr. Leave is Given him to retail Spirituous Liquors on Giving Bond with David Chisholm his Security according to Law.

John Foster   Plaintiff)   Slander
  against   )   Came the Parties into Open
Henry Holcomb Defendant)   Court and then and there dis-
                                missed this Said Suit at Equal
Costs which is ordered accordingly.

Richmond & Sarah Terrell Pltf)   Came the Plaintiff into
  against   )   Open Court and then and
Absalom Petty   Defendant)   there dismissed this Suit
                                   at their costs which is
Ordered accordingly.

Daniel White   Plaintiff)   Attachment
  against   )   Came the Parties into Open
Daniel Howell Defendant)   Court by their attorneys and
                              then and there agreed to discon-
tinue this said suit at the Defendants cost which is
Ordered accordingly.

Adam Thompson   Plaintiff)   Came the Plaintiff into Open
  against   )   Court and then and there
Barlet Whorton Defendant)   Discontinued this Suit at his
                              Costs which is Ordered to be
                              Recorded

David Hopkins Plaintiff)   Attachment
  against   )   Ordered that this case be
Daniel McKee   Defendant)   discontinued at the Plaintiffs
                             Costs.

John Steen   Plaintiff)   Attachment
  against   )   Came the Parties into Open Court
David Stockdon Defendant)   by their attorneys and then and
                              there agreed to Continue this
Suit over untill next Court.

212

John Steen   Plaintiff)   Continued by Consent of the
    against   )   Parties untill next Court Which
Joshua Petty   Defendant)   is Ordered accordingly.

John Steen   Plaintiff)   Continued until next Court by
    against   )   Consent of the Parties.
Joshua Petty   Defendant)

Robert Lusk   Plaintiff)   Continued untill next Court by
    against   )   Consent of the Parties.
Joshua Petty   Defendant)

William Steen   Plaintiff)   Continued untill next Court
    against   )   by the Consent of the Parties.
Adam Goudylock   Defendant)

Robert Montgomery Plaintiff)   Came the Plaintiff into
    against   )   Open Court and then and there
John Meanes   Defendant)   discontinued this said suit
                                 at his costs which is ordered
by the Court accordingly.

Archer Smith   Plaintiff)   Came the Plaintiff into Open
    against   )   Court in his Own Proper Person
Daniel Plummer Defendant)   and then and there discontinued
                             this Suit at his Costs which is
Ordered accordingly.

Thomas Brandon   Plaintiff) Attachment
    against   )   Came the Defendant into Open
George Goodwin   Defendant)   Court by his attorney and the
                              Plaintiff being solemnly called
came not to prosecute his said suit, whereupon a nonsuit
is awarded the defendant and that he recover the sum of five
shillings for his damages and costs of suit which is
ordered accordingly.

Humphrey Bates   )   Continued untill next Court
    vs   )   by the consent of the Parties.
Joseph Bates   Defendant)

Thomas Blasingame Plaintiff)   Came the Plaintiff into
    against   )   Open Court by his attorney
Reuben Ballew   Defendant)   and then and there Discon-
                                 tinued this Said Suit at his
Costs which is ordered accordingly.

Hugh Quinn   Plaintiff)   Came the Plaintiff into Open
    against   )   Court and then and there discon-
Abraham Floyd   Defendant)   tinued this said suit at the
                             plaintiffs costs.

Jeremiah Dyal   Plaintiff)   Came the Plaintiff into Open
    against   )   Court and then and there
John Little   Defendant)   discontinued this suit at his
                             costs which is ordered
                             accordingly.

A Deed of Conveyance from Andrew Jones to John Thompson for
one hundred and Fifty acres of Land proved before a Justice
and Ordered to be recorded.

A Deed of Conveyance from John Montgomery to John Malone
for one hundred and Twelve acres of Land proved before
a Justice and Ordered to be recorded.

A Deed of Conveyance from William Merchant and Wife to
George Harlan proved before a Justice and Ordered to be
recorded.

Chesnut & Company   Plaintiff)   Debt
   against   )   Came the Defendant into
Steens Executors   Defendant)   Open Court by his attorney
                                   James Dohertee Esquire and
the Plaintiff being Solemnly called came not to prosecute
his said suit. Whereupon a nonsuit is awarded the Defendant
against the Plaintiff and further considered by the Court
that the Defendnat recover five shillings damage and costs
of suit, which is ordered accordingly.

Chesnut & Company   Plaintiff)   Debt
   against   )   Came the defendant into
Steens Executors   Defendant)   Open Court by James Doherty
                                   his attorney and the
Defendant being Solemnly called came not to prosecute their
said suit whereupon a nonsuit is awarded the Defendant
against the Plaintiff and further considered by the Court
that the Defendant recover the sum of five shillings for his
damages and costs of suit and the same ordered accordingly.

Jordon Jackson   Plaintiff)   Slander
   against   )   Came the Plaintiff into Open
Edward Goode   Defendant)   Court in his own Proper Person
                                and the Defendant by James
Doherty his attorney, and then and there agreed to dismiss
this suit at the Defendant costs which is ordered
accordingly.

Jordon Jackson   Plaintiff)   Slander
   against   )   Came the Plaintiff in his
Edward Goode   Defendant)   Own Proper Person and the
                                Defendant by James Dohertee his
attorney and then and there dismissed his suit at the
Defendants cost which is ordered accordingly.

255 John McCooll   Plaintiff)   Case
      against   )   Came the Defendant into
    Gabriel Brown & Farr   )   Open Court and Confessed a
                      Defendant)   Judgment according to
                                   Specialty.

Edson & Company   Plaintiff)   Debt
   agt.   )   Came the Defendant Davis
Carlile & David Goudylock   )   Goudylock into Open Court
                  Defendant)   and then and there agreed
                               he owed unto the Plaintiff
the Sum of Fourteen pounds six shillings and eleven pence
Sterling and confessed a Judgment for the Same with Interest
and Costs of Suit which is ordered accordingly.

A Deed of Conveyance from John Nicool and James Vernon to
William Wofford for two hundred acres of Land proved before
a Justice and Ordered to be Recorded.

214

A Bill of Sale from William Merchant and Wife to George Harling for one bay mare and Colt. one feather bed and Furniture three Cows & Two Calfs two yearlings and Twelve head of Hogs and Ordered to be Recorded.

Its ordered that the two sheep that Archibald Kennedy Posted before Thomas Blasingame be sold according to Law at his own house on giving three months credit.

Thomas Brandon	Plaintiff)	Ordered that the Defendant
against	)	Pay Edward Pucket Ten Shillings
Geo. Goodwin	Defendant)	for four days attendance as a Witness for him in the above suit.

Its Ordered that the Sheriff Expose to sale a stray grey Horse posted before Thomas Blasingame by John Goore Immediately according to Law.

Thomas Brandon	Plaintiff)	Ordered that the Defendant
against	)	Pay Alexander McDougal Fifty
George Goodwin	Defendant)	Shillings for Twenty days attendance as a witness for him

in the above suit.

Thomas Blasingame Esqr. high Sheriff of this County Nominated and appointed Samuel Simpson his Deputy in and for the County of Union who met with the Concurrance and approbation of the Court, Ordered by the Court that he take the Oath prescribed by Law. Whereupon he took the oath accordingly in the Execution of his said office and is thereupon admitted as Deputy Sheriff as aforesaid

256 John McCooll   Plaintiff)   Debt
      against   )   Whereupon came a Jury Towit
   Gabriel Brown & Farr   )   Spelsby Glenn Foreman
                  Defendant)   Charles Thompson Jonathan
                           Norman Isaac Hawkins Hugh
Nelson William Martindale Edward Tillman Aaron Fincher
James Wray William Coleman Robert Goode & William Oates
who being duly sworn to well and truly try this Issue
Joined.   On their oathes do say we find for the Plaintiff
two dollars pr hundred Weight of Tobacco. With interest
and costs of suit.   Spilsby Glenn Foreman
Which said Judgment was Ratifyed by the Court and Ordered
to be Recorded.

A Deed of Conveyance from Alexander Hamilton & wife to William Hendley proved before a Justice & Ordered to be Recorded.

A Deed of Conveyance from Alexander Hammelton & wife to William Hendley Proved before a Justice & Ordered to be Recorded.

A Deed of Conveyance from Turner Kendrick to John Gee Proved before a Justice and Ordered to be Recorded.

A Deed of Conveyance from Samuel Scotcher to Joseph McJunkin Proved before a Justice and Ordered to be Recorded.

Thomas Brandon   Plaintiff)   Ordered that the Defendant
    against   )   Pay Josiah Goodwin Twenty five
George Goodwin   Defendant)   Shillings for Ten days
                             attendance as a witness for
him in the above Case.

James Minnis   Plaintiff)   Continued untill next Court
    against   )   by the Consent of the Parties
Gabriel Brown   Defendant)   until next Court.

Thomas Brandon   Plaintiff)   Ptr. & Summons
    against   )   Came the Parties into Open
James Davis   Defendant)   Court and then and there agreed
                             to Put themselves upon a Judg-
ment without a Jury, Whereupon it is Considered by the
Court that the Plaintiff recover against the Deft. the Sum
of Five Pounds and costs of suit, which is ordered
accordingly.

Thomas Brandon   Plaintiff)   Petr. & Sumr.
    against   )   Came the Parties into Open
James Davis   Defendant)   Court and then and there
                             agree to put themselves upon
the Judgment without a Jury. Whereupon it is considered
by the Court that the Plaintiff recover against the
Defendant the sum of Ten Pounds and costs of suit which
is Ordered accordingly.

257 Thomas Brandon   Plaintiff)   Ordered that Thomas Brandon
    against   )   Pay Thomas Crossby Fifteen
James Davis   Defendant)   Shillings for Six days
                             attendance for him in the
above suit.

Aaron Fincher and John Martindale is Exonerated from
their recognizance from Last Court for Forty Pounds on
Paying five Pounds next Court and five Pounds the Court
afterwards & the Same Ordered accordingly.

Ordered that the Court adjourn untill tomorrow 9 o'clock
Signed by   Thomas Brandon
                     Thomas Blasingame
                     Charles Sims

At a Court continued and held according to adjournment at
the Court House of said County on Thursday the Twenty third
day of June One thousand Seven hundred and Eighty nine
Present   Thomas Brandon
               Charles Sims
               Thomas Blasingame   Esquires
               William Hendley
               William Kennedy

A Deed of Conveyance from James Oliphant to John Faucherade
Grimkie for Seven hundred and Fifty acres of Land proved
before a Justice and ordered to be recorded.

A Deed of Conveyance from John McCooll and wife to John
McKibbin acknowledged in Open Court & Ordered to be Recorded.

Robt. Henry Hughes Plaintiff)   Attachment
  against   )   This suit being referred
Jesse Dodd   Defendant)   to Thomas Greer John Martin-
                                dale & Moses Haynes by an
Order of Court, which said arbitrators return their award to
Wit, we do adjudge to the Plaintiff Twenty Pounds Nine
Shillings and Ten Pence Sterling with Costs of Suit, it being
the Ballance of the note to us Delivered and also that the
Plaintiff give the Defendant credit for a certain Waggon sold
by the aforesaid Defendant to Robert Skelton when the Value
of her is assertained by men Chosen for that purpose which
is a Judgment of the Court hereof.

A Deed of Conveyance from John Blasingame Sheriff to George
McWhorter acknowledged in Open Court and Ordered to be
Recorded.

258 Ordered that the Clerks Office be Set fronting the Court
House with the Front Side of said Office in a line with
the back of Samuel Cargoes House and the end with a line
with the Court House.

Ordered that the Plats of the Lots sold out at Union Court
House be drawn a new by the Clerk and recorded in his
Office and that Thomas Brandon Charles Sims and John Birdsong be Commissions to keep the said Town in good regulation
and all streets to be Open and clean agreeable to the Platt
of Said Town, to be known for the future by the Name of
brandonburgh.

Charles Miles   Plaintiff)   Petr.
  against   )   Came the Plaintiff into Open
James Lindsey   Defendant)   Court and Convessed a Judgment
                              for the sum of Four Pounds
Four Shillings and Two Pence and costs of Suit which is
ordered accordingly.

State South Carolina)   Ordered that the fine Inflicted upon
  vs   )   the Defendants be Paid unto John
Cobb & Stribling   )   Haile Clerk as Part of his Extra
                        fees by the County Treasury

A Deed of Conveyance from Henry Long to Ann Robinson
acknowledged in Open Court by the Said Long to the Said
Robinson & Ordered to be Recorded.

John Cambell)   Case
  against   )   Came the Parties into Open Court and
William Young)   then and there agreed to leave all matter
                  of Controversey between them to the
Arbitration of Cold. Thomas Brandon Majr. Otterson and
Andrew Torrence and their award to be the Judgment of this
Court.

Its Ordered that all the Justices in this County be Called
Upon to Settle with the County Treasury and Pay in all the
Money if any they have by the Second Saturday in July.

A Deed of Conveyance from Daniel Jackson to John High
Proved before a Justice & Ordered to be Recorded.

A Deed of Conveyance from Daniel Jackson to John Malone
Proved before a Justice and Ordered to be Recorded.

A Deed of Conveyance from Isaac Haze to William Jackson
Proved before a Justice and Ordered to be recorded.

A Lease and release from the Commissioners of Forfeited
Estates to Daniel Jackson Proved before a Justice and
Ordered to be Recorded.

259 Ordered that the Deposition of Jane Jenkins be recorded
which was Taken before a Justice of the Peace.

Ordered that the Rates be abolished relative to Brand Wines
Ginn & West India Rum which was laid March Term 1789 and the
old Former Rates be Established.

Thomas Holden   Plaintiff)   Continued untill next Court
  against   )   by the Consent of the Parties &
Samuel Cooper   Defendant)   assent of the Court.

Ordered that the fine inflicted on Samuel Little by Thomas
Blasingame Esquire be remitted one half of said fine

Ordered that the Court adjourn untill Court in Course
Signed by   Thomas Blasingame
                   Charles Sims
                   William Kennedy

At a Court begun and held in and for the County of Union
at the Court House of Said County on Monday the Twenty
eighth day of September One thousand seven hundred and
eighty nine:
Present   Thomas Brandon
                 Thomas Blasingame
                 Joseph McJunkin   Esquires
                 Charles Sims
                 William Hendley

The Court Proceeded to draw the Pettit Jury which the
Sheriff is Ordered to Summon to serve next Court Towit.
Frances Fincher, Charles Thompson, William Wright, Jacob
Haild Abel landrick Jesse Pots Abner Pots Ephraim Wilburn
Amos Cook, Richard Minton Amos Hawkins Tulley Davitt Charles
Kelley, James Callwell, William Woolbanks Senr. John
Davidson, Caleb Langston, Malen Pearson Thomas Davis William
Gilkie John Link, John Lancaster, William Edward, Palser
Hugman Robert Wadkins Samuel Cooper Absalom Petty, William
Bogan Thomas Wright & John Prince.

A Deed of Conveyance from Nicholas Lazerous to Jonathan
Peek Proved before a Justice and Ordered to be recorded.

A Deed of Conveyance from John McCooll to William
Goldsmith, Proved before a Justice and Ordered to be
recorded.

260 A Bond from Isaac Edmondson to Caleb Edmondson Proved
before a Justice and Ordered to be recorded.

A Deed from Isaac Edmondson to John Cambell Proved before
a Justice and Ordered to be recorded.

The Last Will and Testament of James Prince Proved in Open
Court by the Oath of Elijah Harrisson Cooper and Ordered
to be recorded.

A Deed of Conveyance from William Smith to Isaac Cook
acknowledged in Open Court and Ordered to be Recorded.

William Parker   Plaintiff)   Attachment
  against   )   Nehemiah Howard being Summoned
Geo Lumkins   Defendant)   as a Garnashee in the above
                              suit who was duly sworn and his
Deposition Filed.

On the Application of Cushman R Edson Leave is Givin him
to retail Spiritous Liquours or Keep Public House on his
Giving Bond with John Blasingame his Security according
to Law for his Lawful Performance.

A Deed from Archibald Howard to John Putman acknowledged
in Open Court by the Said Howard to the said Putman and
Ordered to be Recorded.

261 A Deed from William Comer to John Comer acknowledged in
Open Court and Ordered to be Recorded.

On the application of Ephraim Ramsey Esquire, Leave is
Given him to plead the law in this Court, upon his producing his Commission at our next Court from the Honble.
the associate Judges of this State.

A Deed of Conveyance from Merry McGuire to Charles Brock
Proved before a Justice and Ordered to be Recorded.

Ordered that all the Estrays which are liable for sale be
sold according to Law at Public Auction.

A Deed of Conveyance from John Birdsong Esquire to Elisha
Greer acknowledged in Open Court and Ordered to be
Recorded.

The Worshipful Justices of this County Towit. Thomas Brandon
John Henderson Charles Sims William Kennedy William
McCullock Hugh Meanes, Joseph McJunkin Thomas Blasingame
and John Birdsong Esquires Took the Oath agreeable to the
Sixth Article of the Constitution of this State, in the
Support thereof.

The Grand Jury, Sworn to Serve this Term, Towit, Samuel
McJunkin Alexander McDougal, James Woodson Zachariah Bell,
Henry Millhouse Joshua Palmore Patrick Shaw Joseph Meanes
Thomas Young Thomas Vance Jacob Paulk William Young Robert
Harris Avory Breed and Daniel Comer.

John Cambell   Plaintiff)   Case
  against   )   We the Under Written Person
William Young Defendant)   having been Chosen to Arbitrate
                            this case indifferantly, which
appears by an former order made by this Court, and having
heard the Evidences on both sides, Unanimously agree that
the Defendant Pay the Sum of Seven Pounds Sixteen Shillings
and Six Pence to be discharged within three months with
Cattle Sheep or Wheat to the Plaintiff with Costs of Suit,

219

Given under our hands this first day of August One
thousand Seven hundred & Eighty Nine.
Signed   Thomas Brandon
              Samuel Otterson   Arbitrators
              Thomas Blasingame
              Andrew Torrence

262 A Deed of Conveyance from John Beckham and wife to Moses
Wright Proved before a Justice and Ordered to be recorded.

A Deed of Conveyance from Thomas Wright and Wife to Geo.
Taylor Proved before a Justice and Ordered to be Recorded.

Ordered that the Appearnace Docket be Called for the first
Time which was done accordingly.

A Lease and Release from Moses Winters to Jonas Little
Proved before a Justice and Ordered to be Recorded.

A Deed of Conveyance from Robert Greer to Rebecca Greer
acknowledged in Open Court and Ordered to be Recorded.

A Deed of Conveyance from Robert Lusk to John Hope Proved
before a Justice and Ordered to be Recorded.

John Moore   Plaintiff)   Came the Plaintiff into Open Court
   against   )   and then and there Dismissed this
Isaac Parker Defendant)   Suit at his Costs which is
                            Ordered accordingly.

Holbrook & Uxor. Plaintiff) Slander
   against   )   Came the Defendants by William
Woodson & Gisst. Defendant) Shaw Esquire their attorney &
                              the Plaintiff being Solemnly
called came not to prosecute his said, Whereupon the Court
awarded a nonsuit against the Plaintiff and that the Defendant recover the sum of five shillings damages and costs
of suit, and the same ordered accordingly.

John Williams   Plaintiff)   Debt
   against   )   Came the Defendant into Open
Holland Sumner   Defendant)   Court by his attorney Geo
                              Walker Esquire and the Plaintiff
being Solemnly called came not to Prosecute his Said Suit.
Whereupon a nonsuit is awarded the Defendant against the
Plaintiff and that he recover the sum of five shillings
damage and costs of suit, and the same Ordered accordingly.

A Deed of Conveyance from John Little to Ingrim-
acknowledged in Open Court and Ordered to be Recorded.

A Deed of Conveyance from Thomas Harris to Joseph Harris
acknowledged in Open Court & Ordered to be recorded.

A Deed of Conveyance from John Neederman to John
Martindale acknowledged in Open Court and Ordered to be
263 recorded

John Gregory   Plaintiff)   Attachment
   against   )   Came the Defendant into Open
John Steen   Defendant)   Court by his attorney &c and
                             the Plaintiff being solemnly

220

called came not to Prosecute his Said Suit, whereupon a
nonsuit is awarded the Defendant against the Plaintiff, and
that he recover the sum of five shillings for his damages
& Costs of Suit & the same is ordered accordingly.

William White   Admr Plaintiff)   Debt
  against   )   Came the Defendants into
Beozan & McWhortor Defendant)   Open Court by their
                                  attorney and the Plaintiff
being Solemnly called came not to prosecute his said suit
whereupon the Court awarded a nonsuit against him and that
the Defendants recover the sum of five shillings damage
and costs of suit, & the Same Ord. accordingly.

A Deed of Conveyance from John Martindale to John Nederman
acknowledged in Open Court & Ordered to be recorded.

Nathaniel Davis   Plaintiff)   Debt
  against   )   The Parties came into open
Samuel Osten   Defendant)   Court and then and there agreed
                                to Settle this suit at the
Defendants cost which is ordered by the Court accordingly.

William Philpeck   Plaintiff)   The Parties came into Open
  against   )   Court and then and there
Nicholas Tessincer Defendant)   settled this suit at the
                                 Plaintiffs Cost which is
Ordered accordingly.

Graaff & Company   Plaintiff)   Debt
  against   )   By Consent of the Parties
Thomas Bishop   Defendant)   Ordered that this Suit be
                                dismissed at the Defendants
                                Cost.

William Pattern   Plaintiff)   Ordered that his suit be
  against   )   dismissed at the Defendants
Ford & Little   Defendant)   Cost.

Bernard Glenn Esqr. Took the Oath agreeable to the
Sixth Article of the Federal Constitution in Support
thereof.

Speaks & Montgomery)   Came the Defendant into Open Court
  against   )   by his attorney and the Plaintiff
John Bird   )   being solemnly called but failed to
                        appear to prosecute their suit.
Ordered that they be nonsuited and the defendant recover
five shillings damage and costs of suit.

264 William Farr Esquire having been heretofore appointed
Sheriff for this County Produced his Commission from Under
the hand of his Excellencey the Governor and came into
and took the Oath of Office accordingly.

Mr. Andrew Torrence being appointed Under Sheriff by the
High Sheriff and the Court approving of him as such, he
came into Court and Took the Oath of Office accordingly.

Thomas Blasingame Junr. being appointed Deputy Sheriff by
the High Sheriff and the Court approved of him as such he
came into Open court and took the Office accordingly.

Drewry Gowing   Plaintiff)   Came the Defendant into Open
  against   )   Court by his attorney and the
William Johnstone   Defendant)   Plaintiff being Solemnly
                                   called but came not to pro-
secute his Suit ordered that he be Nonsuited and that
defendant recover the sum of five shillings for his damage
and costs of suit.

Jesse Dodd   Plaintiff   )   Ordered that his suit be
  against   )   Dismissed at the Plaintiffs
Isaac Edmondson Defendant)   Costs

Augustin Wood   Plaintiff)   Ordered that this suit be
  against   )   dismissed at the Defendants
Joshua Scisson   Defendant)   costs.

Lease and Release from William Cunningham to John Bird
Proved before a Justice and Ordered to be Recorded.

William Kennedy   Plaintiff)   Debt P & S
  against   )   Ordered that Judgment be
Gabriel Brown   Defendant)   entered against the Defendant

William Kennedy   Plaintiff)   Petn. & Sums
  against   )   Ordered that Judgment be
William Scisson   Defendant)   entered against the Defendant
                                  agreeable to Specialty and
Costs of Suit.

Nicholas Lazerous   Plaintiff)   Ordered that this suit be
  against   )   dismissed at the Defendants
Luke Carrell   Defendant)   Costs

Henry Holcome   Plaintiff)   The Defendant being dead
  against   )   Ordered that Suit abate.
Samuel Austin   Defendant)

William Kennedy Plaintiff)   Debt
  against   )   Came the Defendant into Open
Danl. & Saml. Jackson   )   Court and then and there
                 Defendant)   confessed a Judgment agreeable
                              to Specialty with Stay of
Execution three months which is Ordered accordingly.

265 Thomas Crosby Plaintiff)   Petr. & Sums.
  against   )   Came the Plaintiff by his
Robert Leverett Defendant)   attorney and the Defendant
                              being Solemnly called but
failed to appear to prosecute his suit, Ordered that
Judgment by default be entered against him which was done
accordingly.

John Blasingame   Plaintiff   )   Came the Defendant
  against   )   into Open Court and
Daniel & Thos. Jacksons Defendant)   then and there con-
                                       fessed a Judgment
agreeable to Specialty which is Ordered accordingly.

Thomas Crosbey   Plaintiff)   Ordered that Judgment be
  against   )   intered up against the
Robert Leverett   Defendant)   Defendant for the sum of

222

Eight Pounds with Interest from the 17th December 1786
and costs of Suit. Condemned in the hands of James Jenkins
Garnashee.

Philip Anderson Proved One days attendance in the above
suit for the Plaintiff.

A Deed of Conveyance from John Blasingame Sheriff of Union
County to Obadiah Olliphant. Proved in Open Court by the
Oath of John George Rainer and Ordered to be Recorded.

A Deed of Conveyance from William Newman to John Stokes
Proved before a Justice and Ordered to be Recorded.

John Haild was Chosen by the Court as Guardian for Elizabeth
White Orphan and he gave bond according to Law, with Aaron
Fincher his Security.

Ann Tanner applied for Letters of Administration on the
Estate of Lewis Tanner deceased, which was granted her and
she gave bond with Adam Thompson and Charles Herrington her
Securities.

Ordered that Joshua Petty Moses Waters James Henderson and
Zachariah Bullock Esquire appraise the Estate of Lewis
Tanner Deceased.

A Deed of Gift from George Goodwin to Josiah and John
Goodwin Proved before a Justice and Ordered to be recorded.

Ordered that the Court adjourn untill Tomorrow 10 o'clock.
Signed by   John Henderson
                     Wm. Kennedy
                     Thomas Blasingame

At a Court continued and held according to adjournment at
the Court House of Said County the Twenty Ninth day of
September One thousand Seven hundred and Eighty Nine.
Present   John Henderson
                     Charles Sims
                     William Kennedy   Esquires
                     Hugh Means

266 A Lease and Release from Wm McCullock and Wife to Nathaniel
    Guiton Proved before a Justice and Ordered to be recorded.

A Deed from Charles Herrington and Wife to Robert Rutherford
Also One other Charles Herrington and wife to Robert
Rutherford both proved before a Justice and Ordered to be
Recorded.

Humphrey Bates   Plaintiff) Debt
   against   ) Ordered that this Suit be
Charles Sims   Defendant) dismissed at the Plaintiffs
                              Cost.

A Bill of Sale from Nathaniel Jefferies and John Steen to
John Trimmier Proved in Open Court by the Oath of John
Haile and Ordered to be Recorded.

A Bill of Sale from Benjr. Clark to John Haile acknowledged
before a Justice and Ordered to be recorded.

                     223

The Grand Jury for the Inquest of the body of this County
Towit Samuel McJunkin Foreman Alexander McDougal James
Woodson Zachariah Bell Henrey Millhouse Patrick Shaw Joseph
Meanes Thomas Young Thomas Vance Jacob Paulk William Young
Robert Harris and Aovory [sic] Breed who being duly Sworn
and having received their Charge and Withdrew.

Benajah Thompson   Plaintiff)   Tresspass
  against   )   Ordered that this suit be
Andrew Gossett   Defendant)   dismissed at the Plaintiffs
                                  Costs.

John Steen   Plaintiff)   Debt on attachment
  against   )   By Consent of the Parties Ordered
David Stockdon Defendant)   that this suit be continued
                              untill next Court.

John Steen   )   Debt
  against   )   Came the Defendant by his
Joshua Petty Administrator)   attorney and the Plaintiff
of John Nuckols Deceased)   being solemnly called but
                                failed to appear to prosecute
his suit. Ordered by the Court that he be nonsuited and that
the Defendant recover the sum of five shillings damage and
costs of suit.

John Steen   Plaintiff)   Case
  against   )   Came the Defendant into Open
Joshua Petty Admr.   )   Court and the Plaintiff being
          Defendant)   Solemnly called but failed to
                            appear. Ordered that he be non-
suited and that the Defendant recover the sum of five
shillings damage and costs of suit.

A Power of attorney from Ann Robinson to Robert Lusk Proved
in Open Court and Ordered to be Recorded.

Robert Lusk Plaintiff   )   Laid over by consent of the
  against   )   Parties untill tomorrow
Joshua Petty admr. Defendant)   12 o'clock.
of Jno. Nuckols decd.

267 John McCooll   Plaintiff)   Atta.
  against   )   Ordered that this suit be
Robert Montgomery Defendant)   dismissed at the Plaintiffs
                                   Cost.

Samuel Jackson   Plaintiff)   Debt on attachment
  against   )   This suit being refered and
William Jackson   Defendant)   the Arbitrators failed to meet
                                and the rule extended.

Ordered that William Kennedy Esquire Swear the appraisers
of the Estate of William Greer deceased and that Letters
of administration be Granted unto Rebecca Greer who enters
into bond with Thomas Vance and Robert Greer her Security
according to Law.

Stephen White Plaintiff)   Debt on attachment
  against   )   By Consent of the Parties.
Mark Jackson Defendant)   Ordered that this suit be dis-
                           missed at equal costs.

224

Robert Gregory   Plaintiff)   Debt on attachment
    against   )   Ordered that this suit be
Thomas Holden   Defendant)   dismissed at the Plaintiffs
                              Cost.

James Minnis   Plaintiff)   Debt
    against   )   Came the Defendant into Open
Gabriel Brown   Defendant)   Court and Confessed a Judgment
                             according to Note and costs of
suit which is Ordered accordingly.

Ordered that James Minnis Pay John Roney Fifty Shillings for
Twenty days attendance as a witness for him against Brown
also the Sum of Thirty Shillings for Miliage. ordered that
James Minnis Pay Nathan Jaggers Forty Shillings for his
attendance as a witness for him against Brown also the sum
of Thirty Shillings for miliage.

David Stockdon)   Case
    against   )   Came the Defendant into Open Court by his
John Steen   )   attorney and the Plaintiff being Solemnly
                    called but failed to appear. Ordered
that he be Nonsuited and that the Defendant recover the sum
of Five Shillings damage and costs of suit.

Gabriel Brown   Plaintiff)   Debt
    against   )   By Consent of the Parties
Thomas Biddey   Defendant)   Ordered that this Suit be
                             Continued untill next Court.

John Thompson   )   Slander
    against   )   Laid over untill tomorrow morning by
Adam Goudylock)   Consent of the Parties.

Jesse Dodd   Plaintiff)   Attachment
    against   )   Continued untill next Court by
Robert Skelton Defendant)   Consent of the Parties.

268 C R Edson & Co.   Plaintiff)   Debt on attachment
      against   )   Ordered that this Suit be
    Thomas Taylor   Defendant)   dismissed at the Plaintiffs
                                 Cost

Humphrey Bates   Plaintiff)   Debt on attachment
    against   )   Ordered that the Land attached
Joseph Bates   Defendant)   be sold by the Sheriff accord-
                             ing to Law to Satisfy the
                             Debt and Costs.

Mark Mitchell   Plaintiff)   Debt
    against   )   Judgment Confessed according to
Benj. Long &   )   Installment on the Defendants
Jesse Maberry   Defendant)   Complying therewith

John Moore   Plaintiff)   Ordered that this Suit be
    against   )   dismissed at the Plaintiffs cost
Isaac Parker   Defendant)

Jonathan Gilbert   Plaintiff)   Case
    against   )   Came the Defendant into
Walter Roberts   Defendant)   Open Court by his attorney
                               and the Plaintiff being

225

Solemnly Called but failed to appear to prosecute his Suit.
Ordered that he be Nonsuited and that the Defendant recover
the Sum of Five shillings damage and costs of suit.

William Farr   Plaintiff)   Tresspass assault and battery
  against   )   Ordered that this suit be
Duncan McCrevin   Defendant)   dismissed at the Defendants
                               Cost.

Geo. & John Parks   Plaintiff)   Ordered that this Suit be
  against   )   discontinued at the Plain-
Daniel Jackson   Defendant)   tiffs costs

Kirkland & Co.   Plaintiff)   Came the Defendant by his
  against   )   attorney and the Plaintiff
John Inlow   Defendant)   being solemnly called but failed
                               to prosecute his suit. Ordered
that they be nonsuited and that the Defendant recover the
Sum of five shillings for his damage and costs of suit.

George Ross   Plaintiff)   Debt
  against   )   Continued untill next Court by
Caleb Gasway   Defendant)   consent of the Parties.

David Hopkins   Plaintiff)   Debt on attachment
  against   )   Ordered that this suit be
Thomas Taylor   Defendant)   dismissed at the Plaintiffs
                              Cost

269 Kirkland & Co.   Plaintiff)   Petition & Summons
      against   )   Came the Defendant into Open
    John Mullins   Defendant)   Court by his attorney and the
                                   Plaintiff being Solemnly called
but came not to Prosecute his Suit Ordered that he be
nonsuited and that the Defendant recover the sum of five
shillings damage and costs of suit.

Evins Winn & Company   Plaintiff)   Came the Defendant into
  against   )   Open Court and the
Warren Hall   Defendant)   Plaintiff being Solemnly
                                     Called but failed to
appear to prosecute his suit. Ordered that he be nonsuited
and that the defendnat recover the sum of five shillings
damage and costs of suit.

Samuel Cathcart   Plaintiff)   Petition & Summon
  against   )   Ordered that this Suit be
Duncan McCrevin   Defendant)   Dismissed and the Defendant
                                Pay the Clerks Fee.

The State So Carolina   Plaintiff)   Larcency
  against   )   The Grand Jury returned
Whitager Shadforth   Defendant)   a True Bill and ordered
                                      that the Defendant
be in Custody who gave Security according to Law.

Daniel Jackson   Plaintiff)   By Consent of the Parties this
  against   )   Suit is refered to the
William Jackson   Defendant)   Arbitration of John
                               Blasingame and Thomas
Blasingame with the Power of Umpiage their award to be the
Judgment of this Court which is Ordered accordingly.

Jonathan Gilkie   Plaintiff)   Came the Plaintiff into Open
   against   )   Court by his attorney and the
John Turner   Defendant)   Defendant being Solemnly
                                called but failed to appear
to prosecute his suit. Judgment by Default is awarded the
Plaintiff and is hereby entered.

Kirkland & Co.   Plaintiff)   Ordered that this Suit be
   against   )   dismissed at the Plaintiffs
James Sims   Defendant)   Cost.

Stockdon   )   Ordered that the Plaintiff pay Littleton,
   against)   Mass Five Shillings as a Witness for him in
Steen   )   this suit also the Sum of Eight Shillings
                and Four Pence for Mileage.

Minor Winn   Plaintiff)   Ordered that this Suit be
   against   )   dismissed at the Plaintiffs Cost.
Caleb Gasway Defendant)

A Deed of Conveyance from Charles Herrington to Robert
Rutherford Proved before a Justice and Ordered to be
recorded.

270 Ordered that the Treasury of this County Pay Major John
Birdsong One hundred and Forty three Pounds which is the
ballance due him for building the Court House Exclusive of
Under pinning of the said Court House.

A Lease and Release from Henry Machem Wood to Adam Potter
Proved before a Justice and Ordered to be Recorded.

A Deed of Conveyance from Adam Potter to John Easterwood
acknowledged in open Court and Ordered to be recorded.

Ordered that the County Treasury Pay John Blasingame the
Sum of Nine Shillings and Four Pence for drawing a County
Tax List which was Given up to the Clerk and Ordered to be
Filed in his Office.

Jeremiah Spiller   Plaintiff)   Trover
   against   )   Ordered that this suit be
Original Hogan   Defendant)   dismissed at the Plaintiffs
                                 Costs.

Ordered that the Court adjourn untill tomorrow 10 o'clock
Signed by   Zachariah Bullock
                        John Henderson
                        Hugh Meanes
                        William Hendley
                        Joseph McJunkin

At a Court continued and held according to adjournment at
the Court House of said County on Wednesday the 30th day
of September in the year of our Lord One thousand seven
hundred and Eighty Nine.
Present   Zachariah Bullock   John Henderson
     William Kennedy   Thomas Brandon   Thomas Blasingame
     & Wm Hendley Esqrs.

A Lease and Release from William Cunningham to James
Lindsey proved before a Justice and Ordered to be recorded.

227

On the motion of William Gilkie for Letters of Administration on the Estate of Samuel Gilkie deceased. Ordered
that a citation Issue to Excite all the kindred and
creditors of the said deceased to appear at Our Next Court.
to shew cause if any why letters of administration should
not be granted to William Gilkie according to Law.

A Deed of Conveyance from Lewis Akins to John Hughey.
Proved before a Justice and Ordered to be recorded.

A Deed of Conveyance from Vardra McBee to Lewis Akins
Proved before a Justice and Ordered to be recorded.

John McKnit Alexander   ) On an appeal the Judgment
  vs   ) of the Justice Confirmed
Jos. Petty Amr. of Jno. Nuckols) with Costs of Suit

271 State So Carolina   Plaintiff) Bastardy
    against   ) By motion of James Dohertee
  Nancy Paulk   Defendant) attorney for the Defendant
                                 and upon proper Investiga-
tion of the matter Whether (as her husband is now alive)
he have access to her or not which appeared to the Court he
had It was therefore Ordered that she be acquited upon her
paying of Costs.

The State So Carolina   Plaintiff) Indictment Came Ephraim
  against   ) on Assault Ramsey Esqr
Robert Gibson   Defendant)   in behalf
                                 of the State and the
Defendant by James Dohertee his attorney whereupon came a
Jury Towit James Gibbs James Raldolph Thomas Allbritien
Stephen Howard Joseph Gault James Harling William Nix William
Woolbanks John Martindale Samuel Wood Benjamin Jones John
High Who being Elected Tried and Sworn on their Oathes do
Say Guilty   James Gibbs   Foreman

Ordered by the Court that he Pay the Sum of One Shillings
and Costs of Suit.

Cushman R Edson Appellee) On appeal
  against   ) Came the Plaintiff by W. Carnes
William Pooll   Appellant) his attorney and the Defendant
                           by William Shaw Esqr. his attor-
ney and upon hearing the Alegations of each Party. Ordered
that the Judt. of the Justice be Confirmed with Costs of
Suit.

John McKnit Alexander) Ordered that the Plaintiff Pay
  against   ) Henry Smith Two Shillings and
Joshua Petty. Admr.) Six pence for one days attendance
                       as a Witness for him in this Suit.

The State So Carolina Plaintiff) Indictment on Riot Came
  against   ) Ephraim Ramsey. in behalf
Samuel Cooper, David Cooper   ) of the State and the
and Elizabeth Cooper Defendant) Defendant by their
                                 Consillers Whereupon
came a Jury as aforesaid and after being sworn on their
Oathes do Say Guilty   James Gibbs foreman
Ordered that they be fined the sum of One Pound each and
Costs of Suit.

228

On the application of James Woodson Leave is Given him to
retail Spiritous Liquor on his Giving Security according
to Law who entered into bond with John Fincher his Security
accordingly.

Mark Mitchell	Plaintiff)	Debt
against	)	Dismissed at the Defendants
Wm Giles &	)	Cost which is Ordered
Joshua Palmore	Defendant)	accordingly.

272
John Thompson Exors	Plaintiff)	Ordered that the Defendants
against	)	give special Bail
Daniel & Samuel Jacksons	)	Immediately or Taken into
	Defendant)	Custody by the Sheriff.

Which John High and Mark
Jackson came into Open Court and entered themselves Special
Bail in the above Suit for the defendants.

Union County	Plaintiff)	Came the Defendant into Open
against	)	Court in his Own Proper Person
Daniel Lipham	Defendant)	and Confessed a Judgment for the
		Sum of Two Pounds Eight Shillings

and Six pence and costs of suit.

Samuel Jackson	Plaintiff)	Debt on attachment
against	)	George Harling Hatter
William Wofford	Defendant)	being summoned as a Garnashe
		who was sworn in Open Court

and his Deposition filed.

Ordered that the Court adjourn untill Tomorrow 9 o'clock
Signed by   Thomas Brandon
                   Hugh Meanes
                   Joseph McJunkin
                   William Kennedy

At a Court Continued and held by adjournment at the Court
of Union in and for the County aforesaid on the first day
of October 1789. Present Zachariah Bullock
                   Thomas Blasingame   Esquires
                   Charles Sims
                   William Hendley

Ordered that the Sheriff do Summons Four Constables to
attend the next and every Succeeding Court and that he
take them in Rotation and Return the Name of those Summoned
to the Clerk and if they fail to appear they Shall be fined
agreeable to the discretion of the Court.

A Bill of Sale from Benjamin Gilbert to James Bell Proved
before a Justice and Ordered to be recorded.

The State So Carolina	Plaintiff)	Larcency Came Ephraim
against	)	Ramsey Esquire in
Robert Gibson	Defendant)	behalf of the County
		and the Defendant

by William Shaw his Counciller Whereupon Came a Jury Towit.
James Gibbs Foreman Joseph Randolph Thomas Allbrition
Stephen Howard Joseph Gault James Harling David Norman
Thomas Harris John Martindale Samuel Wood Willial Nix and
John High who being duly Sworn do say on their Respective
Oaths NOT GUILTY James Gibbs Foreman

John Thompson Exr.   Plaintiff)   Debt
   against   )   Came the Defendants into
Daniel & Samuel Jackson   )   Open Court in their own
                      Defendants)   Proper persons and then
                                    and there Confessed a
Judgment for the Sum of Eighteen Pounds Seventeen Shillings
and Ten Pence and Costs of Suit. Which is Ordered by the
Court accordingly. Payable by Installments on Stay of
Execution three months.

273 The State So Carolina   Plaintiff)   Indictment on Escape
      against   )   The Indictment proved
    Richard Burgess   Defendant)   to be Illegal and
                                          Quashed which is
    Ordered accordingly.

On the motion of Austin Newman he is hereby appointed
Constable for this County who was duly Qualifyed according
to Law.

The State So Carolina   Plaintiff)   Bastardy
   against   )   The Defendant being duly
Milley Sumner   Defendant)   Sworn and doth Say that
                                      Thomas Richardson is the
Father of the Said Child Ordered that She be fined the Sum
of Three Pounds Eleven Shillings and Four Pence with Stay
of Execution three months, and ordered that she give
Security for the Same.

Thomas Blasingame Esqr. Absent

The State So Carolina)   Bastardy
   vs   )   Samuel Saxon came into Open Court
Milley Sumner   )   and enters himself Special bail
                         for the Payment of the fine of the
Defendant which is three Pounds Eleven Shillings and Four
Pence Sterling with Costs of Suit.

William Skelton   Plaintiff   ) Ordered that
   against   ) a Dedimus
James Duncan, Son of Alexander Defendant) Potestion Issue
                                             to any two of
the Justices of Wilks County in the State of Georgia to take
the deposition of Archer Smith in this Suit on giving Legal
Notice.

Reuben Ballew   Plaintiff) Slander
   against   ) On the motion of M. (W?) Shaw
Thomas Blasingame Defendant) attorney for the Defendant
                              for a Nonsuit for the Plain-
tiff not filing his declaration, "Which was Granted, and
Ordered that the Defendant recover against the Plaintiff
the sum of Five Shillings damage and Costs of Suit.
"Ordered that the Plaintiff Pay Elizha Greer 10f. For Four
days attendance as a Witness for him in the above suit.

William Steen   Plaintiff)   Slander
   against   )   Came the Plaintiff by Charles
Adam Goudylock   Defendant)   Goodwin Esquire his attorney
                              and the Defendant by William
Shaw Esqr. his Counseller.   "Whereupon came a Jury Towit

James Gibbs Foreman Joseph Randolph Thomas Allbritten
Stephen Howard Joseph Gault James Harling David Norman
Thomas Harris John Martindale Samuel Wood William Nix
and John High who being duly sworn do say on their Oathes
"we find for the Plaintiff the Sum of One pound and costs
of suit.   James Gibbs   Foreman
Which said Verdict was ratifyed by the Court and Ordered
to be Recorded.

274 William Steen) Ordered that the Defendant Pay Elizabeth
      against   ) Fannin Fifteen Shillings for Six days
    Adam Goudylock) attendance as a witness for him in the
                    above suit also the sum of sixteen
shillings and eight pence for mileage and John Morehead
and William Morehead the sum of Seven Shillings and Six
pence each for their attendance three days a piece as a
Witness also.

William Steen) Ordered that the Plaintiff Pay William
   against   ) Cotter Two Shillings and Six Pence for
Adam Goudylock) One days attendance as a Witness for him
                in this Suit.

William Steen   Plaintiff) Slander
   against   ) William Shaw Esquire attorney
Adam Goudylock Defendant) for the Defendant moved for an
                          arrest of Judgment which was
agreed to and to be argued next Court which was Ordered
accordingly.

Ordered that the Court adjourn untill tomorrow nine o'clock.
Signed by   Zacha. Bullock
                  Hugh Meanes
                  William Hendley
                  Joseph McJunkin
                  William Kennedy

At a Court continued and held according to adjournment at
the Court House of Union on Fryday the Second day of
October one thousand seven hundred and Eighty Nine
Present   John Henderson   Thomas Brandon
          John Birdsong   Thomas Blasingame   Esquires

Charles Miles   Plaintiff) Debt
  against   ) Thomas Brandon Executor
James Steen Exors. Defendant) came into Open Court and
                              Confessed a Judgment,
agreeable to Specialty, after the Plaintiff gives all
Just Credits which is Ordered accordingly.

Burton & Hopkins   Plaintiff) Debt
  against   ) On motion of the Plaintiffs
Edmond Cradock   Defendant) attorney Ordered that a
                              Dedimus Potestatim Issue
directed to any three Justices in Mecklenburg County,
Virginia to take the Examination of Peter Skipwith and
return the Examination So Taken Sealed up under their hands
to the next Court. The Plaintiff to Give the Defendant
Twenty days notice of the time and Place of Examination.

Benjamin Clark   Plaintiff)   Tresspass assault and Battery
   against   )   Ordered that this Suit be
William Dalefield Defendant)   discontinued at the Defendants
                               Cost.

John Hampton   Plaintiff)   Sci Facias
   against   )   On motion of the Plaintiff
Merry McGuire   Defendant)   Ordered that an Execution
                              Issue on the Former Judgment in
this Suit Including the Costs hereon.

275 The Court Proceeded to Lay a Tax for the County of Union
to defray the Necessary Expences of said County which is
ordered to as follows. for the year 1789 which is to be
Collected by the Sheriff Towit. All Low Grounds at three
Shillings per hundred acres, First Quality of up Land at
Two shillings and Six pence Second Quality at One Shilling
and Ten pence half Penny, pr Hundred third Quality at One
Shilling and three pence pr Hundred. All Negroes at Two
Shillings per head, Additional Tax for the Poor
All Negroes Six pence pr head Low Grounds pence per hundred
acres, First Quality at Seven pence half Penny Second
Quality at Five pence third Quality at Four pence for every
hundred. Which the Sheriff is Ordered to Collect. the
above Tax by the Twenty fifth day of December next.

A Deed of Conveyance from Japtha Hollingsworth and Uxor
to William Whitlock proved in Open Court and Ordered to be
recorded.

A Deed of Conveyance from Jeptha Hollingsworth and Uxor
to William Whitlock Proved before a Justice and Ordered
to be recorded.

Ordered that Stephen Scisson Orphan of William Scisson be
bound according to Law to John Murrell according to Law.

A Bill of Sale from Archelous Fore to Cushman R Edson
Proved in Open Court by John Birdsong Esqr. and Ordered to
be recorded.

A Bill of Sale from Archelous Fore to Cushman R Edson
Proved by John Birdsong Esqr. and Ordered to be recorded.

The State So Carolina   Plaintiff)   Bastardy
   against   )   Ordered that a Scie
Valentine Harling   Defendant)   facias against the
                                       Defendant on his
forfeited recognizance.

On the motion of Joseph McJunkin for a Road from this place
crossing Tygar River at John Cooks Bridge to Daniel Liphams
Ordered that Samuel Otterson John Wilson Isaac Hawkins and
Ralph Hunt lay out the most convenient and best way and
make the report thereof to next Court.

Samuel Kelso is appointed Overseer of the Road from
Jacksons Race Ground to the County Line in the Room of
Daniel Jackson which is ordered accordingly.

On the motion of William Farr, Esquire for a Road from
this place to the Charleston Road near Fishdam Ford

232

Ordered that Joseph McJunkin Esqr. John Savage and John
Sartor Lay out the most convenient and best way and make
their report thereof to Next Court which is Ordered to be
done accordingly.

Ordered that James Moseley be Overseer of the Road from
Grindol Shoales to the forks of the Road Towards this
place with the hands of Jesse Maberrys John Henderson
Benjn. Clarks James Maberry John Jasper and Adam Chisholm
in the Room of John Henderson who is now discharged and
that he keep the same in good repair according to Law. with
the hands aforesaid.

276 Ordered that the Court adjourn untill Court in Course
Signed by   John Henderson
                       Thomas Brandon
                       John Birdsong
                       Thomas Blasingame
                       Joseph McJunkin

At a Court begun and held in and for the County of Union
at the Court House of said County on Monday the Twenty
eight day of December in the year of our Lord One thousand
seven hundred and eighty nine.
Present   Thomas Brandon
                       Thomas Blasingame   Esquires
                       John Birdsong

The Court proceeded to draw the Grand Jury for the County
of Union to serve next Court. Ordered that the Sheriff
Summons them accordingly towit. Stephen Layton, John
Sarter, William Plummer Samuel Jackson Federick Crowder.
Arthur Cunningham, John Haild, farmer, Drewry Murrel,
Nathan Hawkins, Edward Denney, Adam Chisholm, Spelsby
Glenn, Thomas Williams, Aaron Fincher, John Beckham Thomas
Lamb Junr. Ralph Hunt, Charles Miles & Richmond Terrell

The Court proceeded to draw a Pettit Jury for the County
of Union, to serve next Court. which the Sheriff is
Ordered to Summon to appear at the time and place
accordingly. Which are as follows Towit.
Thomas Menton, Charles Humpharies, Soloman Whiston
Benjamin Hughey William Smith Richard Hockoboy Robert
Walker Isaac Land James Townsend Henry Hill Benjamin
Darby James Parnell Isaac Gregory Jnr. Thomas Miles
Thomas Wright Thickety Nathan Langstone Samuel Little
Joseph Coleman John Hames, George Harlin (Hatter) John
McPhearson Mark Jackson Ephraim Smith John Kennedy &
John Hammilton.

276 Ordered that John Bailey Robert White and Federick Jackson
appraise the Estate of James Prince Deceased.

A Deed of Conveyance from Isaac McKissick and wife to James
Bankhead proved before a Justice and Ordered to be recorded.

On the motion of Federick Crowder for Letters of
administration on the Estate of William Haild. Deceased
Ordered that a Citation Issue to excite all the Kindred
and Creditors of the said Deceased to appear at our next
Court to shew cause if any they have why Letters of

administration should not be Granted to Said Federick
Crowder &c.

On the application of Benajah Thompson Leave is given him
to retail spirituous liquors on giving bond with Charles
Miles and Landlot Porter his Security according to Law.

A Deed of Conveyance from James Bendington to George
Harling (Farmer) acknowledged in Open Court by the Said
James Bendington and Ordered to be recorded.

277 A Deed of Conveyance from John Goodwin to Robert Woodson
acknowledged in Open Court by the said John Goodwin to the
said Robert Woodson & Ordered to be Recorded.

Ordered that John High be Overseer of the Road in the Place
of George Harling (Farmer) and Jonas Little in the Room
of Richard Powell and Renny Ballew in the Room of William
Plummer and that they keep the Same in Good repair according to Law. with the hands Convenient to said roads.

Ordered that Zachariah Bullock Esqr. Qualify Thomas
Stribling Junr. respecting his Collection of the County
Tax &c. While Deputy Sheriff under William Farr. Sheriff.

Ordered that Letters of Administration be granted to
William Gilkie on the Estate of Samuel Gilkie Deceased
a Citation having been Issue Published and returned
according to Law.

The Last Will and Testament of William Bullock Proved in
Open Court by the Oathes of William Williams John Palmore
and Ephraim Pucket and ordered to be recorded.

A Lease and Release from Marlo Pryor to Hargrove Arther
Proved before a Justice and Ordered to be Recorded.

A Power of attorney from Edward Goode to Hermon Howard
Proved in Open Court by the Oath of Thomas Brandon and
Ordered to be Recorded.

A Power of Attorney from Isaac Brooks to William Birdsong
Proved (in Open Court) before a Justice and Ordered to
be recorded.

A Deed of Conveyance from Alexander McDougal to Thomas
Stribling Junr. acknowledged in open Court by the said
Alexander McDougal and Ordered to be recorded.

An Inventory of the Estate of William Greer Deceased which
is Ordered to be filed in the Clerks Office. and on the
application of Rebeca Greer. Letters of administration is
Granted to her. who entered into Bond and Security according to Law.

An Inventory of the Estate of Lewis Tanner. Being returned
and Ordered to be filed in the Clerks Office.

On the application of Messrs. Alexander Macbeth & Co.
Leave is Given him to retail Spirituous Liquors untill
March Court on his giving bond and security with Jeremiah
Gregory and William Plummer according to Law.

234

A Deed of Conveyance from Isaac Gregory to Margaret
Gregory Proved in Open Court by the Oath of Jeremiah
Gregory and Ordered to be recorded.

278 William Shaw attorney   Plaintiff)   Ordered that this action
     against   )   be dismissed at the
     Jonathan Gilbert   Defendant)   Defendants Cost.

     Jack Lacketure   Plaintiff)   Petn & Summons
     against   )   Ordered that this Action be
     Federick Eisen   Defendant)   dismissed at the Plaintiffs
                                      Cost.

A Deed of Conveyance from James Johnston to Aaron Harling
Proved by the Oaths of Jacob Holemes and Jacob Harling and
Ordered to be recorded.

     Bazel Lee   Plaintiff)   Jeptha White being summoned
     against   )   Garnashee in this suit who was
     Henry Holcome Defendant)   duly Sworn and says, he has one
                                  Feather bed two sheets one
     bolster and one Hymn Book the Property of Henry Holcome.

On the Application of William Hendley Leave is given him
to retail spiritous liquors and keep a Public House on
Giving Bond according to Law who Gave Security with John C
Foster and Alexr. Hammelton accordingly.

A Deed of Conveyance from Samuel Jackson to Mark Jackson
his Son, proved before a Justice and Ordered to be recorded.

Ordered that a Stray Horse Posted before Bernard Glenn
Esquire be Exposed to Sale According to Law.

On the Application of Ann Tanner Letters of Administration
is Granted her on the Estate of Lewis Tanner Deceased.
A Citation being Issued Published and returned according to
Law. And an Inventory of the Appraisement being returned
of the Estate of the Said Deceased and Ordered by the Court
that the Personal Estate of the Said Deceased be Exposed
to Sale for ready Money on the third Monday in January next
according to Law.

Daniel Brown Esqr. formerly County attorney for this County
having declined his Practice in this Court, the Court
Proceeded to the Choice of a Proper Person to be appointed
County Atto. for the County in the Room of Mr. Brown.
Where William Shaw Esquire was duly made choice of to be
County Attorney and is hereby declared County Attorney for
this County. Who was Unanimously chosen by Zachariah
Bullock, Thomas Brandon, William Kennedy, Thomas Blasingame,
Hugh Meanes and John Birdsong Esquires all Personally
Present in Court and a Magority of the Justices of said
County.

Ordered that the Court adjourn untill Tomorrow 10 o'clock
Signed by   Zacha. Bullock, Thomas Brandon, Hugh Meanes,
            Thomas Blasingame.

279 At a Court Continued and held According to Adjournment at
the Court House of Said County on Thursday the Twenty
ninth day of December One thousand Seven hundred and

235

Eighty Nine. Present William Kennedy, Charles Sims and
John Birdsong Esquires

Ordered that the Clerk Provide for the Use of this Court all
the Acts of the General Assembly from the year 1782 to the
this (sic) Date and that is Any Extraordinary Expence is
Incured on Account thereof the Same to be paid by the
Treasury of this County, and that he provide the same by
next Court.

A Deed of Conveyance from John Nicol to Aaron Harling
Proved in Open Court and Ordered to be recorded.

A Deed of Conveyance from Samuel Harling to Aaron Harling
acknowledged in Open Court by the said Harling to the said
Aaron Harling and Ordered to record.

Present Thomas Blasingame, Joseph McJunkin & Hugh Meanes.

John Steen   Plaintiff) Debt on attachment
  against   ) Came the Plaintiff into Open
David Stockdon Defendant) Court by William Shaw his
                           Attorney and the Defendant by
James Dohertie his Attorney Whereupon Came a Jury to Wit,
Jacob Haild Foreman, Jesse Pots, Abner Pots, Richard
Minton, Charles Kelly, William Woolbanks, Malen Pearson,
John Leek, William Edwards, Robert Wadkins, Samuel Cooper,
Absalem Petty who being duly Sworn, do say on their Oathes
"we find for the Plaintiff One shilling and Judgment
accordingly with Costs of Suit.

A Lease and Release from John McCooll and Wife to Cushman R
Edson Proved before a Justice and Ordered to be recorded.

A Lease and Release from John McCooll and wife to Graaff
Seibels Braselmin & Co. Proved before a Justice and
ordered to be recorded.

William Steen   Plaintiff) Slander
  against   ) On motion of W. Shaw attorney
Adam Goudylock Defendant) for the Defendant and argument
                             Ordered that the firmes Verdict
of the Jury be arrested and Judgment entered for the
Defendant.

John Steen   Plaintiff) Debt on attachment.
  against   ) Adam Potter formerly Special
David Stockdon Defendant) bail for the Defendant brought
                           him into Open Court and delivered
him up and thereupon was discharged from his former bail.

280 Gabriel Brown   Plaintiff) Came the Defendant into Open
      against   ) Court and the Plaintiff being
    Thomas Biddy   Defendant) Solemnly called but failed to
                               appear to prosecute his suit
Its ordered that he be nonsuited and that the defendant
recover the sum of five shillings for his damage and Costs
of Suit.

John McKibben   Plaintiff) Debt on attachment
  against   ) By Consent of the Parties
Jesse Dodd   Defendant) Ordered that this Suit be

236

Continued untill next Court.

John Thompson   Plaintiff)   Slander
   against   )   Ordered by the Court that the
Adam Goudylock   Defendant)   Plaintiff in this action be
                              Nonsuited and that the Defen-
dant recover the Sum of Five Shillings damage and Costs of
Suit.

A Bond from Isaac Briggs to Thomas Todd Proved in Open Court
by the Oath of Richard Burgess and Ordered to be Recorded.

Geo Ross   Plaintiff)   Debt
   against   )   Continued untill next Court for
Caleb Gaway Defendant)   the Plaintiff.

Daniel Jackson   Plaintiff)   Ordered that this action and
   against   )   by the Consent of the Parties
William Jackson Defendant)   be referred as before

John Sanders   Plaintiff)   Case
   against   )   Came the Plaintiff into Open
William Clark   Defendant)   Court and the Defendant being
                             Solemnly called but failed to
appear to prosecute his suit. Its Ordered by the Court that
he be nonsuited and that the Defendant recover the Sum of
Five Shillings for his damage and Costs of Suit.

John Bird Assa. Plaintiff)   Debt
   against   )   Came the Plaintiff
John Steen   Defendant)
Whereupon came a Jury Towit Jacob Haild Foreman Jesse
Pots Abner Pots Richard Minton Charles Kelley William
Woolbanks Malen Pearson John Leek William Edwards Robert
Wadkins, Samuel Cooper Absalom Petty who being duly sworn
do say we find for the Plaintiff the sum of eighteen pounds
nine shillings and Eleven Pence with Costs of Suit.
Jacob Haild foreman
Which was ratifyed by the Court and Ordered to be recorded.

John Steen   )   On motion Eleanor Vance as a Witness
   against   )   in this case, on oath in Open Court was
David Stockdon)   allowed the Sum of One pound ten
                   Shillings for Twelve Days attendance
as a witness aforesaid.

281 Nathaniel Burton Plaintiff)   Petition & Summons,
    against   )   On motion of William Shaw
Benjamin Clark   Defendant)   Esquire attorney for the
                                 Plaintiff for a Judgment
which was granted and the Court decreed for the Plaintiff
against the Defendant the sum of Ten Pounds Sterling and
Costs of Suit, and the same Ordered accordingly.

Bazel Lee   Plaintiff)   Debt on attachment
   against   )   Came the Plaintiff by James
Henry Holcome Defendant)   Doherteie his attorney and
                            the defendant being solemnly
called but failed to appear to prosecute his suit. Judgment
by default was ordered and entered accordingly and decreed
for the Plaintiff the sum of Nine pounds Nineteen Shillings

237

and Eleven Pence, which is ordered by the Court accordingly
with costs of suit.

Ordered that all Estrays Liable to be sold at this Court
be Exposed to Saile by the Sheriff agreeable to Law.

Doctor Geo Ross   Plaintiff)   Ordered that the Defendant
   against   )   Give special bail for the
Caleb Gasway   Defendant)   Debt according to
                                 Specialty.

Ordered that a Commission Issue to Colo. Robert Anderson
and Andrew Pickens or any Two. Justices of Pendleton
County to authorize them to cause Esther Grindle to appear
before them to renounce her Right of Dower in a Conveyance
of Land from John Grindle to John Watson and Adam Chisholm
and that he Transmit the same to this Court.

Sarah Gist.   Plaintiff)   Debt on attachment
   against   )   Samuel Simpson and Jonathan
Jesse Dodd   Defendant)   Norman came into Court and
                                enterd themselves Special Bail,
Ordered that the attachment be desolved.

On the application of Edward Tillman for letters of
administration on the Estate of Elijah Davis Deceased
a citation is Granted him on Said Estate to Excite all the
Kindred and Creditors of the Said Deceased to appear at
Our next Court to Shew Cause if any they have why letters
of administration should not be Granted to the Said Edward
Tillman.

A Bill of Sale from Daniel Jackson to Thomas Brandon Proved
before a Justice and Ordered to be recorded.

Adam Goudylock)   Ordered that the Plaintiff Pay Mary
   against   )   Palmore Ten Shillings for four days
John Thompson)   attendance as a Witness in this action
                   for the said Plaintiff.

282 Theodolious Prigmore   Plaintiff)   Petr. & Summon.
      against   )   Came the Defendants
    Phillip Gossett &   )   into Open Court and
    James Gossett   Defendants)   there confessed a
                                          Judgment for the sum
of Six Pounds Shillings with Stay of Execution three months.

John Thompson)   Ordered that the Plaintiff Pay Frances
   against   )   Latimore Twenty Shillings for eight days
Adam Goudylock)   attendance as a witness for him in this
                  action.

Adam Goudylock Plaintiff)   Ordered that the Plaintiff
   against   )   Pay Geo Taylor Fifteen
John Thompson   )   Shillings for Six days atten-
                             dance as a witness for him in
the above Suit also the Sum of Twenty Shillings for Mileage.

Bazel Lee   Plaintiff)   Debt on attachment
   against   )   Ordered that the Property
Henry Holcome Defendant)   attached be Exposed to Sale

238

agreeable to Law to Satisfy the Plaintiff for his Debt and
Costs.

Ordered that the Court adjourn untill Tomorrow 9 o'clcok
Signed by   William Kennedy
                Hugh Means
                Bernard Glenn

At a Court continued and held according to adjournment at
the Court House of said County of Union on Wednesday the
30th Day of December. One thousand Seven hundred and
Eighty Nine 1789. Present Thomas Brandon Joseph McJunkin
Bernard Glenn and William Kennedy Esqrs.

A Deed of Conveyance from William Farr to Thomas Miles
acknowledged in Open Court and Ordered to be Recorded.

A Lease and Release from William Rhoades to Jesse Dodd
proved before a Justice and Ordered to be recorded.

A Lease and Release from Jesse Dodd to Andrew Torrence
proved in Open Court by the Oath of Thomas Brandon Esqr.
and Ordered to be recorded.

A Bill of Sale from John Sanders to Lewis Sanders Proved
in Open Court by the Oath of Henry Gibson and Ordered to
be Recorded.

Holland Sumner   Plaintiff) Petr. & Summon
  against   ) This action being refered
William Blackstock Defendant) & the arbitrators return
                                 their award (Towit) that the
Suit be dismissed at the Plaintiffs Cost.

Ordered that Two depositions of John Pearson Taken before
Thomas Blasingame Esqr. be recorded.

283 Thomas Holder   Plaintiff) Debt
      against   ) Came the Plaintiff into Open
    Samuel Cooper   Defendant) Court by James Dohertee his
                                 attorney and the Defendant by
William Shaw his attorney Whereupon came a Jury Towit.
Jacob Haild foreman. Jesse Pots Abner Pots Richard Minton
Charles Kelley William Woolbanks Caleb Langstone John Leek
William Edwards Robert Wadkins John Prince and Absalom
Petty, who being duly sworn do say on their oaths "We find
it in favour of the Plaintiff One Shilling Jacob Haild
Foreman.
On Motion of W. Shaw attorney for the Defendant the Judg-
ment of the Jury is arrested.

A Deed of Conveyance from John McCooll to Federick Eison
proved before a Justice and Ordered to be recorded.

A Deed of Conveyance from John McCooll to John Whittick
Proved before a Justice and Ordered to be Recorded.

Charles Miles & Co.   Plaintiff) Petr & Summons
  against   ) Came the Plaintiff into
John Tollerson   Defendant) Open Court by Ephraim
                                   Ramsey his attorney and

239

the Defendant by William Shaw his attorney, and after
hearing the Parties on both Sides. Its ordered by the
Court that Judgment be entered up against the Defendant
for the sum of Seven pounds three Shillings to be Collected
by Installments.

Samuel Saxon   Plaintiff) Ptr. & Summons
  against   ) Continued untill next Court
William Jackson Defendant) by Consent of the Parties.

A Deed of Conveyance from Joseph Jones to John Ewart
Decd. acknowledged in Open Court and Ordered to be recorded.

Samuel Jackson Plaintiff) This Suit being refered and
  against   ) the award of the arbitrators
William Jackson Defendant) being returned. Towit. that.
                            the Defendant. Shall Pay Two
pounds and each Pay his Own Costs. which is made a Judgment
of this Court and Ordered accordingly.

Hermon Howard   Plaintiff) Debt on attachment
  against   ) Ordered that the property
Mark Jackson   Defendant) attached be sold by the Sheriff
                            agreeable to Law to satisfy the
Plaintiffs Debt and Cost.

A Deed of Conveyance from Merry McGuire and wife of the
one part and William Bowman of the other Part. Proved
before a Justice and Ordered to be recorded.

A Deed of Conveyance from Thomas Brandon Esquire to
John Palmore acknowledged in Open Court by the Said Thomas
Brandon to the Said John Palmore and Ordered to be
recorded.

284 Braselman & Co.   Plaintiff) Petr. & Summons
      against   ) Came the Defendant into
    Abel Pearson   Defendant) Open Court in his own proper
                                 Person and then and there
Confessed a Judgment for the Sum of Six pounds Ten Shillings
and Seven pence and Costs of Suit and the Same Ordered by
the Court accordingly.

Edson & Co.   Plaintiff) On a Bill
  against   ) The Defendant Came into Open
James Dohertie Defendant) Court and Confessed a Judgment
                           for the Sum of Six pounds, two
shillings and Eleven Pence Sterling and Costs of Suit Which
is ordered accordingly.

The State South Carolina Plaintiff) Pettit Larcency
  against   ) Came the Plaintiff
Whitager Shadforth   Defendant) by William Shaw his
                                      attorney and the
Defendant by his Counseller &C. Whereupon Came a Jury
Towit. Jacob Haild foreman Jesse Pots, Abner Pots Richard
Minton Charles Kelley William Woolbanks Caleb Langstone
John Leak William Edwards Robert Wadkins John Prince and
Absalom Petty who being duly Sworn to well try and True
deliverance make between the State of South Carolina and
the Preseser at the bar. return their verdict and say on

240

their respective Oathes "We find him Not Guilty."
Jacob Haild foreman
And Ordered that he be discharged on Paying of Costs.

Samuel Jackson   Plaintiff)   Debt on attachment
  against   )   Robert White being Summoned
William Wofford   Defendant)   as a Garnshee came into Open
                                Court and on Oath declares
that he is Justly Indebted to William Wofford the Sum of
Thirteen Pounds Six Shillings and Nine Pence to be paid on
Horses. or Waggon ing to the Congaree.

On the Application of George Patterson Leave is Given him
to keep a Tavern or Publick house and retail Spirituous
Liquours untill next Court in this County on his Giving
bond according to Law.

A Title Bond from David Hopkins to Nathan Glenn Proved
before a Justice and Ordered to be recorded.

Samuel Davis and Margarett Montgomery applied for Letter
of administration on the Estate of John Montgomery
Deceased Ordered that a Citation Issue to Excite all the
Kindred and Creditors of Said Deceased.

John Thompson)   Ordered that the Defendant Pay Frances
    vs   )   Latimore Seven Shillings and Six Pence
Adam Goudylock)   for his attendance as a Witness, also
                   John Whelchel the Sum of Twleve Shillings
also.

The Worshipful Court Ordered the Former Order made Last
Court respecting the County Tax be abolished and that a
Tax be laid for One hundred and Fifty Pounds to be
Collected in the Same manner as the State Tax is now
Collected.

Ordered that the Court adjourn untill Tomorrow 9 o'clock
Signed by   Thomas Brandon
                   Joseph McJunkin
                   Thomas Blasingame
                   Hugh Meanes

285 At a Court Coninued and held by adjournment at the
    Court House of Said County of Union on Thursday the Thirty
    first day of December one thousand Seven hundred and Eighty
    Nine.
    Present Thomas Brandon, Chas. Sims & Thomas Blasingame
           Esquires.

Ordered that a Deed of Conveyance Given in this Court and
Ordered to be recorded from Isaac Edmondson to Jesse
Dodd that it be Given up to Isaac Edmondson again.

Humphrey Bates   Plaintiff)   Debt on attachment
  against   )   The Defendant was solemnly
Joseph Bates   Defendant)   called and not answering or
                                any other Person for him to
replevy the attachment by default was ordered to be entered.

241

Humphreys Bates   Plaintiff)   On a Writ of Enquiry
   against   )   Came the Plaintiff by William
Joseph Bates   Defendant)   Shaw his attorney and the Deft
                                 was Solemnly Called but
appearing.   Whereupon came a Jury Towit. Jacob Haild
foreman Jesse Pots Abner Pots Richard Minton Charles
Kelley William Woolbanks Malen Pearson John Leek William
Edwards Robert Wadkins John Prince & Absalom Petty who
being duly Sworn to Execute this writ of Enquiry Between
their verdict and say on their several Oathes "We find
for the Plaintiff the Sum of Seventy three pounds and costs
of Suit.   Jacob Haild foreman
Which was ratifyed by the Court and Ordered to be recorded.

Humphrey Bates   Plaintiff)   Ordered that the Land attached
   against   )   be Exposed to Public Sale
Joseph Bates   Defendant)   according to Law to Satisfy
                                 the Plaintiffs Judgment.

State So Carolina)   Ordered that a bench warrant Issue
   against   )   against Archer Fore on a Charge lodged
Archer Fore   )   against him in this Court.

Ordered that the Clerk write a Letter to the Several
Magistrates of this County requesting them to return all
recognizance returnable to this Court to the Clerks Office
as soon as possible after Such recognizance are Taken and
within four days before the next succeeding Court at the
Fatherest.

Thomas Cook   Plaintiff)   Attachment
   against   )   On a Writ of Enquiry Whereupon
Alexander Chesney   )   came a Jury Towit.
                             Jacob Haild Foreman Jesse Pots
Abner Pots Richard Minton Charles Kelley William Woolbanks
Malen Pearson John Leek William Edwards Robert Wadkins John
Prince and Absalom Petty who being duly Sworn to Execute
this writ of Enquiry return their verdict and say on their
several Oathes "We find for the Plaintiff One Shilling
Jacob Haild Foreman

286 A General Release from John Flenton to Daniel Comer Proved
    in Open Court by the Oath of Cold. Thomas Brandon and
    Ordered to be recorded.

George Taylor   Plaintiff)   Came the Defendant into Open
   against   )   Court by his attorney and the
Robert Smith   Defendant)   Plaintiff being Solemnly Called
                                but came not to prosecute his,
Suit and on motion of the Defendant by his attorney. Ordered
that he be Nonsuited.

Andrew Thompson John Lindsey and Abraham Gray is appointed
to appraise the Estate of William Young Deceased and return
an Inventory of the Said appraisement to Our Next Court.
and the aforesaid appraisers to be Sworn by Some Justice
of Spartanburgh County.

Holland Sumner   Plaintiff)   Came the Defendant into Open
   against   )   Court and the Plaintiff being
Dudley Red   Defendant)   Solemnly Called but bailed to
                                appear to Prosecute his Suit

242

Its Ordered that he be nonsuited and that the Defendant
recover the Sum of Five Shillings for his damage & Costs
of Suit.

William Parker   Plaintiff)   Ordered that a Decree be
  against   )   entered for the Plaintiff
George Lunkins   Defendant)   against the Defendant for the
                                Sum of Seven pounds Seven
Shillings and Seven Pence and Costs of Suit.

Ordered that the Clerk do Provide a Correct and regular
List. and accompt. of all Fines and Forfeitures all
Estrays Tavern Licences Granted. and all other Public
moneys. Whatsoever that have become due to this
County since the First Establishment of this Court against
the next Court and to be delivered to the County attorney
for his Investigation.

A Deed of Conveyance from Walter Holemes to John McCooll
proved before a Justice and Ordered to be recorded.

State So Carolina   Plaintiff)   Bastardy
  against   )   Ordered that Scere Facias
Valentine Harling   Defendant)   Issue the Defendants
                                   Securities to Shew Cause
if any they have why Execution should go against them as
Securities aforesaid.

John McKibbin   Plaintiff)   W. Richard Burgess being Special
  against   )   bail in this Suit. came into
Jesse Dodd   Defendant)   Open and upon motion thereof
                               was discharged from off his bail
Which is ordered accordingly.

287 John McKibbin   Plaintiff)   Debt on attachment
      against   )   Came the Plaintiff into Open
    Jesse Dodd   Defendant)   Court by
                                   Whereupon came a Jury Towit.
Jacob Haild Foreman Jesse Pots Abner Pots Richard Minton
Charles Kelley William Woolbanks Marlin Pearson John Leek
William Edwards Robert Wadkins John Prince and Absalom
Petty who being duly sworn to well and truly try the Issue
Joined returned their verdict and say on their several
Oathes "We find for the sum of Ten Pounds Fourteen Shillings
and Interest and Costs of Suit.   Jacob Haild foreman
Which Said Verdict was ratifyed by the Court and Ordered
to be recorded.

William Darby   Plaintiff)   Debt on attachment
  against   )   The Defendant being Called to
Robert H. Hughes Defendant)   replevy the Property attached
                               and to appear and enter bail
to answer the Plaintiffs Suit and not answering a Judgment
by default is entered against him.

Holland Sumner)   Mill Sumner Proved Seventeen Days
  vs   )   attendance in this Suit as a Witness which
Dudley Red   )   is two pounds two shillings and six pence.

Geo Taylor   )   James McCracken on Oath in Open Court is
  vs   )   allowed the Sum of Ten Shillings For Four
Robert Smith)   days attendance in this Suit also

243

John Albritten is allowed on Oath as aforesaid the Sum of
One Pound for Eight days attendance in the suit as a Witness.

William Darby   Plaintiff)   Attachment
against   )   On a Writ of Enquiry came the
Robert H. Hughes Defendant)   Plaintiff into Open Court by
                              William Shaw his attorney and
the Defendant by   Whereupon came a Jury Towit
Jacob Haild Foreman Jesse Pots Abner Pots Richard Minton
Charles Kelley William Woolbanks Malen Pearson John Leek
William Edwards Robert Wadkins John Prince and Absalom
Petty. Who being duly Sworn return their Verdict and Say on
their Several Oathes "We find for the Plaintiff the Sum of
Eleven Pounds Eleven Shillings. Jacob Haild. foreman.
Ordered that the Property attached in the above Suit be
sold according to Law to Satisfy the Plaintiffs Judgment &c.

Major Birdsong who built. Union Court House came into
Open Court and Gave the Same up to the Justices which was
Received by them and thereon the Said Birdsong is discharged
from the charge of said Court House. and the same Ordered
accordingly.

288 Whitager Shadforth Plaintiff)   Ordered that this Suit be
    against   )   Discontinued at mutual
    William Massey   Defendant)   Cost.

John Briggs   Plaintiff)   Debt on attachment
against   )   Came the Plaintiff into Open
Robert Henry Hughes   )   Court by William Shaw Esquire
                 Defendant)   his attorney and the Defendant
                              by James Dohertee his attorney
Whereupon Came a Jury Towit. Jesse Potts Abner Pots Richard
Minton Charles Kelley William Woolbanks Marlen Pearson John
Leek William Edwards Robert Wadkins John Prince and
Absalom Petty who being duly sworn return their verdict and
Say on their several Oathes "We find the Property attached
to be the Property of Robert Henry Hughes   Jacob Haild
foreman.

A Title Bond from Thos Henderson to John McCooll Proved
before a Justice and Ordered to be recorded.

A Power of attorney from Adam McCooll to John McCooll
proved before a Justice and Ordered to be recorded.

State So Carolina)   Ordered that the Defendant Pay James
against   )   Wodlleton five Shillings for Two days
William Shadforth)   attendance in this Suit also William
                     Wadlleton 5 for two days attendance
as a Witness also.   Eight Shillings and four pence for
mileage.

John Briggs   Plaintiff)   Debt on attachment
against   )   Mr. John McCooll came into
Robert H. Hughes Defendant)   open Court and entered him-
                               self special bail for the
Defendant.

David Stockdon   Plaintiff)   Ordered that the Plaintiff
against   )   Pay Robert Lusk the Sum of
John Steen   Defendant)   Two Pounds Twelve Shillings

and Six pence for Twenty One days attendance for him as a
Witness in this Suit.

John Briggs   Plaintiff   ) Debt on attachment
  against   ) Came the Plaintiff by
Robert Henry Hughes Defendant) William Shaw his attorney
                                 and the Defendant by James
Dohertee his attorney Whereupon came a Jury (Towit)
Jacob Haild Foreman Jesse Pots Abner Pots Richard Minton
Charles Kelley Caleb Langston Malen Pearson John Leek
William Edwards Robert Wadkins John Prince and Absalom
Petty, Who being duly Sworn to well and truly try this Issue
Joined return their Verdict and Say on their several
Oathes "We find for the Plaintiff the sum of Nine Pounds
Nineteen Shillings with costs of suit. and Judgment
accordingly.   Jacob Haild foreman
Which said Verdict was Ratifyed by the Court and Ordered to
be recorded.

289 John Steen   Plaintiff) Debt on attachment
      against   ) Ordered that Execution Issue
    David Stockdon Defendant) against Stockdon for the Penalty
                               of the Bond with Costs of Suit.

Robert Lusk   Plaintiff) Ordered that a Scere Facias
  against   ) Issue against the Defendant
John Jones   Defendant) Laurence County to Shew cause if
                            any he has why Execution should
not Issue on a Former Judgment Obtained by the Plaintiff
against him.

John Briggs   Plaintiff   ) Attachment
  against   ) Ordered that the Property
Robert H. Hughes Defendant) attached be Exposed to Sale
                               at Public auction agreeable
to Law to Satisfy the Plaintiffs Debt and Costs.

Ordered that the Court adjourn untill Tomorrow 9 o'clock
Signed by   Thomas Brandon
                Joseph McJunkin
                John Birdsong

At a Court Continued and held by adjournment at the Court
House of Union, on Fryday the First day of January One
Thousand Seven hundred and Ninety.
Present   Thomas Brandon
                John Birdsong   Esquires
                Thomas Blasingame

Ordered that the Road be Opened and made as Strait as
Possible from Crossleys Old Field to Mr. McBeths Corner
from thence to the Congaree Old road and its hereby
Ordered that the overseers of said road Clear out and keep
the same in good repair according to Law and that Mr. John
McKibbin and Alexander Macbeth is hereby appointed to Lay
out the same in form aforesaid and by Order aforesaid.

Samuel Kelso is hereby appointed Overseer of the Road in
the Room of Daniel Jackson in the Same Road Jackson was
Overseer.

Ordered that Thomas Layton be and is hereby appointed
Overseer of the Road from Where the New Road turns Out of
McJunkens Road to Cooks bridge and that he keep the Same in
Good repair according to Law.

Ordered that the Clerk Call on all the Justices of this
County to Return a List of the Names of the Constables that
serve under them To him beofre Next Court.

A Deed of Conveyance from John McCooll and wife to Cornelius
Dempsey acknowledged by John McCooll and his Wife being
290 Privately Examined by a Justice who reports that she
Voluntarily Does renounce her Right of Dower which was
Ordered to be Recorded.

Ordered that the Minutes be read which was done accordingly
and Signed by Thomas Brandon, John Birdsong, Thomas
Blasingame. The Court then adjourned untill Court in Course

At a Court begun and Holden in and For the County of Union
at the Court house of Said County On Monday the 22.d Day of
March in the year of our Lord One thousand Seven hundred
and Ninety and of the Independance of the United States
of North America the Fourteenth
Present.   John Birdsong
                  Joseph McJunkin   Esquires
                  Thomas Blasingame
                  Thomas Brandon

Ordered that the Sheriff Summon the following persons to
serve next Court as Pettit Jurors for the County aforesaid
which are as follows. Towit Waller Roberts. James Insco.
William Thompson Isaac Norman Adam Potter Thomas Bell
George Harling (Farmer) William Pearson Benjamin Savage
Junr. Gilham Woolbanks Curtis Wood Daniel Crownover William
Martindale Moses Wilder. James Johnstone John Sparks Junr.
William McClennin Samuel Harling Daniel Lipham John Lawson
Garrot Gregory John Palmore Junr. George Gordon. John
Gregory Elisha McGuire John Ray Thomas Evins Samuel
Littlejohn John Roberts & Thomas Skelton.

The Last Will and Testament of Joseph Jolly Deceased Proved
in Open Court by the Oaths of John Brandon and James
Bogan and Ordered to be recorded.

A Lease and Release from Joab Mitchell of the One Part and
Thomas Draper of the other Part. Proved before a Justice
and Ordered to be Recorded.

Rachel Paulk applied for Letters of Administration on the
Estate of Urias Paulk Deceased. Its Ordered that a Citation Issue to Excite all the Kindred and Creditors of the
Said Deceased to appear at our Next Court. to Shew cause
if aney they have why Letters of administration Should not
be Granted unto the Said Rachel Paulk.

A Deed of Conveyance from Randolph Depriest. Proved in
Open Court by the Oath of James Woodson and Ordered to be
recorded.

A Deed of Conveyance from William Whitlock to Handcock
Porter acknowledged in open Court by the Said William

Whitlock to the Said Handcock Porter and Ordered to be Recorded.

291 A Deed of Conveyance from Benjamin Darby of the One Part and Jeremiah Hammelton of the Other Part acknowledged in Open Court by the Said Benjamin Darby to the Said Alexr. Hammilton and Ordered to be Recorded.

Ordered that there shall be no Instrument of writing whatsoever taken into the Clerks Office from Caleb Edmondson unless in Time of Court by reason of his Giving a Power of attorney to Andrew Torrence and John Fincher which is Irrevocable.

Ordered that Letters of administration be Granted unto Fedk. Crowder on the Estate of William Haild Deceased he has returned his Citation Published agreeable to Law Who entered into bond with Samuel Simpson and William Plummer his Securities according to Law in the Sum of One hundred and Fifty Pounds Sterling.

A Bill of Saile from James Sharp to William Thomas Linton and James Sims Proved before a Justice and Ordered to be recorded.

The Grand Juros. for the Inquest of the body of this County Who was Sworn and having received their charge they withdrew Towit Samuel Jackson foreman William Plummer Federick Crowder John Haild Drewry Murrell. Nathan Hawkins Edward Denney. Spilsby Glenn Thomas Williams Aaron Fincher Thomas Land Junr. & Richard Terrell.

Ordered that the Poor Orphan Children of Alexander Fitzpatrick be bound Out (Towit) Elizabeth to Thomas Layton; John, to Cornelius Dimpsey Taylor; Nancey, to Samuel Cooper and Sarah Agreeable to Law.

Ordered that a Road be cleared out from the Cross Road near the Fish dam Ford to where it will Intersect the Road that Leads from Tyger River to Union Court House and that William Farr be Overseer of the Said Road from the Cross roads to the Corner of Richards Barrotts field, and Joseph McJunkin from there to where it Intersects the Court House Road and that they Clear and keep the same in good repair according to Law. With the hands convenient thereto.

A General Releasement from William Farr to Elias Hollingsworth acknowledged in Open Court & Ordered to be recorded.

A Deed of Conveyance from Isaac Holeman to George Taylor. Proved before a Justice and Ordered to be recorded.

Moses Waters Plaintiff   )   Debt. attachment
  against   )   Francis Latimore being
George Henderson Defendant)   Summoned as a Garnashee
                               Who came into Open Court and
after being Sworn as Law directs. Declares On Oath that he hath nothing in his hands belonging to the said Defendant George Henderson.

292 Ordered that the Poor Orphan Children of Thomas Dayfields

Deceased be bound Out as the Law directs. To wit That
Thomas Sunnah and Joel Dayfields be bound to Walter Roberts
&C.,

A Deed of Conveyance from John Langsley to Irby Duebery
Proved before a Justice and Ordered to be recorded.

A Lease and Release from James Timms to James Hawkins
Proved before a Justice and Ordered to be recorded.

Ordered that John Watson Senr. be Overseer of the Road from
Grindals Shoals to Thickety Creek by Charles Miles in the
room of Thomas Cook and that he keep the Same in Good repair

A Deed of Conveyance from Page Pucket to William White
Proved in Open Court by the Oathes of William Buckhannon
and Syazmond Stribling and Ordered to be Recorded.

Ordered that a Citation Issue to Excite all the Kindred
and Creditors of John McPherson Deceased to appear at Our
next Court to Shew cause if any they have why Letters of
administration Should not be Granted to Sarah McPhearson
and Geo Harling Hatter.

A Lease and release from Daniel Trammel to James Carveal
(Carrel?) Proved before a Justice and Ordered to be
recorded.

Ordered that John Pooll be Overseer of the Road from Rockey
Creek to Grindol Shoals in the Room of Abner Coleman and
that he keep the Same in Good repair according to Law.

Ordered that Jesse Dodd be Overseer of the Road from Tyger
River to Enoree River at bobos ford in the Room of W.
Murrell & that he clear and keep the same in good repair
according to Law.

A Bill of Saile from Spencer Brummet to William and Daniel
Brummet Proved before a Justice and Ordered to be recorded.

A Bill of Sale from Spencer Brummet to William Brummet
Proved before a Justice and Ordered to be recorded.

A Deed of Conveyance from John Blasingame Sheriff to
Cushman Edson Proved in Open Court by the Oath of John
Haile & Richard Mitchell and Ordered to be recorded.

A Deed of Conveyance from William Blackstock and wife to
William Edwards Proved in Open Court by the Oath of William
Smith and Ordered to be recorded.

George Parks	Plaintiff)	Debt on attachment
against	)	Ordered that this Suit be
Daniel Jackson	Defendant)	discontinued at the Plaintiffs Cost.

C. R. Edson	Plaintiff	)	Ordered that this suit
against		)	be discontinued at the
William Thomas Linton	Defendant)		Plaintiffs Cost

248

293 William Giles   ) Debt
    against   ) the Defendants Came into
William Watson. John Albritten &) Open Court in their Own
    John Griffeth   ) proper person and
                                       Confessed a Judgment for
the sum of Fifteen Pounds and Costs of suit which is
ordered by the Court accordingly.

Ordered that Phillip Buzan be Overseer of the Road from the
Road from the Old Field road. that leades from Grindle
Shoales to Henry Longs house along the new Cut. road to
the Cross Path that Leads from Clayton Striblings to Snoden
Cains in the room of Charles Humphraes and that he keep the
same in good repair according to Law.

Ordered that all the Estrays that are Liable to be sold
this Court that the Sheriff Expose them to Sale agreeable
to Law.

Ordered that the Court adjourn untill Tomorrow 9 o'clock
Signed by   John Birdsong
                     Thomas Brandon
                     Thomas Blasingame
                     Joseph McJunken

At a Court continued and held by adjournment at the Court
House of Said County on Tuesday the 23d day of March One
thousand seven hundred and Ninety.
Present Wm Kennedy Charles Sims Thos. Brandon & John
Birdsong Esqrs.

A Deed of Convey from John Little to Thomas Palmore Proved
in Open Court by the Oath of William Farr and Ordered to
be Recorded.

A Deed of Conveyance from John Little to Thomas Palmore
proved in Open Court by the Oath of William Farr and
Ordered to be recorded.

William Brandon   Plaintiff) Attachment
    against   ) Continued untill next Court
William Boyd   Defendant) by Order of Court.

Samuel Jackson   Plaintiff) Judgment for Plaintiff for
    against   ) the Sum of Two Pounds and each
William Jackson   Defendant) Pay their own costs.

Daniel Jackson   Plaintiff) Came the Defendant into Open
    against   ) Court and the Plaintiff
William Jackson   Defendant) Altho Solemnly called but Came
                              not to prosecute his Suit.
Its Ordered that he be nonsuited and that the Defendant
recover the sum of five shillings for his damage and costs
of suit.

John Bird Assee. Slappy Plaintiff) The Plaintiff being
    against   ) Solemnly Called but
John Steen   Defendant) Came not to defend
                                     his action its ordered
that he be nonsuited and that the Defendant recover the sum
of five shillings for his damage and costs of suit.

294 John Bird   Plaintiff)   The Plaintiff being Solemnly Called
    against   )   but failed to appear to prosecute
    John Steen Defendant)   his suit. Its Ordered on the motion
                              of the Defendant by his attorney
that he be nonsuited and that the Defendant recover the sum
of five Shillings damage and Costs of Suit.

John Bird   Plaintiff)   Came the Defendants by their
    against   )   attorneys and the Plaintiff.
Steen & Montgomery Defendant)   Altho Solemnly called came
                                    not to prosecute his Suit
Its Ordered on the motion of the Defendant by his attorney
that he be Nonsuited and that the Defendant recover the Sum
of five Shillings damage and costs of suit.

George Ross   Plaintiff)   Debt
    against   )   Came the Defendant into Open Court
Caleb Gasway Defendant)   & then and there confessed a
                            Judgment for the Sum of Eleven
Pounds Sterling to be discharged in One month with costs
of suit which is ordered accordingly.

Jonathan Gilkie Plaintiff)   Came the Defendants into Open
    against   )   Court by their attorneys and
Steen & Smith   Defendant)   the Plaintiff altho Solemnly
                               call failed to appear to
Prosecute his Suit. Its ordered that he be nonsuited and
that the Defendants recover the Sum of Five Shillings
damage and Costs of Suit.

Edson & Co.   Plaintiff)   Petr. & Summons
    against   )   Came the Defendant into Open Court
James Tosh   Defendant)   in his Own proper person and then
                            and there confessed a Judgment
for the Sum of Eight pounds Two Shillings and One penny
and costs of suit with Stay of Execution untill the first
day of January next and the same is ordered accordingly.

Jasper Tommerlin Plaintiff)   Came the Defendant into Open
    against   )   Court by his attorney and the
John Mullins   Defendant)   Plaintiff altho Solemnly
                               called came not to prosecute
his Suit. Its Ordered that he be nonsuited and that the
defendant Recover the sum of five Shillings for his damage
and costs of suit.

William Steen   Plaintiff)   The defendant agrees to Pay all
    against   )   Costs Except the attorneys
Benjamin Clark Defendant)   fee and the cause of action to
                              be left to the determination of
Captain John Thompson Zachariah Bullock and James Terrell.

James Davis Exors   Plaintiff)   Came the Defendant into
    against   )   Open Court by their attorney
Burgess & White   Defendant)   and the Plaintiffs altho
                                   Solemnly called came not to
prosecute his Suit. Its Ordered that they be nonsuited
and that the Defendants recover the Sum of five shillings
damage and costs of suit.

James Timms   Plaintiff   against Humphrey Posey Defendant
Came the Defendant into Open Court by his attorney and the

Plaintiff Altho Solemnly called came not to defend his Suit.
Its ordered that he be nonsuited and that the Defendant
recover the Sum of five Shillings for his damages and costs
of Suit.

295 Kershaw & ComY Plaintiff)   Debt
      against   )   Came the Plaintiff by Ephraim
    Joseph East   Defendant)   Ramsey his attorney and the
                                Defendant by William Shaw his
attorney. Whereon came a Jury Towit. John Martindale foreman. Thomas Minton Charles Humpharies Soloman Whison
Benjamin Crownover Thomas Roberts Richard Huckabey James
Townsend. Benjamin Darby Isaac Gregory Nathan Langstone &
William Smith who being duly sworn well and truly to try
the matter on the Issue Joined upon their Oathes do say
that the Plaintiff recover against the Defendant the sum
of One hundred and Nine pounds Sterling and also his costs
by him about his suit in this behalf expended and the Said
defendant in Money &c.   John Martindale foreman

John Blasingame Sheriff Plaintiff)   Ordered that this
      against   )   action be discontinued
Lusk and Vance   Defendant)   at the defendants costs

A Deed of Conveyance from Thomas Bishop to John Cambell
proved before a Justice and Ordered to be recorded.

Alexander Hammelton Plaintiff)   The Parties came into Open
      against   )   Court and then and there
James Lindsey   Defendant)   agree to refer all matter
                                of Indefferance between
them to the Arbitration of Edward Tillman and William
Beauman and their award to be made the Judgment of this
Court and the Same Ordered accordingly.

State So. Carolina Plaintiff)   On a Bill of Indictment for
      against   )   Larcency the Court having
Archelous Fore   Defendant)   heard the matter properly
                                Chanceled. Its ordered
that he be acquited on paying of costs.

William Hodge   Plaintiff)   Tresspass assault. & Battery
      against   )   This Suit refered to the
Andrew McBride   Defendant)   Arbitration of Captain
                            John Thompson and Andrew Mays
with Power to chose a Third person if they disagree and
their award to be the Judgment of this Court. Which is
ordered accordingly.

David Frazier   Plaintiff)   Ordered that this suit be
      against   )   discontinued at the Defendants
Caleb Gasway   Defendant)   Cost in person.

On the Application of William Darby leave is given him to
retail Spirituous Liquors on his giving bond according to
Law. Who came into Open Court and entered into bond with
John Murrell his Security accordingly.

Jeremiah Thompson   Plaintiff)   Decreed that the Defendant
      against   )   Pay the Plaintiff the Sum
Spencer Brummet & Samuel Saxon)   Six pounds Ten Shillings
              DefendantS)   and eight pence and costs

251

of Suit which is ordered accordingly.

State So Carolina   Plaintiff)   Indictment for Pettit
  against   )   Larcency.
James Spray   Defendant)
                              No bill being found by the
Grand Jury and he is thereon discharged on Paying of Costs.

296 Jasper Tommerlin   Plaintiff)   Willism Conner on Oath in
  against   )   Open Court was allowed the
John Mullins   Defendant)   Sum of One pound Seven
                            Shillings and Six pence
for Eleven days attendance as a Witness in this Suit.

John Henderson Esqr.   Plaintiff)   Debt. attachment
  against   )   decree for the Plaintiff
James Yancey   Defendant)   and that he recover the
                          Sum of Five pounds
fifteen Shillings and Four pence half penny with costs of
Suit. that the property in the hands of the Garnashees
be adjudged the property of the said Yancey and that it be
appropiated to the discharge of the above Debt which is
ordered accordingly.

Ordered that a Commission Issue to Alexander Blair and
Ambrose Arther to take the relinquishment of Dower of
Mrs. Pryor wife of Marlo Pryor in a tract of Land conveyed
by said Pryor to Hargrove Arther Lying in the County of
Union.

John Henderson   Plaintiff)   Attachment
  against   )   James Moseley. John Beekham
James Yancey   Defendant)   William Coleman Abner Coleman
                        Nathaniel Gorden and John
Haile being Summoned as Garnashees in the above suit who
was duly sworn and declares Towit James Moseley confessed
to owe to the Defendant the Quantity of 114½ lb. of Tobacco
John Beekham 271. lb William Coleman 271.lb of Tobacco a
cow calf and one yearling also One deerskin Abner Coleman
100.lb Tobacco Nathaniel Gorden 135.lb Tobacco and hath
Credit for Six Shillings aught of Said Tobacco.
John Haile 271.lb of Tobacco & Twenty Weight of Pork.
Out of which he has Credit for Nine Shillings.

George Wadkins   Plaintiff)   Ordered that this Suit be
  against   )   discontinued at Equal Costs
James Duncan   Defendant)

A Deed of Conveyance from Samuel Jackson to James Meanes
acknowledged in Open Court and Ordered to be recorded.

A Deed of Conveyance from Daniel Jackson to Joseph Meanes
acknowledged in Open Court and Ordered to be recorded.

Jasper Tommerlin   Plaintiff)   Phelimon Bass proved Eleven
  against   )   days attendance. Job. Hamblen
John Mullins   Defendant)   proved Nine days attendance
                        George Russel proved Four-
teen days attendance and Uriah Mullins proved Nine days
attendance all in the above suit which is ordered to be
recorded.

John Crow Foster   Plaintiff)   Came the Parties into Open
   against   )   Court and then and there
James Lindseey   Defendant)   agreed to refer this Action
                                 of Controversey to the
Arbitration of Captain Edward Tilman William Bowman and
Turner Kendrick and their award to be the Judgment of this
Court.

On the application of Samuel Davidson and Margaret
Montgomery Letters of administration is Granted them on
the Estate of John Montgomery Deceased. Who was Qualifyed
in Open Court and that they be bound in a Bond of two
hundred pounds with Security--Charles Clanton Robt. Lusk
and Francis Drake be and is hereby appointed to appraise
the Estate of the Said Decd. and that William McCullock
or the nearest Justice Qualify the Said appraisers.

297 Ordered that the Court adjourn untill tomorrow 9 o'clock
Signed by   Hugh Meanes
                   William Kennedy
                   Joseph McJunken

At a Court Continued and held by adjournment at the Court
House of said County on Wednesday the 24th Day of March
Present Zacha. Bullock John Birdsong & Charles Sims
Esquires.

A Quiet Claim Deed from Elias Hollingsworth to William Farr
proved in Open Court by the Oath of Charles Humpharies and
Ordered to be recorded.

On the application of Geo Patterson leave is given him to
retail spirituous liquors on his giving bond according to
Law who came into Open Court and entered into bond with
William Farr his Security accordingly.

A Deed of Conveyance from John Hughey and Elizabeth Hughey
to James Townsend proved before a Justice and Ordered to be
recorded.

A Lease and Release from Geo Taylor to John Blalock Proved
before a Justice and Ordered to be recorded.

A Deed of Conveyance from John McCooll and Wife to Thomas
Blasingame Esquire acknowledged in open Court by the Said
John McCooll and ordered to be recorded.

Samuel Saxon   Plaintiff)   Petr. & Summons
   against   )   decree for the Plaintiff and
William Jackson Defendant)   that he recover the sum of
                                 five pounds against the
Defendant and that the Plaintiff Pay all costs. that has
occured on this suit.

Samuel Saxon   Plaintiff)   Debt
   against   )   Came the Plaintiff by James
William Jackson Defendant)   Dohertie his attorney and the
                                 Defendant by William Shaw his
attorney Whereupon came a Jury Towit. John Martindale
Foreman Thomas Minton Charles Humpharies Solomon Whitson
Benjamin Crownover Thomas Roberts Richard Ruckebey. James

Townsend Benjamin Darby Isaac Gregory Nathan Langstone
and William Smith Who being sworn well and truly to try the
matter on the Issue Joined upon their Oathes do say that
the Plaintiff recover against the defendant the sum Thirty
Pounds Sterling also his costs by him about this Suit in
that behalf Expended and the said defendant in Money &c
John Martindale foreman

James Barron   Plaintiff) Slander
  against   ) Ordered that the Plaintiff be
Cushman R Edson Defendant) Nonsuited and that the
                             defendant recover the sum of
Five Shillings for his damage and costs of suit.

William Thomas   Plaintiff) Debt
  against   ) Ordered that this Suit be
Albritten & Manley Defendant) dismissed at the defendants
                               cost.

Robert Baitey   Plaintiff) Tresspass
  vs   ) On motion Ordered that the Writ
Nathaniel Cooper Defendant) be amended.

298 Robert Baitey   Plaintiff) Special Action
      against   ) Came the Plaintiff by William
    Nathaniel Cooper Defendant) Shaw Esquire his attorney
                                   and the defendant by Zacha.
Talliafero his attorney. Whereupon came a Jury Towit.
John Martindale foreman Mark Jackson Charles Humpharies
Solomon Whitson Benjamin Crownover Thomas Roberts Richard
Huckaby James Townsend Benjamin Darby Isaac Gregory. Nathan
Langstone and William Smith. Who being Elected Tryed and
Sworn well and Truly to Try the matter on the Issue Joined
upon their oathes do say "that the Plaintiff recover against
the Defendant the sum of Twenty five pounds Sterling also
his costs by him about his suit in this behalf Expended.
John Martindale foreman

The Defendant moves for arrest of Judgment to be argued
before the Court adjourned.

Jonathan Greaves   Plaintiff) Debt
  against   ) Came the defendant into Open
John Henderson   Defendant) Court in his own proper
                                person and then and there
confessed a Judgment for the sum of Thirty one pounds
two shillings and costs of suit with stay of execution
untill the 10 day of November Next--and the Same is
Ordered accordingly.

James Ollephant appellant Plaintiff) On an appeal from a
  against   ) Justice the Court
Charles Bruce appele   Defendant) after hearing the
                                        Investigation of the
matter Ordered that the Judgment of the Justice be
confirmed with costs of suit.

Ordered that Nicholas Curry be Overseer of the Road from
Smiths ford on Borad River to the meeting house Between
Gilkies Creek and Thickety in the Room of Laurence House
and that he keep the same in Good repair according to Law,
with the Hands Convenient thereto.

254

Ordered that David Goulictly receive from the County
Treasury the money that a Stray cow was sold for after the
fees are all Paid which he had proved to be his property.

Ordered that Zachariah Ballew be Overseer of the Road from
Rockey Creek to Elisha Greens in the Room of Evin Thomas.

Ordered that each of the Justices bring in all the publick
moneys that they have in their hands and all Notes given
from persons to the County or County Treasury and also the
Sheriff to Settle his accompt. by Next Court.

James Ollephant) Ordered that James Ollephant Pay Wm
  against   ) Wilder Seven Shillings & Six pence for
Charles Bruce) three days attendance as a Witness for
               him in this Suit also the Sum of Six
Shillings for Mileage.

Robert H. Hughes Plaintiff) Debt
  against   ) Came the defendant into Open
John Haile   Defendant) Court in his own proper person
                       and then and there confessed
a Judgment for the sum of Seventeen Pounds Six Shillings and
Nine pence to be paid in tobacco at the market price where
delivered with Stay of Execution Six months.

Burton & Hopkins Plaintiff) Debt
  against   ) Continued untill next court
Edmond Cradock Defendant) by Consent of the Parties.

299 Robert Baitey   Plaintiff) On motion of Mr. Zachariah
    against   ) Talliafero attorney for the
Nathaniel Cooper Defendant) defendant for a nonsuit but
                     was over ruled.

On the Application of Edward Tillman Letters of administration is granted to him on the Estate of Elijah Davis deceased on his giving bond with Security according to Law.

William Darby   Plaintiff) Hermon Howard being summon as
  against   ) Garnashee who was duly Sworn
Edward Goode   Defendant) in Open Court and declares on
                   Oath he has in his hands four
pounds Nineteen Shillings which is condemned to answer
the Plaintiff.

Ordered that the Court adjourn untill Tomorrow Nine o'clock.
Signed by   Zachariah Bullock
          William Kennedy
          Joseph McJunkin

At a Court continued and held by adjournment at the Court
House of Said County on Thursday the 25th March One
thousand seven hundred and Ninety.

Present   Thomas Brandon
          John Birdsong
          Joseph McJunkin   Esquires
          Charles Sims

On motion of Mr. Shaw Leave is given Alexander Macbeth

to retail Spirituous Liquors on giving bond with William
Shaw his Security.

A Deed of conveyance from Shadrach Lewallen to William
Mitchell acknowledged before a Justice and Ordered to be
recorded.

A Deed of conveyance from Jedethan Porter to Elizabeth
Holmes proved before a Justice and Ordered to be recorded.

Edson & Company   Plaintiff) Debt
  against   ) George Patterson being bail
Caleb Gasway   Defendant) for his appearance at court
                                and gave him up and was from
his recognizance discharged which is ordered accordingly.

A Deed of Conveyance from Zachariah Bullock to John &
Robert Steen proved before a Justice and Ordered to be
recorded.

A Deed of Conveyance & release from George Igleburger to
Thomas Clandennan proved before a Justice and Ordered
to be recorded.

A Deed of Conveyance from Rebecca McNeal to William
Johnstone proved before a Justice and Ordered to be
recorded.

C R Edson   Plaintiff) Petr. & Summons
  against   ) Ordered that the Plaintiff be
James Barron Defendant) Nonsuited & that the defendant
                                recover the sum of five shillings
for his damage and costs of suit.

A Deed of Conveyance from Edward Prince to William Woolbanks proved before a Justice and Ordered to be recorded.

A Deed of Conveyance from Francis Posey to Nehemiah Posey
proved before a Justice and Ordered to be recorded.

300 A Deed of Conveyance from Wm Horrell of the one part and
George Rowden of the other part proved before a Justice and
ordered to be recorded.

A Deed of Conveyance from Nehemiah Posey to George Bowden
proved before a Justice and Ordered to be recorded.

A Deed of Conveyance from Thomas Smith to William Hardwick
proved before a Justice and Ordered to be recorded.

A Deed of Conveyance from William Bryan and wife to John
Little proved before a Justice and Ordered to be recorded.

Charles Miles   Plaintiff) Debt attachment
  against   ) Richard Terrell bail for the
Benjamin Burnet Defendant) property & Judgment for the
                                sum of forty seven pounds
and three pence Sterling and costs of suit with stay of
Execution three months which is ordered accordingly.

David Bailey   Plaintiff   ) Came the defendant
  against Isaac Holeman Defendant) into Open Court by

his attorney and the Plaintiff Altho Solemnly Called came
not to prosecute his Suit and on Motion of the defendant
by his attorney Ordered that he be Nonsuited and that the
defendant recover against the Plaintiff the sum of Five
shillings damage & Costs of suit.

Tabitha Pearson   Plaintiff)   Came the Plaintiff into
   against   )   Open Court by her attorney
Skelton & Smith   Defendant)   and the defendant Altho
                                  Solemnly called came not to
defend their suit and on motion of the Plaintiff by her
attorney Judgment by default is ordered and hereby entered.

Raldolph Alexander   Plaintiff)   Came the defendant by his
   against   )   attorney and the Plaintiff
Isaac Edmondson   Defendnat)   Altho Solemnly called came
                                  not to prosecute his
Suit. Its Ordered that he be Nonsuited and that the Defendant recover the sum of five Shillings damage and costs
of Suit which is ordered accordingly.

301 Larken Wells   Plaintiff)   By consent of the Parties Ordered
      against   )   that this suit be continued
    John Bailey   Defendant)   untill next Court.

John McCooll in behalf   )   Ordered that this Suit be
of Jane Grimes   Plaintiff)   discontinued at the
   against   )   Plaintiffs Cost.
Joseph Jones   Defendant)

John Steen Senr.   Plaintiff)   Came the defendant into
   against   )   Open Court by his attorney
Charles Burton   Defendant)   and the Plaintiff. Altho
                                Called Solemnly came not to
prosecute his Suit and on motion of the defendant by his
attorney a nonsuit is awarded him against the Plaintiff
and that he recover the sum of five shillings for his
damage and costs of suit which is ordered accordingly.

Larken Wells   Plaintiff)   Continued untill next
   against   )   court by Consent of the
John Henry &   )   Parties.
Susannah Baileys   Defendants)

Tabitha Pearson   Plaintiff)   On a Writ of Enquiry
   against   )   Came the Plaintiff by William
Skelton & Smith   Defendant)   Shaw his attorney and the
                               Defendant altho Solmenly
called came not to defend his suit whereupon came a Jury
Towit. John Martindale F. M. Thomas Minton Charles
Humpharies Solomon Whitson Benjamin Crownover Thomas
Roberts Richard Huckebey James Townsend Benjamin Darby
Isaac Gregory Nathan Langstone and William Smith who being
duly sworn to well and truly try this writ of Enquiry
return their verdict and say on their several oathes "We
find for the Plaintiff the sum of five shillings and costs
of suit and Judgment accordingly.   John Martindale
                                      foreman

On a Presentment of the Grand Jury against Henry Burrell
Ordered that he be Suspended from his Office of Constable
and that he be bound in recognizance for his Personal

257

appearance at next Court in September Court in Order to
answer the Charge laid against him by the Grand Jury
Henry Burrow you acknowledge to owe to the State the sum
of Twenty pounds George Harling and Samuel Clowney you and
each of you acknowledge to owe to the State the Sum of
Ten pounds each to be levied on your several goods and
chattles lands and Tenements by way of recognizance
to the States Use. Provided you the said Henry Burrow
shall fail to Personally appear at this Court to be Holden
on the Fourth Monday in September Next to answer to a
charge prefered against you by the Grand Jury.

Isaac Hawkins   Plaintiff) Tresspass
   against   ) On motion of William Shaw
William Hughes   Defendant) Esquire atty for the defendant
                             for a Nonsuit and being Over
Ruled by the Court, Whereupon came Isaac Hawkins by Ephraim
Ramsey his attorney and the defendant by his attorney
aforesaid. Whereupon came a Jury Towit. John Martindale
Foreman Thomas Minton Charles Humpharies Solomon Whitson
Benjamin Crownover Thomas Roberts Richard Huckebey James
Townsend Benjamin Darby Isaac Gregory Nathan Langston and
William Smith who being sworn well and truly to try the
matter on the Issue Joined upon their Oathes do say "that
the Plaintiff recover against the said Defendant the sum
of Eighteen pounds also his costs by him about his suit
in this behalf expended John Martindale foreman
William Shaw Esquire moved for a New Tryal.

On the motion of Hugh Meanes Esquire lease is given him
to retail Spirituous Liquors on his Giving Bond and
Security according to Law. Who came into Open Court and
entered into bond in the Sum of one hundred pounds Sterling
with Samuel Clowney his Security.

Sion Cook   Plaintiff) Debt attachment Granted by a
   against   ) Justice of the peace the Parties
Archer Smith Defendant) came into Open Court and then and
                         there agreed to refer their Suit
to Wm. Farr. James Gibbs and Samuel McJunkin and their
award to be the Judgment of this Court which is Ordered
accordingly.

Edson & Company) attachment
   against   ) Ordered that this suit be dismissed
Robert H. Hughes) at the Defendants cost.

A Mortguage from Jesse Dodd to Andrew Torrence proved
before a Justice & Ord.

Ordered that the Minutes be read which was accordingly
done & signed by   John Birdsong
                      Joseph McJunkin
                      Hugh Meanes
The Court then adjourned untill tomorrow 9 o'clock.

302 At a Court continued and held according to adjournment at
the Court House of Said County on Fryday the Twenty sixth
day of March One thousand seven hundred and Ninety.
Presnet   John Birdsong   Thomas Blasingame
             Hugh Meanes   Joseph McJunkin   Esquires

258

Robert Baitey   Plaintiff)   Special action
  against   )   On motion of the Defendant by
Nathaniel Cooper Defendant)   his Counceller for an arrest
                                of Judgment and after an
Investigation by the Parties Ordered by the Court that the
Judgment be confirmed and Stand Valid.

George Wadkins   Plaintiff)   Tresspass
  against   )   Came the Parties into Open
James Duncan   Defendant)   Court and then and there
                                agree to discontinue their
Suit at Mutual Costs which is ordered accordingly.

Edson & Company   )   Debt attachment
  against   )   The defendant came into Open Court in
Nathaniel Cooper)   his Own proper Person and confessed
                        a Judgment for the Sum of Nine pounds
Nineteen Shillings and Four pence half penny and costs
of suit. which is ordered accordingly.

Sarah Gist   Plaintiff)   Continued untill next Court by
  against   )   Consent of the Parties which is
Jesse Dodd   Defendant)   Ordered accordingly.

James Timms   Plaintiff)   Debt
  against   )   there being a nonsuit entered
Humphrey Posey Defendant)   through a mistake and on the
                             motion of Daniel Brown Esquire
attorney for the Plaintiff for a reinstatement of the case
which was accordingly granted by the Court; and Judgment
was thereupon entered by default for Thirteen pounds Sterling and costs of Suit which is ordered accordingly.

John Henderson   Plaintiff)   Debt attachment
  against   )   Ordered that the property
James Yancey   Defendant)   attached be sold agreeable to
                               Law by the Sheriff to satisfy
the Plaintiffs Judgment.

A Deed of conveyance from John McKibbin to Jane Rogers
acknowledged in open Court by the said John McKibbin and
ordered to be recorded.

William Skelton Plaintiff)   Case
  against   )   Came the Plaintiff by William
James Duncan   Defendant)   Shaw Esqr. his attorney and
                               the defendant by his
Counciller Whereupon came a Jury Towit. John Martindale
foreman Thomas Minton Charles Humpharies Solomon Whitson
Benjamin Crownover Thomas Roberts Richard Huckeboey James
Townsend Benjr Darby Isaac Gregory Nathan Langstone William
Smith who being duly sworn to all and truly to Try the
matter on the Issue Joined Upon their Oathes do say that
the Plaintiff recover against the said defendant The sum
of Fifteen pounds Two Shillings and eight pence and also
his costs by him about his suit in this behalf expended.

303 James Yancey   Plaintiff)   Petr. & Summons
      against   )   Ordered that this Suit be
    Samuel Jackson Defendant)   Discontinued at the defendants
                                  cost and no attorneys fee to
    be Taxed.

259

Samuel Jackson   Plaintiff)   Debt attachment
   against   )   Came the Plaintiff by William
William Wofford   Defendant)   Shaw Esquire his attorney and
                               the defendant being solemnly
called but failed to appear to prosecute his suit Judgment
by default was entered against him on which the plaintiff
proceeded to execute his writ of enquiry Whereupon came a
Jury towit. John Martindale foreman Thomas Minton Charles
Humpharies Solomon Whitson Benjamin Crownover Thomas
Roberts Richard Huckeboy James Townsend Benjamin Darby
Isaac Gregory Nathan Langstone and William Smith Who being
duly sworn to well and truly try this writ of enquiry
return their verdict and say "We find for the Plaintiff
the Sum of Forty Pounds and Costs of Suit
                        John Martindale foreman

Ordered that Charles Hames Senr. James McWhorter, John
Foster John Hames Baxster Moseley, Work on the road from
Grindle Shoals to where the New Road Turnes out of the
Old road that leads to Henry Longs under James Moseley
Overseer of the said road and that they keep the same in
good repair according to Law with the hands aforesaid.

James Olephant)   Ordered that James Ollephant Pay James
   against   )   Gibbs five Shillings for Two days
Charles Bruce)   attendance as a witness for him in this
                  suit.

Hugh Holland   Plaintiff   ) Tresspass
   against   ) Came the Parties into Open
Richardson Rountree Defendant) Court and then and there
                               referred this suit to the
Arbitration of Thomas Brandon and George Harling Hatter and
their award to be made the Judgment of this Court.

A Deed of Conveyance from Charles Jones to William Clark
proved before a Justice and Ordered to be recorded.

Robert Baitey   Plaintiff)   Special action on the case
   against   )   This day came the Parties in
Nathaniel Cooper Defendant)   their own proper persons
                              and then and there agreed to
Settle this suit on the defendant paying all costs which is
Ordered accordingly.

State So. Carolina   Plaintiff)   Bastardy
   against   )   Rebecca Rountree having
Rebecca Rountree   Defendant)   made Oath that she has
                                 been delivered of an
Illegitimate Child and that C R Edson is the Father
thereof--and Ordered by the Court that he the said C R
Edson give Security for his appearance at next Court
whereupon--William Farr and John Sanders came into Open
Court and Severally acknowledged themselves indebted to
the State. Towit the said C R Edson in the sum of Twenty
pounds and each of his Securities in the sum of ten pounds
for his appearnce &c
Signed   C R Edson
                  Wm Farr
                  John Sanders

260

304 William Skelton   Plaintiff)   Ordered that a New Tryal be
       against   )   granted in this Suit.
    James Duncan   Defendant)

    Chesnut & Company)   Attachment
       against   )   Ordered that this Suit be dismissed
    Joseph East   )   at the Plaintiffs Cost.

    Robert Baitey)   Ordered that Nathan Cooper Pay James
       against   )   Townsend the Sum of One pound Twelve
    Nathl. Cooper)   Shillings and Six pence for thirteen
                      days attendance as a witness for him in
    this Suit.

    Ordered that the minutes be read which was done accordingly
    and the Court then adjourned untill Court in Course
    Signed by   John Birdsong
                       Thomas Brandon
                       William Kennedy

    At a Court Begun and Holden in and for the County of Union
    at the Court House of Said County on Monday the Twenty
    Eighth day of June in the year of our Lord one thousand
    Seven Hundred and Ninety and of the Independence of the
    United States of North America the Fourteenth.
    Present   John Henderson   Hugh Meanes
                   William Meanes   Charles Sims   Esqrs.
                   Thomas Blasingame   Thomas Brandon

    The Court proceeded to draw a Grand Jury for this county
    to serve next court which the sheriff is hereby Ordered to
    Summons to attend and serve as aforesaid for the County
    aforesaid. Towit. William Coleman, William Wood, William
    Brummet, Elias Cook William Whitlock William Beckham
    Benjamin Woodson Samuel Shippey Isaac Hawkins James Olli-
    phant, John Putman, Joshua Petty Nathan Glenn, Abadiah
    Howard Edward Tilman, James Maberry Thomas Mays Bartlet
    Whorton Thomas Stribling Senr. and John Brandon

    The Court proceeded to draw a Pettit Jury to serve next
    Court which the Sheriff is ordered to Summon accordingly
    Towit Jesse Spann Roger Pots Thomas Cook William Williams
    Bazel Wheat, Ellis Fowler Hugh McBride David Hudson Joseph
    Little William Hodge Reuben Wilks Freeman Roberts Turner
    Kendrick John Rutledge John Hames James Benson Richard
    Prewet Joshua Martin James Petty Junr. William Barnet.
    James Meanes Junr. Abel Pearson Thomas Draper Junr. Thomas
    Lewis Abner Cain Daniel Hollingsworth Wm. Young. William
    Jackson Richard Barnet and Goven Gordon.

    A Deed of Conveyance from Reuben Landrum to Obadiah Prewet
    proved in open court and ordered to be recorded.

    A Deed of conveyance from Esther Insco to Hannah Insco
    for one hundred acres proved in open court and Ordered to
    be recorded.

305 A Deed of conveyance from Renny Ballew to Zachariah Ballew
    proved before a justice and ordered to be recorded.

    A Deed of Conveyance from Renny Ballew to Reuben Ballew
    proved before a Justice and ordered to be recorded.

A Deed of Conveyance from John Hammelton to John Bankhead
Proved before a Justice and Ordered to be recorded.

A Deed of Conveyance from Ralph Jackson to John Putman
acknowledged in open Court and ordered to be recorded.

John Crow Foster   Plaintiff)   This suit being refered the
  against   )   Arbitrators return their
James Lindsey   Defendant)   award and Say "that the defen-
                                dant pay all costs of suit
which is made a rule of this court and ordered accordingly.

Alexander Hammelton   Plaintiff)   This Suit being refered
  against   )   the Arbitrators return
James Lindsey   Defendant)   their award and say "that
                                   the Plaintiff Pay all
costs of suit which is made a rule of this court and
ordered accordingly.

A Lease and Release from John Haile and Wife to Thomas
Draper Proved in open court by the oathes of John Beckham
and Richard Mitchell and Ordered to be recorded.

A Deed of Conveyance from Andrew Jones to William Lipscombe
proved before a Justice and Ordered to be recorded.

On a Petition of Major Gordon for a Road from Tullingstons
to Hawkins Mill on Tyger River, Ordered that James Blewford
Senr. Capt. Phillip Anderson and Bernard Glenn Esqr. view
it and report the same to our next court.

William Steen   Plaintiff)   Ordered that this suit be
  against   )   discontinued at the defendants
Clark and Steen Defendant)   cost

Edson & Company   Plaintiff)   Ordered that this suit be
  against   )   discontinued at the Defendants
Caleb Gasway   Defendant)   Cost.

A Deed of conveyance from William Mitchell to Isaac Cook
acknowledged in Open Court and Ordered to be recorded.

On motion of Adam Potter he is therefore Exonerated from
Serving as a Juror, and also Samuel Littlejohn.

A Deed of conveyance from John Little to Federick Jones
proved before a Justice and ordered to be recorded.

Ordered that William Anderson be Overseer of the road from
Mitchells Creek to Dining Creek, in the room of Fielding
Curtis and that he keep the same in good repair.

Sarah Gist) Ordered that this suit be discontinued
  against   ) at the Plaintiffs cost.
Jesse Dodd)

306 Braselmin & Company   Plaintiff)   Ordered that this suit be
      against   )   discontinued at the
    David Prewet   Defendant)   Plaintiffs Cost.

William Farr Plaintiff against James Inlow Defendant
A Writ of Enquiry Issued and returned Nonest. Which the

262

plaintiff by William Shaw his attorney prayed for a Judicial attachment which was granted by the court.

Nathaniel Davis	Plaintiff)	Ordered that this suit be
against	)	discontinued at the defendants
Samuel Otterson	Defendant)	cost.

On the application of Sarah McPhearson and Geo Harling Hatter Letters of administration is granted them on the Estate of John McPhearson Deceased, there being a citation returned and published agreeable to Law who entered into bond with George Harling Farmer and Jehue McPhearson agreeable to law.

Edson & Company	Plaintiff)	Debt
against	)	Abel Pearson being bail for
John White	Defendant)	the defendants appearance
		brought him into Open Court

and delivered him up and was Taken into custody by the Sheriff.

On the application of Winney Laurence for Letters of administration on the Estate of John Laurence deceased. Ordered that a citation Issue to Excite all the kindred and creditors to appear at our next Court, to Shew cause if any they have why Letters of Administration should not be granted to the Said Winney Laurence.

Ordered that John Blasingame William Plummer and Renny Ballew appraise the Estate of John McPhearson deceased & make due return thereof Certifyed under their hands. and Inventory and apprisement thereof.

Ordered that the Court adjourn untill Tomorrow 9 o'clock.
Signed by   John Henderson
                 John Birdsong
                 William Kennedy

At a Court continued and held by adjournment at the Court house of said County on Tuesday the Twentyninth day of June One thousand seven hundred and Ninety and of the Independance of the United States of North America the Fourteenth
Present William Kennedy, John Birdsong, Thomas Blasingame Esquires.

On the Application of James Rountree, Ordered that he be a Constable for this County, who came into open court and Took the Oath prescribed by Law.

307 A Renounciation of the Right of Dower of Esther Grindle wife of John Grindle in a certain Tract of Land Granted from said Grindle to Adam Chisholm and John Watson, which said Dower was brought into open Court and Ordered to be recorded.

Ordered that Letters of Administration be granted to Martha Steen and John Steen on the Estate of Thomas Jones deceased.

A Deed of conveyance from John Murrell to Archer Howard being proved before a Justice, Ordered to be recorded.

263

Robert Lusk   Plaintiff)   Ordered that this Suit be
  against   )   discontinued at the Plaintiffs
Joshua Petty   Defendant)   cost.

William Brandon   Plaintiff)   Attachment
  against   )   Ordered that this Suit be
William Boyd   Defendant)   continued untill next Court.

State So Carolina)   Bastardy
  against   )   Ordered that the defendant be fined
Cushman R Edson)   the sum of Three Pounds Eleven Shillings
                      and Four pence and Costs of Suit.

The State So. Carolina   Plaintiff)   Bastardy
  against   )   Ordered by the Court
Rebecca Rountree   Defendant)   that the defendant be
                                         the sum of three pounds
Eleven Shillings and Four pence and Costs of Suit. which
Cushman R Edson came into Open Court, and acknowledged to
Pay the aforesaid fine of three pounds Eleven Shillings and
four pence, also the costs of suit.

State So. Carolina   Plaintiff)   Ordered that the defendant
  against   )   recognizance continue over
John Mullins   Defendant)   untill Next Court

A Lease and Release from John Blasingame and Uxor to
Thomas Bearden Proved in Open Court by the Oath of Ralph
Jackson and Ordered to be recorded.

William Skelton   Plaintiff)   Debt
  against   )   The defendant fileing an
James Duncan   Defendant)   affidavit that he cannot
                                safeley come to Tryal without
the Testimony of Robert Henry Hughes and Prayed a Continuance which was granted by the Court at his costs.

Burton & Hopkins   Plaintiff)   Debt
  against   )   An affidavit being filed by
Edmond Cradock   Defendant)   the Plaintiff and Ordered
                                 that this Suit be continued
untill next court at his the Plaintiffs Cost.

William Skelton   Plaintiff)   Dbt.
  against   )   Ordered that Archer Smith be
James Duncan   Defendant)   shown in open court and his
                                Testimony be admitted at the
Tryal of this Suit.

On the Application of James Holliday leave is Given him to
keep a Tavern or Publick House who came into Open Court and
entd. into Bond with Joseph Hughes and William Hall his
Securities according to Law.

308 Burton & Hopkins   Plaintiff)   Debt
    against   )   The Plaintiff being Out of the
    Edmond Cradock   Defendant)   State Ordered that they give
                                     Security for the Costs of
Suit which Richard Mitchell was formerly Security was not
approved of by the Court as an Officer of the same. Where
Captain Joseph Hughes enters himself Security for the Costs

of Suit, in case the Plaintiffs Should be cast in this
Suit.

William Jackson   Plaintiff)   Ordered that this suit be
   against   )   discontinued at the Plaintiffs
Samuel Saxon   Defendant)   cost.

Braselmin & Company Plaintiff)   Ordered that this suit be
   against   )   discontinued at the
Speller & Anderson Defendant)   Plaintiffs Costs.

Robert Lusk   Plaintiff)   Attachment
   against   )   Ordered that this Suit be
John Liles   Defendant)   discontinued at the Plaintiffs
                                 Costs.

James Hogans   Plaintiff)   Came the Defendant into open
   against   )   Court by his Counceller and
Philip Anderson Defendant)   the Plaintiff Altho Solemnly
                                 Called came not to prosecute
his Suit. Whereon the motion of the defendant by his
attorney, a nonsuit is awarded him against the Plaintiff
and that he recover the Sum of Five Shillings damage and
costs of suit. Which is Ordered accordingly.

Landlot Porter   Plaintiff)   Continued by consent until
   against   )   Tomorrow Morning which is
James Earley   Defendant)   Ordered accordingly.

Thomas Holden   Plaintiff)   Robert Gregory Proved Four days
   against   )   attendance in this Suit on
Samuel Cooper   Defendant)   behalf of the defendant which is
                                 to be Taxed in the bill of costs.

Ordered that an Estray bay horse, Posted before Bernard
Glenn Esquire by Bird Booker be Exposed to Sale by the
Sheriff Immediately according to Law.

A Bond from Joseph Edmondson to Hosea Holcome and assigned
from Hosea Holcome to John Holcome and from John Holcome
to William Woolbanks proven in open court by the Oath of
William Skelton and ordered to be recorded.

William Williams   Plaintiff)   Ordered that this suit be
   against   )   discontinued at the defendants
Luke Carrell   Defendant)   cost

William Hodge   Plaintiff)   Tresspass assault & Battery
   against   )   This Suit being referred and
Andrew McBride   Defendant)   the Arbitrators return their
                                 award and say that the said
McBride Shall pay all costs except one Guinea that Hodge
Paid his attorney which is made a Rule of this Court and the
Same Ordered by the Court accordingly.

309 Luzial Parlor appeler)   On appeal. The Court after
   against   )   Hearing the Allegations of each
Holland Sumner appellant)   Party ordered that the Judgment
                                 of the Justice be confirmed
                                 with costs of suit.

265

Daniel Brown, son of Gabriel Brown minor came into open
court and made choice of Landlot Porter for his guardian
which the Worshipful Court approv'd of. Who entered into
Bond with Job Hammond his Security according to Law.

Ordered that a Stray Cow. Posted before Hugh Meanes
Esquire by Samuel Clowney be exposed to sale at public
auction by the Sheriff according to law.

Edson & Company   Plaintiff)   William Williams came into
  against   )   open Court and entered
John White   Defendant)   himself Special bail for the
                                defendant.

On the motion of Edmond Ellis, he is appointed Constable
for this County, who came into open Court and entered into
office on his Taking the Oath prescribed by Law.

Ordered that the Court adjourn Untill Tomorrow 9 o'clock.
Signed by   William Kennedy
                     Thomas Brandon
                     Joseph McJunkin
                     Bernard Glenn
                     Hugh Meanes

At a Court Continued and Held according to adjournment at
the Court House of Said County on Wednesday the Thirtieth
day of June One thousand Seven hundred and Ninety and of
the Independance of the United States of North America
the Fourteenth.
Present   Thomas Brandon
             William Kennedy
             Charles Sims   Esquires
             William McCullock
             Thomas Blasingame

A Deed of Conveyance from William Jolley to William
McCullock proved before a Justice and Ordered to be recorded

A Deed of conveyance from Jno. McCooll to Allen Holland
Proved in open court by the oath of Thomas Brandon and
ordered to be recorded.

William Coleman   Plaintiff)   On attachment
  against   )   Ordered that the Sheriff
Philip Beozan   Defendant)   Expose to Sale Two Negroes
                                attached in this Suit and that
the Sheriff advertise said Negroes Thirty days and detain
the money arrising from the Saile in his hands untill our
next Court.

James Hogans   Plaintiff)   Attachment
  against   )   Ordered that the Sheriff
Shadrach Lewallen Defendant)   Expose to Sale the property
                                attached in this Suit after
advertising 30 days and detain the money in his hands
untill next Court.

310 William Shaw   Plaintiff)   Petr. & Summons
  against   )   Ordered that this Suit be
Joshua Petty   Defendant)   discontinued at the defendants
                                Cost.

266

```
John Jefferies      Plaintiff)  Debt
  against                    )  Ordered that the defendant
Charles Herrington Defendant)  Give Special Bail Immediately
```

John High being appointed Constable for this County came
into Court and Took the Necessary Oathes of Office accordingly.

```
Landlot Porter    Plaintiff)  The defendant demured to
  against                  )  the Plaintiffs declaration
James Earley      Defendant)  for inconsistencey Between
                              the Original Writ and the
```
declaration which the Court over ruled and Ordered the
defendant to Plead.

```
Landlot Porter    Plaintiff)  On motion of Wm. Dohertie
  against                  )  attorney for the Plaintiff,
James Earley      Defendant)  Ordered that the defendants
                              Plea in this case be Set aside
```
as Insufficient and Unsubstantial and that the defendant
do Immediately put in a sufficient and substantial plea.

```
Landlot Porter    Plaintiff)  On Motion of Wm. Dohertie
  against                  )  attorney for the Plaintiff
James Earley      Defendant)  Ordered that for want of a
                              Substantial and Sufficient
```
Plea in this case the Plaintiff take Judgment by default as
for a Nihil Disit.

```
Landlot Porter    Plaintiff)  On a Writ of Enquiry
  against                  )  Came the Plaintiff by James
James Earley      Defendant)  Dohertiee his attorney and
                              the defendant by his Counciller
```
Whereupon came a Jury. Towit William Pearson Walter Roberts
William Thompson, George Harling, Gilham Woolbanks Daniel
Crownover William Martindale James Johnstone William
McClarin Samuel Harling Daniel Lipham and John Sparks who
being Sworn Well and Truly to Execute this writ of Enquiry
on their Oathes do say "We find for the defendant. William
Pearson foreman.
Which Verdict is ratifyed & by the Court and Ordered to be
recorded.

```
Landlot Porter    Plaintiff)  Nickolas Lazerous proved
  against                  )  Twelve days attendance in
James Earley      Defendant)  this Suit as a Witness for the
                              Plaintiff which is ordered to
```
be Taxed in the bill of Costs.

```
David Hopkins     Plaintiff)  Debt
  against                  )  On Motion of William Shaw Esqr.
Thomas Biddey     Defendant)  attorney for the Plaintiff it
                              appearing there is a Clerical
```
mistake in the Writ Ordered that it be amended to a Writ
of promises and assumptions which was done in open court
accordingly.

```
311 David Hopkins   Plaintiff)  Debt
      against                )  On motion of Wm. Shaw attorney
    Caleb Gasway    Defendant)  it appearing there is a
                                Clerical mistake in the writ.
```
Ordered that it be amended to a writ of Promises and

assumptions which was done in open court and Ordered
accordingly.

David Hopkins   Plaintiff) Debt
  against   ) On motion of Wm. Shaw attorney
David Hudson   Defendant) it appearing there is a Clerical
                             Mistake in the writ. Ordered
that it be amended to a writ of Promises and assumptions.

Ordered that the Sheriff Expose to sale a Stray Mare
Posted by before Charles Sims Esqr. according to Law.

David Stockdon assa.   Plaintiff) Ordered that this Suit
  against   ) be discontinued at the
Herrington & Terrell   Defendant) Defendants cost.

Benjamin Clark   Plaintiff) Tresspass on the case
  against   ) On motion of Zachauas Talleafero
William Giles   Defendant) attorney for the Plaintiff for
                             an allorative of the Writ which
he was Over Ruled and ordered that the Writ Stay as is now
Set Forth.

Larkin Wells   Plaintiff) Trespass assault & Battery
  against   ) Came the Plaintiff by his
John Bailey   Defendant) attorney and the Defendant by
                             his Counceller. Whereupon came
a Jury Towit. Walter Roberts William Thompson George Harling
& William Pearson. Gilham Woolbanks Daniel Crownover William
Martindale James Johnstone William McClarin Samuel Harling
Daniel Lipham and John Sparks who being duly sworn do say
"We find for the Plaintiff One pound   William Pearson
                                                    foreman
Which Verdict is ratifyed by the Court and Ordered to be
recorded.

Ordered that James Townsend be and is hereby appointed
Overseer of the road from Cooks Bridge to Liphams as laid
out by Gentlemen appointed by this Court.

Edson & Company   Plaintiff) Dbt
  against   ) Ordered that this Suit be
John White   Defendant) continued untill next court.

Larken Wells   Plaintiff) Ordered that the Examination
  against   ) of William Hendley Esquire
John Henry & Susannah Bailey) be taken in this case and
              Defendant   ) be admitted in Testimony
                                in case he is Incapable of
attending court.

Ordered that John Gregory be Overseer of the Road from
Hughes Creek to McNeales Creek in the Room of Joseph
Hughes and that he keep the Same in good repair according
to Law with the Hands convenient thereunto.

312 Ordered that Peter Sarter be Overseer of the Road from the
Cross road near the Fish dam to Joseph Hollingsworth
Spring in the Room of Thomas Miles and that he keep the
same in good repair.

Benj.n Clark   Plaintiff)   Continued by consent untill
   against   )   next Court which is Ordered
William Giles   Defendant)   accordingly.

William Skelton)   Ordered that James Duncan Pay Archer
   against   )   Smith Twelve Shillings and Six pence for
James Duncan   )   Five days attendance also the sum of
                    Twenty Six Shillings and Six pence for
Mileage--in the above suit.

Larken Wells)   Philemon Bass proved in open Court Seven
   against   )   days attendance as a witness for the
John Bailey)   Defendant which is Ordered to be taxed in
                 the bill of costs.

James Hogans   )   Jeremiah Speller proved Six days
   against   )   attendance as a witness for the
Philip Speller)   defendant in this Suit which is ordered
                   to be Taxed in the bill of Costs.

Ordered that Daniel Lipham be Overseer of the Road from his
own house to the County Line towards Bookers Ferry &c.

Ordered that Benjamin Savage be Overseer of the Road from
Fannins Creek into the Road to where it Intersects the
Ninety Six Road in the Room of James McCracken.

Ordered that Curtis Wood be Overseer of the Road from
Hammeltons Ford on Tyger River to Hendricks ford on
Enoree River and that he keep the Same in Good repair
according to Law.

Ordered that George Lymen be Overseer of the road from
Hawkins Old Mill to Hammeltons Ford on Tyger River and that
he keep the Same in good repair according to Law.

Ordered that the Court adjourned untill Court in Course
Signed by   Charles Sims
                     Hugh Meanes
                     Bernard Glenn
                     Thomas Brandon
                     Joseph McJunkin

313 At a Court began and held for the county of Union at the
    Court House of said county on Monday the Twenty seventh
    day of September in the year of our Lord one thousand
    seven hundred and Ninety and of the Independance of the
    United States of North America 14t.
    Present   John Henderson
                   Thomas Brandon
                   Hugh Meanes   Esquires
                   William Kennedy
                   Joseph McJunkin

Ordered that the Pettit Jury be drawn to serve next Court
and that the Sheriff Summon them accordingly Towit.
William Sharp Joseph Howard David Leak William Lee Isham
Prince Moses Collier Henry Trevilla John Green Joseph
Cowen John Bennit. William Brandon Charles Brock John
Jasper Sion Murphey James Randol, Jacob Segar. Richard
Thompson Isaac Edmondson Nehemiah Norton William Buckhannon

Rainey Ballew John Steen James Guthries, Robert Chrinshaw
Benjamin Hawkins Page Puckett, Robert Gregory Evin Thomas
John McWhortor & Thomas Cox.

James Spray   Plaintiff)   Slander
   against   )   By consent of the Parties Ordered
William Smith Defendant)   that this case be refered to the
                            Arbitrament of Thomas Brandon
and William Farr Esquires with power of umperage their
award returned to our next Court shall be the Judgment
thereof.

Edson & Company   Plaintiff)   Petr.
   against   )   Debt
James McCracken   Defendant)   The defendant came into open
                            Court in his own proper
person and then and there confessed a Judgment for the
sum of five pounds seven shillings and eleven pence
according to specialty with interest and costs of suit.

A Deed of Conveyance from Shadrack Lewallen to William
Hardwick proven in open court by the oath of George Harling
and ordered to be recorded.

Walter Roberts   Plaintiff)   Trover
   against   )   By consent of the Parties
James Wray   Defendant)   and assent of the court the
                            Tryal of this case is refered
to the Abbitrament of David Smith and William Pearson with
power of Umpirage their award returned to next Court shall
be the Judgment thereof.

A Lease and Release from Charles Brandon to Charles Hamm
proven in open Court by the Evidence of Robert Gault and
Charles Sisson & Ordered to be recorded

A Deed of Conveyance from William Littlefield to Leonard
Smith proven in open Court by the oathes of James Sanders
and Nicholas Keating and ordered to be recorded.

A Deed of Conveyance from Charles Browning to Peter
Laurence proved before Thomas Brandon Esquire and ordered
to be recorded.

Martha Hollingsworth Plaintiff)   Continued by Consent
   against   )   untill next Court which
William Hardwick   Defendant)   is ordered by the Court
                            accordingly.

314 James Hogans   Plaintiff   )   An attachment
   vs   )   Ordered by Consent of the
Shadrack Lewallen Defendant)   Parties that this case be
                            Continued over untill next
                            Court.

A Deed of Conveyance from Frances Wilkie Senr. & Francis
Wilkins Junr. and Martha Wilkins to John Jefferies proven
in open court by the evidence of John Lefever and ordered
to be recorded.

A Deed of Conveyance from James Townsend and wife to
Jeremiah OClain proved acknowledged in Open Court by the

said Thomas & wife & Ordered to be Recorded.

A Deed of Conveyance from James Carvel and wife to Amos Cook acknowledged in Open Court by the said Carvial and Ordered to be Recorded.

A Deed of Conveyance from Thomas Brandon Esquire to Thomas Hightour proven before a Justice and ordered to be Recorded.

A Deed of Conveyance from William Williams to Isaac White proved in Open Court by William Dawkins lane ordered to Record.

A Deed of Conveyance from Amos Cook and wife to John Cook acknowledged in open Court by the said Amos Cook and ordered to be recorded.

A Deed of Conveyance from James Wright to Bazel Wheat acknowledged in open Court by the said Wright and Ordered to be recorded.

John Palmore is appointed overseer of the Road from Hollingsworth mill to the new Road from Grindal shoals to this Court house in place of George Newton.

Ordered that Benjamin Addington a poor Bastard boy of the age of five years be bound unto Moses Weldon untill he arrives to the age of Twenty one.

A Deed of Conveyance from Thomas Blasingame Esquire to John Ham acknowledged in Open Court and Ordered to be Recorded according to law.

David Hopkins Plaintiff	)	P. & Summons
vs	)	The defendant Z. Bell
Zacha. Bell & Patterson Defendants)		Came into Open Court
		& Ack. the source of
this writ.		

315 Ordered that Richard Wood be Overseer of the Road from Fannins Creek to Whitlocks mill on Browns Creek in the Room of Thomas Balley.

Came into open Court Elizabeth Taylor and Alsey Taylor and made Choice of Colo. William Farr their Guardian which met with the approbation of the Court and was appointed accordingly.

Colo. William Farr applied for letters of administration on the Estate of James Taylor deceased, which is granted him who entered into Bond according to Law in the sum of seven hundred pounds sterling.

Jesse Dodd Plaintiff)	Case
against)	The Plaintiff Came into open
Isaac Edmondson Defendant)	Court and dismissed this
	Suit at this own costs which
	is ordered accordingly.

Jesse Dodd Plaintiff)	Case. The Plaintiff came into open
against)	Court and dismissed this suit at his
David Smith Defendant)	Costs which is ordered accordingly.

271

Ordered that the minutes be read which was done accordingly
& the Court adjourn untill tomorrow nine o'clock.
And Signed by   John Henderson
                   Thomas Brandon
                   Hugh Meanes
                   Joseph McJunken

At a Court continued and held according to adjournment at
the Court house of said County on the Twenty Eighth day
of September in the year of our Lord one thousand Seven
hundred and Ninety.
Present   Zachariah Bullock
             John Henderson   Esquires
             Thomas Brandon
             Joseph McJunkin

Captain Edward Tilman applyed for letters of admr. on the
Estate of Elisha Davis deceased and a Citation granted him
and Returned to this Court lawfully published & its therefore ordered that letters of administration be granted to
the said Edward Tilman on the Estate of the aforesaid
Elisha Davis who entered into bond according to law in the
sum of two hundred pounds. sterling.

316 The Grand Juror for this County Towit. James Olliphant
foreman William Coleman William Brummett Eli Cook William
Beckham Benjamin Woodson Samuel Shippey Isaac Hawkins
Joshua Petty Thomas Stribling Nathan Glenn James Maberry
Thomas Mays John Brandon and Obadiah Olliphant being duly
sworn according to Law and received their Charge Withdrew
to Consult their Verdicts &c.

State   )   Larcency
vs   )   Witnesses sworn and bill sent to the
Thomas Edwards)   Grant Juror

The State   )   On Escape
vs   )   Witnesses sworn and bill sent to Grand Juror
Joseph Jones)

The State   )   Larcency
vs   )   The Witnesses sworn & bill sent to the
John Mullins)   Grand Juror.

The State   )   Larcency
vs   )   The Witnesses sworn and the bill sent to
James Robinson)   the Grand Juror & Ordered that a Capias
                   Issue against John Woods as an evidence
on this Indictment.

The State   )   Larcency
vs   )   The Witnesses sworn and the bill sent to
James Robinson)   the Grand Juror.

The State   )   Larcency
vs   )   The Witnesses sworn and the bill given
John Thompson &)   to the Grand Juror.
James Robinson)

The State   )   Larcency
vs   )   The Defendant came into Open Court and
Thomas Edward)   entered into Recognizance.

272

The State   )   On a presentment of the Grand Juror on him
    vs   )   for malpractices as a Constable for this
Henry Runow)   County by order of the Court the County
                 attorney is directed to enter a noleprosique.

The State   )   Ordered that a bench warrant Immediately
    vs   )   Issue against the defendants returnable
John Hogans &)   to this Court or if it cannot be executed
James Robinson)   returnable to any our Justice to give
                   Recognizance to appear at next Cambridge
Court to answer to the said Charge.

317 Edson & Co. Plaintiff)   Debt
      against   )   The defendant came into open Court
    John McNeail Defendant)   in his own proper person and
                             Confessed a Judgment for the sum of
Eighteen pounds Two shillings & four pence according to
specialty with Lawful Interest with stay of Execution until
next Court.

A Deed of Conveyance from Thomas Miles & Wife to John
Peter Sartor proven before a Justice and Ordered to be
recorded.

The State   )   Assault & Battery
    vs   )   Witnesses sworn and the bill given to the
Luzian Parlor)   Grant Juror.

George Patterson   Plaintiff)   Petr.
    against   )   The defendant Linear came
Hopkins & Linear   Defendants)   into Court in his own proper
                                 Person & confessed Judgment
for the sum of Nine pounds nine Shillings and one penny
with Interest.

A Deed of Conveyance from Thomas Miles to John Peter Sartor
Proven before a Justice and ordered to be Recorded.

The State   )   On Charge of Receiving Stolen Goods
    vs   )   Dismissed on paying costs.
Landlot Porter)

The State   )   Assault & Battery
    vs   )   Witnesses Sworn and the bill sent
Caleb & Isaac Edmondson)   to the Grand Juror

Ordered that the Worshipfull Court Adjourn One House
The Worshipful Court met according to adjournment.

A Deed of Conveyance from Colo. Thomas Brandon to James
Johnson Proved before a Justice and Ordered to be Recorded.

On the application of James Wilson leave is given him to
Retail Spiritous Liquors in this County Who enters into
bond agreeable to the Act of Assembly in that case made &
provided.

318 On the application of Samuel Simpson leave is given him to
Retail Spiritous liquors or keep a public house in this
County who entered into bond according to law.

An Inventory of the Estate of John Montgomery deceased
Returned into Court & ordered to be filed in the Clerks
office.

The State South Carolina)   Malicious Mischief
   against   )   True Bill
James Robertson   )   James Olliphant, foreman

The State South Carolina)   Burglary
   against   )   True Bill
Thomas Edwards   )   James Olliphant, foreman

The State South Carolina)   Assault & Battery
   against   )   True Bill
Luzian Parlor   )   James Olliphant, foreman
Ordered that the Defendant Six pence & then be discharged
on her Paying of Costs.

The State South Carolina)   Larceny
   against   )   No Bill
John Mullins   )   James Olliphant, foreman

The State South Carolina)   Escape
   against   )   True Bill
Joseph Jones   )   James Olliphant, foreman

The State South Carolina)   For assaulting the Sheriff in the
   against   )   Execution of his office.
Philip Shivertaker   )   Ordered that the Sheriff take
                      the defendant into Custody and
Commit him Goal unless he give security for his appearance.

The State South Carolina)   Escape
   against   )   Ordered by the Court that the
Joseph Jones   )   defendant Joseph Jones give
                      Security for his appearance at
next Court Whereupon came Daniel Comer and Benjamin Clark
into open Court and acknowledged themselves Indebted to the
State to wit the said Joseph Jones in the sum of Ŀ 100 &
each of his Securities in the sum of Ŀ 50 each for his
appearance &C.

319 Ordered that Major Charles Miles be fined Twenty shillings
for Insult to the Court and that the Sheriff take him into
Custody untill he pay the same

The State So Carolina)   Killing a horse
   against   )   ordered that a bench warrant Issue
James Robinson   )   against the defendant immediately.

A Deed of Conveyance from William Farr Sheriff to Humphrey
Bates acknowledged in open court and Ordered to be recorded.

Ordered that a Road be Cleared from William Darbys Store
the nearest and best way to prewet Town on Dutchmans Creek
then the nearest & best way to where it intersects the road
leading from Spartan Court Co Blackstocks ford on Tyger
River and that Archer Howard and Daniel Parmer View and lay
out the same and Nicholas Keating be Overseer of the Road.

A Lease and release from John Wafford to Isham Clayton
proved before a Justice and Ordered to be Recorded.

Ordered that the minutes be read which was done acc.g and
the Court adjourn untill tomorrow Nine o'clock.
Signed by   John Henderson
                   William Kennedy
                   Thomas Brandon
                   Joseph McJunkin
                   Thomas Blasingame
                   William McCullock

At a Court Continued and held according to adjournment at
the Court house of said County on Wednesday the Twenty
ninth day of September in the year of our Lord One
thousand seven hundred and Ninety.
Present   Thomas Brandon
                 William Kennedy   Esquires
                 Jos. McJunkin
                 Charles Sims

Ordered that the County Treasury pay Samuel Clowney Twenty
one shillings for Wintering a Cow & Earling that was sold
as Estrays in this County.

The State South Carolina   Plaintiff)   Burglary
   against   )   W. William Shaw
Thomas Edwards   Defendant)   County attorney
                                         entered a Nolle
                                         Prosique

320 Richard Mitchell Plaintiff)   Trover
      against   )   The Parties Came into Court
    Joseph Jones   Defendant)   and agreed to refer their
                                   suit to the arbitration of
Thomas Brandon Esquire and William Beckham. With umpirage
of Choseing a third person and their award to be the Judgment of this Court.

Edson & C.   Plaintiff)   Debt
   against   )   The defendant came into open
Edmond Ellis Defendant)   Court in his own proper person
                           and confessed a Judgment for
Thirteen pounds fifteen shillings and six pence with
Interest and costs of suit with stay of execution untill
next Court.

The Last Will and Testament of Aaron Jackson deceased
was proven in open Court by the Oath of Richard Thompson
and Ordered to be recorded.

Ordered that Hugh Meanes Junr. Hugh Meanes & Thomas Mays
appraise the Estate of Aaron Jackson deceased and that
Hugh Meanes Esquire qualify the appraisers.

James Hogans   Plaintiff)   Ordered that the Plaintiff
   against   )   pay Presilla Spiller Ten
Jeremiah Spiller   Defendant)   Shillings for four days
                                attendance as a Witness for
him in this Suit.

William Brandon)   Attachment
   against   )   Ordered that this suit be continued
William Boyd   )   until next Court.

275

John Murphey   Plaintiff)   Petition & Summons On motion of
    against   )   Zachariah Taliaferro Plaintiffs
John Bird   Defendant)   attorney. Ordered by the Court
                             that Judgment be entered up
against the defendant for the sum of Ten pounds & Costs of
suit Subject to the Installment Law.

A Power of Attorney from Isaac Briggs to James Gibbs proven
in Open Court by the Oath of Daniel Comer & Ordered to be
Recorded.

William Coleman   Plaintiff)   On attachment
    against   )   The Plaintiff by James Dohertie
Philip Bogan   Defendant)   his attorney and the defendant

321 Being Solemnly Called but failed to appear. Whereupon came
a Jury Towit Bazel Wheat foreman. Roger Pots William
Williams Hugh McBridge, William Hodge, Turner Kendrick
John Rutledge John Hames James Benson, William Barnet
James Meanes and Thomas Cook, who being duly sworn return
their Verdict upon their several Oathes and say "We find
for the Plaintiff Seventy seven pounds with costs of suit
                        Bazel Wheat   foreman
Which Judgment was ratifyed by the Court & Ordered to be
Recorded.

David Hopkins   Plaintiff)   Debt on assumpett
    against   )   Dismissed by Order of the
Thomas Biddy   Defendant)   Plaintiff

David Hopkins   Plaintiff)   Debt on assumpett
    against   )   Dismissed by order of the
Caleb Gasway   Defendant)   Plaintiff

A Deed of Conveyance from David Robinson and wife to
Richard Waters proven before a Justice & Ordered to be
recorded.

Ordered that the minutes be read which was done accordingly
and the Court adjourn untill Tomorrow Nine o'clock
Signed by   Thomas Brandon
                     Hugh Meanes
                     Joseph McJunkin

At a Court continued and held according to adjournment
at the Court house of said County on Thursday the Thirtieth
day of September in the year of our Lord one thousand
seven hundred and Ninety.
Present   Thomas Brandon
               Thomas Blasingame   Esquires
               Charles Sims
               William McCullock

A Deed of Conveyance from John Little and wife to James
Woodson proved before a Justice and ordered to Record.

The Grand Juror for this County have duly considered the
Indictments given to them by the Court return the following
bills &c Towit.

The State South Carolina against James Robenson Larcency
True Bill James Olliphant foreman

276

The State South Carolina)   Larcency
    against   )   True Bill
John Thompson   )   James Olliphant foreman
and James Robenson   )

322 The State South Carolina)   Assault & Battery
    against   )   True Bill
Caleb and Isaac Edmondson)   James Olliphant foreman

The State South Carolina)   Larcency
    against   )   True Bill James Olliphant
Thomas Edwards   )   foreman

The State South Carolina)   Rescuing property from the
    against   )   Sheriff by direction of William
Philip Shivertaker   )   Shaw Esquire County attorney
                                Ordered that a Nole proseque be
                                entered.

The State South Carolina)   Indictment
    against   )   For Assaulting an officer in the
Philip Shivertaker   )   execution of his office &c
                                By direction of William Shaw
Esquire County attorney Ordered that a Nole prosique be
entered on this Indict.

The State South Carolina)   Assault & Battery
    against   )   The defendant by his attorney
Caleb Edmondson   )   pleads not Guilty and traverses
and Isaac Edmondson   )   this Indictment. Ordered that a
                                Capias Issue against Isaac
Edmondson returnable to the nearest magistrate in order to
enter into recognizance for his appearnace at next Court.

William Darby   Plaintiff)   Attachment
    against   )   Philip Shivertaker together
John Montgomery   Defendant)   with John Steen Junr. came
                                into Open Court and entered
themselves special bail, to try the right of the horse,
attached, on an enterpleader, filed by the said Philip
Shivertaker and that in case the said property be adjudged
to be the property of said montgomery then the said Shivertaker deliver up the said horse to the Sheriff in as good
order as when attached, and if the horse is not considered
Montgomeries, then and in such case the Special bail
discharged and this not considered to the action. The above
bail bound in the sum of Twenty pounds

The State South Carolina)   Larcency
    against   )   Josiah Tanner came into open
John Thompson and   )   Court and acknowledged to owe
James Robenson   )   to the State of South Carolina
                                the sum of Twenty five pounds,
if he shall fail to appear at our next Court to give
evidence in the above suit, or indictment acknowledged in
open court   Josiah Tanner
Rich Mitchell D.C

323 The State South Carolina)   Larcency
    against   )   Ordered that a capias Issue
John Thompson and   )   against Abraham Lemaster and
James Robenson   )   Adam Goudylock returnable to

277

to some Justice, to give recognizance to appear at next
Court to give testimony in the above case.

The State South Carolina) Escape
  against   ) Ordered that a capias Issue
Joseph Jones   ) against James Maberry returnable
                              to some Justice to give recog-
nizance to appear at next Court to give testimony in the
above case.

The State South Carolina) Indictment
  against   ) William Tate Junr. came into
James Robinson   ) Court and acknowledged to owe
                              to the State the sum of Twenty
five pounds to be levied on his goods and Chattles by way
of recognizance, if he shall fail to appear at our next
Court to give testimony in the above case.
acknowledged in Open Court   William Tate
Richard Mitchell D.C.

Burton & Hopkins   Plaintiff) Debt
  against   ) On motion of James Dohertie
Edmond Cradock   Defendant) Esquire attorney for defen-
                               dant for a nonsuit. Its
decreed by the Court there shall be no nonsuit and ordered
that this case continue untill next Court.

The State South Carolina) Ordered that his recognizance
  against   ) Continue untill next Court by
Elijah Melton   ) Consent of his Securities

The State South Carolina) Larcency
  against   ) Wm Nicholas Jasper and John
John Thompson &   ) Nail and James Thompson came
James Robinson   ) into open Court and severally
                              acknowledged themselves to owe
to the State aforesaid the sum of one hundred pounds each
for the defendants John Thompson personal appearance at
our next Court and not depart the said Court without leave
thereof
Acknowledged in open Court   Nicholas Jasper
Richard Mitchell D.C.   James Thompson

Luke Carrell   Plaintiff) Case
  against   ) On motion of William Shaw Esquire
Jeremiah Dyal Defendant) attorney for defendant for a
                           nonsuit which was granted &
Ordered accordingly.

Thomas Brandon   Plaintiff) Ordered that this case be
  against   ) Continued untill next Court
William Speers   Defendant)

324 Jesse Dodd   Plaintiff) Debt
  against   ) Continued untill next Court
John & Sion Cook Defendant) by Consent of the parties.

James Lindsey   Plaintiff) This writ being returned
  against   ) nonest inventus by the
John Crow Foster Defendant) Sheriff ordered that this suit
                             be dismissed at the Plaintiffs
                             Costs.

278

```
John Murphey      Plaintiff)  P. & S.
  against                  )  Judgment being entered up
John Bird         Defendant)  yesterday against the defendant
                              and on motion of William Shaw
Esquire attorney for defendants, the Judgment was reversed
and this suit continued untill next Court.
```

```
Nicholas Lazerus  Plaintiff)  P. & S.
  against                  )  Ordered that this suit be
Luke Carrell      Defendant)  Continued untill next Court.
```

```
Elizabeth Alexander  Plaintiff)  Debt
  against                    )  By Consent of the parties
Harrisson Bell       Defendant)  Ordered that this suit be
                                 Continued over untill our
                                 Next Court.
```

```
Benjamin Johnson  Plaintiff)  Debt
  against                  )  By Consent of the Parties
William Johnson   Defendant)  Ordered that this suit be
                              Continued untill next Court.
```

```
Graaff & Co.    Plaintiff )  Debt
  against                 )  By Consent of the parties
David Chisholm  Defendant)  Ordered that this suit be
                            continued untill next Court.
```

```
David Hopkins   )  Debt
  against       )  By Consent of the parties ordered that
William Speers  )  this suit be continued untill next Court.
```

```
The State South Carolina  Plaintiff)  Larcency
  against                        )  True Bill
Thomas Edwards            Defendant)  James Oliphant foreman
```

```
325 Edson & Co.    Plaintiff)  P. & S.
      against              )  On motion of Wm. Shaw attorney for
    James Yancey  Defendant)  the defendant for discharge of
                              John High. Special bail, who was
    discharged and Judgment entered up against the defendant
    for Four pounds and five pence with costs of suit.
```

```
Edson & Co.      Plaintiff)  Petition & Summons
  against                )  The defendant came into open
Daniel Jackson  Defendant)  Court in his own proper person
                            and confessed a Judgment for the
sum of eight pounds sixteen shillings with interest and
costs of suit with stay of execution six months.
```

```
Josiah Tanner   Plaintiff)  Attachment
  against               )  On motion of Wm. Shaw attorney
John Tanner     Defendant)  for Plaintiff for an order of
                            Saile of the property attached
in this suit which is granted
```

```
Josiah Tanner   Plaintiff)  Attachment
  against               )  Judgment entered up against
John Tanner     Defendant)  The defendant for four pounds
                            thirteen shillings and six
pence with costs of suit.
```

279

Edson & Co.   Plaintiff) Petition and Summons
  against   ) Decreed for the Plaintiff nine
Adam Chisholm   Defendant) pounds eight shillings and five
                            pence Virginia Currency with
interest and costs of suit and Judgment accordingly.

Nicholas Keating   Plaintiff) Petition & summons
  against   ) Decreed by the Court for the
Spincer Brummet   Defendant) Plaintiff, the sum of seven
                               with interest & Costs of suit
and Judgment accordingly.

Mills Sumner proved four days attendance in the above suit.

The State South Carolina   Plaintiff) Larcency
  against   ) The prisoner being
Thomas Edwards   Defendant) arrained at the bar
                                       and Pleads not
Guilty. Whereupon came the State by William Shaw Esquire
County attorney and the defendant by Charles Goodwin
Esquire his Counceller, whereupon came a Jury Towit Basel
Wheat foreman, Roger Pots, William Williams, Hugh McBride,
William Hodge, Turner Kendrick, John Rutledge, John Hames,
James Benson, William Barnett, James Meanes and Thomas
Cook who being duly sworn according to Law Return their
Verdict and Say "We find the Prisoner Guilty, Basel Wheat
foreman
The Court ordered that he receive Twenty Lashes on the
bare back Immediately and then he be discharged on paying
costs.

The Grand Juror for this County, after due consideration
Return the following Presentments. Towit.
326 We Present James Mathews living on the waters of neds
Creek for breaking the thigh bone of a horse the property
of James Gassaway by which the said horse was killed and
for not having a legal fencee by which horses or cattle
might be kept out of his field, the same not appearing on
Prooff to be in the highest place fourfeet.

Ordered that a Capias issue immediately against James
Mathews to appear at our next Court to be holden on the
fourth Monday in December next to answer to a presentment
of the Grand Juror for killing a horse.

Josiah Tanner   Plaintiff) Mr. Nathan Gibson proved three
  against   ) days attendance in this suit
John Tanner   Defendant) which is 7/6 which is ordered
                            to be taxed in the bill of
                            costs.

Sarah Gist   Plaintiff) Debt
  against   ) Judgment confessed for the
Daniel Jackson Defendant) principal and interest due on
                            Specialty with costs of suit
with stay of execution by Instalment. Cold. Thomas Brandon
came into open Court and entered himself Security for the
said debt and Costs   Daniel Jackson
Acknowledged in Open Court   Thomas Brandon
Richard Mitchell D.C.

The State South Carolina)   W. James Gasway Senr. came into
   against   )   Open Court and acknowledged
James Mathews   )   himself indebted to the state of
                             South Carolina the sum of Fifty
pounds Sterling for his appearnace at March Court next to
prosecute James Mathews on a presentment of the Grand
Juror and not depart the same without leave thereof
acknowledged in Open Court   his
Richard Mitchell DC   James   X   Gasway
                                          mark

Ordered that William Farr administrator of the Estate of
James Taylor deceased. Expose to sale all the personal
Estate of the said deceased agreeable to Law.

Ordered that four head of Cattle posted by John Wilkie
before William McCullock Esquire be sold at the said Wilkies
house on the 15 of next month by Isaac Parker Constable.

Ordered that the minutes be read which was done accordingly
The Court then adjourned untill Court in Course.
Signed by   William Kennedy
                   Joseph McJunkin
                   Thomas Blasingame
                   William McCullock

327 At a Court begun and held in and for the County of Union
    at the Court house of said County on Monday the Twenty
    seventh day of December in the year of our Lord one
    Thousand Seven hundred and Ninety and of the Independance
    of the United States of North America the Fifteenth.
    Present   Thomas Brandon
                       William Kennedy
                       John Henderson   Esquires
                       Thomas Blasingame
                       Bernard Glenn
                       Charles Sims

The Court proceeded to draw the Grand Juror to serve next
Court which are as follows Towit. Jacob Haild, James
Parnold Benja. Woodson Ellis Fowler Robert White Thomas
Right, John Huey Samuel Littlejohn, William Woolbanks,
John Bailey, Govin Gordon Turner Kendrick John Lancaster,
Thomas Minton, Adam Potter Thomas Stribling Senr. William
Martindale Junr. Isaac Gregory Hugh McBride & Avory Breed.

Also the Pettit Juror to serve next Court which are as
follows Towit. Philip Holcome, Jos. Hopkins, William
Goldsmith, James Ellit Lott Wood, John Thomas, Jonathan
Cudd Wm. Lawson, John Parks, Edward Prince, John Greffin,
Robert Wallace, Patrick Moore, Robert Millhouse George
Cowen Robert Glover John Kennedy, John Murrell, James
Woodson Robert Gault Obadiah Howard, Thomas Kedwell John
Clark Charles Humpharies, George Crossley Henry Hooff,
William Jinkins Saml. Kelso, John George Junr. & Richard
Cannon.

A Deed of Conveyance from Jonathan Parnell and wife to
Zachariah Nance acknowledged in open Court, Ordered to be
recorded, Upon a Justice reporting that she freely relinquished her dower, when privately examined.

281

A Deed of Gift from Thomas Palmore to William Palmore Junr.
acknowledged in open Court and ordered to be recorded.

The Last Will and testament of John Birdsong esquire
deceased being proven in open Court by the evidence of
Joseph West Richard Davis and Kindro West, who made Oath
that they believed the said deceased, was in his proper
senses at the time of making the same which was thereupon
Ordered to be Recorded.

Ordered that Fredreck Eisen have a Citation in order for
administration on the Estate of John Leepe deceased.

A Deed of Conveyance from Charles Sims Esquire to Reuben
Wilks acknowledged in open Court by the said Charles Sims
Esquire and ordered to be recorded.

328 A Deed of Conveyance from Charles Sims Esquire to Reuben
Wilks acknowledged in open Court by the said Sims and
Ordered to be recorded.

A Deed of Conveyance from Charles Sims Esquire to Ann Veal
acknowledged in open Court and ordered to be recorded.

A Deed of Conveyance from Thomas Brandon Esquire to Abner
Wells proven before a single Justice & Ordered to be
recorded.

The Executors of the Last will and testament of John
Birdsong deceased be qualifyed in open Court Ordered that
they have letters of administration accordingly.

A Bill of Saile from Benajah Thompson to Rayney Ballew
acknowledged in open Court and ordered to be recorded.

Ordered that William Beckham Nathan Glenn and John Sartor
appraise the Estate of James Taylor deceased and make due
Return of the same.

Ordered that John Peter Sartor be Overseer of the Road
leading from the Cross roads near said Sartors to Hills
ford on Tyger River as far as Joseph Hollingsworth Spring
on said Road and that he keep it in good repair according
to Law.

Ordered that Drewry Murrell Rainey Belew and Richard Powell
appraise the Estate of John Birdsong Esquire deceased and
make due Return of the same according to Law.

Ann Gasway and James Gasway made application to the Court
for letters of administration on the estate of Caleb
Gasway deceased which was granted and they entered into
bond with William Beckham & William Farr, their Securities
according to Law.

Ordered that Archer Howard to overseer of the Road from
Cold. Brandons Bridge to Bobos ford on Tyger River, in the
Room of Fredrick Jackson and that he keep the same in
repair accg.

Ordered that William Beckham Nathan Glenn and John Sartor

appraise the Estate of Caleb Gasway deceased and make due
return thereof according to Law.

Ordered that Daniel Malone be Overseer of the Road from
Cooks mill on Tyger River to the Road that leads from
Samuel McJunkins to Thomas Horrells and that he keep the
same in Good repair according to Law.

Ordered that John Stokes be Overseer of the Road from
Dening Creek to the Ford on Tyger River at Adams mill in the
Room of Joseph Little who resigns and that he clear and
keep the same in good repair according to Law.

329 A Deed of Conveyance from Col. William Farr, to John
Underwood acknowledged in open Court and ordered to be
recorded.

William Hogans applied for letters of administration on the
Estate of Oregenal Hogans, Ordered that he have a Citation.

Ordered that Joseph Hollingsworth be Overseer of the Road
from Hollingsworth Spring to Hills ford on Tyger River in
the room of William Hogans and that he keep the same in
good repair.

Sarah Gist   Plaintiff   ) Attachment
   against   ) Aaron Fincher and James
Shadrack Landtrip Defendant) Duncan Son of Alexander come
                                 into Open Court and
entered themselves Special bail to pay the Consideration
and Costs of Suit in Case Judgment goes for the Plaintiff.

Sarah Gist   Plaintiff) Attachment
   against   ) Ordered that the Corn
Shadrack Landtrip Defendant) attached in this case be
                                 sold to satisfy the Plaintiffs
Judgment and also one Cow and Calf.

Ordered that all recognizances to this Court be Continued
over till the next.

Margaret Edmondson and Walter Roberts applied for letters
of administration on the Estate of Isaac Edmondson deceased
Which is granted, and they entered into bond with Samuel
Simpson and Isham Prince their Securities in the sum of
Forty pounds.

Ordered that the minutes be read which was done, accordingly
& the Court adjourned untill Tomorrow ten o'clock.
Signed by   Charles Sims
                 H Meanes
                 Thomas Blasingame

At a Court continued and held according to adjournment at
the Court house of said County on Tuesday the twenty eighth
day of December in the year of our Lord One thousand
seven hundred and Ninety.
Present   John Henderson
               Charles Sims
               Thomas Blasingame   Esquires
               Thomas Brandon
               William Kennedy

Ordered that all the Estrays lyable to be sold this Court
be exposed to public sale by the Sheriff according to law.

A Deed of Conveyance from John McWhorter and wife to John
Jasper acknowledged in open Court, and after the said
wife being privately examined by a Single Justice, who
reported She freely relinquishes her dower, Which is
Ordered to be Recorded.

330 A Lease and Release from John McWhorter and wife to John
Jasper acknowledged in open Court the wife being privately
examined, relinquishes her dower, before a Single Justice.
Ordered to be Recorded.

A Deed of conveyance from Joseph Pearson and wife to John
McKibbin and James McKibbin proven in open Court or before
Thomas Brandon and ordered to be Recorded.

Ordered that William Young, John Addington and Thomas
Roberts appraise the estate of Isaac Edmondson deceased
and make return thereof according to Law.

Ordered that the Rates established by the Court the 26th
day of June 1785 be Strictly adhered to by all tavern
keepers future.

Good West India Rum pr Quart	0.2.0	Toddy pQuart with	
Ditto p Pint	0.1.0	Loaf Sugar	0.1.2
Ditto p½ Pint	0.0.7	Lodging pr Night	
Ditto p Gill	0.0.4		0.0.4
		Stabling for one	
		horse twelve hours	
			0.0.4
Common Rum pr Quart	0.1.4	Corn pr Gallon	0.0.6
ditto p Pint	0.0.9	Oats pr Ditto	0.0.4
ditto p½ Pint	0.0.6	Warm dinner	0.1.0
ditto pr Gill	0.0.3	Cold ditto	0.0.9
		Breakfast with	
		coffee Tea or	
		Chocolate	0.0.8
Wine pr Quart	0.2.4	Cold Breakfast	0.0.6
ditto pr Pint	0.1.4	Pasturage for one	
ditto ½ Pint	0.0.9	horse 12 hours	0.0.3
ditto p Gill	0.0.5		

Batholomew Baker   Plaintiff)   Case
   against   )   By Consent of the parties
Arther Thomas   Defendant)   ordered that this case be
                                   referred to William
Beckham and James Thomas with power of Umpirage their
award returned to next Court shall be the Judgment Thereof.

On the application of John Lancaster. Ordered that he have
a Licencee, to keep a tavern and retail Spirituous Liquors
in this County, who entered into bond with James Gibbs and
John Blassingame Esquire his Securities for his Lawful
performance.

Ordered that Cushman Ruggles Licence continue untill next
Court.

A Deed of Conveyance from William Mayfield to Thomas
Brandon acknowledged in open Court & ordered to be recorded.

284

Ordered that John Wilkie be allowed the sum of Five pounds
for wintering five head of Estray Cattle to be paid out of
the County fund by the Treasury.

331 A Deed of Conveyance from William Edmondson and wife to
Walter Roberts proven before a Justice of the peace and
ordered to be recorded.

William Farr Esquire Sheriff of this County having been
elected as a representative of this County, in the next
General assembly of this State and the said William Farr
Esquire not being Eligible to take his seat, whilst he holds
the said office of Sheriff came into Court and resigned his
commission as Sheriff. Whereupon the Court proceeded to
the recommendation of a proper person to sucesed the said
William Farr Esquire as Sheriff and the Court after ballotting according to Law, do recommend Thomas Stribling Junr.
to be commissioned by his excellency the Governor as Sheriff
of the County of Union for the term of Two years, next
ensuing.
Ordered that the Minutes be read which was accordingly
done and signed by   John Henderson
The Court then adjourned   Bern.a Glenn
untill Court in Course   Thomas Blasingame
  John Haile C.A.C   Charles Simms

FINIS.

332 The State So Carolina)
    Union County   ) Be it remembered that on the
                           Twenty eighth day of March one
thousand seven hundred & Ninety one at the Court House of
the County aforesaid met. John Blasingame & John Henderson
Esqr. who produced their commissions, constituting &
appointing they the said John Blasingame & John Henderson
Judges in & for the County of Union in pursuance of an act
of the General Assembly of the this State passed at
Columbia the   day of   in the year
of our Lord one thousand seven hundred and ninety one
wihch said commission the court ordered to be recorded by
the Clerk.

John Haile was continued as Clerk of the Court by Order
thereof, who took the Oath prescribed by Law, and proceeded
to record the following commissions & likewise to the
duties of his said Office.

The State of South Carolina
                To John Blasingame Esqr.
We, reposing Special trust and confidence in your abilities,
care prudence and integrity, have commissioned constituted
and appointed and by these presents do commission constitute and appoint you the said John Blasingame, to be a
Judge of the County
(LS) Charles Pinckney
Court in and for the County of Union, and you are
hereby vested with full power & Jurisdiction to Hold the
said County Court and to hear and determine all causes
and other matters and controversies properly appertaining
and referred by Law to your Jurisdiction. This
comission to continue in force during good behaviour. Given
under the Seal of the State.

285

Witness his excellency Charles Pinckney our Governor and
commander in chief and over the said State at Columbia this
        day of   in the year of our Lord one thousand
Seven hundred and Ninety one, and of the Sovereignty and
Independence of the United States of America the Fifteenth.
Secretarys Office. Certified by

333 The State of South Carolina.
                To John Henderson Esqr.
We reposing Special trust & confidence in your abilities
care prudence and integrity, have commissioned, constituted, and appointed, and by these presents do commission
constitute & appoint, you the said John Henderson to be a
Judge of the County Court in and for County of Union, and
you are hereby vested with full power & Jurisdiction to
hold the said County Court, and to hear & determine, all
causes & other matters and controversies properly appertaining and referred by Law to your Jurisdiction.   This
commission to continue in force during Good behaviour.
Given under the Seal of the State
Witness his Excellency Charles Pinckney our Governor
and commander in chief in and for the said State, at
Columbia, This Twenty first day of   in the year of our
Lord, one thousand Seven hundred and Ninety One, and of
the Soveriegnty and independence of the United States of
America the Fifteenth.
(LS) Charles Pinckney
Secretarys Office
Certified by.
John Blasingame Esqr. one of the Judges did on the 28th
Instance Qualify John Henderson; as one of the Judges of
this County.

The Court proceeded to the recommendation of a Sheriff
and after ballotting according to Law. Thomas Stribling
Jnr. is recommended to the Governor as a fit person to
serve as Sheriff for this County the ensuing four years.

Richard Mitchell resigned his appointment as Deputy Clerk
of this Court.

On the recommendation of Benjamin Haile, he is appointed
Deputy Clerk of this Court and took the necessary Oath of
Office.

The Court proceeded to draw the Juries to serve at our next
Court, when the following persons was drawn as Grand Jurors
towit. Robert Coleman, William Wood, Robert Gregory Andrew
Mays Thompson Browning Thomas Greer Bird Beuford
334 Frances Drake, John Pearson, William Johnson, Jesse Holcomb,
James Kennedy, William Hollingsworth, Gabriel Patrick,
John Hamm Thomas Palmore, William Mays George Wadkins
Obadiah Howard & Daniel Lipham.

Also the following as Pettit Jurors. Joseph Hart, Page
Puckett William Hardridge John Cole Phillip Holcomb
Aaron Fincher Randol Alexander John Huey David Puckett
John Leah Benjamin Gordon Gedeow Porter Richd. Cox John
Hames James Petty, John Roberts Senr. Alexander Martin
James McWhortor John Bowers Thomas Davis James Puckett,
Mathew Robinson William Hodge Robert Chapman Edward Moore
Hugh Means William Keaton Joseph Davidson William Hayney

& Samuel Shippey.
Ordered that the Sheriff summons the following persons to
serve as Jurors for next June term.

Thomas Davis & Robert Woodson was qualified as Constables
for this County.

Ordered that all Recognizances & other States business
be continued untill next June Court.
The Court then adjourned until tomorrow 10 o'clock
John Henderson
John Blasingame
The Court was Opened & adjourned untill the first Monday
in April next by   Ben. Haile Clerk.

At an Intermediate Court begun to be Holden in & for the
County of Union, at the Court House of said County On
Monday the fourth day of April in the year of our Lord one
thousand seven hundred and Ninety one.
Present their Honors   John Henderson
John Blasingame   Esqrs.

A Deed of conveyance from John Neale to Thomas Moore
proved in open Court by the Oath of Adam Potter & Ordered
to be recorded.

A Deed of conveyance from Robert Thompson to John Easterwood. Proved in Open Court by the Oath of Adam Potter and
Ordered to be Recorded.

A Deed of conveyance from John White to William White
acknowledged in Open Court and ordered to be recorded.

335 A Deed of conveyance from John White Senr. to John White
Junr. acknowledged in Open Court and Ordered to be
recorded.

A Lease & Release from Frances Bremar to Adam Scale
proved in open Court by the Oath of John Hawkins & ordered
to be recorded.

A Deed of conveyance from John Bennet to Jehue McPhearson
acknowledged in open Court & Ordered to Record.

A Deed of conveyance from Lewis & Sarah Bobo to Jas. Duncan
proved in open court before a Justice and Ordered to be
recorded.

The Last Will and Testament of Caleb Edmondson Senr.
deceased, was proved in Open Court by the Oaths of Ralph
Hunt & Caleb Smith who said they believed him to be in his
proper senses at the time of Executing the said Will. and
ordered to be recorded.

A Lease & Release from John McMillon to Joseph Guiton
Proved before a Justice & Ordered to be recorded.

A Deed of conveyance from John Blasingame Sheriff to John
Haile, acknowledged in Open Court & Ordered to be Recorded.

On the application of James Woodson lease is given him to
retail Spiritous liquors & keep public House, during the

term of twelve months from the date hereof who gave bond
with Security accordingly.

On the application of James Darby leave is given him to
retail Spiritous Liquors & keep public House, during the
term of twelve months from the date hereof who gave bond
with Security accordingly.

On the application of James Park leave is given him to
retail Spiritous Liquors & keep, public House, during the
term of twelve months from the date hereof who gave bond
with Security accordingly.

A Lease & Release from John Winn to John White proved in
Open Court by the Oaths of William White & Daniel White &
Ordered to be Recorded.

A Deed of Conveyance from William Farr late Sheriff of
Union County to Thomas Brandon, acknowledged in Open Court
and Ordered to be Recorded.

336 Ordered that James Jeater be appointed to appraise the
Estate of Caleb Gasway deceased, in the room of John Sartor
who refuseth to serve.

On the application of John McKibbin leave is given him to
retail Spiritous Liquors & keep Tavern during the term of
twelve months from the date hereof, who give bond &
Security accordingly.

A Deed of conveyance from William Wofford to George Harling
proved in open Court by the Oath of William Plummer and
Ordered to be recorded.

Ordered that the Coroner Expose to Sale all Estrays now
brought forth that is posted up agreeable to Law.

A Deed of conveyance from Daniel McPheaters to John Thompson
proved before a Justice & Ordered to be recorded.

The Last Will & Testament of Thomas Young deceased proved
in Open Court by the Oath of Thomas Brandon and Ordered
to be Recorded.

On the application of Alex. Macbeth &Co. leave is given
them to retail Spiritous liquors, at Union Court House
during the term of twelve months from the date hereof.
who give Bond with Security accordingly.

On the application of Cush. R Edson leave is given him keep
a Tavern during the term of twelve months from the date
hereof who give Bond with Security according to Law.

A Deed of Conveyance from James Bankhead & Wife to John
Hayney proved before a Justice & Ordered to be Recorded.

On the application of Hannah Haild wife of Jacob Haild late
of this County deceased, Letters of adminstration is
granted her, on the Estate & Effects of said deceased, she
therefore give Bond, with Alexander McDougal & Obadiah
Howard her Securities & was legally qualified as Law directs

Ordered that William Kennedy Esqr. Obadiah Howard Senr. &
James Gibbs view the road from McCools old field to the
Court House & Report to our Court on Thursday if they think
it necessary for a Road to go round Ewarts field on the
Lower side.

337 Ordered that John Brandon Junr. be Overseer of the Road
from Col. Brandons to Union Court House in the room of
Joseph Howard and that he keep the same in good repair.

Ordered that William Steen Joseph Howard and Obadiah
Howard, appraise the Estate of Jacob Haild decd; and that
they be Qualified before Thomas Blasingame Esqr. or any
other Justice of the County.

The Court then adjourned untill tomorrow 10 o'clock
Signed by   John Henderson
                     John Blasingame

At an intermediate Court continued & held according to
adjournment on Tuesday the fifth day of April in the year
of our Lord one thousand Seven hundred & Ninety one
Present His Honor   John Blasingame Esqr.

Ordered that Mr. Samuel Coson be appointed Overseer of the
Road leading from Mr. Darbys Store by James Gibb's along
the old road that Leads to priwit town unto the Spartan
line there forming a Junction with a new cut Road and that
he clear and keep the same in good repair according to Law
with the hands convenient thereto.

Proved in Court a Deed of Conveyance from Benjamin
Covenhoven to William Johnson Junr. proved by the Oath of
William Johnson Senr. & Ordered to be recorded.

A Deed of conveyance from Merry McGuire to Richard Brock
proved before a Justice & Ordered to Record.

A Deed of conveyance from Merry McGuire to Charles Brock,
proved before a Justice & Ordered to be recorded.

On the application of Alexander Macbeth &Co. leave is given
them to retail Spiritous liquors at Grindal Shoals who
entered into Bond with John McKibbin his Security.

Ordered that Joseph Howard View the Road in the Room of Hez.
Rice who refuseth to serve.

338 The Court then adjourned untill Tomorrow 12 o'clock.
Signed   John Blasingame

The Court met according to adjournment on Wednesday the
Sixth day of April 1791.
Present his Honor.   John Blasingame Esqr.

Ordered that the Court adjourn untill Tomorrow 12 o'clock
Signed John Blasingame
The Court met according to adjournment, on Thursday
Present their Honors   John Henderson
                        Wm. Farr   Esqrs.
                        John Blasingame

289

Wihliam Farr Esqr. produced to the Court, a commission from
his Excellency the Governor constituting & appointing him
a Judge of the County Court in & for the County of Union
which commission was Ordered to be Recorded.

The State of South Carolina
        To William Farr Esqr.
We reposing special trust and confidence in your abilities,
care, prudence, and integrity, have commissioned, constituted and appointed, and by these presents do commission
constitute and appoint you the said William Farr to be a
Judge of the County Court, in and for the County of Union,
and you are hereby vested with full power and Jurisdiction
to hold the said County Court and to hear and determine all
matters and other controversies properly appeartaining and
referred by law to your Jurisdiction. This commission to
continue in force during good behaviour.
Given un-er the Seal of the State Witness his excellency
Charles Pinckney, our Governor and commander in chief in
and over the said State at Columbia this twenty first day
of   in the year of our Lord, one thousand Seven hundred
and Ninety   and of the Sovereignty and independence of the
United States of America the Fifteenth.
The said William Farr likewise produced a certificate from
under the hand of John Blasingame Esqr. Certifying that he
took the oath of Office as prescribed by Law.
(LS) Charles Pinckney
Secretarys Office
Certified by
Peter Freneau
Secretary

339 Wm. Farr Esquire having taken the Oath prescribed by Law.
It is Ordered that letters of Administration be granted
him immediately to administer on the Estate of James
Taylor deceased.

Mrs. Ann Gasway & James Gasway having taken the Oath agreeable to Law. It is ordered that letters of administration
issue on the estate of Caleb Gasway deceased.

Ordered that the Rates established last December Court be
stricktly adheared to by all Tavern keepers, also the
following liquors be rated towit. Gin pr Quart two
shillings, pint one shilling, half pint seven pence, Gill
four pence, Whiskey pr Quart one shilling & four pence,
pint Eight pence, half pint Four pence Gill two pence.

A Bond from William Haild to John Still proved before a
Justice & Ordered to be recorded.

Ordered that Mrs. Raby, keep the infant child of John
Leesee & Wife, (both deceased) untill further Orders for
her allowance for keeping said child.

Frederick Eisen applied for letters of adminstration on the
Estate of John Leppe deceased, who gave Bond with Duncan
McCrevan & Abel Pearson his Security, and was duly qualified

Ordered that Obadiah Howard, John McKibbin and James Tosh
appraise the estate of John Leepo deceased.

Ordered that Ben Haile be allowed the sum of five shillings for furnishing a lock to the Court House, and that the Clerk keep the keys thereof.

Ordered that John Goodwin Turner Rountree and John Little, view away for a Road from this place across Fair-forest near the mouth of Sugar Creek, the nearest and best way by Mr. Darbys Store or near the same into the Road leading to Ninety Six and report the same to our next Court.

Ordered that after this Court House is paid for out of the treasury that there be the sum of six pounds, allowed and appropriated, to the use of Thomas Sandwick, his wife & blind daughter, for their Support, and to be put in the hands of James Jeater.

340 Ordered that the Commission of Thomas Stribling Junior Sheriff of This County from under the hand of his Excellency Charles Pinckney esquire be Recorded in the Clerks Office,*likewise a bond from said Stribling to the treasurer of this State. *Bond recorded in Book No. 2.

The State of South Carolina
　　　　To Thomas Stribling Junr. Esqr.
We, reposing special trust and confidence in your abilities, care, prudence, and integrity, have commissioned constituted and appointed, and by these presents do commission constitute and appoint you the said Thomas Stribling Junr. to be the sheriff in and for the County of Union. To have hold exercise and enjoy the said office of Sheriff of the said County, together with all rights privileges profits & Emoluments whatsoever thereunto belonging or in any wise appertaining. This commission to continue in force for four years and no longer.
Given under the Seal of the State
Witness his excellency Charles Pinckney our Governor and commander in chief at Columbia, this Sixth day of April, in the year of our Lord one thousand seven hundred and ninety one and of the Sovereignty and independence of the United States of America the Fifteenth.
(LS) Charles Pinckney
Secretarys Office
Certified by.
Peter Bremar
Pro. Secretary

Thomas Stribling was commissioned, from under the hand of the Governer, as high Sheriff of this County and on his recommendation doth appoint John McNeail as Deputy Sheriff of this county who was Qualifyed according to Law.

Ordered that Joseph Jones be appointed Constable for this County, who was duly Qualifyed according to Law.

On the application of Robert Anderson leave is given him to keep a public House in this County, during the term of twelve months from the date hereof, who give Bond with sufficient Surety accordingly.

341 Ordered that Cushman R. Edson be allowed out of the County treasury, four pounds nine shillings, for furnishing lime,

to underpin the Court house, to be paid as soon as it is
raised by the County.

Thomas Blasingame Esquire was Qualifyed by John Blasingame
Esquire, as a Justice of the peace for this County. the
14 March 1791. John Pearson Esqr. was Qualifyed by John
Blasingame Esqr. as a Justice of the peace for this county
the   day of March 1791.
The Court then adjourned untill Court in Course
Signed   John Henderson
                    Wm. Farr
                    John Blasingame

At a Court begun and held in and for the County of Union
at the Court House of said County, on the first day of
June in the year of our Lord one thousand Seven hundred
and Ninety one, and of the Independence of the United
States of America the Fifteenth.
Present their Honors   John Blasingame
                        John Henderson   Esqr.

Ordered that the Sheriff summon the following persons to
serve as Grand Jurors for a body of Inquest, for this
County, they being drawn according to Law.

1.	James Sims	11.	Joseph Hollingsworth
2.	James Gibbs	12.	Stephen Layton
3.	Robert Harris	13.	George Newton
4.	Ralp Jackson	14.	William Lawson
5.	Thomas Vance	15.	George Harlan Hatter
6.	Samuel Simpson	16.	Joseph McJunkin
7.	James Hawkins	17.	Lewis Ledbetter
8.	William Lipscomb	18.	Cush R. Edson
9.	Joshua Petty	19.	Jesse Mayberry
10.	Isaac Gregory	20.	Basel Wheat

Also the following persons to serve as petit Jurors at our
next Court, they being drawn according to Law.

1.	Joseph Qualls	5.	Daniel Crownover
2.	John Garret	6.	John Thompson
3.	John Steen Jnr.	7.	John Ray
4.	Zachariah Belue	8.	Richard Cannon

342

9.	Thomas Harris	20.	John Rogers
10.	John Veil	21.	Isaac Chapman
11.	William Means	22.	James Thompson
12.	Nathaniel Langstone	23.	Holliway Dimpsey
13.	William White	24.	John Marten
14.	John Thomas	25.	Thomas Wright
15.	William Barnett	26.	Richardson Rountree
16.	Henry Hooff	27.	Stephen Howard
17.	Moses Meek	28.	Thomas Blasingame
18.	Water.n Boatman	29.	Augustan Wood
19.	Charles Humphries	30.	Arthur Brandon

William McCullock Esquire Qualified as a Justice of the
peace for this County, as appears by a certificate from
John Blasingame Esqr. one of the Judges of this date.

Edmond Ellis was appointed by the Court constable & was
Qualified in open Court.

Isaac Parker & Enoch Floyd was Qualified as constables, before John Blasingame one of the Judges for this County.

William Shaw as County attorney of this County by order of the Judges of said Court, took the Oath of office, as County attorney also the Oath to support the constitution of this State & of the United States.

The following persons, appeared & was sworn as Grand Jurors for this Court.
Thomas Greer foreman, Robert Coleman, Robert Gregory, Andrew Mays, Thompson Browning, Bird Beuford, Francis Drake John Pearson, Jesse Holcolm, James Kennedy, William Hollingsworth John Hamm, Thomas Palmore, William Mays, Obadiah Howard, Daniel Lipham.

William Lee	Plaintiff)	Case.
vs	)	By consent of the parties,
Thomas Brandon	)	Ordered that this case be dismissed at Defendants cost.

Cush. R. Edson	)	Debt
vs	)	By Consent of the parties. Ordered that
William McCullock)		this case be dismissed at Defendants costs.

343
Cush. R. Edson	Plaintiff)	Debt
vs	)	Dismissed at Defendants cost
William Johnson	Defendant)	by Consent.

Charles Green	Plaintiff)	Tresspass)	By consent of
against	)	assault &)	the parties
Harrison Bell	Defendant)	Battery)	Ordered that this suit be

Dismissed at the plaintiffs cost.

The following persons appeared to serve this Court as petit Jurors. Joseph Hart, Page Puckett, John Cole, Philip Holcomb, Aaron Fincher, John Huey, David Puckett, John Leep, Richard Cox's, John Hames, James Petty, James McWhorter, John Bowers, Thomas Davis Mathew Robinson, William Hodge, Edward Moore, Hugh Means, William Heaton, Joseph Davidson

The following persons being sum.d but failed to appear William Hardridge, Randolph Alexander, Benjamin Gordon, John Roberts.

Cushman R. Edson & Co.	Plaintiff)	Debt
vs	)	By consent of the
John Watson Senr.	Defendant)	parties Ordered that this case be dismissed

at the defendants cost, except the plaintiffs attorney fee.

John Chandler	Plaintiff)	Trover
vs	)	On motion of Wm. Shaw, Ordered
James Hogans	Defendant)	that the defendant, James Hogans, give Special Bail for

fourteen pounds

Ordered that the Trial & appearance Dockett be called over for the first time, which was accordingly done.

293

Nathaniel Davis   Plaintiff)   Petition & Summons
      vs   )   Came the defendant into Open
Spencer Brummett Defendant)   Court in his own proper person
                                   and confessed a decree for
the sum of seven pounds, with costs of suit, came also the
plaintiff, and then and there agreed to stay the execution.

344 untill the first of October and. Whereupon it is considered by the Court, that the plaintiff recover against the
defendant the debt aforesaid together with the costs in
this behalf expended, in form aforesaid, and the said
defendant in Money &c &c.

Ordered that the minutes be read, which was accordingly
done; & signed by   John Henderson
                       John Blasingame
The court then adjourned Tomorrow 10 OClock.

At a Court continued and held by adjournment at the Court
House of said County, on the Second day of June in the year
of our Lord, one thousand Seven hundred and Ninety one.
Present their Honors.   Wm. Farr
                         John Henderson   Esqrs.

The State of South Carolina)   Ordered that Enoch Floyd
    against   )   Constable do, bring Thomas
John Thompson   )   Wood, Josiah Tanner and
                                   Abraham Lemaster, personally
to be and appear before this Court, now sitting in order to
give testimony in behalf of the State, in the above case.

Mr. Thomas Walker, produced a commission, from the associate
Judges of this State, authorizing him to plead the Law in
the Several Courts of this State.   Ordered that he be admitted to practice in this Court accordingly.

William Brandon   Plaintiff)   Attachment
    versus   )   Came the plaintiff into Court
William Boid.   Defendant)   by William Shaw his attorney
                                   and the defendant being
solemnly called failed to appear to prosecute his suit.
On motion, Judgment is awarded against him by default.
Whereupon the plaintiff by his attorney aforesaid proceeded
to execute a writ of enquiry. When came a Jury, towit.
Aaron Fincher foreman, Joseph Hail Page Puckett, John Cole
Philip Holcomb, John Huey, David Puckett, John Leak,
Richard Cox, William Hayney John Hames and James Petty,
who being sworn to well and truly try this writ of enquiry,
say on their Oathes aforesaid, we find for the plaintiff
Thirty pounds and
345 Costs of suit, Whereupon it is considered by the Court
that the Verdict be Recorded and that the plaintiff recover
against the defendant in form aforesaid, and the said
defendant in Money &c &c.

John Chandler)   Trover
      vs   )   Mr. James Hogans being Ordered to give
James Hogans)   Special bail in this suit for fourteen
                    pounds. Whereon Mr. Thomas Evans came into
open court and entered himself as Special Bail for the debt
& costs of suit in this case, for James Hogans.

294

The State of So. Carolina) Indictment
    vs   ) The Court ordered a
William Bratcher &al.   ) Noleprosique to be entered
                        in this case.

John Jenkins) P. & Sum
   vs   ) Came the defendant into open Court in his
William Davitt) own proper person and confessed a decree
               for the sum of seven pounds, together with
the interest due thereon amounting to the sum of also the
costs of suit...Wherefore it is considered by the Court
that the plaintiff recover against the defendant the money
aforesaid and the said Defendant in money &c &c.

Knox & Harper   Plaintiff) Petition & Sums
 assee of   ) Came the defendant into Open
   vs   ) Court in his own proper person
Charles Sims   Defendant) and then & there acknowledged
                    that he owed the plaintiff
the sum of Eight pounds ten shillings sterling and confessed
a decree for the same, with costs of suit, Wherefore it
is considered by the court that the plaintiff recover against
the defendant the money aforesaid, inform aforesaid, and
the said Defendant in money &c &c
Came also the plaintiff in Open Court, and then agreed to
Stay the Execution against the defendant, untill the first
day of October next, which is hereby Ordered accordingly.

346 John Lusk   Plaintiff) Petition & Summons
   vs   ) Came into open Court the wife of
John Hope   Defendant) the defendant, in her own proper
                 person, and then and there in
behalf of her said husband aforesd. confessed a Judgment
for the sum of Seven pounds, two shillings and four pence
with the Lawful interest, amounting to
and costs of suit, wherefore it is considered by the court
that the plaintiff recover against the defendant the debt
aforesaid & also his costs in this behalf expended in form
aforesd. and the said Defendant in money &c &c.

Burton & Hopkins Plaintiff) Debt
   vs   ) Abated by death of the
Edmond Cradock Defendant) Defendant.

John Thompson Plaintiff) Petr. & Sums.
 vers.   ) The Plaintiff came into open
John Steen Junr. Defendant) Court in his own proper person
                 and dismissed his suit at his
                 Own cost.

Graaff & Co.   Plaintiff) Debt
 vers   ) Came the parties into open
David Chisholm Defendant) Court and then and there
                 agreed to discontinued this
suit at the defendants costs. the same is ordered
accordingly.

John Thompson) P. & S.
 vers.   ) Thomas Vance came into open Court and
John Steen Junr.) proved seven days attendance in this
               suit as a Witness for the defendant
which is Seventeen Shillings & six pence, also James Steece

proved Eight days attendance in this suit for the defendant
which is Twenty Shillings, Ordered that John Thompson pay
the above sum.

The State   ) Indictment for assault, on the
   vs   ) body of David Boshart, the Witnesses
William Williams) being sworn to give evidence before
                      the Grand Jury. Who returned a true
                      Bill.   Thomas Greer foreman

The Grand Jury, returned their presentments, and was
thereupon Discharged.

347 The State So. Carolina) Indict & assault
      vs   ) David Boshart, Cush. R. Edson
    William Williams   ) David Chisholm & Thomas Stribling
                             Junr. came into open Court and
severally acknowledged themselves to owe to the State of
South Carolina (towit) that Capt. Edson in the sum of
Twenty five pounds and each of this Rest in ten pounds for
their appearance in this Suit to give evidence in behalf
of the State.

The minutes were read & the Court adjourned untill
tomorrow 9 OClock.
Signed by   John Henderson
                   Wm Farr
                   John Blasingame

At a Court continued & held by adjournment in and for the
County of Union at the Court House of said County, on the
third day of June, in the year of our Lord, one thousand
Seven hundred and Ninety one.
Present their Honors   Wm. Farr
                       John Blasingame   Esquires

David Hopkins   Plaintiff) P. & S.
   vs   ) Came the defendant into open
Zachariah Bell   Defendant) Court in his own proper
                              person and confessed a Judgment
for the sum of Nine pounds Seven shillings and Eight pence
with Interest due thereon amounting to
and the cost of suit, Came also the plaintiff and agreed
to stay the Execution four months. Wherefore it is considered by the court that the plaintiff recover against the
defendant the debt, aforesaid and his costs in this
behalf expended, in form aforesaid, and the said defendant,
in Mercy &c &c.

William Farr esqr.   Plaintiff) Judicial attachment
   vers.   ) Came the plaintiff by
James Inlow   Defendant) William Shaw esqr. his
                                 attorney, the defendant
being solemnly called, failed to appear to defend his suit.
Judgment was awarded against him by default the plaintiff
proved his case, Wherefore it is considered by the Court
that the plaintiff recover against the defendant the sum
of Five pounds ten shillings, with the costs of suit in
this behalf expended and the said defendant in Mercy &c.
&c.

348 Edson & Com.y   Plaintiff)   Petition & Sums.
        vs   )   Came the plaintiff into open
    John White   Defendant)   Court by William Shaw his
                                    attorney..by petition and the
defendant being solemnly called but maketh default, the
court on hearing the complaint of the plaintiff by his
attorney aforesaid, Decree against the defendant Seven
pounds Nineteen shillings with costs of suit.

    Peter Braselmann & Co. Plaintiff) Petition & Sums
        vers   )   Came the plaintiff
    Robert Glover   Defendant)   into open Court by
                                        William Shaw their
attorney by petition & Sums. and the defendant being
Solemnly called came not to defend his suit, wherefore,
the plaintiff by their attorney aforesaid complains that
the defendant is Justly indebted to them, the sum of Six
pounds four shillings & Eleven pence. Wherefore it is
considered by the court that a decree be entered for the
said debt, together with the costs of suit.

    John Comptey   Plaintiff)   Petition & Sums.
        vers.   )   Came the Defendant into Court
    David Jackson   Defendant)   by William Shaw his attorney
                                    the plaintiff having him called
came not to prosecute his suit, On motion therefore a
nonsuit is awarded against him, Wherefore it is considered
by the Court that the defent..recover against the
plaintiff five shillings damage & costs of suit.

    Abner Potts   Plaintiff)   Slander
        vs   )   The plaintiff being called
    Enoch Garrett   Defendant)   failed to appear to prosecute
                                    his suit, a nonsuit is awarded
against him. Wherefore it is considered by the court that
the defendant recover against the plaintiff the sum of
five shillings damage & costs of suit.

    John Jefferies   Plaintiff)   Debt
        vs   )   On motion of William
    Herrington & Thompson   Defendants)   Shaw Esqr. attorney
                                          for the plaintiff
this case is dismissed at defendants costs which is
ordered accg.

349 Thomas Wood   Plaintiff)   Petition & Summons
        vs   )   Continued by consent, untill
    Torrence & Blasingame   )   next court
    Executors of Jno Ewart   )
    decd.   )

    Charles Sisson   Plaintiff)   Petition & Summons
        vers.   )   The plaintiff in this case
    Patrick Moore   Defendant)   being solemnly called to
                                    prosecute his suit failed to
appear, a nonsuit is awarded against him, wherefore it is
considered by the court, that the Defendant recover against
the plaintiff the sum of five shillings & costs of suit.

    Thomas Brandon Plaintiff   ) Petition & Sums.
        vs   ) On the Oath of Thomas
    Henry Long & Wm. Farr Defendants) Brandon this case is

dismissed at the defendants costs. Col. Wm. Farr discharged
from the costs.

Nicholas Lazeras   Plaintiff)   Petr. & Sums.
   vs   )   On motion of William Shaw
Luke Carrell   Defendant)   attorney for the plaintiff,
                               this case is continued untill
                               next court.

The State So. Carolina)   Indict. assault
   vs   )   The defendant being Ordered to
William Williams   )   give Security for his appearance
                           to stand his tryal. When he came
into open court, acknowledged to owe to the State of
South Carolina the sum of Fifty pounds & each of his
Securities in the sum of ten pounds, which they assigned in
open court.
R Mitchell DC   Wm. Williams
                       Wm. Peles
                       James Hogans

Peter Braselmann & Co   Plaintiff)   Debt
   vs   )   The plaintiff by his
Spencer Brummett   Defendant)   attorney William Shaw
                                  came into open court
and dismissed his suit at his own cost.

350 William Darby   Plaintiff)   Petition & Sums
   vs   )   The plaintiff by William Shaw
Aaron Hart   Defendant)   esquire his attorney came into
                               Open court and the defendant
being solemnly called failed to appear to defend his suit
The Court decreed for the plaintiff against the defendant
the sum of five pounds eight shillings and three pence
with cost of suit.
James Sanders proved three days attendance in this case
for the plaintiff, which is seven shillings & six pence
Ordered to be Taxed in the Bill of Costs

Benjamin Clark   Plaintiff)   Case
   vs   )   On the affidavit of Benjamin
William Giles   Defendant)   Clark, Ordered that this case
                            be continued untill next court
on a preemptory rule.

Holland Sumner   Plaintiff)   Attachment
   vs   )   On motion of Wm. Shaw
Thomas Blasingame Junr. Deft)   Defendants attorney for a
                                nonsuit, the plaintiff
being solemnly called fail'd to appear to prosecute his
suit, a nonsuit is ordered against him, and further
considered by the Court that the defendant recover against
the plaintiff five shillings damage & costs of suit.

David Stockton)   On appeal
   vs   )   Dismissed at the plaintiffs cost.
Wm. Gilkie   )

Benajah Thompson   Plaintiff)   Trover
   vs   )   Came the plaintiff by Zacha.
Andrew Gossett   Defendant)   Talioferro his attorney
                            and the defendant by

298

William Shaw, his attorney; Came also a Jury towit, Aaron
Fincher, foreman, Joseph Hart, Page Puckett, John Cole,
Phillip Holcomb, John Huey, David Puckett, Richard Cox,
William Hayner, John Hames, James Petty & Mathew Robinson
who being duly sworn to try this issue Joined, returned
their verdict & Say "We find for the defendant.
Wherefore it is considered by the court, that the defendant
recover against the plaintiff aforesaid, inform aforesaid,
with Costs of Suit.'

351 John Comer proved 8 days attendance which is Twenty
shillings ordered to be Taxed in the Bill of costs.

William Beckham   Plaintiff)   Debt
vs   )   On motion of William Shaw
Philip Anderson   Defendant)   Esqr. Ordered that the
                                defendant give Special
Bail for the sum of Thirty pounds.

William Skelton   Plaintiff)   Case
vs   )   Came the plaintiff by William
James Duncan   Defendant)   Shaw his attorney and also
                                the defendant by Zach.
Taliaferro his attorney, the issue being Joined, whereupon
came a Jury Towit. Aaron Fincher, Joseph Hart, Page
Puckett, John Cole, Philip Holcomb, John Huey, David
Puckett, Richard Cox, Wm. Hayner, John Hames, James Petty,
Mathew Roberson who was duly empanneled & Sworn, and
ordered to Seal up their Verdict & deliver it in the
morning.

Benajah Thompson)   Thomas Gossett proved Eleven days
vs   )   attendance in this suit as a Witness
Andrew Gossett)   for the plaintiff which is Twenty seven
                   shillings & Six pence which is Ordered
to be Taxed in the Bill of costs.

Richard Mitchell   Plaintiff)   Trover
vs   )   The parties came into open
Joseph Jones   Defendant)   Court and then & there agreed
                                to refer and leave their suit
to the arbitration of William Beckham and Col William Farr,
and their award to be the Judgment of this Court.

Drewry Gowing   Plaintiff)   Debt
vs   )   The plaintiff came into open
Spencer Brummett Defendant)   court and dismissed his suit,
                                at his own cost.

Martha Hollingsworth)   This case is dismissed at the
vs   )   defendants cost by Order of Court.
William Hardwick)

352 Benajah Thompson)   Nicholas Laxerus proved Twelve days
vs   )   attendance in this suit, which is
Andrew Gossett)   Thirty shillings. Ordered to be Taxed
                   in the Bill of Costs.

William Skelton)   Jesse Dodd proved Eleven days attendance
vs   )   in this suit as a Witness. John Martindale
James Duncan)   Eleven Days. William Gamble eight days
                 & two hundred miles, Ambrose Wray proved

nine days and William Woolbanks proved five days attendance
in the above suit Which is ordered to be together in the
Bill of costs.

The State So. Carolina)　Ordered that Elijah Milton, John
　　versus　　　　　　　)　Woods and Abraham Lemaster give
John Thompson　　　　　)　Security to appear and give
　　　　　　　　　　　　　　evidence in this suit, Vz. John
Woods the sum of Fifty pounds and his Security Hugh
Holland in the sum of Twenty two pounds. Abraham Lemaster
in the sum of Fifty pounds, and Thomas Wright his Security
the sum of Twenty five pounds. Elijah Milton the sum of
Fifty pounds and John Lipscomb his Security the sum of
Twenty five pounds. which they acknowledged in open Court.

George Ross　　Plaintiff)　P. & S.
　　versus　　　　　　　　)　The plaintiff by his attorney
Charles Sims　Defendant)　William Shaw came into Court and
　　　　　　　　　　　　　　complained by petition. The
defendant being called failed to appear. Whereupon the
Court decreed for the plaintiff, Seven pounds two shillings
& Nine pence, with Interest on the same amounting to
together with costs of suit.

The Court then adjourned untill tomorrow 9 OClock
Signed　　　　　　Wm Farr
　　　　　　　　　　John Blasingame

353 At a Court continued and held by adjournment in and for the
County of Union at the Court House of said County, the
fourth day of June, one thousand seven hundred and ninety
one and of the Independance of the United States of
America the Fifteenth
Present their Honors　　Wm. Farr
　　　　　　　　　　　　　John Blasingame　　　　Esqrs.

William Skelton　Plaintiff)　Cas.
　　vs　　　　　　　　　　)　The Jury in this case returned
James Duncan　　Defendant)　their Verdict. Sealed up,
　　　　　　　　　　　　　　which was opened, in open
Court and was read as follows (Towit) We find for the
defendant:
Wherefore it is considered by the Court that the defendant
recover against the plaintiff in form aforesaid, as also
the costs, by him in this behalf expended & the said
plaintiff in Mercy &c.

Larken Wells　Plaintiff　)　Trover
　　versus　　　　　　　　)　Came the plaintiff by his
John Bailey, Henry Bailey)　attorney Zachariah Taliaferro
Susannah Bailey Defendants)　Esquire Came also the defen-
　　　　　　　　　　　　　　dants by William Shaw their
attorney. The issue being Joined, whereupon came a Jury
duly drawn Empanneled & Sworn, towit Aaron Fincher,
Joseph Hart, Page Puckett, John Cole, Phillip Holcomb,
John Huey, David Puckett, Richard Cox William Hayney John
Hames, James Petty & Mathews Robinson, returned their
Verdict & Say we find for the defendants
Wherefore it is considered by the Court, that defendants
recover against the plaintiff in form aforesaid, also the
costs of suit by him about his suit in that behalf
expended and the said plaintiff in Mercy &c.

300

Larken Wells   ) Elisabeth Moore proved eight days
      vs   ) attendance in this case which is twenty
John Bailey   ) shillings. William Hall proved seven
Henry Bailey   ) days attendance in this case which is
Susannah Bailey) Seventeen shillings & six pence John
                     Mullins proved Twelve days attendance
which is Thirty Shillings. Fanny Baily proved nine days
attendance which is Twenty two shillings and six pence
and Unity Baily proved nine days attendance which is
Twenty Two shillings & six pence which is ordered to be
Taxed in the Bill of costs.

354 Walter Roberts Plaintiff) Case
      vs   ) This case being referred, but
James Wray   Defendant) no award returned by the
                                 arbitrators. The plaintiff
being called came not in to Court to prosecute his suit.
Ordered on motion of William Shaw that the said plaintiff
be Nonsuited. Wherefore it is further considered by the
court, that Defendant recover against him five shillings
damages & costs of suit.

Robert Wilson   Plaintiff) Case
   against   ) The plaintiff being called
Spencer Brummett Defendant) to prosecute his suit, came
                                not on motion of Zach. Talia-
ferro Esqr. Defendants attorney. Ordered that he be nonsuited, and it is further considered by the court that the
defendant recover against the plaintiff five shillings
damages & costs of suit.

John McColl   ) Attachment
   vs   ) Dismissed by consent of parties & all
Wm. Dalrymple) fees forgiven by the officers of Court.

William Darby   Plaintiff) Attachment
   versus   ) Came the plaintiff by
John Montgomery   Defendant) William Shaw his attorney
                                and moved the court for a
decree in this case, the defendant being called failed to
appear to Defend the suit. Ordered therefore that, the
plaintiff recover against the defendant, a decree for the
sum of Nine pounds Twelve shillings & costs of suit.

The State   ) The court being informed that the
   vs   ) defendant Thompson was inveigling with one
John Thompson) of the States Witnesses. Towit John Wood
                   who was bound yesterday for his attending
to give evidence in this suit, that he could make his
security bring him into open Court & give him up, and he
would be clear of his recognizance whereon the Court saw
cause to have him bound in the sum of one hundred pounds
and two securities towit Adam Thompson & Hugh Holland each
in the sum of Fifty pounds, who acknowledged to owe to the
State of South Carolina the same sums in open Court &
Signed their Names   Adam Thompson
                         Hugh H Holland

355 William Farr, one of the Judges of this Court certified
that Charles Sims Esqr. has taken before him the Oath of
Office as a Justice of the peace for this County & the

Oath to Support the Constitution of this State & the
United States.

James Spray   Plaintiff)   Slander
   versus   )   Came the plaintiff by Z.
William Smith   Defendant)   Taliaferro his attorney &
                                the defendant by William Shaw
his attorney, the issue being Joined, when came also a
Jury towit. Aaron Fincher foreman Joseph Hart, Page
Puckett, John Cole, Philip Holcomb John Huey David Puckett
Richard Cox, William Hayney John Hames James Petty Mathew
Robinson, who being duly sworn, return their verdict and
say we find for the palintiff Forty one shillings & costs
Wherefore it is considered by the court, that the plaintiff
recover against the defendant the damages assessed as
aforesaid and his costs in this behalf expended and the
said defendant in Mercey &c &c.

Richard Mitchell   plaintiff)   Trover
   versus   )   This suit being refered to
Joseph Jones   Defendant)   the arbitration of William
                                Beckham & Col Wm. Farr, who
met and after hearing the matter investigated returned
& could not agree in their award, which is as follows
"June 3rd, 1791. We the arbitrators cannot agree
The award Read &)   Wm. Beckham
Ordered to Record)   Wm. Farr
and that the Suit)
Stand for Tryal)

Ordered that the County Treasurer deliver all notes taken
in behalf of the County from individuals to the sheriff of
this County, and that he shall advertise that all persons
due the County fail to settle the same in thirty days from
the day of advertisment, that the sheriff shall take the
most speediest way to collect the same.

John Blasingame one of the Judges of this County Certifyed
that Hugh Means Esquire took the Oath of Office as a Justice
of the peace for this County, also the Oath to Support the
Constitution of this State, and that of the United States.
2nd. June 1791. Court adjourned untill tomorrow 10 OClock
Signed   John Blasingame
                        Wm Farr

356 At a Court continued and held by adjournment in and for the
County of Union at the Court House of said County, on
Monday the Sixth day of June, one thousand seven hundred
and ninety one and the Fifteenth year of the American
Independence.
Present Their Honors   John Blasingame
                        Wm. Farr   Judges

Adam Scane   Plaintiff)   Debt
   against   )   On motion of William Shaw
Thomas Brandon   Defendant)   Esqr. the Plaintiffs atty.
                                this case is continued
untill next Court.

Brandon & Gregory) On motion of William Shaw the defendants
   vs   )   atty for Mr. Johnsons name to be struck
Johnson & Sims)   off the docket also the note which

302

was granted & Ordered accordingly.

David Boshart came into open Court and petitioned for a
Guardian to be appointed him, to Enable him as an enfant
to prosecute a suit the State vs. William Williams, and
made Choice of Cushman R. Edson which was granted him &
ordered accordingly.

The State   ) Indict
   vs   ) Larcency
John Thompson) Ordered that a Seire facias issue against
                  Josiah Tanner to be and appear before the
Justices of our County Court next January term to shew
cause why his recognizance should not be forfeited, for
not appearing as a Witness in the above case in behalf of
the State.

Ordered that all recognizance be continued over untill
next January Court.

Hugh Holland   Plaintiff   )
   versus   ) The Defendant being solemnly
Richardson Rountree Defendant) called, failed to appear to
                                 defend his suit. Ordered
that Judgment be entered against him by default. on which
the plaintiff proceeded to execute his writ of enquiry.
Whereupon came a Jury Towit. Aaron Fincher Page Puckett,
John Cole, Philip Holcomb John Hughey William Hodge Joseph
Hart, Edward Moore, John Leak.

357 David Puckett James McWhorter and William Hayney. Who
being duly sworn to well & truly this writ of enquiry,
return their Verdict on their oaths aforesaid and say we
find for the plaintiff the sum of sixteen pounds and costs
of suit. Wherefore it is considered by the Court that
the plaintiff recover against the defendant in form aforesaid and the said defendant in Mercy &c &c.

Peter Braselmann & Com.y Plaintiff) Debt
   vs   ) Came the Defendant
David Hudson   Defendant) into open Court in
                                        his own proper person
and acknowledged that he owed the plaintiff twenty seven
pounds four shillings and eleven pence half penny. and
confessed Judgment for the same with costs of suit wherefore it is considered by the court that the plaintiff
recover against the defendant in form aforesaid, and the
said defendant in Mercy &c &c.

Carmical   ) Debt
   vs   ) The plaintiff failed to appear to prosecute
Merry McGuire) his suit, a nonsuit is entered against him
                and its further considered by the court
that the defendant recover against the plaintiff five
shillings damage & costs of suit.

Benjamin Johnson   Plaintiff) Debt
   vs   ) Continued by consent and
William Johnson   Defendant) Ordered that a dedimus issue
                                to any three Justices in
the State of Georgia to take the deposition of Thomas
Johnson, on the defendants giveing Allen Degraffenreedt

303

ten days notice of the time and place of taking the same.

Sion Cook   Plaintiff)   Attachment
  versus   )   The plaintiff being solemnly
Archer Smith   Defendant)   called came not to prosecute his
                            suit. On motion therefore
Ordered that he be nonsuited and its further considered by
the Court that the plaintiff pay the Defendant five
shillings damage & cost of suit.

358 Woodson & Gist) Continued untill next court on motion of
      vs   ) William Shaw Esqr. plaintiffs attorney
    Isaac Edmondson)

William Thomas Linton Plaintiff   ) Case
  versus   ) The plaintiff being
William Williams & others Defendants) solemnly called but
                                        failed to appear,
he is therefore on motion of Zachariah Taliaferro Nonsuited
And it is further considered by the court that the defendant recover against the plaintiff five shillings damage
& costs of suit.

James McMullin Plaintiff)   Attachment
  vs   )   On the motion of William Shaw
Daniel Jackson Defendant)   the defendants attorney Ordered
                            that this case be dismissed
at plaintiffs cost.

James Dohertie   Plaintiff)   Petition & Summon
  vs   )   The plaintiff being solemnly
Shadrack Landtrip Defendant)   called failed to appear to
                              prosecute his suit.
Ordered that he be nonsuited. Wherefore it is considered
by the Court that the defendant recover against the
plaintiff five shillings damage & Costs of suit.

David Hopkins   Plaintiff)   On the motion of Wm. Shaw
  versus   )   Esqr. Ordered that this case
David Hudson   Defendant)   be continued untill next
                            Court.

Lusian Parlor   ) Slander
  vs   ) The plaintiff hath since the
Holland & Ann Sumner) commencement of this suit, married
                        to Wm. Townsend. On motion,
Ordered that he be a party in the action, with his wife
the plaintiff aforesaid.

William Townsend &) Slander
Lusian his wife   ) Came the plaintiff by William Shaw
  versus   ) their attorney and the defendant by
Holland Sumner &   ) Thomas Walker their attorney.
Ann Sumner   )

359 Whereupon came a Jury towit Aaron Fincher foreman Page
    Puckett, John Cole, Philip Holcomb, John Huey, William
    Hodges, Joseph Hail, Edward Moore, John Leak, David Puckett
    James McWhorter, William Hayney, who being duly drawn
    empanneled & Sworn return their Verdict & Say we find for
    the plaintiff the sum of Fifteen pounds & costs of suit.

Wherefore it is considered by the Court that the plaintiff
recover against the defendants in form aforesaid, and the
said defendant in Mercy &c &c.

Holland & Ann Sumner   ) Slander
  versus   ) Came the plaintiffs by William
William Townsend & Wife) Shaw their attorney & the
                            Defendants by their attorney
Thomas Walker it appearing to the Court the action was
brought allegal. Ordered that a Nonsuit be entered.
Wherefore it is considered by the Court that the Defendant
recover against the plaintiffs five shillings damage &
costs of suit.

Thomas Head   Plaintiff   ) Debt
  versus   ) Came the plaintiff by
Fredrick Lenear Defendant) Zachariah Taliaferro and the
                             defendant by William Shaw
his attorney.
Whereupon came also a Jury Towit. Aaron Fincher foreman
Page Puckett, John Cole Philip Holcomb John Huey, William
Hodge, Joseph Hart, Edward Moore, John Leak, David Puckett
James McWhorter and William Hayney. who being duly sworn
according to Law. return their verdict on their Oaths
aforesaid & say we find for the plaintiff, Twenty pounds
sixteen shillings & Ten pence, and the interest due thereon
amounting to
and costs of suit, Wherefore it is considered by the
Court that the plaintiff recover against the defendant, in
form aforesaid, and the said defendant in Money &c &c.

360 James Spray   Plaintiff) Elias Hollingsworth proved eight
      versus   ) days attendance as a witness in
    Wm. Smith   Defendant) the above suit, for the plaintiff.

William Thomas Linton   ) Frederick Thompson proved twelve
  vs   ) days attendance which is Thirty
William Williams & Others) shillings in the above suit, for
                             the defendant.

Alexander McDougal   Plaintiff) Attachment
  versus   ) Samuel Jackson came into
Mark Jackson   Defendant) open Court and entered
                                  himself Special Bail for
the defendant, and to pay the condemnation money and costs
if the said defendant should be cast in the above suit.
Samuel Jackson

Hugh Holland   ) William Gilkie proved one days
  vs   ) attendance which is two shillings &
Richardson Rountree) Six pence, Ordered that the same be
360   Taxed in the Bill of costs.

William Farr   ) Petition & summons. Continued,
  vs   ) but subject to a confession of
Olliphant & Blasingame) Judgment by the defendants if the
                          debts is not satisfied.

Nathaniel Gibson Plaintiff) Petition & Summons
  vs   ) The plaintiff being called
Samuel Gilkie   Defendant) failed to appear to prosecute
                             his suit. Ordered that he be

nonsuited. Wherefore it is considered by the Court that
the Defendant recover against the plaintiff five shillings
damage & costs of suit.

James Hogans   Plaintiff   ) Attachment
    vs   ) On motion of William Shaw
Shadrack Lewallen Defendant) Esqr. & consent of the parties
                                this suit is dismissed at
the defendants costs except the plaintiffs attorneys fee.

Ordered that none of the Judges of this Court act as
arbitrators in any matter that shall be in court, as it is
considered entirely contrary to Law.

361 Thomas Brandon   Plaintiff) Debt
    versus   ) Came the parties into open
    William Speers Defendant) Court and there agreed to
                                refer this suit to the arbi-
tration of Captain Edward Thilman and John Stokes, and their
award to be the Judgment of this Court.

Nicholas Lazerus   Plaintiff) Petition & Summons
    versus   ) The plaintiff by William
Luke Carrell   Defendant) Shaw his attorney and the
                                defendant being called came
not. Whereupon the Court Decreed for the plaintiff three
pounds & costs of suit.

Elizabeth Alexander Plaintiff) Slander
    versus   ) On motion of Zach.
Harrison Bell   Defendant) Taliaferro the defendants
                                attorney Ordered that the
Plaintiff be nonsuited, and its further considered by the
Court that the defendant recover against the plaintiff
five shillings damage & Costs of suit.

George Patterson   Plaintiff) Debt
    versus   ) Came the plaintiff by Thomas
James Sims   Defendant) Walker his attorney and the
                                defendant by William Shaw
his attorney, whereupon came a Jury Towit Aaron Fincher
foreman Page Puckett John Cole, Philip Holcomb John Huey
William Hodge Joseph Hart Edward Moore, John Leak, David
Puckett, James McWhorter & William Hayney who being duly
drawn empanneled & Sworn according to Law return their
Verdict & Say we find for the defendant, Wherefore it is
considered by the Court that the Defendant recover against
the plaintiff in form aforesaid with costs of suit. Jeremiah Kingsland proved four days attendance in the above
suit for defendant which is ten shillings, Robert Glenn
proved five days attendance in the above suit which is
Twelve Shillings & Six pence & John Steward proved two days
attendance for defendant, Which is ordered to be Taxed in
the Bill of costs.

Thomas Head) Elijah Nunn proved four days attendance
    vs   ) as a Witness in the above suit for the
Fred. Lenear) plaintiff which is ten shillings & five
                shillings for mileage.

362 Ordered that the Sheriff expose to Sale, a stray Horse
    Posted by Benjamin Clark before John Henderson Esqr

The Court then adjourned untill Tomorrow 9 O Clock
Signed   Wm Farr
                John Henderson   Esquires
                John Blasingame

At a Court continued and held by adjournment, in and for
the County of Union at the Court House for the said County
on Tuesday the Seventh day of June one thousand seven
hundred and Ninety One, and in the fifteenth year of the
American Independence.

Present their Honors   John Henderson
                              William Farr   Esqrs.
                              John Blasingame

Ordered that the Sheriff, sell all the property taken by
Executions at the following places Towit. at the Court
House, at Mr. Hammeltons on Tyger River, Grindal Shoales
on Pacolate & at Mr. James Woodsons between Tyger & Enoree.

John Murphey   Plaintiff)   Petition & Summons
    versus   )   Came the plaintiff into Court
John Bird   Defendant)   by his attorney Zacha. Taliaferro
                             and the defendant by William
Shaw his Counciller, and after a full investigation of the
matter; the Court decreed for the plaintiff Ten pounds &
Costs of suit, subject to the installment Law.

Richard Mitchell   Plaintiff)   Trover
    versus   )   Came the defendant into open
Joseph Jones   Defendant)   Court in his own proper
                                person and acknowledged that
he owed the plaintiff, Twenty pounds and confessed Judgment
for the same with costs of suit, wherefore it is considered
by the court that the plaintiff recover against the
defendant the debt aforesaid and his costs in this behalf
expenced, in form aforesaid and the said defendant in
Mercey &c.

363 The State So. Carolina)   Indict. for the Escape of a
    versus   )   Negro from Goal.
Joseph Jones   )   The Court after hearing the
                              matter investigated. Ordered that
the defendant be fined the sum of Seven pounds, ten
shillings & Costs of suit with Stay of Execution until
January Court next.

William Beckham   Plaintiff)   Debt
    versus   )   Col. Thomas Brandon came into
Philip Anderson   Defendant)   open Court, and acknowledged
                                himself Special Bail for the
defendant in the sum of Thirty pounds & costs of suit.
Came the parties then into court to wit the plaintiff by
Wm. Shaw his attorney and the defendant by Z. Taliaferro his
attorney and proceeded to try their issue Joined. Whereupon
came also a Jury duly drawn empanneled & Sworn towit
Aaron Fincher Page Puckett, John Cole, Phillip Holcomb,
John Huey, Wm. Hodge, Joseph Hart, Edward Moore, John Leak,
David Puckett, James McWhorter & William Hayney, returned
their Verdict & Say we find for the plaintiff Thirty
pounds with the interest due thereon amounting to

307

Subject to a discount of Six pounds two shillings & four
pence on the defendants producing and delivering to the
plaintiff..Braselmann & Co. receipt for the above sum paid
before the note was assigned over to the plaintiff Wherefore
it is considered by the Court that the Verdict be recorded
and that the plaintiff recover against the defendant in form
aforesaid, and the said defendant in Mercy &c &c.

Ordered that the County Treasurer deliver to Richd.
Mitchell, Adam Potters note, given in behalf of the County
for a Stray Mare, and this order shall be good for the same.

Batholomew Baker) Case
   versus   ) The parties came into open court and
Arthur Thomas   ) referred their suit to the arbitration
                of William Beckham James Thomas &
Jeremiah Gregory and their award returnable to next January
Term shall be the Judgment of Court.

364 On the information of the Sheriff to the towit of Joseph
Jones constable being summoned to attend this court who
neglected. Ordered that he be fined five shillings for
refusing to wait on and attend the Court, and be suspended
from his appointment.

Braselman & Co.   Plaintiff) Petition & Summons
   versus   ) On the motion of William Shaw
William Rogers   Defendant) plaintiff attorney. Ordered
                      that this case be dismissed
at the defendants cost.

Thomas Brandon &   ) Debt came the plaintiff
John Gregory Admrs. Plaintiffs) by Zacha. Taliaferro their
   versus   ) attorney and the defendant
Charles Sims   Defendant) by Wm. Shaw his attorney.
                   Whereupon came also a Jury
towit. Aaron Fincher foreman, Page Puckett, John Cole,
Philip Holcomb, John Huey, William Hodge, Joseph Hart,
Edward Moore, John Leak, David Puckett, James McWhorter,
William Hayney, who being duly drawn empanneled & Sworn
return their verdict & say we find for the plaintiffs the
sum of Ninety pounds, with the interest due thereon
amounting to and costs of suit, subject to the installment
Law.
Wherefore it is considered by the Court that the plaintiffs
recover against the defendant in form aforesaid and the said
defendant in Mercy &c &c.

Alexander McDougal   Plaintiff) Debt on attachment
   versus   ) Came into Court the
Mark Jackson   Defendant) plaintiff by his attorney
                    Wm Shaw & the defendant
by his attorney Z. Taliaferro, the matter being investigated, the Court decreed for the plaintiff against the
defendant according to Specialty which is with the costs
of suit.

Edson & Co.   Plaintiff) Attachment
   versus   ) Came the parties into open Court
George Taylor   ) and dismissed the suit at
                  Defendants cost.

265 George Patterson) Debt
  versus   ) On motion of Mr. Zachariah Taliaferro
  Charles Sims) attorney for the plaintiff, a new Tryal
           is Granted in this case, which is
Ordered accordingly.

John Fincher Plaintiff) The defendant being called and
  vs   ) not answering. Judgment by
Robert Merrick Defendant) default was ordered which is
          hereby entered.

Daniel Lipham) Case
  vs   ) The defendant being called & not
Wm. Barton &   ) answering Judgment by Default was
Elisabeth Barton) ordered which is hereby entered.

Brandon & Gregory) Scifa
  vs   ) By consent of the parties Ordered that
Ann & James Gasway) this case be dismissed at the defen-
          dants cost.

Bolan Godber & Co.) Debt
  vs   ) Continued untill next Court.
Wm. McCullock)

Cushman R Edson & Co. Plaintiff) Attachment
  vers   ) The defendant being
John Hugh   Defendant) called and not answering
            Judgment by default was
ordered. Wherefore its considered by the court that the
plaintiffs recover against the defendants Seven pounds
three shillings & seven pence and costs of suit.

John Fincher) On appeal
  vs   ) Continued untill next Court.
Robert Merrick)

Wm. Clark) Attachment
  vs   ) Ordered that the Land attached be
Isaac Frazier) advertised according to Law.

366 Benjamin Steadham) Attachment
  vers   ) Ordered that the Land attached in this
  Isaac Frazier) suit be advertised according to Law.

The Court then adjourned untill court in course.
Signed: John Henderson
      Wm. Farr
      John Blasingame

At an Intermediate Court begun and holden, in and for the
County of Union at the Court House of said County on
Monday the fifth day of September one thousand Seven hundred
and ninety one.

Present their Honors John Henderson
          John Blasingame Esqrs.

Presented in open Court the last will and testament of
John Hope deceased, which was proved by the Oath of
Nathaniel Thompson, who said he believed the said John
Hope to be in his proper senses at the time of executing

the said will. Ordered that it be recorded.

A Deed of conveyance from William Williams to William Hightour, acknowledged in open court and ordered to Record.

A Deed of conveyance from William Williams to Henry Davis acknowledged in open Court and ordered to Record.

On the application of Martha Kent, letters of administration is granted her, on the Estate & Effects of Mark Kent deceased, "who entered into bond, with James Bankhead & John Bankhead her Securities according to Law & took the oath accordingly. Ordered that John Read, John Cole and Richard Wood appraise the Estate of Mark Kent deceased, and make due return of the same according to Law.

A Deed of conveyance from John Winn attorney for Daniel Hager to George Newton, proved in open Court by John Haile & Ordered to Record.

A Deed of Conveyance from Elias Hollingsworth & Dianna his wife to Bernard Glenn, proved in open Court by Spelsby Glenn and Ordered to be Recorded.

367 A Deed of Gift from Samuel Tarbert to Susannah Logans and Sarah Robinson, acknowledged in open court by the said Tarbert and Ordered to be Recorded.

The Last Will & Testament of Zachariah Bullock deceased Proved in open Court by the Oaths of Adam Potter & John Lipscombe, who said they believed the said Zachariah Bullock deceased to be in his proper senses, at the time of executing the said Will, and Len Henry Bullock and Richard Bullock being appointed executers in the said Will, was duly Qualifyed accg. to Law. Ordered that Adam Potter, Thomas Draper and William Coleman be and are hereby appointed to appraise the Estate of Zach. Bullock deceased, and Return the said appraisement according to Law.

Ordered that a Dedimus Potestatum issue to any two Justices of the County of Newberry to cause Diannah Hollingsworth wife of Elias Hollingsworth, personally to come before them, in order to take the relinquishment of dower, in a certain tract of Land conveyed by the said Elias Hollingsworth to Bernd. Glenn.

Ordered that George McWhorter, Samuel Davidson & William Speers, appraise the Estate of John Hope deceased, and that William McCullock Qualify said appraisers.

On the application of James Bell he is hereby admitted to retail Spiritous liquors or keep public house, who came into open court and give bond according to Law.

On the application of James Wilson, leave is given him to retail Spiritous liquors in this County who entered into Bond according to Law.

Acknowledged in open Court a Deed of conveyance from John Hamm to Amos Martin and Ordered to Record.

Acknowledged in Open Court a Deed of conveyance from Thomas Palmore to Amos Martin, Ordered to Record.

Proved in Court a Deed of conveyance from William Little-field to George Harling. Ordered to record.

368 Proved before a Justice a mortgage Deed of Sundry articles from William Massay to James Townsend Ordered to record.

Proved in Court a Deed of conveyance from Joseph Thomas & Wife to John Palmore, by the oath of John Springer, Joseph Jones & Samuel Quinton. Ordered to Record.

Proved in court a Deed of Gift from Robert Chesney to John Chesney and Ordered to Record.

Proved before a Justice a Deed of Conveyance from James Huey to William Thompson. Ordered to Record.

Ordered that Soloman Smith Orphan of James Smith be bound an apprentice to Cornelius Dempsey according to Law.

John Steen) It appearing to the court that there
vs) was in March term 1789 a Clerical Error
David Stockdon) made in an order for the attendance of
Adam Goudylock. Whereupon it is con-
sidered that the said error be corrected and that David
Stockton, pay the said Adam Goudylock as a witness instead
of John Steen his last claim. agreeable to the former
order.

Ordered that Joseph Connor & Jacob Hollingsworth and Edward Moore appraise the Estate of Original Hogans deceased.

Ordered that Ralph Hunt, William Young & James Addington & Abraham Pott, appraise the Estate of Caleb Edmondson deceased.

A Deed of conveyance from Thomas Stribling to Robert Gibson acknowledged in open Court and Ordered to Record.

On the application of Thomas Evans leave is given him, to retail Spiritous liquors in this County, who give bond with Thomas McDonnell his Security.

Ordered that John Cook Hall orphan of John Cook Senr. deceased be bound to Richard Davis according to Law, untill he arrives to the age of Twenty one years, and that the said Davis give the said John Cook Hall, three months schooling.

Court adjourned untill Tomorrow 9 0 Clock
John Henderson
John Blasingame

369 At an Intermediate Court, continued & held by adjournment in and for the County of Union at the Court House of said County, on Tuesday the Sixth day of September A. D. 1791. Present their Honors
John Henderson
John Blasingame

Ordered that William Cotter be Overseer of the road from
the Skull Shoals on Pacolate River to the Bridge on
Thickety Creek in the room of Moses Meek; and that he keep
the same in good repair according to Law.

Ordered that Samuel Jackson, John High & John Barrit view
and mark out a road from Gibbs old field to Blackstocks
ford on Tyger River the nearest and best way and report the
same to our next intermediate Court.

Ordered that George Harling farmer be Overseer of the road
from Jordon Jackson to Mitchels Creek, and that he keep the
same in good repair in the room of John High.

Ordered that the Sheriff expose to Sale, a Stray heifer
posted before Thomas Brandon Esqr. also Eleven Hogs posted
before Thomas Blasingame Esqr. immediately.

Ordered that William Kennedy Esquire Treasurer of this
County, pay or discount with Cushman. R. Edson the sum of
Eight pounds three shillings & Six pence to it being for
John Blasingame Esquire, extra fees due him by the County
as sheriff also the sum of one pound and two pence as a
debt due Mr. John Putman.

A Deed of conveyance from Thomas Brandon to John Fincher
acknowledged in open Court and ordered to Record.

A Deed of Conveyance from James Campbell to John Fincher
proved before a Justice and Ordered to Record.

A Deed of conveyance from Daniel Wooton to Mary Wooton.
Proved in open Court and ordered to be recorded.

370 On the motion of Thomas Stribling Sheriff of this County
for Thomas Blasingame son John to be appointed Deputy
Sheriff, who met with the approbation of the court and took
the Oath of office accordingly.

Ordered that Jonathan Newman be overseer of the Road from
Jesse Dodds up the Belmount road to the County line.

Ordered that Jesse Dodd Jonathan Newman & David Norman be
and are hereby appointed to view and mark away for a road
from Blackstocks ford on Tyger leading to Jesse Dods at
the cross roads, and report the same to our next Court.

Ordered that John Martindale be Overseer of the road from
Jesse Dodd o Enoree River in the room of said Dodd, and that
he keep the same in repair according to Law.

Ordered that James Duncan be Overseer of the road from
Jesse Dodds to Tyger River and that he keep the same in
good repair according to Law.

Its ordered in pursuance of a petition to us directed,
petitioning for a road from Cooks Bridge to Daniel Liphams
which is granted and that a road be cleared out from said
Bridge to said Liphams to cross padgets creek, at the
Lower end of Clarks plantation and that this way be cleared
out instead of the one already. marked out by commissioners appointed heretofore. James Townsend is appointed

overseer of said Road. Ordered that he clear out & keep
the same in good repair according to Law.

Proved in Open Court a Deed of conveyance from James
Roberson to Elizabeth Hogans, proved by the Oath of William
Wood and ordered to Record.

Acknowledged in open Court a Deed of conveyance from
Archer Howard to John Merrell, Ordered to Record. Acknow-
ledged in open Court a Deed of conveyance from Ditto to
Ditto.

On the application of James Townsend and Sarah Massay
Letters of administration is granted them, on the Estate
of William Massay Junior deceased, who give Bond with
Willm. Townsend and James Caldwell their Securitys according to Law.

Ordered that Geving Girdon Nathaniel Davis, William Rogers
and Samuel Selvy, appraise the Estate of William Massay
deceased and make due return of said appraisement according
to Law.

371 A Deed of conveyance from Richardson Rountree to Ephraim
Wilbourn, acknowledged in open Court by said Richardson
Rountree and Mildred Rountree wife of said Richardson being
privately examined by John Blasingame esquire, voluntarely
relinquished all her right of dower, with her husband.
Which is ordered to be required.

The Last will and testament of John George deceased being
proved in open Court by the Oaths of John McWhorter a
witness thereto, who said he believed the said John
George; to be in his proper senses, at the time of executing
the said will and John Jasper and John George being appointed
executors in the said will came into open court and was
duly qualified acc.g to Law.

Ordered that John Jasper Senr. Nicholas Jasper, Benjr.
Crownover & Charles Hames or any three of them, is hereby
Nominated and appointed to appraise the Estate of John
George deceased and make due return of the said appraise-
ment thereof.

On the application of George Huey, letters of administration is granted him, on the Estate of William Huey deceased
who came into open Court, and entered into bond, according
to Law & took the Oath accordingly.

Ordered that Samuel Spray John Huey, James Townsend and
Jeremiah Hammelton be and are hereby appointed to appraise
the Estate of William Huey deceased, & make due return of
the same thereof.

Ordered that Nathan Thomas be Overseer of the road from
Neds Big Creek to the lower fish dam creek and that he
keep the same in good repair according to Law.

Ordered that John Peter Sartor be Overseer of the Road from
the Lower fish dam creek to Cain Creek and that he keep the
same in good repair according to Law.

Ordered that Joseph Hollingsworth be Overseer of the Road from Cain Creek to Hills ford on Tyger River and that he keep the same in good repair according to Law.

372 Ordered that Spilsby Glenn be overseer of the road from the fish dam ford on Broad River the 96 road that leads to Hammeltons ford on Tyger River to Cain Creek, and that he keep the same in good repair according to Law.

Ordered that Jeremiah Hammelton be Overseer of the Road from Cain Creek to Hammeltons ford on Tyger River and that he keep the same in good repair according to Law.

Thomas Blasingame Junr. was qualifyed as a Constable for this County.

Acknowledged in Open Court, a Deed of conveyance from Thomas Brandon to Reuben Hatter and Ordered to be recorded.

Ordered that William Kennedy Esqr. & Wm. & Henry Birdsong Executors of John Birdsong deceased, Together with the Judges of this Court, do meet together at this Court House on the first Fryday in October next. In order to adjust the accounts concerning building of the Court House and that the Exors of Birdsongs Estate being the said deceased Books in order to Settle as aforesaid.

Court adjourned untill Court in Course
Signed   John Henderson
                John Blasingame

January Term 1792

At a Court begun and held in and for the County of Union at the Court house of said County on Monday the Second day of January in the year of our Lord, one thousand Seven hundred and ninety two, and in the Sixteenth year of the American Independence
Present their Honors   John Blasingame
                        Wm. Farr   Esqrs.

Thomas Blasingame Junr. came into open Court and resigned his appointment as constable for this County which is Entered accordingly.

373 On motion of William Shaw Esqr. Abram Nott is admitted to practice as an attorney in this court. Who produced his commission from under the Hand of the Honorable Hugh Ruttledge & B Burke Esqrs. authorising him to practice Law in the Several Courts of this State.

The Court proceeded to draw the grand Jury for next Court when the following persons was drawn which the Sheriff is ordered to Summons Towit, Isaac Bogan, John Goodwin, Edward Ragsdale, Robert Crenshaw, John Bankhead, William Jackson William Coleman James Townsend, Joseph West, Thomas Pearson William Glenn, Isaac White, Hugh Means, Thomas Young, Benjamin Gregory William Goldsmith Maher Liles James Mosely Isaac Cook, John Bailey.

314

Also the following persons drawn to serve at next Court as petit Jurors, and the Sheriff Ordered to Summons towit James Lindsey, George Parker, William Hames, George McClain Robert Lusk, Thomas Bell, James Mabry, John George Junr. John Grier John Sims, John Petty Pool, James Anderson, John Comer Isaac Newman Daniel Tollerson, Richd. Prewit, Absalom Wood, Thomas Minton Junr. James Steward, Joseph Randal, Nichs. Tassinier, Thomas Minton Senr. George Bowden, William White, Jesse Paty John Ingrim Gilbert Prince, Thomas Horrell, John Kennedy Richard Minton.

A Deed of conveyance from Charles Sims to Tho. McDonnell proved before a Justice & Ordered to be Recorded.

John Thomas) Case
   vs   ) The arbitrators return their award and that
John Stokes) John Stokes pay the sum of Thirteen pounds
             sterling and costs, with stay of Execution,
Three months. Wherefore, its considered by the Court that
the plaintiff recover against the defendant the debt
aforesaid with costs of suit, agreeable to said award &
the said Defendant in Mercy &c &c.

The following persons, sworn to serve this Court as hand
Jurors. Towit. James Gibbs, Ralph Jackson, Tho. Vance,
Samuel Simpson, William Lipscombe, James Hawkins, Isaac
Gregory, Joseph Hollingsworth, Joseph McJunkin, Lewis
Ledbetter Cush. R. Edson, Jesse Mabry.

374 Benjamin Johnson   Plaintiff) Debt
       vers   ) William Hughes, came into
    William Johnson   Defendant) open Court and acknowledged
                       himself Security for the
costs in this case & to pay to the same if the plaintiff is
cast.

William Johnson   Plaintiff) Case
    vers.   ) This suit abated by the death
David Chisholm   Defendant) of the defendant, at the
                  Plaintiffs Costs.

Court adjourned untill tomorrow 10 OClock.
Sign'd   John Blasingame
         Wm. Farr.

At a Court continued and held by adjournment in and for
the County of Union at the Court House of said County on
Tuesday the third day of January in the year of our Lord,
one thousand Seven hundred and Ninety two and the Sixteenth
year of American independency.
Present the Honbl. John Blasingame
                    Wm. Farr   Esqrs.

Batholomew Baker   Plaintiff) Case
       vs   ) This suit being refered
    Arther Thomas Defendant) last Court to arbitrators
                   who return their award &
Say, that the defendant pay the sum of four pounds nine
shillings sterling to be discharged in any kind of Merchantable produce. & costs of suit. Wherefore it is
considered by the Court that the plaintiff recover against
the defendants in form aforesaid & the said Dfdt in Mercy&c.

315

The State of So. Carolina)   Indict.
     versus   )   On motion of Wm. Shaw. County
     Enoch Floyd   )   attorney Ordered that a
                                noli Prosique be entered in
                                this case.

375 John Campbell   Plaintiff)   Debt
     vers   )   Ordered that this suit be
    William Heaton   Defendant)   referred to David Smith,
                                John Addington, James Townsend
    & Eli Cook, and their award returnable to next Court shall
    be the Judgment of this court, and if they cannot agree to
    choose a fifth person.

    The State So. Carolina)   Indict. for breaking the peace.
     vs   )   James Duncan having taken the Oath
    Samuel Cooper   )   prescribed by Law. Its therefore
                                Ordered that the defendant Samuel
    Cooper enter into recognizance of One hundred pounds, with
    two good free holders as his Security in the sum of Fifty
    pounds, cash, for his good behaviour toward the said James
    Duncan for one year.

    The State So. Carolina)   Indict.
     vs   )   Its Ordered that Capt. James
    John Nuckols   )   Torrell give Security in the sum
                                of Fifty pounds sterling to
    personally appear before the Judges of the District Court
    of Pinckney on the first day of April next, to give
    testimony in behalf of the State against the Defendant John
    Nuckols--Who came into Open Court with Adam Potter & Wm.
    Heaton, and acknowledged themselves indebted as aforesaid
    in the sum of Twenty pounds each as witness their Hands
    the 3rd January 1792   James Terrell
                            Adam Potter
    Acknowledged in   Wm. Heaton
    Open Court
    Ben. Haile D.C.

    The State So. Carolina)   Indict.
     vs   )   Its ordered that the Defendant
    John Nuckols   )   John Nuckols give Security to
                                appear before the Judges of the
    District Court of Pinckney to be holden on the first day of
    April next, at the place to answer to a bill of Indict.
    then to be prefered against him, who came into open Court
    with Joshua Petty & Edmond Ellis and acknowledged them-
    selves indebted to the State of South Carolina in the sum
    of Four hundred pounds sterling, that is to say the said
    John Nuckols, in the sum of Two hundred pounds and his
    securities in the sum of One hundred pounds each for his
    personal appearance as aforesaid.
    Acknowledged in Open Court   John Nuckols
    Ben. Haile D.C.   Joshua Petty
                                  Edmond Ellis

376 The State So. Carolina)   Indict.
     vers   )   Its Ordered that John Lipscomb
    John Nuckols   )   and Adam Chisholm give Security
                                in the sum of Fifty pounds each.
    for their personal appearance at the District Court of

316

Pinckney to be holden on the first day of April next, also
Adam Goudylock & Edward Tilman as Securities in Twenty
pounds each. John Lipscomb
              Adam Chisholm
              Adam Goudylock
              Edward Tilman

Acknowledged in Open Court
Ben. Haile D.C.

Ordered that the Estate of William Huey deceased be exposed
to Public Sale, agreeable to Law, by George Huey administrator.

Bolan Godber & Co.)   Debt
     vs   )   On motion of Ephraim Ramsay esquire
William McCullock)   Plaintiffs attorney Ordered that this
                      suit be dismissed at the Defendants
                      cost.

The State of South Carolina)   Indictment
        vs   )   Its ordered that the
Samuel Cooper   )   defendant be bound to the
                                peace for twelve months in
the penalty of one hundred pounds sterling and his Securities
in the sum of Fifty pounds each. Whereupon came Wm. Brandon
and John Sanders and Severally acknowledged themselves
indebted to the State in the sum aforesaid, for his good
behaviour toward James Duncan   his
                                  Samuel X Cooper
Acknowledged in Open Court   Mark
Ben. Haile D.C.   Wm Brandon by mark
                                  John Sanders

Benjamin Clark)   Case
     vs   )   Came the plaintiff by Zachariah
William Giles)   Taliaferro his attorney and the defendant
                  by William Shaw esqr. his attorney and
after a full investigation of the matter the court ordered
that the plaintiff be nonsuited. Wherefore it is further
considered by the Court that the Defendant recover against
the Plaintiff five shillings damage and costs of suit.

377 Cushman R. Edson & Co)   Debt
         vs   )   On motion of Wm. Shaw attorney for
    William Hall   )   the defendant. Its ordered that a
                          nonsuit be enterd, as it appears to
the Court that the action was improperly brought. Wherefore it is considered by the Court that the defendant
recover against the plaintiff five shillings damage and
costs of suit.

Benjamin Clark)   Case
     vs   )   Ordered that the plaintiff pay Joseph
William Giles)   Hughs Twenty shillings for eight days
                  attendance for him as a Witness in the
                  above suit.

Benjamin Johnson   Plaintiff)   Debt
     vers   )   Came the plaintiff by William
William Johnson   Defendnat)   Shaw esquire his attorney,
                               and the Defendant by

317

Ephraim Ramsay & Zachariah Taliaferro his attorney.
Whereupon came a Jury Towit. Moses Meek foreman James
Voel Stephen Howard, Zachariah Belue, John Garrot, Waterman
Boatman, Charles Humphries, Arthur Brandon, Thomas Harris,
William White, Daniel rownover & Richardson Rountree who
being duly sworn to well and truly try this issue return
their Verdict on their oaths & Say. We find for the Plaintiff the sum of Fifteen pounds & Costs of suit.
Wherefore it is considered by the court that the plaintiff
recover against the defendant in form aforesaid and the
said defendant in Mercy &c.

Cushman R. Edson & Co) Ordered that William Hall pay
vs   ) Nathan Jaggers Seventeen shillings
William Hall   ) and Six pence for seven days
                         attendance in this suit, also forty
                         miles mileage.

State So. Carolina) Bastardy
vs   ) Ordered that the defendant give
Edmond Simpson   ) security in the sum of Fifty pounds
                     for his appearnace at our next June
court to answer to the above charge to be prefered then
against him, who gave Samuel Simpson his Security who
acknowledged themselves indebted to the State as aforesaid
for his appearnce: Edmond Simpson
                                   Samuel Simpson
Acknowledged
Ben. Haile

378 Arthur Thomas   ) Detinue
    vers   ) Ordered that this suit be dimissed at
    Daniel Whitehead) the defendants cost.

    State   ) Assault
    vs   ) Ordered this tryal come on tomorrow morning.
    James Inlow)

Court adjourned untill tomorrow 9 0 Clock.
Signed   John Henderson
                John Blasingame
                Wm. Farr

At a Court continued and held according to adjournment in
and for the County of Union at the Court House of said
County on Wednesday the fourth day of January in the year
of our Lord one thousand seven hundred and Ninety one.

Present their Honors.   John Henderson
                         William Farr   Esqrs.
                         John Blasingame

On motion of Ephraim Ramsay esqr. Mr. Michael Barrot is
admitted to practice the law as an attorney in this Court,
who produced his commission from the Honlb. the Judges
of this State, authorising him to practice the Law in their
Several Courts.

The State So. Carolina) Ordered that a Capias Issue to
vs   ) Fairfield County to take the body
John Nuckols   ) of James Huey and him to be
                         personally carried before some

318

Justice of said County, to enter into recognizance for his
personal appearance at the next Court of Pinckney District
at this Court House, on the first day of April next, in
order to give testimony in behalf of the State against said
Defendant.

James Holland   Plaintiff)   Debt
    vs   )   On motion of William Shaw
John Steen   Defendant)   plaintiffs attorney
                               Judgment is entered by default.

379 James Hogans   Plaintiff)   Case
    vs   )   Ordered that the Defendant
Spencer Brummett Defendant)   give Special Bail Before one
                                of the Judges of this Court.

James Holland   Plaintiff)   Debt
    vs   )   Ordered that the defendant give
John Steen   Defendant)   Special Bail, before some one
                               Judge of this Court.

Aaron Fincher & Henry Millhouse   ) Debt
Exors of Armel Fincher decd.   Plaintiff) Came the
    vers.   ) Defendant into
Richardson Rountree   Defendant) Open Court, in
                                            his own
proper person, and acknowledged that he owed the plaintiffs
on a note the Sum of Twenty pounds Sixteen shillings, with
Interest due thereon amounting to Two pounds ten shillings
and nine pence and confessed a Judgment for the Same with
Costs of suit. Wherefore it is considered by the court
that the plaintiff recover against the defendant, in form
aforesaid & the said defendant in Mercy &c.

Joshua Palmore)   Debt
    vs   )   Issue Joined & Continued
Joseph Hughes)

Cush. R. Edson)   P. & S.
    vs   )
Robert Savage)   Issue Joined & Continued

William Farr Esqr.) Debt
    vers   ) The Defendants came into Open Court
James Gasway &   ) and admitted the Bond, on which this
Ann Gasway admrs   ) action is brought as the act and
Caleb Gasway decd.) Deed of her husband in her life time.
                       But in her plea on Out to Saith, that
hath not any of the goods chattles or assetts of the
deceased by which she can satisfy the said debts, having
fully administered the same, but saith there is a tract of
Land of one hundred and Sixty acres lying on the Lower fish
dame Creek in the said County. and it is therefore Ordered
that the said Land be Sold to Satisfy the said debts
agreeable to Law.

380 William Buchanan)   Debt
    vs   )   On motion of William Shaw attorney
Wm. Dalefield   )   Ordered that Judgment be entered by
                     default.

George Salmon   Plaintiff) Seira.
  vers   ) Ordered that this Judgment be
Shadrack Landtrip Defendant) revived and execution issue
                      according to the former
                      Judgment.

John Steen   Plaintiff) Trespass
  vs   )
John Lusk   Defendant) Nonsuit.

John & William Steen) Trespass
  vs   )
John Lusk & Jos. Jolly) Nonsuit.

John Miller   Plaintiff) Debt
  vs   ) Came the Defendant into open
Charles Sims   Defendant) Court in his own proper person
                      and acknowledged to owe to the
plaintiff, on a note One thousand pounds to Tobacco, and
confessed Judgment for the same at fourteen shillings
pr Ct. amounting to seven pounds, with Interest and costs
of suit. Wherefore it is considered by the Court that
the plaintiff recover against the Defendant, in form
aforesaid & the said defendant in Mercy &c &c.

Sarah Gist   Plaintiff) Debt
  vers   ) Came the Defendant into open
Charles Sims Defendnat) Court in his own proper person
                      and acknowledged that he owed the
plaintiff the sum of Thirty five pounds three shillings &
three pence, according to Specialty with Interest due
thereon to the amount of Six pounds eight shillings &
Eleven pence and confessed a Judgment for the same, with
costs of suit, wherefore it is considered by the Court, that
the plaintiffs recover against the defendant, in form
aforesaid and the said defendant in Mercy &c &c.

380 Col. William Farr Plaintiff) Feire facias
    vers   ) On motion of William Shaw
  John Steen   Defendant) esqr. plaintiffs attorney
                      and no cause being revived,
for the balance due, and execution issue for the same.

Ferdinand & P. T. Hopkins Plaintiff) Attachment
  vers.   )
Thomas Lewis   Defendant) Judgment by Default.

John Haile   Plaintiff) Debt
  vers.   ) Came the Defendant into
William Lipscombe Defendant) open Court in his own
                      proper person and confessed
a Judgment for the sum of   according to specialty
with costs of suit. Wherefore it is considered by the
Court, that the plaintiff recover against the Defendant
in form aforesaid, & the said Defendant in Mercy &c &c.

David Hopkins Plaintiff) Debt
  vs   ) Continued untill next Court.
David Hudson Defendant)

Sarah Gist   Plaintiff)   Attachment
vers   )
Shadrack Landtrip Defendant)   Dismissed at Plaintiffs Cost.

Adam Scane   Plaintiff)   Continued
vers   )
Thomas Brandon   Defendant)

Ordered that the Sheriff expose to Sale all Estrays lyable
to be sold, Tomorrow, agreeable to Law.

John Fincher   appelle   )   Appeal, from John Pearson, a
vers.   )   Justice of the Peace. Came the
Robert Merrick appellant)   appelle of Wm. Shaw esqr. his
                               attorney, and the appellant by
Ephraim Ramsay Esqr. and after a Full investigation of the
matter. Its ordered by the court that the Judgment be
affirmed with costs of suit.

John Chandler   Plaintiff)   Trover
vs   )   Ordered that this suit be
James Hogans   Defendant)   dismissed at the defendants
                               cost, except the Plaintiffs
attorneys fee, and plaintiffs Witnesses attendance.

382 Thomas Brandon assigne of Plaintiff)   Debt
vers   )   By order of the
William Speers   Defendant)   Court of Union
                                          County in the State
of South Carolina, dated June term 1791, that the suit
Thomas Brandon against William Speers, should be left to
the Judgment of Edward Tilman and John Stokes as arbitrators, we the Under Written arbitrators have duly examined
and heard the cause as well of the plaintiff as defendant
do Order an award that the Defendant William Speers deliver
up to Thomas Brandon the Plaintiff, a Negro Woman named Sall
which was hired to Robert Gregory in the year 1789, sound
and well, and clear of any impediment, after upon the tenth
of this instant, and also to pay all costs except said
Brandons. Witnesses which said Brandon is to pay. If
said Speers should not deliver said Negro woman then to pay
the sum of Fifty pounds sterling Money.
Given under our hands this 8th, June 1791
                               Edward Tilman, arbitrator
                               John Stokes arbitrator
Wherefore it is considered by the Court that the Plaintiff
recover against the Defendant in form aforesaid, and the
said Defendant in Mercy &c.

Edson & Co.   Plaintiff)   Petition & Summs.
vers   )   Cap. Daniel Comer being
Samuel Pearson   Defendant)   summon bail for the defendants
                                 appearance, came into open
Court with said Defendant & delivered him up. Ordered that
he be discharged from his Bond.

William Smith   Plaintiff)   Petion & Sums.
vers.   )   Continued untill Tomorrow
Tho. Blasingame   Defendant)   morning Ordered that William
                                Smith pay James Wafford five
shillings for two days attendance for him in this Suit

321

also two shillings for mileage, also Wily Williferd five
shillings for two days attendance as a Witness & two
shillings for Mileage, also Rachel Compton five shillings
for two days attendance as a Witness and two Shillings
for Mileage.

John Miller   Plaintiff)   P. & S.
  vers.   )   Ordered that John Miller pay
Charles Sims Defendant)   Joseph Combs Seven shillings &
                           Six pence for three days atten-
dance as a Witness for him in this suit.

383 State So. Carolina)   Indict.
    vs   )   Mr. Shadrack Lewallen being Surety
    James Inlow   )   for the defendants appearance at the
                       Court delivered him up to the same
    for which he is dismissed from his recognizance

The Court adjourned untill Tomorrow O Clock
Signed   John Blasingame
                John Henderson

At a Court continued and held by adjournment, in and for
the County of Union at the Court House of said County, on
Thursday the second day of January one thousand Seven
hundred & Ninety two.
Present their Honors   John Blasingame
                        John Henderson   Esqrs.
                        Wm. Farr

Thomas Blasingame Esqr. Plaintiff) Case
  vers   ) Came the parties into
James Tosh   Defendant) Open Court and agreed
                                      to refer their suit to
the arbitration of John Goodwin and Charles Humphries, and
if they cannot agree to choose a third person, and their
award returnable to next Court shall be the Judgment thereof.

On motion of Nancy McKibbin for administration on the
Estate of John McKibbin deceased which was granted, who
took the Oath according to Law, and entered into Bond with,
Wm. Shaw Esqr. Wm. Farr esq.r John Haile esqr. & Adam
Potter esqr. her securities in the sum of one hundred
pounds sterling.

State So. Carolina) Assault
  vers   ) Came Wm. Shaw Esqr. in behalf of the
James Inlow   ) state and the Defendant being arrained
                     at the bar. Plead Guilty whereof he
stands indicted; and its Ordered that the defendant James
Inlow suffer one months imprisonment and pay ten pounds
fine and cost of suit, and if the said James Inlow at the
experation of said term, shall give security to pay the
said fine of ten pounds & costs of suit at our next
Court, then to be acquitted Otherwise to continue in
Goal for the Space of three months, and then to be acquitted
on paying costs & Charges & afine a two pounds sterling.

Ordered that the Treasurer pay Fredrick Eisen Seven
shillings & Six pence for repairs to the Goal, agreeable
to his acct. filed.

322

385 The State of So. Carolina   Plaintiff)   Larcency
        vers   )   Came Wm. Shae esqr.
    John Thompson   Defendant)   in behalf of the
                                               State & Zachariah
Taliaferro in behalf of defendant, who being arraigned &
upon his Indictment pleads not Guilty. Whereupon came a
Jury Towit. Moses Meek foreman, James Veal, Stephen Howard
Zachariah Belue, John Garrot, Waterman Boatman, Charles
Humphries, Arther Brandon William White David Crownover
and Richardson Rountree, who on their several oaths do say,
"We find the defendant Guilty.
Whereupon the Court proceeded to pass Sentence on the
Defendant John Thompson, and Ordered that he pay to the
clerk of this court immediately the sum of Ten pounds
sterling, or receive on his bare back five lashes Tomorrow
morning at nine OClock.
The Defendant John Thompson came accordingly into open
Court and paid the sum of Ten pounds agreeable to the above
Order, and was therefore acquitted on paying of Costs.

Ordered that the Executors of the last Will and Testament
of John Hope deceased, expose to Sale all the Estate of
the said deceased liable to be sold by the said Will.

Ordered that all recognizances be continued untill next
Court. The Court then adjourned untill Tomorrow 9 OClock
Signed by   John Henderson
                     John Blasingame   Esqrs.

At a Court continued and held by adjournment in and for
the County of Union at the Court House of said County, on
Fryday the Sixth day of January in the year of our Lord
one thousand seven hundred & ninety two.

Present their Honors   John Blasingame
                          John Henderson   Esquires
                          William Farr

Edson & Co   Plaintiff)   P. & S.
    vers.   )
Samuel Pearson   Defendant)   Ordered that Samuel Pearson
                                 be held to Special Bail
386 The presentments of the grand Jury of this County, were
read and the following orders made Towit.
On the Second presentment, relating to the Opening of a
Road from McCools old field to Union Court House, the
following order was made, that the Court have before
considered that such a road was unnecessary and improper
Ordered that no other directions be taken in opening the
said Road.
Ordered that the third presentment; presenting as a greviance the Tax laid on Spirits distilled of the materials
or growth of America; be laid before the Legislature of this
State.
On the fourth presentment, Presenting, Alexander Macbeth
& Cushman R. Edson John Beckham Junr. Thomas Evans & Widow
McKibbin, for se-ling Spiritous liquors for more than is
allowed by Law. Ordered that the several persons mentioned
in the said presentment, enter into recognizance in the
sum of Twenty five pounds each for their personal appearance at our next June Court, to answer to the said
presentment.

On the fifth presentment presenting John Haile clerk of
Union Court for not issuing and furnishing the different
overseers of the Roads with orders whereby several Roads
are almost neglected. Its ordered in pursuance of said
presentment that the Clerk do issue the orders for the
Several overseers of this County. Ordered that the following instructions be included in future orders issued to the
overseers of this County, that in all Public Roads leading
to Market the same be opened Twenty feet wide and Grubbed
Ten feet, and that in all old roads the same be straightened
the nearest and best way, and that new orders be issued to
the different overseers between this Court House and Enoree.

On the Sixth presentment, Presenting as a Greiviance that
the currency of this State passes so very Low to that of
our Northward Sister States.
Ordered that a copy of the foregoing presentment be for-
warded by the Clerk of this Court to the representative
of Ninety Six in Congress to be laid before that House.

On the Seventh presentment, presenting as a greviance that
the Standard for Weights and Measures is not kept by the
clerk for the use of the County.
Ordered that when the clerk collects as much Public
money as will pay for such standards that he apply for and
get the same, having first discharged the former Orders of
this Court.

On the Eighth presentment, presenting that the road from
Cooks bridge leading by Stacy Coopers, thence by Roger
Potts thence the nearest and best way to Liphams, is not
cleared out as was reported by the commissions appointed
for that purpose and recommend John Campbell to be an
Overseer to clean out the same. Ordered that Joseph
McJunkin Esqr. John Pearson Esqr. and John Cook be commissions to Survey the Road above described and also the old
road leading from Cooks bridge, by the lower end of Clarks
plantation thence to Liphams, and make their report to the
next intermediate Court which of the Roads is the best and
most for the public advantage.

387 On the Ninth presentment, presenting James Hogans, living
in adultery and recommend, for the court to have John
Jefferies and Lewis Steadham summoned to prove the same.
Ordered that a Capias issue against James Hogans returnable
before some Justice of this County, in order to give
recognizance for his appearance at our next June Court to
answer to the above presentment and that John Jefferies
and Lewis Steadham be summoned to appear at our next Court
to be held next June, in order to give evidence against the
said James Hogans.

On the Tenth presentment, Presenting as a greivance that
the road does not go the nearest and best way from Mr.
Darbys Store to the Bridge on Sugar Creek, leading through
a corner of Mr. Torrance's field and Ordered that William
Darby James Gibbs and Col. Brandon be commissioners to survey the said Road, and report the same to our next intermediate Court.

On the Eleventh presentment, presenting Adam Thompson for

living in adultery, and recommend, James Thompson and
John Wood to prove the same, and Ordered that a Capias
issue against the said Adam Thompson returnable before
some Justice of this County, to take his recognizance
for his appearnace at our next June Court to answer to the
said presentment, and that a Capias issue to command the
said James Thompson and John Woods and Heth Thompson, to
appear before some Justice to enter into Bond for their
appearance at our next June Court to give testimony against
the said Adam Thompson.

John Campbell   plaintiff)   On appeal
    vers.   )   Came the plaintiff by William
Samuel Cooper   Defendant)   Shaw esqr. his attorney and the
                              defendant in his own proper
person, Wherefore the Court considered. And after hearing
the matter properly argued Its ordered by the Court that the
Judgment of the Justice be confirmed with cost of suit.

(Blank on purpose due to pagination)

```
Samuel Cooper      appellee )  On appeal
     vs                     )  Continued untill next court.
Francis Fincher    appellant)
```

```
Aaron Fincher &     )  Debt
Henry Millhouse     )  Landlot Porter being bail for the
     vs             )  defendants appearance at this court who
Richardson Rountree)  came into open court and delivered him
                       up and was discharged from his bail:
```
And ordered that the defendant give special bail for his
personal appearance at our next June Court.

Ordered that Wm Kennedy Treasury Pay Thomas Stribling ten
shillings for keeping four stray horses.

Mrs. Nancy McKibbin mother of James McKibbin of the age of
Eleven years on the second day of July next came into open court
Together with Jame McKibbin an Uncle of the said James McKibbin
and Andrew Terrence and entered into an Indenture of an apprenticeship of the said James McKibbin untill he attains the age
of Twenty one years: Unto William Shaw Esquire of which the
Court approved: and ordered that such Indenture to be recorded
in the record of this court.

Ordered that the County Treasury pay Edmond Ellis ten shillings
for Guarding the Prisoner as a states Witness.

Ordered that John Haile supply one Halloway Denson with Three
Hundred weight of Parks as on the Information of John High
it appears that the said Holloway Denson is an object of
Charity; and that County Treasury pay the said John Haile
for the said Pork.

Ordered that the sheriff deliver up to Mr. Ballew, Leonard
Smiths note that was given to the County for a stray cow and
Mr. Ballew Proved as his property.

Ordered that Court adjourn untill court in course. And signed
by: Jno Blasingame
               John Henderson

At an Intermediate court begun according to adjournment the
Third day of April one thousand seven hundred and ninety two
Present the Honbl. John Blasingame, William Farr Judges

A Deed from John Blasingame Sheriff of Union County to William
Farr Esquire Proved in open court by Ben. Haile and ordered
to Record.

A Deed from Jesse Liles and wife to John Insco Proved before
a Justice and ordered to be recorded.

Ordered that Ezekiel Spinger be overseer of the Road from
this Court house along the road that leads to Plummers ford
on Fairforest as far as the cross Road that Leads to Grendal
Shoals in the Room of Jonas Little who Resigns.

Ordered that William White son Isaac be overseer from the cross
Path that lead to Clayton Striblings to Hendersons old Road
in the Room of Philip Buzan.

325

The Last Will and Testament of David Chesholm deceased being Proved in Open Court by the Oaths of Jesse Maberry and John Beckham Junr. who said that they believed the said deceased to be in his proper senses at the time of executing the said Will ordered that to be recorded.

Obadiah Trimmier and William Chisholm being appointed Exors. in the said will came into open court and took the oath prescribed by Law as Executers aforesaid also give bond and signed.

Ordered that Charles Miles John Watson Senr. William Coleman and Abner Coleman appraise the Estate of David Chisholm deceased.

On the motion of C R Edson & Co. for a licence to retail spiritous liquors or keep a Public house which was granted. Who give security accd. to law.

The Last Will and Testament of David Stockton deceased being Proved in open Court by the oath of Angelica Mitchell and Ordered to be admitted to Record. William Buckhannon being an Executor to the above will came into open Court and took oath accd. to Law.

A Lease & Release from Terrance OKerrell to James Hughey Proved before a Justice and ordered to be recorded.

A Deed of conveyance from James Hughey to George Lynam Proved in open court by Majr. Otterson and ordered to be recorded.

A Bill of sale from William Whitlock to C E Edson proved in open court by Benjr. Haile and ordered to be Recorded.

Ordered that John Palmore Francis Wilkie and John Wilkie appraise the personal Estate of David Stockton deceased and certify the same under their hands accd. to Law and that Wm. McCullock Esquire qualify the above appraisers.

A Deed of conveyance from John Ingrim and wife to John Putman being Proved before a Justice and ordered to be recorded.

A Deed of conveyance from Archer Howard to John Putman proved before a Justice and ordered to be recorded.

A Lease and Release from Aaron Fincher Mary Fincher and Esther Insco to William Morgain proved before a Justice and ordered to be recorded.

A Deed of conveyance from Aaron Fincher Mary Fincher and Esther Insco to William Morgain and Jemima his wife proved before a Justice and ordered to be recorded.

A Bill of sale from Benajah Thompson to Jesse Farr proved before a Justice and ordered to be recorded.

Ordered that Drewry Herrington be overseer of the Road from Smiths ford on Broad River to the Bridge on Thickety and that he clear the same 20 feet wide and Grub it ten feet and keep it in repair accordingly.

A Lease and Release from Francis Beemar Esquire to Adam
Potter being Proved before a Justice and ordered to be
recorded.

A Deed of Conveyance from John Crittenton and wife to Nicholas
Curry proved before a Justice and ordered to be recorded.

A Deed of conveyance from Robert McMillion to Gabriel Patrick
being proved before a Justice and ordered to be recorded.

A Deed of conveyance from Abraham Miller and wife to William
Wood proven before a Justice and ordered to be Recorded.

A Deed of conveyance from William Hendley to John Mullins
Proved before a Justice and ordered to be recorded.

A Deed of conveyance from Landlot Porter to John Wharton
proved before a Justice and ordered to be recorded.

A Deed of conveyance from Roderick Right to Amos Cook Proved
before a Justice and ordered to be recorded.

A Bill of sale from Anna dorotha Moore to John Jefferies being
proved in open court by Nathl. Jefferies and ordered to be
recorded.

A Deed of conveyance from William Hardwick to Joshua Renworthey
Proved before a Justice and ordered to be recorded.

A Deed of conveyance from Turner Kendrick and wife to John
Gee Proved before a Justice and ordered to be recorded.

A Deed of conveyance from James Terrell to Nathl. Guyton
proved before a Justice and ordered to be recorded.

A Deed of conveyance from Landlot Porter to Thomas Thomas
proved before a Justice & ordered to be recorded.

A Deed of conveyance from John White & wife to William
Mitchell Proved in open court by Wm. White and ordered to be
recorded.

A Deed of conveyance of Bryan White & Judah his wife to Isaac
Edmondson Proved before a Justice and ordered to be recorded.

On motionof Nancy McKibbin for licence to keep a Tavern or
Public house which was granted and she entered into bond
according to Law.

Ordered that Colo. Thomas Brandon Andrew Torrence and James
Tosh appraise the Personal Estate of the late John McKibbin
deceased and return the said apprisement certifyed under
their hand accd. to Law.

On motion of Benajah Thompson for licence to keep a tavern and
Retail spiritous Liquor in this county which was granted and
he entered into Bond accd. to Law.

Its ordered that Ralph Hunt be overseer of the Road from Cooks
Bridge leading by the lower end of Clarks Plantation to Daniel
Liphams agreeable to Report of John Pearson and John Cook
Genl. appointed for that Purpose and that he clear the same

20 feet wide and grub it 10 feet wide and keep it in good
repair according to Law.

On the motion of Thomas Stribling Esquire Sheriff of this
county for Edward Mitchell to be appointed Deputy Sheriff
under him which met with the approbation of the court who
came into open court and took the oathes prescribed by law.

Ordered that William Darby be admitted to Retail Spiritous
in this County on his giving Bond and security according to
Law.

On motion of James Park for licence to Retail spiritous
liquors in this county which was granted and he gave security
according to Law.

Ordered that Samuel Clowney be overseer of the road from
Rockly Creek to Grendol Shoales on Pacolate River in the Room
of John P. Pooll who Resigns and that he keep the same in
repair according to Law.

Ordered that James Townsend admr. of the Estate of Wm Massey
Expose to Public sale at the Plantation of the late deceased
all the Personal Estate of said deceased on his advertising
three week's of such sale and give six months credit.

Ordered that the minutes be read and the Court adjourn untill
Tomorrow 9 OClock and signed by Wm Farr   Jno Blasingame

The Court met according to adjournment on Wednesday the 4th
day of April 1792. Present the Honble
                              William Farr
                              John Blasingame   Judges

A Deed of Conveyance from William Beckham to Richard Farr.
Proved in open court by Colo. William Farr and ordered to be
recorded.

The same to the same Proved by the same and ordered to Record.

A Renounceation and Right of Dower for Ann Gasaway Widow to
Wm. Beckham and ordered to be recorded.

On motion of Frederick Thompson for licence to keep a tavern
or Public house which was Granted & entered into bond according
to Law.

The Last will and testament of William Plummer deceased being
proven in open court by the oath of John Stiles who said that
he believed the said deceased to be in his proper sences at
the time of executing the said Will. Also came into open
court Christian Plummer wife of said Wm Plummer deceased and
acknowledged the said Will to be the last Will and Testament
of his husband Wm. Plummer deceased which is hereby ordered
to Record. Christian Plummen and George Harling Hatter being
appointed executers in the said deceased will came into open
court and entered into Bond: and the oathes as executors
aforesaid according to Law.

Ordered that George Harling Farmer, Rayney Balleu and William
Morgain appraise all the Personal Estate of the above William
Plummer deceased and return their appraisement certifyed under

328

their hands into the clerks office according to Law. and that
Thomas Blasingame Esquire qualify the above appraisers.

On the application of Alexander Macbeth & Co for licence to
retail Spiritous Liquors in this county at Union Court house.
Also a licence to retail spirituous liquors at Grendol Shoals
by John Beekham Junr. which is granted and he entered into Bond
according to Law.

Ordered that John Jenkins be allowed to keep a Tavern or
Retail Spirituous liquors in this county on his giving bond
and security according to Law.

Ordered that William Clark be overseer of the Road from the
Road that leads from Samuel McJunkins toward Fairforest to
the Union Court House in the Room of Mr. Howell.

A General Releasement from John Towns to William Farr Esquire
Proved beofre a Justice and ordered to be recorded.

Ordered that the minutes be read and the court adjourn untill
court in course and signed by Wm Farr   Jno Blasingame
memorial & probates transmitted

At a Court begun and holden in and for the county of Union
at the Court house of said oounty on Fryday the first day of
June in the year of our Lord one thousand seven hundred and
ninety two and of the Independance of the United States of
North America the sixteen
Present the Honble
        John Henderson
        John Blasingame
        William Farr   Judges

Ordered that the Grnad Juror be sworn which are as follows
to Wit.

Ben Hollingsworth	1	Thomas McDonnell	11
Charles Sims	2	John Putmann	12
Hugh Donaldson	3	James Woodson	13
Wm McCullock Esqr	4	Joseph Meanes	14
Wm Buckhannon	5	Nicholas Waters	15
Thomas Saml	6	Joseph Hughes	16
Handcock Porter	7	Adam Potter	17
Bernard Glenn	8	Alex Hammilton	18
John Kennedy	9	Isaac Hollingsworth	19
Charles Hames Senr.	10	Jonathan Prigmore	20

Also the following persons are sworn as Pettit Jurors
ToWit

Henry Hill	1	Wm White son of Isaac	14
Patrick Shaw	2	Patrick Moore	15
John Gilham	3	John Foster	16
William Savage	4	Reubin Wilks	17
David Thomas	5	Wm Newman	18
John Nederman	6	Wm McCown	19
Richd. Huckebey	7	John Hervey	20
John Herrington	8	Richd. Thompson	21
Wm Hughes Snr.	9	Wm Wright	22
Robert Wadkins	10	Edward Prince	23
Richard Menton Junr.	11	Robt. Thompson	24
Thos. Biddy	12	John White	25
John Gibson	13	Ben Woodson	26

Henry Burrow   27   Saml. Spray   29
James Guthery   28   Elisha McGuire   30

On motion of Ephraim Ramsay for William Nibbs and Patrick
Mickey Esquire to be allowed to practice as attorney in this
Court who produced their licence for the same and is thereon
admitted to Practice in this Court as an attorney aforesaid.

Cushman Edson)   P A S
     vs   )   Came the parties into open Court and agreed
Robert Savage)   to Discontinue this suit at defendants cost.

The State   )   Overselling rates
     vs   )   Discharged.
Alex Macbeth)

The State   )   Ditto
     Vs   )   Discharged.
John Beckham Jnr.)

The State   )   Ditto
     Vs C R Edson)   Discharged

The State   )   Ditto
     vs   )   Discharged
Nancey McKibbin)

The State   )   Ordered that the defendant give security in
     Vs   )   the sum Fifty pounds sterling for his appear-
William Foster)   ance at this court now sitting and not depart
                    the Court without leave of the same who
came into open court together with Jepam Foster and John
Woods and acknowledged himself Indebted to the state in the
sum of fifty pounds and the said securities in the sum of
Twenty five pounds each for his appearnace aforesaid.
Witness
Ben Haile   DC   Wm Foster
                     John Wood x his mark
                     Isham Foster

State   )   Ordered that the defendant enter into recog-
     Vs   )   nizance for his appearnace at the next court
Peter Varnier)   and not depart the same without leave of the
                    same answer to bill of Indictment to be
perfered against him who came into open court with John
Thompson and Edmond Ellis and acknowledged himself Indebted
to the state in the sum of one hundred pounds and his securities in the sum of fifty pounds each for his appearnace
aforesaid
Witness   Peter Varnier
Ben Haile D. C.   John Thompson
                         Edmond Ellis

State   )   Bastardy
     Vs   )   Ordered that the defendant be fine in the
Edmond Simpson)   sum of three pounds eleven shillings and
                    four pence and costs of suit credited 12
                    months.

State   )   Bastardy
     Vs   )   Ordered that the defendant be fined three
Elizabeth Newman)   pounds eleven shillings and four pence

330

sterling and costs of suit and ordered that she give security
for the payments of the said sum & costs of suit.

State   )   Bastardy
    Vs   )   Ordered that the defendant give security
Edmond Simpson)   for the payment of the above fine who entered
                       into sec. with Saml. Simpson
Ben Haile D.C.
                          Edmond Simpson
                          Saml. Simpson.

State   )   Ordered that the Indictment be discharged at
    Vs   )   defendants cost.
Henry Burrow)

State   )   Ordered that this Indictment be discharged
    Vs   )   at defendants cost.
Robert Smith)

State   )   Ordered that this Indictment be discharged
    vs   )   at the defendants costs.
Robert Armstrong)

A Deed from Bernard Glenn to Joseph Coleman proved before Wm
Farr Esquire and ordered to Record.

Ordered that the Court adjourn untill Tomorrow nine OClock.

                          John Henderson
                          Wm Farr

The worshipful Court of Union County met according to
adjournment on Saturday the second day of June 1792
Present the Honble
                          John Blasingame
                          William Farr   Esquires

Ordered on motion of William Chisholm Executor of David
Chisholm deceased expose to Public sale all the Pershable
Estate of the said deceased on a Credit of Eighteen month
at the plantation of Adam Chisholm.

Two Deeds of conveyance from John D Young to Fedrick Eison
Proved in open Court by John Haile & subg. witness & ordered
to Record.

The State)   Ordt.
    Vs   )   That the recognizance of George Taylor & others
Wm Foster)   be discharged from of their recognizance.

A Deed of conveyance from Daniel McJunkin to Joseph McJunkin
proved before William Farr Esquire & Ordered to be recorded.

A Powers of attorney from John Taylor & wife to Richard
Bullock also a Deed of conveyance from Richard Bullock to Adam
Potter Esquire proved in open Court by James Bullock and
ordered to be recorded.

A Deed from Geo. Taylor to Lewis Sanders proved by John
Nuckols & ordered to record.

331

The State)   Ordered that a rule be served on John Pearson
Vs   )   Esquire to appear at this court on Monday to
John Cox)   shew cause why he has not returned to this court
                 the recognizance and other proceedings in this
suit against the defendant for Horse stealing.

The State   )   Pettit Larcency
Vs   )   The Grand Juror having considered this case
William Power)   and return their verdict tell Hugh Means
                foreman.

Ordered that all recognizance returnable to this court be
continued untill next January court. being the recognizance
that have not been carried into execution.

The State   )   Pettit Larcency
Vs   )   Came the state by Wm Shaw attorney and the
William Power)   defendant by William Nibbs Esquire his
                Counseller whereupon the deft. being arrained
at the bar and Pleads not guilty whereupon came a Juror to
Wit Robert Lusk foreman, James Lindsey William Hames James
Maberry John George John Greer John Petty Pooll Thomas Menton
Joseph Randol William White Gilbert Price Richard who being
duly sworn according to Law to will and truly try this
Indictment return their verdict on their respective oathes
and say we find the defendant Guilty.
                      Robert Lusk foreman

Its ordered in pursuance of the above verdict that the defendant be removed back to the Goal of this county and there
remain untill Tuesday and then to be taken out and serve
on his case back on the hour of Twelve OClock Twenty lashes
at the whipping Post by the sheriff.

Robert Baitey)   On appeal
Vs   )   Ordered that this suit be dismissed
Robert Williams)   at the appellants cost.

The State   )   Ordered that William Foster be bound over for
vs   )   his appearnace at our next court of Union
Peter Varnier)   aofresaid on the first day of Jany. next
                then and there to give evidence in behalf of
the state against the said Peter Varnier. Who came into open
Court and acknowledged himself indebted to the state in the
sum of Fifty pounds sterling for his appearance aforesaid
                     Wm Foster
Teste
Ben Haile D.C.

Fincher)   Ordered that the Plaintiff pay James Skelton 7/6
Vs   )   for 3 days attendance in this suit for Plff.
Rountree)

Jno Fincher   )   Ordered that John Fincher pay James Skelton
Vs   )   7/6 for 3 days attendance in this suit.
Robt. Merrick)

On motion of Hughe Meanes Esquire Mr. McCarter is appointed
Constable for this county who came into open court and took
the oath according to Law.

State   )   Its ordered that the defendant be bound in
  Vs   )   security in the sum of one hundred pounds
Peter Varnier)   sterling and his securities in the sum of
                 Fifty pounds whereupon came the defendant
into open court Together with John Thompson and Edmond Ellis
and acknowledged himself indebted to the state in the sum of
one hundred pounds and his securities in the sum of fifty
pounds each for the appearnace of the defendant at our next
County Court of Union aforesaid on the first day of January
next then and there to answer to a Bill of Indictment then to
be preferred against the defendant for stealing a negroe and
all charges now alleged against him.
Teste   Peter Varnier
Ben Haile   DC   John Thompson
                         Edmond Ellis

Ordered that William Buckhannon at David Stockton decd.
expose to public sale at the Plantation of said deceased all
the perishable Estate or part of the said deceased and part
of the house hold furniture on a credit of six months ancy. to
Law.

Ordered that the County Treasury pay James Kennedy Twenty
five shillings for keeping a stray horse as soon as all former
orders of this court an discharged.

Ordered that the minutes be read which was done and adjourned
untill Monday 9 OClock
                         Wm Farr
                         Jno Blasingame

The worshipful court of Union met according to adjournment on
Monday the Fourth day of June 1792
            Present the Honble
                         John Blasingame
                         William Farr   Esquires.

A Deed of conveyance from Thomas Brandon to John Haile
acknowledged in open court and ordered to be recorded.

A Deed of conveyance from Christopher Brandon to Aaron Thomas
Hart proved in open court by Thomas Brandon and ordered to
be recorded.

Thomas Wood   )   Petn. & Sums
  Against   )   the defendant pleads administrat
Andrew Terrence &   )   and on proof of the note or acct.
Thomas Blasingame Exors)   filed the court decreed for the
                           Plaintiff seven pounds nine
shillings & eight pence with int. & costs of suit when future
assets come into the hands of the Exors & after satisfaction
of prior Judgments & superior debts.

John Fincher)   On appeal
  Vs   )   Referred to Cold. John Sanders and Andrew
Robert Merrick) Terrance and their award to be made a Judt.
                 of this court.

George Patterson Plaintiff)   Debt on a new Trial came the
  against   )   Plaintiff by Abraham Nott
James Sims   Defendant)   Esquire and the Defendant by
                              William Shaw and Ephraim Ramsay

Esquire his councellers whereupon came a Juror Towit Robert
Lusk fore James Lindsey William Hames James Maberry John
George John Greer John Petty Pat Thomas Minton Joseph Randol
William White Gilbert Prince and Richard Minton who being
duly sworn and affirmed to will and truly this Issue Joined
and a true verdict give according to evidence and upon their
sworn oathes and affirmation return their verdict and say
We find for the defendant.   Robert Lusk Foreman

Ordered that James Sims pay Robert Glenn 7/6 of 3 days attendance also 6/6 for miliage.

Ordered that James Sims pay John Stewart 7/6 of 3 days attendance also 8/4 for miliage.

Ordered that James Sims pay Jeremiah Kingsley 7/6 for 3 days
attendance also 8/4 for miliage for his attendance in the
above suit.

John Fincher)   On appeal
    Vs   )   by consent of the parties this suit is
William Lee)   referred to Captain John Sanders and Andrew
                Terrence with power of chosing an umpire and
    their award to be the Judgment of court.

Frances Fincher) On appeal
    Vs   ) Ordered that this suit be refered to the
Samuel Cooper   ) Arbitration of C R Edson and Joseph Lee
                   with Power to chose an umpire and their
    award to be the Judgment of this court.

John Murphey)   Debt
    Vs   )   Came the parties into open court by their
David McCall)   attorneys and the defendant by Thomas Walker
                his attorney confessed a Judgment accy. to
    specialty with Interest and costs of suit with stay of
    execution untill the first day of September next.

Ordered that the Court Adjourn untill tomorrow 9 OClock
                            Wm Farr
                            Jno Blasingame

The Honble Court met according to adjournment on Tuesday the
fifth day of June 1792
Present the Hbl   John Henderson
                    John Blasingame   Judges
                    William Farr

A Deed of conveyance from Isham Cleaton & wife to Mill Sumner
Proven in open court by Jno McBeth & ordered to be Recorded.

A Deed of conveyance from James Huey to Henry Huey proved
before a Justice & O R
A Deed from Henry Hughey to Geo Hughey acknowledged in open
court & ordered to Record.

James Hogans   Plaintiff) Case
  against   ) Came the Plaintiff by William
Spencer Brummett Defendant) Shaw Esquire his attorney and
                             the defendant by Zachariah
Taleaferro Esquire his counseller whereupon came a Juror
Towit the same as Geo Patterson against James Sims who

being duly sworn return their verdict and say we find for the
Plaintiff seventeen pounds fifteen shillings with interest
& costs of suit.   Robt. Lusk foreman

Joshua Palmore) Debt
    Vs   ) Ordered that a dedimus Polestation Issue
Joseph Hughes) to the James Knox Esquire to take the
                 examination of Jasper Sleeker and return
                 the same to our next January court and his
examination so taken shall be taken as evidence in this suit.

The State   ) Pettit Larceny
    Vs   ) In pursuance of the sentence of court on
William Power) Saturday the second day of this instant for
                 the defendant to receive his sentence of said
Court and this being the time limited was taken out by the
sheriff and received his punishment accordingly being twenty
lashes on his bare back And its therefore ordered by an oath
made. Requiring security for the peace for the defendants
good behaviour and that he give Security in the sum of one
hundred pounds and two securities in the sum of fifty pounds
each for his Good behaviour toward all.

Toward all Good people of this state for the time of Twelve
months and that he be committed to the Common Goal of this
county and thence remain untill he give such security aforesaid.

James Holland) Debt on writ of Enquiry came the Plaintiff
    Vs   ) by Wm Shaw his attorney & the defendant being
John Steen   ) solemnly called but failed to appear whereupon
                came a Juror to Wit the same as Patterson
against Sims return their verdict & say "we find for the
plaintiff according to specialty.
                      Robert Lusk Foreman

Ordered that James Hogans pay Wm Hogans 1010 for 4 days
attendance as a witness for him against Spencer Brummett

The State) Ordered that the Recognizance in this be
    Vs   ) continued untill next January Court 1792.
Thomas Cox)

Henry Miller   ) Debt in a writ of Enquiry came the Juror
    Vs   ) the same as Patterson vs Sims Report their
Benjamin Johnson) verdict and say we find for the Plaintiff
                   Ten pound & with Interest & costs of suit.

Robert Cook) Attachment
    Vs   ) The plaintiff proved the note on which this
Henry Miller) attachment is found Decree for Plaintiff for
               five pounds and Interest from 1st October 1791
and condemned in the hands of Mr. Benjamin Johnson, as
Garnashee and crediter of said Defendant with cost of suit and
ordered that the balance of said Garnashee debt to said
defendant be also condemned in his hands to satisfy a Judgment
given by Charles Junr. Esquire in behalf of John Fott and that
the execution of said John Boott(?) against the Property of
said Garnashee be superseded.

David Boshart by C R Edson his Guardian) T.A.B.
    Vs   ) Came the Plaintiff by
William Williams   ) William Shaw and

335

Ephraim Ramsay Esquire his attorney and the defendant by
Zachariah Taleafero and Alexd. Mickie his Counciller whereupon
came a Juror the same as George Patterson against James Sims
and the Jurors being subj. sworn and affirmed Return their
verdict on their several oaths and affirmations say We fine
for the Plaintiff Forty one shillings & Costs of suit.

Robt. Lusk foreman

Ordered that Adam Scane pay William Williams 10 for four days
attendance as a witness him against Thomas Brandon

Thomas Clark   ) By consent of the parties ordered that this
Vs   ) case be refered to John Stokes Col. Brandon
Daniel McJunkin)   with power of chosing an umpire & their
                   award to be made a Judt. of this Court.

Ordered that Thomas Stribling sheriff pay Federick Eison one
pound nineteen shillings and two pence & this receipt shall
be his fee the same.

Ordered that the Court adjourn untill tomorrow until 9 OClock
John Henderson
Jno Blasingame

The Honbl Court of Union met accy. to adjournment on Wednesday
the sixth day of June 1792.
Present the Hobl.   John Henderson
                        John Blasingame
                        William Farr   Esquires

Adam Scane   ) by consent of the parties ordered that this
Vs   ) suit be referred to Andrew Torrence & James
Thomas Brandon)   Gasaway with power of chosing an umpire &
                   their award to be made a Judt. of this court.

David Boshart by   ) Ordered that C R Edson pay John
C R Edson his Guardian)   Sanders 201 for 8 days attendance as
Vs   ) a witness in this suit ordered that
William Williams   ) C R Edson pay Jno Petty Pooll 251
                          Shillings for 10 days attendance in
the above suit.

Daniel Lipham   ) Case
Vs   ) By consent of the parties
Wm Burton & Elizabeth Burton)   ordered that this suit be
                                    refered to the arbitration of
Maj. Samuel Otterson John Sanders Edward Finck and Bernard
Glenn and if they cannot agree to chose John Pearson Esquire
a fifth arbitrator and their award returnable to our next
January court shall be the Judgment thereof and that the said
parties meet at Wm Burtons in order to Arbitrate the above
suit on any time they shall agree.

John Henderson Esquire being appointed Executor of the last
will and testament of David Chisholm deceased who came into
open court and took the oath of an Exord. aforesaid.

The State) The defendant being indicted for asst. &
Vs   ) Battery Pleas Guilty and shew himself upon the
Wm Williams) mercy of the court & Ordered that he be fined
              one penny & costs of suit.

336

John Cambell   )   Debt.
Vs   )   Ordered that this case be dismissed at the
William Heaton)   defendants cost.

Wm Farr Esquire   )   On writ of enquiry came the Plaintiff by
Vs   )   William Shaw Esquire his atty. and came
Ann & James Gaway)   a Jury the same as Patterson vs James
Sims who being duly sworn to execute this writ of Enquiry
return their verdict and say we find for the Plaintiff thirty
pounds & costs of suit.   Robt. Lusk foreman

Thomas Blasingame)   Case
Vs   )   Came the Plaintiff by William Shaw
James Tosh   )   Esquire and the defendant by his own proper
                     person whereupon came a Juror the same as
Patterson against Sims who being duly sworn say on their
oathes we find for the Plaintiff two pounds fifteen shillings
with two years interest and costs of suit.
                                   Robt. Lusk foreman

Adam Scane   )   Ordered that Adam Scane pay James Gasway
Vs   )   17 /6 for 7 days attendance for him in the
Thomas Brandon)   above suit.

Ordered that Nancey McKibbin admr. of the Estate of John
McKibbin deceased expose to Public sale at Union Court house
all the personal Estate of the said deceased and that she
allow said Purchasers six months credit.

Kirkland & Co.)   P. & S.
Vs   )   On motionof Mr. Shaw attorney for the
William Hall)   defendant and the Plaintiff being solemnly
                  called but not appearing a nonsuit as ordered.

Charles Green)   Non suit
Vs   )
Joseph Jolley)

The Same   )   Nonsuit
Vs   )
Richd. Terrell)

Wm Buckhannon)   Dismissed at Pltff. costs.
Vs   )
Wm Dalefield)

Graff Peebles Braselman Edson)   Debt
   against   )   On a writ of enquiry same
John McCooll   )   Juror as Patterson against
                                  Sims say on their oathes &
affirmations we find for the Plaintiff according to notes with
interest & costs & suit.   Robt. Lusk foreman

Robert Smith)   Dismissed at Plff costs by his order.
Vs   )
Henry Burrow)

Robert Smith   )   Dismissed at the Plff cost.
Vs   )
Robt. Armstrong)

Macael Crawford   )   Debt on Judgt.
  Vs   )
Laurence Easterwood)

The Defendant having been duly called and not answering ordered
that Judgt. be taken by assault & that the Judgment be entered
up for the principle interest and costs of the sd. Judt. and
for the costs of this suit.

Ordered that the clerk do Issue Petition summons and other
process against all defaults that has obtained a licence in
this court and that he Issue Executions for all fines & for
futures that is now due on advertising thirty days of such
order.

Peter Ellis   )   Attacht.
  against   )   Ordered that ther sheriff expose to sale
Peter Varnier)   certain horse now attached to satisfy the
                   debt of said Ellis and that the money remain
in his hands untill further orders of this court.

A Deed of conveyance from James McKibbin to Wm Patten Proved
before a Justice & Ordered to be recorded.

Leonard Smith)   Contd.
  Vs   )
James Gastin)

Peter Varnier)   Desolved
  Vs   )
Geo Taylor   )

Ordered that the Court adjourn untill tomorrow 8 OClock
                         John Henderson
                         Jno Blasingame

The Honble. Court met according to adjournment on Thursday
the Seventh day of June 1792   Present the Honble
                         John Henderson
                         William Farr   Esquires

Ordered that the fees due William Shaw Esquire as County
attorney be paid unto him by Wm Kennedy Treasury by the first
money that comes into his hands.

The Court proceeded to the choice of three proper persons to
fill the vacancys of Magistrates in this county, when Andrew
Torrance Adam Potter and Dr. Harmon Anderson were chosen by
the court and ordered that a copy of this order together with
the Particular recommendation of this court be transmitted
to his excellency the governor in order to obtain from his
excellency the usual commission.

The State)   Ordered that Benjamin Haile pay Frederick Eison
  Vs   )   Twenty shillings & six pence being for the defts.
Wm Powers)   prison Fees agreeable to his acct. filed.

A Deed of conveyance from Charles Sims to his son William
Sims proved before Wm. Farr Esquires & ordered to be recorded.

Frances Fincher)   Ordered that Frances Fincher pay James
   Vs   )   Duncan thirty five shillings for ten days
Samuel Cooper)   attendance as a witness for him also ordered
                    that Frances Fincher pay Elizabeth Duncan
twenty shillings for eight days attendance as a witness in
this suit also.

Ordered that the minutes be read which was done & ordered
that the Court adjourn untill court in course.
                              John Henderson
                              Wm Farr

The worshipful Court met according to adjournment Present the
Hounourable the 3d day of Sept. 1792   John Blasingame
                                        John Henderson

A Deed of conveyance from James Harrison to James Gibbs
ordered to record Proved before a Justice.

A Deed of conveyance from Jeremiah Cooper to Robert Burns
Proved by the affirmation of John Clark O to R

Ordered to be recorded aprobate as appears to be taken before
John Thompson in the year.

Proved in court by Nicholas Lazerous the last will & Testament
of John Lendon Porter & ordered to be record.

Proved before a Justice a Deed of conveyance from John
Weadennben to William Spears O T R

Proved before a Justice a Deed of conveyance from Turner
Kendrick to Lot Wood O T R

Acknowledged in court a Deed of conveyance from Henry Allison
Davis to Robert Bullington, Nancy his wife acknowledged her
right of Dowery in open court.

On the motion of John Sanders & other for the original way
from Bales's ford on Fairforest to Cooks mill to be opened
as a good Bridle way to said Mill, ordered that Joseph Mc-
Junkin Henry Millhouse & Wm Clark or any two of them view
the said way & those now in use & make report to the next
court.

A Deed from James Henry to Joshua Palmer, proved before a
Justice & O. to R.

A Deed from John McKee to James Jackson Proved by John Haile
& O to R.
A Deed and platform D. Huger to James Jackson & O to R.

On motion of Daniel Lipham he has leave to keep a Tavern or
publick house who gave Bond & security accordingly.

Proved before a Justice a Deed of conveyance from Wilson Jolly
& Mary his wife to Abraham Smith O to R.

Proved in court by the oath of Wm Darby a Deed from John &
Mary Bennet to George Harling (Hatter) O to R

339

Acknowledged in court a Deed from John Basingame late sheriff of Union to Nathaniel Jefferies 0 to R

Acknowledged in court a Deed from Jane Rogers to William Davis & 0 to R

Proved before a Justice a Deed from David Akins Jennet Bowden James Hendrick Sarah Henderick & Rebecca Bowden to Robert Savage 0 to R.

Mr. Nevel Holcom is appointed overseer of the road in the room of Archer Howard from Col Brandons to Bobos ford on Tyger.

Ordered that the Road Mark out by James Gibbs Thomas Brandon & Wm Darby be cleared out & kept in good repair by Wm Anderson who is appointed overseer of said Road.

On the petition of the Inhabitants between Packolet Broad River for a road from Union Court House to be the Mouth of Packolate leading by Pinckney court house its ordered that Capt. Palmore Wm Sharp & Ben Savage be & are appointed to Mark & lay out the same the nearest & best way & report the same tomorrow to this court.

A Deed of conveyance from Daniel Huger Esquire to Thomas Stribling Jnr. Esquire proven in open court by Ben Haile & ordered to be recorded.

Ordered William Goldsmith be overseer of the road from Union Courts along the road that leads to Cooks and on Tyger as far as the Cross Road that leads from Magt. McJunkins to Montgomerius old place and Humphrey Bates from said Road to Cooks Bridge on Tyger river & that they clear & keep the same in good repair according to Law with the Hand convenient thereto.

On the Resignation of Thomas Vance ordered that William Cambell overseer of the road from Bogans Creek to Union Court house & that he keep the same in good repair accd.

Ordered that Ralph Hunt be overseer of the Road from Cooks Bridge to Liphams agreeable to his former order &

A Deed of conveyance from William Gilkie to Ralph Roger is proved before a Justice & 0 R

A Deed of conveyance from Ralph Rodgers to Isaac Chapman proved before a Justice & ordered to be recorded.

Ordered that Mahn Pearson be overseer of the Road from Adames ford on Tyger to Townsends shop.

Ordered that George Watkins be overseer of the Road from Townsends shop to Kenedys ford on Enoree.

Ordered that Job Seigler be bound to George Harlin (Hatter) to learn this art and missing as Hatter
Court adjourned untill tomorrow ten oclock.
                                        John Henderson
                                        Jno Blasingame

340

September 4th 1792 the court met according to adjournment
Present the Hounourable Judges &c.

John Henderson
John Blasingame   Esquires

Acknowledged in court a Deed from Abel Kenderick to Jonathan
Cud & O to R.

A Deed of Gifts from Turner Kenderick to his son for a tract
of land proved before a Justice & O to R.

Proved before a Justice a Deed from Lott & Mary Woods to Wm
McCollock esqr. & O to R.

Proved by the oath of Wm Tate a deed from John Tompson & Mary
his wife to James Lorronce & O to R
Proved by the oath of Francis Whelchel a Deed from John
Thompson to William Tate & O to R.

Proved in court by oath of Robert Anderson a Deed from Jesse
Fore to Ezekial Wilburn & O to R.

William Cotter having served his time as overseer of the Road
from the skull shoals on Packolate to Thicketty Bridge
in consequince thereof it is ordered & that Samuel Wood be
& is appointed overseer of the same & that he keep the same
in good repair.

Proved before a Justice a Deed from Richard Bolsen to Robert
Smith & O to R.

Proved before a Justice a Deed from William Thomas to Robert
Smith & O to R.

James Thomas came into court & proved an account against the
Estate of Daniel Thomas decd. which act. is Lodged in the
Clerks office.

William Thomas affsd. proved an account against the same which
is also Lodged in the sd. office.

A Deed of conveyance from William Pooll to Jno McKee proven
before a Justice and ordered to be recorded.

A Deed of conveyance from Charles Lewis to William Sims proven
before Cold. Farr Judge & O to R.

A Deed from James McKelwain to William Palteur(?) proved
before a Justice & ordered to be recorded.

A Deed from John Bennet & wife to Hendley Eaves Proved before
a Justice and ordered to be recorded.

A lease and release from Daniel Prince to Richard Hays proved
before a Justice & ordered to be recorded.

A Deed from Richard Barrot to William Glover proved before a
Justice & ordered to be Recorded.

A Deed of conveyance from John McDonnell to Alexr. Cain
proven in open court & O to R.

A Deed of conveyance from John Gregory to Alexr. Cain acknowledged in open court & O to R.

A Deed of conveyance from Philip Anderson to Capt. Bird
Beuford, proven in open court & ordered to be recorded.

Two Deeds of conveyances from Zachariah Bell Senr. and
Margaret his wife, to William Smith Davis, acknowledged in
open court by the said Zachariah Bell, and the said Marg-
Bell being privately examined by a Judge of court she reports
that she freely relinquishes her right of Dower in the above
conveyances, Which as ordered to be recorded.

Ordered that John Clark Executor of the last Will and testament
of Caleb Edmondson deceased expose to Public sale at the
decd. Plantation all his Parishable Estate, on a Credit of
Six months, after giving Thirty Days notice of such sale.

Ordered that James Jeater be allowed out of the county
Treasury his account filled in open court for maintaining(?)
Thos. Sandeage as soon as money arises by Licences &c &
Ects into the treasury after all former orders are satisfyed.

The application of Renny Ballew for a licences retail spiritous
liquors, which was granted & he entered into Bond according to
Law.

Proved in Court by the Oath of John Martin a Deed from John
McCool to James McKibbin & O to R.

Proved in Court by the oath of James Porter a Deed from Thomas
Biddy to John Biddy & O to R.

Proved in Court by Colo. Wm Farr a Deed from William Johnston
& Susanah Johnston to William Sims & O to R.

Proved before a Justice a Deed from Charles Sims to William
Sims & O to R.

Its ordered that Adam Young orphan be released from his
Indenture, Ewin to James McKilwain Junr. also William Young
or released also from his Indenture given to James McKelwain
senr.
Ordered that the above, James Young and William Young orphans
of Margaret Young be brought to our next court in order to be
bound out according to Law.

Ordered that John Haile to overseer of the Road from Gibbs
old Field to the head of Tanners Creek and that he keep it
in Good repair accd. and James Bankhead from there to
Pinckney Court house & that he keep it in Good repair accd. to
Law.

Ordered that the sheriff expose to sale all stray lyable to
be sold this court. accd. to law.

A Deed from Thomas Biddie to John Biddie proven in open court
by James Porter & Ordered to record.

Ordered that Hugh Means Esquire be overseer of the road from
Gibbs old field to Fairforest.

Ordered that Alexd. McCarter be overseer of the road from Fairforest to the county line.

On motion of Sarah House for letters of administration to be Granted her on the Estate of Lawrence House deceased, which was granted and she came into open court and was duly qualifyed, according to Law. and entered into Bond in the sum of five hundred pounds sterling with security accd.

Ordered that Capt. Palmore be overseer of the road from Jas McCrackeng shop to Pinckney Hill & Benjamin Savage from James Bogans to Jas. McCrackens, agreeable to the report of the Commt. appointed for that purpose.

Ordered that Nathl. Gaiton James Kennedy & Menus Dawson is hereby appointed to appriase the Estate of Lawrence house & that Nicholas Currey Esquire Qualify the said appraisers.

These are to certify that Nickolas Curry was duly qualify as a Justice of the peace for the county of Union and took the oath presented by Law before me John Henderson a Jury U.C.

A Sheriffs Deed from William Farr Esquire to Cushman Ruggles Edson, acknowledged in open court by the said Wm Farr & ordered to record.

Ordered that Hugh Meanes Esquire Capt. Jno. Sanders Stephen Layton Hazekiah Rice, and John Pearson, meet at some time between this & next court and settle the dispute between James Gibbs and Capt. Archer Howard, concerning a Road or Paths and their award, shall be the Judgment of this court.

John Henderson
Jno Blasingame

The court then adjourned untill court in course.

At a Court begun and holden in and for the county of Union at the court house of said county on the first day of January in the year of our Lord one thousand seven hundred and Ninety Three and of the Independance of the United States of North America the seventeenth
Present the Honble John Blasingame Esqr.

Charles Scisson James Kennedy and John High this day made application to be appointed constalbes for this county. Who met with the approbation thereof and they came into open court and took the oaths of office agreeable to Law.

On the application of Cushman R Edson and Jane Edson his wife ordered that letters of Admr. be granted to them on the Estate and effects of Alexr. Fitzpatrick as next of kin to said deceased and ordered that the said Cush R Edson & wife enter into Bond & security in the sum of one thousand pounds sterling agreeable to law.

A Deed of conveyance from Nathl. David & Elizabeth his wife to Jacob Leager proven before a Justice & ordered to record & the said Elizabeth Davis being privately examined by John Blasingame Esqr. who says she freely relinquishes her Dower to said land.

The court then adjourned untill Tomorrow 9 OClock only one
Judge appearing   Jno Blasingame

The Honble court of Union met according to adjournment on
Wednesday the second day of January 1793.
Present the Honbl   John Henderson Esqrs.
                         John Blasingame

The Court proceeded to draw the Grand Jurors for the county
of Union to serve next June court which are as follows:

John George Junr.	1	Richard Beuford	11
C. R. Edson	2	Lewis Ledbetter	12
Thomas Williams	3	Jethn. Porter	13
James Jeater	4	John Kennedy	14
James Harling	5	John White	15
John Gilham	6	Richard Cox	16
William Hodge	7	Thos. McDonnell	17
Obd. Howard	8	James Sims	18
Robt. White	9	Thomas Parmer	19
John Foster	10	Robert Harris	20

Also the following persons are drawn as Pettit Jurors to
serve next June court to wit.

James Davis	1	Barnnet Longstone	16
Joshua Martin	2	Soloman Whitson	17
Thomas Weaver	3	Robert Glover	18
Joseph Gault	4	Isaac Smith	19
Curtis Wood	5	Wm McCown	20
Reubin Wilks	6	James Hawkins	21
John White	7	Wm Blackstock	22
Samuel Jackson	8	Wm Scisson	23
Lewis Bobo	9	David Floyd	24
Wm Hughes H	10	Thomas Lamb Jnr.	25
Aaron Hait	11	Wm Campbell	26
James Smith	12	Ephraim Smith	27
James Ray	13	William Nix	28
George Crossley	14	Freeman Roberts	29
Joseph Coleman	15	James Benson	30

Ordered that Thomas Stribling provide for the Jury Boxe &
Lock and Led for the same & the expences thereof to be paid
by the County treasury.

On motion of Ephraim Ramsay Esquire, for Charles Jones
Colcock and Wm Peater Tennant Esquires for them to be
admitted to practice as attorneys in this court, which is
ordered accordingly on thy producing their licence when
necessary.

Graffs Co.   )   P & S Judges confessed for Ł 5-16-8
    Vs   )   star of Exors six months.
Abel Kendrick)

Graffs & Co.)   Case - Judgt. confessed for Ł 12-0-1½ with
    Vs   )   star of Exors six months.
Abel Kendrick)

A Deed from Hermon Howard to Job Mitchell Provin beofre
a Justice & ordered to Record.

Daniel Lipham Plf   ) Case
     against   ) Pursuant to the within order
William & Elizabeth Burtons) we the arbitrators convinced
                              agreeable to appl. and of
opinion that Wm Buston be Examined from any damage or cost of
suit and we the arbitrators on of opinion that Elizabeth
Buston pay Daniel Lipham ten pounds 5/6 sterling and costs of
suit on her part Given under our hands this 19th day of Oct.
1792.   Saml. Otterson
                              Bernard Finch
                              Edward Glenn
                              John Pearson

The following persons being drawn as Grand Jurors from this
court being duly sworn to wit Wm McCullock foreman Benjn.
Hollingsworth Hugh Donaldson Wm Buckhannon Thomas Lamb
Handcock Porter Bernd. Glenn Charles Hames Thomas McDonnell
James Woodson Joseph Means Joseph Hughes Alexd. Hammolton
Isaac Hollingsworth and John Kennedy.

Charles Berry   ) Attachment
    against   ) Ordered that this suit be dismissed
Randolph Holebrooks)   at the Pltfs. cost.

Charles Kelley) P. & S.
     Vs   ) The defendant came into open court and
John Martendale) confessed a Judgment for the sum of four
                    pounds fifteen shillings & costs of suit
with stay of Exors. untill March next which is ordered
accordingly.

John Edson & al) Slander
     Vs   ) Ordered that this Suit be dismissed at the
Robt. Armstrong) defendants cost.

Robt. Armstrong) T A B
     Vs   ) dismissed at the Plaintiff costs.
John Gibson   )

David Smith   ) On motion of Abm. Nott Esqr. atty for the
     Vs   ) pltf. ordered that this suit be discon-
Benajah Thompson) tinued which is ordered accd.

The State   ) Bastardy
     Vs   ) On motion of William Shaw Esqr. ordered
George Wells &) that the defendants be fined the sum of five
Fanny White   ) pounds each Proclamation money and costs of
                    suit.

The State   ) Bastardy
     Vs   ) Came into open court the defendant George
George Wells &) Wells and William Williams and Abner Wells
Fanny White   ) and confessed a Judgment for ten pounds
                    proclamation money being the fine imposed
on the Defendants George Wells & Fanney White for Bastardy
with stay of execution twelve months.

     And also Bind themselves to the Judges of this court and
their successors in the sum of one hundred pounds Will and
truly to be lived on then Exors and Chattles conditioned thus
that of the above bound Exor Wells shall will and truly clear

the county from the maintainance of the Bastard child then to be void otherwise remain inferee.

Tests   George Wells Seal
Ben Haile D. C.   Wm Williams L. S.
         Abner Wells L. S.

Benjamin Woodson came into open court & took the necessary oaths of office as a Justice of the peace for this County and therefore entered on the Exor of his office accordingly.

James Bankhead applied for licence to Retail spirituous liquors and Publick house in this county which was granted him and he entered into bond and security according to Law.

Capt. John Murrell applied for a licience to keep public house in this county which is granted and he gave bond & secey. accd. to Law.

Ordered that Adam Young Orphan of Margt. Young be bound to John Chesney to learn the art and mastery of Wheel making untill he arrives to the age of Twenty one and that the said John Chesney give the said Adam Young six months schooling and Lodging & clothing accd.

Bryan White) P & S
 Vs   ) By consent of the parties this suit is
Margt. Edmondson) referred to John Martindale and John
       Sanders with power of chosing an umpier
and their award shall be the Judgment of their court.

The court then adjourned untill Tomorrow 10 O'Clock
        John Henderson
        Jno Blasingame

The Honble Court of Union met according to adjournment on Thursday the third day of January 1793 Present. the Honble
        John Henderson
        John Blasingame

Adam Scane Pltf.) I obedience to an order of the Honble
 Vs   ) Judges of Union County Court we have
Thomas Brandon Deft.) examined the dispute between Adam
       Scane and Thomas Brandon and after a
full investigation of the same one of opinion that Cold. Brandon do pay unto Adam Scane Twelve Pounds sterling with half the costs on or before the first day of November next this 10th day of August 1792.
      And. Torrence
      James Gasway

The following persons failing to appear as Pettit Jurors ordered that they be fined David Thomas, John Needennan Richd. Thompson W, Right Robert Thompson Hy Bunow Reuben Wilks Richard Huckaby.

Samuel Littlejohn) P & S.
 Vs   ) By Consent of the parties ordered that
Thomas Thomas) this suit be discontinued at the Deft
       cost.

346

The State) Breaking the Peace
  Vs   ) On motion of William Shaw Esquires ordered that
James Tosh) the defendant James Tosh give security in the
               sum of one hundred pounds sterling for his good
behaviours towards Thomas Blasingame Esquire and all the
good people of this state. Whereupon Came into open court the
defendant James Tosh & his securities Cold. Thomas Brandon
and C R Edson & Ackd. themselves indebted to the state of
the said James Tosh in the sum of fifty pounds and each of
his securities in the sum of twenty five pounds each for
his good behaviour towards the said Thos. Blasingame & all
the good people of this state.

                     James Tosh   Seal
                     Thos Brandon   Seal
                     Cahn. R. Edson   Seal

The State) The defendant came into open court and having
  Vs   ) made acknowledgements to the Prosecutor Thos
Polley Tosh) Blasingame Esqr. Its ordered by direction of
             the County attorney Nole prosiques Entered.

Union County) P & S
  Vs   ) Ordered that this suit be discontinued at
Wm Handley) the counties cost it appearing that the
              record any benefit from his licence obtained
of said court. On which this action was brought.

Union County) P & S
  Vs   ) By consent of the Defendant a decree is
Thomas Evans) entered for one pound ten shillings and costs
             of suit.

Wm Smith Esqr.) P & S.
  Vs   ) The defendant came into open court &
John Martindale) confessed a Judt. for the sum of Ⱡ 6-11-3 &
             costs of suit.

Allen Degraffenrudt) P & S
  Vs   ) Decree for the Pltf five pounds Eight
Daniel Malone   ) shillings on the affivavite of Abraham
                Nott Esquire & costs of suit.

Moncrieffe & Co.) P & S
  Vs   ) Dismissed at the Defendants costs.
Cornelius Dempsey)

Graff & Co.) Debt
  Vs   ) By Consent of the parties ordered that this
Thos. Bishop) suit be referred to Cold. Brandon & James
              Woodson with power of chosing an umpier & their
award to be made a Judgment of this court.

Hugh Holland) T A B
  Vs   ) By Consent of the parties ordered that this
Wm Williams) suit be discontinued at the Defendants costs
              except attorney fees.

John Nuckols) Attacht.
  Vs   ) The defendant being called & failing to appear
Danl. Mathews) ordered that a Judgment be entered against
              him by default.

Thereupon came the Jury Benjamin Woodson foreman Henry Hill
Patricke Shaw William Hughes Robert Wadkins Richd. Menton
John Gibson Wm Newman John Huey Edward Prince John White &
James Guthrie who being sworn & affirmed to execute this writ
of enquiry Return their verdict and say we find for the plain-
tiff Twenty pounds & costs.   Benj Woodson foreman

James Crawford)   Attachment
    Vs   )   Darka Farris being summoned as Garnashee,
David McCall)   declared on oath that she is indebted to the
                  deft. about thirty pounds by note of hand
on which is a Cn. of 15 dols. payable in about two years.
whereupon the court ordered that the said Darka Farris should
pay to the sd.
James Crawford the sum of seven pounds sterling according to
said note and also the costs of suit.

James Huey   )   Debt
    Vs   )   Came the Plaintiff by Aled. Nott Esqr.
Joshua Petty admr.)   and the defendant by his own proper
                        person whereupon came a Juror towit
Benj. Woodson foreman Henry Hill Patricke Shaw William Hughes
Robt. Wadkins Richard Minton John Gibson Wm. Newman John
Huey Edward Prince John White James Guthrie who was duly
sworn & upon their several oaths and affirmations return
their verdict and say we find for the Plaintiff seventy six
pounds 1 of c sterling   Benjr. Woodson   foreman

James Huey)   Debt
    Vs   )   On motion of the Plaintiff attorney ordered
Nuckols &   )   that David Hopkins be struck of the note which
David Hopkins) was done accd.

Ordered that all Estrays lyable to be sold this court exposed
to Public sale immediately.

On motion of Mr. Shaw on the application of Abner Coleman
ordered that Thomas Draper appear at the next court of
ordinary to shew cause why he does not make a full & perfect
return of the property belonging to the Estate of the said
deceased.

Daniel Brown Esqr.)   Debt the Defendant came into open court
    Vs   )   & confessed a Judgment for the sum of
Josiah Culberson   )   twenty pounds sterling & Int. & cost of
                       suit.

The State)   Assault
    Vs   )   True Bill Wm McCullock foreman
James Moore)

The State)   Larcency
    Vs   )   No Bill Wm McCullock foreman
John Martin)

The State   )   Larcency
    Vs   )   No Bill Wm McCullock foreman
Samuel Cooper)

The State)   Assault
    Vs   )   True Bill Wm McCullocke T.M.
James Tosh)

348

The State   ) Assault
    Vs   ) True Bill Wm McCullocke foreman
Peter Philips)

The State   ) Negroe stealing
    Vs   ) ordered that the Witnesses in behalf of the
Peter Varnier) state be bound over for their appearnace at
                the next court of Pinckney Dist.

C. R. Edson & Co.) Attachment
    Vs   ) Decree for the Plaintiff for 1100 1
Mathew Robenson) Tobacco at 8/6 & ct. & interest on also a
                    Book acct. for 241 and costs of suit.

A Lease & Release from Samuel Jackson to John Blasingame and
George Harling Hatter intrust for Jane H Darby & Elizabeth
Mary Darby Proven in open court by the oath of Andrew Torrence
and ordered to be recorded.

Ordered that the sheriff expose to sale three cows & shoats
Posted before Thos. Blasingame Esqr. by Archer Howard on
Saturday next.

Ordered that the minutes be read which was done accordingly &
signed by:
The Court then adjourned untill Tomorrow 9 OClock
                              John Henderson
                              Jno Blasingame

The Court met according to adjournment on Fryday the Fourth
January 1793
Present the Honble   John Henderson
                        John Blasingame

Frederick Thomson)
    Vs   ) By consent of the parties ordered that all
Nichs. Lazerus   ) matters of
Nicholas Lazerus)
    Vs   ) controversey depending between the said
Fred. Thompson   ) parties be refered to the arbitrament of
                    Cold. Brandon & Capt. Duff with power of
chosing an umpier & their award to be made Judgment of this
Court.

The State) T A B
    Vs   ) The defendant came into open court and himself
James Moore) on the mercy of the court & ordered that he be
              fined one penney & costs.

Sthe State) Negroe stealing
    Vs   ) Ordered that a Scera Facias be Issued against
Peter Varnier) Edmond Ellis and John Thompson to Shew cause
                why their Recg. should not be forfeited as
securities for the defendant Peter Varnier & that the Papers
in this suit be Transmitted to the next circuit court at
Pinckney.

The State) Countery.
    Vs   ) Ordered that the Recognizances in this suit
Wm Williams) be continued untill next court and that a Capias
              Issue against Edmond Pagett to appear at next
court to give evidence in the above suit.

349

The State   ) Cheating
Vs   ) ordered that this suit be continued untill
Fred Thompson) Court.

The State) After the usual proclamation & no prosecutor
Vs   ) appearing ordered that the defendant be discharged.
Thos. Cox)

The State   ) Cheating
Vs   ) Ordered that this suit be contd. untill next
Nichl. Lazerus) Court.

The State   ) Ordered that the defendant be discharged on
Vs   ) paying costs.
Thomas Evans)

The State) Travesed continued untill next court.
Vs   )
James Tosh)

The State) Recq. & continued & ordered that a Capias
Vs   ) Issue against Hannah Bryant to appear at next
Wm Merchant) Court to give evidence in the above suit.

The State   ) Ordered that the Defendant be discharged on
Vs   ) paying costs.
John Whitlock)

David Hopkins) Debt
Vs   ) The Defendant being solemnly called and
David Hudson) failing to appear on motion of William Shaw
                 Esquire attorney for the Plaintiff a Judgment
by a default is entered

David Hopkins) Debt
Vs   ) By consent of the Parties, all matters of
William Spears) controversey now depending between them be
                 refered to the arbitration of Cold. Thomas
Brandon & William Kennedy & if they cannot agree to have
leave of chosing an umpier & their award returnable to the
court shall be the Judgment of this court.

Mark Thompson) Debt
Vs   ) On the oath of Thomas Stribling Esqr. ordered
John Bird   ) that this suit be dismissed at Defendants
                costs.

Edson & Co.) P. & S.
Vs   ) C. R. Edson came into open court and having
Saml. Pearson) Proved his acct. on motion of Ephraim Ramsay
                decree for the Plaintiff Ł 7.4.6. & costs of
                suit.

Frances Fincher) On appeal
Vs   ) We C. R. Edson James Bell and Jeremiah
Samuel Cooper) Gregory being chosen to arbitrate a matter
                  in dispute being an appeal from the Judgment
from Thomas Blasingame Esquire on a suit brought by Francis
Fincher vs Samuel Cooper and after hearing the evidence on
both parties and duly considy. therof do award for the
Plaintiff the sum of one pound seventeen shillings & seven
pence sterling together with all costs of suit but in case

350

any payment has been paid by the said Cooper since the Judgment of the said Blasingame to the said Fincher that such
payment at Union Court House 7th June 1792.

C R Edson   Seal

Jame Bell   Seal

Josh. Gregory   Seal

James Rountree   ) Debt
    Vs   ) The defendant being solemnly called but
James Dohartie &) failing to appear whereupon the court
John McCooll   ) ordered a Judgment by default to be
                     entered whereupon came a Juror towit
Benjr. Woodson foreman H. Hill Patrick Shaw Wm Newman John
Huey Edward Prince James Guthrie and Saml. Spray who being
sworn to Execute this writ of Enquiry Returned their verdict
upon their several oaths & affirmations & say we find for
the Pltff twenty one pounds of which sd. verdict was ordered
to be recorded.   Benjn. Woodson

Alexdr. Bootcher   ) Case
    Vs   ) The defendant in this action but
Spencer Brummett & C.) failing to appear its ordered on motion
                        of Wm Shaw Esqr. Judgment by default
is entered against the defendant then the court proceeded to
execute a Writ of enquiry whereupon came the Juror the same
as above & after being sworn to execute all writs of enquiry
return their verdict & say We Find for the Plaintiff fourteen
pounds 13/4½   Benjr. Woodson foreman
Which said verdict was ratified by the court & ordered to be
recorded.

Alexr. Bootcher) Debt the Defendant came into open court and
    Vs   ) confessed a Judgment for twenty one pound
David Hudson   ) two shillings and seven pence with stay of
                  execution untill the first of December next
on his giving bond and approved security to the Plaintiff for
the payment of the above debt as also the costs of suit.

Alexn. Bootcher) Debt
    Vs   ) The deft. came into open court and con-
Thomas Biddie   ) fessed a Judgment for the sum of fourteen
                   pounds fourteen shillings and four pence
with say of exor ten months on the Defendant giving bond &
security for the payment of the sd. Debt as also costs of
suit.

Union County) P. & S.
    Vs   ) Decree for the Pltf. three pounds & costs of
Chas. Miles) suit.

Union County) P & S
    Vs   ) Decres for the Plaintiff the sum of one
Robt. Anderson) pound ten shillings and costs of suit.

Graff & Co) P & S
    Vs.   ) Decree according to note & costs of suit.
Lewis Bobo)

Graff & Co   ) Debt
    Vs   ) Issue joined & contd.
Richd. Rountree)

351

Nancey Rodgers) Slander
Vs   ) on motion of Aled. nott Esqr. attorney for
James Tosh   ) the defendant the court ordered a nonsuit
                the plaintiff failing to appear by an
attorney.

Peter Ellis) Attach.
Vs   ) Came the Plaintiff into open court and
Peter Varnier) Dismissed suit at his own costs.

Alexd. Macbeth & Co.) Debt
Vs   ) By consent of the parties ordered that
John Hugh   ) this suit be discontinued at the
                    Defendants cost.

John Fincher   appellant) On an appeal
Vs   ) Came the appellant by Abraham
Robert Merrick appellee) Nott and Ephraim Ramsay attorney for
                    the appellee, and after a full
investigation of the matter, the court Refered their award
untill Tomorrow.

David Hopkins) Debt
Vs   ) We the arbitrators to whom was referred the
William Speers) suit dpending between Cold. David Hopkins &
                  William Speers having heard all allegations
proofs and accounts upon full investigation of the same award
as Moses David Hopkins remains indebted to Wm Speers the sum
Ł 4.4.10½ therefore David Hopkins pays all cost of suit
Given under our hands Jany. 4th 1793.
                            Wm Kennedy
                            Thos. Brandon

Peter Varnier   ) P & S
Vs   ) Came Abraham Nott Esquire attorney
Geo. Taylor & M. Waters) for Plf and E Ramsay Esqr. attorney
                          on Record for the Defendants, and
after a full investigation of the matter ordered by the court
that the Pltff be nonsuited.

Ordered that the sheriff expose to Public sale the Estrays
lyable to be sold this court delivered him by the Holders
immediately.

John Fincher) Appeal
Vs   ) In obedience to an order of the Honble
Wm Lee   ) Judges of Union County court we have examined
               accompts and witnesses between William Lee
and John Fincher at an appeal from the Judgment of a Justice
and one of opinion that the Judgment of a Justice is confermed
and one of opinion that the Judgment was founded on ecquity
and good conseience and do confirm the same if agreeable to
Law for References to be ruled thereby otherwise if verbal
assumpsits are not held legal we differ in sentiments from the
said Judgment given under our hands this 7th July 1792
                            John Sanders
                            Andw. Torrence
                            John Martindale

The court are of opinion that verbal assumpsits on good &
that the award & Judgment of the Justice be confirmed with
costs of suit.

352

Enoch Floyd Proved eight days attendance in the above suit ordered that the same be taxed in the bill of costs. And Daniel White proved Eight days Attd. as a witness and that he serve in the another county fifteen miles from this court house, ordered that the same be taxed in the bill of costs.

Andrew Torrence) Debt
 Vs   ) Judgment confessed according to Notes
Chas. Sims Esqr.) & cost of suit.

Peter Ellis   )Attacht.
 Vs   ,Ordered that the money that was ordered to
Peter Varnier)remain in the sheriffs hands untill this court
              for the sale of a Horse sold by justice of the
above attachment be transmitted to the Defendant Peter Varnier as the Pltff having Dismissed his attachment against sd. Defendant.

The State   ) Peace Warrant
 Vs   ) James Tosh Praying the peace against the
Chas. Blasingame) defendant Thos. Blasingame Esqr. Its ordered
                  that the said Defendant give Secy. for to
keep the peace to the said James Tosh and all the good people of this state in the sum of one hundred pounds sterling, oweing twelve months and one day. Whereupon came the Thos. Blasingame Together with Thomas McDonnell & James Duncan his security and ackd. themselves indebted to the state the above sum of one hundred pounds to fulfil the above order & prayer of James Tosh.
Ackd. in Open court   Thos. Blasingame Seal
Ben Haile   Thomas M Daniel   Seal
                           James Duncan son of __ Seal

Ordered that the minutes be read which was done & signed by the Court adjourned untill Tomorrow 9 OClock
                           John Henderson
                           Jno Blasingame

The Court met accd. to adjournment on Saturday the 5th January 1793
Present the Honble   John Blasingame
                          John Henderson   Judges

John Fincher) Appeal
 Vs   ) The court having taken time to consider from
Robt. Merrick) yesterday. Judgment of the Justice confirmed
               for two pounds nineteen shillings and eleven
pence & costs of suit.

Joshua Palmore Exor. of   ) Debt
the Estate of Richd. Hughes deceased) Came the Plaintiff by
 Vs   ) Ephraim Ramsay Esquire
Joseph Hughes Exor   ) and the Defendant by
the Estate of Wm Hughes decd.   ) William Shaw his
                                         counceller and after
a full investigation of the matter it appeared for the court that the defendant did not receive the usual notice on the dedimus, issuing from this court to take the Examination of Jasper Sticker Its ordered therefore that this suit be continued untill next court and that a dedimus Potestaim Issue to Doctor Knox and Jos. Brown & J Wm Gastin or any two

of them in Chester County to take the Exam. of Jasper Sticker
on the Plf. to give the usual notice.

On the application of David Ollephant and George Gorden for
letters of Admr. on the Estate of James Ollephant deceased,
which was granted and they came into open court and was duly
qualified accd. to Law & entered into bond & security in the
sum of Two thousand Pounds.

Its ordered that Thomas Todd Stephen Layton & Drewry Murrell
appraise the Estate of James Olliphant decd. & that Thos.
Blasingame Esqr. qualify the aforesaid appraisers.

Agnes Rodgers   Plaintiff)   Slander
    Vs   )   Came the Plaintiff by Ephraim
Nancey McKibbin   Defendant)   Ramsay and Abm. Nott Esquire and
                                William Shaw Esquire counseller
for the defendant.

Whereupon came a Juror Towit Benjamin Woodson Foreman Henry
Hill Patrick Shaw William Hughes Robert Wadkins Richard
Minton John Gibson William Newman John Huey Edward Prince
James Guthrie and Samuel Spray who being duly qualified
according to Law. But the Plaintiff being called but failed
to appear, the Court ordered a Nonsuit.

Ordered that a rule should be issued against
Jane Edson wife of C R Edson to shew cause at next court why
an attachment for a contempt of the authority of this court in
rufusing to attend give testimony between Agnes Rodgers
Plaintiff & Nancey McKibbin Defendant When legally should not
issue against her.

Wm Smith Esqr.   )   P & S
    Vs   )   By consent of the parties & their
Thos. Blasingame Junr.) attorneys, all matters of controversey
                           now depending & undetermined between
them be refered to the arbitration Samuel Lancaster & Britain
Willeford with power of chosing an umpier and their award
returnable to next court shall be the Judgment thereof and if
they cannot agree to be perremptorly tried next court the
arbitration to be on the 2nd day of March next.

Leonard Smith   )   Trover
    Vs   )   Came the Plaintiff by William Shaw
Jas. Gastin & Wm. Jackson) Esquire his attorney and the
                            Defendant by Ephraim Ramsay their
counciller whereupon came a Jury towit Benjamin Woodson
foreman Henry Hill Patricke Shaw William Hughes Robert Wadkins
Richard Minton John Gibson William Newman John Huey Edward
Prince James Guthrie and Samuel Spray and after being duly
qualified return their verdict upon their respected oaths
and afirmations and say we find for the Plaintiff ten pounds
with costs of suit.   Benjr. Woodson   foreman
Which said verdict was ratified by the court & ordered to be
recorded.

William Lee)   P & S
    Vs   )   By consent of the parties ordered that this
C R Edson   )   suit be refered to Hez. Rice and Drewry Murrell
                with power of umpier and their award returnable

354

to this court shall be the Judt. thereof & the arbitrators to
be sworn.

Leonard Smith   ) Trover
    Vs   ) On motion of Ephraim Ramsay Esqr.
Jas. Gaston & Wm. Jackson) for the defendant William Jackson
                         to be struck out of the suit, and
for said Jackson to be admitted to give evidence in this suit
& after a full investigation of the matter as will on the
part if the Pltf. by his attorney Wm. Shaw as on the part of
the Defendant by his attorney Ephraim Ramsay Esqr. The Court
gave their opion that it appearing to them on the evidence
given on both sides that the said William Jackson was not
concernd. in this case, Its ordered that the said Jackson be
discontinued from this action and be admitted to his testimony in the above suit accordingly.

Frances Fincher) Appeal
    Vs   ) David Cooper proved 3 days attendance in
Samuel Cooper) this suit also proved eight days attendance
and James Gibbs) ordered that the same be taxed in the bill
                 of costs.

Woodson Rountree) By consent of the parties by their
    Vs   ) attorneys ordered that thsi suit be
Capt. Jas. Woodson) dismissed at the Plaintiff cost.

Andrew Torrence this day came into open court and took the
necessary oath of office as a Justice of the peace for this
county.

Graff & Co.   ) P & S. It appearing to the court that
    Vs   ) his suit was brought illegal   Its ordered
Jno. Peter Sartor) that a nonsuit be entered.

Smith) Trover
  Vs) Ordered that John Bearden be allowed thirty seven
Gastin) shillings & six pence & 2/4 for miliage & Wm
         Smith Esqr. be allowed 2/1 for 6 days attendance
in this suit and Robert Armstrong 1716 for 7 days attendance
ordered that the above attendance be taxed in the Bill of
costs.

Edmond Ellias Proves six days attendance as a witness in the
suit Peter Sarmon against George Taylor & Moses Waters

Ordered that the County treasury pay Edmond Ellis 24/ for
state services.

Job. Hammond this day came into open court & was duly qualified
as a constable for this county.

John Fincher) Appeal
    Vs   ) Abee Nott Esqr. moved the court for the
Robt. Merricke) Judt. of the Justice to be set asside he
               having given Judt. for a sum beyond his
               Jurisdiction.

Ordered that the minutes be read which was done accd. The
court then adjourned untill Monday 10 OClock & signed by
Jno Blasingame   John Henderson

Monday the 7th Jany 1793 the Court met according to adjournment   Present the Honourable   John Henderson   John Blasingame
Esqr.

Ordered that the way Petitioned for by James Gibbs and others
for a road from William Brownings by Gibbs to Bobos ford on
Tyger River be opened and established as a private road
agreeable to the report of the viewers formerly appointed by
this court for that purpose.

Ordered that the way motioned for by Sanders & others for old
way to be opened from H Bate's to Cooks Mill ordered that the
same be opened through Cooper Fields and by the House of Wm
Woodward agreeable to the said old way and report of the
Gentlemen appointed to view the same.

Leonard Smith) Trover
    Vs   ) Epraim Ramsay Esquire moved the court for
James Gastin) a new Tryal to be granted & on motion of
                William Shaw Esqr. atty for the Plaintiff
for this Deft. motion not to be heard on the Ground of not
giving the Plaintiff attorney the Ground on which he entended
to move for a new Trial but the court over Ruled him, and the
Judgment of the court being divided and new Tryal not granted.

John Fincher) Attachment
    Vs   ) Ordered that the Defendant give special
Robt. Merrick) Bail in this suit, whereupon came John
                Addington and acknowledged themselves special
bail to this action.

Ordered that a Road be opened & cleared out by Colo. William
Farr & Joseph McJunkin leading to the Fish dam on B. River
agreeable to the Former ordered of this court and that all
persons within five miles of said Road work & keep said Road
in repair, Those that are lyable by law.

John Fincher) Attachment
    Vs   ) Came the Plaintiff by Wm Shaw Esqr. and the
Robt. Merrick) defendant by E Ramsay whereupon came a Jury
                towit Benjamin Woodson Foreman Henry Hill
Patrick Shaw William Hughes Robert Wadkins Richard Minton
John Gibson William Newman John Huey Edward Prince James
Guthrie and Samuel Spray who being duly sworn return their
verdict on their respective oathes and affirmations say we,
But the Juror not having returned their verdict untill the
adjournment of court, ordered that they return their verdict
tomorrow morning under seal.

C Leonard Smith) Absalom Littlefield Proved eight days
    Vs   ) attendance as a witness for the Plaintiff
Jas. Gastin   ) Leornd. Smith

Saml. Simpson came into open court and was duly qualified as
a constable for this county.

John Nuckols) Attachment
    Vs   ) Ordered that the property attached on this
Danl. Mathews) attacked be sold to satisfy the Plaintiff.

                    John Henderson
                    Jno Blasingame
                        356

Tuesday the 6th Day of January 1793 the court met according to adjournment.

Presnet   John Henderson
John Blasingame

On motion of William Shaw Esqr. county attorney ordered that he be allowed to Discount with the county treasury the amount of two stray horses that he purchased this count in Part of his fees due from the county being three pounds eighteen shillings.

John Fincher) Attachment
Vs   ) The Juror being called and all appearing
Robert Merrick) delivered their verdict according to the order
                 of court yesterday under seal, which is as
follows We find for the Plaintiff ten pounds & costs of suit.
Benjamin Woodson foreman
Which said verdict was ordered by the court to be recorded.

Mr. Ramsay gave notice that he intended to move the court for a new Tryal.

John Fincher) Detinue
Vs   ) The Plaintiff came into open court &
Robt. Merrick) dismissed this suit at his own costs.

Daniel Brummett) Debt
Vs   ) Ordered that this suit be dismissed at the
Charles Johnson) Plaintiff costs.

John Fincher) Attachment
Vs   ) On motion of Ephraim Ramsay Esquire for a
Robert Merrick) new Tryal on the grounds that the verdict
                 of the Jury was contrast to law or evidence,
and on motion of William Shaw for no new Tryal to be Granted
but he being over ruled and a new Tryal Granted.

John Nuckols) Attachment
Vs   ) It appearing to the court that this suit
Peter Varnier) ord. not come before them being under their
                Jurisdiction, its ordered that the papers
be transmitted to Wm McCullock Esqr. & that this suit be
discontinued at the Plft. cost.

Absalom Littlefield) Trespass
Vs   ) Came the Plaintiff by Abee Nott Esquire
Amos Martin   ) his attorney and the Defendant by William
                      Shaw Esquire his attorney and after a
motion on each side it appeard. to the court that this action
was brought illegal ordered that the Plaintiff be nonsuited.

Thomas Evans) On attachment
Vs   ) By orders of the Plaintiff this suit is
Wm Brummett) dismissed at his costs.

Nuckols   ) Attach.
Vs   ) Richd. Thompson proved three days attendance
Peter Varnier) in this suit.

Absalom Littlefield) Trespass
Vs   ) Mary Springer proved five days
Amos Martin   ) attendance in this suit & thereby have
                      proved 4 days Sarah Brooks 2 days

357

ordered that the same be taxed in the bill of costs.

Henry Wolf)   P & S
  Vs   )
John High)

Ordered on motion of Mr. Shaw that this cause be tried at next
court a Jury at the Defendants cost.

Richd. Hays)   On an appeal
  Vs   )   The appeleses attorney objected to this appeal
Isham Prince)   being heard by the court in as much as an
                execution had issued on the Judgment given by
the freeholders & further that no appeal lay from the appraisment. view & valualied of the freeholders the court being
ordered that his suit be continued

Ordered that the Presentments of the Grand Juror at this Court
be continued over until our Next Intermediate Court the Same
tending entirely to the Police of the County.

Ordered that the Clerk provided by our next Intert. Court the
proceeding of the Court, on the Disputed Road that leads from
Hollans field the lower side of Ewarts field to Union Court
House being the road Presented by the Grand Juror this Court.

On motion of Thomas Stribling Esqr. Sheriff Samuel Simpson
is Appointed Deputy Sheriff for this County, who came into
open Court and took the Necessary Oaths of Office Accg. to
Law.

On a Petition to us directed Ordered that a road be cleared
out to begin about a quarter of a mile above widow littlefields Plantation & on the west side of Leonard Smiths into
the said Road, near Wm. Littlefields Plantation & that Abm
Littlefield be Overseer of the said Road in the room of Jno
Lancaster agree. to Lancasters Order Excepting this
Amendment.

Ordered that Wm Kennedy Esqr treasury of this County Collect
all moneys that is due at this time on the Clerk furnishing
him all the defalters thereof.

Ordered that the County treasury Deliver unto Thomas Stribling
Esqr. a Note due from Cornelius Dempsey on his given His rcpt.
for that amount.

Ordered that the road be opened agreeable to the Petition of
Potter & Cunningham Presented to us this Court & that
Arthur Cunningham Clear out of the same with the Hands
Covt. thereto & be Overseer thereof.

Ordered that the following rates be adhered to relating to
the rates of Whiskey to wit.
All Singles Distilled Whiskey   quart   1
                                Pint   7
                                ½ Pint 4½
                                Gill   2

And all Double distilled Whiskey   quart 1 6   ½ Pint 6
                                   Pint   9   Gill   4½

358

Ordered that the Minutes be read which was done accordingly &
Ordered that the Court Stand adjourned untill Court in
Course & signed by   John Henderson
                          Jno Blassingame

At an Intermediate Court begun and Holden the first day of
April in the year of our Lord one thousand seven hundred and
Ninety three. Present John Blasingame

Proved in Court a Deed of Conveyance from John McCool to John
McKibbin O to Record.

Prov'd in Court a Deed of Conveyance from James Hogen Senr.
to Jas. Hogan Jun. O to R.

Prov'd by the Oaths of James Bell & James(?) Brandon the last
Will and Testament of David Comer Deceased O to record.

Prov'd before a Justice a Deed from John Bogin to Isaac Bogin--
also Prov'd before a Justice a Deed of Conveyance from John
Bogin to Elizabeth Bogin & O to Record.

Proved before a Justice a Deed of conveyance from George
Bailey to John Filback & O to Record.

Cushman R Edson is Granted leave to retail spiritous liquors
at his Tavern on Union Hill & at Daniel Burkes old place
where David Buzard now lives and hath given bonds with Cold.
Brandon & James Bell to each bond as securities.

On the application of Nancy McKibbin she is allowed to keep
public house & retail spirituous liquors at Union Court House
who gave bond and security according to Law in Ⱡ 200.

A Lease & Release from Wm Smith David & wife to Cushman Rugles
Edson proved in open court by Colo. Brandon & ordered to
Record.

A Deed of conveyance from Wm Smith Davis to Abraham Nott
Esquire proven in open court by Cold. Brandon & ordered to
Record.

On the application of Thomas Cook he is allowed to keep a
tavern and retail spiritous liquors in this county and gave
bond & sect.

A Deed of conveyance from Jno Thompson to Jesse Ford proven in
open court and ordered to record.

A Deed from Jesse Fore & wife to Abm. Jones ackd. in open
court & ordered to Record.

A Deed from George Wells to John White ackd. in open court and
ordered to record.

Present John Henderson (Esquire)

Proved in court a power of Attorney from Robert Merrick to
James Woodson & Enock Floyd & O to Record.

John Jasper is appointed overseer of the road from Grindol
Shoals to the fork where long Road turns off in the place of

James Mosely who hath Resigned and that he keep the same in good repair according to law.

Its ordered that John Sanders Hezekiah Price & John Heald be one appointed to appraise the Estate of Daniel Comer Deceased & that Anderson Terrence be & is appointed to qualify the said appraisers & that they render a perfect inventory and appraisment of said Estate within three months in the Clerks office.

Acknowledged in court a Deed of conveyance from Thomas Cook to Benj. Haile & 0 to Record.

Acknowledged in court a Deed of conveyance from Adam Potter to Nehamiah Norten & 0 to Record.

Proved in court the last will & testament of James Hawkins senr. deceased by the affirmation of Henry Millhouse & Thomas Cox and 0 to Record.

Proved before a Justice a Deed of conveyance from Basel Wheat to John Thomas 0 to Record.

Proved in court by the oath of Hugh Cook a Deed of conveyance from Moses Watters to Charles Littlejohn & 0 to Record.

Proved in before a Justice a Deed of conveyance from Abel Kenderick & wife to Lewis Garner and 0 to Record.

Proved before a Justice a Deed of conveyance from William Sisson to William Spears & 0 to Record.

Proved before a Justice a Lease & release from John Little to Fieldin Curtis & o to Record.

Its ordered by the Court that the administration of James Olliphant deceased expose to sale a Quantity of Indian corn.

Proved before a Justice a Deed of conveyance from Daniel McBride to Andsen Mcbride & o to Record.

On the application of Moses Akins He is allowed to keep a tavern or public house in this county & he entered into bond accd. to law at Pinckneyville.

On the application of Robert Miller he is allowed to keep a tavern or public house in this county who gave bond & security at Pinckneyville.

Proved in court a Deed of conveyance from Wilson Jolly & wife to Francis Drak & o to Record.

Proved before a Justice a Deed of conveyance from Joseph Jolly & wife to Nathaniel Jeffries & o to Record.

Proven in open court the last will and test. of Daniel Prince & o to Record.

And that John Addinton & Soloman Whitson took the oath of Execuloship to the above will.

On the application of Mathew Ross he is allowed to keep a

tavern or public house in this county at Pinckneyville &
he entered into bond accd.

A Bill of sale from Jno. Henderson & wife Adam Potter &
Jno. Beckham Junr. to Hy. ONail for one negroe Girl named
Edee acknd. in open court & ordered to record.

A Bill of sale from Lemuel James Alston to Jno. Jasper proven
by Jno. Henderson Esqr. & ordered to Record.

On the application of Alexd. Macbeth & Co. he is allowed to
retail spirituous liquors at Union Court House & he gave bond
& secy. accd. to Law.

On the motion of Alexd. McBeth & Co. for Jno. Beckham Junr. &
Co. to retail spirituous liquors Grindal Shoals on their
givg. bond & security accd. to law.

On motion of Alexd. McBeth & Co. for Richd. Farr & co. to
retail spirituous liquors at the Fish dam on Bd. River on
their giving Bond & security accd. to law.

A Deed from Jno. Crittenden to Jno. Jeffries proven in open
court & o to R.

On the resignation of Renney Ballew ordr. that Moses Collier
be overseer of the road from Jorden Jacksons also Fairforest
at Plummers ford to the Cross roads.

Ordered that Charles Browning to overseer of the road in the
room of Cold. Littlefield.

Ordered that Jos. Howard be overseer of the road from Union
Court House to Cold. Brandon in the room of Jno. Brandon.

On Resignation of John Haile former clerk of this court,
the court after proclamation being publicly made by the
sheriff at the door of the Court House, proceeded to chose a
clerk of this court, Benjamin Haile being unanimously chosen
as clerk of this court during Good Behaviour, which is ordered
accordingly and was qualified according to law & gave bond
in the sum of one thousand pounds with Adam Potter, John
Haile and Joseph Howard his securities accordingly & thereupon
entered upon the execution of his office.

A Renounciation & right of Dower from Mary Jackson wife of
Samuel to Jno. Blasingame Esqr. & Geo. Harlan & ord. to record
as trustees of James H Darby & Eliz M. Darby.

Ordered that the minutes be read which was done & the court
adjourned untill court in course & signed by
                         John Henderson
                         Jno. Blasingame

At a court before and Holden in and for the county of Union
at the court house of said county, on Saturday the first day
of June in the year of our Lord one thousand seven hundred
and Ninety three and of the Independance of the United States
of North America the seventeenth.

Present   John Blasingame

361

The court ordered that the court adjourned until Monday 10
OClock & signed by   Jno Blasingame

The Court met according to adjournment on Monday the third
day of June in the year of our Lord one thousand seven
hundred and ninety three.
Present   John Henderson
              John Blasingame

The court proceeded to draw the grand Jury for our next
court to be holden on the first day of January next court.

William White son Isaac	1	John High	11
Nevel Holcomb	2	Alexd. Hamilton	12
Abel Pearson	3	Jno. Peter Sartor	13
Samuel Harlan	4	Moses Waters	14
Thomas Draper Senr.	5	William Sharp	15
Patrick Shaw	6	John Sartor	16
Thos. Blasingame Esqr.	7	Capt. Tom Johnson	17
Moses Meek	8	[18 omitted]	
Robt. Woodson	9	George Gordon	19
Thos. Hightower	10	Moses Wilson	20

Also the following persons to serve next court as Petty Jurors

Randol Jonas	1	Wm Hightower	16
Jacob Seiger	2	Thomas Gossett	17
Robt. Wadkins	3	Jas. Rountree	18
Daniel Bain	4	Abory Breed	19
Wm Bryant	5	Jesse Dodd	20
John Whilchel	6	James Mathews	21
Alexd. Prince	7	James Harris	22
Abm. Jones	8	John Taylor	23
John Hopkins	9	Wm Heaton	24
Henry Bray	10	Jonathan Gilkie	25
John Haney	11	Joshua Martin	26
Andrew McBride	12	Leory Hollingsworth	27
Wm Perdy	13	Thomas Harris	28
Richd. Hays	14	William Hames	29
Wm Hawkins	15	Daniel Holder	30

The State   )   Ordered that the defendants recognizance
    Vs   )   continue over untill next intermediate court
Edmond Simpson)

Warran Hall)   P & S
    Vs   )   William Sims being common bail for the appear-
John Martin)   ance of the defendant came into open court
                and delivered him up to the court and was
therefore discharged from off his bail and ordered that the
said defendant give special bail, whereupon came into open
court Samuel Cooper and acknowledged himself special bail for
the Defendants appearance at our next court.

The State   )   Jeremiah Gregory came into open court and
    Vs   )   delivered up the defendants in discharge
William Williams)   of his bail, which is ordered accordingly.

Proclamation being made by the sheriff that all recognizances
continued over from last court to this and all recognizances
returnable to this court, stand continued over untill next
court, which is ordered accordingly.

```
James Harrison    Plaintiff)   Debt
  Vs                      )    Judgment Confessed according to
Charles Sims      Defendant)   note which is ordered accordingly.
```

```
Henry Burors )    P & S
  Vs         )    Decree for the Plaintiff the sum of Five
Edward Denny )    pounds and cost of suit.
```

Ordered that the Estray horses lyable to be sold this court
be sold Tomorrow by the sheriff.

```
The State         )    Came the Defendant into open and entered
  Vs              )    into bond and acknowledged himself
William Williams)      indebted to the state in the sum of fifty
                       pounds sterling for his personal appearance
at our next court.
```

Also came into open court James Veil and David Stewart
and acknowledged themselves indebted to the state the sum of
twenty five pounds sterling for the defendants appearance at
our next court as witness their hands & seals.
```
Ben Haile  C C    Witness    Wm Williams    Seal
                             Jas. C Veil    Seal
                             David Steward  Seal
```

```
John Leek    )    Judgment confessed accd. to note with interest
  Vs         )    costs of suit.
John Quinton)
```

```
John McDonnell    )    P & S
  Vs              )    Judgment confessed accd. to note with
Fielding J. Gregory)   interest and costs of suit.
```

```
John Effingham)   P & S
  Vs          )    Judgment confessed according to note with
Wm Rogers     )    interest & cost of suit.
```

```
John Steen )    By consent of the parties ord. that this suit
  Vs       )    be refered to John Thompson and John Bird with
James Clark)    power of chosing an umpeir and their award
                returnable to next court shall be the Judgment
                thereof.
```

```
John Steen        )    Debt
  Vs              )    The defendant being solemnly called but
Mathew Roberson)      failing to appear on motion of Abne. Nott
                       atty for the Plaintiff, ordered that
Judgment by default or entered
```

```
John Clark Exr. Edmondson)   Debt
  Vs                     )    Judgment confessed accd. to note
Caleb Smith              )
```

```
Alexd. MacBeth & Co.)   Attachment
  Vs                )    Decree for the Plaintiff for the sum
Robert Armstrong    )    of four pounds seventeen shillings and
                         one penny half penny & costs of suit.
And ordered that the property attached be sold by the
sheriff to satisfy the debt & costs
```

```
The State  Vs James Depoister)   Bastardy   James Depoister
Robert Chesney and Joseph Golt came into open court and
```

acknowledged themselves indebted to the state the said James
Depoister in the sum of fifty pounds and his securities in
the sum of twenty four pounds each for the defendants appearance at our next court to be holden on the 1st Jany. next.

```
                        James Depoister  (Seal)
                        Robt  his  Chesney  (Seal)
Teste                         R
B. Haile                      mark
                        Joseph Gault  (Seal)
```

Henry Coon   )   P & S
   Vs   )   Decree for the Plaintiff accd. to
Austin & Wm Newman)   specialty with stay Exor. untill Christmas

Thomas Blasingame)   Attachment
   Vs   )   Came the plaintiff by Ephraim Ramsay
William Moody   )   Esquire and the defendant by Samuel
                        Farrar Dudly Reed being summoned as
Garnashe & the sum of ten pounds twelve shillings and con-
demned in his subject to the debt of the Plaintiff in case
he Establishes the same against the Defendant William Moody.

Danl. Hollingsworth)   Pet. & S
   Vs   )   Decree for the Plaintiff the sum of
Collins Johnson   )   six pounds and costs of suit.

Wm Lee   )   Debt
   Vs   )   Judgment confessed according to note with
Colo. Maberry &)   interest & cost of suit with day of
James Gibbs   )   execution six months which is ordered
                        accordingly.

The court adjourned untill tomorrow 10 OClock
                             John Henderson
                             Jno. Blasingame

The Court met according to adjournment on Tuesday the fourth
day of June 1793
Present   John Blasingame
             John Henderson   Esquires

Allen Degraffenriedt)   Case
   Vs   )   By consent of the parties, and on
William Giles   )   motion of their attorneys this suit is
                        dismissed and each man pay his own
costs, which is ordered accordingly.

William Smith Esquire)   P & S
   Vs   )   Came the plaintiff by William Shaw
Thomas Blasingame Junr.)   Esquires his atorney for the
                            Plaintiff and the Deft. by Abraham
Nott Esquire, and the witnesses in this case being sworn and
having given in their evidence as will on the part of the
plaintiff as on the part behalf of the defendant and after a
full investigation of the matter in dispute, by their attorneys
the court gave their opinion and say Decree for the Plaintiff
the sum of five pounds fifteen shillings and eight pence and
costs of suit.

Wm McJunkin Vs Geo Huey Admr. Wm Huey decd. P & S.
Dismissed at the Plaintiff cost.

A Deed from Thomas Clandenning to Jehue Wilson proven before a Justice and ordered to be recorded.

William Smith Esquire) P & S
   Vs   ) James Wafford proved nine days
Thomas Blasingame Junr.) attendance in this suit & also is
                         allowed miliage for 123 miles
going & coming
Wiley Willeyford proved eight days attendance in this suit and that he lives fourteen miles from this court house in Spartanburgh & that he has attend this courts by subpoena.

John Bearden proved nine days attendance in this suit and that he levis fourteen miles from this court in Spartg. County and he hath attend at three courts, ordered that the above be taxed in the Bill of costs.

William Trammell) P & S
   Vs   ) Came the plaintiff by Abraham Nott and
William Farr   ) the defendant by William Shaw Esquire and
                  it appearing to the court on the Testimony
of Cold. Thomas Brandon that the note on which this suit was brought has previously been satisfied & paid and Judgment for the Defendant which is ordered accordingly.

Ordered that John Smarr be overseer of the Road from the negroe grave to Hammeltons ford on broad river and that he keep the same in good repair accd. to law.

Ordered that a citation Issue on the Estate of Nehemiah Miller to all the kindred and creditors of said deceased to shew cause if any they have why letters of administration should not be granted to Cold. William Farr.

A Deed of conveyance from John McCooll to Abraham Nott to show proven in open court and ordered to be recorded.

Charles Miles asse. Wm Graham) Sci Fa
   Vs   ) The rule on this case
Thomas Brandon and   ) made absolute & judgment
Wm Steen Exors. James Steen decd.) revived which is ordered
                          accordingly.

James Cambell   ) On appeal
   Vs   ) Judgment of the Justice confirmed with
Joseph Howell &) costs of suit.
Canl. Howell   )

Ordered that Colo. Farr furnish Massay Sandredge & the necessary provisions for her support & clothing for the term of six months & his bill then rendered in shall be paid out of the County Treasury.

And that Richard Prewett be allowed for his charge to be rendered in at the same time for attending & nursing the said Massay Sandredge during 6 months.

Wm Lee   ) P & S
   Vs   ) By consent of the parties all matters now
C R Edson) depending between them on the aforesaid

C R Edson & Exor)   Case
   Vs   )   Suits is refered to the arbitration of
Wm Lee   )   Hezikiah Rice and Drewry Murrell with power
                       of chosing an umpier in case they cannot
agree, and their award to be make a Judt. thereof, returnable
to our next court.

Ordered that Wm Bowman and James Lindsay, View the nearest
and best way for a Road leading from Pinckney court house
across Pacolate to Sharps ford then to Bullocks Creek ford
on Broad river, and make their report to our next court at
Sept. Court.

Ordered that the County Treasury discount with Alexd. Macbeth
& Co. the sum of six pounds to be placed to Thos. Striblings
acct in part of his Extra fees.

Ordered that the minutes be read which was done & the court
adjourned untill court in course & signed by
                              John Henderson
                              Jno Blasingame

At an Intermediate court begun and Holden in and for the
county of Union at the court house of said county the second
day of September 1793.
Present   John Henderson Esquire

A Deed of conveyance from James Hogans Junr. to Robert Kennedy
proven before a Justice and ord. to be recorded.

A Deed of conveyance from James Hogans & wife to Stephen
Comer, proven before a Justice and ordered to be recorded.

A Deed of conveyance from James Hogans senr. to Robert Comer
proven before a Justice and ordered to be recorded.

The last will and testament of John Herrington deceased,
proven in open court by the oaths of Drewry Herrington and
Abraham Guiton and ordered to be recorded, and David Smith
being appointed in said will one of the Executors thereof
came into open court and took the necessary oaths according to
law.

A Deed of conveyance from Thomas Stribling sheriff of Union
County to Michael Crawford acknowledged in open court and
ordered to be recorded.

A Bill of sale from Robert Anderson & wife to Henry O. Nail
proven in open court by C R Edson and ordered to be recorded.

A Deed of conveyance from John Ham to Thomas Brooks acknowledged in opne court and ordered to be recorded.

Ordered that Wm Clark be overseer of the road from Union Court
House to Caleb Fraziers in the Room of Wm. Goldsmith and that
he keep the same in Good repair according to law, with the
hands convenient to thereto.

Ordered that Amos Cook be overseer of the road from Edward
McNeals Begg Creek to the forks of the road in the Room of
Asther Thomas, and that he keep the same in Good repair
according to Law with the hands convenient thereto.

Ordered that Mahers Liles be overseer of the Road from the
county line to the top of the Hill between Arther Cumminghams
& Nicks Harris and that he keep the same in good repair
according to law with the hand convenient thereto.

Ordered that Samuel Shippey be overseer of the Road in the
Room of Joshua Petty who resigned from the county line into
the old road leading from smith ford to Grendel Shoals near
Thomas Cooks and that he keep the same in Good repair according
to law with the hands convenient thereto.

Talley Davit to Jeremiah Cooper a mortgage proven in open court
by James Townsend and ordered to be recorded.

Ordered that Daniel Glenn be overseer of the Road from the
Ninety six road to the Charleston Road near Shockleys old
place and that he keep the same in good repair according to
Law. with the hands allowed by law.

Ordered that John Wilson, John Hawkins and J. Peter Sarter,
be and are hereby appointed to view and mark out a cert road
from Cooks Bridge on Tyger River to the Fishdam ware house
and make their report to our next court.

Ordered that Wm Sartor James Jeater and Cold. Wm Farr view
and mark out a certain road from Hardwicks old field to the
Fish.

Ordered that George Story and Capt. Saml. Jeater view and mark
out a road the nearest and best way from Col Shaws old Place
to the county seat leading by Story mill and make their report
to the next court.

Ordered that John Giffey be overseer of the road from Jas
Bogans creek to James McCrackens, in the room of Benj. Savage
Senr. and that he keep the same in good repair with the hands
allowed by law.

Ordered that John Loggins be overseer of the road from Tanners
Creek to where it interesects the road leading from sover
ford to Union Court house, and that he keep the same in good
repair, with the hands allowed by law.

A Deed of conveyance from Mathew Robinson & Susannah Robenson
to Joshua Potty proven in open court by John Nuckols and
ordered to be recorded.

A Deed of conveyance from [William Goldsmith] to Benjamin
Haile, acknowledged in open court by the said Goldsmith and
ordered to be recorded.

A Deed of conveyance from Obadiah Ollephaint & wife to Joshua
Scisson, proven before a Justice and ordered to be recorded.

A Deed of conveyance from [Tom Scisson] to Joshua Scisson
proven in open court and ordered to be recorded.

A Decd of conveyance from Wm Scisson to ___ Scisson proven
in open court and ordered to be recorded.

A Deed of conveyance from Wm Clarke & wife to Josh. Cooper
proven in open court by Izrael Frazier & ordered to be recd.

A Deed of conveyance from John Murrell to Wm Browning acknowledged in open court and ordered to be recorded.

A Deed of conveyance from John Robinson to Robert Cook,
proven in open court by Wm B Farr, and ordered to be recorded.

A Deed of conveyance from William Scisson to Joshua Scisson
proven before a Justice and ordered to be recorded.

A Deed of conveyance from Daniel Lipham to Joseas Darby,
proven before a Justice and ordered to be recorded.

A Deed of conveyance from Daniel Lypham to Jonas Darby proven
before a Justice and ordered to be recorded.

A Bill sale from James McKibbins to Elizabeth Potter, acknowledged in open court and ordered to be recorded.

A power of attorney from Robert Merrick to George Newman and
James Parnell proven before a Justice and ordered to be
recorded.

On the application of James D Puckett for licence to retail
spirituous liquors in this county at Pinckneyville which was
granted and he gave bond & security according to Law.

On the application of William Darby leave is given him to
retail spiritous liquors at his own house, and he gave bond
& security according to law.

On the application George Gordon Admrs. the state of James
Olliphant deceased, ordered that he give leave to make sale
of the personal property of said deceased, according to Law.

Ordered that Lewis Pinnion be overseer of a road from Wm
Darbys to aposite Leonard Smiths, in the room of Garrner
Gibbs and that he keep the same in Good repair according to
law with the hands allowed thereby.

Ordered that all Estrays lyable to be sold this court sold
on tomorrow.

Ordered that Colo. William Farr, being a cause to be brought
to our next January court, four orphan Blacks children to wit
Anthony, Staford, Robin & Francis, Children of a free woman
called Beckee now in the possession of Benjamin Hawkins.

Ordered that a certain orphan girl, called Amy daughter of a
free woman called Becka be bound unto Robert Cook, until
she arrive to the age twenty one, who is to learn her the art
of spinning and household business.

Ordered that the court adjourn untill tomorrow 9 OClock &
signed by   John Henderson

The Court met according to adjournment on Tuesday the third
day of September 1793 Present John Henderson
                                John Blasingame Esquires

A Deed of conveyance from Wm Eaves & wife to John Crittenden
proven before a Justice and ordered to be recorded.

368

A Deed of conveyance from Merry McGuire to Obadiah Kendrick
proven before a Justice and ordered to be recorded.

A Deed of conveyance from Merry McGuire to Obadiah Kendrick
Proven before a Justice and ordered to be recorded.

On the application of Andrew Torrence, letters of administration is granted him on the Estate of Herman Howard deceased,
who entered into bond in the sum of twenty five pounds with
Colo. Wm Farr his securities.

Ordered that William Buckhannon be allowed out of the county
Treasury, ten pounds for supporting a poor blind man, named
John Reive Jnr. at the rate & annual.

Acknowledged in open court a Deed of conveyance from Thomas
Stribling sheriff of Union County to William Shaw Esquire &
ordered to be recorded.

Ordered that James Moseley, Abel Kendrick & George McWhortor,
be and are hereby appointed to lay out a certain road the
nearest and best way Grindol shoals to Pinckney ville and
report the same to our next court.

The last will and testament of George Crossleys returned in
open court and was duly proven according to law by Thomas
Smarr & John Stokes, Colo. Thomas Brandon and Lydia Crossley
being Executors in the said will, came into open court &
was duly qualified accordingly as executors aforesaid.
and ordered that John Stokes, John Heald, and Jos. Reeder.
appraise the Estate of the said George Crossley decd. and make
their return to our next court & that Andrew Torrence Esqr.
qualify the aforesaid appraisers.

A Deed of conveyance from George Crossley to Colo. Thomas
Brandon, proven in open court by the oaths of John Stokes and
Thomas Smarr, and ordered to be recorded.

Ordered that Colo. Thomas Brandon supply Elizabeth Crossley
and Levey Crossley with sufficient support and that he being
in his acct. for the same convenient.

Ordered Robert Summerel be overseer of the Road from Rockey
Creek to Grindol Shoals in the Room of Saml. Clowney and that
he keep the same in Good repair with the hand allowed by Law.

Ordered that William Kennedy Esquire, collect with all convenient speed all the fines & for feteues and debts due the
county Treasury to defray the expences of said county.

Ordered that Wm Darby, Nevel Holcomb, and Frederick Jackson
appraiser the Estate of Herman Howard deceased, and return
their appraisment according to Law.

Ordered that Hezekiah Rice deliver to Samuel Cooper an Indenture of Nancey Fitchpatrick an Orphan Child of Alexr. Fitzpatrick at the said Cooper deliver up the said Orphan to
C R Edson & be exonerated from the said Indenture.

A Deed of conveyance from Jedithan Porter to Hancock Porter
Proven in open court by the oath of John McDonnell and
ordered to be recorded.

A Deed of conveyance from William Whitlock to Hancock Porter
Proven in open court by the oath of Landlot Porter and ordered
to be recorded.

Ordered on a former order of this court, for a road to be
opened from McCools old field the lower side of Ewarts field
to Union Court House be referred for consideration untill
our next Intermediate court.

Ordered that Jonathan Norman, David Norman and Jesse Dodd,
be and are hereby appointed to view and mark out a way for a
Road from Blackstock ford, Round into Belmont Road & to
intersect the road by Jesse Dodd and make their report to our
next court.

Ordered that the minutes be read which was done & signed by &
the court adjourned untill court in course.

John Henderson
Jno Blasingame

At a court begun & holden in and for the county of Union at
the Court house of said county, on Wednesday the first day of
January in the year of our Lord, one thousand seven hundred
and ninety four, and of the Independance of the United States
of North America the 18th.

Present   John Blasingame
           John Henderson

The court proceeded to draw a Grand Juror to serve next court
as Grand Jurror

Wm Farr	1	Isaac Bogan	9
Wm McCullock	2	Alex Macbeth	10
Wm Park	3	John Beckham Jnr.	11
Wm Woolbanks	4	John Oslin	12
Wm Martendale	5	John Stowers	13
James Sims	6	Bathw. Baker	14
Richd. Terrell	7	Geo. Lynam	15
Ambrose Ray	8	Nathl. Davis	16
		John Stokes	17
		Jos. McJunkin	18
		Danl. Parmor	19
		Wm McJunkin	20

Also the following persons for Petty Jury

John Strange	1	Joseph Dawson	17
Lewis Ledbetter	2	Archibald Kennedy	18
Samuel Little	3	Charles Hames Junr.	19
Philip Holcomb	4	Samuel Thompson	20
Nathl. Guiton	5	Abner Potts	20
John Ham	6	Leond. Smith	21
Robt. Gibson	7	James Gibbs	22
Thomas Dean	8	Wm Campbell	23
Moses Collier	9	David Scisson	24
Thomas Thomas	10	John Brandon	25
Wm Lockhart	11	Fredrick Whitmon	26
Robert Summorelle	12	Thomas Taylor	27
Josiah Wilson	13	Woodson Rountree	28
Robt. Gregory	14	John Cook	29
John Thompson	15	John Hutten	30
Thomas Lusk	16		

The State   ) Ordered that this recognizance be continued
   Vs   ) untill next court by consent of the
Cristian Plummer) security.

Richard Burgess, qualified as constable for this county,
before John Blasingame Esquire.

John Beckham Junr.)Case
   Vs   )Came the defendant into open court in his
Nicholas Murray   )own proper person and confessed a Judgment
                   for the sum of fifty pounds sterling &
costs of suit.

John Clark) By consent of the parties, ordered that this
   Vs   ) suit be referred to H Reece & Thomas Young
Thomas Lee) with power of chosing an umpeir and their award
              lible to our next court shall be the Judgment
              thereof.

John Fincher) P &
   Vs   ) Continued on the application of the defendant
Benj Rash   ) on a presomplosely Rule to be tried next court.

John Lancaster) T A B
   Vs   ) Dismissed at Defendants cost.
Mill Sumner   )

Exors Ballock) P & S
   Vs   ) Judgment confessed according to note with
George Story) stay of Exor. one month.

Ordered that John Wilson be overseer of the road from Cooks
Bridge to Cain Creek and clear out said road agreeable to the
marked trees done by Compr. appt. for that purpose as
annexd. repott & that he keep said road in good repair
according to Law with the hands convenient thereto.

And John Peter Sartor from Cane Creek to the cross Roads
leading to the fish dam & that he clear out and keep the same
in good repair according to Law with the hands allowed by Law.

Ordered that Henry Stevans be overseer of the road from Cain
Creek to the lower fish dam Creek, in the room of Jno P.
Sarter and that he keep the same in good repair accd. to Law.

Nicholas Curray came into open court and took the necessary
oaths as an executor of the last will and testament of John
Herrington decd.

Ordered that Joseph Guiton James Petty Junr. & Drewry
Harrington appriase the Estate of John Herrington decd. and
make due return thereof & that Wm McCullock qualify the
aforesaid appraisers.

Ordered that Robert Anderson be overseer of the road from
Caty Spears to George Storys & from there to Saml. Kelsos.
and that he clear out & keep the said road in good repair,
agreeable to marked trees, marked by Compr. for that purpose
appointed.

The court adjourned until tomorrow 9 OClock & signed by
      John Henderson   Jno Blasingame

The Honble court of Union County met according to adjournment
on Thursday the 2d day of January 1794.
Present The Honble   John Henderson
                      John Blasingame   Judges

The State   ) Ordered on motion of the county attorney,
   Vs   ) that this indictment be dismissed.
William Sims &)
Mathew Sims   )

The State) On motion of the county attorney the defendant
   Vs   ) is discharged on paying the costs.
Wm Marchant)

The State   ) Bastardy
   Vs   ) Ordered that the defendants be fined five
Ralph Hunt &   ) pounds each & costs.
Esther Roberts)

The State   ) Bastardy
   Vs   ) The defendant Ralph Hunt came into open
Ralph Hunt   ) court and acknowledged to pay the fine of
Esther Roberts) Esther Roberts, Its ordered therefore that
                    Execution Issue against the defendant
Ralph Hunt for ten pounds proclamation money & costs of suit,
also ordered that the said Defendant give security for the
maintaince of the Bastard child.

The State   ) Bastardy
   Vs   ) Agreeable to the above order we Ralph Hunt,
Ralph Hunt   ) Saml. Hunt & Jas. Addington have come into
Esther Roberts) open court and acknowledged ourselves indebted
                    to the Judges of the county court of Union
and their successors in office in the sum of one hundred
pounds sterling to be leved on our several goods and chattels
lands and tennements, that in case it shall appear the
county stands chargeable for the maintaince of the bastard
child of the Defendant Esther Roberts untill its attains the
age of Ten years. Witness our hands the 2d January 1779
Ralph / O Hunt Seal
   his mark
Samuel Hunt Seal
James T Addington Seal
   his mark

The State) Peace Warrant
   Vs   ) On the oath of the prosecutor, Nancy Belue,
Esther Insco) ordered that the recognizance be continued
               untill next court.

The State) T A B
   Vs   ) Ordered that this suit be dismissed at the
Wm Coleman) Defendants cost.

The State   ) Bastardy
   Vs   ) Ordered that a Capias Issue so the
Wineford Steward) security to cause why the defendant does
                    not appear to answer to the above.

The State   ) Cheating Ordered that the rule of refer-
   Vs   ) ence between the parties be extended and
Shedrick Thompson) the recogn be continued until next court.

372

```
State      )
  Vs       )
Nichs. Lazerus)
```

```
The State   )  Larcency
  Vs        )  Ordered that this case & the recognizance
Alexd. Hammilton)  stand continued untill with next court.
```

On the application of Elizabeth Greer and Ralph Jackson for administration on the Estate of John Greer deceased which is granted & ordered that he enter into bond with security accd. to Law in the sum of four hundred pounds sterling which is done & took the necessary oaths as Admrst.

Ordered that the overseer of the road from Grendol Shoals leading to Union Court House turn & clear out part of the same to begin Clarks old field leading by James Maberry thereby Moonlys there into the main road below Majr. Henderson & that he keep the same in good repair accd. to Law.

```
The State   )  Bastardy
  Vs        )  After a full investigation of the matter
Winney Jones & )  ordered that the defendant be fined five
James Depoister)  pounds each & costs of suit ordered that
               the defendant give security Immediately
for the support of the said Bastard child & the said fine.
```

Ordered that Col. Brandon, Benjamin Holcombe & Robert White appraise the Estate of John Greer decd and make due return thereof, to our next court.

```
Graffe & co.     )  Debt
  Vs             )  Judgment confessed according to note
Richardson Rountree)  & costs of suit, with stay of execution
                 two weeks.
```

```
The State   )  Bastardy
  Vs        )  Ordered that Execution be stayed six
Winney Jones)  months for the fine.
```

```
The State   )  Bastardy
  Vs        )  Ordered that the defendants, come into
James Depoister)  open court and give security to Indemnify
Winney Jones  )  the county from the maintaince of the said
               Bastard child likewise the payment of the
said fines. By virture of the said order, came the said
defendants and acknowledged themselves indebted to the
county in the sum of fifty pounds each also came John
Thompson Adam Thompson & Lewis Sanders, Sion Clanton acknow-
ledged themselves indebted to the county in the sum of
twenty five pounds each to be levied on our certain goods
and chattels lands & tennements,
In case we do not answer & comply with the intention of the
above order signed, in open court.        her
              James Dupyster    Winney   X   Jones
              John Thompson            mark
              Adam Thompson     Lewis Sanders
Witness                         Sion Clanton
Ben Haile clerk
```

Came into open court George Cook minor of 18 years of age son of Hugh Cook and make choice of Thomas Cook his Guardian,

who is ordered to enter into bond & secy accd. to law which
was done accordingly.

The State   )   Larceny
   Vs   )   The Grand Jury returned no bill and is
Daniel Howell)   thereupon discharged.
Joseph Howell)

The State   )   Larceny
   Vs   )   The Grand Jury returned True Bill & travered
Joseph Howell)   by Mr. Nott ordered that the securities in
                     this case stand bound by their recognizance
untill next court.

The State   )   Hog Stealing
   Vs   )   The Grand Jury returned true Bill traversed
Meshack Inman)   by Mr. Nott, ordered that the securities in
                  this case stand bound by their recognizance
                  untill next court.

The State   )   The Grand Jury returned no bill & is therefore
   Vs   )   discharged.
James Inlow)

Thomas Whitehead)   Case
   Vs   )
Arthur Thomas   )

By consent of the parties, this case in refered to James
Thomas & Wm Sartor, with power of chosing an umpeir & this
award returnable to next court shall be the Judgment thereof.

Edward Tilmore)   Debt
   Vs   )   Dismissed at Defendants cost
Chas. & Wm Lewis)

Ordered James Maberry be overseer of the road from James
Moseleys to Portmans Creek and that he clear out the same &
keep it in good repair the way that is marked out by Mosely
& others.

And George McWhorter from Portmans Creek to the reedy branch
above Gees.

And Alex. Kendrick from the reedy branch to Pinckneyville,
have reference to the first order.

Samuel Simpson, came into open court & took the necessary,
oath as a Justice of the peace for this county.

James Mathews)   Case
   Vs   )   By consent of the parties ordered that this
Thomas Hays   )   suit be refered to Cold. Brandon, Col. Farr,
                  and if they cannot agree to chose Elijah
Nunn and their award returnable to next court shall be the
Judgment thereof.

Ordered that the court adjourn untill tomorrow 9 OClock
                              Jno Blasingame
                              John Henderson
Signed by

374

Fryday the 3d. day of January 1794
The Honble court met according to adjournment
Present   John Henderson, John Blasingame, Judges

Renny Belue)   Attachment
    Vs   )   It appearing to the court that the papers
Zach Gibbs)   in this case is mislaid, ordered therefore
               that the clerk write to Mr. Nibbs, who was
attorney for the defendant, to demand those papers if in his
hands or make his affidavite thereof.

John Fincher   Plaintiff)   On a New Tryal, from last court,
    Vs   )   Attachment
Robert Merrick Defendant)
Came the plaintiff by William Shaw Esquire attorney for the
Plaintiff, and the defendant by Ephraim Ramsay Esquire, where-
upon came a Jury Towit Avery Breed foreman, Daniel Bain Henry
Bray James Mathew James Rountree, John Huey, John Hopkins
Wm Hightower, Thos. Harris James Harris Levy Hollingsworth &
Wm Hawkins, who upon their oaths & affirmation, say we find for
the Plaintiff nine pounds 21lE with costs of suit.
                    Avery Breed   foreman

Which verdict is ratified by the court & ordered to be
recorded.

Ordered that all the personal Estate of the late James
Olliphant deceased be sold on the second monday in February
next for cash at the plantation of the said decd. as the
Exeqences of said Estate appears to require such sale, and
public notice to be given the creditors of said Estate, by
the Admrs.

William Johnson)   Debt
    Vs   )   Judgment confessed for fifty pounds with
Charles Sims)   Jnr. and costs of suit.

The State   )   Bastardy
    Vs   )   Came the defendant into open court and
Robert Wallace &) agreed to pay the sum of five pounds
Tabitha Pennell) proclamation money for his fine & costs of
                   suit which is ordered accordingly. Also
ordered that he give security to indemnify the county from
the maintaince of the said Bastard child of Tabitha Pennall
by virtue of said order came said Robert Wallace Ralph Jackson
and Joshua Petty, and bound themselves in the sum of one
hundred pounds sterling in case the county stands chargeable
for supporting the said Bastard child and more compliance of
the above order.   Robert Wallace
                          Ralph Jackson
                          Joshua Petty

Braselman & Co.)   P & S
    Vs   )   Decree for the Plaintiff for seven pounds
Thomas Beddie)   ten shillings with Int. & costs of suit.

Peter Carns   )   P & S
    Vs   )   Dect. for five pounds & costs of suit.
Mathew Roberson &)
others   )

375

B John Fincher)   By consent of the parties ordered that the
    Vs   )   examination of Wm Addington senr. to taken
Wm Addinton   )   before a Justice on the Plaintiff lending
                    & his examination shall be taken as evidence.

James Gasway   )   P & S
    Vs   )   Decree for the plaintiff for 1180 Tobacco
Jno. P. Sartor)   at 221 & hundred and cost of suit.

Edson & Co.   )   P & S.
    Vs   )   Decree for the Plaintiff Eleven shillings
Jno. P. Sartor)   & 3d. & costs of suit.

Danl. Brammett)   Attachment
    Vs   )   By consent of the parties this suit is
Jno. & Wm Marten) dismissed at the Plaintiffs costs

Edson & Co   )   P & S
    Vs   )   Decree for the Plaintiff Eleven shillings
Jno. Peter Sartor) & 3d & costs of suit.

Danl. Brammett)   Attachment
    Vs   )   By consent of the parties this suit is
Jno & Wm Marten)   dismissed at the Plaintiffs costs.

Edson & Co.   )   P & S
    Vs   )   James Parnell proved 5 days attendance
Jno. Peter Sartor) on this suit.

James Gibbs   )   Decree for eight pounds & costs of suit &
    Vs   )   ordered that the property attached be sold
Saml. Savage &)   to satisfy the above debt.
Abn. Jones   )

The court adjourned untill tomorrow 9 OClock
                              John Henderson
                              Jno. Blasingame

The Honble court met according to adjournment on Saturday
the 4d. day of January 1794
Present   John Henderson   Jno. Blasingame   Judges

Ordered that all Recognizance to this court stand continued
untill next court.

Union County) P & S.
    Vs   ) Dismissed at the countys cost.
James Bell   )

Jesse Birdsong)   T A B
    Vs   )   Continued at the defendants cost. Ordered
Thos. Springer)   that Col. Brandon & Jno. Comer Exr. Danl.
                   Comer decd. bring the orphans of said decd.
in order to have them bound according to Law.

Nicholas Keating) P & S
    Vs   ) Came the Plaintiff by Wm Shaw Esquire
Mill Sumner   ) his attorney and the defendant by Abraham
                    Nott. Esqr. Whereupon came a Jury the
same Fincher vs Lee, who being duly sworn and say on their
several oaths & affirmation, we find for the plaintiff four

pounds four shillings of 10 d. law & costs.
Avery Breed foreman
The court ratified the verdict & ordered to be recorded.

Alex Macbeth & Co.) Debt
  Vs   ) Came the defendant into open court and
John High &   ) confessed a Judgment for the debt & costs
Mark Jackson   ) according to specialty with interest.

On the application of C R Edson he is appointed Guardian of
John Fitchpatrick nephew of Alexd. Fitchpatrick decd who
entered into bond with secy accg. to law.

Charles Waters) P & S Sptg.
  Vs   ) the plaintiff being solemnly called but
Bishop & Fincher) failing to appear, ordered that he be
             nonsuited.

Ordered that all Estrays liable to be sold this court, be
delivered to the sheriff & sold accg. to Law.

John Steen   ) Ordered that a demius Potestatum Issue
  Vs   ) to any 2 Justices in North Carolina to take
Mathew Roberson) the examination Francis Latimor on giving
            the Plf. the usual notice allowed by law
of the time of place of taking each examination.

Wm Euburgh   ) Case
  Vs   ) Nonsuit on being solemnly called but failing
Jno. Steen Ex.) to appear.

Edson & Uxor) Dismissed at the Plaintiff cost excepting
  Vs   ) the defendants attorneys case fees.
Wm Lee   )

Braselman & Co.) P & S
  Vs   ) Judgment confessed with stay of levy
Hammilton & Jenkins) untill next court.

Coulter & Stewart) P & S
  Vs   ) Decree for the Plaintiff for seven pounds
Wm Davis   ) 9 3 with Inst. & costs of suit.

Braselman) Shad. Lewalleir proved 2 days attendance.
  Vs   )
Beddie   )

Brummett) Shad. Lewallier proved 2 days attd.
  Vs)
Martin)

C R Edson   ) Attachment
  Vs   ) Richard Mitchell being sumd. as Garnashee
Jos. Buffington) in this attachment came into open court
           & was qualified accordingly and his
affedavitte ordered to be filed.

Ordered that the county treasury pay Edmond Ellis fourteen
shillings & three pence sterling & for new license don(?)
the county & bill filed.

Keating) Wm Brittain proved 4 days atty. in this Just. &
Vs) lives 16 miles from this place is Spartg. county.
Blammer)

The court adjourned untill court in course & signed by
John Henderson
Jno Blasingame

At an Intermediate court begun and holden in an for the
county of Union at the court house of said county on Monday
the 7th day of April 1794
Presnet   John Henderson
              John Blasingame   Judges

Colo. Thomas Brandon being commissioned from the Governor as
a Judge of this court was duly qualified according to the
constitution of this state and of the United States.

Ordered that John Cook be overseer of the road from Books
Bridge to Caleb Frazers in the room of Humphrey Bates; who
resigned

A Mortgage from William Mayfield to John Critten Proved before
a Justice and ordered to be recorded.

Proved in open court a Deed from Chalton Shockly to Henry
Stevens & ordered to be recorded.

Acknowledged in open court a Deed of conveyance from Philip
Anderson to John Jenkins & ordered to Record.

Proved in open court a Deed of conveyance from Alex Wilson to
Jos. Brock & ordered to be recorded.

Proved in open court a Deed of conveyance from Danl. Brown to
Casper Ruggles Edson & ordered to Record.

Presented in open court a will said to be the Last will and
testament of William Hendley deceased, which was duly
proven by the oath of Turner Kendrick, which is ordered to
be recorded.

Came then into open court, Mary Hendley, Edward Tilman and
William McCullock thy being appointed Executors in the said
Will, and was daily qualified as Exors. according to Law,
ordered therefore that letters testamony with the will
annexed be granted to them on the said Estate.

Ordered also that James Bankhead, Turner Kendrick, Richard
Cole & Geo McWhorter or any three of them be and are hereby
appointed to appraise the Estate of the said deceased, and
return their appraisement according to Law, they to be
first sworn by Benjamin Woodson Esqr. who is hereby appointed
to qualify them.

Ordered that the sale Bill of the Estate of Cap. Danl. Comer
decd. return by Colo. Brandon one of the Exors. be filed in
the clerks office.

Ordered that the sale Bill of the Estate of James Olliphant
deceased be filed in the clerks office as returned to us by
the admr. thereof.

Presented in open court will said to be the last will and
testament of Colo. William Farr deceased which was duly
proven in open court by the oath of Capt. William Johnson,
who said he believed the said deceased to be in his proper
senses at the time of Executing the same, Richard Farr, Wm B
Farr.

Thomas Stribling Junr. and Elizabeth Taliaferro Farr being
appointed executors and executrix in the said will came into
open court and was duly qualified according to law, Ordered
therefore that letters testamony with the will annexed be
granted to them.

Ordered that Col. Brandon, John Sartor Wm Johnson and Joseph
Coleman or any three of them be and accg. hereby appointed to
appraise the Estate of the said decd. and they to be first
sworn by Capt. Charles Sims and that they return their
appraisement according to Law.

Ordered that James Benson be overseer of the road from Cooks
Bridge to Danl. Liphams in the Room of R. Hank, and that he
keep the same in good repair, according to law with the hands
allowed thereby.

On the application of Graff Edson & Co. leave is granted him
to keep a public house, at Union Court House, likewise at his
place at Psaank occupied by John Grastey, he gave bond &
security according to law.

On the application of Tho. Stribling Esqr. leave is given him
to keep Public house at this place who gave bond according
to law.

Presented in open court an Instrument of writing said to be
the last will and testament of Charles Clanton deceased, which
was duly proven in open court by the oath of Absalom Petty
according to law, Sion Clanton being appointed executor in
the said will came into open court and was duly qualified
according to law.

Also ordered that letters testamontory with the will annexed
be granted to the said executors and that Moses Guiton John
Steen Junr. Absalom Petty and Drewry Herrington or any three
of them appraise the said Estate, being first sworn by Wm
McCullocke Esqr. who is hereby appointed to qualify the said
apprs.

Ordered that Francis Fincher be overseer of the road from
Adams old Mill to James Townsend shop in the room of Malon
Pearson and that he keep the same in good repair according to
law with the hands allowed by law.

Ordered that William Kennedy Treasury pay Wm Lawson eight
shillings for ___ a Heifer.

A Deed of conveyance from Col. Brandon to Wm Brandon proven
before a Justice and ordered to record.

Presented the last will and testament of John Huey deceased,
which was duly proven in open court by the oath of Majr.
Saml. Otterson which is ordered to be recorded.

Thomas Huey being appointed in the said will Executor came into open court and was duly qualified according to law as executor thereof.

Ordered that letters Testamontory be granted to the said Thomas Huey with the will annexed, on the said Estate.

Ordered that Majr. Otterson Benjr. Gordon Thomas McDonnell be and are hereby appointed to appraise the Estate of the said Estate to be first sworn by Charles Sims Esqr. who is hereby apptd. to qualify the above appraisers.

Proved in open court a Deed of conveyance from Jas. Johnson to Shepperd Mize & ordered to record.

Ordered that William Parmer be overseer of the road from Michells Creek to Dining Creek, In the room of Wm Anderson and that he keep the same in good repair according to law, with the hand allowd. by law.

Ordered that all the personal Property of the late John Greer deceased be exposed to Public sale according to a law at the Plantation of the said deceased, by the admrs. on their advertiseing thirty days of Luck sale, and a credit of six months to be given.

Ordered that Landlot Porter be overseer of the road from Loves ford to sharps Creek, in the room of Richard Hugh and that he keep the same in good repair according to Law with the hand allowed by Law.

The admr. accot. concerning the Estate of Robert Farris deceased was returned into open court & qualified to by Hugh Means Esqr. admr. and ordered to be filed in the clerks office.

The account of John Clark executor of Caleb Edmondson decd. against the said Estate was duly proven and allowed by the court & ordered to be filed amongst the best of said decd. acct.

On the application of James Bankhead leave is given him to retail spirituous liquors and keep a Public house at his house, who gave bond & security according to Law.

A Deed of conveyance from Col. Brandon to Jeremiah Lucas proven before a Justice and ordered to be recorded.

A Deed of conveyance from Abner Wills to William Fowler & Proven before a Justice & ordered to be recorded.

Ordered that a Bridge be built with all convenient speed across Tyger River at Bobos Ford or near the same, as it appear to us subscription for that purpose is raising, and that the undertaker thereof shall receive from this county Treasury after all debts due by the county are satisfied, the sum of twenty pounds for the encouragement of the same, to be paid in twelve months from this date.

Ordered that William Edward keep and support Suckey Girley who appears to be an object of charity untill next court and that he then bring in his bill as proven and will be made for the payment thereof.

380

Ordered that Majr. Otterson, Jeremiah Hamilton and Benjamin
Gordon view and mark out a road to begin at Cooks bridge
thence to the Fish dam ford on Broad River the nearest and
best way & make their report to our next Intermediate court.

Edward Nixon filed an account against the Estate of Edward
Nixon which was sworn to & ordered to be filed.

Ordered that the county Treasury pay Col. Tho Brandon three
pounds six & eight pence for supporting widow Crossley &
as his Bill filed.

Ordered that John Foster be overseer of the road from Grendol
Shoals leading to Union Court House as far as the forks of
the road, in the room of John Jastor, and that he keep the
same in good repair according to Law, with the stand allowed
by Law.

Ordered that the county treasury pay John Blasingame Esquire
the sum of eight pounds 3/0 which amount being the balance due
the said John Blasingame Esquire for his Extra services as
former sheriff, if this county he being qualified to the said
balance being due.

Ordered that a former order of the court respecting the
maintaince of John River be discontinued and that Wm Buck-
hanon supported him make out a new account of his expences
from the date of said order, likewise his acct. for supporting
him hereafter, and that he render said acct. to him over
convenient In order to be paid by the county.

Ordered that Richard Thomson be overseer of the road from the
county line, to the top of the Hill between Arthur Cunningham
and Nicholas Harris, and that he keep the same in good
repair according to Law, in the room of M Liles

Richd. Farr & Co. made application for Tavern Licence which
is granted, and he gave bond & security according to Law.

Ordered that all Estray, lyable to be sold be exposed to sale
tomorrow according to Law.

Ordered that the court adjourn untill tomorrow 10 Oclock &
signed by   John Henderson
                             Jno Blasingame

The court met according to adjournment at the court house
of said county on Tuesday the eight day of April 1794
          Present   John Henderson
                         John Blasingame   Judges

A Deed of conveyance from R Rountree & wife to James Ezell
Proven in open court & ordered to Record.

A Bill of sale from Thomas Rider to John McCullock proven in
open court & ordered to record.

Acknowledge in open court a Deed of conveyance from James
McCullock to Wm David & O to R.

Ordered that David Floyd be overseer of the road from Samuel
Simpsons to Enoree River in the room of Jehu Martindale and

381

that he keep the same in good repair according to law with
the hands allowed thereby

Proven in open court a Deed of conveyance from Thomas Stribling
sheriff to Abraham Nott Esqr. and ordered to record.

Acknowledge in open court a Deed of conveyance from Abraham
Nott Esquire to John Nuckols & ordered to be recorded.

Proven in open court a Deed of conveyance from David Prewitt &
wife to Geo Harling and ordered to Record.

A Mortgage from Jesse Dodd to John Martindale Proven before a
Justice & O to R.

Ordered that the Clerk advertise & give the most public notice
thats convenient, to all persons who has taken up Estrays in
this county, and has not make the due return of them according
to Law that they shew cause at our next intermediate court why
the same is not done.

On the application of Alexd. Macbeth & Co. & Wm Darby leave is
given them to Retail spirituous liquors at their stores, each
came into open court and gave bond & security according to
Law   Present Col Brandon

Ordered that Bastard child of Milley Sumner named Patsey be
bound into Enoch Floyd untill she arrives to the age of
eighteen to learn the art of spinning weaving & household
business.

Ordered that Zachariah Goodwin, orphan boy of Thomas Goodwin
deceased minor of Nine Shears years old be bound unto Lewis
Bobo untill he arrives to the age of twenty one, in order to
learn the trade & master of a Cooper

Ordered that two orphan children, anmely Mary Goodwin, six
years old, and Hyram John Goodwin, minor of five years old
orphans of Thomas Goodwin deceased, be bound unto Jonathan
Norman, the said Mary Goodwin untill she arrives to the age
of eighteen to learn the art of spinning & other household
employment, the said Hyram John Goodwin untill he arrives to
the age of twenty one to learn the business of a farmer.

Ordered that Given Gordon be overseer of the road from Keesers
old place to Gordons ford alias Anderson Ford on Enoree River
and that he keep the same in Good repair accg. to law with the
hands allowed thereby.

Ordered that John Martindale be overseer of the road from
Saml. Simpsons to the county line in the room of Jonathan
Norman and that he keep the same in good repair according
to law, with the hands allowed by law.

Ordered that David Norman be overseer of the road from Blackstocks Ford to Samuel Simpsons the old Road and that he keep
the same in good repair according to law with the hands allowed
thereby.

Ordered that Thomas Downey orphan boy of Julian Downey, Minor
of Twelve years of age be bound unto Thomas Hollingsworth

untill he arrives to the age of twenty one to learn the trade
of stocking & mounting guns.

Ordered that the county treasury discount with Thomas Stribling
the balance which appears to be due to him for his extra
services as sheriff.

Ordered that Robert Miller and Arthur Ross have leave to keep
a Public house at Pinckneyville on their giving bond and
security to the clerk according to Law

Saml. Simpson applied for Tavern licence which is granted and
he gave bond & secy according to Law.

On the application of C R Edson, on a Petition for a road, to
begin at Wm Eaves from thence the lower side of Ewarts old
field to Union court house, agreeable to the comrs. appointed
to mark out the same

The Court ordered that the said C R Edson have leave to open
the same & keep it in good repair, with those who petitioned
for the said road, so as not to Invalidate the main Charleston
Road leading by Macbeth store.

Ordered that the Clerk's sheriffs and Treasurer cause to be
made out all their accounts, against the county and have
them ready at Union Court house on the last Fryday in May
next in order to make a final settlement and that the clerk
furnish each of them with a copy of this order.

In an amendment of an order for Birdsong three orphan
children to Lewis Bobo & Jonathan Norman, Namely Zack. Goodwin
Mary Goodwin & Hyram John Goodwin, Its ordered therefore that
the said Lewis Bobo and Jonathan Norman give or cause to be
given the above orphans eighteen months schooling, each also
ordered that Thomas Hollingsworth give or cause to be given
the boy Thomas Downey, an orphan eighteen months schooling
and a horse & saddle at the experation of his apprentice ship
to be valued at seven pounds & a And the said Lewis a good
suit cloathes.

Bobo and Jonathan Norman allow to their 2 orphans boys at
the experation of their apprenticeship sack a Horse & saddle
to be valued at seven pounds and a suit good cloaths.
The court then adjourned untill court in course & signed by
                    Thos Brandon   Jno Blasingame

        South Carolina
At a court begun and holden in and for the county of Union at
the court hosue of said county, on Monday the second day of
June in the year of our Lord one thousand seven hundred and
ninety four; and of the Independance of the United States
of North America the eighteenth
Present the Honble
                    John Henderson
                    John Blasingame   Judges

The court preceeded to draw the Jurors for the next court,
which are as follows, and ordered that they serve as Grand
Jurors. Viz

383

Jeremiah Hammelton	1	Bernard Glenn	12
Nathaniel Gordon	2	Arthur Thomas	13
John Hammelton	3	Archer Howard	14
Bennet Langstone	4	Edward Tilman	15
Charles Sims	5	Batte Birdsong	16
James Park	6	Francis Fincher	17
Thomas Blasingame Junr	7	John Martindale	18
Jeremiah Gregory	8	Philip Blasingame	19
George Story	9	Bird Beuford	20
Thomas Lamb	10		
William Morehead	11		

Also the following as Petty Jurors

Nathl. Jackson	1	Malen Pearson	17
Avery Howard	2	Chas. Humphries	18
John Easterwood	3	Roger Potts	19
Jonathan Field	4	Wm Browning	20
Henry Long	5	James Savage	21
Enoch Floyd	6	Robert Bailey	22
Thomas Williams	7	John Greer	23
James Jackson	8	David Stewart	24
Wm Hayney	9	Jesse Maberry	25
Joseph Tucker	10	Jas. Smith	26
John Whorton	11	Jesse Sile	27
Saml. Gilkie	12	Thomas Blasingame	28
Robt. Thompson	13	Jacob Harlan	29
Lewis Sanders	14	Joseph Reder	30
Thomas Bell	15		
Jos. Hopkins	16		

Acknowledged in open court a deed from Job Hammond to William White & ordered to be recorded.

The State) Larcency
 Vs) Wm Brandon being bail for the defendant
Joseph Hart) appearance came into open court and delivered
 him up, and ordered that he be released;
Ordered that the said defendt. give other bail for his appearance at this court.
 Wherefore came Joseph Howard & John Willard and acknow-ledged themselves indebted to the state in the sum of twenty five pounds each to be levied on their certain goods and chattels in case the defendant fails to appear and abide to all ordered make by this court on the above indictment.

Wm Clark) Attachd.
 Vs) Ordered that this suit be dismissed being
Isaac Frazier) levied on Land, and appears this court has
 not recognizance of the same.

Thorogood Chambers) Abated by death of the defendant
 Vs)
Col William Farr)

James Beuford) Abated by death of the defendant
 Vs)
Col Wm Farr)

Oldes Neail) On appeal Dismissed at Kennedys costs as &
 Vs) his setts for the same.
Wm Kennedy)

Graff Edson & Co) P & S
Vs   ) Judgment confessed for four pounds twelve
Thomas Winn   ) shillings and 5, with costs of suit.

Alex. Macbeth & Co.) Debt
Vs   ) Judgment confessed for fourteen pounds
Wm Anderson   ) five shillings and three pence; with
                 int. and costs of suit.

Daniel Jackson) On an attachment
Vs   ) Ordered that the defendant give special bail
William Gist) to this suit and that the former securities
                 be released, wherefore came Aaron Fincher
and Enoch Floyd, and acknowledged themselves special bail
for the defendant Wm Gist and that the sheriff release the
property now in his custody taken by virtue of this attachment.

Genl. Sumpter) P & S
Vs   ) Judgment confessed for three pounds eighteen
John Beckham) shillings and ten pence with costs of suit.

Alexander Macbeth & Co.) Debt
Vs   ) Judgment confessed according to
Job Hammond   ) specialty with interest and costs of
                 suit.

Alexander Macbeth & Co.) Debt
Vs   ) Judgment confessed according to
Joshua Palmore) specialty with interest and costs
                 of suit.

Alexander Macbeth & Co.) Debt
Vs   ) Judgment confessed according to
Wm Hammond   ) specialty with interest and costs
                 of suit.

Graff Edson & Co) Debt
Vs   ) Judgment confessed accg. according to note
Lewis Bobo   ) with interest and costs of suit with stay
                 of execution untill the 1st September
                 next

Graff Edson & Co.) P & S
Vs   ) Judgment confessed for one thousand
Lewis Bobo   ) pounds, at eleven shillings & 8 p with
                 int. and 6 cts assuit: with stay of execu-
                 tion untill the 1st day of Sept. next.

James Gurtis) P & S
Vs   ) Judgment confessed for two pounds twelve
Graff Edson & Co) shillings and one penny with costs of
                 suit.

Thomas Johnson Executors) Debt
of John Boswell   ) Judgment confessed in this case
Vs   ) for thirteen pounds five shillings
David Brock   ) sterling with costs of bail the
                        Plaintiff staying levy of execution
for two months and sale thereon till the twenty seventh of
December next, which is ordered.

Julias Nichols   apl.)   P & S
  C Goodwin   )   Dismissed by consent of the Parties
  Vs   )   at the defendants costs.
John Fincher   )

The State   )   Ordered that the defendant be discharged on
  Vs   )   paying costs.
Esther Insco)

The state   )   Ordered that the defendant be discharged
  Vs   )   on paying costs.
Christ. Plummer)

Ordered that the county treasury pay William Edwards two
pounds for maintain Susannah Gousley as p his accot. filed.

Alexander Macbeth & Co)   Debt
  Vs   )   Judgment confessed accg. to note
Isaac Hollingsworth   )   with

Interest and costs of suit, stay of execution three months
which is ordered accg.

The State   )   Breaking the peace
  Vs   )   Maher Siles, came into open court and took
William Dasefield)   the necessary oath prescribed by Law and
Robert Gibson   )   prayed the court for a continuance of the
John Gibson   )   defendant recognizance, whereforce came
Wm Gibson   )   the said defendants, together with James
                      Lockhead, Thomas Dean, James Maberry,
John Beckham, Senr. Their securities and acknowledged themselves indebted to the state in the sum of viz the said
defendants in the sum of twenty five pounds and their securities
in the sum of ten pounds, to be levied on their certain goods
and chattels, for their good behavior towards Maher Liles
and his son Delmar Liles for the term of twelve months and
one day.

Presented in open court the last will and testament of
Francis Drake deceased, which was duly proven in open court
by the oath of James Thompson, which is ordered to be
recorded.

Richard Drake came into open court being appointed in the
said Will one of the Executors thereof as was duly qualified
according to Law as executor aforesaid.

Ordered that Nathl. Jeffries James Thompson and John Jeffries
be and are hereby appd. to appraise the said Estate and make
their return thereof according to Law, and that N. Cerry
Esquires attend and qualify the said appraisers.

John Hank   )   On attachment
  Vs   )   Thomas Blasingame Esquire being second as
Thomas B. Hunt)   Garnashee made oath, that he is justly
                   indebted to the defendant the sum of twenty
pounds which is ordered to be condemned in his for the
satisfaction of the Plff debt in case he establishes the
same.

Presented in open court the last will and testament of Samuel
Coopers deceased, which was proven in open court by the

oaths of Jeremiah Cooper, which is ordered to be recorded.

Elizabeth Cooper being appointed Executrix in the said Will came into open court and took the necessary oaths according to Law, as Executrix.

Ordered that John Sanders, Thomas McDonnell and Thomas Layton be and are hereby appointed appraisers, to appraise the said Estate, and that they make a due return thereof accg. to Law and the Col. Brandon qualify said appraisers.

Richard Brock was qualified in as a constable for this County

The court then adjourned untill tomorrow 9 Oclock signed by
John Henderson
Jno Blasingame
Thos. Brandon

The Court met according to adjournment on Tuesday the Third day of June 1794.
Present   John Henderson
               John Blasingame   Judges

The State   ) Ordered that the defendant enter into
Vs   ) recognizance for his appl. at Pinckney Court
James Campbell) next to be holden on the first day of
              November next to Answer to a Complaint
lodged against him for passing counterfeit Money.

The State)   Bastardy
Vs   )   Discharged for want of proof.
Sarah Law)

Joshua Palmore) Debt
Vs   ) On motion of Wm Shaw Defendant attorney the
Joseph Hughs) Plttf. being solemnly called out failed to
                 appear ordered that he be nonsuited.

John Chesnat & Co.) Case   Nonsuit
Vs   )
Edward Tilmore   )

Elizabeth Wilson   Plaintiff) Trover
against   ) Came the Plaintiff by William
Enoch Floyd   Defendant) Shaw Esqr. and the defendant
                               by Ephraim Ramsay, whereupon
came a Jury towit James Gibbs foreman, Thomas Dean, John
Brandon, Robt. Gibson, Moses Collejoe David Sisson John
Strange Robt. Gregory, Leonard Smith, Abner Potts Archer
Kennedy John Cook, who being duly sworn according to Law.
but on motion of Wm Ramsay for a nonsuit, which was ordered
accg.

Thomas Brandon) Debt
Vs   ) Judgment confessed according to note, with
Jesse Dodd   ) interest and costs of suit.

James Bell) Debt
Vs   ) Judgment confessed by the Deft. according to
Wm Campbell) note with interest and costs of suit.

387

John Steen   ) Attacht.
Vs   ) Ordered that this cause be continued, and that
Isham Saffold) the plaintiff have leave for a commission.

John Fincher) Larceny
Vs   ) Ordered on motion of the county attorney that
Benj. Rush   ) the recognizance to continued untill next court.

The State   ) Larceny
Vs   ) Discharged on motion of the Pl. attorney
Alexd. Hammelton) for want of Prosecution

The State So. Carolina) Hog stealing
Vs   ) Came the state by William Shaw
Meshick Inman   ) Esquire and the defendant by Abraham
                         Nott Esquire, Whereupon came a Jury
the Same as Wilson Against Floyd who being duly sworn to will
and truly try and true delivery make; return their verdict
on their several oaths and affirmations & say we find Meshick
Inman Guilty.   James Gibbs   foreman

It appeared to the court that the constables for this county
fails to attend, the court which sitting, and neglect their
duty in several respects, ordered that each of said
constables be fined twenty shillings unless they make some
lawfull excuse for their nonattendance.

Wm Hogans Admr.) Debt
  Wm Hogans   ) Judgment confessed according to note with
  Vs   ) interest & costs of suit.
James Sims   )

Ordered that the Presentments of the Grand Jury be laid over
untill Sept. Intermediate Court for ordered to be make thereon.

John Steen   ) Debt
Vs   ) We the under named Arbitrators was indiffer-
James Clark) ently chosen to deliver a cause which was in
                court between John Steen Plf. and James Clark
defendant, we therefore after hearing such proof with their
allegations do adjudge that Clark owe the Plaintiff nothing
and is by this adjudged to pay the costs of suit.
                                    John Thompson
                                    John Bird

The State   ) Larcency
Vs   ) Came the defendant into open court, with
Mesheck Inman) William Hodge and John Thompson and confessed
                a Judgment for Five Pounds being the fine
or fleated on the said Inman, also cost of suit with stay of
execution three months, which is ordered accordingly.

Robert Wallace) P & S
Vs   ) Decree for the Plaintiff according to note
Wm Hagan   ) with interest and costs of suit.

Jesse Dodd) Attachment
Vs   ) On motion of Abrm Nott ordered that this
Wm Gist   ) attachment be discontinued

388

The State   ) The defendant demanded his Tryal but
  Vs   ) continued untill next court.
J. P. Shattleford)

The State) Continued untill next court
  Vs   )
Wm Gist)

The State) Continued untill next court.
  Vs   )
John Gambler)

The State   ) Assault
  Vs   ) Came the State by Wm Shaw Esqr. atty
Peter Philips   ) and the defendants by Ephraim
Gabriel Philips Junr.) Ramsay Esqr. whereupon came a Jury
John Philips   ) to wit, the same as Wilson Vs Floyd
                    who being duly sworn as Law requires
return their verdict & say we find all three of the Philips
guilty   James Gibbs foreman

The court ordered in consideration of said Verdict that the
said defendants be fined three pounds & costs of suit

The State) Assault
  Vs   ) The defendant came into open court & plead
James Tosk) guilty and shew himself on their mercy, Its
            considered therefore that he be fined six pence
and costs of suit.

James Mathews) The Parties consented to refer this case to,
  Vs   ) the Brandon Anderson Thomas & Elijah Nunn,
Thomas Hays) and their award returnable to next court,
             shall be the Judgment of this court, also
ordered that either two of said arbitrators may be allowed to
settle the case.

John Steen Junr.) By consent of the Parties ordered that
  Vs   ) this case be refered to the arbitration of
Drewry Herrington) Wm Kennedy and Moses Guiton, with power of
                chosing an Umpire, and their award return
to next court shall be the Judgment of this court.

Nathaniel Jefferies) Debt
  Vs   ) The Defendant came into open court and
William Steen   ) confessed a Judgment according to
              specialty, with interest and costs of
              suit.

Warran Hall) P & S
  Vs   ) By consent of the parties by their attorneys
John Martin) ordered that this case be refered to the
            arbitration of Doctor Herman Anderson and
Anderson Thomas with Power of chosing an Umpier, and their
award returnable to next court shall be the Judgment of this
court.

Fed. Thomas) Case
  Vs   ) The defendant being called but failed to appear
N. Lazerius) Ordered that he be nonsuited.

Joseph Howell)   Case
Vs   )   Came the Plaintiff by Wm Shaw & Samuel Farrar
Thomas Evans)   and the defendant by Abraham Nott Esquire,
                 Whereupon came a Jury towit the same as Wilson
vs Floyd, who being duly sworn, say on their several oaths
and affirmation We find for the Plaintiff fourteen pounds
16/9/4   Jas. Gibbs foreman

Zach. Hays)   Ordered that this case be refered to, Thomas
Vs   )   Blasingame Wm Martindale and Saml. Simpson and
Wm Newman)   their award returnable to next court shall be
              the Judgment thereof.

David Hopkins)   Debt
Vs   )   Abated by death of the defendant.
James Hawkins)

Thomas Brandon & Joseph Hughs   )   Debt
  Administrators of Benj. Jolley decd.)   Came the Plaintiff by
Vs   )   Abm. Nott Esqr. his
James Burnley and John Sanders   )   attorney and moved
                                           that Charles Sims
Esquire be admitted to prove the bond who being & called &
duly sworn, deposeth and sayeth, that he saw the said James
Burnby sign seal & deliver the said bond & saw the said
John Sanders, subscribe his name & affix his seal as security
to the same.
          Whereupon came a Jury Towit, the same as Wilson Vs
Floyd and say we find for the Plaintiff accg. to specialty
with interest and costs of suit.   James Gibbs foreman

Thomas Word qualified as a constable.

Thomas Bishop)   On attachment
Vs   )   Mark Jackson came into open court and
Tho C Russell)   acknowledged himself special bail for the
                 defendant.

Hugh Means)   Attachment
vs   )   Robert Summerell came into open court, and
Wm Jackson)   acknowledged himself special bail for the
               defendant

Hezekiah Terrell)   P & S
Vs   )   Judgment confessed for ten pounds &
John Leek   )   costs of suit to be discharged with 2000
                    lb tobacco.

The court adjourned untill tomorrow 9 OClock & signed by
                              John Henderson
                              Jno Blasingame

The court met according to adjournment on Wednesday the Fourth
day of June 1794 Present John Henderson
                           John Blasingame
                           Thomas Brandon

The State   )   Ordered that the recognizance of the defendant
Vs   )   be discharged it appearing that she has been
Fanny Penny)   resident of Spartanburgh.

390

Charles Goodwin Esquire)   P & S
Vs   )   On motion of the Plaintiff; the
Josias Woods   )   court decreed for the Plaintiff
                              the sum of six pounds ten shillings
and six pence with interest & costs of suit with stay of
execution untill next court, subject to all discounts that
shall be brought in by the defendant.

John Fincher   )   Slander
Vs   )   On an affidavet made by the Pltff. ordered
Robert Merrick)   that this suit be continued untill next
                   court on Peremptorily rule

The State   )   Larceny
Vs   )   Came the state by William Shaw, Esquire,
Joseph Howell)   and the defendant by Abraham Nott his
                    attorney; whereupon came a Jury the same as
Wilson vs Floyd who being duly sworn to will & truly try
this case return their verdict on their several oaths and
affirmations & say We find Joseph Howell guilty.
                              James Gibbs foreman

The court proceeded to pass sentence on the said Joseph
Howell on consideration of the verdict of the Jury, and say
that the said Howell receive on his bare back twenty five
lashes, immediately, which is ordered accordingly.

The Sheriff made his return, that he be duly executed the
sentences of the court on the said Joseph Howell, ordered
that he be discharged on paying costs;
                    Absent   John Henderson

Nicholas Lazerus   Plaintiff)   Case
Vs   )   Nonsuit
Fredrick Thompson   Defendant)

Jesse Birdsong by John Murrell)   Dismissed at the Pltff cost
Vs   )   except the defendants
Tho Springer   )   attorneys fee & six dollars

Gabriel Philips Plaintiff)   P assault & battery came the
Vs   )   Plaintiff by William Shaw and
Thomas Minton   Defendant)   Epm. Ramsey Esquire and the
                              Defendant by Abraham Nott Esq
Whereupon came a Jury to wit the same as, Wilson against
Floyd, Who being duly sworn & say on their oaths & affirma-
tions We find for the defendant. James Gibbs foreman

Nicholas Lazerus)   Slander
Vs   )   Refered by Consent of the parties to
Joshua Palmore   )   Wm Kennedy and Charles Sims with power
                      of chosing an umpier, and their award
returned into court shall be the Judgment hereof.

Christian Cradock)   Debt
Vs   )   Judgment confessed according to note
Samuel Otterson)   with interest & costs of suit.
Benjamin Gorden)

John Steen   Plaintiff)   Debt
Vs   )   Came the Plaintiff by Mr. Michie
Nathl. Jefferies Defendant)   & William Smith; and the

defendant by Abraham Nott and Ephraim Ramsay Esquire whereupon came a Jury to wit the same as Wilson vs Floyd who being
duly sworn to will and truly try this cause, return their
verdict and say we find for the defendant with costs of suit.
James Gibbs foreman

Which said Verdict was ratifyed by the court and ordered to
be recorded.

Jno Nicholas Lazerus) Slander
Vs   ) This action being refered the
Joshua Palmore   ) Arbitrators, returned their award &
                         was of opinion, that the Plaintiff
had no sufficient cause of action, and agreed that it be
therefore dismissed at Plaintiff cost which is ordered
accordingly.

John Martindale and William Hogan being qualified as Justice
of the peace for this county by Col. Brandon & John Blasingame
Esqr. who ask for the future considered as such.

The Court then adjourned untill tomorrow 9 OClock.
Jno Blasingame
Thos. Brandon

The Court met according to adjournment on Thursday the fifth
day of June 1794   Presnet   John Blasingame
Thomas Brandon   Judges

On motion of Thomas Stribling Esquire for Enoch Floyd to be
appointed deputy sheriff who mett with the approbation of
the court and was duly qualified according to law.

John Steen   ) Debt
Vs   ) James Thompson proved six days attendance
Nathl. Jefferies) in behalf of the deft. in this case,
                      ordered that the same be taxed in the
bill of costs.

Henry Coon   ) P & S
Vs   ) Decree for the Plaintiff for one
Austen & Wm Newman) thousand pounds of tobacco at fourteen
                      shillings & cent.

Jesse Dodd   ) On attachment
Vs   ) On motion of Mr. Farrar that the attachment
William Gist) should be qualified on the ground of not being
                agreeable to law; the attachment having
been issued in term & returned the same term but the court
overruled the motion the deft. having replevied the property
by giving bond to the sheriff.

Hogan   ) Consented by Mr. Nott atty for pet. and Mr. Shaw
Vs   ) atty for Deft. notwithstanding this case that
James Sims) Mr. Sims shall appoint one man & the Plaintiff
             another before whom Mr. Sims shall bring all the
payments & accts. he can set up in disch. ag the sd. Judge &
that the said two now allow him thereout what shall appear
to them to be just and right the amount of which shall be
deducted out of the said Judgment.

John Cunningham Admr.) Debt
    Wm Cunningham) Judgment confessed according to note
  Vs   ) with interest & costs of suit
James Lindsay   )

Robert Merrick) Debt
  Vs   ) The difendant came into open court and
John Taylor) confessed a Judgment according to bond
           with interest & costs of suit.

James Howard   ) Debt on Bond
  Vs   ) On motion of the defendants attorney;
Joshua Petty Admr.) for a nonsuit being band by the
John Nuckols   ) Limitation act which was granted &
           Ordered accg.

Gordon & Co) Debt
  Vs   ) Judgment confessed according to note with stay
John Fincher) of sale six months with interest and costs of
        suit.

John Steen   ) Debt
  Vs   ) By consent of the parties ordered that this
Mathew Robenson) suit be refered to Nich Corny and Wm
          McCullock with power of umperage, and their
award returnable to next court shall be the Judgment hereof.

Thorogood Chambers) Debt
  Vs   ) Dismissed at the Plaintiff costs.
Danl. McElduff)

Thomas Brandon) Judgment confessed for eight pounds eleven
  Vs   ) shillings and three pence, but subject to all
Samuel Jackson) just credits, with stay & execution untill
         next court, with costs of suit.

Nathaniel Jefferies Plaintiff) Debt
  Vs   ) Dame the Plaintiff by Abraham
John Bird   Defendant) Nott Esquire and the defendant
                    by Ephraim Ramsey Esquire
whereupon came a Jury towit Wilson against Floyd, who being
duly sworn return their verdict on their several oaths and
affirmations, return their verdcit & say We find for the
Defendant James Gibbs foreman.

John Steen) Case
  Vs   ) Nonsuit
John Bird)

John Steen) Nonsuit
  Vs   )
Wm Giles)

John Steen   ) Nonsuit
  Vs   )
The admr. Nuckols)

Wm Williams) on attachment
  Vs   ) Charles Brock; Thomas Palmore came into
Edward Brown) open court and acknowledged themselves
           special bail in this active and the property
           be released.

Thomas Brandon) Debt
Vs) Judgment confessed for twelve pounds eighteen
Daniel Jackson) shillings & one Penny, subject to all jsut
credits that shall be brought in by the
defendant, with stay of Exor, six months with costs of suit.

John Compty) Case
Vs) The Plaintiff being solemnly called but failed
Rod. Wright) to appear ordered that he be nonsuited.

Wm Hammond) Case
Vs) Continued untill next court at the Plaintiff
William Giles) costs on Pesemptorily rule.

Samuel Bell) By consent of the Parties Preforce to John
Vs) Alexander and Richard Pounds with power of
John Popham) umperage and their award, returnable to this
court shall be the Judgment thereof.

Samuel Otterson) Debt
Vs) Judgment confessed according to note with
William Brummett) interest & costs of suit.

Daniel Jackson) Contd. untill next court with leave for a
Vs) dedemus for pltff on his giving the usual
Wm Gist) notice to the defendant's attorney.

Samuel Cooper) Abated by death of the Pltff.
Vs)
Filby Davett)

Nathl. Jefferies) Joseph Jolley Wilson Jolley and Sarah
Vs) Gilliam each proved four days attendance
John Bird) in this suit; ordered that the same be
taxed in the bill costs.

Wm Chisholm) Debt
Vs) By consent of the parties ordered that this
Wm Giles) suit be refered to the arbitration of Wm
Thompson & Wm Kennedy with power of umpirage;
and their award returnable to this court shall be the
judgment hereof.

C R Edson & Co) On attachment
Vs) Came the Plaintiff by Abraham Nott
Joseph Buffington) Esqr. and the defendant failing to appear
whereupon came a Jury towit the same as
Wilson vs Floyd who being duly sworn say on their oath we
find for the plaintiff, Twenty pounds seven shillings and two
pence & costs of suit. James Gibbs foreman

C R Edson & Co) Attachment
Vs) Richard Mitchell being summoned as
Joseph Buffington) Garnashee in this action, made oath as
p his affidavite that he owes the defen-
dant eighteen dollars, & three quarters; also some papers
lodged in his hands by said defendant.
Its ordered therefore that the said sum of eighteen &3/4
dollars be condemned in the hands of said Mitchell; also
ordered that the said papers mentd. in this affidavitt be
delivered to the Plaintiff he accounting for said papers;
to the defendant as far as debt & costs.

394

```
John Steen    )  Debt
   Vs         )  The Jury being sworn on this cause; but the
Wilson Jolley )  Pltf suffered a nonsuit before verdict was
                 returned.


John Steen      )  Sci fa
   Vs           )  On motion of Mr. Nott the rule made
The Exors.      )  absolute & the Judgment revived
  David Stockton)


Thomas Whitehead)  Writ Case
   Vs           )  Dismissed at Plaintiff cost
Arthur Thomas   )


Thomas Bishop      Plaintiff)  On attachment
   Vs                       )  Came Plaintiff by Abraham Nott
Thomas C Russell   Defendant)  William Shaw & the defendant by
                               Ephraim Ramsay esquire Whereupon
came a Jury to wit the same as Wilson vs Floyd, who being
duly sworn say on their several oath & affirmations We find
for the Plaintiff twenty nine dollars and the interest from
1784.      Jas. Gibbs foreman


John Clark )  P & S
   Vs      )  In obedience to an order of the worshipful
Thomas Lee )  court of Union we the subscribers being
              appointed to settle a dispute, between John
Clark & Thomas Lee on hearing the witnesses it appears that
the Deft. was indebted to the Plaintiff the sum of Ŀ4 in
trade and that the defendant was ever ready and willing to
pay a cow & calf and we do award that the said defendant pay
unto the Plaintiff the above sum of four pounds in a good
cow & calf corn at 2/2 P Bus. pork 20/ p lb or credit in
one of the stores at Union court house.
Certified this 5 day of June 1794    Hez. Reece
                                     Tho. Young
```

In amandment of the above award ordered that the defendant pay
the costs.

John Comer proved seven days attendance in the suit; ordered
that the same be taxed in the bill of costs.

Ordered that all Estrays lyable for sale this court be
delivered to the sheriff and sold immediately.

The court then adjourned untill tomorrow 9 OClock
                              Jno Blasingame
                              Thos. Brandon

The Court met according to adjournment on Fryday the sixth
day of June 1794.   Present   John Henderson
                              John Blasingame   Judges

```
Gabl. Philips)
   Vs        )
Thomas Menton)
```
James Townsend proved six days attendance in this suit,
ordered that the same be taxed in the bill of costs.

John Fincher   )   P & S
Vs   )   On motion of Mr. Nott for the Plaintiff to
Thomas Justice)   be nonsuited on the ground; that the defendant
                  was arrested at Pinckney court while attend-
ing as a Prosecutor in behalf of the State; the court were of
oppinion that he was under protection in that case, and
ordered nonsuit. Present Thomas Brandon

Exors John Hope   )   P & S
Vs   )   Judgment for the Plaintiff according
Cristopher Johnson)   to note, with stay of execution
                        four months.

Charles Kelley)   P & S
Vs   )   The sheriff made his return that he had
Stephen Huff   )   duly executed the within writ on Henry Hugg
Henry Huff   )   decree for the Plaintiff against the
                   defendant Henry Huff for twelve hundred weight
of Good merchantable tobacco at nine shillings with interest
and cost of suit.

Richd. Fryer Proved 3 days attendance.

Alexander Macbeth & Co.)   P & S
Vs   )   Judgment confessed by Col. Brandon
Andrew Mays &   )   according to note with int. with
Thos. Brandon   )   stay of sale; untill the first day
                           of Nov. next with costs of suit.

Wm Whitlock)   P & S
Vs   )   Decree for the Plaintiff for twelve hundred
Danl. Manley)   weight of tobacco at nine shillings & costs of
                 suit.

David R. Evans   )   P & S
Vs   )   Decree for the Plaintiff according to
Benjn. Hollingsworth) note with interest and costs of suit.

Hugh Gourley)   P & S
Vs   )   The suit being brought illegal ordered that
Robert Patton)   he be nonsuited.

Nathl. David)   Dismissed the Plaintiff paying the clerks
vs   )   fees & by the parties consent.
John Jenkins)

Nelson)   Judgment by default
Vs   )
Biddie)

C. R. Edson & Co)   P & S
Vs   )   Decree for the Plaintiff according to note
Geo Taylor   )   with interest & costs of suit.
Robert Greer   )

C R Edson & Co   ) Attachment
Vs   ) The plaintiff came into open court &
Jeptha Hollingsworth) dismissed this suit at his costs

James Woodson)   Debt
Vs   )   Ordered that the defendant give special bail
Sarah Gist   )   in this case whereupon came Mill Sumner and

396

acknowledged himself special bail for the defendant.

Charles Sims) Trover
 Vs   ) Mr. Farrarr attorney for the defendant moved
William Gist) the court for the writ to be qualified on the
             ground that the process was served legal;
ordered that the sheriff cause to be made a fuller return on
this process at our next court.

Archer Howard) P & S
 Vs   ) By consent of the parties ordered that this
James Gibbs) suit be refered to the arbitration of George
             Harlan (Hatter) and William Kennedy, and if
they can not agree to chose an umpier; and their award returnable to next court shall be the Judgment thereof.

Joshua Petty) On appeal
 Vs   ) Ordered that the Judgment of the Justices
John Hogan) be sett aside on the grounds; he having given
            Judt. for a sum larger than his Jurisdiction.

Daniel Lepham) On appeal
 Vs   ) Ordered that the Judgment of the Justice be
Geo. Wadkins) sett aside on the grounds, he having given
             Judgment beyond his Jurisdiction.

James Townsend proven two days attendance in the above suit.

Ordered that the treasury pay Edmond Ellis for serving a
Warrant on Thompson.

John Morehead   ) On appeal
 Vs   ) From the Judgment of N Corry Esqr.
Drewry Herrington) Wherein he had given a nonsuit, against
                 the Plaintiff, ordered that the nonsuit
before the magistrate be sett aside and a New tryal granted,
at the deft. cost.

On motion of Thomas Stribling Stokes for Henry Farnandis to
be appointed deputy sheriff who met with the approbation of
the court and was duly qualified accg. to Law.

Then the court adjourned untill court in course.
Signed by: Jno Blasingame
                 Thos Brandon

At an Intermediate court begun and holden on Monday the first
day of September 1794
Present   John Henderson
             Thos Brandon   Esquires

Acknowledged in open court a Deed conveyance from Jeremiah
Lucas to James White & ordered to record.

A Deed from Bird Booker to Joseph Coleman Proven before a
Justice & ordered to be recorded.

The last will and testament of John Wilson, Present in open
court which was duly proven in open court by the affirmation
of Rebecca Milhouse & Henry Milhouse being qualified to the
same before a Justice & ordered to record

Jehue & Seth Wilson being appointed executor of the said will came into open court, and was duly qualified to as executors,

Ordered that Henry Milhouse, James Townsend and John Hawkins appraise the Estate of John Wilson decd. and Mahie their return accg. to law.

Presented in open court the last will and testament of Tho. Henderson decd. which was duly proven by the oath of Saml Hardy & ordered to record.

Nathl. Henderson & John Henderson being appointed exors in the said Will came into open court & was qualified accg. to Law.

Ordered that Robt. Crenshaw, Byrd Beauford Saml. Hardy & Danl. Brummet or any three of them appraise the Est. of Tho. Henderson Dc.

Presented in open court the last will and testament of Thomas Wright deceased, which was proven in open court by the oaths of Anner Taylor and Wm Wright which was ordered to be recorded.
　　Dylla Wright & William Wright being appointed executors on the said Will came into open and was duly qualified according to Law.

Ordered that Adam Potter, John Watson and John Beckham Junr. appraise the Estate of Tho Wright deceased and make due return thereof accg. to Law.

Acknowledged in open court a Deed from Col Brandon to Fredrick Eison & ordered to be recorded.

Proven in open court a Bond from Herman Anderson to Chris. Johnson & ordered to Record.

Proven in open court a Deed from Robert Gault to John Jasper & Ordered to be recorded.

Acknowledged in open Court a Deed from Benjr. Convehoven to John Jasper & ordered to be recorded.

Presented in open court the last Will and Testament of James Gibbs which was duly proven in open court by the oath of Jacob Holmes & ordered to be recorded.

Jesse Connell, Zachareas Gibbs & Ann Gibbs, being appointed executors in the said will came into open court and was duly qualified according to Law.

Ordered that Robert Wallace, John Goodwin & George Harlan (Hatter) appraise the Estate of the said decd. & make their return accg. to law.

Proven in open court a Deed from James Jackson to Joseph Jackson & ordered to be recorded.

A Deed from Jesse Brown to Richd Hughs Proven in open court and ordered to be recorded.

Acknowledged in open court a Deed from Tho. Stribling to Charles Webb & ordered to be recorded.

On the motion of John B. Anderson, Wm. Johnson & Abm. Nott, admor is granted them on the Estate of Doct. Harmon Anderson decd. who gave bond & security accg. to Law.

It is ordered that Christ. Johnson & James Thomas & Warren Hall or any three of them appriase the Estate of Doct. H. Anderson decd. & make their return to next court, ordered that Charles Sims qualify them.

James Barron is appointed overseer of the Road in the room of John Gregory.

Arthur Thomas is appointed overseer of the road in the room of Amos Cook.

On the application of James Townsend, letters of administration is granted to him on the Estate of Isaac Cook senr. who gave bond & security and was duly qualified according to Law.

Ordered that Amos Cook, John Cook, Seth Wilson & Ely Cook appraise the Estate of Isaac Cook senr. decd. and that they make due return thereof to Law.

Ordered that Robert Savage, son Wm Be overseer of the road in the room of John Greffy, from James Bogan Creek to Jas. McCrakens & that he keep the same in Good repair accg. to law with the hands allowed thereby.

John B Anderson and Abraham Nott Esquire came into open court and was duly qualified as administrators of the Estate of Herman Anderson deceased.

Ordered that Thomas Wilbourn be overseer of the road from the Cross road leading to Grendol Shoals, to Union Court House in the room of Ezekiel Springer.

On the application of Ralph Jackson letters of Administration is granted him on the estate of Amy Jackson decd. who gave bond & security & was duly qualified accg. to Law.

Ordered that Drewry Murrell John Baily and Robert White appraise the Estate of Amy Jackson deceased & make due return thereof accg. to Law.

Ordered that the county treasury pay Wm Buckhannon ten pounds for supporting John Reeves an object of charity as p his account filed; to be paid as soon as the Public Building is settled for.

Ordered that the county Treasury pay John Eison for an Estray sold last court & bought by Wm Wm the sum of four pounds nine shillings, as soon as it become due to the county.

Ordered that all Estrays lyable to be sold this court, be sold on tomorrow.
Ordered that the court adjourn untill tomorrow 10 oclock
                              Jno Blasingame
                              Thos Brandon

The Court met according to adjt. on Tuesday the 2d. September 1794. Present Tho Brandon, Jno Blasingame, John Henderson

Wm Johnson came into open court and was duly qualified as administrator of the Estate of Herman Anderson deceased.

Ordered that Wm Kennedy Treasury pay Fredrick Eisen the sum of forty shillings being for goalers fees & repairs to the goal he being qualified to the same.

Proven in open court by Benj Haile a Power of attorney from Danl. Hagen esquire to Abraham Nott Esquire & ord. to be recorded.

Acknowledged in open court by deed from Abm Nott Esquire attorney for Danl. Huger Esqr. to John Eisen & ordered to be recorded.

Acknowledged in open court a deed from Abm Nott Esquire Attorney of Danl. Huger Esquire to Wm Jones & ord. to record.

A Deed from Isaac Gregory senr. to Isaac Trammel & ordered to record.

Ordered that Seth Wilson be overseer of the road from Cooks Bridge to Cain Creek in the room of his father and that he keep the same in good repair accg. to Law with the hands allowed thereby.

James Farr son of Colo. Farr deceased a Minor came into open court and made choice of Daniel McElduff his guardian who entered into bond & security accg. to Law.

On the motion of Capt. James Woodson for letters of adminis- tration on the Estate of Sarah Gist decease, its considered by the court that a citation issue to all the kindred and creditors of said deceased to shew cause at our next January Court, why letters of Admr. should not be granted said Jas. Woodson.

Acknowledged in open court a sheriffs Deed from The Stribling to Abm Nott and Benj. Haile & ordered to record.

Acknowledged in open court a sheriff deed from Tho. Stribling Esquire to James Hawkins & ordered to record.

A Lease and release from Daniel Trammel to Thomas Trammel Presented for Record, "The subscribing witnesses being dead, came into court Tho. Stribling Richd. Farr & Jno. Peter Sartor who was qualified to the hand writing of the witnesses the court ordered said title to be recorded.

On the application of the Executors of the last Will and Testament of Colo. William Farr deceased, for a sale of Property to the amount of three hundred pounds, to discharge the exigences of said Estate, which they represent to be about that amount, Its ordered therefore that the said Executors expose to public sale at the Plantation of said decd. for cash, Property to that amt. on giving timely notice of such sale.

On the application of the admr. of the Estate of Herman Anderson deceased.

400

Ordered that they expose to Public sale at the Plantation
of Wm Johnson, all the perishable property of said deceased,
on giving the usual notice of such sale negroes accepted for
ready cash.

Ordered that the minutes be read which was done accg & signed
by   Thos Brandon
              Jno Blasingame

The court then adjourned untill tomorrow 10 oclock.

The court met according to adjournment on Wednesday the 3d
September 1794.
Present Thomas Brandon Esqr.

The court being called to business, appeared Its ordered that
the court adjourn untill tomorrow 10 oclock.
                              Thos. Brandon

The court met according to adjournment on Thursday the Fourth
day of September 1794
Present   John Blasingame, Thomas Brandon

Ordered that the county Treasury deduct 31/ out of an order,
give to John Eisen for the amount of a stray sold last court
for wintering said stray, as p. Bell Brought in by Mill
Sumner.

On the application of Mrs. Sarah Darby for Letters of administration on the Estate of William Darby, deceased, which was
granted her, who entered into bond with Daniel Parmer &
John Bailey her security in the sum of fifteen hundred
administratrix.

Ordered that Alexander Macbeth, Andrew Torrence, James Woodson,
& Thomas Greer and Thomas Blasingame Esquire or any three
of them appraise the Estate of William Darby deceased, and
make due return of such appraisement according to Law, & that
Col. Brandon qualify the said appraisers.

Ordered that immediately after an inventory & appt. of the
above Estate is made & filed in the clubs office, that the
admr. expose to Public sale at the late dwelling House of
the said decd. also the Personal Estate of said deceased, on
a credit of twelve months for all sums above twenty shillings
on giving security to be approved of by the admrs. and all
sums under twenty shillings for cash.

On the oath of Mrs. S. Darby, ordered that an indenture of
Nelly Baker to Mrs. Jean Actor, be recorded & filed in the
Clerks office.

Ordered that letters of admr. Al Colligendum be granted to
James Woodson, on the Estate & effects of Issiah Gist deceased
he entering into bond & security for the delivery of all the
deceased property to the Person, to whom legal letters of
admr. shall be granted.

Ordered that the county Treasury pay Mill Sumner Three Pounds
two shillings for wintering two estray colts.

401

Ordered that Benjamin Haile Clerk be allowed out of the
county Treasury the sum of sixteen pounds 16/2d as p his bill
filed for extra services & other charges

Ordered on application of George Bailey that he be appointed
Guardian of an orphan boy Jordon Bailey, son of Thomas Bailey
deceased, and that the said George Bailey be authorized to
bind said orphan to some good trade.

Ordered that the court adjourn untill court in course which
was signed by   Thos. Brandon   Jno Blasingame

At a county court begun an holden in an for the county of
Union at the court House of said county, on Thursday the first
day of January in the year of our lord one thousand seven
hundred and ninety five and of the Independance of the United
States of North America the Nineteenth
Present the Honble   Thomas Brandon   John Blasingame   Judges

The Court proceeded to draw the Grand Jury for next, and
ordered that the sheriff summon the following persons to serve
as such viz. &

Nathan Lanstone	Wm Steen Junr.
John Gregory	Turner Kendrick
Hezekiah Rice	Aaron Fincher
William Sims	Joseph Coleman
Given Gordon	Ephraim Fowler
John Jefferies	Taylor Stribling
Nicholas Jasper	Willis Fowler
Spelsby Glenn	John Speers
Robert Burns	Richd. Hughs
Wm Bowman	Stephen Layton 20 G Jurors

The following persons are drawn as P. Jurors to serve next
court viz.

Perry Evans	Elisha Bond
John Coleman	Isaac Chapman
Thomas Lamb	John Ruttledge
John Howell	John Brandon
William Williams	Henry Burrow
James Townsend	Reuben Ballew
James Parnell	Jesse Palmore
James Lindsy	James Bogan
Gillion Woolbanks	Benjr. Darby
Andrew Thompson	Danl. Tollerson
Edward Denny	Thomas Grier
Hugh Donaldson	John Sisson
Wm White (son Isaac)	Robert White
Jonathan Roberts	Richd. Cannon 31 Jurors
John Kennedy	
John Ray	

Abraham Nott Christopher Johnson, and James A White was
returned by Col. Thomas Brandon duly qualified according to
Law as Justice of the peace for this county.

John Taylor deceased will being returned into open court, and
was duly proven by the oath of James May Jun: which was
approved of by the court and ordered to be recorded.

402

Susannah Taylor and Majr. Moses Guiton being appointed and the said will executors thereof came into open court and took the oath of executors prescribed by Law.

Jeremiah Cooper deceased will being returned into open court and was duly proven by the oath of Gabriel Philips senr. which was approved of by the court and ordered to be recorded.

David Cooper being appointed in the said will executors thereof came into open court and took the oath of executor prescribed by law.

On the application of Annes Morehead and Wilson Jolly for letters of administration on the Estate of John Morehead, deceased, which was granted by the court on their giving bond & security according to law, which was done and both duly qualified according to the form prescribed by law as admt. & admr.

On motion of the admr. of John Morehead dead. Moses Guiton and John Jefferies and Charles Carviena, be and are hereby appt. to appraise the Estate of the said deceased, and that Wm McCullock esqr. qualify the said appraisers.

The Last will and testament of Elizabeth Miller deceased being returned into open court, and proven by the oath of Emanuel Hollums which was appointed of by the court and ordered to be recorded; Jeremiah Gregory and John Gregory qualified as executors in the above will.

The last will and testament of James Sims deceased, being returned into open court by John Sanders one of the Executors was proven to the satisfaction of the court by the oath of Cornelius Wilson which was ordered to be recorded.

On motion of the Exors of Elizabeth Miller deceased, Majr. Jos. Hughs Richard and William Adair; appraise the Estate of the above deceased and make due return thereof and that Benj. Woodson qualify said appraisers.

On motion of Charles Brock for letters of administration on the Estate of Elias Brock deceased, ordered that a citation issue to all the kindred and creditors of said deceased to shew cause if any they have, at one next intermediate court, why letters of administration should not be granted to the above named Charles Brock.

Edson & Co	)	P & S	By consent of the parties ordered
Vs	)		that all matters of controversey
John Campbell	)		now depending in court between
Graaff Edson & Co	)		them be refered to the Judgment
Vs	)	Case	of John Clark and his award
John Campbell	)		returnable to next court shall be
			the Judgment thereof.

Wm Coleman) Dismissed at Pltf cost
Vs   )
Abner Coleman)

Abner Coleman & wife) Dismissed at Plttf cost.
Vs   )
Wm Coleman   )

403

Ferdinand Hopkins) Dismissed at Defendants cost
  Vs   )
Wm Johnson   )

John Haile Asse   ) Dismissed at defendants cost
   A Macbeth & Co   )
   Vs   )
Wm Coleman & John Gibson)

William Williams) Dismissed at defendants cost
  Vs   )
Edward Brown   )

Thomas Lyman is qualified as constable for this county on motion of William Hogans Esquire

Proven in open court by the oath of John Lucas a Deed of Gift from William Williams to Charles Humphries and ordered to be recorded.

On motion of Captain Palmore; George Baily is appointed overseer of the road from Pinckney Court House to James McCrackens and that he keep the same in repair accg. to law with the hand allowed thereby.

Ordered that the minutes be read which was done, the court then adjourned untill tomorrow 10 OClock
                              Thos. Brandon
                              Jno Blasingame

The court met according to adjournment on Fryday the 2d January 1795 Present Tho. Brandon Jno Blasingame Judges

Sarah Darby Admx.) By consent of the parties, ordered that
   Wm Darby decd.) this suit be dismissed at Deft. cost.
   Vs   )
Jeremiah Spann   )

Graff Edson & Co) By consent of the parties ordered that this
   Vs   ) suit be dismissed at deft. cost.
Hugh Nelson   )

Wm Mitchell asse.) Dismissed at defendants cost
      Wm White   )
   Vs   )
Philip Anderson)

Sarah Darby Admx.) Dismissed at defendants cost.
      Wm Darby decd.)
   Vs   )
John Harmon   )

Graff Edson & Co) Debt
   Vs   ) Judgment confessed according to note
Gidion Shelton) allowing all just credits, with interest
                   & costs of suit; with stay of execution
                   untill 1 June next.

Renny Belue) On attachment
   Vs   ) Ordered this suit be dismissed the original
Zacha. Gibbs) papers being mislaid or casually lost

404

John Fincher) Slander
    Vs   ) On oath of Enoch Floyd ordered that this cause
Robert Merrick) be continued at Defts. cost untill next
               court.

Gabriel Philips) Slander
    Vs   ) On oath of the Pltf. this suit stand over
Tho. Minton   ) untill next court at his costs.

Warran Hall) P & S
    Vs   ) By consent of the parties, ordered that this
John Martin) cause be referred to Hez. Rice and Anderson
            Thomas with power of chosing an umpier, and
their award returnable to next court shall be the Judgment
thereof.

Archer Howard) P & S
    Vs   ) Abated by death of the defendant
James Gibbs)

John Steen   ) Debt on Bond under seal
    Vs   )
Mathew Robinson)

Mr. Shaw moved the court for a nonsuit on the following ground
that the paper oblg. on which this action was brought was not
under seal, but was a penal note & further the statute of
limitations on
Which the court over ruled him, and ordered that the cause
to be determined by the Jury/ Whereupon came the Plaintiff by
Abraham Nott his attorney and the defendant by William Shaw
attorney by defendant whereupon also came a Jury to wit
Nathaniel Jackson for Jonathan Cudd Henry Long Thomas Williams
James Jackson Joseph Tucker

Malan Carson, Charles Humphries, William Browney David
Stewart, Thomas Blasingame, and Jacob Harlan who being duly
sworn and return on their verdict on their several oaths
and affirmation say we find for the plaintiff one shilling
damage   Nathl. Jackson Pltff.
Which was ordered to be recorded.

Graaf Edson & Co) Dismissed at the defendants cost
    Vs   )
Robert Greer   )

Elizabeth Sims, Peter Braselman, and John Sanders being
appointed Ext. and executors of the last will and testament
of James Sims deceased, came into open court, and took the
oath of executors prescribed by Law.

The Admr. of) P & S
Doct. Henning) The defendant confessed a Judt. accg. to
    Vs   ) note with stay of execution untill the first
Tho. Stribling) day of August next.

Alex. Bookter   ) P & S
    Vs   ) Dismissed at Pltf cost being served on
Spencer Brummett) the wrong person

405

Elijah McGuire)   P & S
Vs   )   Decree for the Plaintiff for 1 Thousand
William Eaves)   pounds of tobacco at seven shillings
                & six pence & cent with int. & cost of suit.

On motion of the Executors of James Sims decd. ordered that
Robert Crenshaw Bird Bluford and Danl. Brummett appraise
the Estate of said deceased, and make due return accg. to
law. and that Wm Hogans Esq. qualify said appraisers.

Charles Waters)   P & S
Vs   )   Dismissed at Plaintiff cost
Tho. Bishop &)
John Fincher   )

Silas Bell)   P & S
Vs   )   This action dismissed each party paying their
Wm Campbell)   own costs, agreeable to an award filed.

Clayton Rodgers   Plaintiff   )   Case
Vs   )   Came the Plantff. and the
James Lockart Admr. Defendant)   defendant by Wm Shaw Esqr.
John Mills decd.   )   whereupon came a Jury towit
                                    the same as Steen against
Robenson who being duly sworn and after a full investigation
of the matter return their verdict on the several oaths &
say we find for the Plaintiff eight pounds with interest.
                               N. Jackson foreman
Which verdict is ordered to record.

On motion of the administrators of Doct. Herman Anderson
deceased ordered that they expose to public sale at the
plantation of William Johnson, all the remainder of the
personal Estate of the said deceased; on their giving the
usual notice of such sale, for cash.

On motion of the Exors. of Thomas Henderson deceased, ordered
that they expose to sale the personal Estate of said deceased
on their giving the usual notice of such sale at the plantation of said deceased; on a credit of six months.

Graff Edson & Co)   Debt
Vs   )   Judgment confessed by the plaintiff
William Whitlock)   according to specialty with interest and
                   costs of suit.

Graaff Edson & Co)   Case
Vs   )   Judgment confessed according to acct.
Robert Gibson   )   filed with costs of suit, with stay of
                   Exors untill 1 June next.

Same   )   Judgment confessed according to note, with stay
Vs   )   of exor 2 months & costs of suit.
Robert Smith)

Same   )   Judgment confessed accg. to note; with
Vs   )   interest & costs of suit on stay of execution
Lewis Sanders)   untill the 1 June next.
  Dd Brock   )

John McElnulty) Case
  Vs   ) Came the defendants in open court and
James Johnson &) confessed a Judgment for the sum of fourteen
Hugh Wilson   ) pounds sterling with interest & costs of
                 suit.

John Fincher Asse   ) P & S
     Saml. Martendale) Nonsuit
  Vs   )
Thomas Elliott   )

Ordered that all estrays lyable to be sold this court be
exposed to public sale on tomorrow.

The court adjourned untill tomorrow 10 oclock signed by
                         Thos Brandon
                         Jno Blasingame
                         John Henderson

The court met according to adjournment at the court House of
said county, on Saturday the third day of January 1795.
     Present   John Henderson   Tho Brandon

Andrew Torrence, Charles Sims, John Martindale, Benjamin
Woodson & Thomas Blasingame, Esqr. came into open court and
took the oaths prescribed by Law as Justices of the peace
for this county.

John Speers came into open court and took the oath prescribed
by Law, as constable for this county.

The State) Mr. Farrar, in behalf of the deft. moved for
  Vs   ) tryal & ordered that this case stand continued
Shuttleford) untill next court.

Ordered that all recognizances returnable to this court stand
over untill next court.

William Hammond) Case
  Vs   ) The plaintiff not being prepared in this
William Giles) action the defendants attorney moved for a
                 nonsuit which was granted & ordered
                 accordingly

Graaff Edson & Co) Debt
  Vs   ) The Defendant came into open court and
Henry Birdsong   ) confessed a Judgment according to specialty
                   with interest & costs of suit, on stay of
Exors untill 1 June next.

Graaff Edson & Co) P & S
  Vs   ) The defendatn came into open court and
Wm McJunkin   ) confessed a judgment according to note
                   with interest & costs of suit on stay of
exors untill last June next.

Graaff Edson & Co) P & S
  Vs   ) The defendant came into open court and
James Bogan   ) confessed a Judgment according to note
                   with interest and costs of suit.

Alexander Bookter) Debt
   Vs   ) The defendant confessed a Judgment accord-
Hollis Biddie   ) ing to note with interest and costs of
               suit.

Wm Chrisholm) Debt
   Vs   ) Contd. untill next court at the defendants
Wm Giles) costs.

John Morehead) On an appeal
   Vs   )
Drewry Herrington)

Its ordered that the execution in the hands of the sheriff
for costs in this case, be suspended it appearing to the court
an error being made in the order of Last court inspection
this costs and that Moorehead is adjudged to pay the same and
said Herrington Leberated from the execution & his property
released.

Wm Furgus) Debt on note
   Vs   ) Came the plaintiff by William Smith his attorney
Wm Brummett) and the defendant by Abm Nott whereupon came a
             Jury the same as Steen against Wm Bethue
Robinson, who being duly sworn return their verdict and say
we find for the plaintiff accg. to specialty with interest
and costs of suit.   M. Jackson foreman
Ordered that the verdict be recorded.

Christ Degraffenreid) Debt
   Vs   ) Came the defendant into open court
John McNeal   ) and confessed a Judgment accg. to note
                   with int. & costs on the execution
untill 1 June next.

Ordered that the county treasury pay SN Caster 14/ & keeping
its mare & bill when collected.

Arthur Brandon) P & S on note
   Vs   ) Samuel Jackson was called and proved the
Wm & Dudly Redd) note on which the above suit was brought
               Decree for the plaintiff the sum of three
pounds ten shillings with interest & costs of suit.

Graaff Edson & Co) P & S
   Vs   ) Judgment confessed accg. to account filed
Arthur Ross   ) with stay of exor untill 1st April next
              with costs of suit.

Wm Nelson) Trover
   Vs   ) Contd. untill next court at the defendant
Tho. Biddie) cost.

John Murrell   ) Case
   Vs   ) Judgment confessed with int. &
Wm Rogers & Majr. Dupre) costs of suit.

Graff Edson & Co) P & S
   Vs   ) Judgment confessed accg. to note with
Ebenezer Pickett) stay exor untill March & costs of suit.

Hugh Means came into open court and was qualified as Justice
of the peace for this county.
The court then adjourned untill Monday 10 OClock.
                           Jno Blasingame
                           John Henderson
                           Thos Brandon

The court met according to adjournment on Monday the fifth
day of January one thousand seven hundred and ninety five
            Present Thomas Brandon, John Henderson Judges

Wm Shaw Esqr.   ) Debt on note
    Vs   ) On motion of Mr. Saxon attorney for the
John Nail &   ) plaintiff and leave of Abraham Nott
Thomas Brandon   ) attorney for the Deft. Judgment is awarded
                      against the said defendants accg. to
specialty with interest & costs of suit, on stay of sale untill
next court which is ordered accg.

Evans Winn & Co.) Debt on Bond
    Vs   ) Came the plaintiff by Abraham Nott Esqr.
William Hall   ) their attorney and the defendant by Mr.
                   Saxon & Mr. Leak attorney for him, whereupon
came a Jury towit the same as Steen vs Roberson who being
duly sworn, and on the evidence of N. Jaggers who proved
payment on said bond, return their verdict on their several
oaths and affirmations say we find for the plaintiff accg. to
bond after deducting the sum of nine pounds 15/8 with interest
on the full of said bond 28 Feby .86 at which time the above
deed thought to been given & Int. on the Col. with costs of
suit.   Nathl. Jackson foreman
which verdict is ordered to record.

Wm Holder) Dismissed at Plaintiff cost
    Vs   )
Wm Williams)

John Campbell   ) Atty.
    Vs   ) Dismissed at the Plaintiff costs
Jeremiah Kingstand)

Graaff Edson & Co) Debt
    Vs   ) The defendant came into open court and
Saml. Bogan   ) confessed a Judgment accg. to specialty
                    with stay exon. untill the first day
March 1795 next with costs of suit.

Graff Edson & Co) Case
    Vs   ) The defendant came into open court and
James Depoister) confessed a Judgment for the sum of nine
                   pounds six shillings and nine pence with
costs of suit with stay of execution untill 1st Oct. next.

John Hunt) On attachment
    Vs   ) Dismissed at Pltfs costs.
Thomas Hunt)

Jesse Dodd   ) On attachment
    Vs   ) Came the plaintiff by Abraham Nott and Wm
William Gist) Smith Esqr. and the defendant by Saml
                Torrence Benj C Saxon whereupon came a Jury

409

Towit; the same as Steen against Roberson who being duly
sworn to will and truly the above attachment return their
verdict on their verdict on several oaths and affirmations
say we find for the plaintiff one hundred and fifty pounds
old currency with interest.   Nathl. Jackson   foreman
Which verdict is ordered to record.

Evens Winn & Co)   Nathan Jaggers proved 5 days attendance in
    Vs   )   this suit ordered that the same be taxed
Wm Hall   )   in the bill of costs, also 6/8 for milage

Ordered that the court adjourn untill tomorrow 10 oclock.
                            John Henderson
                            Tho. Brandon

The court met accg. to adjournment on Tuesday the 6th day of
January 1795   Present   John Henderson
                           Tho. Brandon

Graff Edson & Co)   P & S
    Vs   )   Judgment confessed by the plaintiff accg
Joshua Gault   )   to note with interest & costs of suit.

Graaff Edson & Co.)   P & S
    Vs   )   Judgment confessed accg. to note with
Wm Hightower &   )   interest & costs of suit.
Epm. Fowler   )

Graaff Edson & Co)   P & S
    Vs   )   Wm B Farr sworn to prove the note Decree
Reuben Hatton   )   for the Plaintiff according to note,
                    allowing all just credits, with costs of
suit, on stay of execution untill next court at which time the
deft. is to bring forward all his payments & credits on said
note.

James D. Puckett)   P & S
    Vs   )   Ordered by consent of the parties this
John McDonnell)   case be referred to Majr. Jos. Hughs &
                    Edward Tilmon with power of chosing an
umpier & this award returnable to next court shall be the
Judgment thereof.

Graaff Edson & Co)   Contd. untill next court.
    Vs   )
Robert L. Miller)

James D. Puckett)   P & S
    Vs   )   The defendant by Josias Leak confessed a
James a Whyte   )   Judgment for the sum of four pounds six-
                    teen shillings and two pence half penny
sterling the Plaintiff paying the sheriff & the defendant the
clks fees.

Graaff Edson & Co)   P & S
    Vs   )   Contd. untill next court
Charles Thompson)

Thomas Word   )   P & S
    Vs   )   On note for one thousand pounds of tobacco
James Dickerson)   Decree for the Plaintiff at two dollars
                    p. ct. with int. & costs of suit.

                        410

```
Alex. Macbeth & Co)    P &
       Vs           )    Decree for the pltf. accg. to note with
Adam Kilpatrick     )    interest & costs of suit.


Alexander Bookter)      Debt
       Vs          )      Came the pltff. by Abm Nott the defendant
Henry Mitchell     )      being called failed to appear, ordered
                          that Judgment by default be entered
against him.


Alexander Bookter & Co.)   Writ
       Vs              )    Came the plaintiff by Abm Nott &
Daniel Lake            )    the defendant being solemnly called,
                           failed to appear, ordered that
Judgment be entered accg. him by default.


Elijah Wilbourn )    The defendant came into open court and
       Vs        )    confessed a judgment accg. to note with
John McAnulty   )    interest & costs of suit.


Graaff Edson & Co)    Debt
       Vs        )    The defendant came into open court and
Joseph Howard    )    confessed a Judgment accg. to specialty
                      with int. & costs of suit.


Alexander Macbeth & Co)    Debt
       Vs             )     The defendant came into open court
Thomas McCaffarty     )     and confessed a Judgment for the sum
                            of ten pounds 13/5 with int. &
costs of suit.


Alexander Macbeth & Co)    Debt
       Vs             )     The notes being proved in court by
Joseph Simmons        )     Ben Haile & confession of Judgment
          ·                 of the back of the process, Judgment
against the defendant for the sum of eight pounds 15/6 with
int and costs of suit which is ordered accg.


Alexander Macbeth & Co)    Debt
       Vs             )     The note being proven on which this
James Rountree        )     suit was brought & confession of
                            Judgment on the back of the process
Judgment is awarded the plaintiff ag. the dft. for the sum of
eighteen pounds 1/4/2 with int. & costs of suit.
Which is ordered accg.


John Haile        )    Debt
       Vs         )    Came the Plaintiff by Abm Nott and the
Cap. James Marten )    defendant being solemnly called, but
                       failed to appear, Judgment is awarded
the plaintiff against the defendant for the sum of seventeen
pounds seventeen shillings & five pence sterling with
interest & costs of suit. which is ordered accg.


Joshua Marten    )    Debt on note under seal came the Plaintiff
       Vs        )    by Abm. Nott and the defendant being
James Dikerson   )    called but failed to appear Judgment is
John Dickerson   )    awarded.
                          the plaintiff against the defendant accg
to specialty with interest & costs of suit.
```

Alexander Bookter & Co.) Writ
Vs   ) Debt and the plaintiff by Abm.
Samuel Jenkins   ) Nott and the defendant being
                         solemnly called failed to appear
ordered that Judgment be entered against him by default.

Jesse Dodd) Case
Vs   ) Ordered that the defendant give special bail
John Fincher) to the pltf. in this case.

Joseph Kershaw & Al   ) Debt or Bond
Vs   ) Judgment confd. by Thomas
The Exors Col Wm Farr decd.) Stribling one of the Exors,
                               according to Bond with interest
& costs of suit.

Geo Hood   ) Dismissed at Defendants cost
Vs   )
Wm McCulloch)

Alexr Macbeth & Co.) On Note
Vs   ) The defendant confessed judgment by the
Wm Whitlock   ) Deft. and the notes of said confession
                     being proved Ordered that Judgment be
entered against the defendant accg. to note with 2d
Interest & costs.

Isham Prince) On attacht.
vs   ) The bond of this attacht. not being returned
Francis Barnett) Mr. Nott moved the court on that ground
                 for the attachment to be dismissed. The
court was divided on their opinion.

Nathaniel Davis qualified by Col. Brandon as a Justice of the
Peace for this County.

John McNulty   Plaintiff) Case
Vs   ) Came the plaintiff by Abraham
James Johnson Defendant) Nott his attorney and whereupon
                          came a Jury to wit the same again
Steen against Robinson who find for the plaintiff fourteen
pounds & Costs of suit. Nathaniel Jackson foreman

Thomas Elliott) Ordered that this suit be dismissed at the
vs   ) plaintiffs cost.
John Fincher)
Enoch Floyd   )

Ordered that the court adjourn untill Tomorrow 9 OClock
                              J. Henderson
                              Thos Brandon

The court mett according to adjournment on Wednesday the
Seventh day of January A. Domini 1795
          Present   Thomas Brandon
                     John Henderson Judges

Jesse Dodd) Case
Vs   ) James Bell came into Court and acknowledged
John Fincher) himself Special Bail for the Defendant in the
              above suit. Together with Thomas Bishop.

412

An Inventory sale appraist. and sale of the Estate of William
Darby decd Ordered that the same be filed in the Clerks
office.

On motion of Samuel Farrar, letters of administration is
granted him on the Estate and effects of Sarah Gist deceased
during the minority of Joseph Gist, minor of the said
deceased, Who took the oath prescribed by law, and gave bond
and security in the sum of one thousand pounds accordingly.

Col. Thomas Maberry has leave to retail Spirituous liquors
and keep public house he gave bond & security accg. to Law.

Ordered that Ambrose Ray, William Woolbanks, and Saml. Simpson
appraise the Estate of Sarah Gist deceased and make their
return accg. to Law; being first sworn by John Martindale

Joseph Gist minor of Sarah Gist decd. came into open court and
make choice of Samuel Farrow to be appointed his guardian who
met with the approbation of the court and gave bond & security
accg. to Law.

Ordered that the county treasury pay referred to T. Eison the
Admt. of an estray sold him last court, which appears to have
been proven away by Tho. Hames.

Ordered that the court stand adjourned untill Saturday next
John Henderson
Thos. Brandon

The court met according to adjournment on Saturday the Tenth
day of January 1795
Present   Thomas Brandon
John Blasingame
John Henderson   Judges

On the application of Jno. Peter Sartor and William Sartor,
letters of administration is granted those on the Estate of
John Sartor deceased, who gave bond & security, and took the
oath prescribed by Law.

Ordered that James Townsend Admr. Isaac Cook deceased Senr.
expose to sale all the personal Estate of said deceased, on
a credit of twelve months.

Ordered that Jos. Coleman, Bird Booker & Wm Glenn & Wm
Hollingsworth, appraise the Estate of John Sartor deceased
and make due return thereof accg to Law and that Capt.
Johnson qualify said appraisers.

The Court proceeded to the election of a sheriff for this
county to succeed Thomas Stribling Esquire after his
commission expires, and after ballotting according to Law,
do find that John Henderson Esquire is duly elected as
sheriff aforesaid for the term of four years.

Col. Brandon voted for Wm B. Farr one of the candidates for
the sheriff & desired the same entered on the records.

John Henderson Esquire being elected sheriff for this county,
came into open court and resigned his commission as Judgd
of this county.

413

The court then adjourned untill court in course & signed by
Jno Blasingame
Thos. Brandon

At an intermediate court begun and holden in and for the
county of Union on Monday the sixth day of April 1795
Present   John Blasingame Judges

Proved in open court by Wm Morgan a deed of conveyance from
John Stiles to Renny Belue, And ordered to record.

A Sheriff deed from Saml. Saxon to Nathan Langstone, proven
before a Justice and ordered to record.

Proved in open court by Wm Rogers a Deed of conveyance from
Danl. Lipham to Chas. Jenkins & o to R.

Proved open court by Wm Rogers a Deed of conveyance from
Josias Darby & Drusilla his wife to Chas. Jenkins & o to R.

Proved in open court by Reuben Knight a Deed of conveyance
from Jas. Shockley to Jas. Knight & o to R.

Proved before a Justice a Mortgage from Richd. Crittenden
to John Crittenden & ordered to record.

A Deed from Turner Kendrick and wife to John Crittenden,
proved before a Justice and ordered to recrd.

Nicholas Waters being appointed executor in the last will and
Testament of William Bullock deceased, came into open court
and to be the necessary oath as executor thereof.

A Deed from Robert White & wife to John Lawson, proven in
open court by Wm Lawson and ordered to record.

Ordered that a citation issue to John Cook on the Estate of
John Christian Creese to shew cause why letters of administration should not be granted him on said Estate.

Proceed before a Justice a Deed from John Herrington to
Richd. Terrell, and ordered to record.

Presented in open court the last will and Testament of Aaron
Fincher deceased, was duly proven by the oath of Hezekiah
Rice and ordered to Record.
    Mary Fincher being appointed executrix of the above will,
came into open court and was duly qualified according to Law,
as executrix thereto.

Also Moses Fincher being qualified as executor accordingly to
the above will.

Ordered that Thomas Greer, John Clarke, John Stokes and
Hezekiah Rice or any three of them appraise the Estate of
the said Aaron Fincher deceased, and make due return accg
to Law and that any Justice of the peace qualify the said
appraisers.

A Deed from Hugh Means to William Dewitt, proven in before
a Justice and ordered to record.

Ordered that the executors expose to sale all the personal
Estate of John Morehead deceased at the House of said deceased
on their giving a credit of six months the purchasers giving
Bond with approved security to the executors.

Ordered that Joseph Reeder be appointed overseer of the road
from Col Brandons to Union Court House in the room of Joseph
Howard and that he keep the same in good repair according to
law with the hands allowed thereby.

A Deed from John Thompson to Benjn. Jones proved before a
Justice and ordered to record.

Acknowledged in open court a Deed from Ellis Foster to John
Kigar acknowledged in open court and ordered to record.

Proved in open court by Jesse Palmore a Deed from Wm Hightower
to Charles Humphries & ordered to record.

The court adjourned untill tomorrow 9 OClock
                              Jno Blasingame

The court met according to adjournment on Tuesday the 7 Oct.
1795 Present Tho. Brandon Judges

Acknowledged in open court a Deed of conveyance from Robert
Coleman to John Coleman for 150 acres land with the place
annexed & O to record.

Nicholas Corry this day was qualifyed in open court as a
justice of the peace for this county.

Proved before a Justice a Deed of gift from Sarah Bogan to
Elizabeth Bogan and ordered to be recorded.

Proved before a Justice a Deed of Gift from Sarah Bogan to
her Daughter Elizabeth Bogan and ordered to record
Present   John Blasingame Judge

Acknowledged in open court a Deed from Adam Potter to Richd.
Kirby.

Presented in open court the writing said to be the last will
and testament of James Thomas deceased, James Tate being
qualified to prove the same, says on his oath that he saw
the said will presented to the said James Thomas, and heard
him acknowledged the same to be his last, will and testament
and farther sayeth he believed the said James Thomas to be in
his proper senses at the same time, when he acknowledged the
same
      Which proof the court thought satisfactory ordered the
same to be recorded, and letters granted the exors appointed
therein.

Ordered that Woodson Rountree be overseer of the road from
Col Brandons to Bobos Ford on Tyger River in the room of
Nevel Holcomb and that he keep the same in good repair
according to Law, with the hands allowed thereby.

Ordered that a citation issue against Mrs. Sarah Darby
administratrix of Wm Darby decd to cite her to personally
be and appear before the Judges of this court on the first

day of June next. To shew cause if any she has why Daniel
Palmore and John Bailey should not be released from their
present securityship and give other security for her faithful
administration on the above decd. Estate.

Also ordered that the said John Bailey and Daniel Palmore be
sumd. to attend at the same time.

Ordered that Alex Macbeth & Co. have leave to retail spirituous
liquors in this county.

Ordered that all Estrays lyable to be sold this court be
exposed to sale immediately by the owner.

A Bill of Sale from Aaron Fincher to John Martindale, Proved
before Justice & ordered to record.

James Barron applied for licence to retail spirituous
liquors & keep public house, he gave bond & security accg
to Law.

A Deed from Wm Sims & James Fanning to Richd. Terrell proven
in open court and ordered to record.

A Deed from Robert Gilham to John Bird & ordered to record
Proved before a Justice.

A Deed from Richd. Ferrell to John Bird proved before a Justice
& ordered to record.

A mortgage from John Thompson, to Abm Smith & ordered to record

A Sheriff bond from John Henderson to the treasurers of the
state taken in open court and ordered to be recorded, and
transmitted to the said treasurers office.

Ordered that a citation be granted to Seth Wilson on the
Estate of Rachel Penny.

By consent of the Court & the parties ordered that an orphan
boy Thomas Thickpenny son of Rachel Thickpenny decd. be
bound unto Seth Wilson untill he attain the age of twenty
one,
        Provided the said Wilson does on his part give the said
Boy one years schooling, and learn him the art and mastery
of a Blacksmith, and provide for the said Boy in other
respects according to Law, and also at the expiration of his
said indentures to allow to the said orphan boy two suits
of good cloaths

On the application of Nichs. Corry Esquire one of the Executors of John Herrington deceased ord. that they permited to
expose to public sale, such of the personal Estate of said
decd. as the executors , may suppose will be perishable by
detaining in their hands.

Their being no sheriff at this time committed for this
county the Business revoling on William Kennedy corsoner,
On motion of the said corsoner for Henry Farnandis to be
appointed his deputy untill their shall be a sheriff the said
Henry Farnandis met with the approbation of this court, and
was duly qualified.

416

Ordered that the court adjourn untill court in course and
signed by   Jno Blasingame
                 Thos Brandon

At a county court begun and holden in and for the county of
Union on Monday the first day of June 1795 Present
                 John Blasingame
                 Tho. Brandon

John Henderson Esquire being commissioned from the Governor
as sheriff of this county, came into open court and took the
oaths of office prescribed by Law.

On motion of John Henderson, Henry Farnandis was qualified
as Deputy sheriff accordingly.

Ordered that the following persons serve next court as Grand
Jurors, and that the sheriff summon the same fiz.

Capt. John Murrell	1	James Woodson Jur.	11
Moses Guiton	2	Wm Morgan	12
Daniel McBride	3	Tho. Draper Jur.	13
Nich. Corry	4	Wm Lawson	14
Abm. Petty	5	John Cole	15
Wm Tate	6	Ben Hawkins	16
Elisha Hayoon	7	Robt. Harris	17
Joshua Petty	8	Reuben Landrum	18
Richd. Powell	9	Mark Murphy	19
Turner Rountree	10	Abel Kendrick	20

Also the following persons to serve as P. J.

Wm D. Lane	1	Joshua Sisson	6
Geo. Little	2	Absalom Wood	7
Wm Clark	3	Daniel Noghor	8
Robert Lusk	4	Joseph Huey	9
Reuben Wilks	5	Tho. Lee	10
Marshall Chandler	11	Peter Laurencee	21
John Gibson	12	Richd. Huckoby	22
Epm Wilbourn	13	Augustus Wood	23
Mark Jackson	14	Tho. Hollingsworth	24
Benj. Nix	15	Wm Wilbanks senr.	25
Freeman Roberts	16	Jonathan Peak	26
Jonathan Whitsoh	17	John Foster	27
David Smith	18	Benj. Cooper	28
Tho. Wright Tyger	19	Joseph Covenhover	29
John Hill	20	Daniel Langstone	30

William Shaw Esquire County attorney came into open court and
resigned his appointment as such.

The following persons was qualified as Grand Jurors for this
court. Stephen Layton, Nathan Langstone, John Gregory, Wm
Sims John Jefferies, Nichs. Jasper, Robert Burns, Wm. Bowman,
Turner Kendrick, Jos. Coleman, Epm. Fowler, Willis Fowler,
Richd. Hughs and Wm Steen Junr.

On the resignation of Wm Shaw Esquire county attorney. Abraham
Nott Esquire was nominated and appointed in his room who
took the oath required by law.

Graaff Edson & Co)   P & S
  Vs   )   The defendant confessed a Judgment accg.
David Liles   )   to specialty with costs of suit, on stay
                    execution three months.

On the application of Charles Brock letters of administration
is granted him on the Estate of Elias Brock deceased, who
gave bond accd. security accg to Law and took the oath accg.
by law.

Olive Cook and Ann Cook orphans of Isaac Cook came into open
court and made choice of John Cook their guardian, the said
John Cook entered into Bond & security accg. to Law.

Danl. Jackson)   Atta.
  Vs   )   Dismd. at Plts. costs.
Wm Gist   )

Wm Thomas and Reuben Wilks being appt. executors of the last
will and testament of James Thomas deceased, came into open
court and took the oath required by law.

Ordered that Wm Johnson Christ. Johnson, John Murrell &
Wm Sims or any three of them appraise the Estate of the said
deceased.

Thomas Farrow   )   Debt
  Vs   )   Judgment confessed accg to specialty
John Martindale & at)   with costs of suit. stay ex. 1 due next

Wm Farrow   )   Debt
  Vs   )   Judgment confessed for twenty pounds
John Martindale & al)   13/8 with costs of suit, stay ex. 1
                        due next

William Chisholm)   Debt
  Vs   )   Dismissed at defendants costs
Wm Giles   )

Ordered that Wm Brummett, Joshua Martin, Richard Farr, Peter
Sartor and Wm Glenn be and are hereby appointed to view and
mark out a way for a road from Union Court House the nearest
and most convenient way to David Sims Ferry on Tyger and make
their report, to our next intermediate court.

Aaron Hart)   TAB
  Vs   )   Dismissed at Defts. cost
Mill Sumner)

Gordon   )   Attacht.
  Vs   )   Dismissed at Plt. cost.
Jos. Howell)

On motion of Adam Potter Wm Darsfield qualified as constable
for this county.

Edson & Co.)   P & S
  Vs   )   Dismissed at mutual costs by consent of
John Campbell)   parties.

418

Graff Edson & Co.) Case
Vs) Dismissed at mutual costs by consent.
John Campbell)

Ordered that Joshua Palmore, Geo. Bailey, Edward Tilman &
Wm. Sharp view and mark out away for a road from with of
John Reeds Mills the nearest & best way to Pinckney court
House.

Ezekiel Gilham) Debt
Vs) Judgment confessed accg to specialty with
Wm Johnson) interest and costs of suit on stay of exors
& six months.

Alex. Bookter) P & S
Vs) Judgment confessed accg to specialty with
Wm Brummett) interest & cost of suit on stay of execution
six months.

On the application of John Cook letters of administration is
granted to him on the Estate of John Christian Creese, who
gave bond and security accg to Law and was duly qualified.

Ordered that Ralph Hunt, Seth Wilson and James Townsend
appraise the Estate of John Christian, Crews, deceased and
make their return thereof according to Law.

On motion of Seth Wilson Letters of administration is granted
him on the Estate of Rachel Thockpenny deceased who gave
bond & security accg to Law and took the oath prescribed by
Law.

Ordered that John Clark John Cook & James Townsend appraise
the Estate of the said Rachel Penny decd. and make the return
thereof accg to Law.

Ordered that Josias Woods be overseer of the road as marked
out by comrs. from David Sims Ferry four miles from the same
toward Union Court House and Ned Moor from there to where it
interesects the main road leading to said court House.

Ordered Fielding Curtis be overseer of the road from Mitchels
Creek to Dining Creek in the room of Wm Pamer and that he
keep the same in good repair accg. to Law.

The court then adjourned untill tomorrow 10 oclock.
signed by Thos. Brandon
Jno Blasingame

The court met accg to adjournment on Tuesday the 2d. June 1795
Present John Blasingame
Tho. Brandon

On the application of Margaret Wadkins letters of administration is granted her on the Estate and Heck of Geo. Wadkins
deceased, she having entered into bond & security according
to Law & took the necessary oath accordingly.

Ordered that Nathl. Davis, Goven Gordon and James Townsend
be and hereby appointed to appraise the Estate and effects
of the above deceased Geo Wadkins and that they make due
return thereof accordingly.

Joseph Hart)   T.A.B.
Vs   )   Ordered that this case be dismissed at defts
Wm Springer)   cost.

On motion of Abraham Nott Esquire, ordered that all Recognizances returnable to this court, stand continued untill next
January Court.

Graaff Edson & Co.)   Debt
Vs   )   The defendant came into open court and
Henry Long   )   confessed a Judgment according to
                       specialty, with costs of suit stay of
Exor. 1 Sept. next.

Ordered that the county treasury pay Mr. Fredrick Eisen
Thirteen shillings & 5d/ for repairs to the Goal & his Bill
filed with the Clerk.

Graaff Edson & Co)   Debt
Vs   )   Judgment confessed according to specialty
John McDonnell)   with costs of suit allowing all Just.
                     credits with stay of execution untill
1st November next.

John Fincher   Pltf)   Slander
Vs   )   The Plaintiff came by Mr. Dunlap his
Robert Merrick   )   attorney and the defendant by Abraham
                    Nott Esquire, whereupon came a Jury towit
James Townsend foreman Robert White, Andrew Thompson, John
Scisson, Reuben Belue, Elisha Bond, John Ruttledge, Wm. White,
John Coleman, Hugh Donaldson, Henry Burrow and Thomas Lamb
who being duly sworn according to Law, return their verdict
and say we find for the defendant.   James Townsend foreman
Which verdict was ratifyed by the court and ordered to be
recorded.

Graaff Edson & Co)   Debt
Vs   )   Judgment confessed accg to specialty
Wm Hammond   )   with costs of suit with stay execution
Job Hammond   )   untill the 1st December.

John Steen Junr.)   P & S
Vs   )   Ordered that Wm Kennedy and Majr. Guiton
Drewry Herrington)   be and are hereby appointed as arbitra-
                    tors to settle the above controversy,
with power of chose an umpier and their award returnable to
next court shall be the Judgment thereof.

Ordered that Licences be granted to John Speers and Robert
Miller to keep public House & retail spirituous liquors
each having given bond and security according to Law.

Robert G. Harper)   P & S
Vs   )   Decree confessed accg. to note with
Samuel Jackson)   Interest & costs of suit.

Whereas it appears that the sum of nine pounds two shillings
and eight pence has been collected on an execution that issued
from this court in favour of Lenard Smith against James
Gastin and paid into court and it appearing that John Steel
is entitled to receive the same by an assignment of said
Judgment to him by said Smith, therefore, ordered it is

the said money be paid to said steel.
Ordered that the court adjourn untill tomorrow 10 oclock
                                    Jno Blasingame
                                    Thos. Brandon

The court met according to adjournment on Wednesday the 3d.
June 1795 Present   John Blasingame
                        Tho. Brandon
Isaac Parker was qualified as constable for this county.

On the application of Margaret Watkins admr. Geo. Wadkins
deceased, ordered that he expose to sale all the personal
estate of said deceased, after an appraisement of the same
is returned, she giving the usual notice of such sale on a
credit of six months.

On the application of Warran Hall leave is given him to retail
spirituous liquors and keep public house he given bond &
sec. accg to Law.

James Hogans   ) Case
   Vs   ) The defendant being solemnly called &
Henry Miller &) failed to appear on motion therefore, of
Josias Wood   ) Mr. Dunlap, Judgment is entered against
                  them by default.

Graaff Edson & Co) P & S
   Vs   ) The defendant came into open court and
John McCaffarty   ) confessed a Judgment accg to specialty
                    with interest and costs of suit; with
stay of exors untill 15 Nov. 1795.

Gabriel Phillips   Pltf.) Slander
   Vs   ) Came the plaintiff by Mr. Dunlap
Thomas Minton   Deft.) his attorney and the defendant by
                          Abm Nott whereupon came a Jury
towit. James Townsend foreman, Robert White, Andrew Thompson,
John Sisson Reuben Belue Elisha Bond, John Ruttledge, Wm.
White, John Coleman Hugh Donaldson Henry Burrow and James
Parnell who being duly sworn according to Law. Return their
verdict and say we find for the defendant
                        James Townsend Foreman

John Fincher   Pltf.) Slander
   Vs   ) Mr. Dunlap moved the court for a new
Robt. Merrick   Deft.) Tryal in this case on the following
                       grounds; 1st that the facts in the
allegation of the plaintiff were fully proved as well as the
slanderous words, and that the verdict is contrary to law
and evidence, 2nd, that he had not an opportunity of getting
witnesses forward to court at the present session, who would
clearly and substantially prove Zack which are materially
pertinent to his case, and that at the formen Tryal he had
not in his power to adduce them. The court took the above
grounds into consideration and were of opinion the same are
good, Its ordered thereofre that the plaintiff be entitled
to a new tryal on his paying the costs of the above suit.

Gordon & Co   ) Debt
   Vs   ) Judgment confessed according to specialty
Thomas Bishop &) with interest and costs of suit on stay of
Thomas Brandon   ) Exor. three months.

421

George Hood   ) Debt
  Vs   ) Judgment confessed by the defendant, according
Wm McCullock) to specialty, with costs of suit, subject to
                 a credit of thirty one dollars on stay of
execution six months.

Alexander Macbeth & Co) Debt
  Vs   ) Judgment confessed according to
Barbar Millard and   ) specialty with interest and costs of
John Willard   ) suit with stay of sale untill the
                         1st November next.

John Taylor   ) On attachment
  Vs   ) By consent of the parties this attachment
Robert Merrick)   is refered to John Martindale Esqr. and
                   James Townsend Walter Roberts and their
award returnable to this court shall be the Judgment thereof.

James D. Puckett) P & S
  Vs   )   Dismissed by consent of Plaintiff at his
John Murrell   )   costs.

James D. Puckett) Attachment
  Vs   )   The plaintiff came into open court and
Thomas Hooper)   proved his acct. against the defendant
                   ordered that decree be entered for the
plaintiff for the sum of four pounds 18/3 with costs of suit.
Ordered thereupon that the property attached be exposed to
sale accg to law to satisfy the above debt & costs.

Graaff Edson & Co) P & S
  Vs   )   Decree for the plaintiff according to
Andrew McBrock)   specialty with costs of suit.

The exors. Daniel Thomas) Case
  Vs   )   Dismissed at the Plaintiff cost.
James Hogans   )

Samuel Bell) Case
  Vs   ) Ordered that this case be contd. untill next
John Popham) court at defendant cost.

Graaff Edson) P & S
  Vs   ) The defendant confessed a Judgment accg to
John White) specialty with costs of suit stay exor 1 Sept.
               next.

Graaff Edson & Co) P & S
  Vs   )   The defendant confessed a decree accg to
Nichs. Lazerus)   specialty with interest and costs of suit.

Charles Sims) Trover
  Vs   ) Dismissed at Plf cost
Wm Gist   )

Peter Varnier vs Peter Ellis) Nonsuit

Peter Varnier Vs Bart Whorton) Nonsuit

Bird Beuford Vs Nolles Biddie) Dismissed at Pltfs costs.

422

Ordered that all estrays lyable to be sold this court are
ordered to bring them forward tomorrow before court adjourns.

Zack. Hays)   Trover
  Vs   )   Dismissed at Plf cost
Wm Newman)

Graaff Edson & Co)   Case
  Vs   )   Came the plaintiff by Abr. Nott and the
John Willard   )   defendant not appearing whereupon came a
                     Jury the same as Phillips vs Minton, being
duly sworn say on the oaths, we find for the pltff twelve
pounds 14 4/2 and costs of suit.   J Townsend foreman

Ordered that the County treasury pay Thomas Stribling Esquire
former sheriff twenty one pounds 18/S deducting all just
credits due the county by said Stribling as p/ his Bill filed

Ordered that the court adjourn untill tomorrow 10 oclock
Signed by   Jno Blasingame
                 Thos Brandon

The Court met according to adjournment on Thursday the 4d.
day of June 1795 Presnet   John Blasingame
                      Thomas Brandon

William Chisholm   Plaintiff)   Debt
  Vs   )   Came the Pltff by Abraham
William Giles   Defendant)   Nott Esquire his attorney and
                      the defendant by John Dunlap.
Whereupon came a Jury the same as Graaff Edson & Co. Vs John
Wilalrd who being duly sworn return their verdict and say on
their several oaths we find for the defendant.
                 James Townsend foreman

Which verdict being ratifyed by the court and a deed to be
recorded.

Jesse Dodd)   By consent of the parties ordered that this
  Vs   )   case be referred unto. Richd. Burgess, Samuel
John Fincher)   Simpson and William Pearson and their award
           returnable to next court shall be the Judgment
thereof.

Nicholas Lazerus)   P A B
  Vs   )   By consent of the parties, ordered that
Tho. Draper Junr.)   this case be referred to Col Brandon and
              Wm Kennedy with power of chosing an
umpire and their award returnable to this court shall be
the Judgment hereof

Graaff Edson & Co)   P & S
  Vs   )   John Nuckols proved three days attendance
A. McBride   )   in this suit.

Graaff Edson & Co)   Debt
  Vs   )   John Nuckols proved three days attendance
John Willard   )   in this suit.

William Nelson   )   Trover
  Vs   )   Came the plaintiff by Abr. Nott attorney
Thomas Biddie Jnr.)   and the defendant by William Smith Esqr.

his attorney whereupon came a Jury towit the same as Chisholm
vs Gils who being duly sworn Return their verdict on their
several oaths and say we find for the plaintiff ten pounds
ten shillings withcost of suit.   James Townsend foreman

Which verdict was ratified by the court and ordered to be
recorded.
Mr. William Smith prayed an appeal

Elizabeth Wilson) P & S
 Vs   ) The Plaintiff claimed a tryal by Jury which
Enoch Floyd   ) is granted at his costs.

Ordered that the court adjourn untill tomorrow 9 oclock
                    Jno Blasingame
                    Thos Brandon

The court met according to adjournment on Fryday the 5th day
of June 1795 Present   John Blasingame
                    Thos Brandon

Elizabeth Wilson Plaintiff) P & S
 Vs   ) Trover Came the plaintiff by
Enoch Floyd   Defendant) Samuel Farrow her attorney and
                    the defendant by Abraham Nott
Esquire whereupon came a Jury Towit James Townsend Foreman
Robert White Andrew Thompson John Sisson Elisha Bond, John
Ruttledge William White Hugh Donaldson Henry Burrow, James
Parnell James Woodson and Joshua Palmore who being duly sworn
say on their oaths we find for the defendant.
                    James Townsend foreman

James Mathews) Case
 Vs   ) In obedience of an order of court we the
Thomas Hays) arbitrators have examined the evidences of
               both parties and after a full investigation
of the matter we find for the plaintiff one pound one
shilling and nine pence & costs of suit given under our hands
this 12d. day of July 1794.   Thos. Brandon
                    Anderson Thomas
                    Elisha Nunn

John Taylor   ) Attachment
 Vs   ) We the arbitrators appointed by order of
Robert Merrick) Court to arbitrate a matter of controversy
                 between John Taylor and Enoch Floyd attorney
for Robert Merrick on an attachment after a full investigation
of the matter and duly considering the same we do adjudge
and award that the said John Taylor shall have credit for the
sum of twelve pounds sterling on a Judgment that the said
Merrick obtained against the said Taylor last April court at
Pinckney and that the said attachment be dismissed at the
Plaintiff cost given under our hands this 3d. day of June
1795   Jno Martindale
               Walter Roberts
               James Townsend.

Graaff & Edson & Co) P & S
 Vs   ) Dismissed at the costs being paid
Robert Miller)

424

William Davitt   ) P & S
Vs   ) Decree for the plaintiff for 1000 lb
Spencer Brummett) tobacco at ten shillings p. cent with
Daniel Brummett   ) int. and costs of suit.

Graaff Edson & Co) Debt
Vs   ) Came the plaintiff by Abr. Nott and the
Jehue McPhearson) defendant not appearing whereupon came a
                    Jury towit James Townsend foreman Robert
White, Andrew Thompson, John Sisson Elisha Bond, John Ruttled
Wm White, Hugh Donalson, Henry Barrow James Parnell Reuben
Belue, Joshua Palmore who being duly sworn say on their oaths
we find for the plaintiff according to specialty with cost of
suit.   James Townsend foreman

Alex. Bookter   ) Debt
Vs   ) Judgment confessed by Mr. Dunlap the
Daniel Brummett) defendants attorney, according to specialty
                   on stay of execution untill the 1st. November
                   next.

Nathaniel Davis) Debt
Vs   ) Judgment confessed according to specialty
John McCooll   ) with interest and costs of suit on stay of
                  execution three months.

The State   ) Larcency
Vs   ) The prosecutor being not bound over the
Nich Lazerus) defendant therefore is discharged from his
               recogn.

Joseph Gibson) On an appeal
Vs   ) The court taking this case into consideration
Joseph Gill) are of opinion that the proceedings of the
               Justice is illegal ordered that the Judgment
of the Justice be reversed.

Capt. Lewis Hogg) Debt
Vs   ) Ordered that a Commissnor De. Bene-esse,
Wm Brummett   ) do issue to take the examination of for
                 George Loving and his examination so taken
shall be admitted as evidence in the above case.
    The examination to be taken before Wm Kennedy & Nathaniel
Davis Esquire.

Graaff Edson & Co) Seifa
Vs   ) Ordered on motion of Abraham, that the
Daniel Jackson) Rule be made absolute

Jesse Dodd   ) On an appeal
Vs   ) Ordered that this case be referred back to
Robt. G. Harper) the Justice for another consideration.

Alexd. Macbeth & Co.) P & S
Vs   ) The note being proved by William
John Willard &) Cunningham decree for the Pltf. accg
Barbary Willard) to specialty with interst.and costs
                 of suit.

Elizabeth Wilson) P & S On motion for a new tryal by the Plf
Vs   ) attorney and after hearing the objections
Enoch Floyd   ) of the defendants attorney, Ordered that

no new tryal be granted.

Jesse Dodd	)	Appeal
Vs	)	On consideration of the case its ordered
Robert G. Harper)		that the Judgment of the Justice in the
		case aforesaid be confirmed with costs of
		suit.

John Moorehead	)	On an appeal
Vs	)	Mr. Wm Smith attorney for Moorehead gave
Drewry Herrington)		notice that he entended to move the
		Judges of the superior court for a

Mandamus unless they shew cause to the contrary.

William Chisholm)		Debt
Vs	)	On motion of Abraham Nott Esquire Ptf.
William Giles	)	Atty. for a new tryal in this case and
		after hearing the objection of the opposite

party by his attorney Mr. Dunlap. The court was divided in
their opinions.

The court then adjourned untill court in course and signed by
Jno Blasingame
Thos Brandon

At an Intermediate court begun and holden in and for the
county of Union on the first Monday in September otherwise
7th day 1795   Present   John Blasingame
Thomas Brandon   Judges

On motion
Ordered that the administrators of John Sartor deceased have
leave to expose to public sale all the personal Estate and
effects of the said deceased on giving the usual notice of
such sale at the plantation of said decd. allowing a credit
of six months for all sums above twenty shillings then under
cash. The purchasers giving bond & security to Law

On motion of William Sartor, we do hereby nominate & appoint
him the said William Sartor Guardian.

Guardian to George Washington Sartor; a minor of about eight
years of age; son of John Sartor & deceased during the time
that he is incapable of chosing & guardian himself.

Proved in open court by the oath of John Ennis a Deed of
conveyance from Nathl. Alexander to Landlot Porter; & ordered
to be recorded.

Ordered that Margaret Wadkins admr. of George Wadkins deceased
expose to public sale all the personal estate & effects of
said deceased on giving a credit of nine months for all sums
above twenty shillings those under to be paid in cash, on
giving the usual notice of such sale at the plantation of said
deceased.

Presented in open court the last will and testament of Thomas
Layton deceased, which was duly proved by the oath of John
Goodwin one of the subscribing witnesses, which is ordered
to be recorded.

426

Humphrey Bates being appointed executor to the above will came into open court and took the necessary oath prescribed by law.

Acknowledged in open court a Deed of conveyance from Jonas Little & his wife Rebecca Little to John Springer & ordered to be recorded the said Rebecca Little was also privately examined & relinquished her Dower to the said land.

On the application of Richard Cox. Its ordered that his mark of his stock be inserted on the records which are as follows, a swallow fork in the right ear a half cross out of the upper side of the left ear & under keel in the same ear.

On motion ordered that John Haile Arthur Cunningham & Nicholas Harris, be and are hereby appointed to view the way for a road from Harris place paths to Major Edson plantation, and make their report to the overseer of the road leading to Spartanburgh if any better way than the present road can be marked out who is hereby required to clear out the same immediately as they mark.

On motion of John Haile, ordered that Danl. White be appointed overseer of the road in his room from the forks of the road leading by Gikhold field to Pinckneyville as far as Ellis Fowlers, and that he keep the same in good repair according to Law.

On the application of Mary Taylor widow of John Taylor deceased, letters of administration is granted her on said estate, who entered into bond & security accordingly & took the oath prescribed by Law.

Ordered on motion of Mary Taylor admr. Jno Taylor decd. & Wm Marshal, Walter Potter & Solomon Whiter that John Addington or any three of them be & are hereby appointed to appraise to the Estate & effects of John Taylor deceased and make their return thereof accg. to Law being first qualifyed by John Martindale Esquire.

Proved in open court by the oath of Jacob Paulk a Deed from Abr. Nott for Danl. Heifer to John Springer & ordered to be recorded.

On a petition presented to court for a road from Pinckney-ville to Samuel Sprays hedges after taking the same into consideration find that the prayer thereof ought to be granted, we do hereby order, that Joseph Hughs; William Sharp.

___ & John Savage are hereby appointed to view and mark out a way for a road from Pinckneyville to the Quaker meeting House on Cain Creek the most nearest & best way, and make their report ot our nearest court.
Also ordered that Samuel Otterson Thomas McDonald and William Rogers John Campbell be and are hereby appointed to view and mark out the way for a road beignning at the quaker meeting house to Saml. Sprays hedge on Tyger and from said Bridge to Kennedys Ford is Hendricks Mill on Enoree River also to mark out a way for a road out of the ninety six road to said Bridge, and make their report to our next court.

Acknowledged in open court a Deed of conveyance from Cush. R
Edson to Abraham Nott Esquire and ordered to be recorded.

Ordered that the court stand adjourned untill tomorrow 10
oclock   Signed by   Jno Blasingame
                          Thos Brandon

The court met according to adjournment at the court house of
said county on Tuesday the eighth day of September 1795
Present   John Blasingame
                Tho Brandon

John Gibbs & Reuben Sanders came into open court & took the
oath of office as constables
Robert Woodson was qualified as constable for this county

Proved in open court a Relinquishment from Elizabeth Wells &
Lewis Mills to Humphrey Bates by the oath of Col Brandon &
John McNeail & ordered to be recorded.

Proved in open court by the oath of Robert Woods on a Deed
from John Goodwin & wife to Sampson Goodwin & ordered to be
recorded.

Ordered on motion of John Cook admr. of John Cristian Crews
decdl that he expose to sale all the personal Estate of the
said deceased on giving the usual notice of such sale on a
credit of six months.

On motion of David Leeck for Tavern Lice. which was granted &
he gave bond & security according to law.

Presented in open court the last will and testament of Magnus
Simonson deceased, which was duly proved by the oath of John
Austin & Bird Booker & ordered to record.
Magnus Simonson & Richard Cox being appd. executors to the
said Will came into open court & took the oath prescribed by
law.

Ordered on motion of Magnus Simonson Arthur Thomas & Richard
Cox Exors of the last will & testament of Magnus Simonson
decd. that Adam Skane, William Sartor & Jehue Wilson & Jno
Peter Sartor or any three of them appraise the estate of the
said deceased, and make their return according to Law & that
Charister Johnson Esqr. qualify the said appraisers

On motion of Jesse Connell Exor. of James Gibbs deceased
ordered that he expose to public sale at the plantation of
said deceased, all the personal Estate and effects of said
deceased, or as much thereof as may satisfy all debts due by
the Estate on the following terms or credits for all sums
under five pounds, a credit to be given of three months & all
above five pounds, one third to be paid in three months & the
balance in six months from the day of sale, with approved
security, the executors giving the usual notice of such sale.

Proved in open court, A Bill of Sale from Polly Jones to Patty
& Sary Jones & ordered to be recorded.

Whereas it appears that the personal property belonging to the
Estate of Col William Farr decased has not been sold in such
a manner as to do Justice to the creditors and heirs of said

428

Estate, and it being represented to us that the terms of the
sale have not been complied with it is therefore ordered that
the whole personal Estate be exposed to sale by the executors
on the third Monday of October next to satisfy the demands
against the Estate and also that the said executors have time
untill next January court, to render to the court on account
of the receipts & expenditures of said estate as the law
requires.

Ordered that Barnet Lights an orphan of Barnet Lights decd.
be bound unto Turner Kendrick untill he arrives the age of 21
to learn the art & mastery of a Sadler the said Barnet
Lights being present & consented to the same, and the said
Kendrick shall on his part allow the said appentice during
the said term six months schooling and at the end of his
servitude shall allow him two suits of common good cloaths

Ordered that William Bolding be overseer of the road from
Union Court House to James Bogans Creek and that he keep the
same in good repair accg to Law.

Ordered that Richard Fossett be overseer of the road from
Bogans Creek to Major J. Hughs and that he keep the same in
good repair accg. to law.

Ordered that Thomas Hughs be overseer of the road from Major
Hughs to Lovesford on Road river and that he keep the same
in good repair according to Law.

Ordered that Margaret Wadkins admr. of the estate of George
Wadkins decd. expose to sale all the personal property of
said deceased on a credit of six months, she giving the usual
notice of such sale at the plantation of said deceased.

Upon application of the executors of the last will & testament
of Col William Farr deceased & representing to this court, that
property belonging to the said Estate of which they did not
know at the time of the former appraisement has come to
their knowledge, Ordered that William Glenn be appointed in
the room of John Sartor deceased, to assist the other
appraisers in appraising that part of the Estate.

Ordered that the Executors of the last will and Testament of
John Ewart deceased be summoned to personally be and appear
at our next court to be holden on the first day of January
next, to under an account of their proceedings on said Estate
according to law.

Whereas Danl. Palmore is bound in a bond as security to Sarah
Darby admr. of the estate & effects of William Darby decd. for
the faithful discharge of her administration. The said
Parmer Petitioned the court to be relieved from his said
bond. Its therefore ordered that he be exorinated and cleared
from his said security ship from this date.

The said Sarah Darby Admr. as aforesaid brought into court
Capt. John Murrell who entered himself as her security in the
room of said Parmer

Ordered that Wm Kennedy pay Benjr. Haile seven pounds 11/10d
being the amt. of his bill render in this day proven in open
court.

429

Ordered that the clerk issue summones to all these persons
who was noted in as commissioners of the poor at our last
election, which the sheriff is ordered to summoned to appear
before the Judges of this court on the last saturday in this
month at Union Court house.

Ordered the clerk issue out orders to the sheriff to notify
the Executors of the estate of Col William Farr deceased,
John Murrell the executors of John Birdsey deceased, Thomas
Stribling Junr. late sheriff & William Kennedy treasurer of
this County to appear at Union Court House on the last
Saturday of this month, in order to come to a settlement with
those before mentioned persons and the county.

Then the court adjourned untill tomorrow 12 oclock.
                                        Jno Blasingame
                                        Thos. Brandon

The court met according to adjournment on Wednesday the 9
September 1795 Present   Tho. Brandon Judge

Presented in open court an acct. of Nancy Conyers against the
Estate John Nuckels decd. for ₤151.13.11¼ which was sowrn to
& ordered to be recorded.

The court then adjourned untill court in course   Thos Brandon

At a Call Court on Thursday the 14 Oct. 1795
            Present Tho. Brandon

Presented in open court the last will and testament of
Benjamin Holcomb deceased which was proven in open court by
the oath of Elijah H Copen & ordered to be recorded
Nevil Holcomb being appointed executor in the said will was
duly qualified according to Law.
                        Ordered that Robert White
Joseph Little Elijah H. Copen and John Bailey is any three of
them appraise the estate and effects of Benjamin Holcomb
deceased and return the same accg to law and that a Terrance
qualify the said appraisers
                        Signed by Thos. Brandon
                                   State of South Carolina

At a county court begun and holden in and for the county of
Union at the court house of said county on Fryday the first
day of January in the year of our Lord one thousand seven
hundred and ninety six and of the independance of the United
States of America the twentyeth.
                        Present His Honor Tho. Brandon Judge

On a petition of a number of inhabitants on Enoree, Ordered
that William Wood have leave to erect a toll Bridge across
Enoree river below the ninety six road intersect the said
river.

John Hugh minor of Wm Hughs decd. come into open court & made
choice of Benjamin Woodson Esquire his guardian who gave bond
& security accg in the sum of one hundred pounds.

On the application of John Moore ordered that Letters of
administration be granted him on the estate of Edward Moore
deceased, who took the oath & gave bond & security accg. in

the sum of one hundred pounds sterling.

Ordered that Andrew Terrence Esqr. admr. of H. Howard
decd. expose to sale all the personal estate and effects of
said decd, for ready cash on the 3d. Monday in this month.

Ordered that John P. Sartor Henry Stevens & John Massay
appraise the Estate & effects of Edward Moore decd. and make
due return thereof accg to Law. Bat first duly sworn by Wm
Hogans Esqr. or Nath. Davis Esqr.

Thomas Vance came into open court and took the oath as Justice
of the peace of this county.

On the application of Hugh McBride & Andrew Thompson, ordered
that they have leave to take out letters of adminstration on
the Estate and Hecks of Andrew McBride decd. who took the oath
required by law & gave bond in the sum of five hundred pounds
with Wm Kennedy & Robert Harris secury.

Ordered that Robert Harris, Arthur Cunningham, Richard
Thompson and James Parks be and are hereby appointed to
appraise the Estate and effects of Andrew McBride decd. and
that they make due return accg to law being first duly sworn
by H. Means Esquire.

Ordered that the Executors of Magnus Simonson deceased expose
to sale all the personal Estate and effects of said deceased,
on giving a credit of nine months and the usual notice of such
sale.

On motion of Joshua Sisson, ordered that letters of administration be granted him on the Estate and effects of Willism
Sisson deceased who gave bond & security accg to law & took
the oath accordingly.

Ordered that Wm McCullock, Nathl. Dabbs & John Cole appraise
the Estate & effects of Wm Sisson deceased, and make due
return thereof accg to Law--being first sworn by Doct. White
or Nick, Corry Ordered that the court adjourn untill
tomorrow 10 oclock & signed by   Thos Brandon

The court met according to adjournment on Saturday the second
day of January one thousand seven hundred and Ninety six
Present their Honors   John Blasingame
                              Thomas Brandon   Esquires

The court proceeded to draw the grand Jury to serve at our
next June court, who are as follows, which are ordered to be
duly summoned by the sheriff Viz

James Petty Junr	1	Wm Sartor	11
Adam Seave	2	John Goodwin	12
Wm Whiteson John	3	John Beckham Jur	13
Isaac Parker	4	John Sanders	14
Geo. Harlan Hatter	5	Joseph Hollingsworth	15
Wm Hughs	6	Jeremiah Lucas	16
James Veail	7	Obd. Howard	17
Robert Millhouse	8	George Newton	18
John Moorehead	9	Hancock Porter	19
Nathan Glenn	10	Thomas Parmer	20

Also the following as Petty Jurors

John Jenkins	1	Ephraim Smith	16
Edward Brown	2	Randal Alexander	17
John Hamm	3	John Cook	18
Wm Gossett	4	Jesse Potts	19
George Bailey	5	Henry Thickpenny	20
John Patrick	6	William Cotter	21
Richard Wales	7	Wm Bennet	22
Zadock Roberts	8	Allen Davis	23
Mahu Liles	9	Thomas Parmer Jur	24
James Mayberry	10	Wm Jackson	25
Henry Stevens	11	Joshua Palmer	26
Isham Prince	12	Drewry Herrington	27
Sion Murphey	13	Aaron Hart	26
John White son John	14	John Eisen	29
Jas. Dekerson	15	Wm Pearson	30

Lewis Sanders qualifyed in open court as constable for this
county under John J Hines Esquire

State   ) Bastardy
Vs   ) On motion of the county attorney ordered
Levena Rachlay &) that the recognizances stand contd. untill
Saml. Fowler   ) next court.

James A. Whyte) P & S
Vs   ) The defendant confessed Judgment accg. to
Wm Pratt   ) note with costs of suit.

Hancock Porter) John Bogan buy Bail for the defendant came
Vs   ) into open court and good stand him ap.
John Howell   ) ordered that he be released from his said
              Bail and that the sheriff take atty, into
custody untill he give special bail.

Alexd. Bookter   ) Judgment confessed in open court by
Vs   ) John Jenkins according to note
John & Randolph Jenkins) with costs of suit.

The following persons qualifyed as Grand Jurors for this court
Viz.
Nicholas Corry Esqr. foreman   John Cole
John Murrell   Ben Hawkins
William Tate   Robert Harris
Elisha Heador   Mark Murphey
Richd. Powell   Abel Kendrick
James Woodson Jur.
Thos. Draper

The State   ) Indict Prosecutor Elizabeth Huey Riot witness
Vs   )   Tho. Enlow
Hollis Biddie)   Sworn &
                   Bill given to the Grand Jury
Shad. Lewallen
Jesse Jenkins

Graaff Edson & Co) Debt
Vs   ) Judgment confessed accg to note with
Nathl. Jefferies) interest and costs of suit on stay of
                  execution untill the first day of June
                  next.

The State   ) Indict
Vs   )   Hog stealing   Zachariah Belue Wm Morgan
Shadrack Johnson) & Reuben Belue, sworn as witnesses & bill
                  delivered to the grand Jury.

Ordered that all Estrays lyable to be sold this court shall be
sold on Tuesday next.

The State   ) Indict
Vs   )   Riot.
Hollis Biddie) Joseph sec. being security for the defendant
Shad. Lewallen) appear as at this court who delivered them
                up ordered that he be discharged from his
recognizance. Shadrack Lewallen with Wm Glenn his security
acknowledged themselves indebted to the State in the sum of
twenty pounds for him at the said Hollis Bidie personal
appearance at the court now sitting.

Graaff Edson & Co) Debt
Vs   )   James Tish & Joseph Reeder being Bail
Thomas McCaffarty) for the defendant appearance came into
                    open court and delivered said defendant
up. Ordered that the said securities be exonerated from their
said Bond. And that the sheriff take said defendant into
custody untill he give special bail.

John Bogan and James Turk came into open court and acknowledged
themselves special bail for the defendant in the above case.

Ordered that John Clark John Stokes & Henry Thickpenny be
and are hereby appointed commrs. to view and mark out a way
for a road from Union Court House to Fairforest between Rices
& Sanders from thence to Tyger River to Mich Lees Ford from
thence to Enoree to the nearest and best way & make their
report to our next intermediate court.

Ordered that Daniel Blair be overseer of the road from the
Spartanburgh line to Blackstocks ford on Tyger River, in the
room of Bennet Langstone who has moved off and that he keep
the same in good repair according to Law.

The State   ) Indict.
Vs   )   P. Larceny
Jasper Tommerlin) The Grand Jury returned true Bill

The State   ) Indict
Vs   )   Riot
Hollis Biddie   )   No Bill Nich by from G. J.
Shadrack Lewallen)
Jesse Jenkes   )

The State   ) Indict.
Vs   )   Hog stealing
Shad, Johnson)   True Bill   Nich. Curry foreman G.J.

Ordered that the court adjourn untill Monday 9 oclock

                        Thos. Brandon
                        Jno Blasingame

The Court met according to adjournment on Monday the Fourth
day of January 1796

433

Present their Honors   John Blasingame
                        Tho Brandon   Esquires

The State   ) Indict.
 Vs   )   Hog stealing
Shad. Johnson)   The State by Abraham Nott & attorney
             and the defendant appeared by John Dunlap
whereupon came a Jury to wit Robert Lusk foreman Wm Clark
Joshua Sisson, Joseph Huey, Mischack Chandler Ephraim Wilbourn
Benjamin Nix. Benjamin Nix, Jonathan Whitson, David Smith,
Peter Laurence, Augustan Wood & John Foster, who being
severally duly sworn in due form of Law after hearing the
Evidence as well as on the part of the state as on the part
of the prisoner return their verdict on their oaths & say we
find the defendant guilty.   Rob. Lusk foreman

The State   ) Indictment
 Vs   )   assault. Sarah Philips
Thomas Menton)   Joseph Cooper   Witnesses
  &   )   Richd. Burges   Sworn
Thomas Davis) True Bill N. Corry foreman

The State)
 Vs   )
Joseph Hart) Indictment
          Hog stealing   Robert Gregory) Witnesses
                      Barba Willard) sworn
                      Wm Steen Junr)
                      Jn Thomas   )
The grand Jury returned   True Bill
                            Nich. Corry foreman

Alexander Macbeth & Co) Debt
 Vs   ) Judgment confessed accg to note with
George Harlan   Hatter) Interest and cost of suit.

The State   ) Indictment
 Vs   ) Petit Larceny
Jasper Tormerlin) Came the State by Abm. Nott and the
                 defendant by John Dunlap whereupon came
a jury towit. Robert Justin foreman, Wm Clark Joshua Sisson
Joseph Huey Michack Chandler Ephraim Wilbourn Benj. Nix
Jonathan Whitter David Smith Peter Laurence Augustin Wood &
John Foster who being duly sworn return their verdict & say
not guilty   Robert Justin foreman

On the application of James A. Whyte Esquire Thomas Neighbours,
was qualified by constable for this county under him

Alexander Menifrow) Attachment
 Vs   ) Dismissed at Pltf. costs.
James D. Puckett)

The court adjourned untill tomorrow 9 Oclock & signed by
                        Thos Brandon
                        Jno Blasingame

The court met according to adjournment on Tuesday the 5th
January 1790 Present their Honors Tho. Brandon
                         Jno Blasingame   Esquires

Ordered that the sheriff Summon Thos. Greer; Hugh Means. Wm McCullock Charles Sims Goom Gordon & Robert Harris, personally to attend the court now sitting to shew cause why they do not qualify as commissioners of the poor for this county.

Elizabeth Cooper) On appeal
  Vs   )
Thomas Pearson) Ordered that the papers be returned back
                  to the Justice, who is hereby signed to
                  excuse the matter.

The State   ) Indict
  Vs   ) On motion of the defendants attorney
Joseph Shuttlesworth) ordered that he be discharged as no
                      prosecution appeared.

Jesse Dodd   ) Case
  Vs   ) The defendant not appearing ordered that he
John Fincher) be nonsuited

John Fincher) P & S
  Vs   ) Ordered that the Plaintiff be nonsuited he
Benj. Rush   ) not appearing.

Mr. W. Eaves was granted a tavern licence who give bond & security accg. to Law.

Samuel Bell Plf.) Case
  Vs   ) The plaintiff appeared by Abraham Nott
John Popham Deft.) and the defendant by John Dunlap
                     attorney whereupon came a Jury to wit
Robert Lusk foreman, Wm Clark, Joshua Sisson, Joseph Huey Michach Chandler Benjamin Nix, Jonathan Whitton David Smith Peter Laurence Augusta Wood John Foster & Mark Jackson who being duly sworn return their verdict & say we find for the Plaintiff one pound 17/14d.   Rob. Lusk   foreman

Ordered that James Parks be overseer of the Iron Works road from the county line to Jacksons and that he keep the same in good repair according to Law.

The State) Indict.
  Vs   ) Assl. & Battery
Jno Gamblin) A True Bill N. Corry foreman

Robert Lithgow assue) Debt
  Excert. Col Farr   ) Judgment confessed accg to note
  Vs   ) with cots of suit on stay of Exor
John McNeail   ) untill the 1 Apl. next.

Wm Hancock   ) Case
  Vs   ) Came the Plaintiff by Abr. Nott Esqr. and
Thomas Biddie) the defendant by B. H. Saxon whereupon came
                a Jury the same as Bill Vs Popham who being
duly sworn return their verdict & say we find for the plaintiff seven pounds 2/7 with interest from due with costs.
                    Robert Lusk   foreman

Warran Hall Plaintiff) P & S
  Versus   ) Decree for the plaintiff for sixteen
John Martin Defendant) Barrels corn at seven shillings &
                        six pence & barrel with interest

435

and cost of suit.

Ordered that the clerk issue an attach to a constable to summon Barba Willard to attend court on tomorrow morning to give evidence in behalf of the state against Joseph Hart.

Elizabeth Thomas & Catherine Thomas came into open court and make choice of James Tillit Thomas their guardian who is ordered to give Bond & security accg to Law.

Dennis Miller orphan of Nehemiah Norton came into open court and make choice of B Woodson Esq. his guardian who is ordered to give bond & security accg. to Law

The court then adjourned untill tomorrow 9 Oclock
                              Jno Blasingame
                              Thos Brandon

The court met according to adjournment on Wednesday the 6th dya of January 1796 Present their honors Thos Brandon Esqrs.
                              John Blasingame

Graaff Edson & Co.) Case
      Vs   ) Discontinued by the Plaintiff at his costs.
Thomas Bishop   )

On motion of John Henderson Sheriff Enoch Floyd was appointed Deputy sheriff under him who took the oaths of office presented by Law.

Geo. Walker   ) Debt
      Vs   ) The Plaintiff being without the limits of
Cush R. Edson) this state ordered that security be entered
                  for costs, whereupon came Capt. Wm Johnson
into open court and acknowledged himself security for costs
in case the Plaintiff fails in his action in the above case.

George Walker   Plaintiff) Debt
      Vs   ) Dame the plaintiff by Abraham
Cushm. R. Edson Defendant) Nott Esquire and the defendant
                             by Wm Smith whereupon came a
Jury to wit. Robert Lusk foreman Wm Clark Joshua Sisson,
Mechack Chandler Ephraim Wilbourn Benj. Nix Jonathan Whitton
David Smith Peter Laurence Augustin Wood Tho. Hollingsworth
and Mark Jackson who being duly drawn empanneled and sworn
return their verdict and say we find for the Plaintiff
eleven pounds 13/4d with costs   Robert Lusk foreman

Which verdict the court ordered to be recorded.

The State   ) Indict.
      Vs   ) Disfiguring a Hog The witnesses sworn &
Tho. V. Nance) bill that to Grand Jury who return No Bill
                              Nick Corry foreman

The State   ) Indictment
      Vs   )   Hog stealing No Bill
Tho. V. Nance)   Nick Corry foreman

The State   ) Indictment asst. & battery
      Vs   ) The same Jury as Walk Vs Edson who being
John Gamblin) duly sworn do say on their oaths do say

436

guilty of assault.   Rob. Lusk   foreman

Ordered that John Savage be overseer of the road from Bogans
place to the Green Pond on the new road lately marked out &
James Gregory be over of the Green Pond to the quaker meeting
house and John Smith from the quaker meeting house to Sprays
Bridge.
     And David Prescott from Sprays Bridge to Danl. Liphams
and that they keep the same in good repair accg. to Law.

Isaac Trammell came into open court and took the oath as
constable for this county under Tho. Vance Esquire.

The court then adjourned until tomorrow 9 Oclock
                              Jno Blasingame
                              Thos Brandon

The court met according to adjournment on Thursday the 7th
1796. Present their Honors   John Blasingame
                              Thomas Brandon   Esquires

Geo. Patterson   ) Case
  Vs   ) Judgment confessed for thirty pounds
The Exors Col Wm Farr) 13/9d with costs of suit subject to
                           debts of superior nature & the pled of
plene administravit

Doctor Robert Kendricks)   Judgment confessed for fifteen
  Vs   )   pounds fifteen shillings with costs
The Exors Col Wm Farr)   of suit, subject to debts of
                            superior nature & the plea of
plene administravit

Jehue Wilson   ) Case
  Vs   ) Judgment confessed for sixteen pounds
The Exors Col Wm Farr) 3/7d with cost of suit, subject to
                           debts of superior nature & the
plea of administravit.

Wm Ore   ) Debt
  Vs   ) Judgment confessed according to
The Exors Col Wm Farr) specialty with interest & cost of
                           suit, subject to debts of superior
nature & the plea of administravit.

Wm Johnson   ) Debt
  Vs   ) Judgment confessed for four pounds
The Exors Col Wm Farr) 13/1d subject as above.

James A. Whyte) P & S
  Vs   ) Richard Farr confessed Judgment for four
Dodd Ryan   ) pounds 12/3 & entered himself security for
                 payment with equal costs

Cap. Lewis Hogg) Debt
  Vs   ) Contd. untill next court at Dft. costs
Wm Brummett   ) and the deposition of Cap Avery taken in
                  evidence next court.

Danl. McElduff Asse Baner Hall) Debt
  Vs   ) Nonsuit
James Barron   )

```
The State    )   Indict
   Vs        )     Hogstealing
Joseph Hart)   Mr. Wm Smith appeared by the state and the
                 defendant by Jno Dunlap Ab Nott  & Leak
Esquires whereupon came a Jury who being duly drawn empanneled
& sworn towit.
```

Robert Lusk foreman	Jonathan Whitton
Wm Clark	David Smith
Joshua Sisson	Peter Laurence
Mechach Chandler	Thomas Hollingsworth
Ephraim Wilbourn	Mark Jackson
Benjamin Nix	John Foster

Return their verdcit & say not guilty Robert Lusk foreman

```
Braselman & Co     )   P & S
   Vs              )   Decree for the plaintiff according to
Katherine Jenkins)   specialty with interest & cost of suit.

Geo. Walker    )   John Nuckols proved six days attendance in
   Vs          )   this case, ordered that the same be taxed in
Cush. R. Edson)   the bill cost.

Graaff Edson & Co)   P & S
   Vs              )   Decree for the Plaintiff according to
Charles Thompson )   specialty with interest & costs of suit.
```

Jno Nuckols proved 3 days attendance on the above case.

```
Robert G. Harper)   P & S
   Vs            )   Decree for the plaintiff accg to specialty
John Thompson   )   with interest & costs of suit.
```

Then the court adjourned untill tomorrow 9 oclock & signed by
                         Jno Blasingame
                         Thos Brandon

The court met accg to adjournment on Fryday the 8th day of
January 1796 Present their honors John Blasingame
                              Tho. Brandon Esquires

```
Alex. Macbeth & Co)   P & S
   Vs             )   Decree for the plaintiff accg to note
James Hoard (?)   )   with interest & costs of suit.

Alex. Macbeth & Co )   P & S
   Vs              )   Decree for the plaintiff accg to
Wilson Jolley      )   specialty with interest & costs of suit

Alex. Macbeth & Co)   P & S
   Vs             )   Decree for the plaintiff accg to
Joshua Petty      )   specialty with interest & costs of suit
                      stay of execution untill 1st April
                      next.

Alex. Macbeth & Co  )   P & S
   Vs               )   Decree for the pltf accg to specialty
Tho. Blasingame Junr.)   with interest & costs of suit.
```

438

Graaff Edson & Co) P & S
  Vs   ) decree for the plaintiff & accg to note
David Smith   ) with interest & costs of suit on stay
                    execution 3 months.

Thomas Stribling) P & S
  Vs   ) The defendant confessed Judgment according
James Martin &) to note with interest & costs of suit,
John Martin   ) on stay of execution 3 months.

Michael Montgomery) P & S
  Vs   ) Judgment confessed for 82 bushels corn
John Leake   ) at 1/6 p. bushel on stay of execution
                   untill execution untill 1st April next
with int. & costs of suit.

John Robertson   ) P & S
  Indorsa D. Brown) Decree for the Plaintiff accg to notes,
  Vs   ) with interest and costs of suit, stay
Wm Johnson   ) of execution 3 months.

Josiah Wood   ) P & S
  Vs   ) Nonsuit
Wm Brummett &   )
Spencer Brummett)

Wm Kennedy Tanner) P & S
  Union County) Decree for the plaintiff accg to note,
  Vs   ) with interest & costs of suit.
Danl. McElduff   )

Graaff Edson & Co) Debt
  Vs   ) The defendant being called & not appeared
Josiah Tanner   ) ordered that Judgment be entered against
                   him by default.

C R Edson & Co) Debt
  Vs   ) Judgment by default
Joshua Petty)

Graaff Edson & Co) Debt
  Vs   ) Judgment by default
Jno Beekham   )

Henry O Nail) Debt
  Vs   ) Dismissed by order of Pltf.
Hugh Means)

Alex. Macbeth & Co) Case
  Vs   ) The defendant being called & not
Hancock Porter   ) appeared Jud. by default is entered
                   against him.

John Jasper) Attachment
  Vs   )   Dismissed
John Thompson)

Lusk   ) Attachment
  Vs   )
James Martin)   Dismissed

John Morris   ) Appeal
    Vs   )   Judgment reversed
Gordon & Monisson)

John Morris   ) Appeal
    Vs   )   Judgment reversed
Gordon & Monisson)
John Leak   ) Appeal
    Vs   )   Judgment of the justice confirmed with
Randal Laurence)   costs.

James Lyon) Appeal
    Vs   )   Abated by death of penalty from original
Thomas Weer)   proceedings before the magistrate.

James D. Pucket) By consent of the parties Joseph Hughs &
    Vs   ) Bay Woodson Esquire is appointed to
John McConnell) arbitrator in this case, with power of
                  umpirage.

State   ) Indict.
    Vs   ) Mr. Farraw moved an arrest of Judgment, ordered
John Gamblin) that the same be contd. untill next court.

Wm Kennedy Treasurer Union County) P & S
    Vs   ) Decree for Plaintiff accg
The Exors Col Farr decd.   ) to note with interest &
        Ben Haile   ) costs of suit.

Saml. Jackson   ) Appeal
    Vs   ) Judgment of the Justice confirmed with
Daniel Brown Esq.)   costs of suit.

John Jolley was qualifyed as constable for this county.

Geo. Walker   ) Debt
    Vs   ) Ordered that a New tryal be granted on the
Cushman R. Edson)   grounds ordered in court by Cush. R. Edson
                     in writing at Defendants cost.

Christopher Johnson on motion of Benjamin Haile was qualified
as Deputy Clerk for this county who took the oath prescribed
by Law.

Ordered that the clerk issue orders for the defendant
overseers of the road as presented by the Grand Jury.

The court then adjourned untill court in course.
                              Jno Blasingame
                              Thos Brandon

At a court of ordinary for the county of Union, met on Fryday
the 22d. day of January 1790 Present Jno Blasingame
                                       Tho. Brandon

On the application of Mary Prewet & Daniel Palmer, Letters of
administration is granted them on the Estate and effects of
Obadiah Prewett deceased, who entered into Bond with security
according to Law and took the oath prescribed accordingly.

440

On the application of the administrators of Obadiah Prewitt
deceased, Ordered that Robert Wallace Amos Marton & Thomas
B Hunt appraise the Estate and effects of the said deceased,
and make due return thereof according to Law. being first sworn

The court then adjourned   Jno Blasingame
                                   Thos Brandon

At a court of ordinary for the county of Union met on
Saturday the 30th day Jany. 1796
               Present   Thomas Brandon

Ordered that the Admr. of Andrew McBride decd. expose to sale
all the personal Estate of Decd. on a credit untill the first
of Nov. next and that they make due return according to law.
                                   Thos Brandon

State of South Carolina
　　At a Intermediate Court begun and Holden in and for the
County of Union at the Court House of said County on Monday the
fourth day of April in the year of our Lord one thousand seven
hundred and Ninety Six and of the Independence of the United
States of American the Twentyeth.

　　　　　　　　Present　John Blasingame, Thomas Brandon, Judges.

　　Presented in open Court an Instrument of writing said to be
the last will and testament of Elizabeth Cooper deceased which
was duly proved according to Law by the Oaths of Capt. John Sanders & Ezekiel Frazier subscribing evedences thereto.
Ordered therefore that the said Will be Recorded.

　　Ralph Hunt Junr & Col. Thomas Brandon being nominated Executors to the above will by the said deceased came into open court
and took the oath prescribed by Law.

　　On Motion of the Executors aforesaid　Ordered that Captain
John Sanders Joseph McJunkin, Ralph Hunt & John Cook or any three
of them be and are hereby appointed to Appraise the Estate and
effects of Elizabeth Cooper deceased and that they make due return accordingly, being first duly sworn by Nathl. Davis Esquire.

Proved in open Court by the oath of John Savage a Deed of Conveyance from Wm Sims & Betsey Sims to Isaac Hawkins.　Ordered therefore that the same be Recorded.

Proved in open Court by the oath of Arthur Thomas a Deed of conveyance from Jn. P. Sartor to William Glenn.　Ordered therefore
that the same be Recorded.

Presented in open Court an Instrument of writing said to be the
Last Will and Testament of Jesse Patty deceased which was duly
proved by the Oaths of Jacob Woolright and James Patty subscribing evidences thereof.　Ordered therefore that the same be Recorded.
　　Deliah Patty & Turner Kendrick qualified as Exors thereto.

A Deed from Tho. Brandon Esqr. to Wm Whitlock proved by the oath
of James Woodson & O to R.

Nathan Sims & Ann G. Sims came into Cot. & made choirce of Eliza.
Sims their Guardian the said Elizabeth was also appointed Guardian
to Reuben Sims orphans of James Sims decd. who gave Bond & security according to Law.

Acknowledged in open Court a Deed of conveyance from Stephen Howard & wife to Timothy Ezell Ordered therefore that the same be
Recorded.

On Motion of John Moore Ordered that he Expose to Sale all the
personal Estate and effects of Edward Moore deceased, giving the
Usual Notice of such Sale on a Credit of Six Months taking bond &
good Security.

Ordered that the road leading from Tyger River to Bobo's be continued the way it was formerly to wit turning out the left hand
way by Bobos fence from thence into the old road, and that the
Overseer thereof keep it in repair accordingly.

On Motion of Wm Hogans Admr. of Original Hogans deceased, Ordered
that Joseph Brock, Wm. A. Brock, and Jacob Hollingsworth, be and
are hereby appointed to appraise the Estate & effects of said
deceased & that they make due return accg. being first duly sworn
by Nath Davis Esqr.

On the application of Samuel Clouney Letters of Administration
is granted him on the Estate and effects of Archibauld Clouney
deceased, who entered into Bond & Security accordingly and took
the Oath prescribed by Law.
Ordered on Motion of Samuel Clouney that John White, Arthur
Cunningham & Richard Thompson appraise the Estate and effects of
Archibauld Clouney, deceased and that they make due return according to Law, first duly sworn by H Means, Esqr.

On the Resignation of Robert Savage (son Wm) William Adier is appointed overseer of the Road from James Bogans Creek to James
McCrackens Shop.
Ordered therefore that he keep the same in good repair according
to Law with the hands allowed thereby.

On the Resignation of Francis Fincher, Edward Prince Snr is appointed overseer of the Road from Adams Old Mill to Townsends
old Shop.
Ordered therefore that he keep the same in good repair according
to Law, with the hands allowed thereby.

Ordered that Nathan Cooper be overseer of the Road from Townsends
old Shop to Kennedys old ford on Enoree, and that he keep the
same in good repair according to Law with the hands allowed
thereby.

Presented in open Court a petition praying that a Ferry may be
established at or near to Bobo's ford on Tyger River, Ordered
therefore that the Ferry be vested in Ralp Jackson at the said
Place petitioned for; who is to observe & abide by the former
Rates Established by this Court on said River. Provided the
said Jackson can make it appear he has leave from the owner of
the Land on the opposite side of the River.

Ordered that the County Treasurer pay Jno Price on his order the
amount Sale of a certain Sorrell Horse posted before Tho. Blasingame Esqr and sold by order of this Court at last January Court.
provided Substantial prooff is brought from the said owner of
the horse, Otherwise Ordered that if the purchaser will deliver
up the said before mentioned horse to the said Jno Price on his
order after the prooff aforesaid, the order shall be a full discharge against his said note given the Wm. Kennedy Esqr. treasurer, after the Necessary Lawful charges are paid.

Ordered that Caleb Frazier be Overseer of the Road from his house
to Union Court House and that he keep the Same in Good repair
according to Law.

Proved in open Court by the Oath of Adam Potter Esquire the last
will and testament of Adam Goudylock deceased, Ordered therefore
that the same be Recorded.

Ordered the the minutes be Read, which was done accordingly.
The Court then Adjourned untill Court in Course & Signed by
Thos Brandon, Jno Blasingame.

443

At a Court of Ordinary Mett for the County of Union on Saturday
the 7 May 1796.
Present   Tho. Brandon, Judge.

On the Application of Mathew M Patton & Thomas Patton Letters of
administration is granted to them on the Estate & Effects of
William Patton decd. who gave Bond & Security accg. to Law.

Ordered that Hugh Means, Alex McCarter, Saml Kelsey & James Mays
Junr or any three of them appraise the estate & effects of Wm
Patton deceased and make due Return according to Law, being first
duly swron by Hugh Means Esquire.   Thos Brandon.

At a Court begun & Holden in and for the County of Union at the
Court House of said county on Wednesday the first day of June
A Domini 1796. Present   Thos Brandon, John Blasingame, Judges.

William Kennedy Esquire being commissiond by the Governor as a
Judge of this Court Was duly Qualified according to Law & took
his Seat.

The court proceeded to draw the Grand Jury to serve at our Next
January term: to wit.

Isaac Hawkins	1	Henry Millhouse	11
John Bailey	2	Wm Buchanan	12
Richard Cox	3	Dd. Norman	13
Saml Otterson	4	John Jasper Jnr	14
Wm Hays	5	Ralph Hunt	15
Tho McDaniel	6	Stephen Chrinshaw	16
John Reed	7	Jas. Kennedy	17
John Clark	8	Robt. Chrinshaw	18
Benj. Hollingsworth	9	Henry Goode	19
Alex. McDougal	10	James Means Snr.	20

Pettit Jury

John George	Jarrot Gregory
Saml Turner	Michl. Lee
John Huey	Benjn. Burns
Thos. Hill	Nathl. Summons
Randal Jinkins	Wm. Horrell
John Fincher	Wm. Rogers
Edward Prince	Richd. Addis
McCormet McCaffarty	John Townsend
Watern. Boatman	Nichs. Rochester
Longshore Lamb	Nichs. Harris
Moses Right	Jas. Johnson
James Gutterie	John Lee
Saml Clouney	Renny Belue
John Steen Junr.	James Benson
	Wm. Thompson
	Hugh Nelson

Presented into open Court the last Will and testament of Thomas
Harris decd which was duly proved by the Oaths of Richard & Thomas Harris, and Ordered to be Recorded, & the Executors therein
Sally Harris & James Townsend came into open Court & took the
Oath required by Law as Excuts. thereto.
Ordered that John Cook Ralph Hunt Ely Cook & Thomas McDonnell appraise the Estate & effects of Thomas Harris decd. & make their
return according to Law, beign first sworn by Some Justice of the
peace.

444

Peter Philpeck applied for tavern License which was granted him
he having given bond & secy.

Daniel Hollingsworth applied for tavern license which was granted
he giving bond & secy. accg.

Alexr Macbeth & Co)   Debt
    vs   )   Judgment confessed for Ł 16 s 10 d 4 sterling
Alexander Kendrick)   with Interest & Costs of suit.

Alex Macbeth & Co)   Debt
    vs   )   Judgement confessed according to Notes with
Abel Kendrick   )   Interest & Costs of suit.

On the application of Joshua Sisson admr. of Wm Sisson deceased
he has leave to expose to Public Sale all the personal Estate of
the said deceased, on his giving the usual Notice of such Sale
& giving 12 Mo Credit.

On the application of Lydia Hollingsworth & Richard Farr Letters
of Administration is Granted them on the Estate of Jos. Hollingsworth deceased, who give bond & security according to Law.
    Ordered that John P. Sartor, Wm. Sartor Saml Hardy & Robuck
Comer or any three of them appraise the Estate & effects of Jos.
Hollingsworth decd & that they make due return accg. being first
swron by W Hogans Esqr.

Alex Macbeth & Co)   P & S
    vs   )   Judgement confessed accg. to Acct. for Ł 3
John ---(?)   )   8/5 with costs of suit.

Alexander Macbeth & Co) Debt
    vs   ) Judgment confessed according to Specialty
Josiah Wilson   ) with Interest & Costs of suit On Stay
                      of execution until 1st Octr next.

Alexander Macbeth & Co) Debt
    vs   ) Judgment confessed by the defendant,
Charles Thompson &) Chs. Thompson according to Specialty
Turner Kendrick   ) wtih costs of suit.

John Steen   ) P & S
    vs   ) By consent of the parties this case is refer-
Drewry Herrington) red to Wm Kennedy & Moses Guyton with power
                      of Chosing & umpire & their award returnable
to this court shall be the Judt. thereof.

James Martin   ) Case
    vs   ) Ordered that the plaintiff give
The Exors of Herrington) security for costs in this case, he
                           being not a Citizen of this State.

Thos Renalds) P & S
    vs   ) Contd untill next court by consent
Joseph King)

Seibels & Co) The defendant Robert Rogers with Wm Rogers con-
    vs   ) fessed a Judgment according to Specailty with
Robert Rogers) Interest & Costs of suit On Stay of Execution
                Six months.

```
Graaff Edson & Co)   Debt
      vs           )   Judgment confessed by the defendant for Ł 10
Tho. McCaffarty    )   11/1 with Interest & Costs of suit
```

The Court then adjourned untill Tomorrow 9 o'clock.
Jno Blasingame, Thos Brandon.

The Court Mett according to adjournment on thursday the 2nd day
of June 1796. Present John Blasingame, Tho Brandon, Wm Kennedy.

```
The State   )   Indict  asst. & Battery
   vs       )
Tho. Elliott)   dismissed at Defendants cost.
```

The Grand Jury towit being duly sworn to serve the Court. Jeremiah Lucas foreman, Wm. White, Isaac Parker, Geo Harlan hatter,
John Morehead, Nathan Glenn, Wm. Sartor, John Goodwin, Jno. Beckham Senr, Obd. Howard, Geo. Newton & Hancock Porter.

James Porter & John Gibson was qualified as Constables for this
County.

```
John Steen        )P & S
      vs          )We Moses Guiton & Wm Kennedy chosen to Settle a
Drury Herrington)Dispute Between John Steen Plaintiff & Drewry
                  Herrington having heard all the allegations on
```
both sides award that Drewry Herrington pay unto John Steen
Eight Dollars and Cow and calf to their value also all costs now
due concerning said suit Given under Our hands the 1st Jany 1796
```
                                            Wm Kennedy
                                            Moses Guiton
```

```
The State        )   Bastardy
   vs            )   Ordered that the defendants be fined the sum
Saml Fowler &    )   of Ł 5 each pro. Money & Costs of suit & that
Lavinah Rachley)     the defendant five Security to the County to
                     pay Forty shillings sterling yearly into the
```
hands of Levinah Rackly untill sd. Bastard child attains the
age of Ten years.

On the present't of the Grand Jury, Ordered that the following
persons be appointed overseers of the road & that they keep the
same in Good repair According to Law---viz.
      John Cole from the Skull Shoals to Fannin Creek
      Jeremiah Lucas from Fannins Creek to Whitlock's Mill
      George Newton from Whitlock's Mill to the Duck pond.

```
James D. Puckett) P & S
      vs        )   On Motion of Mr. Smith & Oath of the defendant
James Hanna     )   Ordered that the plaintiff five Security for
                    payment of Costs.
```
      Whereupon came Christr. Johnson into open Court & Acknow-
ledged himself security for the payment of costs in the above
case.

```
Cap. James Martin      )   Case
      vs               )   Contd. untill Next Court
The Exors of Herrington)   the Plaintiff giving Secy. for payment
                           of costs to the Clerk within thirty
```
days, Else to Suffer a Nonsuit.

Captain Lewis Hogg) Debt
         vs   ) Came the Plaintiff by Abraham Nott Esqr. his
William Brumett) attorney and the defendant by Mr. Smith,
                   Jury being Sworn but contd. by consent of
parties without going to Them.

The Exors James Gibbs) P & S
         vs   ) Judgment confessed according to Specialty
John High & Al   ) with Interest & Costs of suit, on Stay of
                       Execution until the last of October.

Alex Macbeth & Co   ) P & S
         vs   ) Judgment confessed for Ł 7 18/3 with
The Exr. of Tho: Wright) Interest & Costs of suit.

Alex Macbeth & Co) P & S
         vs   ) Judgment confessed for Ł 4 s 6 sterling with
Delia Wright   ) costs of suit.

Graaff Edwon & Co) Debt
         vs   ) Came the plaintiff by Abm Nott & the Defen-
William Bowman   ) dant by Wm Nibbs, whereupon came a Jury to
                    wit , Joshua Palmore, foreman, Geo Bailey,
Maher Lils, Sion Murphey, Ephraim Smith, John Cook, Henry
Thickpenny, Wm. Cotter, Wm. Jackson, Aaron Hart, Wm Pearson, John
Nelson, who being duly sworn Return their Verdict & Say we find
for the Plaintiff according to Note with Interest & Costs of suit
                    Joshua Palmore, foreman.
Which Verdict was ratifyed by the Court & O to R.

On the Application of Saml Clouney, Admr. of Arch. Clouny decd
Ordered that he have leave to expose to Public Sale all the personal Estate & Effect of the deceased, giving Nine Months Credit.

E R Edson   ) Debt
         vs) Same Jury as Graaff Edson vs Wm Bowman who being
Wm S. Davis) sworn Return their Verdict & say we find for the
               Plaintiff Ł 18 s 15 d 5 & costs of suit.
                    Joshua Palmore, foreman.
Which Verdict was ratifyed by the Court & Ordered to be Recorded.

Washington Brown orphan of Gabl. Brown deceased, came into open
Court & Made choice of Majr. Jas. Hughs, his Guardian, who gave
Bond of Security accord. to Law.

Ordered that a Citation issue to excite all the kindred & Creditors of Gabriel Brown decd. to shew cause if any they have why
letters of administration should not be granted to Majr. Jas.
Hughs---at Next Intr. Court.

    Whereas Samuel Farrow Esqr was appd. by the County Court of
Union, administrator to the Estate of Sarah Gist decd. till
Joseph C Gist, her son should come to the age of 21 years, & it
now appearint to the said Court that the said J C Gist has ar-
rived to the age of twenty one years, it is Ordered that the
said Samuel Farrow deliver up to the said Jos. B. Gist all the
bonds, notes, accot. moneys, Debts due & demands belonging to
the Estate of the said Sarah Gist decd which has come to his possession.

Cush R Edson) P & S
      vs   ) Decree for the defendant with costs of suit except
Christr. Johnson) his attorneys fee.

On Motion of Abraham Nott Esquire for Stephen Heard Esquire to
have leave to practice as an Attorney in this Court, who produced
his commission of his being Legally Licensed, Ordered that he
have admittance accg.

Ordered that the Court adjourn untill tomorrow 9 0 Clock & Signed
by Thos Brandon, Wm Kennedy.

The Court Mett According to adjournment on Fryday the third day
of June 1796. Present Thos Brandon, John Blasingame, Wm. Kennedy.

Sarah Darby Admx)   Case
Wm Darby decd   )   Discontinued at the Plaintiff costs
   vs   )
Archer Howard   )

Graaff Edson & Co)   Debt
   vs   )   Same Jury as Graaff Edson & Co against Bow-
Robert Anderson)   man, who being duly drawn, empaneled & sworn
                     Return their Verdict & Say we find for the
Plaintiff according to Note with Interest & Costs of suit
                                 Joh. Palmore, foreman.

Graaff Edson & Co)   Debt
   vs   )   Writ of Enquiry
Josiah Fannen   )   Same Jury as above, Who being duly drawn &
                     Empaneled & Sworn Well & truly to execute all
writs of enquiry &C Return their Verdict & Say we find for the
Plaintiff accg. to Note with Interest & cost of suit.
                                 Joshua Palmore, foreman.

C R Edson & Co)   Writ of Enquiry
   vs   )   Debt
Joshua Petty   )   Same jury as above. Return their Verdict & Say
                   we find for the Plaintiff accg. to note with
Interest & costs of suit.   Joshua Palmore, foreman.

Graaff Edson & Co)   Writ
   vs   )   Debt
John Grastey   )   Judgment confessed according to Specialty
                     with Interest & Costs of suit.

Ordered that the amount sales of some Hogs Posted before Wm
Hogans Esquire & Sold at this Court be refunded to Solomon
Anderson(?) who has filed his affidavit that the said Hogs is
his property.

John H Gee vs Abel Kendrick) P & S Dismissed at Defendants
                                       cost

Same vs the Same) Debt Settled at Plaintiffs cost

Hancock Porter)   Debt
   vs   )   Same Jury as Graaf Edson & Co against Bowman
John Howell   )   who being duly sworn Return their Verdict & say
                   we find for the Plaintiff the Principle of the
Notes & Costs of suit.   Joshua Palmore, foreman.

John Reed   ) P & S
   vs   ) Stands over untill Tomorrow
John Murrell)

448

```
John Reed         )  P & S
    vs            )  Continued untill next court on affidavit filed
Christr. Johnson) by the defendant at his costs.


James D. Puckett) P & S
    vs            )  Pursuant to an Order of the County court of
John McDannell   )  Union to us directed We have settled & deter-
                    mined all disputes in an action brought by
James D. Puckett against John McDonnell and hereby award that the
plaintiff pay to the defendant the sum of Ł 3 s 14 & d 5 sterling
with the costs of suit.  Given under our hands the 3d day of
June 1796.  Benj. Woodson, Jos. Hughes.  Which award the Court
Ordered to be final.


Drury Murrell     )  Debt
    vs            )  Same Jury as Graaff Edson & Co against Wm
John Martindale &) Bowman who being duly drawn empanneled & sworn
Samuel Simpson   )  return their verdict & say we find for the
                    plaintiff the Balance of the Bond deducting
Six months interest at Forty pounds agreeable to the credits of
the Bond with costs of suit.    Jos. Palmer, formn.
```

Mr. Farrow gave Notice that he intended to move for a new Trial
in the above case.

Whereas Thomas Brandon & Samuel Simpson, the Securities for the
faithful administration of the Estate & Effects of James Oliphant
deceased by David Oliphant and George Gordon to whom administration was granted by this Court, have preferred their humble petition stating they conceive themselves in danger of being injured
by such their sd. Suretyship from the way & manner in which the
said David Oliphant hath conducted himself in the Management of
the said Estate, he having possessed himself of the greatest
part of the said Estate and removed the same to Charleston without having at any time rendered to this Court a true & Just account upon Oath of his receipts and expenditures of the said
Estate or the manner in which or the persons to whom he hath
administered applied or appropriated the said Estate or the
Moneys arising therefrom And that the said David Oliphant hath
been Guilty of a Devastavit(?) in the said Estate and pray relief
    It is therefore Ordered that a Citation or Summons do issue
from this Court and a Copy thereof be personally served on the
said David Olliphant by the Sheriff of Charleston District,
Summoning & requiring him without fail personally to be & appear
before a Court of Ordinary to be held in and for this County on
Saturday the Sixteenth day of July next at the Court house of
said County to answer to the said petition and to receive, abide
by and perform such order or decree as shall then & there be
made by the said Court to give relief to the said Securities and
as to the said Court seem meet and the Nature of the case requires.

    Whereas it appears by the Records of this Court that admini-
stration of the Estate & effects of James Oliphant late of this
County deceased on the Fifth day of January 1793 was Granted to
David Oliphant & Geo Gordon as next of kin to the said deceased
and whereas by the decree or Sentence of the said Court the personal Estate of the said deceased was ordered to be publicly sold
for Costs on the second Monday in February 1794 following to answer the Exeginces of the said Estate. And it appearing Satisfac-
tory to this Court that the greatest part of the said Estate came
to the hands and possession of the said David Oliphant and he having neglected to make any return or render to the Court an accompt
of his receipts or expenditures or in what manner he has applied

or appropriated the said Estate. And it being necessary that such return should be made and rendered to the Court without further delay.

It is therefore Ordered that a Citation do issue from this Court and a Copy thereof be personally served on the said David Oliphant by the Sheriff of Charleston District. Summoning and requiring him without fail or further delay personally to be and appear before a Court of ordinary to be held in and for this County on Saturday the Sixteenth day of July next, at the Court House for said County and that he come prepared then & there to make & render to the said Court a Just & true Accompt upon Oath of his receipts & expenditures of the said Estate & the manner in which and to whom he hath applied & appointed the said Estate or the Moneys arrising thereupon and to abide by such further order or Decree as the said Court may seem right thereupon.

The Court then adjourned untill Tomorrow 9 O Clock & Signed by Jno Blasingame Wm Kennedy.

The Court Mett According to adjournment on Saturday the 4 day of June 1796. Present John Blasingame, Tho. Brandon, Wm Kennedy.

On Motion of Mr. Saml Farrow & upon the administration of Sarah Gist decd being given to J C Gist (her son) according to a former order, Ordered that the said Samuell Farrow be released from his said administration and his bond given up to him. And that the said J C Gist enter into Bond with Sufficient Security for the faithful administration of the remaining part of the said Estate & effects of the said deceased.

John Reed   ) P & S
    vs   ) Same Jury as Graaff Edson & Co against Wm Bowman
John Murrell) who being duly sworn Return their Verdict & say we
find for the Plaintiff Ł 6 s 19 d 6 with costs of suit.
                         Joshua Palmore, foreman.

Graaf Edson & Co) Debt
    vs   ) Same jury as Graaff Edson & Co against Bowman,
John Beckham Senr) who being duly sworn, return their Verdict &
                    say we find a Verdict for the Plaintiff, sum
of Ł 45 s 17 d 9 1/2 with Interest from the time it becomes due
with costs of suit.   Jos. Palmore, foren.

Sarah Darby Admx   ) Case
  Wm Darby decd   ) Continued untill next court on an affida-
    vs   ) vit filed by the Defendant.
Tho Blasingame Esqr.)

Ordered that a Dedimus Potestatum issue to North Carolina to take the deposition of John Blasingame son (tom)(?).

James D Puckett) P & S
    vs   ) Decree for the plaintiff for s 6 d 2 with
James Hanna   ) costs of suit

Graaf Edson & Co) Writ Debt
    vs   ) Same Jury as Graaf Edson & Co against Bowman
Robert Armstrong) who being duly sworn return their Verdict &
                   Say we find for the Defendant d 11 with costs
of suit   Joshua Palmore, foreman.

Joseph Coleman) Case writ of Enquiry
        vs   ) Same Jury as Graaf Edson & Co against Bowman
Wm Giles   ) who being duly swron &C Return their verdict &
                   Say we find for the Plaintiff Ŀ 21 and costs
of suit   Joshua Palmore, foreman.

Richard Farr proved four days attendance in the above case &C.

Judge Blasingame certifyed that Batte Birdsong was Legally qualified as Constable for this County.

The State   ) Indictment   Ass. & Battery
     vs   ) On Motion of Samuel Farrow Esqr the Verdict of
John Gamblin)   the Jury in the above case at last Court be Sett
                aside as the Indictment was defective

The State   ) Indict   The State   ) Indict
     vs   ) Discharged on   vs   ) Discharged
Thomas Mintor) Motion Mr. Dunlap   Sarah Phillips) Recogce
                                                  being _?_

Graaff Edson & Co) P & S
        vs   ) Decree for the plaintiff accg. to note with
McCormit McCaffarty) costs of suit.

James D Puckett)   P & S
     vs   )   Richard Burgess enters himself security for
Turner Kendrick)   the cost in this case the plaintiff being
                   absent & out of the State

James D. Puckett) P & S
     vs   )   Same order as above
Willis Walker &)
Turner Kendrick)

Graaff Edson & Co) Attachmt
     vs   ) Cont untill next court
Adam Thompson   )

Ordered that the Minutes be read which was done & the Court then
adjourn untill Court in Course. Signed by Jno Blasingame,
Thos Brandon, Wm Kennedy.

At a Court of Ordinary for the County of Union Held on Saturday
the Sixteenth day of July in the year of our Lord one thousand
Seven hundred and Ninety Six. Present their Honors, John Blasingame, William Kennedy, Esquires.

Whereas Thomas Brandon & Samuel Simpson Securities for the faithful administration of the Estate & Effects of James Oliphant
deceased by David Oliphant...[see last term of court] David Oliphant hath failed to appear before this Court according to the
Tenor of the said Citation to answer the Allegations contained
in the said Petition...And this court being satisfied of the mal
administration of the said David Oliphant...relief is granted
the sd. Thomas Brandon & Saml. Simpson the securities....& decree
that administration of the Estate and Effects of the said James
Oliphant unadministered by the said David Oliphant & George Gordon be granted to the said George Gordon solely he taking the
usual oath and giving approved Security for his faithful administration....

The court then adjourned until Saturday the 23d Instant....

Signed by Jno Blasingame, Wm Kennedy.

At a Court of Ordinary Held for the County of Union at the Court House of said County on Saturday the 23d July 1796. Present Jno Blasingame, Judge.

Whereas at a Court of Ordinary Held for the County of Union on Saturday the 16th of July instant, the said Court decreed & Ordered that the administration of the Estate & Effects of Jas. Oliphant deceased, unadministered by David Oliphant & George Gordon, to whom the Letters of Admn. was granted by the Court, be granted to the said George Gordon solely....Whereupon came the said George Gordon, with John Martindale & Thomas Blasingame Esquires his Securitys, & Entered into Bond Accordingly in the sum of Ł 1000 for his faithful administration & took the Usual Oath prescribed by Law. Its therefore ordered that letters of administration be granted the said George Gordon...Signed by Jno Blasingame.

At a Court of Ordinary Held for the County of Union on Monday the 23d July 1796. Present Wm Kennedy, Esq.

On the application of the administrators of the Estate & Effects of Wm Patton decd, Ordered that they have Leave to expose to Sale all the personal Estate of the said deceased, at the plantation of the said Wm. Patton decd on Wednesday the 27 Instant, as it appears the Administrators having duly advertised to Sell on that time previous to this date and that they give Seven months Creditt from the day of Sale taking Bond with approved Security from the purchasers Thereof. Wm Kennedy, J. C. C.

At an Intermediate Court begun & Holden in and for the County of Union at the Court House of said County on Monday the 5th day of September 1796. Present: Thos Brandon, Wm Kennedy, Judges.

Ordered that Leonard Smith be Overseer of the Road from William Darbys Store (alias Mrs. Darbys) untill he gets opposite Leonard Smith, in the room of Lewis Pennion, and that he keep the same in good repair accg. to Law, with the hands allowed thereby.

Ordered that Elisha Bond be overseer of the road from Mitchells Creek to Dining Creek in the room of __?__ Curtis and that he kepp the same in good repair according to Law with the hands allowed thereby.

Present John Blasingame Esqr   Absent T. Brandon

Proved in Open Court a Deed of conveyance from Thomas Draper & Lucy his wife to Wm. Chisholm & Ordered to be Recorded.

Acknowledged in open Court a Deed from Wm. Smith to Ann Smith-- & One from said Wm. Smith to John Smith & Ordered to be Recorded.

Proved in open Court a Deed of conveyance from John Lewis to Philip Coleman & O to R.

A Mortgage from Henry Long to John Henderson & ordered to be Recorded--proved.

Bernard Glenn an agent for Walter Goodman applied for License to Retail Spirituous Liquor in this County at Liphams plantation who gave bond & Security accg. to Law.

452

On the application of Lydia Hollingsworth admx. & Richard Farr admr. of the goods chattles & Credits of Joseph Hollingsworth deceased for a Sale of the Estate of the said deceased. Ordered that they expose to Public Sale at the plantation of said deced. all the personal Estate & Effects belonging to sd. deceased, On the Last Saturday in October next, giving Twelve Months Credit to the purchasers thereof.

Ackd. in open Court, a Deed of conveyance from Enoch Floy atty. for Robert Merrick to Jnth. Newman. & O to R.

Ackd. in Open Court a Deed of conveyance from Wm. Martindale & wife to David Norman & O to R.

Ackd. in open Court a Deed of conveyance from Samuel Simpson to David Floyd & Ordered to Record.

Ackd. in Open Court a Deed of conveyance from John Martindale Esquire to David Floyd & O to R.

Ordered that Moses Meek, Henry Goode, John Bailey & Henry McCann or any three of them, appraise the Estate and effects of Jesse Patty deced, and that they make due Return thereof according to Law, and that Doctr. White qualify the said appraisers & Certify the same on the back of the Order.

The last Will & testament of George Norman deceased, proved before John Martindale Esqr & Ordered to be Recorded.

Upon the petition of Majr. Jos. Hugs(sic), guardian of Washington Brown & On stating that the orphans Estate (is he has any) lies in such a situation that he cannot support him without commencing Litegeous Lawsuits. Ordered that the said Petitioner be discharged from his Bond in that case given & that his bond be given up to him.

On the application of Wm Hogans admr. of Original Hogans decd Ordered that he Expose to Public Sale at the plantation afsd. Wm Hogans on the Last Saturday in this Month, for Cash, a Certain Bay Mare belonging to the Estate of said deceased.

Account of Expenditures against the Estate of Wm Darby decd. return by the admn. Ord. to be filed.

All Estrays lyable to be sold this Court, Ordered to be sold immediately.

On Motion of the Exors. of Thomas Harris Ordered that they expose to Public Sale at the plantation of said deceased, One Negroe Boy named Jacob, on the first Monday in October ensuing, on a Credit of Six months.

Ordered that John Reed be fined One pound One shilling & nine pence for Obstructing the road leading to Pinckneyville, & that the clerk issue against him for the same.

Ordered that William McCulloch be overseer of the road from the Skull Shoals to Gilkies Creek and that he keep the same in good repair according to Law.

Ordered that Isaac Parker be Overseer of the Road from Gilkies Creek to Smiths ford on Broad River and that he keep the same in good repair according to Law.

Upon the petition of a Number of Inhabitants Ordered that Captain Wilbourn, Samuel Jackson & Richard Powell be and are hereby appointed to view & mark out a way for a road from Mark Jackson's ford on Forrest(?) [Fair Forrest?] to Union Court House the nearest & best way and that they make their Report to next Court.

Ordered that Jesse Young, Malan Ceason & John Garrot be and are hereby appointed to View and Mark out a way for a Road from Cooks Bridge on Tyger River to Garrots Bridge on Enoree and that they make their report to next Court.

The Court then adjourned untill Court in Course & Signed by Jno Blasingame, Wm Kennedy.

At a Court of Ordinary Held for the County of Union at the Court House of said County, on Tuesday the Eighth day of November 1796. Present Thos Brandon, Esquire.

On the Application of Jacob Harlan, Its Ordered that Letters of Administration be granted him on the Estate and effects of Aaron Harlan late of This County deceased. who entered into Bond with George & Samuel Harlan his Securities in the sum of Ł 200 sterling, & took the Oath prescribed by Law.
 Ordered that Solomon Spann, George Harlan hatter & Samuel Harlan, be and are hereby appd. to Appraise the Estate & Effects of Aaron Harlan deceased, and that they make due Return acog. to Law being first sworn by Tho. Blasingame Esqr.

[Signed]   Thos Brandon

At a Court of Ordinary held fro the County of Union at the Court House of said county on Thursday the 24th day of November 1796. Present Tho. Brandon.

On the application of Jacob Harlan, Administrator of all & Singular the goods chattles and Credits of Aaron Harlan late of this County deceased. Ordered that he expose to Sale all the personal Estate and effects of said deceased, on the 13th day of December next, at the plantation of said Jacob Harlan, giving Twelve Months credit to the purchasers thereof, and that he return a true accot. of the same according to Law.
Signed by   Thos Brandon.

At a Court of Ordinary held for the County of Union at the Court House of said County on Saturday the 3rd day of December 1796. Present   Tho. Brandon.

Present in Open Court the Last will and Testament of William Lee, which was duly proved by the Oath of Hezekiah Rice, and Ordered to Record.
Signed by   Thos Brandon.

At a Court begun and Holden in and for the County of Union at the Court House of said County, on Monday the second day of January 1797.   Present their Honors Jno Blasingame, Thos. Brandon, Esqrs.

Ordered that the Grand Jury be draw'd for next Court, who are as follows.

Arthur Cuningham	1	Philip Anderson	11
John Bankhead	2	Jonathan Norman	12
Josiah Darby	3	Geo Harlan farmr	13

Abner Coleman	4		Tho. Palmer snr	14
Joseph Hughs	5		Jacob Hollingsworth	15
Andw. Torrance	6		Isaac Hollingsworth	16
John White	6		Humpr. Bates	17
John Palmer Snr	7		Joseph Means	18
Drury Murrell	8		Benj. Woodson	19
Hugh McBride	9		Saml Littlejohn	20
Jonas Little	10			

Petty Jury

Danl Crownover	1		James Duncan	18
Robt. Chapman	2		Joseph Randol	19
John Adington	3		Edmd. Ellis	20
Philip Bass	4		Leroy Beuford	21
Jo. Thomas	5		John Smith	22
James Mays	6		Alexr Kendrick	23
John Lancaster	7		Saml Selby	24
Wm McCown	8		Jno McNeail	25
James Laurance	10 (sic)		Thomas Young	26
John Crittenden	11		Zacka. Belue	27
James Addington	12		Ebenezer Hale	28 [stricken]
Ingrim(?) John	13		John Hawkins	28
Saml Jackson [stricken]			Robt Greer	29
Amos Cook	14		Arthur Brandon	30
Wm Parmer	15		John Hayney	31
Saml Huey	16			

Potter Inlow   ) Slander
           vs   ) dismissed by consent of the parties
Amos & Danl Hollingsworth) the defendant pay one fourth of the
                                    Costs & the Pltff. the Balance

Presented in Open Court the last will & Testament of Mary Frost
which was duly proved by the Oath of James Benson Snr & Ordered
to Record.
        James Benson and James Townsend appd. Executors to the said
will, came into open Court & took the oaths prescribed by Law.
        Ordered the Henry Penny, Ralp Hunt, James Addington & John
Townsend Jnr. or any three of them be and are hereby appointed
to Appraise the Estate & Effects of Mary Frost decd. and make
due Return thereof accg. to Law. to be first Swron before Capt.
David Esqr or the next hearest

Present in open Court the last will and Testament of John Clark
late of this County deceased, which was duly proven by the Oath
of Henry Thickpenny, A witness thereto, which is Ordered to be
Recorded.
Henry Clark & John Clark being appointed Executors in the above
Will came into Open Court, and was Qualified according to Law.
        Ordered that Henry Penny, Francis Fincher, James Andington &
Ralph Hunt be and are hereby Appointed to Appraise the Estate and
effects of John Clark deceased, and that they make due return
according to Law. being first sworn by a Justice of the peace

Rebecca Fincher Daughter of Sarah Fincher came into open Court
and made Choice of John Fincher her Guardian, who is Ordered to
give Bond with sufficient Security accordingly.

On the Application of Richard Powell & Zacha. Belue for letters
of administration on the Estate and effects of James Pickett
deceased, which was granted them, Who entered into Bond with
Richd. Burgess & Fielding Carter in the sum of Ł 100 sterling

and the said Richd. Powell & Zacha. Belue was duly qualified accg. to Law.

Ordered that Wm. Morgan & James Doan, Steven Howard & Saml Harlan or any three of them be and are hereby appointed to appraised the Estate & Effects of James Pickett deceased, and that they make due return accg. to Law..being first duly sworn by some Justice of the peace for this County.

On the application of Saml. Simpson Leave is given him to keep a public House & Retail Spirituous Liquors in the County during One year from the date hereof who entered into Bond in the sum of Ł 100 with John Martindale & Richd. Burgess secy.

Upon the application of Saml Simpson & Jo. Duncan, Ordered that John Martindale, Ambrose Ray, Wm. Woolbanks, Drury Murell & Robt White be appd. to View the Road Between Tyger River & Saml Simpsons and make their report to our Next Intermediate Court, if they think it Neccessary, to turn the Road from what it now Stands.

Richard Farr & Co) P & S
　　vs　　　　　) Judt. confessed by Thomas Hardy his Security
John Stowers　　) in behalf of the defendant accg. for Ł 3
15/ 8½ & Cost of suit.

Wm Kennedy Esquire produced a commission from under the hand of his Exl. Thos. Pinckney Esqr. authorising him as a Judge for the County of Union Who took the oath agreeable to Law.

Thomas Lee came into open Court & was qualified as an Executor to the last will and testament of William Lee late of this County deceased.

Arthur Dillard on Motion of Wm Hogans Esquire, was qualified as a Constable for this County.

Ordered that Thomas Word & James Porter Constables for this County, be Suspended from their Office.

Proven in Open Court a Deed from John Martin to Charles Humphries & Ordered to Record.

The State　　) Ass. & Battery
　　vs　　　　) Richard Farr & Daniel McElduff Securities for
Shad. Lewallen) the Appearance of the defendant to this Court
　　　　　　　　came into open Court & delivered him up...
said Shadrack Lewallen acknowledged himself indebted to the State for Ł 50 with James Spray his Security...In case the above named Shadrack Lewallen fails to atten the Court....

The State) Ass. Battery
　　vs　　) James Jeater Security for the defendt. appearance
Eliz. Brown) came into open Court and delivered her up...Came into open Court Job Hammond & James Campbell, who acknowledged to owe to the State the sum of Ł 25 each for her appearance.

Jeremiah Lucas having been appointed as one of the Justices of the County of Union, who took the Oath prescribed by Law.

On Motion of Jeremiah Lucas Esquire Wm Gossett took the Oath prescribed by Law as a Constable for this County.

the Court adjourned untill Tomorrow 9 OClock.
Jno Blasingame, Thos Brandon, Wm. Kennedy.

The Court Mett According to adjournment At the Court House of
said County on Tuesday the third day of January 1797. Present
their Honors John Blasingame, Thomas Brandon, Wm. Kennedy, Esqrs.

The State)
   vs   ) Discharged from his recognizance
John Pooll)

State   ) Ordered that a Bench Warrant issue against the
   vs   ) defendant returnable to next Court directed to some
James Inlow) officer to Execute.

Graffe Edson & Co Plaintiff) Debt
   vs   ) Came the Plaintiff by Abraham Nott
Job Hammond Defendant   ) Esquire attorney and the Defendant
                        by John Dunlap Esquire whereupon
came a Jury to wit, Samuel Clouney, foreman, John Lee, Edward
Prince, Jarrot Gregory, James Guthrie, Longshore Lamb, McCormit
McCaffarty, John Huey, James Johnson & Randol Jenkins, on their
Oaths and James Bensons & John Townsends on their Solemn affir-
mation, return their Verdict & Say we find for the plaintiff
Ł 14 9 0½ with interest from the date, with costs of suit
                     Samuel Clouney, foreman. Which
verdict was ordered to be recorded.

Graaff Edson & Co) Case
   vs   ) Dismissed at Pltf Cost
James Parnell   )

A Macbeth & Co) P & S
   vs   ) Judgment confessed according to note deducting
Jesse Birdsong &) all Just Credits with Cost of suit.
Batte Birdsong)

Graaff Edson & Co) Debt
   vs   ) Judgment confessed according to note with
Landlot Porter) Interest & Costs of suit.

Graaf Edson & Co) Debt
   vs   ) Judgment confessed by the Plaintiff together
John White Junr.) with John White Senr & Daniel White Jr. his
                Security, according to note with costs of suit.
Stay of execution till the 25 Decr next.

William Giles) Case
   vs   ) Came the plaintiff by John Dunlap & Abm Nott
Bayles Earle) Esquires and the defendant by Samuel Farrow Es-
            quire whereupon came a Jury The same as Graaff
Edson & Co vs Job Hammond who on their Several Oaths & affirmations
return their verdict & Say We have all agreed that the plaintiff
has Ł 12 and costs of suit. Saml Clouney, foreman. Ordered that
the verdict be Recorded.

Mr. Hudson came into open Court & took the Oath prescribed by Law
as a Constable for this County.

The Court then adjourned untill Tomorrow 9 0 Clock. Jno Blasingame, Wm Kennedy.

457

The Court mett according to adjournment at the Court House of
said County on Wednesday the fourth day of January 1797. Present their Honors, John Blasingame, Tho. Brandon, Wm. Kennedy,
Esqrs.

Lewis Hogg) Debt
    vs   ) Came the plaintiff by Abm Nott esqr and the defen-
Wm Brummett) dant by Wm Smith Esquire Whereupon came a Jury
               to wit Samuel Clouney, foreman, John Lee, Edward
Prince, Jarrot Gregory, James Guttrie, Longshore Lamb, John Fincher, John Huey, James Johnson, Randol Jenkins, Wm. Horrell, who
on their several Oaths, and John Townsend on his Selmn affirmation, return their Verdict & Say we find for the plaintiff Ł 15
s 11 with Interest and costs of suit. Samuel Clouney, forem.
Ordered that the Verdict be recorded.

Capt. James Martin) Case
     vs   ) The plaintiff having failed to give Secur-
The Exors Herrington) ity for costs in this case agreeable to
              an order made by this Court at Last term,
Ordered therefore that he suffer a Nonsuit.

James Kennedy proved twelve days attendance in the above suit.
Ordered that the same be Taxed in the bill of Costs.

Richard Farr applied for a Licence to Retail Spirituous Liquors
and keep a public House at Union Court House which is Granted
him dureing the term of 12 months from the date hereof the said
Richard Farr give Bond with Christr. Johnson & Richard Burgess
his Security.

Graaff Edson & Co) Debt
    vs   ) Judgment confessed by the defendant for Ł 8
Alex Kendrick   ) s 1 d 9 sterling: with interest & Cost of
             suit, Stay of Execution Six months.

Warren Hall applied for a Licence to retail Spirituous Liquors
and keep a public House at Pinckneyville, which is granted him
dureing the term of one year from the date hereof, the said
Warran Hall give bond with John Martindale his Security.

John Murrell   ) Debt
    vs   ) Judgment confessed by the Deft. Whyte for
Tho Wood & J A Whyte) Ł 6 s 6 d 8 & Cost, staying Execution
             three months.

Wm Giles) Richard Farr & Wm Fossett proved one days attendance
  vs   ) in this Suit.
B. Earle)

Graaff Edson & Co) Debt
 asse. Steen   ) Nonsuit
    vs   )
John Thompson   )

Graaff Edson & Co) Debt
    vs   ) Contd. untill next court by consent of the
Edmond Ellis   ) parties

Graaff Edson & Co) Case
    vs   ) Came the plaintiff by A Nott Esquir their
Batte Birdsong) attorney & the Deft. by John Dunlap Esquire
             whereupon came a Jury the same as Hogg vs

Brummett who being Sworn, but the plaintff suffered a nonsuit without the cause going to them.

Eas. Fincher) P & S
    vs) By consent of the parties the cause is summitted
Humphrey Bates) to the Arbitrament of Adw Torrance & James Duncan with power of Chosing an Umpire, and their
Award returnable to this Court shall be the Judgment hereof.

Graaff Edson & Co) Case
    vs) Came the plaintiff by Am Nott & the defendant
Jesse Birdsong) by John Dunlap, whereupon came a Jury the
    same as Hogg against Brummett, who was Sworn,
& by consort of the parties this caus stands over untill Tomorrow.

William Henderson came into open Court & took the necessary oath of office as a Deputy Sheriff for the County of Union.

Jeremiah Gregory) Attacht.
    vs) David Prewitt having been sumd. to attend
James Henry Jnr.) this Court to declare on Oath any property
    in his possession belonging to James Henry
and if he is indebted to him. Say, on his Oath that he has no property in his possession belonging to the said Henry & is nowise indebted to him. But that he owes James Henry Jnr Ten pounds due by his note fiven to him.

The Court then adjourned until Tomorrow 9 O Clock.
Thos Brandon, Wm. Kennedy, Jno Blasingame.

The Court mett according to adjournment on Thursday the fifth day of January 1797. Present their Honors John Blasingame, William Kennedy, Esqrs.

John Fincher) Case
    vs) By Consent of the parties, Ordered that this
David Smith) cause be referred to Archer Howard & Wm Martindale
    with power of chosing an Umpire, and their award
returnable to next Court shall be the Judgt. thereof.

Thomas Runnels) P & S
    vs) On motion of Mr. Dunlap Ordered that the plain-
Joseph King) tiff in this Action do give Security for costs
    in thirty days or a Judgment of a Nonsuit will
be entered against him.

Enoch Floyd) P & S
    vs) Decree confessed by the plaintiff According
John Martindale) to Note with Costs with Stay of Execution
    three months.

Ordered that a Citation issue to Saml. Simpson on the Estate of James White late of this County decd. to be made returnable to next In. Court.

Graaff Edson & Co) Ordered that the Sheriff Bring Lydia Bird-
    vs) song into Court Immediately to give evidence
Jesse Birdsong) in this case

John Hunnycutt) P & S
    vs) Nonsuit
Drury Herrington)

459

The Admrs. Doctr. H. Anderson) Case
vs   ) Came the plaintiff by Abraham
The Exors Col. Wm. Farr decd.) Nott Esqr & the defendants by
                                John Dunlap Esquire, Whereupon
came a Jury the same as Hogg vs Brummett, who on their Oaths &C
Affirmations return their Verdict & Say we find for the plaintiff Ł 7 s 18 d 8 with costs of suit. Saml Clouney, foreman.
    Ordered that the Verdict be recorded.

James Bankhead came into Court and applied for a Licence to
retail Spirituous Liquors & keep a public House at Pinckney
Court House Which was Granted him, who give Bond with James
McElroy & Peter Philpeck his Security in the sum of Ł 100 sterling.

Exors. Fincher) P & S Settled by Award
    vs   ) We the undernamed being appd. according to the
Humy. Bates   ) within order to settle a dispute Between the
                 Exors of A. Fincher plts and Humphrey Bates
defendant after hearing the Evidence on both sides we are of the
opinion that the defendant pay to the Exors of A Fincher Ł 2 s
17 d 7 and discharge all costs of Court, Witnesses excepted
Jany 5 1797. Andw Torrance, James Duncan son Alex.

Col Wm Bratton applied for a license to retail Spirituous Liquors
and keep a public House at Pinckneyvill, who give Bond with
Security according to Law.

Ordered on Motion of Mr. Farrow, that an attachment issue against
Wm Heaton to be delivered to the Sheriff who is Ordered to bring
the said Wm. Heaton before this Court on Tomorrow.

Gregory) Shad Lewallen proved two days attce in this case.
  vs   )
Hughs)

The Court then adjourned untill Tomorrow 9 0 Clock. Thos Brandon, Wm Kennedy.

The Court mett according to Adjournment on Fryday the Sixth day
of January 1797. Present Their Honors Thomas Brandon, Wm.
Kennedy, Esqrs.

A Macbeth & Co) Debt
    vs   ) Judgment confessed by the Defendants attorney,
Nathl Dabbs   ) according to Note with Costs of suit.

Patrick H Sims   ) Case
    vs   ) Judgment confessed by Richd Farr for Ł 8
The Exors Col. Farr) s 12 d 10 with Stay of Execution till the
                      15 Novr next Subject to the plea afsd. Ad-
ministravit. Each party paying his own cost.

Major Joseph McJunkin came into open Court and took the Oath of
office as a Justice of the peace for the County of Union.

On the application of Elizabeth Henderson for letters of administration on the Estate & Effects of John Cole late of this County
deceased, who produced a Citation which having been read three
times in a public meeting, Its Ordered that letters accordingly
be granted her. She therefore took the Oath prescribed by Law &
Entered into Bond in the sum of Ł 100 with Joseph McJunkin her
Security.

460

Ordered that Thomas Vance, John Savage & Jarrot Gregory be and are hereby appointed to appraise the Estate & Effects of John Cole late of this County deceased, and that they make the Legal Return required by Law, to be first sworn by some Magistrate.

On the applicatoin of the Executors of the Last will and Testament of David Chisholm late of this County deceased. Ordered that they have leave to Expose to Public Sale at the plantation of Adam Chisholm, on the third Monday in this Month, all and Singular the Personal Estate of the said David Chisholm according to the Will of the said deceased, And that they return a just Accot. of the same according to Law.

Present   John Blasingame Esq.

Graaff Edson & Co) Case
vs   ) This action continued from Yesterday. The
Jesse Birdsong) Jury the same as Hogg against Brummett Who
being previously sworn return their Verdict
& say we find for the plaintiff Ł 10 s 6 d 1¼ with costs of suit
Samuel Clouney, foreman.
Ordered that the Verdict be Recorded.

John Reed   ) P & S
vs   ) Same Jury as Hogg vs Brummett Sworn return their
Chr. Johnson) Verdict & Say we find for the plaintiff Ł 4 s 19
d 11 with costs of suit. Saml Clouney, foreman.
Ordered that the Verdict be Recorded.

Jeremiah Gregory) Spal. acnt
vs   ) Came the Plff by Mr. Leak Esqr his Attorney
Hessian Wm Hughs) & the Deft by Abm Nott Esqr his attorney
whereupon came a Jury to wit Samuel Clouney,
foreman, John Lee, Edward Prince, Samuel Simpson, James Guttrie,
Longshire Lamb, John Fincher, John Huey, James Johnston, Randol
Jenkins, Wm. Horrell, who on their segeral oaths and John Townsend on his solemn affirmation the following Verdict. We find
for the plaintiff Ł 10 and costs of suit. Samuel Clouney, foreman.
Shad. Lewallen proved one days attendance.

Sarah Lee   ) P & S
vs   ) Decree for the Defendant with Costs of suit
Thomas Heaton)

Graaff Edson & Co) P & S
vs   ) Judt. confessed according to Note with
John High   ) Costs of suit and Stay of Execution Six
Months.
Thos Brandon, Wm Kennedy.

The Court met according to Adjournment on Saturday the 7th day of January 1797. Present Their Honors, John Blasingame, Wm. Kennedy, Tho Brandon.

Cush R Edson) Appeal
vs   ) Judgment affirmed by consort of both Plaintiff
Daniel Manly) and Defendant, Execution to be Stay'd until next
Court

461

Geo & John Parks) P & S
    vs   ) Decree for the defendant with costs of suit
Patrick Shaw   )
    Wm. Thompson proved Eleven days attce. in the above case,
Ordered that the same be Taxed in the Bill of costs.

Wm Hall was qualifyed as a Constable for this County.

A Macbeth & Co) Debt
    vs   ) Same Jury as Hogg vs Brummett Sworn who return
John McNeail) their Verdict we find for the plaintiff accg.
                to Note with Interest & Costs of suit.
                        Saml Clouny, foreman.

A Macbeth & Co) Debt
    vs   ) Same Jury as Hogg vs Brummet Sworn who return
Adam Chisholm) the following Verdict, We find for the plain-
                tiff according to Note with Interest & Costs
of suit.   Samuel Clouney, foreman.

Thomas Stribling junr.) Debt
    vs   ) The plaintiff by A Nott The Defts by
Warren Hall &   ) J E Gist. Jury Sworn same as Hogg vs
William Sims   ) Brummett we find for the plaintiff Ł 22
                    s 18 d 4 with Costs of suit.
                    Samuel Clouney, foreman.

Graaff Edson & Co) P & S
    vs   ) decree for Richard Cole for s 16 d 5 with
Richd Cole   ) costs of suit
    John Reed proved Seven days attendance in the above case
Ordered that same be Taxed.

Wm Speers proved Seven days attendance in the above case, Ordered
that the same be Taxed in the Bill of costs.

Abner Wells) Debt
    vs   ) Dismissed at the Plaintiffs Cost
John Speers)

    Ordered that the Court adjourn untill Monday next 9 O Clock
signed by Thos Grandon, Wm Kennedy.

At a Court Mett According to adjournment on Monday the 9th day
of January 1797. Present Their Honors, John Blasingame, William
Kennedy, Judges.

Graaff Edson & Co) Attacht.
    vs   ) decree for the plaintiff for Ł 3 s 17 d 4½
Adam Thompson   )

Graaff Edson & Co) Debt
    vs   ) Judgment confessed accg. to Note with Inter-
John Martindale) est & costs of Suit on Stay of Execution
                   till next Court

Wm Anderson   ) Debt
    vs   ) Continued untill next Court at the defendants
Thomas B. Hunt) cost.

James Campbell   ) Debt
    vs   ) Contd. on an Affidavit at Defen-
Marg. Edmondson & David Smith)   dants Cost

                        462

Warran Hall   ) Debt
    vs   ) Contd. on oath of Dft. at Defts costs.
James Barron)

Graaf Edson & Co) Debt
    vs   ) Judgment confessed acg. to note with Interest
John ---ail   ) & costs of Suit.
    Wm. B.Farr proved Seven days attendance.

Jasper Tomerlin) Trover
    vs   )
Cush R Edson   ) Contd. untill Tomorrow.

Alex Macbeth & Co) Debt
    vs   ) Judgment confessed by the Defendant accg.
John Bird   ) to Note with Stay of Execution Six Weeks

Jeremiah Gregory) Case
    vs   ) Mr Nott attorney for the defedant, moved for
William Hughes   ) a new Tryal in this case on the following
                    Frounds, first
That the Verdict of the Jury was Contrary to Evidence
2nd That the Verdict of the Jury was Contra to Law & the direction of the Court
3rdly that New Evidence has come to his knowledge that is pertinent to his case & Which he had it not in his power to adduce.
4thly That a Riot happening during the Tryal which drew the atten-
tion of the Jury from the Suit under their immediate consideration.
    And after a full investigation of the Matter By the attorneys
on each Side, Ordered the Matter on hand be posponed untill a
further Consideration
    Signed by   Tho. Brandon, Wm Kennedy.

At a Court mett according to adjournment on Tuesday the Tenth
day of January 1797. Present Their Honors John Blasingame, Thomas Brandon, William Kennedy, Esqrs.

Jeremiah Gregory) Case
    vs   ) An affidavitt having been made by the Deft.
William Hughes   ) in this case Stating that he has a material
                    witness, who resides in the State of Georgia,
whose Testimony he could not procure at the former Tryal, Its
Ordered that a New Tryal be Granted him in the above Case and
taht a Dedimus Potestatum issue to the State of Georgia to take
the Examination of Barnabas Paine, directed to any two Justices
of the peace of that State and his evidence so taken & returned
to our next Court under their Seals shall be read as evidence in
the above case.

Graaff Edson & Co) Debt
    vs   ) Wm B Farr proved five days attce. in this
John High   ) case

Graaff Edson & Co) Debt
    vs   ) Wm B. Farr proved two days attendance in
Landlot Porter   ) this case.

John Puckett) Attacht.
    vs   ) By Consent of the parties This case is summitted
John Murrell) to the Arbitrament of Andrew Torrance Esquire
                 & Samuel Simpson, with power of Umpirate & their
award returnable to next Court shall be the Judgement thereof.

463

Warran Hall   ) Debt
    ads   ) Mr. Gist attorney for the defendant moved
Thomas Stribling) the Court for a New Tryal on the following
                   Grounds
1st Taken by Surprise
2nd New Evidence discovered since the Tryal

The Court were of Opinion that the grounds were good. Ordd.
that a new Tryal be granted on payment of the Costs of the suit.

James D Puckett) P & S
    vs   )   The Plaintiff claimed a Jury in this case
Arthur Ross   )

a Macbeth & Co) P & S
    vs   ) decree for the plaintiff accg. to Note with
James Hughs   ) Interest & Costs of suit

James Duncan   ) P & S
    vs   ) decree for Ŀ 3 18/6 with costs of suit
The Exors Col. Farr) subject to the plea of Pleni administra-
                      vit Saml. Simpson proved six days atten-
dance in this case.
John Gamblin proved four days att. also
Tho. Kitson Tanner proved Eight days attence also.

On the application of James Daily & Capt John Murrell for letters of administration t be granted them on the Estate & Effects
of Sarah Darby late of this County deceased who produced a Citation which was read three times in a public metting on that occasion.
    Its ordered that letters &C be granted them on said Estate,
Wherefore came Jas Darby and John Murrell and Entered into Bond
in the sum of Ŀ 1500 with Richard Farr, Enoch Floyd, Mark Jackson, John Martindale, James Bell & Christopher Johnson their
Securities & likewise took the oath of administration required
by Law.
    And further the said James Darby & John Murrell applied for
letters of admn. on the remaining part of the Estate & Effects
of William Darby deceased unadministered by Mrs. Sarah Darby
Administratrix on the said Estate. It is therefore ordered that
letters &C be granted them accordingly.
    The said James Darby & John Murrell came into Open Court &
Entered into Bond in the sum of Ŀ 1500 with Richard Farr, Enoch
floyd, Mark Jackson, John Martindale, James Bell and Christopher
Johnson their Security And likewise took the Oath prescribed by
law.

Robert Miller applied for a licence to retail Spirituous Liquors
& keep a public House at Pinckneyville which is granted him one
year from the first Novr last.

Graaff Edson & Co) P & S
    vs   ) Judgment confessed for Ŀ 2 9 2½ with Costs
Wm Hodge   )

Joshua Petty) P & S
    vs   ) decree for the plaintiff for the sum of Ŀ 5 s 18
Joseph Jones) with Interest & Costs of suit

Sarah Massay) P & S
    vs   ) Dismissed at the Pltfs costs.
Wm McJunkin)

464

Sarah Massay)   It appearing to this Court than an appeal was
       vs   )   demanded by Sarah Massay of Charles Sims & Benj.
Wm McJunkin   )   Woodrow, in this case at the time they decided
                   on the matter; Its ordered this the said Chas.
Sims & Benj. Woodrow Esqr Certify their proceedings up to the
next Court or then & there shew cause to the Contrary and that a
Copy of this Order be served on them.
       John Massay proved Eight days attce.

Richard Drake   )   P & S
       vs   )   Party claimed a Jury
Arthur Ross & Lusk)
       Batte Birdsong proved Nine days attendance in this case.

Ordered that Andrew Torrance, Capt. James Woodson, Robert Wallace
and John Goodwin or any three of them be and are hereby appointed
to appraise the Estate and Effects of Sarah Darby late of this
county deceased and that they make thier return according to law
Being first sworn by some Magistrate.

On motion of Abm Nott Co Attorney
       Thomas Blasingame, Thomas Vance & Majr. McJunkins, be and are
hereby appointed to enquire into the Situation of the Goal of
this County, & to propose a plan of a New one, together with
the Estimate of the Expences and report the same at next Intermediate Court.

Ben Haile took the oath of a Justice of the peace for the County.

The Court then adjourned untill Court in Courtse & Signed by
wm Kennedy, Jn Blasingame, Thos Brandon.

At a Court of Ordianry Mett for the County of Union on Thursday
the Second day of February 1797.
Present Thos Brandon, Esqr.

Returned by the admrs an Inventory & appraisement of the Estate
of Mrs. Sarah Darby deceased. Ordered to be filed.

On the application of Mr. James Darby & John Murrell admrs. of
the Estate of Mrs. Sarah Darby Deceased. Ordered that they expose to public Sale all the personal Estate & Effects of the
said deceased at the house of the said deceased on Monday next
as it appears they have given previous notice of the same giving
nine months credit taking bond with approved Security from such
persons who become pruchasers at the said Sale And that they
make the due return thereof accordingly
                                          Thos Brandon

At an Intermediate Court begun and holden on Monday the third
day of April 1797. Present their Honors Thos Brandon, Wm Kennedy, Esqrs.

On the application of Rebecca Roberts & Thomas Roberts Letters of
administration is granted them on the Estate and Effects of John
Roberds late of this County deceased, who give bond inthe sum of
Ł 200 sterling with Thomas Roberds Jnr & Jonas Randal their
Security Also took the Oath prescribed by Law.

Ordered on Motion of Rebecca Roberds & Thomas Roberts Admrs. of
John Roberds decd that John Addington, Joseph Randol & Solomon
Whitson be and are hereby appointed to appraise the Estate and
Effects of the said deceased & make due return accg. to Law to

be first sworn by a Justice of the peace

Present in open Court the Last will and Testament of Isaac Gregory late of the County decd which was duly proved by the oath of Nathan Sandage & Josiah Tyree and Ordered to be Recorded.
Gerard Gregory & Isaac Gregory was appointed Executors to the Will aforesaid, came into open Court and took the Oath required by Law.

· Present John Blasingame Esqr.

Presented in open Court the Last Will and Testament of Susannah Bailey deceased, which was duly proved by the Oaths of John Crittenden a Witness thereto, and Ordered to be Recorded.
George Bailey was appointed Executor to the above Will came into open Court & took the Oath reqd. by Law.

Ordered that John Crittenden, Edward Tilman, Wm. Smith & James Bankhead be and are hereby appointed to appraise the Estate & Effects of Susannah Bailey decd & that they make due return accg. to Law--to be first sworn by a Magistrate.

Ordered that the County Treasurer pay unto Mary Bramlett, the amount of the Sale of a certain horse sold as an Estray unto John Glasgow deducting all the charges of Postage commission &c on her filing with the Clark, the affidavits respecting said horse being her property.

James Tosh applied for a Licence to Retail spirituous Liquors & keep a public house in the County aforesaid during the term of 12 Months from the date hereof who give Bond with Thomas Greer his Security.

Wm Eaves applied for a Licence to Retail Spirituous Liquors & keep a public House in the County aforesaid at his house in Union Village during the time of 12 Months who give Bond &C according to Law.

The Verbal Will of Elijah H. Cooper decd being duly proven by the Oaths of Thomas Greer & Susannah Cooper and a Certificate thereof presented to the Court Its therefore Ordered to be Recorded.

Susannah Cooper came into open Court and was Qualifyed according to Law as an Executrix to the above Will of her husband Elijah H Cooper decd

Ordered that Joseph Little, Thos Greer, Jno & Joseph Mitchell be and are hereby appointed to appraise the Estate & Effects of Elijah H Cooper decd and that they make due Return according to Law to be first sworn by some Justice of the peace for this County.

Ordered that Alexr Macbeth & Co have leave to retail Spirituous Liquors in the County aforesaid in Union Village, during the term of 12 Months, who give Bond & Security accg. to Law.

A Bill of Sale from Adam Chisholm to Watson Chisholm proved by Wm Chisholm & Ordered to Record.

Presented in open Court the Last will & Testament of Nathl Davis Esqr late of this County deceased which duly proved by the Oath of James Caldwell Senr & Ordered to be Recorded.
Elizabeth Davis being appointed Executrix and John Valentine & James Caldwell Junr Executors to the above will came Severally

into open court and took the Oath prescribed by Law

Ordered that James Caldwell Senr, Thomas Davis Senr, & Given gordon be and are hereby appointed to appraise the Estate & Effects of Nathl Davis Esquire late of this County decd and that they make due return according to Law to be first sworn by some Justice of the peace for this County.

Ordered that a Licence be granted unto John Cooper to retail Spirituous Liquors and keep a Public House at his own house in the County of Union, during the term of 12 Months who give bond & Security according to Law.

On the application of Joseph Harris, Letters of administration is granted them on the Estate and effects of Thomas Harris late in this county decd who took the Oath prescribed by Law & give bond with David Norman & David Floyd as her Security in the sum of Ł 150 stg.

Ordered on Motion of Joseph Harris, Jonathan Norman, Solomon Bobo & Ephraim Smith, be and are hereby appointed to appraise the Estate and effects of Thomas Harris late of this County decd and that they make due Return according to Law being first sworn by some Justice of the peace for this County.

Ordered that Tilman Bobo & Wm Edward, be and are hereby appointed to view and Mark out a way for a Road from Blackstocks ford on Tyger, to the Belmount road, and make their report at our Next Court.

Ordered that a Citation be granted unto Capt. Lewis Hogg on the Estate of Capt Danile Horsey decd returnable to this Court

Acknowledged in open Court a Deed of conveyance from Adam Potter to Abm Nott; And Ordered to be recorded.

Acknowledged in Open Court a Deed from A Potter to Richd Kerby and Ordered to be recorded.

Acknowledged in open Court a Deed from A Potter to John Kerby and Ordered to be recorded.

Proved by Batte Birdsong a Mortgage from John Grastey to A Nott & Ordered to be Recorded.

Proved by Batte Birdsong a Bond from John Grastey to Abm Nott & Ordered to Record.

Proved by Adam Potter a Deed from John Henderson to Abm Nott & Ordered to be recorded.

The Court then adjourned untill Tomorrow 9 OClock.
                Thos Brandon, Wm Kennedy, Jno Blasingame.

The Court Mett According to adjournment on Tuesday the 4th April 1797. Present their Honors John Blasingame, Thomas Brandon, William Kennedy, Esqrs.

Ordered that, Adam Potter Esqr furnish by our Next June Court an exact List of all the free holders in this County for the purpose of makeing a New Jury List.

On the application of Daniel McMahen by James McElroy, a Licence is Granted him to Retail Spirituous Liquors at Pinckneyville dur-

467

ing the term of 12 Months.

Ordered that the following Established rates be Adhered to by all Publicans & Retailers in this county. vis

Dinner	1.2	Northward or Taffie rum qt	2.4
Breakfast with Coffee)		pint	1.2
tea or Chocolate)	1.	½ pint	.7
Supper	10 d		
Horse for 24 hours well)		Whiskey Dble Distilled qt	2.
fed with Oats or Corn)		pint	1.
with Foder or Hay)1.2		½ pint	.7

Corn P Gallon	.6	Single Distilled Whiskey qt	1.
Oats P Gallon	.6	pint	.7
		½ pint	4
Jama. Rum P Quart	4.		
Pint	2.1	Lodging P Night	4 d
½ Pint	1.2		
		Peach & Apple Brandy qt	2.
West India Rum qt	3.6	Pint	1.
Pint	1.9	½ Pint	.7
½ Pint	10½		
		Porter P Bottle	1.8

Cogniac Brandy same as Jama Rum

Medira & Port Wine P Quart   4/8
Tennessee Wine   P Quart   2/4

Ordered that John Haile have leave to keep a Public House and Retail Spirituous Liquors in the County aforesaid, at his own house during the term of 12 Months on his giving bond & Security to the Clerk

        Whereas it appears that   A Number of the Overseers of the Roads in this County have failed doing their duty in opening and keeping in good repair the roads under their Jurisdiction, on whose neglect the Judges of this Court have been cited to appear before the Judges of the Court of Pinckney to Shew cause why the Roads is not kept in repair according to Law. Its there- fore Ordered that each Overseer of the roads in this County, clear out & open their respective roads immediately according to Law. Otherwise the Law will be put in force against all the defaulters in the Most regorous Manner And that each Overseer be served with a Copy of this Order And at the same time be summoned to attend at our Next June Court to be holden on the first day of June next to shew cause, why they should not be fined, for their Neglect heretofore, in not working on their roads.

        Ordered that Wm McCulloch be summoned to appear before the County Court of Union on the first day of June next to shew cause why he should not be fined in the sum of Ⱡ 5 for refusing to qualify in as one of the Comrs of the poor for the County.

Ordered that all Estrays lyable for Sale at this Court be sold immediately by the Sheriff.

The Court then adjourned untill Court in Course & Signed by Thos Brandon, Jno Blasingame, William Kennedy.

At a Court of Ordinary held on the Eleventh day of April 1797. Present Tho Brandon, Esqr.

The Last will & testament of Henry Clark late of this County
deceased being proved by the affirmation of Francis Fincher and
Ordered to be ,Recorded.

John Campbell being appointed one of the Executors to the above
will, came into open Court and took the Oath prescribed by Law.

Ordered that Majr. Otterson, Ralph Hunt and Francis Fincher, be
and are hereby appointed to apraise the Estate and Effects of
Henry Clarke decd and that they make due return according to
Law to be first Sworn by some Justice of the peace for this
County.
                              Sign'd Thos Brandon.

At a Court begun and Holden in and for the County of Union at the
Court House of said County on Thursday the first dya of June 1797.
Present their Honors Thos Brandon, Wm Kennedy, Esqrs.

Ordered that the following persons be summoned to appear at our
Next Court to serve as Grand Jurors, for Said County vizt.

Frederick Crowder   Thomas Vance
Wm Johnson   John Park
James Jeater   James Tosh
Robert Goode   Wm Chisholm
John Jasper (B.S.)   Hugh Means Jnr
Richard Drake   Samuel Davidson
Joseph Howard   Henry Cuningham
James Calwell   Cush R Edson
John Putman   Wm Coleman
Landlot Porter
Eli Cook

        Also the following persons as Pettit Jurors

John Savage   Jesse Pool   James Tracey(?)
Jordon Jackson   Jnthn Cudd   Richd Fossett
Edward Prince   Wm Brandon   John Massey
Samuel Spray   James Shealds   Joseph Comer
Elijah Wilbourne Wm Smith   Wm Nix [stricken]
Wm Hodge   James Moseley   Richd Brock
John Prigmore   Jesse Young   Amos Martin
Absalom Posey   George Huey   John Lusk
Chs Woods   Wm Giles   Jedithon Porter
Samuel House   Dd Prewett   James Barrow
Joseph Randol   Thomas Weaver   John Huey
Wm Townsend   Jas Jennins
John Springer

Ordered that Wm White (son Jno.) be Overseer of the Road from
Whitlocks Mill to Jeremiah Lucas Mill, and that he keep the same
in good repair according to Law, with the hands allowed thereby

Ordered that Shepperd Mize be Overseer of the Road from Jeremiah
Lucas Mill to Fannin's Creek and that he keep the same in good
repair accog. to Law with the hand allowed thereby.

Proved in open Court by the oath of Samuel Hardy, The Last will
and testament of James Beuford late of this County decd. & Ordered to be Recorded.
     Warren Beuford, Tavinor Bird Beuford & Mary Beuford being
appointed Executors & Executrix to the said Will came into open
Court and took the Oath required by Law.

Ordered that Robert Crenshaw Senr, Leroy Beuford & Samuel
Hardy & George Lyman or any three of them, be and are hereby appointed to appraise the Estate and effects of James Beuford decd
and that they make due return according to Law.

Ordered that Joseph Harris admr. of Thomas Harris decd have leave
to expose to public sale all the personal Estate of said decd
at the plantation of said decd on the Third Monday in this Instant giving Twelve Months Credit.

John Puckett)   Attacht.
        vs   )   In Obedience to the within order We have mett and
John Murrell)   after a full investigation of the dispute Between
the parties within named we are of the opinion that the plaintiff
pay the Defendant Thirty Shillings with cost of suit, Given
under our hands this 20th day of May 1797. Signed Andw Torrance,
Saml. Simpson.

Ordered the Executors of Elijah H. Cooper decd have leave to expose to public Sale, all the personal Estate and effects of said
decd at said decd plantation, giving the Usual notice, on a Credit of Three months.

Alexr Booker & Co)   Writ Debt
        vs   )   The defendant being solemnly called but
Thomas Sherriff   )   failed to appear Its therefore Ordered that
                      Judgment be entered up against him by default.

Wm Coleman vs John Petty Pool   Case Discontinued.

Richard Farr & Co)   P & S
        vs   )   Decree confessed by A Thomas according to
Chs Charity &   )   Note on Stay of Exon. three months with
Arthur Thomas   )   cost of suit

John Blasingame Esq) Attacht.
        vs   ) Daniel Bain being summoned as a Garnishee
John Glasgow   ) in the above case, came into open Court
                       and declares on his Oath that he has in
his possession the property of the above John Glasgow to wit;
Four Salt Casks, two old Chests, one Keg Butter about 11, 1 Black
Bottle & One Gimble, 1 P Scales & One four pound weight. Its
therefore ordered that the above property be condemned as the
property of the said John Glasgow, and that the said Daniel Bain
deliver unto the Sheriff the said property, who is Ordered to
expose to Sale the same the Money arising therefrom to be aplyed
first to the discharge a debt for rent due to the said Daniel
Bain amounting to 20/ 7d the balance to be appropriated to discharged the debt due the plaintiff

John Blasingame Esqr) Attacht.
        vs   ) decree for the Plaintiff accog. to
John Glasgow   ) note with Interest & Cost of suit.

Its Ordered that Elizabeth Henderson admr of John Cole decd expose to public Sale all the personal Estate and effects of said
decd on a credit of Six months giving the usual Notice of such
sale, and that she make due return according to Law.

Its ordered that the Court adjourn untill Tomorrow 10 o Clock.
Signed by Thos Brandon, Wm Kennedy.

470

The Court mett according to adjournment on Fryday the Second day of June 1797. Present Their Honors, John Blasingame, Wm Kennedy, Esqrs.

Proved in open Court by the affirmation of Eli Cook A Bond & Mortgage from Cush R Edson to Joseph Jones and Ordered to be Recorded

Proved in open Court by the oath of Thomas Lee The Last Will & Testament of Daniel Howell and Ordered to be Recorded.
Ordered that John Stokes, Thomas Lee & Michael Lee appraise the Estate and effects of Daniel Howel decd and that they make due return according to Law to be first sworn by some Magistrate.

John Blasingame Esqr) Attacht.
    vs   ) Daniel Bowen being Summoned as a Gar-
John Glasgow   ) nashe in this action, came into open
                  court and declares on his Oath that he
has in his possession a Black Horse, the property of the Defendant. Its therefore ordered that the said Horse be condemned as the property of the Defendant: And further Ordered that the said Daniel Bowen deliver up the said Horse to the Sheriff who is Ordered to Sell, the money arising therefrom first to pay unto the said Daniel Bowen the sum of Six Dollars for keeping said horse, the Balance to be appropriated towards the Extinguishment of the plfs Debt.

Andrew George) Attacht.
   vs   ) Ralph Hunt was summoned as a Garnashe in this
Shad. Landtrip) suit came into open Court and declared on his
              Oath he had no property in his possession belonging to the defendant, and was in nowise indebted to the defendant.

The State   ) Indict.
  vs   ) Hog Stealing
Daniel Tollerson) A true Bill against Daniel Tollerson &
David Harris Jnr) David Harris Junr. No Bill vs Dd. Harris
David Harris Snr) Senr.
                    A Torrence, foreman.

The State   ) Indict.
  vs   ) Hog Stealing.
Daniel Tollerson) Abraham Nott County attorney in behalf of
David Harris Junr) the State and the Defendants by John Dunlap
             & Jo C Gist   Wherein came a Jury to wit
John Cirttende, Arthur Brandon, John Ingrem, Alex Kendrick, Leroy Beuford, John Smith, Daniel Crownover, Thomas Young, Samuel Huey, Zacha. Belue, Edmond Ellis & Josep Randol, who being duly Empand. & Sworn say on their several Oaths & affirmations we the Jury say Not Guilty.
                  Rd. Crittenden, foreman.

Magnes Simonson) Slander
  vs   ) Dismissed by consent of the plaintiff at his
Arthur Thomas   ) costs.

Wm Lipscombe Jnr) Writ
  vs   ) covenant
Josiah Wilson   ) Judt. confessed by the deft. for Ł 1000 of
               Tobacco at Ten shillings P ct. with Interest
& Cost on Stay of Execution untill the first January next.

Graaff Edson & Co) Debt
vs) Came the plaintiff by A Nott and the deft
Wm Speers) by Jo C Gist Whereupon came a Jury
to wit John Crittenden fn., Arthur Brandon,
Alexr Kendrick, Leroy Beuford, Philip Bass, Daniel Crownover,
Thomas Young, Samuel Huey, Zacha. Belue, Amos Cook & Joseph
Randol, John Ingrim who being duly Sworn return their Verdict &
Say we find according to Note.
John Crittenden, foreman.

John Nuckols proved two days attendance in This case.

Graaff Edson & Co) P & S
vs) Dismissed at Pltf Cost
Rd Harris)

Graaff Edson & Co) Case
vs) Dismissed pltf cost
Chs Green & Nichs Haus(?))
Exors Fincher) Debt
vs) Dismissed at the Dfts Cost.
The Exors Sims)

Beckham & Co) P & S
vs) Decree confessed by the defandants according to
James Bedwell) Specialty with Interest & Costs of Suit. Stay
& Josiah Wilson) of Execution until 1st Jany. next.

Beckham & Co) P & S
vs) Decree confessed by the defendant accg. to Spe-
Josiah Wilson) cialty with Interest & Costs of suit, Stay of
Exon untill 1st January next.

Bekcham & Co) P & S
vs) Decree confessed by the defendants accog. to
Josiah Wilson &) Specialty with Interest & Costs of suit Stay
James Bedwell) of Exon untill 1 January next

Beckham & Co) Case
vs) Judt. confessed by the Defendant for Ł 6 18/4½
Fields Blaney) with costs suit, on Stay of Execution untill
first January next.

Ordered that the County Treasurer pay unto old Mr. McDaniel Ten
shillings for Wintering a Stray Heifer.

Richd Gilbert) Case
vs) By consent of the parties this case is re-
Christr. Johnson) fered to Judge Kennedy & Judge Blasingame
with power of chosing an umpire, and their
award returnable to next Court shall be the Judt. hereof.

Ruth Gwin) Attachment
vs) George Harlan hatter having been summoned as a
Daniel Plummer) Garnishe in this case, came into open Court and
and declared on his Oath that he was indebted
to the Defendant the sum of Ł 37 s 2 d 8 with interest thereon
from the 14th Feb 1796., Whereupon came a Jury the same as
Graaff Edson & Co against William Speer, who being duly Sworn
return their Verdict & say we find for the Plaintiff according
to Note with Interest. John Crittenden, foreman.
It is therefore Ordered that the Verdict be Recorded and that
the sum of Ł 37 2/8 d with the Interest thereon be condemned in

472

the hands of the Garnashe Geo Harlan, who is further Ordered
to pay the same to the plaintiff Ruth Gwin.

Wm Lipscombe assee) Debt
   John Watson   ) Judgment confessed by the Defendt. accor-
      vs   ) ding to Specialty with Interest & Costs of
John Bird   ) suit. Stay of Exon untill first December
                next

Joseph King) Writ of Inquiry
   vs   ) Same Jury as Graaf Edson & Co vs Speers, who
John Stowers) being sworn return their Verdict & Say we find
for the plaintiff One thousand Wt. of Tobacco @ 14/6 with Interest and costs of suit.   Jno Cirttenden, foreman.

James Martin   ) Case
   vs   ) Robert Miller came into open Court and ack-
The Exors of Jno) nowledged himself Security for the Costs in
Herrington decd) the Action in case the plaintiff becomes
                lyable

Wm Chisholm assee) Writ Debt
      T Shelley) Judgment confessed according to Note, allow-
   vs   ) ing refund it of thirty one dollars agree-
John Bird   ) able to his Receipt given to the Defendant
                With interest & costs of Suit Stay of Exon
untill first day of August next.

Thomas Stribling) Debt
   vs   ) Ordered that the plaintiff have leave to
Warran Hall &) proceed to enter up his Judgment in this case.
Wm Sims   )

Wm Smith Esqr) P & S
   vs   ) Decree for the plaintiff According to Specialty
James Hicks) with interest and Costs of suit

The State   ) Indict
   vs   ) Hog Stealing
Richd Lee   ) A True Bill A Torrence foreman.

A MacBeth & Co) Trover
   vs   )
Warren Hall)
  Wm Chisholm Common Bail in this case delivered the Deft in
Court, Wm Sims came in & entered himself Spl. Bail for Deft. &
Continued.

Wm Steen   ) Attachment
   vs   ) Decree for the plaintiff the sum of ₺ 9 with
James Strawn) costs of suit Jeremiah Gregory was summoned
               as a Garnashe declared on his Oath that he has
in his possesion of the property of the Defendant One hand Saw,
on Rifle Barrel Moles & Wipers one Jack plain & one turners
wheel. Its ordered that the said specified property Together
with the property attached by Condemned & to go towards satisfying the above decree

The State   ) Indt.
   vs   ) Stealing Cows
Jos. Simmons) No Bill A. Torrence, foreman.

Ordered that Jo Tucker be Overseer of the road from Cane Creek to Tyger Crenshaws ford and that he keep the same in good repair accg. to Law.

Ordered that the Court adjourn untill Tomorrow 10 0 Clock.
Thos Brandon, Wm. Kennedy

The Court mett according to adjournment on Saturday the Third day of June 1797. Present their Honors John Blasingame, Thomas Brandon, Wm. Kennedy, Esqr.

Ordered that the property Bought in for The Orphan's of Mrs. Sarah Darby decd at the Sale of said Estate, stand untill next Court for a further consideration.
[above entry stricken]

Richard Farr) P & S
     vs   ) Decree confessed by the Defendant for Ƚ 4 s 4
Cush. R. Edson) with costs of Suit. Stay of Execution till
              last day of December next

Jno Peter Sartor) P & S
     vs   ) Decree for the plaintiff for One thousand
Absalom Posey   ) pounds of Tobacco Ten shillings with Interest
                 and costs of suit.

Mark Jackson applied for a License to keep public House & retail Spitiruous Liquors in this County at his own house, which was granted he therefore give Bond & Secy. Accog. to Law.

Robert McCrery assee) P & S
         Smith   ) decree confessed by the Defendant accg.
         vs   ) to Note, with interest & Costs of Suit
John Martindale   )

Robert McCrery assee) P & S
         Taylor   ) Decree confessed by the Defendant accg.
         vs   ) to Note with Interest & Costs of Suit.
John Martindale   )

A Macbeth & Co) Writ Debt
     vs   ) Dismissed by consent at the Defendants Cost.
John Murrell &)
Andw Torrence)

Graaff Edson & Co) Case
     vs   ) Came the plaintiff by Mr. Shaw & Jno Dunlap
John McCooll   ) and the defendant by Wm Smith Esqr
Whereupon came a Jury To wit, John Crittenden, Arthur Brandon, John Ingrim, Luroy Beuford, Philip Bass, David Crownover, Thomas Young, Samuel Huey, Zacha. Belue, Amos Cook, Joseph Randol & Edmond Ellis Who being duly Sworn, Return their Verdict and Say on their Several Oaths & affirmations, we find for the Plaintiff Ƚ 32 s 8 d 4   John Crittenden, foreman. Which Verdict the Court Ordered to be Recorded &C.

Richd. Drake) P & S
     vs   ) decree confessed by Arthur Ross according to
Arthur Ross &) Specialty with Interest & Costs of suit Stay
John Lusk   ) of Exon 3 Months.
   B. Birdsong proved three days attendance in This case.

Granted to John Parham a Licence to Retail & keep a Publi House who give Bond & Secy. accg. to Law.

Proved in open Court by H Farnandis, A Mortgage from Adam Chisholm unto Wm Chisholm & Obadiah Trimmier & John Henderson Exors
of Dd. Chisholm decd & Ordered to be Recorded.

Proved in open Court by H. Farnandis, A Bill of Sale from John
Henderson Obd Trimmier & Wm Chisholm to F W Chisholm & Ordered
to be Recorded.

Proved in open Court a Acct(?) from Watt Chisholm to John Henderson, Obadiah Trimmier & Wm Chisholm & Ordered to be Recorded.

Wm Anderson   ) Debt
    vs   ) Came the pltf. by A Nott and The defendant by
Thomas B Hunt) Jno Dunlap Whereupon came a Jury The same as
                  Graaff Edson & Co vs John McCooll who being
Sworn Return their Verdict & Say we find for the plaintiff Ł 3
14/4 d and the costs of the suit. John Critten, foreman.

Order'd that Andrew Torrence Esqr, Christr. Johnson and Majr.
Means be and are hereby appointed to attend At the clerk's office
of this County on the first Monday in July next, then & there to
continue from day to day untill they make an Examination of the
Clerk's Office and also the Treasurers Books of this County, and
to make their report at our Next Court, what has become of the
Public Moneys arising from Estrays sold, Licenses granted & fines
& forfeitures in sd. County, and how it has been appropriated.
Also Ordered that the Treasurer attend with his Books on that day
and that each be sumd by the Sheriff.

Ordered that the Court adjourn untill Monday 10 O Clock Signed by
Tho Brandon, Wm Kennedy.

The Court mett according to adjournment on Monday the fifth of
June 1797. Present their Honors, Thomas Brandon, Wm Kennedy,
John Glasingame, Esqrs.

James D. Puckett) P & S
    vs   ) On motion of J Dunlap attorney for plaintiff
Arthur Ross   ) Ordered that this case be continued untill
                    next court And that a commission issue to
take the Examination of Jas D Puckett, to be heard in evidence
in the above case at Next Court

Jeremiah Gregory) Action on the case
    vs   ) Came the plaintiff by Samuel Farrow & the
Wm Hughes   ) Defendant by A Nott, Wm. Smith & John Dunlap
                   Whereupon came a Jury to wit John Crittenden,
foreman, Arthur Brandon, John Ingrim, Leroy Beuford, Philip Bass,
Daniel Crownover, Samuel Huey, Zacha. Belue, Amos Cook, Joseph
Randol Edmd Ellis and Alexr Kendrick, who being duly sworn return
their Verdict & Say we find for the plaintiff Ł 10 and costs of
suit.   John Crittenden, foreman.
    Ordered that the Verdict be recorded.

Thomas Evans   ) P & S
    vs   ) decree for the plaintiff for 12 hundred weight
Thomas Beddie &) of Tobacco, at Twelve shillings P ct. with
Peter Beddie   ) Interest & Costs of suit.

Graaf Edson & Co) P & S
    vs   ) Decree for the defendant for five shillings &
John Miller   ) nine pence with costs.

John McCool   ) Case
    vs   ) A Nott for Plaintiff
Nancy Conyers) John Dunlap for Deft
          Same Jury as Gregory vs Hughes who being Sworn return
their Verdict & Say we find for the plaintiff Ł 4 & s 4 & Costs
                              John Crittenden, foreman.

Ordered that the Verdict be Recorded Subject to the plea of
Plene administravit.

Ordered that the Court adjourn untill Tomorrow 10 0 Clock.
Jno Blasingame, Wm Kennedy.

The Court met according to adjournment on Tuesday the Sixth day
of June 1797. Present their Honors Thomas Brandon, Wm Kennedy,
Esqrs.

Graaf Edson & Co   ) P & S
    vs   ) Continued for Deft at his Cost
James Townsend admr. Cook)

Warran Hall) Debt
    vs   ) Same Jury as McCooll vs Conyers who being Sworn
James Barron) return their Verdict and say we find for the
                plaintiff the Costs of Suit.
                              John Cirttenden, foreman.

James D. Puckett) P & S
    vs   ) Decree for the plaintiff for Ł 6 4/5 d with
Wm Bowman   ) costs of suit.

John Marin   ) Debt
    vs   ) Same Jury as Hall vs Barron who being duly sworn
Warren Hall) Return their Verdict & Say we find for the plain-
                tiff Ł 10 s 4 d 9 & costs. John Crittenden, fore-
man. Which Verdict the Court Ordered to be Recorded.

Thomas Bishop) Case
    vs   ) Judgment confessed by the Defendant in open
Cush R Edson) Court for Ł 23 s 14 d 6 with Costs of suit.
                Subject to all Legal discounts said discounts
to be left to Col. Brandon & James Woodson Snr and their Judgment upon the same to be Returned to Next Court or Judgmt. to
be final for the above sum.

Basel Trail) Debt
    vs   ) Judgment confessed accg. to Note, with Interest
Cush R Edson) & Costs of suit. Stay of Execution untill the
                fourth day of November Next. deducting Legal
discounts.

The Admrs. Anderson   ) P & S
    vs   ) decree for the deft with costs of
The Exors of Col. Wm. Farr) suit

Alexr Macbeth & Co) P & S
    vs   ) decree for the Plaintiff for Ł 3 s 8 with
John Miller   ) costs of suit
     Richd. Farr proved Seventeen days attce in the above case.
Ordered that the same be Taxed in the Bill of Costs

Graaf Edson & Co) P & S
    vs   ) Richd Farr proved Sixteen days attendance in
John Miller   ) this case Ordered that the same be Taxed in
               the Bill of Costs

Alexr Macbeth & Co) P & S
    vs   ) decree for the plaintiff for Ł 5 7/8 with
John McNeail   ) costs of suit.

Graaf Edson & Co) Case
    vs   ) Came the plaintiff by A Nott & the defendant
Jacob Holms   ) by J. Dunlap Whereupon came a Jury to wit
               the same as Martin vs Hall who being Sworn
Return their Verdict & Say we find for the Plaintiff 8/1½ &
Costs. John Cirttenden, foreman.

Jas. A. Whyte) P & S
    vs   ) Decree for the Plaintiff for Ł 3 11/ 3d with
Wm Steen   ) costs of suit.

Graaff Edson & Co) P & S
    vs   ) Decree for the Defendant with costs of
James Steen   ) suit

Jno Steen proved five days attce in this case.
Thomas Vance proved fifteen days atte. in this case.

The Court then adjourned untill Tomorrow 10 0 Clock.
Thos Grandon, Wm Kennedy.

John Beckham & Co) Case
    vs   ) Came the deft into open Court in his own
Alex Kendrick) proper person and acknowledged that he owed
               the plaintiff Ł 35 s 17 d 2½ and confessed
Judgment for the same with Costs of suit. Amounting to Ł 1 s 14
d 6 Wherefore this considered by the court that the plaintiff
Recover against the defendant in from aforesaid, and the said
Defendant in Mercy &c &c.

The Court mett according to adjournment on Wednesday the seventh
day of June 1797. Present their Honors Thomas Brandon, Wm
Kennedy.

Jno Beckhan & Co) Case
    vs   ) The Defendant came into Open Court and con-
Alexr Kendrick) fessed a Judgment for the sum of Ł 35 17/2½
               with costs of suit.

Graaff Edson & Co) P & S
    vs   ) Dismissed at Deft cost.
Danl McElduff)

James D. Puckett) P & S
    vs   ) Same Jury as Graaff Edson & Co against Jacob
Willis Walker) Holms, who being sworn, return their Verdict
Turner Kendrick) & say we find for the plaintiff Ł 7 8/5 d
with Interest and Costs accog. to Note. John Crittenden, foreman.
    Doctr. White proved Nine days attene. in this case
    Ordered that the Verdict be Recorded.

Joseph Jones) Attacht.
  vs   ) Same Jury as above, who being duly sworn return
Daniel Bowen) their Verdict & Say we find for the Plaintiff
             Ł 17 with costs. John Crittenden, foreman.
        Ordered that the Verdict be Recorded

Betsey Brown) Case
  vs   ) Write of Enquiry
James Porter) Same jury as aboev return their Verdict & say
             we find for the Plaintiff Ł 12 14/9 with costs
     Ordered that the Verdict be Recorded John Crittenden, foreman.

James D. Puckett) P & S
  vs   ) Decree for the plaintiff accg. to Note with
Turner Kendrick) Interest & costs of suit.
        Doctr Whyte proved Nine day attce in the above case.

John Heald   ) Case
  vs   ) Judgment confessed for Ł 5 18/ with Interest
Barba Willard &) and costs of suit. Stay of Execution till 1st
John Willard   ) Jany next

The state   ) Recognce.
  vs   ) Bastardy
Isaac Gregory &) On Motion of Abraham Nott Ordered that a Rule
Jerem. Gregory) be served on the Defendants to Shew cause at
                 next Court why their Recogce. should not be
forfeited in the above case

Joshua Petty) Debt
  vs   ) Came the plaintiff by A Nott & the Defendant by
Alex Love   ) Wm Smith Whereupon came a Jury to wit the same
             Graaf Edson & Co vs Holms, who being duly sworn
Return their Verdict & say we find for the plaintiff according
to Note, allowing a credit of Six pounds 13/ d 5 agreeable to
the credit on said Note.   John Crittenden, foreman.
     Ordered that the Verdict be Recorded
Wm. Nichols proved Eleven days attce in ths above case.

Graaff Edson) P & S
  vs   ) Decree for the Defendant for Ł 1 s 11 d 7 with
Peter Ellis) costs of suit
Henry Littlejohn proved four days attce in this case
Edmond Ellis proved four days attendance in this case.

Gasper Tomerlin) Trover
  vs   ) Came the plaintiff by John Dunlap and the
Cush R Edson   ) defendant by Abraham Nott Whereupon came a
                 Jury to wit John Crittenden, foreman. Arthur
Brandon, Edmond Ellis, John Ingrim, Philip Bass, Daniel Crownover,
Samuel Juey, Zacha. Belue, Thomas Young, Abel Kendrick, Amos Cook,
& Joseph Randol who being duly Empanneled and sowrn, Return their
Verdict & Say   [verdict not recorded]

Richard Farr & Co) Debt
  vs   ) Judgment confessed in open court by the
Josiah Wood   ) Deft accg. to Specialty with Interest &
                   Costs of suit Stay of Execution untill
25th Decr next.

Shad Rowls) D & L
  vs   ) The plaintiff on the affidavit appears now to
Arthur Ross) reside out of the State. Its Ordered that the

                        478

Plaintiff five Security for costs in this action on or before
the first day of Jany next.

Graaff Edson & Co) P & S
    vs   ) Discontinued
John Palmore   )

John Nuckols proved Six days attc. in the above case.
John Palmore Senr proved Sixteen days attce in this case.

Doctr. Whyte)
    vs   ) Dismissed
Jas Gath   )

Jasper Tomerlin) Trover
    vs   ) Ordered that the Jury who hsa been sworn in
C R Edson   ) this case Seal their Verdict up & return it
                  in Open Court on Tomorrow if they agree

Then the Court adjourn untill Tomorrow 8 0 Clock Thos Brandon,
Wm Kennedy.

The Court met according to adjournment on Thursday the eighth
day of June 1797. Present their Honors John Blasingame, Thomas
Brandon, Wm Kennedy. Esqrs.

Richd Duckett   ) Slander
    vs   ) Ordered that a commission issue to North Ca-
James Martindale) rolina to take examination of   in the
                above

J. D. Puckett   ) P & S
    vs   ) On Motion of J. C. Gist Ordered that a New
Willis Walker &) Tryal be granted on paymt. of costs.
Turner Kendrick)

Jeremiah Gregory) Spl Action the Case
    vs   ) The Defendant having prayed an appeal in
William Hughes) this case, which is granted according who
                give bond & Security according to Law to
prosecute the same

Graaff Edson & Co) Case
    vs   ) On Motion of Wm Smith atty. for the defen-
John McCooll   ) dant. Its ordered that a New Tryal be
                granted in this case on payment of costs.

Jasper Tomerlin) Trover
    vs   ) The Jury being call'd to deliver their Ver-
Cush R Edson   ) dict in this case, Thomas Young & Philip
                Bass being solemnly call'd but fail'd to
answer to their names, The other Ten Jurors to wit John Crittenden, Edmond Ellis, John Ingrim, Daniel Crownover, Samuel Huey,
Zacha. Belue, Alexr Kendrick,Amos Cook, & Joseph Randol appeared
& brought in their Verdict Sealed as Ordered yesterday and say
we find for the plaintiff Ł 15 & costs. John Crittenden, foreman. Its considered that the above verdict is not lega (on
account of the absence of the two Jurors)
Its therefore Ordered that Thomas Young & Philip Bass be summoned
to appear at our next court to shew cause if any they have why
an attachment should not issue against them for a contempt of
this court in refusing to appear in open Court with the other
Jurors to deliver in thier Verdict as they were ordered.

The court then adjourned untill Court in Course & signed by
Jno Blasingame, Wm Kennedy.

At an Intermediate Court begun & Holden in & for the County of
Union On Monday the 4th day of September 1797.
Present their Honors, John Blasingame, Wm Kennedy, Esqrs.

Acknowledged in open Court a Bond from Adam Kilpatrick to Alex
Mcdonnell & Ordered to be Recorded.

On Motion of Amy Yarborough, Administration is granted her on the
Estate & Effects of Jeremiah Yarborough late of this County decd
she complied with the law by giving bond in the sum of Ł 100 with
Jos. Mitchell & Wm. Lawson her Securities also took the Oath
prescribed accordingly.

Ordered that James Putman, Joseph Kelly & Benj. Nix be and are
hereby appointed to appraise the Estate & Effects of Jeremiah
Yarborough late of this County decd and that they amke due
Return thereof acog. to Law. to be first sworn by some Magistrate
for this County.

Proved in Open Court by H Farnandis a Deed of conveyance from
Wm Lipscombe & Ad Chisholm to John Watson & Ordered to be Recorded.

Granted to Walter Goodman Licence to Retail Spirituous Liquors
at D. Liphams plantation in this County for One year who give
Bond.

A Bill sale from James Beuford to Moses & Warren Beuford & Orded
to record proved by Bird Beuford.

On Motion of Daniel White, Ordered that Ellis Fowler be Overseer
of the Road from the forks of the Road leding by Gibbs old field
to Pine __ as far as Ephraim Fowlers, and that he keep the same
in good repair accg. of Law.

Ordered that John Martindale, Tho Lamb & Edmond Simpson be and
are hereby appointed to view & Mark out a way for a Road from
Saml Simpson to Musgroves old Mill, the Nearest & best Way
& Make their Report to our Next Court.

Ordered that Joseph Jones be Overseer of the Road from Union
Court House to his own plantation and Claton Stribling from there
to the Pinckney Road and that they keep the same in good repair
according to Law.

Ordered the Jesse Mayberry Adam Potter & John Haile View the
Roads from Jesse Mayberys to Grindal Shoal and the Road leading
from Gibbs old Field to Grindals Shoal as far as the mill creek
and the Road leading from Spartg. to Grindal Shoal within one
mile of said Shoal, if the proprietors of the Land on said Roads
agree, that the said Commrs make such alterations in the Roads as
Appear most convenient or Necessary and if the parties shall
not agree they should report to Next Janry Court, such alterations
as they recommend.

Ordered that Thomas Woodson be Overseer of the Road from Mitchels
Creek to Darbys Store in the room of Elisha Bend and that he keep
the same in good repair accg. to Law.

Ordered that Wm Littlefield be Overseer of the Road from Leond. Smith to Dining Creek in the room of sd. Smith and that he keep the same in good repair accg. to Law.

Ordered that Avery Howard be Overseer of the Road from Col. Brandons to Union Court House in the room of Jos. Reeder and that he keep the same in good repair according to Law.

Ordered that the Executors of James Beuford Snr late of this County decd Expose to Public Sale at the plantation of afsd. decd. on the first Monday in December Next, all the personal Estate & Effects of said decd giving Twelve months credit and that they make due Return accg. to Law.

Ordered that the Roads leading from Beuford & Tilmans Ferry to Pinckneyville be Opened & kept in repair, also the fork of the Road into the Main road leading to Pinckneyville.

A Sheriffs Deed from John Henderson to Cornelius Wilson Acknd. in open Court & Ord. to Record.

Ordered that the County treasurer pay John Henderson Esqr Sheriff his Extra fees for two years which become due on the first day of June last

On Motion of Abraham Nott in behalf of the Securities of James Darby & Capt John Morell Admrs. of Sarah Darby decd. Ordered that the said admrs. be sumd. to appear at our Next Court to Shew cause why the security should not be relived from their Security-ship.

Ordered that Jos Brock be Overseer of the Road from Grangers ford on Tyger to Cain Creek and that he keep the same in good repair accg. to Law.

Ordered that Jeremiah Rackly be Overseer of the Road from the county line to Leonard Smiths in the room of Chs. Browning, and that he keep the same in good repair accg. to Law.

On the Application of Timothy A Edson, Letters of Administration is granted him on the Estate & Effects of Majr. Cush R. Edson, late of this County decd who give Bond in the sum of Ł 400 ster-ling with James Bell, Avery Howard, Stephen Howard & Wm Brandon his Securities & took the oath prescribed by Law.

Ordered that Richard Powell, James Tosh & Joseph Reeder be and are hereby appointed to appraise the Estate & Effects of Cush R Edson decd and that they make due Return of the same accg. to Law to be first sworn by some Magistrate for this county.

The Court then adjourned untill Tomorrow 10 0 Clock. Thos Brandon, Jno Blasingame, Wm Kennedy.

The Court Mett According to adjournment ton Utesday the Fifth day of September 1797. Present their Honors John Blasingame, Thomas Brandon, Wm. Kennedy, Esqrs.

Ordered that Robert White be Overseer of the Road from Tyger River to Fairforest in the room of Woodson Rountree. And that he keep the same in good repair According to Law.

Ordered that Joseph Kelley be Overseer of the Road from Bobos ford on Tyger River to Samuel Simpson in the room of James Duncan (son of Alexander) and that he keep the same in good repair accg. to Law.

Ordered that Jonathan Cudd be Overseer of the Road from the Reedy branch to Pinckneyville in the room of Alex Kendrick and that he keep the same in good repair accg. to Law

Ordered that the County Treasurer pay the Sheriff of this County two Dollars for furnishing two Locks.

Ordered that Zachariah Belue be Overseer of the Road from Plummers Ford to the main road leading to Union Court House and that he keep the same in good repair accg. to Law.

Ordered that Samuel Clouney be Overseer of the Road from Williamson's Creek to John Hailes And that he keep the same in good repair accg. to Law.

Ordered that the admrs. of Sarah Darby decd Expose to Public Sale the remaining part of the personal Estate of said dec'd, which was sold at the former Sale & Not complied with by the purchasers✳ Giving the Usual Notice and Credit taking Bond & Security Accg. to Law.
✳ Also the remaining part of the property unsold.

Ordered that Daniel Nogher be Overseer of the Road from Loves Ford to Hughes Creek in the room of Thomas Hughes and that he keep the same in good repair according to Law.

Ordered that David Norman be Overseer of the Road from Blackstocks ford to Samuel Simpsons, the Way it was Marked out by the Commissioners Also the Sandy ford Road as far as the County Line and that he keep the same in good repair according to Law.

Acknowledged in open Court A Deed of conveyance from Edward Williams to Thomas Wright & Ordered to be Recorded.

Ordered that James C Veal, James Gasway & Bartholomew Baker be and are hereby appointed to View & Mark out a way for a Road Leading from Cooks bridge on Tyger River the nearest & best way to Rodrick Wrights plantation, and make their report to our Next Court.

Ordered that the Estray be sold by the Sheriff which is now liable.

Ordered that as soon as the Inventory & Appraisement of the Estate & Effects of Majr. Cush R. Edson decd is returned by Timotyy A. Edson the admrs. that he shall have leave to Expose to Public Sale all the personal Estate & Effects of the said decd giving the Usual Notice of such Sale giving a Credit until the first day of March next taking Bond with approved Security.
    [above entry stricken]

The Court then adjourned untill Court in Course.   Jno Blasingame, Wm Kennedy, Thos B randon.

At a Court of Ordinary Mett for the County of Union on the 22nd day of September 1797. Present their Honors, Thomas Brandon, Wm. Kennedy, Esqrs.

Ordered that Timothy A Edson administrator of the Estate & Effects of Majr. Cush R. Edson late of this county decd Expose to Public

482

Sale all the personal estate and effects of said decd at his
dwelling house, on Thursday the Twelfth day of October next on
a credit untill The first day of March next, taking Bond or Notes
with good Security for all sums above Twenty shillings, under
That Cash.   And that he make due return of the same according to
Law.   Wm. Kennedy J. U. C., Thos Brandon, J. U. C.

At a Court of ordinary mett for the County of Union on the 24th
day of October 1797.   Present their Honours, Thos Brandon, Wm.
Kennedy, Esqrs.

On the application of Nancy Simson admx. and William Wilbanks
letters of administration is Granted them on the estate and effects of Samuel Simson late of this County deceased who give bond
in the sum of $2500 with Sampson Bobo, Andrew Torrence Esqr
and Ambrose Ray their Securities and took oath Prescribed by
Law.

Ordered that Andrew Torrence, Ralph Jackson and Robt White and
Thomas Greer appraise the estate of Samuel Simpson Deceasd or
any three of them being first legally Qualifyed.   October 24,
1797.   Thos Brandon, Wm Kennedy.

Att a Court of ordinary mett 4th Novr 1797   Present his honor
John Blasengame Esqr.

Proven in Open Court by the affirmation of Samuel Hunt the last
will and Testament of James Purnell deceased
Ordered that Henry Thick Penny, Samuel Hunt, Mahlon Pearson, John
Townsend apprase the estate and effects of James Parnell decead
and that they make a True return thereof and that George Parnell
and James Townsend to be sworn by some Justice of the Peace

Then the Court adjourned untill Court in Course.   Signed
Jno Blasingame.

At a Court of Ordinary mett for the County of Union on Wednesday
the 8th day of Novr 1797.   Present Thos Brandon, Wm Kennedy, Esqr.

Ordered that the admrs. of Samuel Simpson late of the County
decd. expose to public Sale on Tuesday the fourteenth day of this
instant at the plantation of said decd.,all the personal Estate
& Effects belonging to the said decd. Estate, giving Twelve Months
Credit, Taking bond with approved Security, & that they make due
Return of the same according to Law.   Thos Brandon, Wm. Kennedy.

At a Court begun and Holden in and for the County of Union at
the Court House of said County on Monday the first day of January
One thousand and Seven hundred and Ninety Eight.   Present their
Honors   Thomas Brandon, Wm. Kennedy, Esqrs.

The Court proceeded to draw the grand Jury to Serve at next Court
who are as follows   vizt.

George Park	John Palmore
Tho Hollingsworth	Wm. Buchanan
J P Sartor	John Hamm
Benj. Savage	Abner Coleman
Beo Lyman	Tho Palmore
Tho Parmor	Geo Harland hatter
James McKibben	Patrick H Sims
John Parke	John Portman [stricken]
John Jasper	Walter Roberds

Bartlet Whorton   Adam Potter
                                Ralph Jackson
                                Wm McCulloch

        Also the Following person to serve as Pettit Jurors.

Robert Savage   Jacob Paulk
Nathl. Rogers   Wm. Browning
Jas. Townsend   Wm. Laurence
Isaac Hollingsworth   George Bailey
James Tracey   Philip Philpeck
John Prigmore   George Harlan farmer
Augustus Wood   Arthur Thomas
Peter Philpeck   Robert Huckaby
Peter Thomas   Samuel Paulk
Peter Laurence   Nathan Langston
Arthur Ross   John Weeks
Nathl. Simmons   James Harris
Barnett Woolbright   John Townsend
Daniel Lipham   Chs. Thompson
James Moseley   John Strange

On the Application of Olive Cook Letters of Admn. is granted her
on the Estate & Effects of John Cook late of this County deceased
who give Bond with Eli Cook & Benjamin Smith her Securitys in the
sum of Ł 250 Sterling, & took the Oath required by Law.

Ordered that James Townsend Amos Cook & Ralph Hunt be and are
hereby appointed to appraise the Estate & Effects of John Cook
late of this County decd. and that they make due Return of the
same According to Law. to be first sworn by Majr. McJunkin.

Peter Philpeck is granted a tavern License who give Bond with
Security accg.

Proven in Open Court by the Oaths of Robert Woodson, James Woodson, James Whitlock & Jedithan Woodson, the Last will & Testament of Turner Rountree late of this County decd. & Ordered to
be Recorded.

Proved in Open Court by the Oath of George Harlan hatter the
Last will and testament of Renny Belue Senr late of this county
deceased and Ordered to Record.
        Ordered that Geo. Harland hatter Wm Morgan & Samuel Harlan
be and are hereby appointed to appraise the Estate & Effects of
Renny Belue Senr decd and that they make due Return accg. to
Law to be first sowrn by Tho: Blasingame Esqr.

Zachariah Belue Reuben Belue & Renny Belue being appointed Executors to the last Will and Testament of Renny Belue Senr came
into open Court & took the Oath require by Law as Executors accordingly.

The Court then adjourned untill tomorrow 10 0 Clock.   Thos Brandon, Wm. Kennedy.

The Court Mett according to adjournment at the Court House of
said County on Tuesday the Second day of January 1798. Present
their Honors, Thomas Brandon, Wm. Kennedy, Esquires.

Graaff Edson & Co) P & S
     vs   ) Ordered on Motion of J. C. Gist that a Com-
John Burgess   ) mission Debene Esse issue in this case to

                            484

take the examination of Moses Weldon, to be taken before John
Martindale & Joseph McJunkin Esquire.

Graaff Edson & Co) P & S
    vs   ) Decree for the Defendant, with costs of suit
James Townsend)
Admr. Isaac Cook)

Warren Hall) Writ Debt
    vs   ) Judgment confessed accog. to Note, with Interest
Archlaus Fore) & Costs of suit

Richd. Farr & Co) P & S
    vs   ) Judgement confessed by the Defendant
Christr. Degraffenreidt) for Ƚ 5 s 8 d 7 sterling on Stay
                      of Execution untill next Court with
costs of suit.

Daniel Huger Esquire) Debt
    vs   ) came the plaintiff by A Nott and the de-
James Jackson) fendant being Solm. called but fail to
                    appear Whereupon came a Jury to wit, Sam-
uel Spray, foreman, Jordan Jackson, James Moseley, John Springer,
Jesse Petty Pooll, George Huey, Jonathan Cudd, David Prewett,
John Savage, Richd Fossett, John Massay, & Amos Martin, Who being
duly sworn Return their Verdict & say we find for the pltf.
according to Note with Interest & Costs of suit.
    Ordered that the Verdict be Recorded.   Samuel Spray, fore-
man.

Jeremiah Gregory) Attachment
    vs   ) Same Jury
James Henry   ) Return their Verdict & say we find for the
                  Plaintiff according to Note, with Interest &
costs of suit.

Alexander Bookter & Co) Debt
    vs   ) Settled each party paying their own cost.
The Exors of James Sims)

Mills Sumner) Appeal
    vs   ) Settled at Sumners cost.
Ambrose Dollar)

Ordered that all Recognizances returnable to this Court, Stand
continued untill next Court

Graaff Edson & Co) P & S
    vs   ) Nonsuit
John White, son   )
        Isaac)

Barram Bobo applied for a licence to Retail Spirituous Liquors
and keep a public House at the late dwelling House of Samuel
Simpson decd during the Term of Twelve Months who give Bond &
Security accg. to Law.

Stephen Jones) Appeal
    vs   ) Judt. of the Justice affirmed
Thos. B. Hunt)

John Peter Sartor applied for a licence to Retail Spirituous
Liquors & keep a public House in the County, during the term of

12 Months who give Bond with Security accg. to Law.

The Court then adjourned untill Tomorrow 10 0 Clock.   Jno
Blasingame, Wm. Kennedy.

The Court mett according to adjournment at the Court House of
said County on Wednesday the Third day of January A D 1798.
Present their Honors Thomas Brandon, John Blasingame, William
Kennedy, Esquires.

State   )   Indict.
vs   )   Came the State by A Nott Esqr Co Atty. & the
Betsey Brown)   defendant by John Dunlap Esqr. Whereupon came a
             Jury to wit the same as Daniel Huger Esqr vs
James Jackson who say on their Several Oths   Guilty.
                           Samuel Spray, foreman.

A Macbeth & Co) P & S
vs   ) Settled at Defendants Cost.
John Bird   )

Alexander Macbeth & Co) Debt
vs   ) Judgment confessed according to Spe-
Ferdinand Hopkins   ) cialty with Interest & Costs of suit
                    on Stay of Execution Three Months.

A Licence is granted to John Blair to keep a public House &
Retail Spirituous Liquors at his own house during the Term of
12 Months who give Bond with Security acog. to Law.

Henry Farnandis & Co are permitted to Retail Spirituous Liquors
at Grindal Shoals, during the term of 12 Months who give Bond
with Secy. Accg.

Graaff Edson & Co) Case
vs   ) The plaintiff by A. Nott. The defendant by
Edmond Ellis   ) J. Dunlap. On Motion of the Defendants
                   attorney a Nonsuit was granted him.

Alex Macbeth & Co) Case
vs   ) Judgment confessed by Jo C. Gist esqr. atty.
Warren Hall   ) for the defendant for Ŀ 7 s 10 d 3 sterling
                   with costs of suit.

The State   ) Indict.
vs   ) Ordered that the defendant be fined in the
Elizabeth Brown) sum of Ŀ 1 s 1 d 9 with costs.

The Court then adjourned untill Tomorrow 10 0 Clock. Signed
Jno Blasingame, Thos Grandon, Wm Kennedy.

The Court mett according to adjournment on Thursday the Fourth
day of January 1798. Present their Honors Thomas Brandon, John
Blasingame, William Kennedy, Esqrs.

A Letter of Guardianship from the Court of Equity to Wm. Roun,
as Guardian to Jane Harriot & Elizabeth Darby, minors of Wm.
Darby decd 0 to R

John Gibson) On attachment
vs   ) The defendant being solemnly call'd but failed
John Garner) to appear.
                On Motion of A. Nott atty. for the plaintiff,

Ordered that Judgment be entered against him by Default. Also
ordered that the property attached in this case be condemned &
sold by the Sheriff

James D. Puckett) P & S
        vs   ) Discontinued
Arthur Ross   )

Admrs Anderson) P & S
        vs   ) Dismissed at Defendants cost
Robert Cook   )

Graaff Edson & Co) Case
        vs   ) The plaintiff suffered a Nonsuit
Exors Dan. Comer)

Alexander Macbeth & Co) On Attachment
        vs   ) The defendant being Solemnly call'd
John Thompson   ) but failed to appear, On Motion of
                         Abraham Nott Esqr Judgment is Entered
against him be default.

Alex Macbeth & Co) On Attachment
        vs   ) The plaintiff by Wm Shaw J Dunlap & A Nott
Abm. Smith, Sumd.) their Attorneys, and the Garnsahe by Sm.
as Garnashee to) Smith esqr his attorney.
John Thompson   ) Whereupon came a Jury to wit the same as
                   Huger vs Jackson who being sworn accordingly
Return their Verdict & say we find for the plaintiff Ł 31 Costs
included.   Samuel Spray, foreman.
        Ordered that the Verdict be Recorded.

A Macbeth & Co) John Macbeth proved Three days attendance this
        vs   ) case & is entitled to 100 Miles as Milage for
Warren Hall   ) coming & Returning home, Ordered that the
                   same be taxed in the bill of costs.

Wm Cuningham also proved three days attendance and is entitled
to 200 miles Milege fro coming & returning home. Ordered that
the same taxed in the Bill costs.

Richd Farr & Co) Case
        vs   ) Judgment confessed by John Dunlap Esqr Defts
Hugh Thomas   ) attorney for the sum of Ł 11 s 19 d 6 ster-
                    ling with costs of suit on Stay of Execution
untill the first June next.

The Court then adjourned untill Tomorrow 10 O Clock & Signed by
Jno Blasingame, Wm Kennedy.

The Court met according to adjournment on Fryday the Fifth day
of January 1798. Present their Honors John Blasingame, Wm.
Kennedy, Esqr.

John Bird) P & S
    vs   ) Dismissed at the defendants costs, except the
Wm Maxfield) pltfs attorneys fee.

David Smith) Attacht.
    vs   ) Dismissed at Plaintiffs cost.
Landon Waters)

487

Thomas Runnels) P & S
   vs   ) Decree for the plaintiff for Ł 3 sterling with
Joseph King   ) Interest & Costs of suit.

State   ) Rule to Shew cause
   vs   ) Discharged
Thos Young &)
Philemon Bass)

Graaff Edson & Co) P & S
   vs   ) Decree for Plaintiff for Ł 3 s 5 d 5 & costs
Joshua Hammond) of suit.

Ordered that John Cunningham be paid out of the County treasury
ten shillings for beeding a stray Bull through one Winter.

Abraham Nott) P & S
   vs   ) decree according to Note with costs of suit
Jas Carwail(?)

Cuningham & Haile   ) P & S
   vs   ) Referred by consent of the parties to
Doctr. Richd. Gilbert) Capt. Sanders & Doctr. White with power
                   of Umpirage & their award Returnable to
next Court shall be the Judt. thereof.

John Beckham & Co   ) P & S
   vs   ) Judgment confessed by the Defendant ac-
Doctr. James A. Whyte) cording to Specialty with costs of suit
                   on stay of Execution Three months.

A Macbeth & Co   ) P & S
   vs   ) Judgment confessed by the Defendant for
Doctr. J. A. Whyte) Ł 4 s 2 d 9 with costs of suit
               Stay of execution Three months.

Josiah Leake Esqr) Debt
   vs   ) Discontinued at Pltfs. cost
Thomas Word   )

A Macbeth & Co) P & S
   vs   ) Decree for the plaintiff according to Notes
Richd. Mayfield) with Interest & Costs of suit.

James McClure) On attachment
   vs   ) The plaintiff by J. Dunlap
Doct: Gilbert) The defendant by J. C. Gist
Same Jury as Huger vs Jackson, return their Verdict & Say, we
find for the plaintiff the account of 24 dollars & 8½ Cents and
costs of suit.   Saml. Spray, foreman.

The Court then adjourned untill tomorrow 10 0 Clock & Signed by
Jno Blasingame, Wm. Kennedy.

The Court mett according to adjournment on Saturday the Sixth
day of January 1798.   Present their Honors John Blasingame,
William Kennedy, Esqrs.

Doctr. Richard Gilbert) atta.
   vs   )
James Sprouls   )
   Nicholas Lazarus sworn as a Garnishee acknowledged himself
indebted to the deft. in the sum of s 15 and d 10½.

William Eaves being also sworn as a garnishee in the above
case says on oath that he owes the deft. nothing. Decree
for the Plaintiff for the sum of Twenty four Dollars & Cost.

Richard Farr & Co) Case
        vs   ) Settled at defendants cost.
Obadiah Trainham)

Richard Ducket   ) Slander
        vs   ) The defendant in his plea among others plead
James Martindale) infancy, the Court were of opinion that he
                    should plead Infancy under Gardian, And that
Saml Farrow Esqr appear as Such. Whereupon came the defendant
into open Court and prayed that Samuel Farrow be appointed his
Guardian to Defend his suit which was Ordered accordingly.

Richard Duckett) Slander
        vs   ) Came the plaintiff by Abm. Nott esqr. his
James Martindale) attorney and the defendant by Samuel Farrow
                  his attorney whereupon came a Jury to wit
the same as Huger vs Jackson who being duly swron return their
verdict & say we find for the plaintiff Ł 10 with costs of suit
                        Samuel Spray foreman.
      Ordered that the Verdict be Recorded.

Isaac Cannon   ) Debt
     vs   ) Judgment confessed according to Spe-
Genl. Thomas Brandon) cialty with Interest & Costs of suit
  atty for Wm. Hendrick)

Shadrack Lewallen) P & S
     vs   ) Referred by consent of the parties to Thomas
Thomas Word   ) Hardy & John Underwood with power of Umpirage
               and their Award returnable to next court
shall be the Judgment hereof.
             [above entry stricken]

John Crittenden) Debt
     vs   ) Judgment confessed by the Defendant according
James A. Whyte) to Specialty with Interest & costs of suit,
              on stay of Execution 2 MOs.
Ł 13:8:2d

Wm Simpson) P & S
    vs   ) Judgment confessed according to Note with costs
Thos Brandon) Stay of Exon untill March next
Ł 6:12:3d

Daniel Brown Esqr) P & S
     vs   ) Judgment confessed according to Note with
Col. Thos Brandon) costs Stay Exon until March next
Ł 5:14:1½

Shadrack Lewallen) P & S
     vs   ) Decree for the plaintiff for Ł 2 s 10 with
Thomas Word   ) costs of suit

Beckham & Co) P & S
    vs   ) Decree for the plaintiff Ł 6 s 7 d 1 with costs
Wilson Jolley)

The Court then adjourned untill Monday 10 0 Clock. Jno Blasingame, Wm Kennedy.

The Court mett according to adjournment on Monday the Eighth
day of January 1798. Present their Honors Thomas Brandon, Wm
Kennedy, Esqrs.

Genl Richard Winn) P & S
    vs   ) Decree confessed according to Note, on Stay
John Bird   ) of Execution Six Months with Interest and
               Costs of suit

A Macbeth & Co) P & S
  assee Stokes) Decree for the plaintiff according to Note,
    vs   ) with Interest & Costs of suit
John Martindale) Ł 7:6:2

Walter Goodman) P & S
    vs   ) Decree for the plaintiff according to Note,
The Admrs Doctr) with Interest & Costs of suit
H. Anderson   ) Subject to the plea of Plene administravit
                    Ł 5:13:4d

Graaff Edson & Co) P & S
    vs   ) Settled at Defendants cost
Thomas Hughes   )

Graaff Edson & Co) P & S
    vs   ) Nonsuit, on motion of Wm S. Esquire attor-
Chs Ruff &   ) ney for Defts.
John Jaco   )
    Wm. B. Farr proved 10 days attce. in this suit.

Alexander Macbeth & Co) Debt on Note
      vs   ) Judgment confessed by the Defendant
John Murrell   ) accg. to note, with Interest & cost
                  of suit   Ł 12.7.4

Alex Macbeth & Co) Case, Open Account
    vs   ) The plaintiff by A Nott, the Defendant by
John Murrell   ) J C Gist. Same Jury as Huger vs Jackson
               who being duly sworn, return their Verdict
& Say we find for the Plt Ł 15 s 13 d 4½ & costs of suit.
                    Saml Spray, fn.
Ordd. the same be entered.

Wm. Cuningham proved seven days attendance in this case &
Lives 100 miles from this Court.

Graaf Edson & Co) P & S
    vs   ) Decree for the plaintiff for Ł 1 s 1 d 3
James Towntree) with costs

Thomas Cox) P & S
    vs   ) Decree for the plaintiff for Ł 5 s 12 d 8 with
Richard Farr) cost of suit

Alex Macbeth & Co) Trover
    vs   ) Settled at Defendants cost
Warren Hall   )

The court then adjourned untill tomorrow 9 0 Clock. Signed by
Thos brandon, Wm. Kennedy.

The Courtmett according to adjournment on Tuesday the 9th day
of January 1798. Present their Honors. Thos Brandon, Wm Kennedy.

```
Richd Farr & Co )  P & S
     vs          )  The defendant being solemnly called but failed
James Dillard    )  to appear Ordered that Judgment be Entered up
Ł 19:1:10           against him by default with costs of suit.


Alex Macbeth & Co )  the plaintiff by A nott
     vs           )   The defendant being called but failed to
Alex Cane         )   appear, Judt. is End. by default.
     Same Jury as Huger vs Jackson, return their Verdict & say
we find for the plaintiff Ł 5 17/11 with costs of suit.
                                        Saml Spray, foreman


Reuben Sims Exor  )  Debt
of Mathew Sims    )   The plaintiff by N. Nott
     vs           )   The Defendant by W̄. Smith
Daniel Brummett   )   Same Jury Return their Verdict & say we find
                      for the plaintiff according to Note with
costs of suit.  Saml Spray foreman.  Ł 37:7:5


Reuben Sims Exor)  Debt
Mathew Sims     )  The plaintiff by A Nott
     vs         )  The defendant by J C. Gist
Wm Hall & Wm Sims)  Same Jury return their Verdict and Say we find
                    for the plaintiff according to the Note with
Interest & costs of suit.   Saml Spray foreman.   Ł 12:3:5


A Macbeth & Co  )  Debt
     vs         )  The plaintiff by A Nott
Benj. Woodson   )  The defendant by J. C. Gist
                   Same Jury who return their Verdict and Say we
find for the plaintiff according to the Note with Interest &
costs of suit.  Saml Spray foreman.


Richd Farr & Co)  Debt
     vs        )  The plaintiff by A Nott
Wm Johnson     )  The Deft. P self.  Same Jury who return their
                  Verdict & Say we find for the plaintiff accor-
ding to Note with Interest & Costs of suit  Saml Spray, foreman
Ł 25.6
     Wm. B. Farr proved 3 days attendance in this case.


Shadrack Rawls)  Debt
     vs       )  The plaintiff by A Nott and the defendant by
Arthur Ross   )  J. C. Gist.  Same Jury who Return their Verdict
                 & say we find for the plaintiff according to Note
with interest & Costs of suit.  Saml Spray, foreman
     Ordered that the Verdict be Recorded.


The Admrs. S. Darby )  Debt
     vs             )   Dismissed at Pltfs. cost
James Duncan son    )
    Alexander       )


Graaff Edson & Co )  Case
     vs           )   Referred by consent of the parties to A.
James Bell        )   Torrence & James Darby And their award to
                      be the Judgment hereof.
               [above entry stricken]


John McNeail )  Debt
     vs      )  Continued untill Next Court
Wm Johnson   )
```

Ordered that a Commission issue to the State of Virginia to take the examination of Thomas Johnson directed to two Magistrates in that State and his examination so taken shall be read as evidence in the above case.

On Motion of John Henderson Esqr. Sheriff Enoch Floyd Deputy Sheriff is Dismissed from his Office, as acting under him.

Dedimire Tradiway) Case
    vs   ) The plaintiff by Jos C. Gist Esqr & The
Stephen Neail   ) Defendant by Jno Dunlap Esqr. The same
                   Jury who being duly sworn Return their
Verdict & say we find for the plaintiff the Award of 45 shillings with costs of suit.   Samuel Spray, foreman

Josiah Woods   ) Attachment
    vs   ) Quashed by Order of Court
Wm. Brummet   )

Thos Runnels) Richard Farr proved three days attendance in this
   vs   ) case
Joseph King)

Graaff Edson & Co) Richd. Farr proved two days attce. in this
   vs   ) case
Ruff & Jaco   )

Ordered that the Executors of Nathaniel Davis have leave to expose to public Sale at the plantation of said decd. all the personal Estate and effects of said decd. on a Credit of twelve Months giving the Legal Notice of such Sale, and taking bond with approved Security.

On an affidavit of Fred Eison read in Open Court Ordered that Edwin Porter be Suspended from his appointment as a Constable for this county.

Daniel Holder came into open Court and took the Oath of office as constable for this County.

The court then adjourned untill Court in Course. Thos Brandon, Wm. Kennedy.

At a Court of Ordinary Mett on Thursday the 18th January 1798. Present his Honor Tho. Brandon, esquire.

Its Ordered that the Administratrix of Jeremiah Yarborough decd. Expose to public Sale on the Second Monday in Next March at the plantation of said decd. all the Personal Estate & Effects of the said Jeremiah Yarborough decd giving Six Months Credit & taking Bond with approved Security and they are further Ordered to make the legal Return Thereof.

Its Ordered that the Executors of Renny Belue Senr decd expose to sale on Monday the 22nd of this Instant at the plantation of said decd all the person Estate & Effects belonging to the said Estate, on the terms & conditions as is specified in the Last Will & Testament of the said decd. And they are further Ordered to make the legal Return thereof.
              Signed by Thos Brandon.

At a court of Ordinary mett on Monday the fifth day of February 1798. Present his Honor. Thomas Brandon, Esqr.

Its Ordered that the administratrix of John Cook late of this County deceased expose to public Sale on the Nineteenth of this instant all the personal Estate and effects of the said John Cook decd at his late dwelling house giving twelve months credit taking bond with good Security from the purchasers, and she is further Ordered to make the Legal return thereof. Signed by
Thos Brandon

At a court of Ordinary Mett for the County of Union on Wednesday the Seventh day of February 1798. Present his Honor Wm Kennedy, Esquire.

The Last Will & testament of Benjamin Johnson late of this county deceased, was proven in open Court by the Oath of Presley Williams, in the due from of Law, and Ordered to be Recorded.
Charles Johnson being appointed as one of the Executors to the above will, came forward & took the Oath prescribed by Law.

Ordered that Henry Stevens, Spilsby Glenn, Daniel Glenn and John P. Sartor or any three of them appraise the Estate & Effects of Benjn. Johnson late of this County deceased and that they make this Legal return required by Law.
To be first Sworn by Wm. Hogans Esqr.
Wm Kennedy, J. U. C.

At an Intermedaite Court begun & Holden on Monday the Second day of April 1798. Present their Honors John Blasingame, Thomas Brandon.

Ordered that the administration granted to Joseph C. Gist esquire on the Estate and effects of Mrs. Sarah Gist deceased, be revoked. Thos Brandon, Jno Blasingame.

Ordered that Col: Wm. Bratton be licenced to retail Spiritous Liquors & Keep public House at Pinckneyville during the term of 12 Mo. from this date who is Ordered to give bond with Sureties accordingly.

David Johnson came into open Court and was Qualifyed as Executor to the Last will & Testament of Benjamin Johnson deceased.

On the application of the Exors of Benja. Johnson deceased, Ordered that they expose to public all the remaining part of the personal Estate & Effects of the said decd. which was not Willed on a Credit of 9 Months at the plantation of said decd. on the 10th day of this Instant.

James Mooreman Johnson, Orphan of Benjamin Johnson decd came into Court and made Choice of David Johnson his guardian who gave bond in the sum of Ł 150 accordingly.

William Johnson & Judith Johnson orphans of Benjamin Johnson came into Open Court and made choice of Charles Johnson their guardian who give Bond with Security in the sum of Ł 300 sterling accordingly.

Ordered that Richd Minton be Overseer of the road from Cooks Bridge to Daniel Liphams, and that he keep the same in good repair according to Law.

Ordered that Jesse Young be Overseer of the Road from Adams ford on Tyger River to said Youngs to the intersection of the Road from Cooks Bridge to Liphams and that he keep the same in good

493

repair according to Law.

Ordered that Charles Jenkins be Overseer of the Road from Hendricks Mill to Hammeltons ford on Tyger, in the Room of Curtis Wood who has resigned, and that he keep the same in good repair according to Law.

On the petition of a Number of inhabitants its Ordered that Samuel Otterson, Tho. McDonnell and Shad. Lewallen be and are hereby appointed to View and Mark out a way for a Road from Isaac Hawkins the nearest and best way to Robert Crenshaws ford on Tyger River and that they make their report to our Next Court.

Nicholas Lazerus aplied for License to Retail Spiritous Liquors and keep public house at his house during the term of 12 Months who give bond with Surety for his due compliance with Law &C.

Ordered that Robert Gault be Overseer of the Road from Longs Road to Grindal Shoals in the room of John Foster who resigned and that he keep the same in good repair according to Law

Ordered that Thomas Littlejohn be Overseer of the road from Grindal Shoals to the forks of the road, beyond Thomas Cook, and that he keep the same in good repair according to Law.

Ordered that Isaac McKissick, James Cuningham and James Hayney be and are hereby appointed to View and Mark out a way for a Road from Grindal Shoals to Pinckneyville the nearest and best way as it appears by this Court the present way is almost impossible and the road Commission are Ordered to make their return to Next June Court.

On the application of John Blasingame Esqr Letters of administration is granted him on the Estate and effects of Thomas Blasingame decd who gave Bond with Reubin Belue and Wm Morgan his Sureties in the sum of Ł 50 sterling for his faithfull admn. and also took the Oath prescribed by Law.

Ordered that Daniel Farmer, Jehue McPhearson, Daniel Bain & John Ingrim or any three of them be and are hereby appointed to appraise the Estate & Effects of Thomas Blasingame decd to be first sworn by some Justice.

Ordered that Nancy Simpson (now Colbert) who was an administratrix to the Estate and Effects of Samuel Simpson decd be Suspended as Admx. in consequence of her Mariage with John Colbert and that she be served with a Copy of this order.

On Motion of B. Haile, Batte Birdsong was qualified as deputy clerk of this Court.

Nancy Conyers is Licensed to Retail Spirituous Liquors and keep public House in Union Village during the term of 12 Months who give bond with Security accg.

Wm Eaves is Licenced to retail Spiritous Liquors and keep public House in Union Village during the term of 12 Months who give Bond Accg.

The Court then adjourned untill Court in Course.
Thos Brandon, Wm. Kennedy

At a Court of Ordinary mett for the County of Union on Saturday the twenty first day of April in the year of our Lord 1798. Present Thos Brandon, esqr.

Ordered that John Blasingame Esqr admr. Tho. Blasingame decd expose to public Sale on the 26th Instant all the personal Estate & Effects of the said decd. giving Six Month Credit and That he make Due Return Accg. to Law. Thos Brandon.

At a court of Ordinary Mett on Saturday the 13th of October 1798. Present his Honor Thomas Brandon, Esqr.

[The following three entries stricken.]

Present in Open Court the Last will & Testament of George Harland deceased proved by the Oath of Solomon Spann & Wm Morgan And Order to be Recorded.

Rebecca Harland & George Harland was quallified as Executors of the Last will and Testament of George Harland decd.

Ordered that Elijah Wellbourn & Elisha Bond & Obadiah Howard are appointed to appraise the Estate & Effects of George Harland decd. and to be sworn before any Justiceof sd. county to appraise the same.

At a Court begun & Holden in & for the County of Union at the Court House of said County on Fryday the first day of June One thousand Seven hundred & Ninety Eight. Present their Honors. John Blasingame, Wm Kennedy.

The following persons drawn   grand Jurors to serve at our next court.

Benj. Woodson	John Roberds
James Means	Chs. Sims
Hugh Means Esqr.	Stephen Layton
Joshua Palmore	George Newton
Given Gordon	Isaac Edwards
Chs. Hames	Tho. B. Hunt
Alex McDonnell	Edward Tilman
John Gregory	Hancock Porter
Landlot Porter	Robert Hanes
Thomas Green	Nathl Guiton

Also the following as Pettit Jurors.

Thos K. Tanner	Joseph King	Tho. Roberds
John Thomas [stricken]	Jas McWhorter	Ephraim Welborn
James Savage	Tho. Bishop	
Richd. Humpries	Wm McNeaice	
Lott Wood	David Kenworthy	
Jno McPretridge	Jos. Randal	
Christr. Young	Jnothn Roberds	
Gilleon Willbanks	Jas. Lochart	
John Hopkins	Hugh McBride	
Powers Lambkin	John Keiger	
Jacob Harlan	John Lawson	
James White	Tho. Brooks	
Turner Sesson	John White Jnr	
Mahor Lile	Bennet Tankesley	
John Hill		

Robert Crenshaw is licenced to Retail Spiritous Liquors & Keep public House at the fish dam on Broad River during the term of 12 Mo. who give Bond with Secy. accog.

Jno Beckham Jnr asse.)   Debt
   Stephen Clanton   )   Judgment confessed by the deft. accg. to
        vs   )   Specialty with In & Costs of suit
Robert Waltern &   )   Ł 138.17.8
Sion Clanton   )   Int. Ł 3.3.9

Proved in open Court by the Oath of Elizabeth Weer, the last will & testament of Saml Torbert deceased. At the same time Samuel Torbert one of the Executors appointed in the said Will came into open Court & took the Oath as such accog. to Law.

Woodson Rowntree one of the Executors appointed in the last Will & testament of Turner Rountree deceased, came into open Court & took the Oath of Executor thereto as prescribed by Law.

The Court then adjourned untill Tomorrow 9 0 Clock. Signed by Jno Blasingame, Wm Kennedy.

The Court met according to adjournment at the Court House of said County on Saturday the Second day of June 1798. Present their Honors John Blasingame, Wm. Kenendy & Thomas Brandon, Esqrs.

State   )   On Motion of A Nott County Attorney a Nili Prosi-
  vs   )   que is Entered in this case.
Mahor Liles)

State vs Richd Thompson   Same Order

State vs John Liles   Same Order

State vs John Thompson   Same Order

State vs Mahor Liles   Same Order

The State)   Indict. Assault & Battery
   vs   )   Mathew Robinson, John Robinson, Witnesses sworn.
John Lusk)   true Bill,   Wm. Buchanan, foreman.

The State) Indict.
   vs   )   Asl. & Battery.
John Lusk) Abraham Nott Co atty   Jo C. Gist for Defendant
          Whereupon came a Jury to wit.
James Townsend, foreman, Nathl Simmons, Rob. Savage, Augusten Wood, John Prigmore, Phillip Philpeck, Geo. Harland farmer, John Strange, Jacob Paulk, Daniel Lipham, Peter Philpeck, James Trasey. who being duly drawn empanneled & Sworn return their Verdict on the Several Oaths & affirmations Say Nott Guilty. James Townsend, foreman.

Thomas Stribling   ) Debt
     vs   ) Judgment confessed by The defendant accg.
Archs. Fore   ) to Note with Interest & Costs of suit.

Richd Farr & Co)   Debt
    vs   )   Judgment confessed by the defendant according
John Vanlew   )   to specialty with Interest & Costs of suit.
             Stay of Execution thirty days.

496

```
The State        )  Indictment
   vs            )  Asl & Battry.
Daniel McElduff )  Witnesses sworn   John Inlow, Potter Inlow,
                   Jas. Inlow.
                         True Bill, Wm. Buchanan.

The administrators Sarah Darby )  P & S
           vs                  )    Judgment confessed for the Sum
James Howard                   )    of Ł 4 s 5 d 9 with stay of
                                    execution five months and costs
   of suit.

The State        )  Indict.
   vs            )  Assl. & Baty. The State by A Nott Esqr. County
Daniel McElduff )  attorney the Defendant P Self.  Whereupon
                   came a Jury  the same as the State vs Lusk.
Return their Verdict & Say  Guilty.  Jas. Townsend, foreman.

The Court then adjourned untill Monday 10 0 Clock.  Jno Blasin-
game, Wm. Kennedy, Tho Brandon.

The court met according to adjournment at the Court House of
said County, on Monday the fourth day of June A D 1798.  Present
their Honors  John Blasingame, Tho. Brandon,Wm. Kennedy, Esqrs.

The State   )  Indict.
vers.       )  Killing a Hogg.  A Nott county atty. in behalf of
Amos Martin)   the State  Jo C Gist for Defendant  Whereupon came
               a Jury the same as the State vers. Lusk.  Return
their Verdict & Say  Guilty of Killing the Hogg.
                         James Townsend, foreman.

Proved in Open Court by the Affirmation of John Burgess the last
Will & Testament of Moses Weldon late of this County deceased,
& Ordered to Record.
     Mary Weldon, an Executrix of the said Will, came into open
court & took the Oath prescribed by Law, as such.

William Sharp  )  Debt
   vs          )  The defendant came into open court Acknowledged
John Inlow     )  to owe to the plaintiff the sum of        being
                  the amount of a Judgment obtained by the plain-
tiff against the said Defendant heretofore in this Court & con-
sents for Execution to issue against him for the said sum with
costs of suilt & Waves all exceptions.

The State    )  Indict.
   vs        )  Asst. & Battry.  A Nott County atty. in behalf of
John Foster )   the State.  Jo C. Gist in behlaf of the defendt.
                Whereupon came a Jury to wit the same as the
State vers Lusk, Return their Verdict & Say Guilty.
                         James Townsend, foreman.

Graaf Edson        )  Case
   vs              )  On motion of Samuel Farrow for a Nonsuit,
Thomas Blasingame )   in this case, on the grounds that the plain-
                      tiff did not file his declaration according
to Law.  The court were of Opinnion that the ground was good &
Ordered a Nonsuit to be Entered.

John Nuchols proved five days attendance in the above case.
```

A Sheriffs Deed from Wm Barton Esqr to Benj. Haile, Proven in Open Court by the Oath of John Nuchols, a Witness thereto & Ordered to Record.

Mills Rachley & Wife) Slander
    vers   ) Refered by consent to John Blasingame &
Thomas Parmer &   ) Wm Kennedy Esqr. with power of umpirage
Peter Laurence   ) & their award returnable to Next court
                    shall be the final Judgment of Court.

The Court then adjourned untill Tomorrow 9 O Clock. Signed by Wm Kennedy, Jno Blasingame, Thos Brandon.

The Court mett according to adjournment at the Court House of said County, on Tuesday the fifth day June 1798. Present their Honors John Blasingame, Wm Kennedy, Esqrs.

Richd Farr & Co) John S Sims, a witness in this case, proved
    vs   ) that he has attended Six days at last June
John Vanlew   ) Court & One day at the present Court & Attended from Charleston & is entitled to 360 Miles
as Mileage. Ordered that the Same be Taxed in the Bill of Costs.

Richd Farr & Jno Stokes) Judgment confessed by the Defendant
    vs   ) for Ŀ 11 with costs of suit, Stay Exon.
Wm Johnston   ) Six months.

On Motion of Samuel Farrow Esqr., Ordered that all persons concerned in the Administration of Samuel Simpson decd be cited to a-pear before the Judges of this Court at our next intermediate court to shew cause if any the can why Mrs. Nancy Simpson (now Colbert0 should not be reinstated in her administration on said Estate.

Jeremiah Gregory) Case
    vers   ) On motion of Mr. Nott atty for defendant
Wm Hughes   ) Ordered that a commission issue to the
                  State of Kenrucky, directed to any two Justices of the peace of sd. State to take the examination of John Hall & his examination so taken directed to this court under their seal shall be read in evidence in the above case.

A Nott   ) P & S
    vs   ) Dismissed at Defendants cost
Wm. Johnson)

A Nott vs Wm Johnson   Debt Dismissed at Defendants cost

Admrs S. Darby   ) P & S
    vs   ) decree for the plaintiff accg. to Note,
Jas. White & Tho. Hays) with costs of suit.

Admrs. S. Darby) P & S
    vs   ) The defendant by her atty in this case claim'd
Wm Eaves   ) a Jury & Contd.

Admrs. S. Darby) P & S
    vs   ) Decree for the Plaintiff acg. to Note, with
Henry Birdsong) Int. & Costs of suit
Jesse Birdsong)

Richd. Farr & Co) Debt
    vs   ) the plaintiff by A Nott The defendant being
Joseph King   ) called But failed to appear to answer to
                 his suit. Judgment is Entered by default
against him.

Adam Potter) D
    vs   ) The defendant being calld but failed to appear
Abner Wright) Ordered that Judgment be entered against him by
            default.

Elizabeth Nance) Slander
    vs   ) dismissed at Defendants cost except the Pltfs
Jeremiah Spann) atty fee

Graaff Edson & Co) Case
    vs   ) The plaintiff in this case pray'd an Appeal
Tho Blasingame Jr.) to the Court of Common pleas Pinckney Dis-
             trict from the decision of this court, the
same was granted & they give bond to prosecute the same

Elizabeth Hughey) Appeal
    vs   ) Ordered that the Judgt of the Justice be
Elizabeth Brown) affirmed

Mr. Smith give Notice in writing, that he would Move the Associate Judges at the Court of Genl Sessions of the Peace &C to shew
cause why a writ of Mandamus should not be granted against the
Judges of this Court, commanding them to grant letters of admn.
to Henry Birdsong upon the residue of the Estate of Turner Rountree deceased of which he died intestate & which notice was filed.

Woodson Rountree) Attachment
    vs   ) Decree for the plaintiff for Ł 6 s 4 with
Richd Gilbert   ) costs of suit.

Ordered that Capt. Daniel McElduff do make out a true & fair
Shedule (sic) of the property of Doctr. Richard Gilbert, in his
possession and also a fair Statement of the debts due to him
from the said Richd Gilbert also Ordered that he deliver the
said Schedule to the Clerk, and the goods to the Sheriff who is
to expose them to public Sale on the first Saturday in August
next and that the sheriff retain the money arising from the
Sales, in his hands, untill further Ordered.

Jno McNeail) Debt
    vs   ) Ordered that a commission issue in this case
Wm. Johnson) accg. to an Order of last Court.

Thomas McDonnell) Ordered on Motion of A Nott that a Commission
    vs   ) Debene Esse issue to take the Examination of
Ralph Hunt   ) Judith Bearden to be taken before some Jus-
             tice of the peace of this county.

The State   ) Indict.
    vs   ) Assault & Battery
Danl McElduff) The defendant being found Guilty Ordered there-
             fore that he be find Fifteen dollars & Costs of
suit to be paid into...and that Exon issue for the same.

The State)Ordered that a Sci fa issue vs the Securities of the
    vs   ) Defendant to appear at our Next court to shew cause
Richd Lee) why their Recogce should not be forfeited.

The Court then adjourned untill Next Court. Signed by Jno Blasingame, Wm. Kennedy.

At an Intermediate Court begun & holden in and for the County of Union at the Court house of said County on Monday the 3rd day of September 1798. Present their Honors Wm Kennedy.

Henry Littlejohn on Motion of John Henderson esqr Sheriff, was qualifyed as Deputy Sheriff.

Whereas Mrs. Nancy Simpson (otherwise Nancy Colbert) at our last intermediate Court was suspended from the administraton of the Estate of Samuel Simpson decd. whereof she was an administratrix in consequence of her marriage, On application thereof of the said Nancy Simpson (otherwise Nancy Colbert) Its Ordered that she be reinstated in the said administration, Andrew Torrence one of the Securities on Motion was struck off from the bodn, & Burrel Bobo came into open Court and acknowledged himself as security in his room & signed his name to the bond accordingly.

A Petition was presented to the Court, praying that a Road may be opened & kept in repair from the County line crossing thickety Creek at the widow Rights ford & leading by Maj. Miles old place to Union Court House, Ordered that James Laurence, Saml Sheppy, Charles Littlejohn & Wm Tate View the same, Mark out the road & report to our next Court.

Present to the Court an instrument of writing said to be the last will and testament of Solomon Whetson, which was proved by the Oaths of Marsel Wilbanks & Edward Prince, who said they believe that the said decd. was in his proper senses at the time he executed the same. Ordered to Record.

The Last will and testament of James Townsend deceased was presented to the Court, Ralph Hunt & Josiah Darby witnesses thereto was qualified to prove the same, and said they believed him to be in his proper senses at the time he executed the said Will, Ordered to be Recorded.

Acknolwedged in open Court a Deed of conveyence from John Henderson to Abraham Nott Esq & Ordered to be Recorded.

Acknowledged in open Court a Deed of conveyce. from Abraham Nott esqr to Henry Farnandis & Ordered to be Recorded.

Ordered that Hez. McDougal be appointed in the Room of A Cuningham Overseer of the Road from the forks of the Road below Rockey Creek as far as the top of the Hill oposite Arthur Cuningham's and that he keep the same in good repair accg.

Ordered that Nathaniel Dobbs be appointed overseer of the road leading from Pinckneyville to Grindals Shoals in the room of Geo. McWhorter (viz) of that part of the road which was under the care of Geo. Wherter that he keep the same in good repair

Order, the Wm Easterwood be appointed overseer in lieu of Adam Potter on the Road from the County line leading from the old Iron works to Jesse Mabrys & that he keep the same in good repair

Ordered that John Lee be appointed overseer of the road from Kenedys ford on Enoree to Finchers ford on Tiger & that he keep the same in good repair

500

David Pew & Richd Thompson is granted leave to Retail Spiritous Liquors & Keep Public house who give bond according to Law.

Eli Cook & John Townsend appointed executors in the last will and testament of James Townsend decd came each into open Court as was qualified as such accg. to Law.

Ordered that Jesse Young, Josiah Darby and Ralph Hunt appraise the Estate & Effects of James Townsend decd and make due return accg. to Law to be first sworn by some Justice.

David Whetson, Willis Whetson, & Thomas Roberds being appointed executor to the Estate of Solomon Whetson deceased came into open Court & took the Oath as such prescribed by Law.

Ordered that Esqr Lucas & Ellis Fowler view a way for a Road from the Skul Shoals to Union Court house & Mark out a way on any part of said Road that will in their belief make a better track & make their report to our next Court.

Ordered on Motion of Charles Johnson Exr. to the Estate of Benj. Johnson decd Expose to public Sale at the plantation of said decd on the first Monday in October next, all the remaining part of the perishable property belonging to said Estate, which was not sold at the former Sale, giving a credit of Eighteen Months, taking bond with approved security according to Law.

The Court then adjourned until Tomorrow 10 0 Clock   Thos Brandon, Wm. Kennedy.

The Court mett according to adjournment on Tuesday the 4th of September 1798. Present their Honors, Tho Brandon, Wm. Kennedy, Esqrs.

Ordered that John Addington, Joseph Randol & Walter Roberts be appointed appraisers of the Estate of Solomon Whetson deceased and that they make the legal Return according to Law, to be first sworn by a Justice of the peace.

Ordered that all Estrays lyable to be sold this Court, that they be exposed immediately by the Sheriff.

Ordered that James Traysey be Overseer of the Road from the Loves ford Road to McCrackens old Shop, in the room of Wm. Adair, and that he keep the same in good repair according to Law.

Joshua Stroud, Orphan of   Stroud deceased came into open Court and made choice of John McDonald his Guardian, Who give bond with Security accordingly.

Ordered that Samuel Smith & Landlot Porter be appointed commissioners to mark out a way for a road from Landlot Porters on Browns Creek to the Grindal Shoals Road, the nearest & best way to said Shoals, and make their report to our next Court.

The court then adjourned untill Court in Course.   Thos Brandon Wm. Kennedy.

The Court of Ordinary met on Saturday the 13th of October 1798 Present his honor Thomas Brandon.

Presented in open Court the Last Will and Testament of George Harland deceased late of this county was proved by the Oath of

Solomon Spann & William Morgan & Order to be Recorded.

Rebecca Harlan and Samuel Harland being appointed the Executors of the above will came into Court & took the Oath prescribed by Law.

Ordered that Elijah Welbourn Elisha Bond & Obediah Howard be appointed appraisers of the Estate & Effects of George Harland decd and that they be quallified by any Justice of said County.
                                                    Thos Brandon.

At a Court of Ordinary met on Fryday the 9th of November 1798 Present his honor Thos Brandon.

Ordered that Rebecca Harland Executrix and Saml Harland Executor of George Harland Deceased Expose to sale all the Personal Estate of said decd which was appointed & Return to Court giving Twelve months Credit on the sale.   Thos Brandon.

At a Court begun and Holden in and for the County of Union at the Court House of said County on Tuesday the first day of January in the year of our Lord, one thousand seven hundred and Ninety Nine and of the Independence of the United States of North America the Twenty third.   Present their Honors Thomas Brandon, wm. Kennedy Esqrs.

The Court proceeded to draw the Jury to serve for our Next Court when the following persons were drawn as Grand Jurors accordingly To wit.

Moses Meek	1	Benjamin Darby	11
Tho Blasingame Esqr	2	Leroy Beuford	12
John Martindale	3	Neville Holcomb	13
William Hogan	4	Bird Beuford	14
Robert Woodson	5	Joseph Gayton	15
Tho McDaniel	6	Joseph McJunkin	16
Jonas Little	7	Samuel Clouney	17
Joshua Petty	8	Peter Ellis	18
John Henderson	9	Abner Coleman Snr.	19
Batte Baker	10	Stephen Crenshaw	20

      Also the following persons were drawn to serve at Petit Jurors to Wit

Joshua Wilbourn	1	Abner Wells	16
Epaphroditus Porter	2	John Hopper	17
Nicholas Rochester	3	John Sanders	18
Moses Wirght	4	John Smarr	19
Wm Howard	5	Joseph Little	20
Joshua Kenworthy	6	Seth Strange	21
Richd Addis	7	Isaac Hawkins	22
Joseph Tucker	8	Thos Lenear	23
Jacob Holms	9	Jesse Boatman	24
Nichs Harris	10	Geo Story	25
Elijah Wilborn	11	Wm Tate	26
Sterling Strange	12	John Wallace	27
John McNole(?)	13	Daniel Parmer	28
Wm Litlefield	14	Daniel Bain	29
Jacob Hollingsworth	15	Wm Burnett	30

Ordered that the foregoing persons, be summoned to appear at our next court to serve as Jurors.

John Jefferees came into open court and took the oath of Office
as a Justice of the peace for this County.

Ordered that the Court adjourn untill Tomorrow 9 0 Clock. Signed
by Thos Brandon, Wm Kennedy.

The Court met according to adjournment on Wednesday the 2nd day
of January 1799. Present Thomas Brandon, Wm. Kennedy, Esqrs.

Mark Jackson came into open Court and took the oath of office as
constable for the County.

Mills Rachley & wife   ) Slander
       vers   ) By consent of the parties Ordered
Tho Parmer & John Laurance) that this be discontd. at the
                             Defendants costs

Andrew Torrence Esqr. produced a commission from under the hand
of his Excellency Ed. Rutledge, appointing him a Judge of the
County Court, in & for the County of Union, Ordered that the
said commission be Recorded the said Andrew Torrence Esqre.
took the Oath of Office according to Law.

On the Resignation of A Nott esqre. as County Attorney, Joseph
C. Gist was nominated & appointed in his room, who took the Oath
of Office accg.

The Admrs. S. Darby) Debt
       vs   ) By consent of the parties, Ordered that
Alex & Abel Kendrick) this suit be discontd. at the Defendants
                       cost

Proven in open Court by the Oath of Samuel Bell the Last will and
testament of William Blackstock late of this County deceased, &
Ordered to be Recorded.
     James Blackstock was appointed executor to the above will,
came into open Court & was duly qualified.

The State) Indict.
    vs   ) Asst. & Battery
John Lusk) A Nott esqre in behalf of the State. John Dunlap
             & Jo C. Gist in behalf of the Deft. Whereupon
came a Jury to wit Hugh McBride, foreman, Bennet Tankersley,
David Kenworthy, Wm McNeial, Lott Wood, Tho Bishop, Richd. Thompson, Maher Liles, Ephraim Wilbourn, John Hopkins, Tho K. Tanner,
and James McWhorter who being duly drawn empanneled and sworn
Return their Verdict & Say Guilty. Hugh McBride, foreman.

The State   ) Indict for stealing Tobacco
    vers   ) The Grand Jury Returned a true Bill
Moses Prince &)   Hugh Means, foreman.
Aaron Prince   )

Barrom Bobo came into open Court & give Bond & Secy. for a Licence to Retail Spiritous Liquors & Keep a public House at the
late swelling of Samuel Simpson deceased during the term of 12
Months from the date hereof. Ordered that the same be granted
him accg.

John McNeail) Debt
    vers   ) By consent of the parties Ordered that this suit
Wm Johnson   ) be dismissed the plaintiff paying the Sheriffs
                fee & the Defendant the Clerks fee each party

503

paying his own attorney.

Jesse Stroud   )   Case
    vs   )   By consent of the parties, Ordered that this
James Steen   )   case be refered to Wm. McWright, Col. Jos.
           Hughes, Wm Sims and Landlot Porter, Wm. Sharp,
Capt. Palmore, Wm. Kennedy, John Haild, Chs. Humphres, Daniel
Noghor, Jas. McKibbins and Richd. Hughes, and their award shall
be the Judgt. of the Court.

Sampson Hays)   On Motion of Jo C. Gist esqr Ordered that a com-
    vs   )   mission issue to take the examination of Hugh
Leond. Smith)   Donalson in the State of Georgia.

Josiah Wilson)   Attacht.
    vs   )   Dis missed at Defendants cost, except the attor-
P Laurance   )   neys fee

Thomas Brandon)   Debt
    vers   )   Judgment confessed by the defendant accg. to
Mark Jackson   )   Specialty with Interest & Costs of suit, Stay
                    of Levy three Months. Ł 21.6.7

The Court then adjourned untill Tomorrow 9 0 Clock Signed by
Thos Brandon, Wm. Kennedy.

The Court mett according to adjournment on Thursday the 3rd day
of January 1799. Present their Honors Thomas Brandon, Wm.
Kennedy, Andw. Torrance.

John Simpson took the Oath of office as a Constable for the
County.

Alexr Boockter)   P & Summons
    vs   )   Dismisd. Defts. Costs
Wm Banister   )

Shadrach Lewallen took the Oath of Office as a Constable for
this County.

John Fincher   )   Judgment confessed by the Defendant, ac-
    vers   )   cording to specialty with Interest &
John Martindale esqr)   Cost of suit. Stay of Execution three
                         Months.

John Lockert)   P & S
    vs   )   Decree for the plaintiff for Six pounds two
Arthur Ross   )   shillings & Six pence with Costs of suit

Wm Kennedy Treasurer)   P & S
  of Union County   )   Decree for the plaintiff accg. to Note
    vers   )   with interest Ł9/19/9
Wm Eaves(Taylor)   )

Leonard Smith)   P & S
    vers   )   Judgment confessed by the Deft. Accg. to Note
Wm Eaves   )   with Interest & Cost of suit Ł5/13/2

The State   ) Indict
    vs   ) Stealg.   A Nott Coty attorney
Moses Prince) Tobacco
Aaron Prince) Same Jury as in the case of State vs John Lusk
               continued over untill Tomorrow

504

The following bills of Indictment were given to the Grand Jury, which they return Viz.

```
The State        )                         Witnesses
   vs            ) Indict.
David Williams   )                         Wm F Linton
Jno Williams     ) Cow                     Margt. Robison
Wm Williams      ) Stealg.                 Ann Robison
   &             )
Presly Williams)      A true bill, Hugh Means, foreman.


The State        )  Indict               Wm F Linton
   vs            )                        Margt. Robison
David Williams   ) Cow                    Ann Robison
Presly Williams  ) Stealg.
   &             )
John Williams    )    a true bill, Hugh Means, foreman


The State        )                       Lewis Hunt
   vs            )                        Jos McJunkin
David Williams   ) Cow                    Benjn. Jolly
John Williams    ) Stealg.                Peter Thomas
   &             )                        Ann Robison
Presly Williams )                         Margt. Robison
                                          W T Linton
        a true bill, Hugh Means,          W Robison
                       foreman


The State    )  Indict.                  Ignatius Turley
   vs        )  Marking
Mills Sumner )  Sheep          No Bill Hugh Means, foreman


The State    )  Indict                  David Smith, presecutor
vs           )  Asst. & Battry
Richd Burgess )                          a true bill, Hugh Means,
                                                         foreman
```

The Court then adjourned until Tomorrow 9 0 Clock. Wm Kennedy Andw Torrance.

The Court mett according to adjournment on Fryday the 4th day of January 1799. Present their Honors Tho. Brandon, Wm. Kennedy, Esqrs.

Daniel Brummett made application for Letters of administration on the Estate & Effects of Wm Brummett decd. who produced a Citation legally published, Its Ordered that the said Administration be granted him, who give Bond & Security according to Law, & was duly Qualifyed.
    Its Ordered that Majr. Beuford, Wm. Hogans, Moses Ashford & Joshua Martin or any three of them, appraise the Estate and Effects of Wm Brummett late of this County deceased and make due return according to Law, to be first duly sworn by some Justice of the Peace for this County.

```
The State    )  Indict     The case was contd. over from
   vs        )  Stealing   yesterday, the same Jury appeared
Moses Prince &) Tobacco    & Sat on the Tryal and delivered in
Aaron Prince )             their Verdict        Guilty
                                Hugh McBride, foreman.
```

Ordered that William Gossett a constible for this County, be
fined in the sum of Twenty shillings for a contempt to this Court
in refusing to attend the same, when specially Ordered so to do
by the said Court and that the clerk issue the execution for the
same, And further Ordered that he the said Wm Fossett be suspended from his appointment as a Constable.

Jeremiah Gregory)Special action on the case
   vers   ) Ordered on Motion of A Nott deft attorney
Wm Hughes   ) that this suit abate, the proceeding being
               irregular.
    Mr. Farrow attorney for plaintiff give Notice that he would
appeal.

Ordered that the Court adjourn untill Tomorrow 9 0 Clock.
William Kennedy, Andw Torrance.

The Court met according to adjournment at the Court House of
said County on Saturday the 5th day of January 1799. Present
their Honors Thos Brandon, Wm. Kennedy, Andw Torrence, Esqrs.

The State   ) Indict.
   vs   ) Ordered that a Sic fa issue in this case against
Moses Prince) the Securities of the defendants to appear at
Aaron Prince) next court to shew cause why their recogce should
            not be forfeited.
    It is also Ordered that Berram Bobo deliver up to Morgan
Darnall the parcel of the Tobacco proven to be his on the above
indictment.

The State   ) Bound over for a contempt
   vs   )   The Defendants appeared and summittd. them-
Danl McElduff)   selves to the mercy of the Court, Ordered
Landlott Porter)   that each be find Five Dollars, with costs
Robert Smith)   of suit.
John Inlow   )

The State) Indict.
   vs   ) A Scire facias having been issue against the
Richd Lee   ) securities in this case and which was served on
           Wm Littlefield, and no cause having been shewn
by the securities, Ordered therefore the execution issue against
them, and Wm Wafford, for the sum of Ł 25 each with costs of suit.
    [above entry stricken]

The State) Indict. Ordered that the Defendant pay a fine of
   vs   ) Ass. & Two hundred & fifty mills & Costs
John Lusk) Batt.

James Carveal came into court and took the Oath of Office for
this county as a constable.

Ordered that Wm McCulloch & Isaac Parker view & Mark out a way
for a Road from Smiths ford to the Skull Shoals & make the report to our next Court.

Ordered that Davis Goudylock be overseer of the Road from Thos
cooks to Thickety creek & that he keep the same in good repair
accg. to Law.

Ordered that Wm. Steen be Overseer of the Road from Thickety
Creek to Stratons & that he keep the same in good repair accg.
to Law.

Ordered that David Smith be Overseer of the road from Strators
to Broad River & that ht keep the same in good repair accg. to
Law.

The State   ) Sic fa
   vs   ) The Scire facias having been issue & return and
Richd. Lee   ) no cause shewn why their recogce. should not be
                forfeited, Ordered that the Clerk issue Exon against
the Deft. & his Securities agreeable to their Recognizance.

The Court then adjourned untill Monday 9 0 Clock. Thos Brandon,
William Kennedy.

The Court met according to adjournment on Monday the 7th of January 1799. Present their Honors, Tho. Brandon, Wm. Kennedy,
Andw. Torrance.

The State   ) Indict.
   vers   ) Asst. & Battry
Thomas Word)   Ordered that the defendant pay a fine of Five
                  Dollars with costs.

Graaff Edson & Co) P & S
   vs   ) Decree for the plaintiff for fifteen
Geo Story   ) shillings with costs of suit.

John Bynum   ) Debt
   vers   ) The defendant came into open Court and confessed
Danl McElduff) a Judgment according to Specialty, say for
                 Ł 200 sterling with costs of suit.

Jonathan Gilkie) Appeal
   vs   )   Ordered that Wm McCullock certify the pro-
John B Holms   )   ceedings had before him in this case, to
                     our next court.

Richd Farr & Co) P & S
   vs   ) Contd. untill next Court at Defts. cost
The Admrs. Moore)

Graaff Edson & Co) P & S
   vs   ) Decree for the plaintiff for Ł 3 12/6½
Solomon Spann   )

James Martin   ) Debt
   vs   ) The plaintiff by A Nott Deft by J C Gist
The Exors of John) Sworn & Charged with the Same Jury as State
Herrington   ) vs Lusk. Verdict, we find for the plaintiff
                    Ł 12 7/10 with costs. H McBride, foreman.

Jesse Birdsong) Case
   vs   ) The plaintiff by A Nott. The defendt. by Jo
Wm Eaves   ) C. Gist. Sworn & Charged with the Same Jury
                  as James Martin vs the Exors of John Herring-
ton, Verdict, we the Jury, find for the plaintiff Ł 5 s 13 d 11
                                  Hugh McBride, foreman.

Isaac White) P & S
   vs   ) By consent of the parties Ordered that this case
Wm Williams) be referred to Tho Brandon, Wm. Kennedy and Wm
                Buchanan, and their award returnable to this Court
shall be the Judgment hereof.

Jesse Birdsong   ) Debt
        vs   )   The plaintiff by A Nott
Wm Eaves   )   The deft. by Jo C. Gist.
                         Sworn & Charged with same Jury as James
Martin vs the Exors of John Herrington and Ordered to stand over
untill Tomorrow

Graaff Edson & Co   )   Case
        vs   )   Stands over by Consent of the parties
The Exors James Gibbs)

The Court then adjourned untill Tomorrow 10 0 Clock. Thos
Brandon, wm. Kennedy.

The Court met according to adjournment on Tuesday the Eighth day
of January 1799. Present their Honors Thos Brandon, Wm. Kennedy,
Andw Torrance.

Admrs of S Darby) P & S
        vs   ) Decree for the ptff for Ł 3 16/1 with costs
Enoch Floyd   ) of suit

John Mays   ) Debt
   assee Martin   ) The plaintiff being called & failed to appear
        vs   ) Ordered that he be Nonsuited.
John High   )

Stephen Jones   ) Appeal
        vs   ) Justices Judgment confirmed with costs of
The admn. Simpson) suit

Wm Craig   ) Debt
        vs   ) Judgment confessec by the defendant according
John Martindale   ) to Specialty with interest and costs of suit,
                      stay of Execution Six Months.

The Admr. S Darby) Case
        vs   ) Judgment confessed by the Defendant for
Woodson Rowntree   ) Ł 7 1/6 with costs of suit.

Jesse Birdsong) Debt
        vs   )   This cause was contd. over from Yesterday
Wm Eaves   )   when the Jury appear'd, and sat on the Tryal
                   the same as Jas Martin vs The Exors Herrington
Verdict, we the Jury do find for the plaintiff Ł 1 18/1d
     Ł 2:3:5   Hugh McBride, foreman.

Jeremiah Gregory) Special Action on the case
        vs   )   Mr Farrow give Notice in behalf of the plain-
William Hughes)   tiff that he would appeal from the decision
                    of this Court Wherefore came the plaintiff &
Entered into Bond with John Landus his Secy. to presecute the
same Ordered that the Appeal be Granted & the proceedings be
Certified up by the Clerk.

Cuningham & Haile) P & S
        vs   ) Ordered that the former __?__ of __?__
Richd Gilbert   ) be ended in this case

Admr S Darby   ) P &
        vs   ) Decree confessed by Dt. for Ł 3 8/9 with
Henry Birdsong) costs of suit

Admr W Darby) Case
vs   ) Abated, the action brought Unny.
Enock Floyd)

The Court then adjorned untill Tomorrow 9 0 Clock, Andw Torrance,
William Kennedy, Thos Brandon.

The Court met according to adjournment on Wednesday the Ninth
day of January 1799
Present their Honors, Thomas Brandon, William Kennedy, Andrew
Torrance.

The State) Ordered that a second Sci fa issue vs Wm Wafford
vs   ) one of the Securities in this case And Execution
Richd Lee) be stay'd vs Wm Littlefield Six months.

On the application of Andrew Torrance Esqr leave is given him
to retail Spiritous Liquors & keep public House on his entering
into Bond accg. to Law.

The following persons appointed Justice of the Peace for this
County was Qualified according to Law.
  John Martindale   Hugh Means
  Joseph McJunkin   Tho. Blasingame
  Wm Johnson   Josiah Darby
  John P Sartor   Batte Birdsong
  Nichs Corry

Cuningham & Haile) P & S
vs   ) Pursuant an Order of Union County Court to
Richd Gilbert   ) us directed, We the subscribed appointed to
                   settled the differences on a suit by Petition
& Summons, Between the parties, do award that the Defendant pay
to the plaintiff the sum of Ł 1 d 11 with costs of suit. Witness our hands this 8th day of January 1799. John Sanders
                                              J. Whyte

Ordered that the above award be made a Judt. of this Court.

Graaff Edson & Co) Case
vs   ) John Dunlap, plts. atty
John McCooll   ) Wm Smith, Defts. atty.
     Sworn & charged the Jury
  viz 1. Hugh McBride, foremn.   7. Rd. Thompson
      2. Bennet Tankesly   8. Maher Liles
      3. David Kenworthy   9. Ephraim Wilbourn
      4. Wm McNeill   10. John Hopkins
      5. Lott Wood   11. Tho K. Tanner
         Tho Bishop [stricken]   12. James Mcwhorter
      6. John Murrell
  Verdict, Court were divided & no verdict.

Alex Macbeth & Co) Case
vs   ) The plaintiff executed a writ of enquiry
Ralph Hunt Junr.) Same Jury as Graaff Edson & Co vs Jno
                   McCooll, Return their Verdict & Say, we
find for the plaintiff according to Speacialty with interest &
Costs of suit.   Hugh McBride, foreman.

Adam Potter) Case
vs   ) Writ of enquiry executed Same Jury Return their
Abner Wright) Verdict and say, we find for the plaintiff Ł6
               s 4 d 2 with interest & cost of Suit. Ł 6.13.6

Shaw & Dunlap) P & S
    vers   ) decree for the plaintiff ιccg. to Specialty with
Wm Steen   ) interest & Costs of suit.

The State   ) Case
    &   ) Ordered on Motion of A Nott that an Order to take
Tho McDaniel) the evidence of Judy Bearden Debene esse be ex-
    vs   ) tended.
Ralp Hunt   )

Alex Macbeth & Co) Attacht.
    vs   ) Ordered that the property attached in this
Ralph Hunt Jnr.) case be sold, to satisfy the plaintffs Debt
                    the over plus if any to remain in Shffs hand,
subject to further Ordered.

Ordered that the Sheriff apply out of the Money arising from the
Sale of certain goods Sold by Order of this Court as the property
of Richard Gilbert as much as will satisfy an Execution in his
hands Jas McClure vs sd. Gilbert.

Graaff Edson & Co) Attacht.
    vs   ) The defendant was call'd & faile'd to appear,
Ralp Hunt Jnr.   ) Ordered that Judgment be entered by Default

Tho V. Nance) Debt
    vs   ) The defendant was call'd and fail'd to appear,
James Lanham) Ordered that Judgment be entered by default.

John Fincher)By consent of parties, Ordered that this case be
    vs   )refered to Genl. Brandon & Capt. Martindale with
Enoch Floyd)power of umpirage & their Award returnable to next
              court shall be the Judgment thereof.

Ignatius Turley) S. A.
    vs   ) The defendant was call'd & fail'd to appear
Alex Martin   ) Ordered the Judgment be entered by Default.

Admrs. S. Darby   ) Attacht.
    vs   ) Mr. Smith mov'd to have the attacht.
Tho. Blsaingame Jr.) Quash'd, But was over Rul'd by the Court,
                       with leave to make his objections at
next court.

Darby & Parham   ) Attacht.
    vs   ) Mr. Smith mov'd to this Attt. Quash'd but
Tho Blasingame Jr.) was over rul'd by the Court.

Ordered that the Overseer of the Road presented by the Grand
Jury at this term be summond to appear at next intermediate
Court to shew cause why they ahould not be fined for not keeping
their respective road in good Repair, also the Overseer of the
Road from this place to Genl. Brandons.

Richard Burgess took the oath prescrib'd by Law, as Deputy
Sheriff for this County.

Ordered that the Clerk advertise that the repairing of the Court
House will be lett to the Lowest Bidder on Fryday next. Further
Ordered that the kees of said Court House, be delivered to Fed.
Eison.

510

The Court proceeded to the Election of a Sheriff for this County to succeed John Henderson esqr the present sheriff after his commission expires. After ballotting according to Law, Col. Joseph Hughes was duly Elected. Ordered that the said Joseph Hughes be recommended to his Excellency the Governor to be commissioned for the next four years, as Sheriff for this County.

Then the court adjourned untill Court in Course. Tho Brandon, Wm Kennedy, Andw Torrance.

At an Intermediate Court begun & Holden on Monday the first day of April in the year of our Lord one thousand seven hundred & Ninety Nine. Present Wm Kennedy, Esqr. Thomas Brandon.

A licence was granted to Wm. Johnson to retail Spirituous liquors & keep public House during the term of Twelve Months, who give Bond as law directs.

Presented into Court an instrument of writing said to be the last will & Testament of James Bankhead late of this County deceased which was proven by the Oath of John Reed a witness thereto and Ordered to be Recorded.
 Elizabeth Bankhead & John Bankhead Executrix & Executor to the above Will came personally into Open Court & Took the oath prescribed by Law.

Presented into Court an instrument of writing said to be the last will & Testament of Robert Good decd which was proved in Open Court by the Oath of James Bankhead, a witness thereto as law directs & Ordered to be Recorded.
 Elizabeth Good & John Bankhead, being appd. Extx & Exor to the above Will came Personally into open Court & took the Oath prescribed by Law.

Presented to Court an instrument of writing said to be the last Will and Testament of James Woodson late of this County decd which was proven by the Oaths of Wm Rowntree & Sampson Goodwin Witnesses thereto & Ordered to be Recorded.
 Thomas Woodson one of the Executors Appointed in the above Will came Personally into Open Court and took the Oath prescribed by Law.

A licence granted to Henry Littlejohn to keep public House for 12 Mo. from the date hereof who gave Bond as law directs.

Letters of administration was granted unto Elizabeth Ray & Hosea Ray on the Estate and Effects of Ambrose Ray decd who took the Oath as the Law directs & give Bond in the sum of Ł 250 with Wm Ray & Wm Potts, their Security.

Ordered that Ralph Jackson, Wm. Willbanks and Tho. Greer be and are hereby appointed to Appraise the Estate & Effects of Ambrose Ray decd and that they make the legal return of the same as is required by Law, to be first sworn by some acting Justice of the peacefor this County.

Presented to Court an instrument of writing said to be the last will & Testament of Wm McJunkin late of this County decd Robert Bevil, William Hollingsworth & Thomas Vance Witnesses to the said will came personally into Open Court and made Oath that they were present & saw the said decd Execute the said writing and deliver it as his last Will and Testament, and that they believed

511

him to be of a sound & disposing Mind & Memory at the time he Executed the same. Its Ordered that the said Will be Recorded.

Thomas Vance & Mary McJunkin being appointed Executor & Executrix to the above Will came into Open Court & took the Oath as prescribed by Law.

Ordered that Jarrod Gregory, Jeremiah Gregory & John Wallace(?) be and are hereby appointed to appraise the Estate & Effects of Wm McJunkin late of this County decd and that they make due return of the samd as law directs, to be first sworn by some Justice of the peace for this County.

John Henderson esqr came into open Court and resigned his appointment as Sheriff of this county.

Letters of administration Granted to Mary Huey on the Estate & Effects of Joseph Huey decd who give Bond with David Prewett & Wm Leverett her Security in the sum of Ł 150 sterling and took the Oath prescribed by Law.

Ordered that Bernd Glenn, Philip Anderson and John McNeail be and are hereby appointed to appraise the Estate & Effects of Joseph Huey decd and that make due return accog. to Law, to be first sworn by some Justice of the peace for this County.

Col. Joseph Hughes presented to the Court his commission from under the hand of his excellency Ed. Rutlege Governor of the State aforesaid, as Sheriff in and for the County of Union, who entered into Bond with Security according to Law, and took the Oaths of Office as prescribed by Law.
Ordered that the commission be Recorded, Also the Bond.

On the recommendation of Col. Joseph Hughes, Richard Burgess was appointed Deputy Sheriff for this County, & was Qualified accog. to Law.

Its Ordered that James Darby & John Murrell administrators of the Estate & Effects of William & Sarah Darby be cited to appear at our next Court, and to render to the said Court a Statement of their accounts on said Administrations & the manner in which & to whom they have applied the Moneys belonging to said Estate.

Ordered that Landlot Porter be Overseer of the Road from his House to Pinckney Road and that he keep the same ingood repair according to Law.

Ordered that Robert Bullington be Overseer of the road from Pinckney Road to Union Road and that he keep the same in good repair accg. to Law.

The Court then adjourned untill Court in Course & Signed by Wm Kennedy, Thos Brandon.

The Court of Ordinary Mett the 1st April 1799. Present Tho Brandon, Wm. Kennedy.

Ordered that Daniel Burmmett have leave to expose to Public Sale on the first Monday in May next, all the personal estate and effects of William Brummett late of this County deceased at the plantation of said deceased, giving Six Months Credit & Taking sufficient Security.

Proved in Open Court by the Oath of Jesse Liles the last
will and testament of Renny Belue Jnr late of this County deceased, & Ordered to be Recorded.

Keziah Belue & Reuben Belue executrix & Executor to the above
will came forward & took the Oath prescribed by Law.

Ordered that Wm Morgan, Saml Harlan & Geo. Harland hatter
appraise the estate & Effects of Renny Belue Jnr decd and make
due return according to Law to be firest sworn by some Justice.
Thos Brandon, Wm. Kennedy.

At a Court begun & Holden in and for the County of Union at the
Court House of said County the first day of June, in the year of
our Lord one thousand Seven Hundred and Ninety Nine. Present
their Honors   [not given]

The Court proceeded to draw the Juries to serve at our next
Court when the following persons was drawn to serve as Grand
Jurors.

Nicholas Corry	1	Henry Good	11
Saml Patton	2	Hezekiah Rice	12
Woodson Rowntree	3	Lewis Pennion	13
Ephraim Fowler	4	Richd Prewett	14
Aaron Hays	5	John Haile	15
Tho. Vance	6	Wm Clark	16
Henry Foster	7	Enoch Floyd	17
Thomas Dean	8	William White esqr.	18
Jeremiah Lucas	9	William White	19
Daniel McBride	10	James Gasway	20

Also the following as Pettit Jurors

John Huey	1	Fredk. Davis	11	Sion Murphy	21
Saml Kelso	2	Wm Goudylock	12	Joseph Nix	22
John McDaniel	3	Jesse Jinkins	13	Amos Martin	23
Hugh Nelson Jr.	4	Job Hammond	14	John Sparks	24
James Park	5	Robert Galt	15	John Means	25
John Hutton	6	Sampson Goodwin	16	Henry Millhouse	26[stricken]
John Nelson	7	John Weederman	17	Rucker Maulden	26
John Fowler	8	Robert Norman	18	Leonard Smith	27
Henry Gee	9	Mark Murfee	19	Robert Millhouse	28
Isaac Gregory	10	James McCord	20	James Mathews	29

The Admrs of   ) Debt
Saml Simpson decd) The Defendant confessed Judt. according to
     vs   ) Specialty with Interest & Cost of Suit, Stay
Moses Guiton   ) of Execution till the first day of January
                    next.

The Admrs. of) Debt
Saml Simpson) The defendant confessed Judgt. according to
     vs   ) Specialty with Interest & Costs of suit, stay of
Moses Guitnn) execution till the first day of January next

James Kennedy was sworn as constable for this county, before
Judge Kennedy.

The last will & Testament of Thomas Haselwood late of this
county, deceased, was proven by the Oath of Brittan Williford
& Isaac Wafford & Ordered to be Recorded.

Isaac Pearson is Licenced to keep Public House in this County
for Twelve Montsh who give Bond with Security.

The Court adjourned untill Monday 10 C. Signed by Thos Brandon, Wm. Kennedy.

The court met according to adjournment on Monday the third day of June 1799. Present their Honors, Thos. Brandon, Wm. Kennedy, Andw. Torrance, Esqrs.

Ordered that Zachariah Nance be allowed out of the County treasuer two Dollars for Wintering a Stray Cow.

Ordered that the sum of Two Hundred Dollars be laid as a Tax on the Taxable property in this County, & collected by the Tax Collector for this County for the purpose of defraying the expence of building the Goal for this County.

Wm Alexander) Ordered on Motion of A Nott attorney for the
vs   ) Defendant that the Plaintiff in this case give
Saml Patton) Security within Thirty Days or suffer the nonsuit.

The State   ) Indict.   Shadh Lewallen, prosecutor
vs   ) Killing a Mare Philip Inlow
James Inlow)   Wm Hutson
                 No Bill, Thomas Blasingame, foreman.

Mary Fincher) Attacht.
vs   ) Genl Thomas Brandon summond as Garnashe was
Jesse Fincher) sworn & saith he is indebted to the Defendant
              the sum of Ł 10 3/7d Ordered that the said sum
be condemned in the hands of the said Thomas Brandon to be appropriated toward satisfying the Plaintiffs debt.
    Also came a Jury to wit, Isaac Hawkins, foreman, Daniel Parmer, Jesse Boatman, Seth Strange, Joseph Little, John Smarr, Wm Littlefield, Jacob Holms, Joseph Tucker, Wm. Howard, Elijah Welbourn and Joshua Welbourn, return their Verdict & Say we find for the plaintiff agreeable to Note, with costs. Isaac Hawkins, foreman.

The State   ) Indict.
vs   ) Cow
David Williams   ) Stealing
Presley Williams) Jos. C. Gist & John Williams in behalf of
John Williams   ) the state. Wm. Smith & S. Farrow, for Defts.
    Ordered that a Nole Prosique be Entered.

The State   ) Indict.
vs   ) Cow
David Williams   ) Stealing
John Williams   ) J. C. Gist in behalf of the State.
Wm Williams   ) Wm. Smith, S. Farrow & Mr. Traylor for
Presley Williams   ) Defendants.
    Ordered that a Nole Prosique be Entd.

John Hayney) P & S
vs   ) Defendant confessed Judt. for Ł 7 with Stay of
Wm Mayfield) Exon till 1st day of December with costs.

Its Ordered that the Admrs. of Ambrose Ray decd be permitted to expose to Sale all the personal Estate belonging to said decd. on the fourth Monday in this instant at the plantation of said decd., giving Six Months Credit.

Its Ordered that the Money Arising from the Sale of a Negro boy Sold by the Sheriff as the property of Ralph Hunt by Order of this Court be paid to the persons who had said property attached according to the Seniority of their Levies.

John Lusk   ) Attacht.
     vs   ) The plaintiff came into open Court & discontued
Robert Lusk) this Attact. at his costs.

The State   ) Indict
     vs   ) Cow
David Williams   ) Stealing
Presley Williams)   Ordered that a Nole Prosique be Entered.
John Williams   )

The Court then adjourned untill Tomorow 10 0 Clock. Signed
Thos Brandon, Wm. Kennedy, Andw Torrance.

The court met according to adjournment on Tuesday the fourth day of June 1799. Present their Honors Thomas Brandon, Wm. Kennedy, Andrew Torrence, Esqrs.

Graaff Edson & Co   ) Case
     vs   ) The plaintiff by A Nott. The Deft. by
Thos. Blasingame Jnr.) Saml Farrow.
Jury Sworn & Charged
Isaac Hawkins, foreman   1   Jacob Holms   7
Daniel Parmer   2   Joseph Tucker   8
Seth Strange   3   Wm Howard   9
Joseph Little   4   Epaphros. Porter 10
John Smarr   5   Joshua Welbourn   11
Wm Littlefield   6   Joseph Boatman   12

Verdict We find for the Defendant. Isaac Hawkins, foreman.

John Nuchols proved Twelve days atte. in the above case.

On Motion of the Executors of Nathl. Davis decd permission is given them to expose to public Sale at the late dwelling of said decd on the fourth Monday in this instant, One Negro woman named Jean & Child, one brown mare named flint, one side Saddle and bridle, also one feather bed and furniture, it being that part of the deceased estate which he willed to his wife during her life or widowhood, she having since married, giving Twelve Months credit, taking Bond with approved Security.

John Beckham & Co) P & S
     vs   ) decree confessed according to Note, deduct-
James Clark   ) ing all Just credits with cost of suit.
                    Stay of Exon. till 25th Decr next.

Richard Farr & Co) P & S
     vs   ) Decree for the plaintiff for Ŀ 8 16/11½
John Moore, admr.) with costs of suit.
of Edward Moore decd)

Richd. Farr & Co) Case
     vs   ) Referred by consent of parties to James Tosh
Ebenezer Pickett) & Benj. Haile and their award returnable to
                   this court shall be the Judt. thereof

Alex Macbeth & Co) P & S
     vs   ) decree for the plaintiff for Ŀ 1.8d with
John Speers   ) costs of suit

515

```
The State        )   Ordered that the defts. be discharged from
    vs           )   their recogce.
David Williams)
Wm Williams   )
John Williams )

Graaff Edson & Co.          )   Case
    vs                      )   Ordered that a Nonsuit be entered
The Exors James Gibbs decd)     in this case

John Nuchols proved Twelve days attce in the above suit.

H Farnandis & Co is Permitted to retail Spiritous liquors at
G. Shoals for 12 Months, who give Bond & c. accog. to Law.

Joshua Gurnage)   Appeal
    vs         )   Ordered that the Judt. of the Justice be
John Bird      )   affirmed with costs

Graaff Edson & Co )  P & S
    vs            )  decree for the Deft.
John Burgess      )

Woodson Rowntree )  P & S
    vs           )  Settled at Defts. costs
Rd. Gilbert      )

Timothy Haynes  )
    vs          )  Contd. on affidavit of the Deft. at his costs
Philip Felpeck  )  for this court.

The Court then adjourned untill Tomorrow 10 0 Clock.   Thos
Brandon, Wm. Kennedy, Andw Torrance.

The Court met according to adjournment on Wednesday the Fifth
day of June 1799.  Present their Honors Tho. Brandon, Wm. Kennedy,
Andw. Torrence.

David Harris Jnr.       )   Malicious Prosecution
    vs                  )   John Dunlap & Jo C Gist for Pltf.
Eli Cook & John Savage)     A Nott & Wm Smith for Defts.
    Jury Sworn & Charged to wit
1. Jon Sanders   foreman   s       7. Wm Littlefield   s
2. Danl Parmer          s          8.  Jacob Holmes    s
3. Jesse Boatman        s          9. Joseph Tucker    s
4. Seth Strange         s         10. Wm Howard        s
5. Joseph Little        a         11. Elijah Wilbourn  s
6. John Smarr           s         12. Joshua Wilbourn  a

On motion made by the Deft Attorneys for a Nonsuit, after the
evidence was closed, on the Grounds that no Express Malice was
proven, the Court therefore Ordered a Nonsuit to be Entered

Daniel Tollerson        )   Mal
    vs                  )   pros.
Eli Cook & John Savage )   The plaintiff suffered a nonsuit.

The Executors named in the last will & Testament of Thomas Hasel-
wood decd, regusing to Qualify, On Application therefore of Mary
Haselwood & Lancaster Haselwood, Ordered that letters of admini-
stration be granted to them on the Estate & Effects of said
deceased with the will annexed who give Bond in the sum of
$1000 with John Lancaster & Mark Jackson their Security, & Took
```

516

prescribed by Law.

Ordered that John Blasingame Esqr., Ebenezer Pickett, Isaac Bogan & Philip Blasingame or any three of them be and are hereby appointed to appraise the Estate & Effects of Thomas Haselwood decd. who are further Ordered to make due return accog. to Law, to be first sworn by a Justice of the Peace for this County.

Wm Johnson   ) Debt
vs   ) Judt. confessed by the Deft. accg. to Specialty
William Eaves   ) the plaintiff paying Clerks & Sheriffs fees on
                    condition the debt is paid in Two Weeks to the
Clerk.

John Steel   ) Case
vs   ) A Nott for Pltf.
Leond. Smith   ) S Farrow for Deft
    Jury sworn & charged
Isaac Hawkins, foreman 1   Wm Littlefield 7.
Daniel Parmer   2   Jacob Holms   8.
Jesse Boatman   3   Joseph Tucker 9.
Seth Strange   4   Wm. Howard   10.
Joseph Tucker   5   Elijah Wilbourn11
John Smarr   6   Joshua Welbourn12.
    Verdict, We find for the Defendant. Isaac Hawkins, foreman.

Wm Whitlock   ) Slander
vs   ) Settled at Defendants cost
Hugh Norville   )

Joseph Simmon   ) Mal: pros.
vs   ) contd. over till Tomorrow
Jeremiah Gregory)

Court adjourned untill 9 O Clock.   Thos Brandon, Wm. Kennedy.

The Court met according to adjournment on Thursday the Sixth day of June 1799. Present their Honors Thomas Brandon, William Kennedy, Esqrs.

Saml Farrow esq   ) P & S
vs   ) Decree for the Plaintiff accog. to Special-
Wm Tho Linton   ) ty, with Interest & Costs
& Presley Williams)

John Dunlap   ) P & S
vs   ) Decree confessed for Ł 5 8/9 with Int. & Costs
Danl Mc Elduff   ) of suit.

Patrick H Sims   ) P & S
vs   ) Decree for the Pltf Accog. to Specialty with
Richd. Farr   ) Int. & Costs.

Union County   ) Sci fa
vs   ) The Defendant shew no cause. Ordered that
Jeremiah Gregory) his recognizance be forfeited and that exe-
                    cution issue with costs.

Adam Potter   ) P & S
vs   ) Decree confessed according to Specialty with
John Martindale esq) Interest & Costs, Stay Exon four weeks

Thomas Petty) Debt
   vs   ) Judt. confessed accg. to Specialty with Interest
Warren Hall) & costs.

Thomas Woods) Debt
   vs   ) Judgt. confessed according to Specialty with
Warren Hall) Interest & Costs

Timothy A Edson) Debt
   vs   ) Judgment confessed accg. to specialty with
Daniel McElduff) interest & Costs of suit.
Thomas Brandon)

Timothy A Edson) Debt
   vs   ) Judgmt. confessed according to Specialty,
James A Whyte &) with Interest & Costs of suit. Stay of
Jos. C. Gist   ) Execution till 10th November next.

Adam Potter) Debt
   vs   ) Judt. confessed according to Specialty with
John McNeail) interest & Costs of suit.

The Exors Daniel Comer decd) P & S
      vs   ) Decree for the plaintiff for Ł 4
James McClure   ) with costs.

Joseph Simmons) Mal prosn.
   vs   ) The plaintiff by Mr. Dunlap The Deft by S.
Jeremiah Gregory) Farrow. Jury sworn & Charged (same jury as
                  John Steel vs Leond. Smith)
Verdict, We find for the Plaintiff Ł 15 with costs.
                      Isaac Hawkins, foreman.

The State So Carolina) Quitam
     vs   ) Abated by the death of the Defendant.
Thomas McDaniel)
   vs   )
Ralph Hunt   )

On Motion of the administrators of Joseph Hughey decd Permission
is given them to expose to Public Sale on the fourth Monday in-
stand, all the personal Estate of said deceased at the plantation
of said Joseph Hughey decd giving Six months Credit, taking bond
with approved Security.

John Sanders) Case
   vs   ) Settled by the paries
John Lee   )

Abraham Markley) P & S
    vs   ) Decree confessed accg. to Specialty with costs.
Fields Blakey)

John Mullins) P & S
   vs   ) Contd. at Pltfs. Costs
William Speers)

Graaff Edson & Co) Case
   vs   ) John Dunlap for Pltf.
John McCooll   ) Wm Smith for Deft.
Jury sworn & Charged

```
a  Isaac Hawkins, foreman 1      s John Smarr      7
s  Daniel Parmer         2      s Wm Littlefield  8
s  Elijah Welbourn       3      s Jacob Holms     9
s  Jesse Boatman         4      s  Joseph Tucker 10
s  Seth Strange          5      s  Wm Howard     11
a  Joseph Little         6      a Joshua Welbourn12
      Verdict, we find for the Defendant Ł 34 d8
                              Isaac Hawkins, foreman
```

Shaw & Dunlap) P & S
      vs   ) Decree according to Specialty with costs of
John Fincher) suit

Graaff Edson & Co) Case
      vs   ) The plaintiff prayed an Appeal from the
John McCool   ) Verdict of the Jury to the Court of common
                   Please which was granted and they give Bond
accordingly.

Thos. Hancock) Attacht.
      vs   ) Mr. Nott, atty for Deft.
Reuben Pitcher) moved for the attacht. to be Quashed. The
                 Court over Ruled him & Contd.

The Court then adjourned untill Tomorrow 7 0 Clock. Thos Brandon, Wm Kennedy, Andw Torrance.

The Court met according to adjournment on Fryday the 7th day of
June 1799. Present their Honors Thomas Brandon, Wm Kennedy,
A. Torrence, esqrs.

Graaff Edson & Co   ) Case
      vs   ) A Nott Esquire petition for a new Trial
Thos Blasingame Jur.) in this case and the Corut granted it
                       on paying the costs by the first day
of Jany next.

On the application of Henry Birdsong for Letters of Administration
to be granted on the Residue of the Estate & Effects of Turner
Rountree late of this county deceased. Ordered that Letters of
Administn. be granted to the widow of the decd. at our next
Intermediate Court.. The non Cupative will of said decd as far
as respect to the Money therein Mentioned to be good.

John Murrell   ) Case
      vs   ) Dismissed by consent of the parties each
Saml Farrow Esqr.) paying his own cost.

David Murrell   ) Case
      vs   ) Dismissed by Consent of the parites each
Saml Farrow Esqr.) paying his own cost.

Mary Fincher) Attachment
      vs   ) On Motion of Mr. Farrow Ordered that the Money
Jesse Fincher) condemn'd in the hands of the Garnashe, in
                this case be not paid as was Ordered, And all
proceeding stand over to our Next Court, and the heirs of Jesse
Fincher be suffered to make their defence to shew that the
said Jesse Fincher was dead before the issuing the above attacht.

James Harrison) Sci Fa
    vs   ) Rule made absolute by Order of Court
Charles Sims)

Wm Hancock   ) Attacht.
    vs   ) On Motion of Mr. Nott Ordered that a Commission
Reuben Pitcher) issue in this case to take the examination of
Witnesses who reside out of this State

Ordered that the presentment of the Grand Jury at this Court,
a Copy thereof be laid before the Legislature at their next
meeting.

Ordered that the Executors of Renny Belue Jnr decd expose to pub-
lic Sale at the plantation of said decd. on the Tenth day of
July next all the personal Estate of said deceased, giving Six
Months Credit.

Jeremiah Gregory) Case
    vs   ) On Motion of Mr. Smith Defendt. atty. that
William Hughes) the writ be quashed on the following grounds,
                that the defendant was Notoriously without
the limits of this state at that time, the writ was Served &
had been in & about ten months before the service, and that
the sehriff left a Copy at his most notorious place of residence.
Ordered that it be quashed in as much as leaving a Copy at his
Usual place of abode is not Sifficient to ground at Action when
out of the State.
The plaintiff therefore prayed an appeal which was granted on
Conditions bond & Security is given according to Law And that
the proceedings be certified by the Clerk.

The Court then adjourned untill Court in Course and Signed by
Thos Brandon, Wm. Kennedy.

At an Intermediate court begun & Holden on Monday the Second
day of September in the year of our Lord one thousand Seven
hundred and Ninety Nine   Present his honor Wm Kennedy, Esqr.

Acknowledged in Open Court a Deed from Adam Potter to Bolling
Kirby for one hundred acres of land also one deed to Francis
Kerby for one hundred & 24 acres. Also one deed to Wm Kirby for
one hundred and seventy six acres land. Ordered to be recorded.

Proved in Open Court the Last will & Testament of Joseph Hughs
late of this County decd. by the oath of Col. Joseph Hughes
and Order to be Recorded.

Proved in open court the last will and Testament of Daniel
Norton late of this County decd by the oaths of James Johnson &
Robert McWright and Ordered to be recoded. John Norton, James
Norton and Wm McWright being appointed Executors of the above
will came into open Court & took the oath prescribed by Law.

Proved in open Court the last will & Testamt. of John Cole late
of this County decd by the Oath of James Fowler and Ordered to
be recorded, Mary Cole & Richard Cole being appointed Executrix
& Executor of the above will came into open court & took the
Oath prescribed by Law.

On the application of Thomas Hughes for letters of Administration
on the Estate & Effects of Joseph Hughes late of this County
decd. Order the same be granted him with the last will & Testa-

ment of said Joseph Hughes decd. annexed who give bond with
Joseph Hughes security in the sum of $500 and took the oath
prescribed by Law.

Ordered that Colo. Joseph Hughes, Benjamin Woodson, Esqr., Wm
Adair and Joshua Palmore or any three of them be appointed to
appraise the Estate & Effects of Daniel Norton (Norhor?) decd
and that they be sworn before any Justice of the peace for said
county. and make due return thereof according to Law.

Ordered that all the Estrays of this County subject to be sold
shall be Exposed to sale by the sheriff this Court, and that an
estray horse brought to be sold by Daniel Jackson be Exposed to
Sale today.

On the application of Josias Wood & Lewis Wood for Letters of
Administration on the Estate & Effects of Josias Wood late of
this County decd. Ordered that Letters of Administration be
granted them on the Estate & Effects of said decd. who give bond
with Richd Cox and Warren Hall their securities for the sum of
$2500 and took the oath prescribed by Law.

Ordered that Saml Hardy Esqr, Wm. Hogans, Nathan Glenn, Joshua
Martin or any three of them be appointed to appraise the Estate
& Effects of Josias Wood decd and that they be qualified by any
Justice of the peace in Said County. And make due return thereof
according to Law.

Granted to Daniel Lovett a Licence to retail Spitirous Liquors
for the term of Twelve Months, who Gave bond with Saml Hardy
Security.

The Court adjourned till tomorrow 10 O Clock. William Kennedy,
Thos Brandon.

The Court met according to adjournment on Tuesday the 3 day of
Septr. 1799. Present his honor William Kennedy, Esq.

Ordered that Colo. Joseph Hughes, Wm. Sharp, Joshua Palmer &
William Adair or any three of them be appointed to appraise the
Estate & Effects of Joseph Hughes decd and that Benjamin Woodson
Esqr. qualify them according to Law.

On the application of Sarah Rountree Letters of Administration
is granted her on the Residue Estate of Turner Tountree decd
which was not mentioned in his will & noncupative will who give
bond with Elijah Wilbourn & Wm Brandon her Securities for the
sum of $1000 and took the oath prescribed by Law.

Ordered that James Bell, Robt Woodson, Joseph Reeder, James
Brandon or any three of them be appointed to appraise the Resi-
due Estate of Turner Rountree Decd and that any Justice of the
County aforesaid do qualify the appraisers.

William Rountree an Executor appointed in the last will & Testament of Turner Rountree late of this County decd came into open
Court and took the Oath prescribed by law.

Ordered the County Treasurer pay unto Federick Eison the sum of
Ł 1 for Repairing the bolts & puting on the locks with sufficient
Screws of the Public Goal of this County.

On Motion of William Kennedy Esqr County Treasurer, Ordered that
Joshua Petty, Landlot Porter & Danl McElduff be appointed to
Examine the Clerk and Treasurer office on the 2 Monday in Octo.
and make a Return to next Court thereof and that the Sheriff
notify them of the same.

The Court adjourned till Court in Course. Signed by Thos
Brandon, Wm Kennedy.

At a Court of Ordinary met on Wednesday the Sixteenth day of October 1799. Present William Kenedy, Esqr.

Its order that the Executrix of Turner Rountree Deceased Expose
to public Sale on Saturday the Twenty sixth of this Instant all
the Residue Estate of said Decd which was not mentioned in his
last will & Testament Giving three Months Credit taking bond
with approved Security to be sold at the late Dweling house of
said Decd. and that she make due return thereof according to Law.
Signed Wm Kennedy.

At a Court of Ordinary met on Monday the Twenty eighth day of
October in the year of our Lord one thousand Seven Hundred and
Ninety Nine. Present Wm Kennedy, Andw Torrence, Esqrs.

The Last Will and Testament of Joshua Beuford decd was proved
by the oath of John R Beuford and Ordered to be Recorded. Leroy
Beuford being appointed Executor be the above will refused
to Qualify. Its therefore Ordered that the Administration of all
and singular the goods & Chattles & effects of the said decd be
Granted to Rebecah Beuford the wife of the said Joshua Beuford
and Genl. Thos Brandon with the will annexed Wherefore came the
said Rebecah Beuford & Genl Tho. Brandon into open Court and
took the Oath as required by Law & Also give Bond in the sum of
$2000 with Maj. Saml Otterson & Josiah Darby their secy.
    Its Ordered that Maj. Bird Beuford, Given Gordon & Robert
Crenshaw Senr be and are hereby appointed to appraise the Estate
and effects of Joshua Beuford late of this County decd and make
due return thereof to be first sworn by some acting Justice of
the peace for this County.
                              Andw Torrance, Wm. Kennedy.

At a Court of Ordinary met on Saturday the Sixteenth day of
November in the year of our Lord one thousand seven hundred &
Ninety Nine. Present Wm Kennedy, Andw Torrence, Esqrs.

Present to the Court an instrument of writing said to be the
last Will & testament of John Jasper late of this County deceased,
which was proved by the oath of John Foster & Ordered to be Recorded.
    Its ordered that John Beckham, Ellis Fowler & Capt. John
Prigmore be and are hereby appointed to appraise the Estate &
Effects of John Jasper late of this County deceased & that they
make due return of the same according to Law, to be first sworn
by a Justice of the peace
    John Jasper Jnr & Benjamin Covenhoven appointed executors
to the last will & testament of John Jasper late of this county
deceased, came into open court & took the Oath Prescribed by Law

Rachel Harlan & George Harlan applied for letters of administration on the estate & Effects of Jacob Harlan late of this County
deceased which was granted them who took the oath Prescribed by
Law & Entered into Bond in the sum of $2000 with Obadiah Howard
and Joseph Howard their Securities.

Ordered that Stephen Howard, Joshua Wellborn and William
Brandon be and are hereby appointed to appraise the Estate and
Effects of Jacob Harlan late of this County deceased and make
due return of the same according to Law. To be first sworn by
some Justice of the peace for this County. Wm Kennedy, Andw
Torrance.

At a court of ordinary met for the County of Union on Monday the
18th of Novr 1799. Present [not listed]

Ordered that the administratrix (with the Will annexed) & Admr.
of Joshua Beuford decd Expose to public Sale at the plantation
of said decd all the personall Estate & Effects of the said Joshua Beuford, deceased on this ____ day of ____, giving Fourteen
months credit for all sums above ten shillings those under Cash.
It appearing to the Court that the Sale was duly advertiser according to Law.

On the application of the administrators of the Estate and effects
of Jacob Harlan late of this county deceased, Ordered that they
be permitted to expose to public Sale, on Fryday the Sixth of
Next month, at the late dwelling of said deceased, all the personal property belonging to said Estate giving   credit taking
bond with good & Sufficient Security from the purchasers, and
that the admrs. return a Just account thereof according to Law.
It appearing to the Court the same was advertised.

                              Signed [no names]

List constables Sworn in Since the year [torn]

     Constables   Justices

Shad Lewallen
Presley Williams
James Kennedy
Mark Jackson   Tho. Blasingame
Benjamin Jolley   Maj. McJunkin
Daniel Holder   Batte Birdsong
John Campbell   Josiah Darby

        Ben Haile Esqr
        Deceased in Columbia

        1815

        Wm F Gist C C C Pls
                   Union District
                   So Carolina
                   No America
                   America
                   1815

Other volumes in this series of Minutes of the County Court
include

Winton (Barnwell) County, South Carolina Minutes of the
County Court and Will Book 1 1785-1791

Newberry County, South Carolina Minutes of the County
Court 1785-1798

Chester County, South Carolina Minutes of the County Court
1785-1798